Mean-Variance Analysis in Portfolio Choice and Capital Markets

Harry M. Markowitz

with a chapter and program by
G. Peter Todd

Frank J. Fabozzi Associates

First published in 1987

Printing of Revised Reissue with new Chapter 13 in 2000

FJF

Frank J. Fabozzi Associates
New Hope, Pennsylvania

ISBN: 1-883249-75-9

Printed in the United States of America

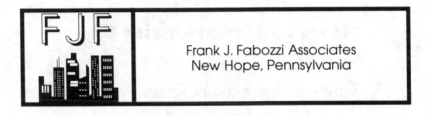

For Barbara, my wife and companion.

H.M.M.

About the Authors

HARRY MARKOWITZ

Dr. Markowitz has applied computer and mathematical techniques to various practical decision making areas. In finance: in an article in 1952 and a book in 1959 he presented "modern portfolio theory," now a standard topic in college courses and widely used by institutional investors for tactical asset allocation, risk control, and attribution analysis. In other areas: Dr. Markowitz developed "sparse matrix" techniques for solving very large mathematical optimization problems, now standard in production software for optimization programs. He also designed and supervised the development of the SIMSCRIPT programming language which has been widely used for programming computer simulations of systems like factories, transportation systems, and communication networks.

In 1989 Dr. Markowitz received The John von Neumann Award from the Operations Research Society of America for his work in portfolio theory, sparse matrix techniques, and SIMSCRIPT. In 1990 he shared The Nobel Prize in Economics for his work on portfolio theory.

G. PETER TODD

Dr. Todd is a Director at Riverview International Group, Inc., where he is responsible for software development. From 1990 to 1998 Dr. Todd was a Vice President at Daiwa Securities Trust's Global Portfolio Research Department (GPRD), where he worked with Harry Markowitz, GPRD's Director of Research. Dr. Todd received a Ph.D. in Biochemistry from Cornell University and a B.S. in Chemistry from Utah State University.

Contents

Foreword ix
Preface to Revised Reissue xv
Preface xvii

Part I The General Portfolio Selection Model

1 PORTFOLIO SELECTION MODELS 3
The Standard Mean-Variance Portfolio Selection 3
Standard Analysis with Upper Bounds 7
The Tobin-Sharpe-Lintner Model 8
Black's Model 11
Model Requiring Collateral for Short Positions 11
Nominal versus Real Returns 13
Appendix to chapter 1 15
Mean and variance of weighted sums 15
General sample spaces 20
Exercises 20

2 THE GENERAL MEAN-VARIANCE PORTFOLIO SELECTION MODEL 23
Three Forms of the General Model 24
Nonlinear Examples 28
Historical Note 36
Exercises 40

3 CAPABILITIES AND ASSUMPTIONS OF THE GENERAL MODEL 42
Semidefinite Covariance Matrices 42
Portfolio Constraints in Theory and Practice 43
Industry Constraints 44
Models of Covariance 45
Exogenous Assets 48
Tracking an Index 50
Turnover Constraints 51
Why Mean and Variance? 52
Bayesian Inference 56
Implied Single-period Utility Maximization 57

Quadratic Approximations 59
Research on EV Approximations 63
Related Matters 68

Part II Preliminary Results

4 PROPERTIES OF FEASIBLE PORTFOLIO SETS 73
Notation 74
The Limit of a Sequence 77
Convergence in R^n 80
Closed Sets 81
Spheres, Balls, and Open Sets 82
Compact Sets 86
Convex Sets 89
Unbounded Constraint Sets 92
Disallowed Directions and Bounded Feasible Directions 94
Conical Sets 98
Appendix to chapter 4 100
Exercises 105

5 SETS INVOLVING MEAN, VARIANCE, AND STANDARD DEVIATION 107
Relationships Involving E 107
Relationships Involving V 109
Compensating Transformations 113
V along a Straight Line 114
σ along a Straight Line 116
Convex Functions 117
Minimum Obtainable V and σ 120
Exercises 122

6 PORTFOLIO SELECTION MODELS WITH AFFINE CONSTRAINT SETS 125
Minimization Subject to Constraints 125
Efficient Portfolios with Affine Constraint Sets 127
Postscript 139
Exercises 143

Part III Solution to the General Portfolio Selection Model

7 EFFICIENT SETS FOR NONDEGENERATE MODELS 151
Kuhn-Tucker Conditions 152
Critical Lines 154
Efficient Segments 157

Adjacent Efficient Segments 161
The Nonsingularity of $\overline{M}$ 166
Nonnegativity of X and η 171
Finiteness of the Critical Line Algorithm 174
The Efficient EV Set 176
Choice of Axes 178
Exercises 179

8 GETTING STARTED 184
The Simplex Method of Linear Programming 185
Prices and Profitabilities 191
Starting the Critical Line Algorithm 193
Exercises 195

9 DEGENERATE CASES 199
Simpler "Good Enough" Methods 200
Efficient Sets when E is Bounded 202
Lexicographical Ordering 214
Unbounded E 216
Related Matters 219
Exercises 223

10 ALL FEASIBLE MEAN-VARIANCE COMBINATIONS 225
The Top of the Obtainable EV Set 229
Comparison of the Top and Bottom of the EV Set 236
The Sides of the Feasible EV Set 238
Exercises 239

Part IV Special Cases

11 CANONICAL FORM OF THE TWO-DIMENSIONAL ANALYSIS 243
The Standard Three-security Analysis 244
Canonical Form when Rank is 2 248
Efficient Sets in the Canonical Analysis (Rank 2) 253
Kinks in the Set of Efficient EV Combinations 257
Linear Segments in the Set of Efficient $E\sigma$ Combinations 259
τ^* of Rank 1 262
The k Dimensional Canonical Analysis 265
Appendix to chapter 11 270
Exercises 272

12 CONICAL CONSTRAINT SETS AND THE EFFICIENCY OF THE MARKET PORTFOLIO 275
The Market Portfolio 276
Conical Constraint Sets 277
Efficiency of the Market Portfolio 280
A Simple Market Equilibrium Model 282
How Inefficient can the Market Portfolio Be? 284
Expected Returns and Betas 286
Exercises 288

Part V A Portfolio Selection Program

13 PROGRAM DESCRIPTION (BY G. PETER TODD) 301
Notation 302
Statement of the Problem 303
Program Inputs 304
The Main Module 305
The Simplex Method 306
The Critical Line Algorithm 312
Appendix A to Chapter 13: Program Listing 318
Appendix B to Chapter 13: Integration with Spreadsheet 334
Appendix C to Chapter 13: Sample Problem 335

APPENDIX ELEMENTS OF MATRIX ALGEBRA AND VECTOR SPACES 339
Mathematical Prerequisites 339
Uses of Matrix Notation 339
Matrix Operations 341
Inverses 343
Substitution of Variables 344
n Dimensional Geometry 346
Orthogonality 348
Independence and Subspaces 348
Change of Coordinate Systems 350
Change of Coordinates in R^n 357

References 361

Index 367

Foreword

Harry Markowitz (1952)* revolutionized the field of finance with his seminal *Journal of Finance* paper "Portfolio Selection." (Interestingly, the paper was the last one in the issue.) In it he argued for the explicit recognition of risk and its quantification in terms of variance. He also introduced the notion of a (mean-variance) efficient portfolio as one that (1) provides minimum variance for a given expected return and (2) provides maximum expected return for a given variance. Finally, he provided a preliminary description of the key aspects of one approach for solving what is now termed the "standard" portfolio selection model.

Markowitz (1956) presented an algorithm for solving a more general class of portfolio selection problems. Markowitz (1959) brought all this material together and discussed at some length the basis for concentrating on the mean (expected value) and variance (or standard deviation) of portfolio return when selecting securities.

In recent years Markowitz has investigated the efficacy of mean-variance analysis when utility functions are not quadratic (Levy and Markowitz (1979)), considered special cases involving factors and scenarios (Markowitz and Perold (1981a)), and investigated ways to exploit sparse matrices when solving portfolio selection problems (Markowitz and Perold (1981b)).

Now Markowitz has collected the majority of this material and much more in *Mean-Variance Analysis in Portfolio Choice and Capital Markets*. Here the reader will find a complete treatment of the most general possible portfolio selection model, efficient solution algorithms, characteristics of possible solutions, aspects of various important special cases, and more.

The exposition follows Markowitz's usual pattern. Practical aspects are introduced first, at a relatively accessible level. Then some fairly heavy mathematical artillery is brought to bear on the subject. This facilitates rigorous proofs of previously known results and generalizations to cover previously unanalyzed cases. The reader who is unable or unwilling to bear the cost

---

* The references are provided at the end of the book.

of following the more difficult parts of the book will still find much of value, however, for highly readable summary statements are provided throughout.

Markowitz defines the task of portfolio selection as one of finding *all* efficient E,V combinations that can be provided by portfolios meeting a set of constraints. Thus, all cases covered share an objective function that can be written as

$$\text{Maximize } \lambda_E E_p - V_p, \text{ for all } \lambda_E \text{ from } +\infty \text{ to } 0, \qquad (1)$$

where E_p is the expected return and V_p the variance of return on the portfolio.[1] Throughout the book, emphasis is placed on the entire set of solutions rather than a particular one.

Thus, no mention is made of the possibility of prespecifying a value of λ_E (such as an investor's risk tolerance) and then solving for a single portfolio. Instead, the problem is approached in two steps: (1) find all efficient portfolios, then (2) select the one that is best for a given investor. "One-step" solutions can be obtained as special cases of the more general approach covered in the book and are thus analyzed implicitly.

Since Markowitz assumes that all portfolio selection problems have the same objective function, cases are differentiated only by the nature of the constraints that determine the feasible set of portfolios. The most general form can be written as

$$Ax \geq b, \qquad (2)$$

where x is an n-element vector that indicates the proportions invested in the various securities plus (perhaps) auxiliary variables, A is an m by n matrix, and b is an m-element vector. The jth row of A and the corresponding value of b define a constraint of the form:

$$a_{j1}x_1 + a_{j2}x_2 + \cdots + a_{jn}x_n \geq b_j.$$

Judicious use of this format allows the inclusion of "less than" inequalities (by reversing all the relevant signs) and equalities (by including two inequalities that together bound the values to be the same).

Equation (2) defines Markowitz's "Form 1" of the general portfolio selection model. An important special case arises when all the constraints are, in effect, equalities. Here one can write

$$Ax = b. \qquad (3)$$

---

[1] In some cases there may be multiple solutions when $\lambda_E = 0$, only one of which may be efficient; however, the algorithm presented in the book handles these cases without difficulty.

Markowitz terms this an *affine constraint set*. Such a case is extremely important for the development of equilibrium theory, for it allows "two-fund separation" (in Markowitz's terms: one critical line). With such a constraint set, every efficient portfolio can be expressed as a combination of two preselected efficient portfolios. This ensures that the aggregate of all investors' holdings (the "market portfolio") will itself be efficient. This, in turn, guarantees that every security will conform to the linear relationship between expected return and beta (measured relative to the market portfolio) of, for example, the Capital Asset Pricing Model.

If the constraint set is not affine (that is, there is one or more inequality constraint), the market portfolio need not be efficient, and simple, economically meaningful relationships between expected returns and beta values need not obtain. Markowitz discusses these relationships at length and provides more general conclusions than were previously available.

The distinction between models with affine constraint sets and those with inequalities is central to both the organization and the focus of this book. Markowitz dichotomizes applications of mean-variance analysis on p. 43 into two groups: *money management*, in which "actual portfolios are selected and money allocated, based on mean-variance analysis," and *economic analysis*, in which "the economy is analyzed assuming all investors seek mean-variance efficiency." More traditional terminology would call the first set *normative models* and the second *positive models*.

Portfolio selection problems with affine constraint sets require little effort on the part of a computer programmer. Inversion of a matrix will often suffice. However, problems with inequality constraints can be much more difficult to solve. A quadratic programming algorithm is needed, and special cases may require considerable sophistication.

A survey of recent journal articles with portfolio selection content would surely reveal much more emphasis on models with affine constraint sets than on those with inequality constraints. In this book the emphasis is reversed. While Markowitz maintains an apparently even-handed approach, his practical experience can be discerned in quotation such as this one from pp. 43-44:

> . . . Surely J. Tobin, W. Sharpe, and J. Lintner knew, as well as you and I know, that if your net worth is $1,000,000 the bank will not loan you $1,000,000,000. Surely F. Black and J. Mossin knew that if you have $10,000 at a broker, you cannot short $1,000,000 of security A and use the proceeds plus your own money to buy $1,010,000 worth of security B, as the Black model allows.

> The reason for models incorporating such assumptions is that they imply simple relationships among interesting economic magnitudes. In chapter 12 we will see that some of the simple relationships implied by these models also hold for somewhat more general constraints, albeit they do not hold generally.

Markowitz's concern with the most general class of portfolio selection problems is also reflected in the location of material on models for "economic analysis." Portions of the Capital Asset Pricing Model are first introduced in exercises at the end of Chapter 6, but detailed discussion is deferred until the penultimate chapter. This makes great sense since the goal of the book is to enable the reader to truly understand the general case before dealing with the relatively simple special cases that arise with affine constraint sets.

The book is divided into five parts and an Appendix.

Part I introduces the subject, starting with simpler models and then proceeding to the general case. It is by far the most readable and should appeal to all who are interested in the subject.

Part II provides preliminary results. It begins with a chapter containing mathematical material needed for the detailed discussions that follow. Next, properties of both general cases and those with affine constraint sets are derived.

Part III deals with solution procedures. Here the critical line method developed by Markowitz in the 1950s is extended to cover potential problems and the resulting algorithm proven to work, in principle, in all possible cases. (Limitations on numeric accuracy resulting from fixed computer word lengths may, however, cause problems in some applications.)

Part IV introduces the notion of a canonical form for analyzing a portfolio selection problem and then applies it to a discussion of the conditions under which the market portfolio will be efficient.

Part V presents and discusses a computer program for solving the general portfolio selection problem.

The Appendix provides elements of matrix algebra and vector spaces that are used in various parts of the book.

The book is full of gems, many of which occur in unexpected places. It is also contains some idiosyncratic behavior. One of the gems is the fascinating "historical note" at the end of Chapter 2. Here, Roy (1952) is given its due although one might reasonably quarrel with Markowitz's overly modest characterization of Markowitz (1952) as "the *other* paper opening the era of modern portfolio theory" (emphasis added). Among other things, we also learn here that Leavens (1945) proposed variance as a measure of the riskiness of a bond portfolio.

Additional gems are found in Chapter 3. Here, Markowitz's original justification for the mean-variance approach (the use of quadratic *approximations* to an investor's utility function) is spelled out in detail and a surprisingly long list of papers measuring its effectiveness cited. Also, a discussion (unfortunately terse) of multiperiod strategies is given, along with a slightly different axiomization of the expected utility maxim from that used in Markowitz (1959).

Idiosyncratic behavior can be found in some places. For example, Markowitz insists that mean-standard deviation and mean-variance diagrams be drawn with expected return on the horizontal axis, although current practice places it on the vertical axis. He provides a valid argument for doing so (based partly on mathematical purity) but thereby imposes added costs on readers familiar with now conventional approaches.

While some discussion of the Lemke and Wolfe quadratic programming algorithms is included, Markowitz deals primarily with the critical line algorithm, which "provides the whole solution, nothing but the solution, and (in the nondegenerate case) the only solution to the portfolio selection problem." No mention is made of the widely used gradient methods, perhaps because they provide only approximate solutions and are not as efficient for parametric programs (that is, with λ_E varying), which Markowitz defines as portfolio selection problems.

The program in Chapter 13 was originally written in EAS-E, a database management language developed by Markowitz but generally unavailable at this time. In this edition it is written in Visual Basic for Applications, which is less elegant but widely used. This change makes a well-tested algorithm available to many at little or no cost — a major contribution for both teachers and practitioners of investment management.

How much mathematics is required to fully understand this book? In the Appendix, Markowitz states, "It has been assumed, as a prerequisite to this book, that the reader has had a course in matrix algebra and two semesters of the calculus." To help those who are a bit rusty, however, the Appendix reviews the former and states that only the first-order conditions for maximization of a function are needed from the latter. Perhaps more important than background is a willingness to "pay particular attention to definitions of concepts such as sphere, ball, open set, closed set, and the like" if the formal proofs are to be followed in detail.

Happily, one need not do even this to get a great deal of good from this book. The essence of Chapters 1, 2, 3, and 12 can be gained without much mathematics, and these cover many of the concepts in the book.

Markowitz's early works have suffered the fate of those of other pioneers: often cited, less often read (at least completely). Indeed, in this book he evidences his concern that "many scholars interested in such matters apparently never found [the discussion of fundamentals in the back of the 1959 book]" This book is organized somewhat differently, to better serve those who will read only the earlier chapters.

My advice to the reader whose interests are relatively pragmatic: Don't be frightened by the formal proofs, canonical forms and so on. Read what you can and skip over what you cannot.

No matter what your level of training, if you are seriously interested in investment theory or practice, you will be well rewarded for having purchased this book.

William F. Sharpe

Preface to Revised Reissue

This reissue is identical to the original except for a Foreword by William Sharpe and a new Chapter 13 provided by Peter Todd. The original Chapter 13 presented a "critical line algorithm" program, for tracing out a complete efficient frontier, written in the EAS-E programming language. (See Markowitz, Malhotra and Pazel (1984).*) The present Chapter 13 is written in VBA (Visual Basic for Applications) for access from EXCEL. The program, presented and described here, is also available from Dr. Todd as noted in his chapter.

Chapter 4 is a stumbling block for some readers. I emphasize the point made in its introduction that "It is not essential for the reader to master every detail of this chapter before moving on to the rest of the book." On the other hand, the reader who has had a course in real or functional analysis will find much of the Chapter redundant. The Chapter was developed for Ph.D. classes whose students mostly had basic courses in matrix algebra and calculus but none in real analysis.

A working knowledge of matrix notation and some results from matrix algebra are prerequisite for this book. These are reviewed in the Appendix. Markowitz (1959) illustrates the ideas presented here for the reader without such background.

The objectives of this book are described in the original Preface and, more completely, in Part I. These need not be repeated here. The original Preface also contains various acknowledgments. What needs to be added here is heartfelt thanks to Frank Fabozzi for suggesting this reissue, to Bill Sharpe for supplying, a Foreword and to Peter Todd for the new Chapter 13. Many thanks also to my secretary, Ruth Sirota. Whenever I received an inquiry about the availability of this book while it was out of print I would send a photocopy to the interested party. I imagine that Ruth is almost as happy as I am at the reissue of this book, since she no longer has to produce small batches of this book on our photocopier from time to time.

Harry Markowitz

San Diego, California
November 1, 1999

---

* The references are provided at the end of the book.

Preface

The principal contents of this book include something old and something new. The something old is what we will refer to as the "*General* mean-variance model." It seeks mean-variance efficient portfolios subject to any system of linear equality or inequality constraints. It was defined and solved under somewhat restrictive assumptions in Markowitz (1956), and under more general assumptions in Appendix A of Markowitz (1959).

Certain special cases of the general model have become widely known, both in academia and among managers of large institutional portfolios. They are part of the standard contents of any modern financial textbook.

But nowhere is the general solution explained except in terse accounts such as the two cited above. In particular, to my knowledge the existence and characteristics of the general solution are presented in no finance text for students at any level.

It is not that the general solution is without connection to modern financial practice. For example, André Perold's widely used portfolio optimizer allows investment institutions to compute mean-variance efficient sets subject to any system of linear equality or inequality constraints, for very large populations of securities. Part of the efficacy of Perold's code results from exploiting properties of efficient sets as determined by the solution to the general model.

But the solution to the general model is not only a computing procedure. It is a body of propositions and formulas concerning the shapes and properties of mean-variance efficient sets. I believe that these propositions and formulas have implications for financial theory and practice beyond those of the already widely known special cases.

My initial objective in writing this book was to present an accessible account of the general mean-variance analysis. Most of the book still reflects this original intent. Specifically, the first part presents the general model. It illustrates the scope of the model in terms of well-known special cases and kinds of constraints used in practice. It also discusses topics such as the approximation of nonlinear constraints, the relationship between the one-period and the many-period analysis, and the reasons for using mean and variance as criteria.

The second part of the book develops preliminary results to be used in the general analysis. Chapter 4 contains an introductory but rigorous exposition of such mathematics - beyond matrix algebra and elementary calculus - needed for the analysis to follow. The appendix to the book (as opposed to two appendices of individual chapters) summarizes such material on matrix algebra and vector spaces as is required. It is intended for the reader who has had a course on the subject but is a "bit rusty." It is hoped that the arrangement of material in part 2 and the appendix will allow readers of different mathematical backgrounds to find suitable paths through the book.

The third part solves the general model for all possible inputs. Chapters 7 and 8 treat the "easy" case in which it is assumed, e.g., that a unique portfolio maximizes expected return, and other such "nondegeneracy" assumptions. In chapter 9 all such assumptions are removed. (Nonsingularity of the covariance matrix is not required, even in chapters 7 and 8.)

The principal new material appears in chapters 11 and 12 which comprise part 4. Like the Black and the Sharpe-Lintner Capital Asset Pricing Models (CAPMs), chapter 12 assumes that all investors have the same beliefs and seek mean-variance efficiency subject to the same constraint set. Unlike these CAPMs, chapter 12 explores the implications of more general portfolio selection constraint sets. For example it shows a larger class of portfolio selection models for which certain implications of the Black and the Sharpe-Lintner models still hold; and also illustrates that these implications do not hold in general.

Chapter 11 presents a "canonical" graphical analysis which is considerably more powerful than the original graphical methods of Markowitz (1952) and (1959). Canonical graphs can easily be drawn to illustrate various cases, e.g., wherein the set of efficient EV combinations does, or does not, have a kink where two pieces of the set of efficient portfolios join; where the set of efficient $E\sigma$ combinations has a straight line segment at one end or other; and so on. The means, variances, and covariances of the securities involved can be read from the graph. Exercise 11.4 presents a remarkable possibility which is counterintuitive in terms of the old graphical method, and easy to construct with the new. Canonical graphs are used in constructing certain CAPM examples in chapter 12.

I find that if one omits purely historical or incidental topics and does not attempt to cover every proof in class, the contents of this book can be taught in a one-semester Ph.D. course on mean-variance analysis. Perhaps professors of finance who must cover some mean-variance analysis in more general investments courses, quantitative analysts in the financial industry who work with inputs to and outputs from portfolio optimizers, and quantitatively oriented consultants to the financial industry may find this book of value for their own background reading.

Some of the exercises at the ends of chapters are purely pedagogical, to emphasize or illustrate material already presented in the chapter. Other exercises present new material of value in itself. In particular, certain classic results in financial literature – a "two funds" separation theorem, a proof that the market is an efficient portfolio given a certain model, some Elton, Gruber, and Padberg algorithms, and so on – are left to be derived as exercises. In general, extensive "hints" are provided, especially when the assignment is not an easy corollary of more general results presented in the chapter.

Marshall Blume, Richard Cheung, Haim Levy, and William Ziemba have read all or large parts of the manuscript of this book and have made many extremely valuable suggestions. The fact that this particular book was written at this time, or the way certain material was handled, is the result of various conversations, recent and less recent, especially with Nusret Cakici, Lawrence Fisher, Alan Hoffman, André Perold, Joel Segall, William Sharpe, and Ming Wang. Thanks to one of the generous grants to Baruch College by Marvin Speiser, I have been able to pursue my writing and research without need to seek support from the organizations frequently acknowledged at this point in technical books. I am delighted to thank Ms Barbara Gautier who has cheerfully and efficiently typed an unbelievable number of drafts of the chapters herein and, as my administrative assistant, has kept the world neatly arranged for me. Finally, but not the least, I would like to thank the two ladies of my home, Barbara Markowitz and her aunt, Satche Shulkin, now 96, who have been most patient with a housemate heavy-laden with book.

Harry Markowitz
Baruch College

Part I

The General Portfolio Selection Model

1

Portfolio Selection Models

This chapter presents several specific portfolio selection models. The following chapter presents a general mean-variance portfolio selection model which includes as special cases the models of this chapter. Chapter 3 contains additional examples of models encompassed by the general portfolio selection model of chapter 2. The principal objective of the remainder of the book is to derive and illustrate the solution to the general model, and hence to its specific instances including those discussed in chapters 1 and 3.

This chapter, and those that follow, use a few concepts and results from probability theory. These concepts can be defined easily and the results proven for finite sample spaces. This is done in the appendix to this chapter. Results for the general case are stated without proof and a standard reference is given. It is suggested that the reader who is not already familiar with formulas such as those for the mean and variance of a weighted sum of random variables, read the appendix to the chapter before proceeding to the next section.

Chapters 1-3, including the appendix to chapter 1, assume that the reader is familiar with certain elementary uses of, and operations with, vectors and matrices. These are reviewed in the appendix to the book through the middle of page 351. The balance of the appendix is not needed until part II.

The Standard Mean-Variance Portfolio Selection Model

In the "standard" portfolio selection model, an investor is to choose fractions $X_1, X_2, \ldots, X_n$ invested in n securities subject to constraints

$$\sum_{i=1}^{n} X_i = 1 \tag{1.1a}$$

$$X_i \geqslant 0 \qquad i = 1, \ldots, n \tag{1.1b}$$

We suppose that the returns this period on individual securities $r_1, r_2, \ldots, r_n$ are jointly distributed random variables, and the return on the portfolio is

$$R = \sum_{i=1}^{n} X_i r_i \tag{1.2}$$

The expected (mean) return on the portfolio as a whole is

$$E = \sum_{i=1}^{n} X_i \mu_i \tag{1.3}$$

where

$$\mu_i = E(r_i) \tag{1.4}$$

In (1.4), E is used as the expected value operator. Where E appears by itself as in (1.3) it refers to the expected value of the return on the portfolio, i.e. $E = E(R)$.

The variance of return V on the portfolio is

$$V = \sum_{i=1}^{n} \sum_{j=1}^{n} X_i X_j \sigma_{ij} \tag{1.5}$$

where

$$\sigma_{ij} = E[(r_i - \mu_i)(r_j - \mu_j)] \tag{1.6}$$

is the covariance between r_i and r_j. In particular,

$$\sigma_{ii} = E(r_i - \mu_i)^2 = V(r_i) \tag{1.7}$$

is the variance of r_i. As with E, when V is followed by a random variable it stands for the variance of the random variable. When V appears by itself it refers to the variance of the portfolio, i.e. $V = V(R)$. Equations (1.3) and (1.5) are true for any jointly distributed $r_1, r_2, \ldots, r_n$ as long as they have finite variances. In particular it is not - repeat, not - required that they be joint normally distributed. The appendix to this chapter derives equations (1.3) and (1.5) for r_i which can take on only a finite number of values, and cites a standard reference for the general case.

Definitions A portfolio $X_1, \ldots, X_n$ which meets requirements (1.1a) and (1.1b) is said to be a *feasible portfolio* for the *standard model.* Synonymously, it is called an *obtainable* or a *legitimate* portfolio. A *feasible* or *obtainable EV combination* is one provided by some feasible portfolio; and a *feasible (obtainable) Eσ combination* is defined similarly, where σ is the standard deviation of the portfolio.

In matrix notation if we let

$$\mu' = (\mu_1, \ldots, \mu_n) \tag{1.8a}$$

$$X' = (X_1, \ldots, X_n) \tag{1.8b}$$

$$C = \begin{pmatrix} \sigma_{11} \ldots \sigma_{1n} \\ \vdots \quad\quad \vdots \\ \sigma_{n1} \ldots \sigma_{nn} \end{pmatrix} \tag{1.8c}$$

then

$$E = \mu' X \tag{1.9}$$

$$V = X'CX \tag{1.10}$$

The set of feasible *EV* combinations will depend on μ and *C*. The area on and in the curve *abcda* in figure 1.1 is a rough sketch of a possible *EV* obtainable set, as we shall see in subsequent chapters.

For any obtainable *EV* combination except those on the arc *bc* it is possible to find a feasible portfolio with at least as much *E* and less *V*, or to find one with less *V* and no less *E*, or both. Any such portfolio is considered inefficient.

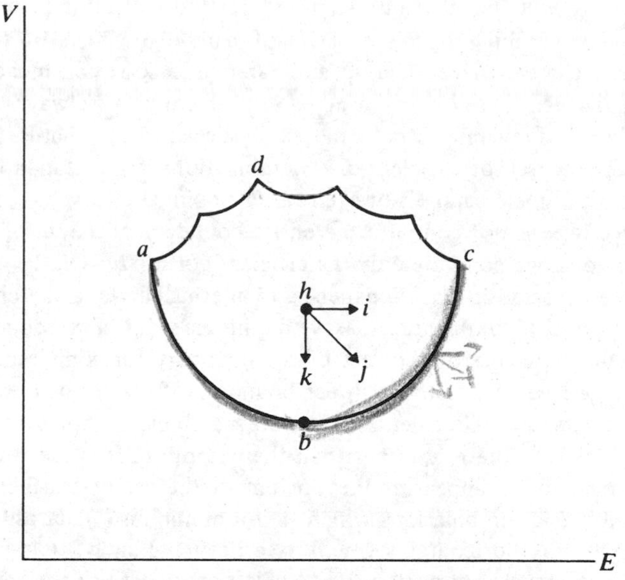

Figure 1.1 Obtainable EV combinations

For example, we can move to the right from h to i obtaining more E and no more V. We can move from h down to k to obtain less V and no less E, or we can move diagonally from h to j obtaining both more E and less V. We cannot move downward from an EV combination on the arc ab but, except for b, these are considered inefficient, since we can move to the right from any such point to obtain higher E and no less V.

Definitions An obtainable *EV combination* is *inefficient* if another obtainable combination has either higher mean and no higher variance, or less variance and no less mean. An obtainable *Eσ combination* is *inefficient* if its E and $V = \sigma^2$ is an inefficient EV combination. An obtainable *portfolio* is *inefficient* if its EV combination is inefficient, where E is given by equation (1.3) and V by equation (1.5). *Efficient portfolios, efficient EV combinations*, and *efficient Eσ combinations* are those which are not inefficient.

In figure 1.1, any EV combination on the arc bc is efficient since any move to the right or downward, or a combination of the two, will move us out of the set of obtainable EV combinations. The corresponding $E\sigma$ combinations and the portfolios which give rise to these are also efficient.

A principal objective in this book will be to determine the shape of the EV efficient sets and provide an economical method for computing these, for a class of portfolio selection models including the standard model as a special case. In particular, we will find that in a standard portfolio selection problem the set of efficient EV combinations is a series of parabolas which fit together so smoothly that there is never a jump and rarely a kink as you move from one parabola to another. Thus bc is typically a smooth curve and always continuous, though made up of several parabolic pieces. In special cases - that is, for particular μ and C - the set of efficient EV combinations for a standard portfolio analysis may be a single parabola or even a single point.

In practice, we do not compute the entire boundary of the set of obtainable EV combinations; we compute only the efficient portion bc. On the other hand, since we have occasion in books, papers, and briefing charts to sketch the entire set of obtainable EV combinations, as we did in figure 1.1, a subsequent chapter will determine the shape of the rest of the boundary for completeness's sake. For example, we will see that the upper boundary of the set of obtainable EV combinations consists of segments which are parabolic or horizontal line segments, and kinks are the rule rather than the exception. It is also possible for a horizontal segment to appear at the bottom of the set of feasible portfolios (among feasible EV combinations which tie for minimum V) but only the rightmost point of this horizontal segment is efficient. Finally, it is possible for vertical segments to appear on the right- or left-hand sides of the set of obtainable EV combinations, containing EV combinations which tie for maximum or minimum E.

Figure 1.1 is drawn here, as it was in Markowitz (1952), with E on the horizontal axis and V on the vertical axis. It is now customary to reverse the axes, placing V or σ on the horizontal and E on the vertical. I shall argue later, in the last section of chapter 7, that certain basic formulas are much more convenient if E is the independent variable, and V and σ are among the dependent variables. Therefore, if we abide by the usual convention of putting the independent variable on the horizontal, the original convention is preferable.

Standard Analysis with Upper Bounds

By law or by policy some portfolios are restricted in the amounts which can be invested in any one security. If, for generality, we allow this restriction to vary from one security to another, we have the following constraint set:

$$\sum_{i=1}^{n} X_i = 1 \qquad (1.11a)$$

$$X_i \geqslant 0 \qquad i = 1, \ldots, n \qquad (1.11b)$$

$$X_i \leqslant U_i \qquad i = 1, \ldots, n \qquad (1.11c)$$

These are the same constraints as in the standard portfolio selection model, except for the upper bounds (given constants) U_i required on the fractions invested in each security.

The expected return and variance of any portfolio is still given by equations (1.3) and (1.5); the objective is still to find efficient portfolios, as defined in the preceding section. The difference between the standard portfolio selection problem and the present one is in the definition of feasible portfolio.

Figure 1.2 shows a possible relationship between the EV combinations obtainable when portfolios are constrained by (1.1a) and (1.1b), enclosed in the outer curve labelled "boundary for standard constraint set", and those obtainable when portfolios are constrained by (1.11), given the same μ and C. If all the U_i are sufficiently large, constraints (1.11c) will have no effect on the set of obtainable EV combinations. In particular, if U_i is greater than 1 for all i then the obtainable set is unaffected. It may also be unaffected if some U_i are less than 1 provided that the corresponding X_i, in the solution to (1.1), are less than U_i at every point on the boundary. As the U_i are decreased the set of obtainable EV combinations will eventually shrink. For example, if $n = 100$ and $U_i = 0.01$ for $i = 1$ to 100, then only one portfolio and one EV combination is obtainable.

It is possible for constraints (1.11) to allow no feasible portfolios. For example, if n is less than 100 and $U_i = 0.01$ for $i = 1$ to n, then no portfolio can satisfy these constraints.

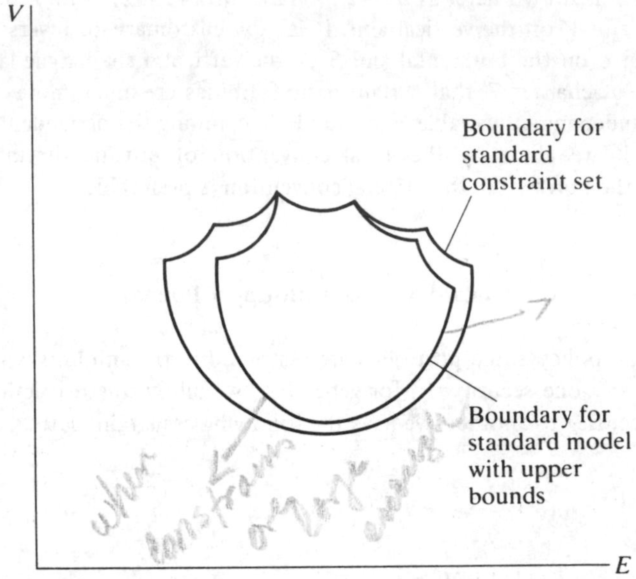

Figure 1.2 Possible effect of upper bounds on obtainable EV combinations

Definition A model is *infeasible* if no portfolio can meet its constraints.

We will see in later chapters that, if a particular standard analysis with upper bounds is feasible, then its set of obtainable *EV* combinations has the same form as that of the standard analysis without upper bounds. The numerical solution may differ, as illustrated in figure 1.2, but the boundary again consists of pieces of parabolas, and perhaps horizontal and vertical line segments. Only parabolic segments can be contained within the efficient portion of the feasible *EV* set. In some cases the boundary, or its efficient portion if not the entire boundary, may consist of just one such segment, or may be a single point.

The standard analysis with upper bounds, like the standard analysis without upper bounds, is a special case of the general portfolio selection model. The shapes of their obtainable *EV* combinations, among other things, will be one of the results of our general analysis.

The Tobin-Sharpe-Lintner Model

As in the two preceding examples, and indeed in the portfolio analysis problem generally, we seek efficient *EV* combinations as defined previously. In the present example the portfolios are to be chosen subject to the following constraints:

$$\sum_{i=1}^{n} X_i = 1 + X_{n+1} \tag{1.12a}$$

$$X_i \geqslant 0 \qquad i = 1, \ldots, n \tag{1.12b}$$

$$X_{n+1} \geqslant -1 \tag{1.12c}$$

Equation (1.12a) may be brought into a standard form to be used later by writing it as

$$\sum_{i=1}^{n} X_i - X_{n+1} = 1 \tag{1.12a$'$}$$

Note that X_{n+1} is bounded by -1 rather than 0. In the analyses of Tobin (1958), Sharpe (1964), and Lintner (1965) the variable referred to here as X_{n+1} is the amount borrowed (if X_{n+1} is positive) or lent (if X_{n+1} is negative). $V_{n+1} = \sigma_{n+1,n+1}$ is assumed to be zero, and hence so is $\sigma_{n+1,i}$ for $i = 1$ to n. The rate of return received (with certainty) by the investor on moneys lent and paid on moneys borrowed is usually referred to as the ***risk-free rate*** and denoted r_0. Since X_{n+1} in (1.12) denotes amount borrowed, $\mu_{n+1} = -r_0$.

A possible set of obtainable *EV* combinations for the Tobin-Sharpe-Lintner model is shown in figure 1.3. (Alternate possible shapes of this set are explored in exercise 12.10.) In the case illustrated here, the lower boundary of the obtainable set consists of two branches. The right branch *ab* is "half" of a parabola beginning at $(E, V) = (r_0, 0)$, the point *a*, and extending without limit to the

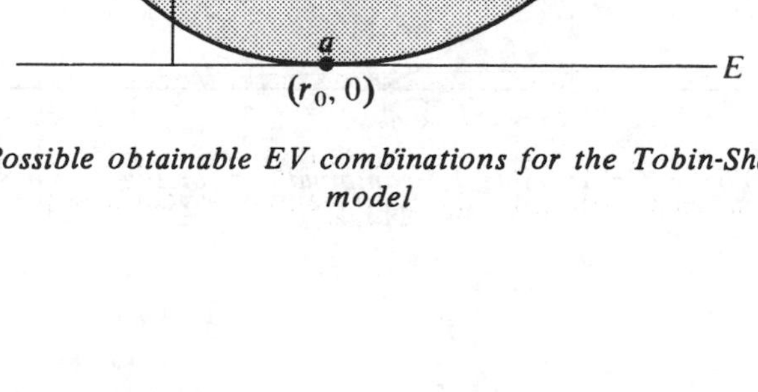

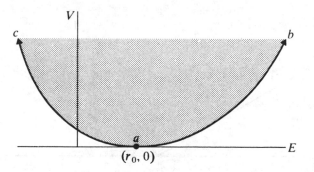

Figure 1.3 Possible obtainable EV combinations for the Tobin-Sharpe-Lintner model

right for all $E \geqslant r_0$. The left branch is also "half" of a parabola beginning at a, but this time extending to the left for all $E \leqslant r_0$. The left and right halves of the lower boundary may be two halves of the same parabola or two halves of different parabolas. The right branch contains all the efficient EV combinations. The left branch, excluding the point a, contains only inefficient EV combinations.

In the case illustrated, the set of obtainable EV combinations has no upper boundary. For any fixed $E = E_0$, obtainable (E_0, V) combinations can be found for every $V \geqslant V_0$, where V_0 minimizes V among obtainable (E_0, V) combinations.

The set of obtainable $E\sigma$ combinations, corresponding to the EV set in figure 1.3, is illustrated in figure 1.4. Its lower boundary consists of two straight line segments. One extends without bound to the right from $(E, \sigma) = (r_0, 0)$; the other extends to the left without bound from the same point. The one straight line segment may or may not be a reflection of the other. There is no upper boundary since the set continues indefinitely upwards in the case illustrated.

The set of efficient combinations for a Tobin-Sharpe-Lintner model, as illustrated in figure 1.3, is like that of the standard model or a standard model with upper bounds (provided it is feasible), in that the efficient set is piecewise parabolic. In the Tobin-Sharpe-Lintner model there is only one such parabolic piece and, in the typical case, it extends to the right indefinitely. It is possible, in a case not illustrated here, for the efficient set to consist of a single point. (When we speak of the "possible" we refer to mathematical possibility - for example, what can happen for arbitrary choice of μ.)

Limited borrowing can be modeled by adding to (1.12) the constraint

$$X_{n+1} \leqslant U_{n+1} \tag{1.12d}$$

In this case the solution to the model becomes as in figure 1.1 rather than as in figure 1.3. When we refer to the Tobin-Sharpe-Lintner model, constraint (1.12d) is not included.

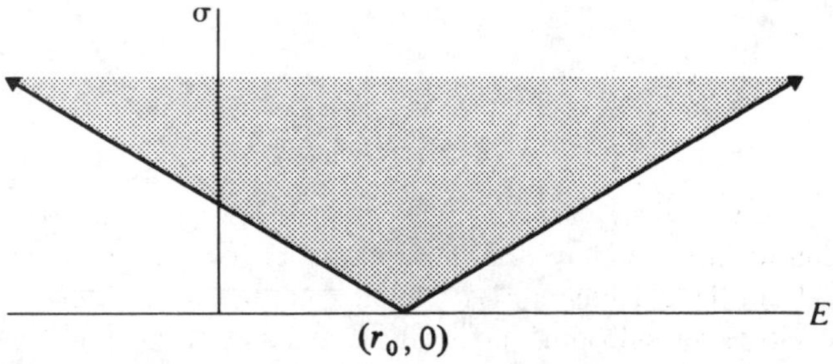

Figure 1.4 Possible obtainable $E\sigma$ combinations for the Tobin-Sharpe-Lintner model

Black's Model

The formulas for E and V and the concept of efficiency are as in the preceding models; however, in what we will call Black's model, portfolios are to be chosen subject to the following constraint:

$$\sum_{i=1}^{n} X_i = 1 \tag{1.13}$$

This is like the standard model except that the nonnegativity constraints (1.1b) are omitted. Negative X_i are spoken of as *short positions* in the ith security; positive X_i are spoken of as *long positions*. As we shall see in the historical note at the end of chapter 2, the phrase "Black's model" is ambiguous; nevertheless:

Definition In the present volume, when we speak of *Black's model* we refer to a portfolio selection model with (1.13) as its sole constraint.

In Black's model a typical set of obtainable EV combinations is like that of the Tobin-Sharpe-Lintner model shown in figure 1.3, with two exceptions. In the Tobin-Sharpe-Lintner model the lower boundary of the set of obtainable EV combinations may consist of two distinct parabola segments - one extending to the right from a, the other extending to the left from a. In Black's model these are two halves of the same parabola. Further, in Black's model $V = 0$ is not necessarily obtainable, whereas it is in the Tobin-Sharpe-Lintner model. ?

Model Requiring Collateral for Short Positions

Since $\Sigma X_i = 1$ is the only constraint in Black's model, the following is a feasible solution:

$$X_1 = -1{,}000$$

$$X_2 = +1{,}001$$

$$X_i = 0 \qquad i = 3 \text{ to } n \tag{1.14}$$

Since "1" represents the investor's equity, for an investor with wealth equal to say 1 million dollars the above solution represents going short 1 billion dollars in security 1 and long 1 billion plus 1 million in security 2. This is not in fact feasible for either an individual, an investing institution, or a brokerage house. If you, as an individual, short 100 shares of stock A the procedure is as follows. The stock is borrowed from some investor or investment institution, and sold in the market. The proceeds are credited to the lender of the stock who can earn interest on these proceeds. That is why the lender loaned the stock. When you choose to close (cover) the short position your broker will buy the stock in the market, return the stock to the lender, and get back the original proceeds credited to the lender. Your gain or loss will be the difference between what you sold (shorted) the stock at originally and what you bought (covered) the stock at subsequently, less commissions. You gain if the stock goes down; you lose if the stock goes up. To be sure that you can pay your losses if you cover at a higher price than you shorted, you are required by law to put up collateral. If there were no such law, this requirement would be a prudent practice anyway on the part of the broker. The collateral can be in the form of certain securities held at the broker, e.g. treasury bills (T-bills) or bonds, as well as the excess of the equity in the account over the securities held.

These constraints can be expressed as follows:

$$\sum_{i=1}^{K+G} X_{iL} \leq A \tag{1.15a}$$

$$\alpha \sum_{i=1}^{K+G} X_{iS} \leq A - \sum_{i=1}^{K} X_{iL} \tag{1.15b}$$

$$X_{iL} \geq 0 \qquad i = 1 \text{ to } K+G \tag{1.15c}$$

$$X_{iS} \geq 0 \qquad i = 1 \text{ to } K+G \tag{1.15d}$$

In the present instance it is convenient to express the constraints in terms of the total equity of the investor. We use A for assets rather than E for equity in equations (1.15a) and (1.15b) since the letter E is preempted. The variable X_{iL} represents a long position in the ith security; a positive value of X_{iS} represents a short position in the ith security. Constraints (1.15c) and (1.15d) express the fact that meaning is assigned only for positive values of X_{iL} and X_{iS}. Constraint (1.15a) says that the sum of the long positions must not exceed the available equity. (To simplify the present discussion we neglect the possibility of borrowing.) Constraint (1.15b) says that the sum of the short positions times α, which here represents the collateral requirement for shorts, must not exceed the equity minus the value of the positions which cannot be used for collateral (i.e. the first K securities).

Constraints (1.15) can be brought into a standard form to be defined later by writing them as:

$$\sum_{i=1}^{K+G} X_i \leq A \tag{1.16a}$$

$$\sum_{i=1}^{K} X_i + \sum_{i=K+G+1}^{2(K+G)} \alpha X_i \leq A \tag{1.16b}$$

$$X_i \geqslant 0 \qquad i = 1, \ldots, 2(K+G) \tag{1.16c}$$

where we write X_i $(i \leqslant K+G)$ for X_{iL} and X_i $(i > K+G)$ for $X_{i-K+G,S}$.

Actual constraints on short positions are more complex than represented in (1.16). First, there is the possibility of borrowing, which can be represented by a variable representing the amount borrowed. The fact that borrowing is limited can be represented by an upper bound on this variable.

Second, some long positions can serve as part of the collateral for specific short positions, even though they cannot serve as collateral generally. For example, a convertible bond which can be converted into, say, 100 shares of stock A can serve as most of the collateral on a short position in the stock. This can be modeled by introducing a variable X_i which represents the combination of long bond and short stock, in addition to variables which represent the bond long only and the stock short only.

Another complexity has to do with the difference between the collateral requirement α_1 which must be put up initially and that α_2 which must be maintained subsequently as the stock price moves. In chapter 3 we will see how current positions can be treated differently from changes in these positions. Such a treatment can be used in the present case.

Also, some securities cannot be shorted at all, either because it is prohibited or because the security cannot be borrowed. Because of these neglected complexities, we refer to (1.15), or equivalently (1.16), as a "more" realistic model of short sales (i.e. more realistic than (1.13) alone) rather than as an (absolutely) "realistic" model.

Nominal versus Real Returns

The random variables R and r_i in equation (1.2) represent *nominal returns* - dollars gained or lost per dollar invested. We have assumed that the investor seeks a good probability distribution of R, where "good" entails high E and low V. Our assertions concerning the efficient sets of various models are, in most cases, little changed if we assume instead that the investor seeks high E and low V of *real return* - the gain or loss in the real value of the portfolio. The present section explores the effects of seeking mean-variance efficiency in terms of real return.

In the standard model, the standard model with upper bounds, and Black's model the return on the portfolio is given by (1.2). Since $\Sigma_{i=1}^{n} X_i = 1$ in these models,

$$1 + R = \sum_{i=1}^{n} X_i(1 + r_i) \tag{1.17}$$

If we let E and V represent the expected value and variance of $1+R$, and let μ_i and σ_{ij} represent expected $(1+r_i)$ and $\text{cov}(1+r_i, 1+r_j)$,[1] then the relationships between E, V, X_i, μ_i, and σ_{ij} are still as given in (1.3) and (1.5) or, equivalently, (1.9) and (1.10). If we compute EV efficient sets using expected $(1+r_i)$ for the μ_i, all results are as described previously. The only difference is that each obtainable, and therefore each efficient, portfolio has its E greater by 1.0 than when μ_i equals expected r_i.

If we let W^b be the value of the portfolio at the beginning of the investment period and W^e be that at the end, then

$$W^e = (1+R)\,W^b \tag{1.18a}$$

If P is an index of prices appropriate for the particular investor, and if P^b and P^e are the values of P at the beginning and end of the period, then real return $\tilde{R}$ is given by

$$\tilde{R} = \frac{(W^e/P^e) - (W^b/P^b)}{W^b/P^b}$$

$$= \frac{1+R}{P^e/P^b} - 1$$

Thus defined, $100\tilde{R}$ is the percentage change in the real value of the portfolio. If we define π so that

$$1+\pi = P^e/P^b$$

then

$$1+\tilde{R} = (1+R)/(1+\pi)$$

$$= \sum_{i=1}^{n} X_i[(1+r_i)/(1+\pi)]$$

Thus if we let E and V represent the expected value and variance of $1+\tilde{R}$, let μ_i represent the expected value of the random variable $(1+r_i)/(1+\pi)$, and let

$$\sigma_{ij} = \text{cov}\,[(1+r_i)/(1+\pi), (1+r_j)/(1+\pi)]$$

then the relationship between E, V, X_i, μ_i, and σ_{ij} will again be as in (1.3) and (1.5) or, equivalently, (1.9) and (1.10). Therefore conclusions concerning the shapes and computation of efficient sets which hold for arbitrary μ and C are true for real returns as well as for nominal returns.

[1] The former equals $1 + E(r_i)$ and the latter equals $\text{cov}(r_i, r_j)$.

The above discussion fails to apply to the Tobin-Sharpe-Lintner model in two respects. First, the return to the portfolio is given, not by (1.2), but by

$$R = \sum_{i=1}^{n} X_i r_i - X_{n+1} r_0$$

where $r_{n+1} = -r_0$ with certainty. Second, the assumption that the $(n+1)$th security is risk-free, i.e. $V_{n+1} = 0$, assumes E and V refer to nominal rather than real return, since $V[(1+r_{n+1})/(1+\pi)] > 0$ even though $V(r_n) = 0$.

One could construct a "real" Tobin-Sharpe-Lintner model by assuming that the investor contracted to borrow or lend at an interest rate proportional to P^b/P^e. But this is not the usual assumption. In any model – such as the Tobin-Sharpe-Lintner model – in which a risk-free asset is required, we will assume that E and V describe the probability distribution of nominal return. When we refer to the standard model (with or without upper bounds) and to Black's model, each of which permits but does not require the existence of a risk-free security, our statements apply equally to the case in which E and V describe the probability distribution of nominal returns and that in which they describe real returns.

Appendix to Chapter 1

Mean and variance of weighted sums

This appendix defines some concepts and derives some formulas of probability theory used throughout this book. The formal discussion assumes a finite sample space. In addition, results are stated and a standard reference cited for a general (i.e. possibly infinite) sample space. Exercises 1.5 and 1.6 apply to this appendix.

We are concerned with jointly distributed random variables. For random variables which can only take on a finite number of values, the notion of a joint distribution can be defined in terms of the vectors and matrices illustrated in table 1.1. Imagine that the values of m random variables are written on n slips of paper. To not sound unsophisticated, we will refer to them as sample points rather than slips of paper. We will deal with probability spaces containing only a finite number of sample points, which we label sample points number 1 through n. One and only one sample point is chosen at random, but not necessarily with each point having the same probability of occurrence. Let p_j be the probability of selecting the jth point. Since the p_j are probabilities,

$$\sum_{j=1}^{n} p_j = 1 \tag{1.19a}$$

$$p_j \geqslant 0 \qquad j = 1, \ldots, n \tag{1.19b}$$

Table 1.1 *Description of joint distribution with finite sample space*

Random variable names	Sample points 1 p_1	2 p_2	3 p_3	.	.	.	n p_n
r_1	v_{11}	v_{12}	v_{13}	.	.	.	v_{1n}
r_2	v_{21}	v_{22}	v_{23}				v_{2n}
r_3	v_{31}	v_{32}	v_{33}				v_{3n}
⋮							⋮
r_m	v_{m1}	v_{m2}	v_{m3}	.	.	.	v_{mn}

The random selection of a sample point determines the values of all m random variables. In table 1.1 the columns refer to sample points, the rows to random variables. Probabilities $p_1, p_2, \ldots, p_n$ are written above each column. The symbols written to the left of each row – $r_1, r_2, \ldots, r_m$ – are the names of the random variables. We could instead write names such as "return on a long position in security 1" rather than r_1; but the present notation is more convenient here. The entry v_{ij} in the ith row and jth column of the table is the value which the ith random variable takes on if the jth sample point is drawn. In a specific instance of such a joint distribution, p_3 would be a number, the probability of drawing the third sample point; $v_{2,3}$ would be a number, the value which the second random variable takes on if the third sample point is chosen; whereas r_2 is a name, like "return on xyz" or just "r_2".

Let $p' = (p_1, \ldots, p_n)$ be the probability distribution of sample points, $r' = (r_1, \ldots, r_m)$ be the vector of names of random variables, and $W = (v_{ij})$ be the matrix of values which each random variable takes on if a particular sample point is chosen. Let $a' = (a_1, \ldots, a_m)$ contain any m real numbers. We define a new random variable whose name is "$\Sigma a_i r_i$". In a specific case its name might be "0.3 times the return on the first security plus . . .". We define $\Sigma a_i r_i$ to be a random variable which takes on the value $\Sigma a_i v_{ij}$ if the jth sample point is chosen. Since the choice of sample point determines the value of $\Sigma a_i r_i$, the latter is said to be jointly distributed with $r_1, \ldots, r_m$, even though its value is not written on the slip of paper. If we let "r_{m+1}" be a synonym for "$\Sigma a_i r_i$" then

$$\begin{aligned} w'_{m+1} &= (v_{m+1,1}, v_{m+1,2}, \ldots, v_{m+1,n}) \\ &= a'W \end{aligned} \tag{1.20}$$

where $v_{m+1,j}$ is the value of $\Sigma a_i r_i$ if the sample point j is selected; w'_{m+1} is the row vector containing $v_{m+1,j}$ for $j = 1$ to n; and $w'_{m+1} = a'W$ expresses in matrix notation the fact, implied by the foregoing, that

$$v_{m+1,j} = \sum_{i=1}^{m} a_i v_{ij}$$

For finite sample spaces, the *expected value* of a random variable is a weighted sum of its possible outcomes, with the probabilities of the outcomes as weights; for example,

$$\begin{aligned} \mu_i &= E(r_i) \\ &= \sum_{j=1}^{n} p_j v_{ij} \end{aligned} \tag{1.21}$$

where $E(\ )$ stands for the expected value of the random variable in parentheses, and μ_i is defined as $E(r_i)$. The terms *mean* or *arithmetic mean* are synonymous with expected value. The vector $\mu' = (\mu_1, \ldots, \mu_m)$ is

$$\mu = Wp$$

(Confirm by multiplying the ith row of W by the column vector p.)

A basic result of probability theory used throughout this book is that the expected value of a weighted sum of random variables equals the same weighted sum of their expected values:

$$\begin{aligned} E\left(\sum_{i=1}^{m} a_i r_i\right) &= \sum_{i=1}^{m} a_i E(r_i) \\ &= \sum_{i=1}^{m} a_i \mu_i \end{aligned} \tag{1.22}$$

In other words, for any choice of $a' = (a_1, \ldots, a_m)$ we have

$$E(a'r) = a'\mu$$

This is shown as follows: (1.20) tells us that the vector of values of the random variable called $a'r$ is $a'W$; hence

$$\begin{aligned} E(a'r) &= (a'W)p \\ &= a'(Wp) \\ &= a'\mu \end{aligned}$$

where the first step applies the definition of expected value to $r_{m+1} = a'r$, and the last step applies it to the other r_i.

Another basic result needed in this book is the formula for the *variance* of $a'r$. For this we need the definitions of the variance of a random variable and the covariance between two random variables. The variance of a random variable r_i is defined to be

$$V(r_i) = E[(r_i - \mu_i)^2] \tag{1.23a}$$

In other words, given a random variable r_i, define a new random variable $(r_i - \mu_i)$. This is jointly distributed with r_i. Now define another new random variable equal to $(r_i - \mu_i)^2$. This is the random variable whose value is $(v_{ij} - \mu_i)^2$ if sample point j is chosen. The expected value of $(r_i - \mu_i)^2$ is defined to be $V(r_i)$. The *standard deviation* of r_i is

$$\sigma_i = V_i^{1/2} \tag{1.23b}$$

The *covariance* between r_i and r_j is defined as

$$\sigma_{ij} = E[(r_i - \mu_i)(r_j - \mu_j)] \tag{1.24a}$$

It is the expected value of (r_i minus its mean) times (r_j minus its mean). In particular, $V(r_i) = \sigma_{ii}$ equals the covariance between r_i and itself. The sign of σ_{ij} will be positive if r_i tends to be above μ_i when r_j is above μ_j; it will be negative if r_i tends to be below μ_i when r_j is above μ_j.

Note that σ with one subscript is a standard deviation; with two subscripts, a covariance. If $\sigma_i > 0$ and $\sigma_j > 0$ then the *correlation coefficient* between r_i and r_j is defined as

$$\rho_{ij} = \sigma_{ij}/\sigma_i\sigma_j \tag{1.24b}$$

Always $-1 \leqslant \rho_{ij} \leqslant +1$; see exercise 1.5. When $\rho_{ij} = 0$ we say that the random variables are uncorrelated.

We will frequently use the fact that the variance of a weighted sum is

$$V(a'r) = a'Ca \tag{1.25a}$$

where

$$C = \begin{pmatrix} \sigma_{11} & \sigma_{12} & \cdots & \sigma_{1m} \\ \sigma_{21} & \sigma_{22} & \cdots & \sigma_{2m} \\ \vdots & \vdots & & \vdots \\ \sigma_{m1} & \sigma_{m2} & \cdots & \sigma_{mm} \end{pmatrix} \tag{1.25b}$$

is the *matrix of covariances*. We will occasionally use the fact that the covariance between two weighted sums $a'r$ and $b'r$ is

$$\text{cov}(a'r, b'r) = a'Cb \tag{1.26}$$

Since $V(a'r) = \text{cov}(a'r, a'r)$ implies that (1.25a) is a corollary of (1.26), we will show (1.26). The argument, annotated (a)–(g) below, goes as follows:

$$\text{cov}(a'r, b'r) = E\{[a'r - E(a'r)]\,[b'r - E(b'r)]\} \tag{a}$$

$$= E\{[a'r - a'\mu]\,[b'r - b'\mu]\} \tag{b}$$

$$= E\{[a'(r-\mu)][b'(r-\mu)]\} \tag{c}$$

$$= E\left\{\sum_{i=1}^{m}\sum_{j=1}^{m} a_i b_j (r_i-\mu_i)(r_j-\mu_j)\right\} \tag{d}$$

$$= \sum_{i=1}^{m}\sum_{j=1}^{m} a_i b_j E(r_i-\mu_i)(r_j-\mu_j) \tag{e}$$

$$= \sum_{i=1}^{m}\sum_{j=1}^{m} a_i b_j \sigma_{ij} \tag{f}$$

$$= a'Cb \tag{g}$$

Step (a) is the definition of covariance applied to the random variables $a'r$ and $b'r$. Step (b) uses (1.22). Step (c) uses the fact that, for example, for every sample point the random variable $a'r - a'\mu$ has the same value as the random variable $a'(r-\mu)$. Step (d) uses the fact that for any numbers $(c_1, \ldots, c_m)$ and $(d_1, \ldots, d_m)$ we have

$$(\Sigma c_i)(\Sigma d_i) = \sum_{i=1}^{m} c_i\left(\sum_{j=1}^{m} d_j\right) = \sum_{i=1}^{m}\sum_{j=1}^{m} c_i d_j$$

This is applied in step (d) to $\Sigma_{i=1}^{m} a_i(r_i-\mu_i)$ and $\Sigma_{j=1}^{m} b_j(r_j-\mu_j)$ or, strictly speaking, to $\Sigma_{i=1}^{m} a_i(v_{ij}-\mu_i)$ and $\Sigma_{k=1}^{m} b_k(v_{kj}-\mu_k)$. Step (e) applies (1.22) treating $a_i b_j$ as a single constant and $(r_i-\mu_i)(r_j-\mu_j)$ as a single random variable. Step (f) applies the definition of covariance. Finally, step (g) expresses (f) in matrix notation.

For given constants α and β, consider

$$u = [r_2 - E(r_2)] - \{\alpha + \beta[r_1 - E(r_1)]\} \tag{1.27a}$$

This is a random variable jointly distributed with r_1 and r_2. Squaring both sides and taking expected values yields

$$E(u^2) = V(r_2) + \alpha^2 + \beta^2 V(r_1) - 2\beta \operatorname{cov}(r_1, r_2) \tag{1.27b}$$

(We have used here the fact that $E(a+r) = a + E(r)$ and, in particular, $E[r - E(r)] = 0$.) $E(u^2)$ is minimized by choosing $\alpha = 0$ and (solving $d[E(u^2)]/d\beta = 0$ and checking the second-order condition) by setting

$$\beta = \beta_{r_2 r_1} = \frac{\operatorname{cov}(r_1, r_2)}{V(r_1)} \tag{1.27c}$$

This is the *beta* or the *least square regression coefficient* of r_2 against r_1. Similarly,

$$\beta_{r_1 r_2} = \frac{\operatorname{cov}(r_1, r_2)}{V(r_2)} \tag{1.27d}$$

is the regression coefficient of r_1 against r_2. Equations (1.27c and d) are defined for any jointly distributed random variables, provided that the respective denominators are not zero. Neither implies that variation in one of the r_i "causes" variation in the other.

General sample spaces

For arbitrary (not necessarily finite) sample spaces, expected value is defined in terms of a generalized Lebesgue integral which includes the sum and the Riemann integral of college calculus as special cases. See for example Halmos (1950). For us, the principal results are as follows. Some random variables do not have (finite) expected values, because the value of the integral is either infinite or undefined. The same statement applies to variance, of course, which is an expected value. Any random variable which has a finite variance also has a finite expected value. If $r_1, \ldots, r_m$ each have finite variances then they also have finite covariances. For random variables with finite expected values it is always true that

$$E(a'r) = a'\mu$$

even if the random variables are correlated. For random variables with finite variances it is always true that

$$V(a'r) = a'Ca$$

and

$$\text{cov}(a'r, b'r) = a'Cb$$

Also, the least squares relationships of (1.27) hold. These various relationships do not depend on any assumption of normality or symmetry.

Exercises

Some possible properties of obtainable and efficient sets may be seen in the easily solved case of $n = 2$. This case is explored in exercises 1.1–1.4.

1.1 In general when $n = 2$, we have

$$E = \mu_1 X_1 + \mu_2 X_2$$

$$V = V_1 X_1^2 + V_2 X_2^2 + 2\sigma_{12} X_1 X_2$$

Throughout this question we assume $n = 2$ and Black's model.

(a) Show that

$$E = \mu_2 + (\mu_1 - \mu_2) X_1$$

$$V = V_2 - 2X_1(V_2 - \sigma_{12}) + X_1^2(V_1 + V_2 - 2\sigma_{12})$$

Note that when $X_1 = 0$, $E = \mu_2$ and $V = V_2$.

(b) Since the variance of the random variable $(r_1 - r_2)$ is

$$V(r_1 - r_2) = V_1 + V_2 - 2\sigma_{12}$$

and variance is always nonnegative, we note that $V_1 + V_2 - 2\sigma_{12} \geqslant 0$. The equality holds if and only if $(r_1 - r_2)$ has zero variance. Show that if $V_1 + V_2 - 2\sigma_{12} = 0$ then $V_2 - \sigma_{12} = 0$. Use the formula for V in (a), and the fact that variance must always be nonnegative, whatever the sign of X_1. Conclude that if

$$V(r_1 - r_2) = V_1 + V_2 - 2\sigma_{12} = 0$$

then $V = V_2 =$ a constant not depending on X_1. (This case is ruled out if C is nonsingular; for in this case $X'CX = 0$ for $X' = (1, -1)$, which cannot happen with nonsingular C.)

(c) Under what conditions is E a constant not depending on X_1?

(d) Show that if $V_1 + V_2 - 2\sigma_{12} = 0$ and $\mu_1 \neq \mu_2$ then the set of obtainable EV combinations is a horizontal line containing points (E, V_2) for every value of E. Furthermore show that, while there are feasible portfolios, there are no efficient portfolios in this case.

(e) If $V_1 + V_2 - 2\sigma_{12} > 0$ show that V is minimized at

$$\hat{X}_1 = \frac{V_2 - \sigma_{12}}{V_1 + V_2 - 2\sigma_{12}}$$

When does $\hat{X}_1 = 0$? Note that every value of V is obtainable for $V \geqslant \hat{V}$ where $\hat{V}$ is the V at $\hat{X}_1$. What is the value of $\hat{V}$?

(f) Show that if $\mu_1 = \mu_2$ and $V_1 + V_2 - 2\sigma_{12} > 0$ then the set of obtainable EV combinations is a vertical line segment extending upward indefinitely from $(E, \hat{V})$, where $E = \mu_1 = \mu_2$ and $\hat{V}$ is given in (e). In this case, what is the efficient set?

(g) When $\mu_1 \neq \mu_2$ and $V_1 + V_2 - 2\sigma_{12} > 0$ express V in terms of E. Show that the relationship between V and E is of the form

$$V = a_0 + a_1 E + a_2 E^2$$

with $a_2 > 0$. Complete the square to show that this can be expressed as

$$V = V_{\min} + a_2(E - E_{\min})^2$$

where $V_{\min}$ and $E_{\min}$ are constants. Thus, for $n = 2$ at least, the lower boundary is as asserted in the text. In the present case the upper boundary is the same as the lower boundary.

1.2 (a) For $n = 2$, the standard model is like Black's model except that

$$0 \leqslant X_1 \leqslant 1$$

Use the results in exercise 1.1 to find examples of standard models whose EV obtainable sets are:

(i) A vertical line segment
(ii) A horizontal line segment
(iii) A parabolic segment with minimum within the interval $0 < X_1 < 1$
(iv) A parabola which rises throughout the interval $0 \leqslant X_1 \leqslant 1$
(v) A parabola segment which falls throughout the interval $0 \leqslant X_1 \leqslant 1$.

(b) In cases (iii), (iv), and (v) of (a) the top of the obtainable set (which is also the bottom of the obtainable set) is a parabola. Compare with figure 1.1.

1.3 Analyze the standard model with upper bounds, for $n = 2$.

1.4 In the model requiring collateral for short positions whose constraints are given in (1.15) or (1.16), what is the nominal return on the portfolio? Describe the expected return vector and covariance matrix. Does the form of the model change if E and V describe the probability distribution of real return?

The following exercises apply to the appendix to this chapter. Unless you are conversant with Lebesgue integrals, in these exercises assume that the random variables can take on only a finite number of values.

1.5 (a) Use the definition of expected value to show that if a random variable r takes on only nonnegative values, then $E(r) \geqslant 0$.

(b) Use (a) and the definition of $V(r)$ to show that - for any random variable r - $V(r) \geqslant 0$.

(c) Use (b) and equation (1.25a) to show that the covariance matrix C is positive semidefinite.

1.6 (a) Without using matrix notation or summation signs, write out

$$V(a_1 r_1 + a_2 r_2) =$$

(b) Assume $\sigma_1 > 0$ and $\sigma_2 > 0$. Show that

$$V[(r_1/\sigma_1) + (r_2/\sigma_2)] = 2 + 2\rho_{12}$$

$$V[(r_1/\sigma_1) - (r_2/\sigma_2)] = 2 - 2\rho_{12}$$

Here $(r_1/\sigma_1) + (r_2/\sigma_2)$ is a random variable of the form $a_1 r_1 + a_2 r_2$ where a_1 happens to equal $1/\sigma_1$, etc. (Hint: use (a) and the definition of correlation.)

(c) Show that, if $\sigma_1 > 0$ and $\sigma_2 > 0$, then

$$-1 \leqslant \rho_{12} \leqslant +1$$

(Hint: use exercises 1.6(b) and 1.5(b).)

2

The General Mean-Variance Portfolio Selection Model

All the models described in chapter 1 use the same definitions of obtainable and and efficient EV combinations, $E\sigma$ combinations, and portfolios. They differ only in the constraints imposed on the choice of portfolio. Each model includes choice variables $X_1, \ldots, X_n$. These variables may be required to be nonnegative, as are the variables in the standard model, and most but not all of the variables in the Tobin-Sharpe-Lintner model. On the other hand a variable may have a lower bound other than zero, as does X_{n+1} in the Tobin-Sharpe-Lintner model, or may have no lower bounds, as with the variables in Black's model. The variables may also be constrained by upper bounds.

In addition to the upper and lower bounds on individual variables, combinations of variables may be constrained by one or more linear equations - as in the standard, Tobin-Sharpe-Lintner, and Black's models (with one equation each) and in the model with collateral required for short positions (with two equations). Examples to be presented in the next chapter, based on more complex modeling considerations, show that additional linear equalities and inequalities may be required.

The general portfolio selection model (at least, as general as we shall consider in this volume) will allow any (finite) number of variables. These variables may or may not have lower bounds, and may or may not have upper bounds. Where lower bounds exist their values may or may not be zero. In addition to the possible lower and upper bounds, the choice of portfolio may be constrained by a (finite) number of linear equalities or linear inequalities. While the general model requires at least one variable, it allows there to be no constraints. Typical current applications may contain only a few variables (when analyzing broad classes of assets) or many hundreds of variables. Usually there are a relatively small number of constraints, but this is not required by either the theory or current computational capability.

Three Forms of the General Model

We shall present three versions of the general portfolio selection model, to be referred to as forms 0, 1, and 2. Form 0 repeats the description given above. Forms 1 and 2 seem simpler, but we will see that each of these forms is equivalent. It is sometimes more convenient to derive results using form 1, sometimes using form 2. Results derived using one form can be translated to either of the other forms without difficulty.

Definition The *general portfolio selection model, form 0*, consists of $n \geqslant 1$ variables subject to zero, one, or more constraints of the following types:

$$\begin{array}{lll} \text{(i)} & X_i \geqslant L_i & \text{for some } i \\ \text{(ii)} & X_i \leqslant U_i & \text{for some } i \\ \text{(iii)} & \alpha' X \geqslant c & \\ \text{(iv)} & \alpha' X \leqslant c & \\ \text{(v)} & \alpha' X = c & \end{array} \tag{2.1}$$

where α is a (constant) vector, and L_i, U_i, and c are (constant) scalars.

The definitions of obtainable and efficient EV combinations, obtainable and efficient $E\sigma$ combinations, and efficient portfolios, in terms of feasible portfolios and their E and V, remain as in chapter 1. A model is feasible if there exists at least one X which satisfies all constraints, and is infeasible otherwise.

Defintion The *general portfolio selection model, form 1*, is as follows. Let m and n be any integers such that $m \geqslant 0$ and $n \geqslant 1$. If $m = 0$ then every vector $(X_1, \ldots, X_n)$ is called "feasible." Otherwise let A be any m by n matrix

$$A = \begin{pmatrix} a_{11} & a_{12} & \cdots & a_{1n} \\ a_{21} & a_{22} & \cdots & a_{2n} \\ a_{m1} & a_{m2} & \cdots & a_{mn} \end{pmatrix} \tag{2.2}$$

and b be an m component vector

$$b' = (b_1, b_2, \ldots, b_m)$$

A portfolio $X' = (X_1, X_2, \ldots, X_n)$ is feasible if it satisfies

$$AX \geqslant b \tag{2.3}$$

Other definitions - of obtainable sets, efficient sets, and feasible model - are as in the model of form 0.

Definition The *general portfolio selection model, form 2*, is as follows. Let integers m and n be given such that both $m \geqslant 1$ and $n \geqslant 1$. Let A be any m by n

matrix, and b be an m component vector. Then a portfolio X is feasible if it satisfies

$$AX = b \tag{2.4a}$$

$$X \geqslant 0 \tag{2.4b}$$

Other definitions - of obtainable sets, efficient sets, and feasible model - are as in forms 0 and 1.

A model of form 1 consists of zero, one, or more constraints of type (iii), and is therefore already in form 0. We shall show, conversely, that for any model of form 0 there is an equivalent model of form 1. Similarly a model of form 2, consisting of constraints of types (i) and (v), is already in form 0. We shall show, conversely, that there is an equivalent model of form 2 for any model of form 0.

Definitions Two models are *equivalent* if they have the same set of efficient EV combinations. They are *strictly equivalent* if they have the same set of obtainable EV combinations.

The following are immediate consequences of the definitions of equivalence and strict equivalence. If two models are strictly equivalent then they are equivalent, but not necessarily vice versa. Equivalent models have the same set of efficient $E\sigma$ combinations; strictly equivalent models have the same set of obtainable $E\sigma$ combinations. If models A and B are equivalent (strictly equivalent) and X is an efficient (obtainable) portfolio of model A, then there is a portfolio of model B with the same E and V.

Theorem 2.1 Every model of form 0 is strictly equivalent to some model of form 1.

Proof We will prove the theorem by showing how to construct a strictly equivalent model of form 1 for any given model of form 0. Since a model of form 1 allows any number of constraints of type (iii), we need only show that models including constraints of types (i), (ii), (iv), and (v) can be transformed into strictly equivalent models with type (iii) constraints only. Since constraints (i) and (ii) are special cases of constraints of type (iii) and (iv) respectively, we only need be concerned with transforming constraints of types (iv) and (v). But a constraint of type (iv) can be transformed into one of type (iii) by multiplying both sides by -1; and any constraint of type (v) can be replaced by two constraints of type (iii) thus:

$$\alpha' X \geqslant \beta \tag{2.5a}$$

$$\alpha' X \leqslant \beta \tag{2.5b}$$

i.e.

$$-\alpha' X \geqslant -\beta \tag{2.5c}$$

These transformations do not change which X are feasible and infeasible, and therefore do not alter the set of obtainable EV combinations. ###

Theorem 2.2 Every model of form 0 is strictly equivalent to some model of form 2.

Proof Of the five types of constraints in form 0, only constraints of type (v) and of type (i) with $L_i = 0$ are immediately accommodated by form 2. In addition form 2 requires that $X_i \geqslant 0$ for every i, and that $m \geqslant 1$. We will first prove that every model of form 0 is strictly equivalent to some model of form 0 in which all variables are required to be nonnegative. We will then show that every model of the latter form is strictly equivalent to a model of form 2.

For every variable X_i which is not already constrained by $X_i \geqslant 0$, replace X_i by $Y_i - Z_i$ and add the requirements

$$Y_i \geqslant 0, \qquad Z_i \geqslant 0$$

We will refer to the given model of form 0, before the substitution of $Y_i - Z_i$ for X_i, as the *original model*, and that after the substitution as the *intermediate model*. (Eventually the list of variables, including new variables and excluding removed variables, can be relabeled as X_i for $i = 1, 2, \ldots, \tilde{n}$; but for the time being it is convenient to distinguish between the original X_i and the new Y_i and Z_i.) The substitution of $Y_i - Z_i$ transforms constraints of types (iii), (iv), and (v) into constraints of the same respective types, and transforms constraints of types (i) and (ii) into types (iii) and (iv). Further, it leaves E a homogeneous linear form in the variables, and V a homogeneous quadratic form. Thus the intermediate model is a portfolio selection model, at least of type 0 if not yet of type 2, with all of its variables required to be nonnegative. The intermediate model is strictly equivalent to the original model since: if $(Y_1, Z_1, Y_2, Z_2, \ldots, Y_n, Z_n)$ is a feasible portfolio for the intermediate model, then $(X_1, X_2, \ldots, X_n)$ with $X_i = Y_i - Z_i$ is feasible for the original model and has the same EV; and conversely if $(X_1, \ldots, X_n)$ is feasible for the original model, then $(Y_1, Z_1, Y_2, Z_2, \ldots, Y_n, Z_n)$ with $Y_i = \max(X_i, 0)$ and $Z_i = \max(-X_i, 0)$ is feasible for the intermediate model and has the same EV. (The argument here assumes that $Y_i - Z_i$ has been substituted for X_i, for all i. The general case is left as an exercise in notation.) Thus an EV combination is feasible for the intermediate model if and only if it is feasible for the original model.

We next show that the intermediate model is strictly equivalent to a model of form 2. (We now assume that the variables of the intermediate model have been relabeled $X_1, X_2, \ldots, X_n$, for suitable n.) Since constraints of types (i) and (ii) are instances of constraints of types (iii) and (iv), and a constraint of type (iii) can be transformed into one of type (iv) by multiplying through by -1, we need only show how a model consisting of constraints of type (iv) and (v) in nonnegative variables can be transformed into a strictly equivalent model conaining constraints only of type (v) in nonnegative variables. A constraint of type iv) may be written as

$$\alpha' X + X_{n+1} = c \tag{2.6a}$$

$$X_{n+1} \geqslant 0 \tag{2.6b}$$

'here

$$\mu_{n+1} = 0 \tag{2.6c}$$

$$\sigma_{i,n+1} = 0 \qquad \text{for } i = 1, \ldots, n+1 \tag{2.6d}$$

his introduces a new nonnegative variable, denoted here as X_{n+1}, usually called *slack variable*. Since there exists $X_{n+1} \geqslant 0$ which satisfies

$$\alpha' X = c - X_{n+1} \tag{2.7}$$

and only if

$$\alpha' X \leqslant c \tag{2.8}$$

e have not changed the set of $X = (X_1, \ldots, X_n)$ which are feasible. Since the lue of X_{n+1} does not affect the value of E and V, we have not altered the set ` obtainable EV combinations. We have thus produced a strictly equivalent odel. Repeating as necessary, perhaps introducing new variables $X_{n+2}, X_{n+3}, \ldots$, e obtain a model of form 2 which is strictly equivalent to the intermediate odel and therefore to the original model of form 0.

One final difference between form 0 and form 2 is that form 0 allows $m = 0$ ilc form 2 requires $m \geqslant 1$. The latter condition can be met by adding a ımmy variable and dummy constraint $X_{n+1} = 0$. (The purpose of the $m \geqslant 1$ quirement in the form 2 definition is to avoid having to distinguish, especially chapters 7-9, between cases in which the A matrix exists and those in which does not.) ###

strictly equivalent form 2 version of a form 0 model can be constructed in a ferent manner than in the above proof. In particular, rather than multiplying constraint of form (iii) through by -1 we can transform it into an equality by

$$\alpha' X - X_{n+1} = c \tag{2.9a}$$

$$X_{n+1} \geqslant 0 \tag{2.9b}$$

linear programming model (see chapter 8 and Dantzig, 1963) seeks to maxize a linear function subject to constraints (2.4a) and (2.4b). Thus the general rtfolio selection model seeks mean-variance efficiency for portfolios chosen bject to the same constraints as in a linear programming model. The set of sible X is the same for both models; the objectives are different.

Nonlinear Examples

This section provides an example of models which are equivalent but not strictly equivalent. At the same time it illustrates the possibility of constructing a linear model (i.e. a general portfolio selection model of form 0, 1, or 2) equivalent to a model with certain nonlinearities. Finally, the section contains a nonlinear model which is not equivalent to any linear model. While the examples and results of this section illustrate an interesting and valuable adjunct to the main results of this book, they are not required for reading the chapters which follow.

Suppose that an investor can borrow funds at a rate which increases with the amount borrowed. The total cost of borrowing $f(Y)$ is given as follows (see figure 2.1):

$$f(Y)=\begin{cases} c_1Y & \text{for } 0\leqslant Y\leqslant u_1 \\ c_1u_1+c_2(Y-u_1) & \text{for } u_1\leqslant Y\leqslant u_2 \\ c_1u_1+c_2(u_2-u_1)+c_3(Y-u_2) & \text{for } u_2\leqslant Y\leqslant u_3 \\ c_1u_1+c_2(u_2-u_1)+c_3(u_3-u_2)+c_4(Y-u_3) & \text{for } u_3\leqslant Y\leqslant u_4 \end{cases} \tag{2.10}$$

Credit is not available for $Y\geqslant u_4$. c_1 may in fact be the cost to the investor of "borrowing" from his or her own savings account which would otherwise draw c_1u_1 in interest. Conceivably, $f(Y)$ could be a piecewise linear approximation to some smooth function $g(Y)$.

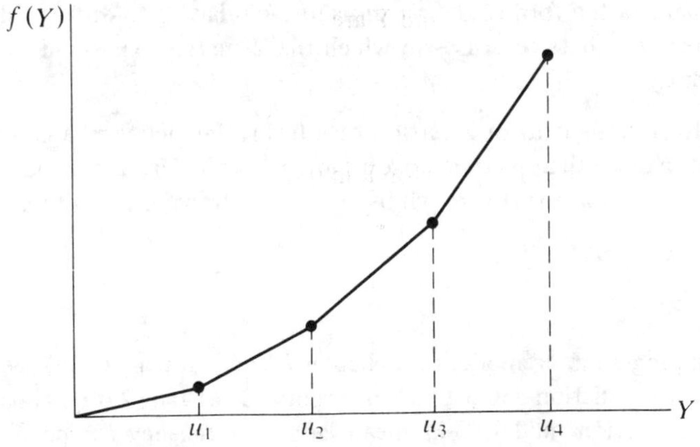

Figure 2.1 Nonlinear cost of borrowing

In this simple model we assume that Y, the proceeds of the borrowing, will be invested in a single security with mean μ_s and variance V_s. If we include the interest on the u_1 in the savings account, then the expected return to a plan which borrows Y is

$$E = u_1 c_1 + Y\mu_s - f(Y) \tag{2.11a}$$

If we ignore the interest on the savings account we have

$$E = Y\mu_s - f(Y) \tag{2.11b}$$

This subtracts the same constant from the E of every feasible EV combination, but otherwise does not alter the feasible and efficient EV combinations or the Y values associated with them. Using (2.11b), as we shall, only shifts the origin of the E axis in the analysis.

The variance associated with a particular investment Y invested in the one security is

$$V = V_s Y^2 \tag{2.12}$$

In the first instance we will assume that

$$c_1 < c_2 < \mu_s = c_3 < c_4 \tag{2.13}$$

Our first task is to find the feasible and efficient EV combinations and their corresponding Y for

$$0 \leqslant Y \leqslant u_4$$

For

$$0 \leqslant Y \leqslant u_1$$

the relationships between V, E, and Y are

$$V = V_s Y^2 \tag{2.14}$$

$$E = (\mu_s - c_1)\, Y \tag{2.15}$$

Since $(\mu_s - c_1) > 0$ we may solve for Y in terms of E to obtain

$$V = \frac{V_s}{(\mu_s - c_1)^2} E^2 \tag{2.16}$$

and

$$\frac{dV}{dE} = \frac{2V_s E}{(\mu_s - c_1)^2} \tag{2.17}$$

In particular, at $E = (\mu_s - c_1) u_1$ we have $dV/dE = 2u_1 V_s/(\mu_s - c_1)$.

For $u_1 \leqslant Y \leqslant u_2$, V remains as in (2.12), whereas E is

$$E = (\mu_s - c_1)\,u_1 + (\mu_s - c_2)\,(Y - u_1) \tag{2.18a}$$

i.e.

$$Y = \frac{E - (c_2 - c_1)\,u_1}{(\mu_s - c_2)} \tag{2.18b}$$

Thus

$$V = \frac{V_s}{(\mu_s - c_2)^2}\,[E^2 - 2E(c_2 - c_1)\,u_1 + (c_2 - c_1)^2 u_1^2] \tag{2.19a}$$

and

$$\frac{dV}{dE} = \frac{2V_s}{(\mu_s - c_2)^2}\,[E - (c_2 - c_1)\,u_1] \tag{2.19b}$$

Evaluating this at $Y = u_1$, i.e. at $E = (\mu_s - c_1)\,u_1$, we have

$$\left(\frac{dV}{dE}\right)_{Y=u_1} = \frac{2V_s u_1}{\mu_s - c_2}$$

$$> \frac{2V_s u_1}{\mu_s - c_1}$$

Thus the parabola which relates V to E between

$$0 \leqslant E \leqslant (\mu_s - c_1)\,u_1$$

has a smaller slope at $E = (\mu_s - c_1)\,u_1$ than does the parabola relating V to E for

$$(\mu_s - c_1)\,u_1 \leqslant E \leqslant (\mu_s - c_1)\,u_1 + (\mu_s - c_2)\,(u_2 - u_1)$$

Figure 2.2 shows a kink at a where the two parabolas meet.

For

$$u_2 \leqslant Y \leqslant u_3$$

V continues to increase according to (2.12), while E is given by

$$E = (\mu_s - c_1)\,u_1 + (\mu_s - c_2)\,(u_2 - u_1) + (\mu_s - c_3)\,(Y - u_2)$$

Our assumption that $\mu_s = c_3$ implies that E is a constant for $u_2 \leqslant Y \leqslant u_3$, and the curve showing the EV combinations for each Y rises vertically from $(E^*, V_s u_2^2)$ to $(E^*, V_s u_3^2)$, where E^* is the value of E at $Y = u_2$. On this segment only the point at $(E^*, V_s u_2^2)$ is efficient.

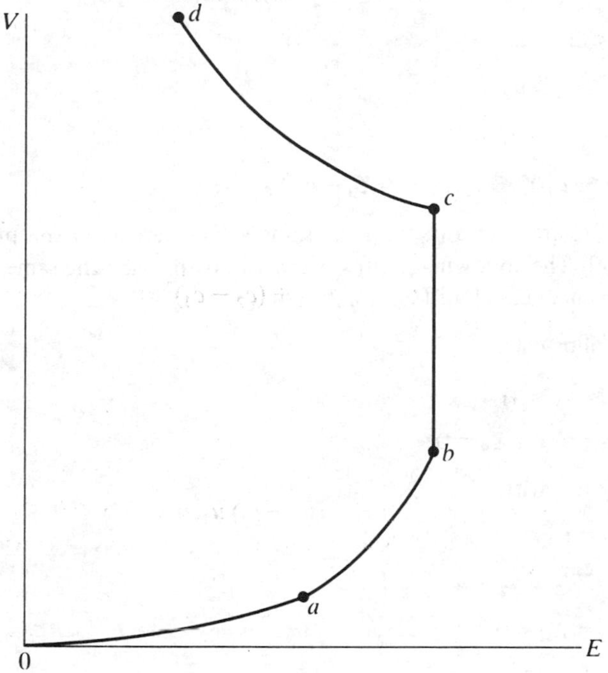

Figure 2.2 Obtainable EV combinations for nonlinear model

For

$u_3 \leqslant Y \leqslant u_4$

V continues to rise, but E falls since $c_4 > \mu_s$. No point on this segment is efficient.

The entire obtainable set, as shown in figure 2.2, consists of two rising parabolic sections meeting at the kink a, a vertical section, and a parabolic section moving up and to the left from the top of the vertical section. Only the arc $0ab$ is efficient.

We next exhibit a general portfolio selection model - written in form 0, but it could be written in form 1 or 2 - which is equivalent to the above nonlinear model. We will then show that no general portfolio selection model can be strictly equivalent to the above nonlinear model.

Consider the following portfolio selection model. Choose X_1, X_2, X_3, X_4, Y subject to constraints

$$Y = X_1 + X_2 + X_3 + X_4 \tag{2.20a}$$

$$0 \leqslant X_1 \leqslant u_1$$

$$0 \leqslant X_2 \leqslant u_2 - u_1 \tag{2.20b}$$

$$0 \leqslant X_3 \leqslant u_3 - u_2$$

$$0 \leqslant X_4 \leqslant u_4 - u_3$$

$$V = V_s Y^2 \tag{2.20c}$$

$$E = \mu_s Y - c_1 X_1 - c_2 X_2 - c_3 X_3 - c_4 X_4 \tag{2.20d}$$

The u_i and c_i are constants with the same values here as in the preceding nonlinear model. The following groups of portfolios provide the same EV combinations as the curve $0abcd$ of figure 2.2:

(1) Portfolios with

$$0 \leqslant X_1 \leqslant u_1$$

$$X_2 = X_3 = X_4 = 0$$

(2) Portfolios with

$$X_1 = u_1$$

$$0 \leqslant X_2 \leqslant u_2 - u_1$$

$$X_3 = X_4 = 0$$

(3) Portfolios with

$$X_1 = u_1$$

$$X_2 = u_2 - u_1$$

$$0 \leqslant X_3 \leqslant u_3 - u_2$$

$$X_4 = 0$$

(4) Portfolios with

$$X_1 = u_1$$

$$X_2 = u_2 - u_1$$

$$X_3 = u_3 - u_2$$

$$0 \leqslant X_4 \leqslant u_4 - u_3$$

The reader can confirm that portfolios in group (1) provide the same E and V as the portfolios in the nonlinear model with $0 \leqslant Y \leqslant u_1$; those in group 2 provide the same EV combinations as the portfolios in the nonlinear model with $u_1 \leqslant Y \leqslant u_2$; those in group (3) the same as the nonlinear model for $u_2 \leqslant Y \leqslant u_3$; and those in group (4) the same as for $u_3 \leqslant Y \leqslant u_4$. Furthermore, V depends only on Y, and no combinations of X can produce the same Y with higher E

than those listed in the above groups. Thus the EV combinations which maximize E for given V in model (2.20) are the same as the solutions to the nonlinear model. In particular, model (2.20) and the nonlinear model (2.10)-(2.12) have the same set of efficient EV combinations and are therefore equivalent.

We now show that they do not have the same set of obtainable EV combinations and therefore are not *strictly* equivalent. Consider the following groups of portfolios which are feasible for model (2.20):

(1′) Portfolios with

$$0 \leqslant X_4 \leqslant u_4 - u_3$$

$$X_1 = X_2 = X_3 = 0$$

(2′) Portfolios with

$$X_4 = u_4 - u_3$$

$$0 \leqslant X_3 \leqslant u_3 - u_2$$

$$X_1 = X_2 = 0$$

(3′) Portfolios with

$$X_4 = u_4 - u_3$$

$$X_3 = u_3 - u_2$$

$$0 \leqslant X_2 \leqslant u_2 - u_1$$

$$X_1 = 0$$

(4′) Portfolios with

$$X_4 = u_4 - u_3$$

$$X_3 = u_3 - u_2$$

$$X_2 = u_2 - u_1$$

$$0 \leqslant X_1 \leqslant u_1$$

Since $c_4 \geqslant \mu_s$, portfolios in group (1′) have negative E. In fact the portfolios in group (1′) provide minimum E for given V for $Y \leqslant u_4 - u_3$; and, generally, the groups (1′), (2′), (3′), (4′) provide the left-hand boundary of the set of obtainable EV combinations for model (2.20). The entire boundary of the set of obtainable EV combinations is the curve 0*abcdefg*0 in figure 2.3. The segments of this boundary, reading counter-clockwise, correspond to portfolio groups, (1), (2), (3), (4), (4′), (3′), (2′), (1′). Furthermore, we will show later (theorem 10.1) that, in any general portfolio selection model, if both (E_0, V_0) and (E_0, V_1) are obtainable then so is (E_0, V) for all V between V_0 and V_1. So the set of

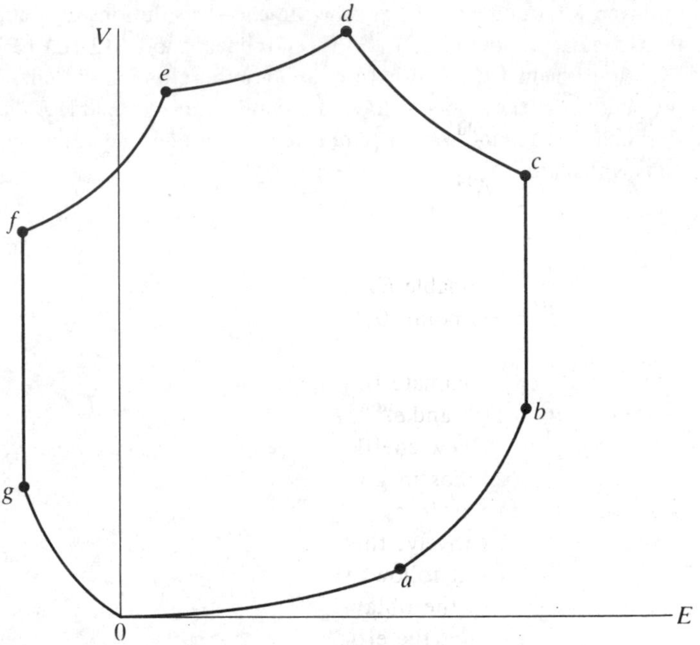

Figure 2.3 *Obtainable EV combinations for linear model (2.20)*

obtainable EV combinations for (2.20) includes not only the boundary of figure 2.3, but its interior as well.

The set of obtainable EV combinations for the nonlinear model (2.10)-(2.12) differs, therefore, from that of the portfolio selection model (2.20), but their sets of efficient EV combinations are identical. These models are equivalent but not strictly equivalent.

The nonlinear model (2.10)-(2.12) could be solved without transforming it into a linear model (2.20). This is not always possible in more complex models. In models with dozens or hundreds of variables, the method illustrated above can sometimes be used to incorporate nonlinear relationships into a linear model.

However, for a given nonlinear model it is not always possible to create an equivalent portfolio selection model (of form 0, 1, or 2). Consider a nonlinear model like that in (2.10)-(2.12) except with new c_i and u_i related to the old ones as follows:

$$c_1^{\text{new}} = c_4^{\text{old}}$$

$$c_2^{\text{new}} = c_3^{\text{old}}$$

$$c_3^{\text{new}} = c_2^{\text{old}}$$

$$c_4^{\text{new}} = c_1^{\text{old}}$$

$$u_1^{\text{new}} = u_4^{\text{old}} - u_3^{\text{old}}$$

$$u_2^{\text{new}} - u_1^{\text{new}} = u_3^{\text{old}} - u_2^{\text{old}}$$

$$u_3^{\text{new}} - u_2^{\text{new}} = u_2^{\text{old}} - u_1^{\text{old}}$$

$$u_4^{\text{new}} - u_3^{\text{new}} = u_1^{\text{old}}$$

In this case the set of obtainable EV combinations is the curve 0*gfed* in figure 2.3. The efficient set is the point (0, 0) and that part of the curve *fed* which lies to the right of the V axis.

Suppose we try to approximate this nonlinear model by (2.20) with the new u_i and c_i now equal to u_i^{new} and c_i^{new}. By construction, portfolios in groups (1), (2), (3), and (4) with the new coefficients will provide, respectively, the same EV combinations as portfolios in groups (1′), (2′), (3′), and (4′) with the old coefficients. Also, portfolios in groups (1′), (2′), (3′), and (4′) with the new coefficients provide, respectively, the same EV combinations as those in (1), (2), (3), (4) with the old. It follows that we again have the entire area within 0*abcdefg*0 of figure 2.3 as the obtainable set; and therefore have 0*ab* as the efficient set. Since this is not the efficient set for the nonlinear model, in this case the two models are not equivalent.

One way to view why model (2.20) is equivalent to (2.10)-(2.12) for the old coefficients and not for the new, is to consider which X_i should be used first and which next if our objective is to maximize E for given V in model (2.20). With the old coefficients - if we are given the constraints of model (2.20), told nothing of model (2.10)-(2.12), and asked to maximize E for given V - we should use X_1 first, since it supplies Y for the smallest cost c_1, X_2 second, X_3 third, and X_4 last. Portfolio group (1) uses X_1 only, with $X_2 = X_3 = X_4 = 0$; portfolio group (2) uses X_1 to the maximum extent permitted, $X_1 = u_1$, uses X_2 as required, and keeps $X_3 = X_4 = 0$; group (3) uses X_1 and X_2 to the maximum extent permitted, uses X_3 as required, and keeps $X_4 = 0$; group (4) uses X_1, X_2, and X_3 to the maximum extent permitted. These four groups provide, respectively, segments 0*a*, *ab*, *bc*, and *cd* of the right-hand boundary of the set of obtainable EV combinations. (Only segments 0*a* and *ab* are efficient, but all four maximize E for given V.) By using X_1 first, X_2 second, etc. among the portfolios which maximize E for given V - and, in particular, among the efficient portfolios - model (2.20) in effect uses the nonlinear borrowing function (2.10).

Next suppose we are given model (2.20), told nothing of model (2.10)-(2.12), and again asked to maximize E for given V - but this time for the new coefficients. To maximize E for given V in model (2.20) using the new coefficients, X_4 should be used first since this provides Y at the smallest cost c_4^{new}; X_3 should be used next; then X_2; then X_1. But when the X are used in this sequence, the cost of Y is not the same as $f(Y)$ in (2.10) for the new coefficients. (*Exercise* Draw $f(Y)$ for the new coefficients. Note that it is a concave function with decreasing costs, rather than a convex function with increasing costs as with the old coefficients, as shown in figure 2.1. Confirm that if X_4 is used first, X_3 second, etc. (with the new coefficients) then the cost of Y in model (2.20) is not $f(Y)$ in (2.10) with the new coefficients. In fact, it is $f(Y)$ with the old coefficients.)

Whether we intend model (2.20) as an approximation to the first or second nonlinear model, the X_i with the lowest c_i is "used first" (by an algorithm that generates EV efficient sets for the general portfolio selection model) to maximize E for given V; that with the second lowest is used second; etc. In one case this is in accord with the specifications of the nonlinear model; in the other it is not. In more complex models, if nonlinear relationships are incorporated in the above manner it must be demonstrated that there is a particular order in which the new variables (X_i above) will be used, and that this corresponds to the nonlinear relationships.

It might be thought that if we worked harder we could find a portfolio selection model (with linear constraints) which would be equivalent (if not strictly equivalent) to the nonlinear model with the new c_i. But no such equivalent model exists. In chapter 5 we define the concept of a convex function and show that min V as a function of E is a convex function for any instance of a general portfolio selection model; but the efficient set for (2.10)–(2.12) with the new c_i does not have V as a convex function of E.

Historical Note

This section briefly sketches the genesis of the models defined in chapters 1 and 2. Hicks (1962) describes portfolio theory as "a formalisation of an approach with which economists have been familiar since ... 1935," referring to Hicks (1935). Hicks (1935) states that

> Now in a world where cost of investment was negligible, everyone would be able to take considerable advantage of [the following] sort of risk-reduction. By dividing up his capital into small portions, and spreading his risks, he would be able to insure himself against any large total risk on the whole amount. But in actuality, the cost of investment, making it definitely unprofitable to invest less than a certain minimum amount in any particular direction, closes the possibility of risk-reduction along these lines to all those who do not possess the command over considerable quantities of capital.

Thus Hicks believed that the reason an investor could not diversify away risk was because of the indivisibility of assets. He had either not seen that investment returns are often correlated, or not realized that diversification among correlated risks does not make portfolio variance approach zero. (For a portfolio with equal percentage invested in each security, as the number of securities increases the variance of the portfolio approaches the average of the covariances among investments; Markowitz, 1959, chapter 5.)

While Hicks did not properly identify the reason why diversification could not eliminate risk from a portfolio of risky assets, he did to an extent anticipate the Tobin (1958) analysis of how the remaining risk in the portfolio of risky assets causes a demand for riskless assets:

> ... since most people do not possess sufficient resources to enable them to take much advantage of the law of large numbers, and since even the large capitalist cannot annihilate his risks altogether in this manner, there will be a tendency to spread capital over a number of investments, not for this purpose, but for another. By investing only a proportion of total assets in risky enterprises, and investing the remainder in ways which are considered more safe, it will be possible for the individual to adjust his whole risk-situation to that which he most prefers, more closely than he could do by investing in any single enterprise.

Hicks (1962) includes an appendix showing some details along these lines, assuming independent returns:

> It can, I believe, be shown that the main properties which I hope to demonstrate remain valid whatever the r's; but I shall not attempt to offer a general proof in this place. I shall simplify by assuming that the prospects of the various investments are uncorrelated ($r_{jk} = 0$ when $k \neq j$): an assumption with which, in any case, it is natural to begin.

Curiously, Hicks (1962) does not cite Tobin (1958) as having presented a general proof allowing any nonsingular C matrix.

Another forerunner of modern portfolio theory is Dickson Leavens (1945). Leavens uses variance as a measure of the riskiness of a bond portfolio, and shows how risk declines with the number of bonds held, assuming uncorrelated returns.

The era of modern portfolio theory opened with two papers published in 1952. Roy (1952) uses the same constraint set as does what we call Black's model. (Had his objective been to trace out mean-variance efficient sets we would have called it Roy's model.) Roy prescribes that we pick from his constraint set the specific "safety-first" portfolio which maximizes $(E-d)/\sigma$ where d is some disastrous level of return. Later, after the notion of an EV efficient set had been introduced, Baumol (1963) argued that a safety-first portfolio with minimum $E - k\sigma$ (for k equal to 2 or 3, for example) has as low an E and V as the investor should choose from the EV efficient set, since $E - k\sigma$ is a more reasonable measure of risk than σ itself. In fact, Levy (1985) shows conditions under which any EV efficient portfolio with smaller E and V than the safety-first efficient portfolio, with $k = 1$, will be "stochastically dominated" (Hadar and Russell, 1969; Hanoch and Levy, 1969) by an EV efficient portfolio with greater E and V, reinforcing Baumol's argument.

Markowitz (1952), the other paper opening the era of modern portfolio theory, defined EV efficiency, assumed what we call the standard portfolio selection model, and illustrated with graphical analysis the piecewise linear nature of the set of efficient portfolios. The general portfolio selection model described in chapter 2 was presented in Markowitz (1956), along with the critical line algorithm for computing efficient sets.

While modern portfolio theory may be dated from 1952, it did not stir a great visible interest until after the works of Tobin (1958), Sharpe (1963, 1964), and Lintner (1965). For example, William Baranek (of Weston and Baranek, 1955) tells me that he was asked to read and report on Markowitz (1952) when he was a graduate student at UCLA in the early 1950s. He proposed that he work on portfolio theory for his dissertation, but was advised to work on something more practical instead.

Tobin (1958) uses portfolio theory to analyze "liquidity preference." While the assumption of unlimited borrowing is not realistic, it has the virtue that the model (which we call the Tobin-Sharpe-Lintner model) can be solved analytically, as compared with the general model for which an algorithm exists but no single set of equations describes all solutions. A crucial property of the Tobin-Sharpe-Lintner model, as shown in Tobin (1958), is what is now called the *Tobin separation theorem*. Typically the set of efficient portfolios for this model consists of: (1) a portfolio X^* containing risky assets only, without borrowing or lending, and (2) portfolios consisting of portfolio X^* plus borrowing, or portfolio X^* plus lending. Thus the choice of proportions among risky assets, portfolio X^*, may be considered a *separate* decision from the choice of borrowing or lending. X^* is determined by C and μ only. The choice of amount to borrow or lend depends, in addition, on the risk preferences of each investor.

Sharpe (1964) and Lintner (1965) apply portfolio theory to the problem of equilibrium pricing of capital assets generally. Since they assume Tobin's constraint set they obtain the Tobin separation theorem. Since all investors hold the same proportions X^* among risky assets plus more or less borrowing or lending, X^* must be the market portfolio. In particular, the market – i.e. the portfolio whose proportion in the ith security equals the ratio of the security's total market value to that of all securities – is an efficient portfolio. In addition Sharpe and Lintner derive the dramatically simple formula that

$$\mu_i - r_0 = k\beta_i \qquad (2.21)$$

for every security i, where r_0 is the expected return on the riskless asset and β_i is the regression of r_i on the market portfolio. Mossin (1966) shows that these Sharpe-Lintner results are also true in equilibrium if we drop the requirement $X_i \geqslant 0$ from the Tobin constraint set - that is, if we assume "Black's model" plus a riskless asset.

Tobin's separation theorem shows that every efficient portfolio is a mixture

$$X = \alpha X^* + (1 - \alpha) X^{\mathrm{C}}$$

where X^{C} is a portfolio consisting only of cash; X^* is a portfolio - or "mutual fund" - consisting only of risky assets; and α is a scalar, $\alpha \geqslant 0$. Sharpe (1970, pp. 59-62) and Merton (1972) show that if the only constraint is $\Sigma X_i = 1$ then - whether or not there is a riskless asset - every efficient portfolio is of the form

$$X = \alpha X^* + (1 - \alpha) \hat{X}$$

with $\alpha \geqslant 0$, where $\hat{X}$ is the efficient portfolio with minimum variance. This result is called the *two-funds separation theorem*. Black (1972) further shows that (2.21) is true when $\Sigma X_i = 1$ is the only constraint, whether or not there is a riskless asset, except that now r_0 is the expected return on a zero β portfolio.

We shall frequently refer to the portfolio selection model whose only constraint is $\Sigma X_i = 1$, since it is a simple special case of an important class of models, namely models whose constraint set is *affine*. (The importance of such affine models is due, at least in part, to their role in the analysis of the general model, as presented particularly in chapters 6 and 7.) I refer to the model whose only constraint is $\Sigma_i X_i = 1$ as Black's model, for ease of reference and because the results of Black (1972) are frequently cited in connection with this model. It would probably be more accurate to name it Roy-Sharpe-Merton-Black, but that is a lot of name for a simple, frequently cited model.

Black (1972) also analyzes a model in which

$$\sum_{i=1}^{n+1} X_i = 1 \tag{2.22a}$$

$$X_{n+1} \geqslant 0 \tag{2.22b}$$

(only the one security has the nonnegativity constraint) where r_{n+1} has zero variance. This model is explored later in this book - specifically in exercises 7.8 and 12.9 - and is there called the Black (1972) second model.

The first "more realistic" model of short sales in portfolio theory appears in Lintner (1965). In addition to analyzing a model with short sales prohibited, Lintner describes actual constraints on short sales, and notes that "the short seller will receive interests at the riskless rate r^* on the sales price placed in escrow, and he may or may not also receive interest at the same rate on his cash remittance to the lender of the stock. To facilitate the formal analysis, we *assume* that *both interest components* are *always received* by the short seller, and that margin requirements are 100%"[1] (italics in original). Lintner then derives the optimum portfolio for the individual investor, assuming unlimited borrowing or lending at the rate r^*. Since the latter assumption implies the Tobin separation theorem, Lintner (1965) concludes that there will be no short sales in equilibrium when all investors believe the same C and μ.

Exercises

2.1 Rewrite the following portfolio selection models in form 1:

(a) The standard model
(b) The standard model with upper bounds
(c) The Tobin-Sharpe-Lintner model
(d) Black's model.

2.2 Which model(s) in exercise 2.1 are already in form 2? Rewrite the others in form 2.

2.3 Let $AX \geqslant b$ be the constraints of a model in form 1. Choose a new coordinate system for the space of portfolios so that

$$Y = HX$$
$$X = KY$$

where $HK = I$; X is the portfolio in terms of the old coordinate system; and Y is the corresponding portfolio in terms of the new coordinate system. Show that there are $\bar{A}, \bar{C}, \bar{\mu}$ such that the constraints on Y are

$$\bar{A}Y \geqslant b$$

and E and V in terms of Y are

$$E = \bar{\mu}'Y$$
$$V = Y'\bar{C}Y$$

Conclude that a linear transformation of coordinates transforms a model in form 1 into a strictly equivalent model, *still in form 1*.

2.4 Suppose that a model requires $AX = b$, $X \geqslant 0$, and has $V = X'CX$. However,

$$E = \sum_{i=1}^{n-1} \mu_i X_i + f(X_n)$$

where $f(X_n)$ is piecewise linear with a finite number of pieces.

[1] In the model of short sales requiring collateral in chapter 1, the fact that "the short seller ... may or may not also receive interest ... on his cash remittance to the lender of the stock" is reflected in the expected return associated with X_{iS}.

(a) If the slope of $f(X_n)$ decreases with X_n, is there always an equivalent portfolio selection model (e.g. a model in form 2)?

(b) If the slope of $f(X_n)$ increases with X_n, is there always an equivalent portfolio selection model?

2.5 Show that, if $\mu_i \neq \mu_j$ for some i and j between 1 and n in a standard portfolio selection model, then there is no equivalent model with constraint set

$$AX = b$$

Conclude that it is not true that, for any model of form 0, there is an equivalent (much less a strictly equivalent) model whose constraints are $AX = b$. (Hint: note that E is bounded in the standard model, but if two feasible portfolios have different E, then E is unbounded in a model whose constraint set is $AX = b$.)

3

Capabilities and Assumptions of the General Model

Chapter 1 contains certain specific portfolio selection models, namely the standard, standard with upper bounds, Tobin-Sharpe-Lintner, Black's, and a more complex but still simplified model requiring collateral for short sales. In chapter 2 we saw that each of these is a special case of a general portfolio selection model allowing any number of variables which may or may not have upper and lower bounds and, in addition, may be subject to any number of linear equalities and/or inequalities. The principal objective of the remainder of this book is to solve and apply this general portfolio selection model.

The present chapter further explores the assumptions and capabilities of the model of chapter 2. We first consider why we trouble ourselves with the more general assumption that the covariance matrix is positive semidefinite rather than restrict ourselves to the somewhat more convenient assumption that it be positive definite. Next, we further illustrate how systems of linear equalities and inequalities can be used to model various financial situations. Finally, we summarize the arguments supporting our fundamental assumption – the use of mean and variance as criteria for portfolio selection.

Semidefinite Covariance Matrices

It is sometimes assumed in financial theory that the covariance matrix C is nonsingular, and therefore positive definite. In this book we shall assume only that C is positive semidefinite, admitting the possibility that it is either singular or nonsingular. We shall note, however, that certain results can occur only when C is singular.

One reason for assuming semidefinite C, rather than definite C, is that the former includes the latter as a special case; the central results of mean-variance theory are obtainable for the former generally as well as the latter in particular. Even if we had no immediate applications with singular C, it would nevertheless be valuable to solve the general problem, in case a singular C were someday encountered.

But in fact there already exist applications in theory and practice with singular C. We will describe three of these.

(1) Sometimes practitioners or research analysts use historical covariance matrices, sometimes computing these with fewer periods than there are securities. In this case C must inevitably be singular. Perhaps it would be wiser to use a model of covariance, discussed below, but in any case we note that the critical line algorithm for computing EV efficient sets still succeeds, and most of the salient geometric facts about efficient sets hold true for such singular C matrices.

(2) In transforming a portfolio selection model in form 0 to a strictly equivalent one in form 2, which is standard for computation, we introduce slack variables with zero variances. Their introduction makes any C singular. Such slack variables are also introduced in the piecewise linear approximation of nonlinear relationships.

(3) To a close approximation, the return from buying a call plus the return from writing (selling) a put on the same stock is perfectly correlated with the return from holding the stock. Thus if puts, calls, and stock are each allowed in the portfolio, and the aforementioned approximation is made in estimating their variances and covariances, C will be singular.

In sum, a positive semidefinite as opposed to a positive definite C is assumed in case some reader would like a theory or computing procedure which applies (1) when covariances equal historical observations for fewer periods than there are securities, or (2) the constraint set requires introduction of slack variables, or (3) the list of securities includes the writing and/or buying of puts and calls as well as the buying or shorting of the underlying security, or (4) for some currently unforeseen need for greater generality.

Portfolio Constraints in Theory and Practice

Mean-variance analysis is used in at least two ways: (1) actual portfolios are selected and money allocated based on mean-variance analysis; and (2) the economy is analyzed assuming all investors seek mean-variance efficiency. We will refer to these as the *money management* and the *economic analysis* uses, respectively, of mean-variance analysis.

Economic analysis using mean-variance typically assumes highly simplified constraint sets. In particular the Tobin-Sharpe-Lintner and the Black model (requiring a riskless asset as in Mossin, 1966, or not requiring one as in Black, 1972) are most commonly assumed. Surely J. Tobin, W. Sharpe, and J. Lintner knew, as well as you and I know, that if your net worth is \$1,000,000 the bank will not loan you \$1,000,000,000. Surely F. Black and J. Mossin knew that if you have \$10,000 at a broker, you cannot short \$1,000,000 of security A and use the proceeds plus your own money to buy \$1,010,000 worth of security B, as the Black model allows.

The reason for models incorporating such assumptions is that they imply simple relationships among interesting economic magnitudes. In chapter 12 we will see that some of the simple relationships implied by these models also hold for somewhat more general constraints, albeit they do not hold generally.

When mean-variance is used for actual money management, more complex constraints are imposed on the choice of portfolio reflecting either legal requirements or management policy. Upper bounds on individual holdings of securities, as discussed in chapter 1, are a frequent requirement. Some further examples of constraints which do or could arise in practice are discussed in the next few sections. Our examples will be concerned with the choice of a portfolio of stocks, bonds, or other readily marketed securities, although mean-variance analysis has also been applied to other areas such as capital budgeting, agricultural planning, and selecting the assets and liabilities of insurance companies.

Industry Constraints

Upper bounds are sometimes imposed on the percent of the portfolio which may be invested in any one industry. If $S_1, S_2, \ldots, S_K$ are subsets of the numbers $1, 2, \ldots, n$, with S_k containing all i for securities in the kth industry, then industry constraints take the form

$$\sum_{i \in S_k} X_i \leqslant w_k \qquad \text{for } k = 1, \ldots, K \tag{3.1}$$

where w_k is the upper bound on the investment in the kth industry, and the sum in the kth constraint is taken of those X_i in industry S_k. While constraints (3.1) are usual in practice, one can imagine more complex industrial constraints. Many firms are in more than one industry. The general portfolio selection model permits industry constraints of the following form:

$$\sum_{j=1}^{n} a_{kj} X_j \leqslant w_k \qquad \text{for } k = 1, \ldots, K \tag{3.2}$$

where a_{kj} represents the contribution which the jth security makes to the portfolio's "being into" the kth industry. Constraint (3.1) is a special case of (3.2).

It is reasonable that constraints such as (3.1) and (3.2) are omitted from economic models in which investors are assumed to act rationally on the basis of probability beliefs μ and C. Diversification across industries should be a consequence of beliefs rather than an input to the model.

On the other hand, the use of constraints of type (3.1) and (3.2) in practice is also understandable and defensible. For example, in an analysis with say 200 securities, a portfolio management team cannot consider carefully, one at a time, the roughly 20,000 covariances needed as input to the model. Frequently some kind of model of covariance is used, such as those described below, with parameters fit to historical data. But even if a model fit well in the past it may have to be amended in the future. Maybe the present will be the period in which some event causes a major revision of the model. The management team would like to take advantage of the model as long as it works, but not stick their neck out too far in case it fails. Constraints (3.1) and (3.2), and the upper bounds on individual securities discussed in chapter 1, allow the model to seek optimum diversification given the estimates, but not exceed the team's "comfort level" with respect to prudent portfolios. After all, low portfolio variance requires avoidance of systematic risk, and the methodology of the statistician who supplies the estimated C matrix can itself be a source of systematic risk.

Constraints (3.1) and (3.2) are of type (iv) in the general portfolio selection model, form 0 (see equation (2.1)), and are thus allowed in the general analysis of the following chapters. Instead of – or in addition to – relations (3.1) and (3.2), the general model could include constraints of type (iv) involving other categories of securities such as "growth stocks" or stocks of large companies versus stocks of small companies, etc. These categories may overlap each other and overlap the industry categories; a particular X_i may appear in several such constraints. Nevertheless, any collection of such constraints is permitted in the general model defined in chapter 2; its efficient sets have the properties derived in chapters 7-9, and these sets can be computed by the algorithm in chapter 13. If the constraints ask "too much", so that no portfolio meets all constraints, then the algorithm will announce that the model is infeasible.

Models of Covariance

We have seen that a portfolio analysis may include "fictitious" securities such as the slack variables discussed in chapter 2. Fictitious securities, plus constraints which assure that the amounts "invested" in these securities are in accord with the meaning of these "securities," often arise from the way in which a model of covariance is incorporated into a mean-variance analysis. In this section we consider some models of covariance and the portfolio constraints which they generate.

In an analysis with 200 securities, for example, it may be reasonable to expect a portfolio management team to prepare 200 carefully considered estimates of expected return and 200 carefully prepared estimates of standard deviation of return, but it is not reasonable to expect the team to prepare $199 \times 200/2 = 19{,}900$ individually considered estimates of covariances. On the other hand, the use of historical covariances as estimates of the covariances among forthcoming returns has at least two problems. First, unaltered history may lack information currently known about the status of specific securities; and second, sometimes the number of periods of relevant data is less than the number of securities analyzed. If we calculate a 200 by 200 covariance matrix from fewer than 200 periods the resulting C matrix will be singular. This implies that there will be a set of weights $W \neq 0$ such that

$$W'CW = 0$$

These weights may not constitute a feasible portfolio. But even if the portfolios which are actually chosen do not have zero estimated variance, the fact that the C matrix used would ascribe a zero V to a weighted sum $\Sigma W_i r_i$ of (perhaps positive and negative) "bets" among risky securities, is cause for concern as to the accuracy of the C matrix.

One approach to this difficulty has been to use one or another model of covariance. For example, suppose that the return on each security were generated as follows:

$$r_i = \alpha_i + \beta_i F + u_i \tag{3.3}$$

where the u_i are random variables with $E(u_i) = 0$ for $i = 1, \ldots, n$; $\text{cov}(u_i, u_j) = 0$ for $i \neq j$; $\text{cov}(u_i, F) = 0$ for $i = 1, \ldots, n$; α_i and β_i are constants, and F is a random factor which may affect any of the r_i. This model was suggested by Markowitz (1959); Sharpe (1963) and Cohen and Pogue (1967) concluded that it did as well as more complex models of covariance. This conclusion was disputed by King (1966) and Rosenberg (1974). Originally historical β_i were used to estimate forthcoming β_i. Better methods of estimation have been explored by Blume (1971) and Vasicek (1973).[1]

One way to incorporate (3.3) into a portfolio selection model is to compute the $V(r_i)$ and the $\text{cov}(r_i, r_j)$ explicitly. Applying the definition of variance and covariance to the random variables $\alpha_i + \beta_i F + u_i$ and $\alpha_j + \beta_j F + u_j$ and using the assumptions listed following (3.3), we obtain

$$V(r_i) = \beta_i^2 V(F) + V(u_i) \tag{3.4}$$

$$\sigma_{ij} = \beta_i \beta_j V(F) \qquad \text{for } i \neq j \tag{3.5}$$

The computing procedures described in chapters 7-9 and 13 provide efficient sets for any portfolio selection model with constraints as defined in the previous

[1] It is beyond the scope of this book to review the statistical aspects of these models or, more generally, recommend procedures for estimating μ and C. Ongoing refinements of the Rosenberg model seem to be the most common source of C in practice. Some current procedures for estimating μ are described in Farrell (1983).

chapter, with any μ and any positive semidefinite C. In particular they apply to variances and covariances computed by (3.4) and (3.5).

However, a more economical approach is based on the following considerations. The return R on the portfolio as a whole may be written as

$$\begin{aligned} R &= \Sigma X_i r_i \\ &= \Sigma X_i \alpha_i + (\Sigma X_i \beta_i) F + \Sigma X_i u_i \end{aligned} \tag{3.6}$$

where $\Sigma \alpha_i X_i$ is a constant, rather than a random variable, equal to the α of the portfolio; and $\Sigma \beta_i X_i$ is a constant equal to the β of the portfolio. It follows from equation (1.26) that

$$\text{cov}(\Sigma X_i u_i, F) = 0 \tag{3.7}$$

An application of (3.4) yields

$$\begin{aligned} V(R) &= (\Sigma X_i \beta_i)^2 V_F + V(\Sigma X_i u_i) \\ &= (\Sigma X_i \beta_i)^2 V_F + \Sigma X_i^2 V(u_i) \end{aligned} \tag{3.8}$$

The last step uses the fact that

$$\text{cov}(u_i, u_j) = 0 \qquad \text{for } i \neq j$$

If we wish to incorporate equation (3.8) into (for example) a standard portfolio selection model we can write the model as follows:

$$\sum_{i=1}^{n} X_i = 1 \tag{3.9a}$$

$$X_i \geqslant 0 \qquad i = 1, \ldots, n \tag{3.9b}$$

$$\sum_{i=1}^{n} \beta_i X_i - X_{n+1} = 0 \tag{3.9c}$$

$$E = \sum_{i=1}^{n} \mu_i X_i \tag{3.9d}$$

$$V = \sum_{i=1}^{n} V(u_i) X_i^2 + V(F) X_{n+1}^2 \tag{3.9e}$$

where (3.9c) constrains X_{n+1} to equal $\Sigma \beta_i X_i$, so X_{n+1} is indeed the β of the portfolio $(X_1, \ldots, X_n)$. For this model, (3.9a), (3.9b), and (3.9d) constrain the first n of the X_i and define E as in chaptér 1. V is written in (3.9e) according to the formula in (3.8).

The one-factor model (3.3) only requires the estimation of n each of μ_i, β_i, and $V(u_i)$, and one $V(F)$, rather than n of μ, n of V_i, and $n(n-1)/2$ covariances.

The advantage of writing the model as in (3.9a) through (3.9e), rather than computing the σ_{ij} explicitly, is twofold: first, it saves the computation of the (for example) $200(199)/2 = 19{,}900$ covariances; second, the covariance matrix in (3.9e) is

$$C = \begin{pmatrix} V(u_1) & 0 & 0 \;\ldots & 0 & 0 \\ 0 & V(u_2) & 0 \;\ldots & 0 & 0 \\ 0 & 0 & V(u_3)\ldots & 0 & 0 \\ & & \ddots & & \\ 0 & 0 & 0 \;\ldots & V(u_n) & 0 \\ 0 & 0 & 0 \;\ldots & 0 & V(F) \end{pmatrix}$$

The efficient set computation can be much speeded by the use of a "sparse" covariance matrix, such as the diagonal matrix above, in which most matrix entries are zero (see exercises 6.3–6.7 and the references cited there). Models of covariance involving several factors can be treated similarly. As a rule, one variable and one new equation are introduced per underlying factor. See, for example, Cohen and Pogue (1967) and Rosenberg (1974).

Another type of model which leads to a sparse covariance matrix is the "scenario model" (see for example Hobman, 1975; Markowitz and Perold, 1981a). It assumes that one of K future scenarios can occur, and if scenario k occurs then the expected return and variance of return of the ith security is μ_{ik} and V_{ik}. One type of scenario model assumes that there is zero covariance between the r_i given that the kth scenario has occurred. The r_i are correlated because, as a rule, the scenarios which raise μ_i also raise μ_j. $V(r_i)$ and $\text{cov}(r_i, r_j)$ can be computed explicitly from the μ_{ik}, the V_{ik}, and the probabilities p_k that the kth scenario will occur. The other way adds one variable and one constraint per scenario, producing a much simpler but strictly equivalent model.

The one-factor model in equations (3.9), the many-factor models, the scenario models cited above, and combination (factor and scenario) models described in Markowitz and Perold (1981a), all conform to the assumptions of the general portfolio selection model defined in chapter 2. They continue to do so if additional linear equalities or inequalities are included, such as the industry constraints of equations (3.1) or (3.2). Therefore their efficient sets have the properties derived in chapters 7–9 and can be computed by the algorithm of chapter 13.

Exogenous Assets

Consider an investor with a source of income in addition to the return on his or her portfolio. Assume that this income is a given random variable which may be correlated with the returns on securities. As argued for example in chapter 13 of Markowitz (1959), and in Tsiang (1972), the mean-variance set (from which a portfolio is to be selected with approximately maximum expected utility) should be computed in terms of the sum of portfolio return and nonportfolio income. Nonportfolio income can be introduced into, for example, the standard model as follows. Let X_i represent the number of dollars, rather than the percent invested, in the ith security; and let W_0 be the dollar value of the portfolio. Then

$$\sum_{i=1}^{n} X_i = W_0 \tag{3.10a}$$

$$X_i \geqslant 0 \qquad i = 1, \ldots, n \tag{3.10b}$$

$$X_{n+1} = 1 \tag{3.10c}$$

$$E = \sum_{i=1}^{n+1} \mu_i X_i \tag{3.10d}$$

$$V = \sum_{i=1}^{n+1} \sum_{j=1}^{n+1} \sigma_{ij} X_i X_j \tag{3.10e}$$

Here E and V are the mean and variance of the total return from both portfolio and nonportfolio sources. Equations (3.10d) and (3.10e) follow from the fact that total return R_{T} - which is the sum of portfolio return R_{P} and nonportfolio return R_{N} - is given by

$$\begin{aligned} R_{\mathrm{T}} &= R_{\mathrm{P}} + R_{\mathrm{N}} \\ &= \sum_{i=1}^{n} X_i r_i + R_{\mathrm{N}} \\ &= \sum_{i=1}^{n+1} X_i r_i \end{aligned}$$

where $r_{n+1} = R_{\mathrm{N}}$ and $X_{n+1} = 1$ as required by (3.10c). We speak of X_{n+1} as an *exogenous asset*. The term $\mu_{n+1} X_{n+1}$ in (3.10d) has no effect on whether or not a portfolio is efficient. It could be omitted during the computation of efficient portfolios, and added later if desired to the E of each efficient portfolio. The terms in X_{n+1} in the computation of V in (3.10e), on the other hand, do typically affect the set of efficient portfolios. Inclusion tends to favor securities with low covariance with r_{n+1}. The model in (3.10) conforms to the assumptions of the general portfolio selection model, and would continue to do so if additional linear equalities or inequalities were included.

Tracking an Index

The performance of a money manager is often compared with an index such as Standard and Poor's 500. The money manager may wish to avoid randomly falling behind the index, especially in the first year or two with a client, lest these be his or her only years with the client. Let

$$W' = (W_1, \ldots, W_n)$$

be the weights of

$$r' = (r_1, \ldots, r_n)$$

in an index of returns.[2] Suppose that the investment manager seeks a portfolio X so as to minimize $V(X'r - W'r)$ for given $E(X'r - W'r)$. That is, among portfolios which beat the index by a given amount on the average, the manager prefers a portfolio which does so more assuredly, where $E(X'r - W'r)$ and $V(X'r - W'r)$ measure "beat on the average" and "assuredly." If we express the constraints on the manager's choice of portfolios as in a portfolio selection model of form 1, then the manager's problem is to be efficient in terms of

$$V = (X - W)'C(X - W) \qquad (3.11a)$$

$$E = \mu'X - \mu'W \qquad (3.11b)$$

subject to

$$AX \geqslant b \qquad (3.11c)$$

If we write

$$Y = X - W$$

then

$$V = Y'CY \qquad (3.12a)$$

$$E = \mu'Y \qquad (3.12b)$$

$$AY \geqslant b - AW \qquad (3.12c)$$

Since $b - AW$ is a constant, (3.12c) like (3.11c) is a constraint set of form 1. Thus (3.12a), (3.12b), and (3.12c) constitute a general portfolio selection model written in form 1.

[2] An index of returns includes dividends as well as price appreciation for the securities in the index. A somewhat different analysis, but still a special case of the general portfolio selection model defined in chapter 2, is required to choose X efficient in terms of $E(X'r - W'\tilde{r})$ and $V(X'r - W'\tilde{r})$, where $\tilde{r}$ excludes dividends.

Turnover Constraints

Partly because of transaction costs and partly for precautionary reasons, portfolio managers hesitate to move too quickly from an existing portfolio to a new one suggested by a mean-variance analysis.[3] Sometimes their reluctance to move too far too fast is incorporated into the analysis by a constraint on turnover, as in Perold (1984). Let X_i^{C} be the current holding of security i. Let X_i^{I} be the amount by which the position in the ith security is increased; let X_i^{D} be the amount by which it is decreased. The problem may then be set up as follows. For a given upper bound U, find "portfolios" $(X, X^{\mathrm{I}}, X^{\mathrm{D}})$ subject to

$$X - X^{\mathrm{I}} + X^{\mathrm{D}} = X^{\mathrm{C}} \tag{3.13a}$$

$$\Sigma X_i^{\mathrm{I}} \leqslant U \tag{3.13b}$$

$$X \geqslant 0, \qquad X^{\mathrm{D}} \geqslant 0, \qquad X^{\mathrm{I}} \geqslant 0 \tag{3.13c}$$

which are efficient in terms of

$$V = X'CX \tag{3.13d}$$

$$= (X, X^{\mathrm{I}}, X^{\mathrm{D}}) \begin{pmatrix} C & 0 & 0 \\ 0 & 0 & 0 \\ 0 & 0 & 0 \end{pmatrix} \begin{pmatrix} X \\ X^{\mathrm{I}} \\ X^{\mathrm{D}} \end{pmatrix}$$

$$E = \mu' X \tag{3.13e}$$

$$= (\mu, 0, 0) \begin{pmatrix} X \\ X^{\mathrm{I}} \\ X^{\mathrm{D}} \end{pmatrix}$$

The model in (3.13) is another instance of the general portfolio selection constraint set defined in chapter 2, to be solved in the following chapters. The covariance matrix in (3.13d) is singular, further illustrating the need to allow semidefinite covariance matrices in our analysis.

[3] Our discussion later in this chapter of the relationship between mean-variance analysis and the theory of rational behavior under uncertainty, implicitly ignores transaction costs including commissions, bid-asked spread, and taxes. Since currently a large-scale dynamic investment model cannot be solved precisely including transaction costs, two approaches are taken: simplified models are solved analytically, or heuristic amendments to mean-variance analysis are evaluated by simulation. See Kallberg and Ziemba (1981) for an example of the former and references to studies of both kinds; also see Schreiner (1980). In practice I have used the simulation/heuristic approach and have found that transaction costs are not a great problem for tax-exempt investing institutions such as pension funds. The addition of taxes significantly complicates the problem.

Why Mean and Variance?

The fundamental premises of Markowitz (1959) were presented in the last four chapters of that book. First principles were presented last because of a concern that starting with a discussion of axioms of rational behavior and related matters might lead many readers to conclude that the subject of the book was of theoretical interest only, not for managing money. Therefore the early chapters of the book speak of mean and variance as measures of return and risk on the portfolio as a whole; promise a subsequent discussion of the choice of these criteria; and promise a review of arguments as to why "probability beliefs" should obey the same rules as objective probabilities. In the intervening chapters the book speaks as if probability distributions are known and takes mean and variance as criteria without question.

The tactic of treating first principles last had its advantages and disadvantages. On the one hand, I have since met many men and women, responsible for the supervision of large corporate and municipal pension funds, who learned portfolio selection from Markowitz (1959). I imagine that many of these would have been "turned off" if chapters 10–13 had come first.

A disadvantage of putting fundamentals in the back was that many scholars interested in such matters apparently never found this discussion. There are a number of papers on fundamentals which cite Markowitz (1959) but attribute to it views which it does not contain. Some assert that Markowitz (1959) justifies mean and variance in the same manner as Markowitz (1952); others that it justifies it as in Tobin (1958). Neither is the case.

Markowitz (1952) argued that to act on the basis of E alone would lead to absurd results (no diversification), suggested mean and variance as measures of return and risk on the portfolio as a whole, and argued that the minimization of variance for given E "led to the 'right kind' of diversification for the 'right reason'." For the most part the exercise of reconciling mean-variance with expected utility and personal probability was not undertaken until the academic year 1954–5 when the author visited the Cowles Foundation, on leave from the Rand Corporation, and drafted most of what was to be Markowitz (1959).

Tobin (1958) offered two alternate bases for assuming mean and variance as the investor's criteria: (1) "the investor evaluates the future of consols [also, the future of portfolios of "bonds and other debt instruments"] only in terms of some two-parameter family of probability distributions" such as the normal; or (2) "the assumption that the utility function is quadratic", and returns do not exceed the point at which the quadratic reaches its maximum. Normal distributions or other two-parameter families of probability distributions were not part of the Markowitz (1959) justification for mean and variance. Nowhere in chapters 10–13 of that book is "normal" or "Gaussian" or "two-parameter family" mentioned.

Approximation of a utility function by a quadratic in a certain neighborhood is central to the Markowitz (1959) rationale for mean and variance, as will be discussed below. Since Tobin clearly did not believe that utility was really quadratic, and therefore his assumption of an investor with a quadratic utility function was clearly an approximation, it might seem to be academic hair splitting to distinguish between Tobin's investor with a quadratic utility function and Markowitz's quadratic approximation. The crucial nature of this distinction will emerge below, when we reconcile two apparently contradictory facts: (1) it has been shown repeatedly that for various utility functions and empirical distributions of portfolio returns, if you know the mean and variance of a distribution you can guess its expected utility almost exactly; whereas (2) the objections of Pratt (1964) and Arrow (1965) show that a quadratic utility function has absurd implications even "in the small."

The justification of mean and variance in chapters 10–13 of Markowitz (1959) is for the most part an application to portfolio selection of the results and methods of Von Neumann and Morgenstern (1944), L. J. Savage (1954), and R. Bellman (1957). Further work along these lines has been assembled in Ziemba and Vickson (1975), including Samuelson (1969), Fama (1970), and Hakansson (1971).

We will give a brief outline of these matters, without proofs. For a more complete exposition of the author's views on these matters see Markowitz (1959, chapters 10–13) and Levy and Markowitz (1979), which extends the former and speaks to certain objections raised by Borch (1969), Pratt (1964), and Arrow (1965). A reader without background in the matters to be discussed – e.g. axioms of rational behavior, Bayes rule, dynamic programming, and its implied single-period utility functions – may find the following synopsis too condensed. If so, the reader is encouraged to skim or skip the remainder of this chapter. The present discussion considers *why* we seek mean-variance efficiency and is not prerequisite to the main topic of this book: *how* to obtain mean-variance efficiency assuming that we want it.

We will consider the actions of a rational investor who does not know the future with certainty, but has the computational and intellectual capacity to act consistently with certain axioms of behavior, and does so act. We will find that while the rational investor is assumed to be able to compute at essentially zero cost and unlimited speed, in certain ways this investor's actions follow quite simple rules. The simplicity of these rules makes it easier for our own actions to approximate those of the mythical rational investor in certain respects.

We assume that the rational investor holds as possible a finite number of hypotheses about the nature of the world. The assumption that there are only a finite number of hypotheses simplifies the analysis. For analyses which derive essentially the same conclusions but allow an infinite number of hypotheses see Savage (1954) or Fishburn (1969) and other studies cited in the latter.

In the present discussion we assume that at the beginning of each period t the investor splits wealth W_t between consumption C_t and investment I_t, and allocates I_t to various securities $X_{1t}, \ldots, X_{kt}$. The returns on the various securities, $r_{1t}, \ldots, r_{kt}$, determine the next period's starting wealth $W_{t+1} = \Sigma r_{it} X_{it}$; this is again split $W_{t+1} = C_{t+1} + I_{t+1}$, and the process is repeated. We assume that the rational investor's objective is to obtain a "good" sequence of consumption $C = (C_1, C_2, \ldots, C_T)$, where T is assumed to be the investor's maximum lifetime. At this point we make no assumptions as to the nature of the preferences for one C vector versus another.

We assume that there are only a finite number of possible C values, e.g. the product of a finite number of possible C_t for each t, where C_t ranges from $C_{t\min}$ to $C_{t\max}$ by steps of \$0.01. We will refer to the C vectors as *outcomes* and label them $O_1, O_2, \ldots, O_m$. Thus an outcome is an entire C vector $(C_1, \ldots, C_T)$. For an analysis not restricted to a finite number of outcomes again see Savage (1954) or Fishburn (1969) and studies cited therein.

We assume that the rational investor chooses a *strategy* in the sense of Von Neumann and Morgenstern (1944). A strategy is a rule which specifies how action at any time will depend on opportunities available at that time and information which has accumulated up to that time. Rather than having the rational investor survey available options and information at time t, and "think things over", Von Neumann and Morgenstern assume that the rational investor can decide now what he will do then, as a function of what circumstances - opportunities and information - obtain at time t.

With this view, the rational investor has only one decision to make: the choice of strategy to follow for the whole "game of life", from time 1 to time T. Given the assumptions of Markowitz (1959), the decision to follow a particular strategy is characterized by an m by n matrix (d_{ij}), where m is the number of possible outcomes, n is the number of hypotheses about the world, and d_{ij} is the probability that the ith outcome will occur if the jth hypothesis is true and the particular strategy is followed. We assume that the rational investor likes some conceivable (d_{ij}) better than others, and that his preferences among (d_{ij}) satisfy four axioms. Altering axiom I slightly, to give simplicity at the expense of generality, the Markowitz (1959) axioms may be summarized as follows:

I The rational investor has a simple ordering of the (d_{ij}) matrices. For example, if $d^1 = (d^1_{ij})$ is at least as good (in terms of the rational investor's preferences among d) as d^2, and d^2 is at least as good as d^3, then d^1 is at least as good as d^3. Also, it is not true that the d are all considered equally desirable.

II If d^1 is preferred to d^2, and d^3 is any other (d_{ij}) matrix, then it is better to: (a) flip a coin and follow d^1 if heads and d^3 if tails, than to (b) flip the same coin and follow d^2 if heads and d^3 if tails. Thus if the rational investor were required to flip the coin to choose a strategy, line (a) of the following table is preferred to line (b), assuming d^1 is preferred to d^2:

	If heads	*If tails*
(a)	Follow d^1	Follow d^3
(b)	Follow d^2	Follow d^3

This statement is true if the probability of heads is any number greater than zero.

III If d^1 is preferred to d^2 and d^2 is preferred to d^3, then there is some probability p of having to follow (the strategy which provides) d^1 and $(1-p)$ of having to follow d^3 which is exactly as good as having to follow d^2.

IV If, for each possible state of nature, d^1 has at least as good a probability distribution of outcomes as d^2, then (d^1_{ij}) is at least as good as (d^2_{ij}).

The reader is referred to Markowitz (1959) for further exposition and justification of these axioms, and their algebraic restatements. From this algebraic restatement the following theorem is shown there. (We label the theorem here for ease of reference, but not in the manner of theorems which are proved in the present volume.)

Theorem A A ranking of d matrices is consistent with axioms I, II, III, IV if and only if

(i) There are m numbers $u_1, u_2, \ldots, u_m$, referred to as the *utility* of each outcome, and $u_i \neq u_j$ for some pair;

(ii) There are n numbers $\pi_1, \pi_2, \ldots, \pi_n$, referred to as the *subjective probabilities* of the various hypotheses, with every $\pi_i \geqslant 0$ and $\Sigma \pi_i = 1$;

such that d^1 is at least as good as d^2 if and only if

$$\sum_{j=1}^{n} \pi_j \left(\sum_{i=1}^{m} u_i d^1_{ij} \right) \geqslant \sum_{j=1}^{n} \pi_j \left(\sum_{i=1}^{m} u_i d^2_{ij} \right) \tag{3.14}$$

The inner summation on the left of (3.14), $\Sigma_{i=1}^{m} u_i d^1_{ij}$, is the expected utility of decision d^1 assuming that hypothesis j is true. The entire expression on the left is a weighted average of such expected utilities using the π_j as weights. We summarize (3.14) by saying that the rational investor whose preferences are in accord with the four axioms maximizes expected utility using probability beliefs where objective probabilities are not given. The theorem does not tell us what utilities the rational investor should assign to outcomes or what probabilities the rational investor should assign to hypotheses. It asserts rather that if one assigns such u_i and π_j and chooses among strategies according to (3.14) then choice will be consistent with the four axioms; and, conversely, unless there exists numbers

u_i and π_j such that choice is given by (3.14), then choice is inconsistent with the four axioms.

We define an outcome O_i to be a time series of consumptions

$$C^i = (C_1^i, C_2^i, \ldots, C_T^i)$$

Theorem A allows any assignment of u_i to C^i. It does not require, for example, that the assignment of u_i be of the form $u_i = \Sigma f_t(C_t)$; this is permitted but not required.

Mossin (1968) has analyzed situations in which the investor's objective is to maximize the expected value of some function of final wealth. In other words Mossin assumes $u_i = f(C_T^i)$. The importance of Mossin's work is due in part to the existence of intervals of time in which actions are to be planned but no consumption is to take place; and in part to the substantial insight Mossin's work has brought to this class of situation. But it is to be emphasized that this is a subset of the cases covered by theorem A.

Bayesian Inference

We will refer to a strategy that maximizes (3.14) for given u_i and π_j as a solution to a *T period lifetime game*. This solution can be viewed in what Von Neumann and Morgenstern refer to as *normalized form* - the choice of a single d matrix. Alternately, it can be viewed in *extensive form* as a choice of an action (usually many dimensional) at the start of time 1, here denoted as ACT_1; plus a function showing action at the beginning of time 2 which may depend on information accumulated during period 1, here denoted as $ACT_2(INF_1)$; plus a function showing action at the beginning of time 3 depending on information then available, $ACT_3(INF_1, INF_2)$; and so on through $ACT_T(INF_1, \ldots, INF_{T-1})$. INF_t includes C_t as part of its vector of information. Let us consider a time at the beginning of some period t, and let $INF_1^*, INF_2^*, \ldots, INF_{t-1}^*$ be possible values which the vectors $INF_1, \ldots, INF_{t-1}$ could have at this time. Consider what happens to the extensive form of the optimal solution to the T period game if we fix

$$INF_1 = INF_1^*, \ldots, INF_{t-1} = INF_{t-1}^*$$

and only consider $ACT_t, ACT_{t+1}, \ldots, ACT_T$. ACT_t is now determined:

$$ACT_t(INF_1^*, \ldots, INF_{t-1}^*)$$

ACT_{t+1} is a function only of INF_t, yet to be determined:

$$ACT_{t+1} = ACT_{t+1}^*(INF_t; INF_j^*, \ldots, INF_{t-1}^*)$$

where our new $ACT_{t+1}^*(INF_t)$ function is like our old $ACT_{t+1}(INF_1, \ldots, INF_t)$ function except with constant vectors INF_τ^* substituted for the variable vectors

INF_τ for $1 \leqslant \tau \leqslant t-1$. Similarly ACT_{t+2} is now a function of INF_t and INF_{t+1}, yet to be determined:

$$ACT_{t+2} = ACT^*_{t+2}(INF_t, INF_{t+1}; INF^*_1, \ldots, INF^*_{t-1})$$

or generally

$$ACT_{t+\tau} = ACT^*_{t+\tau}(INF_t, \ldots, INF_{t+\tau-1}; INF^*_1, \ldots, INF^*_{t-1}) \tag{3.15}$$

for $t \leqslant t+\tau \leqslant T$.

In other words, the set of remaining $ACT^*_{t+\tau}$ functions has the same form as a strategy for a $T-t+1$ period game. It can be shown that it is in fact the optimum strategy for a particular such game. We will refer to this $T-t+1$ period game - the game for which (3.15) is the optimum solution - as the *remaining game*.

The original T period game and the remaining $T-t+1$ period game are related in important ways. First, and not surprisingly, the utility u_i attached to each outcome $(C^i_t, C^i_{t+1}, \ldots, C^i_T)$ of the remaining game may be taken to be the same as the utility assigned in the original game to the outcome

$$(C^*_1, C^*_2, \ldots, C^*_{t-1}, C_t, C_{t+1}, \ldots, C_T)$$

where $C^*_i (1 \leqslant i < t)$ are the components of the consumption vector already determined by time t. Less obvious and of greater significance is that the π^*_j for the remaining game are obtained from that of the original game according to *Bayes rule*:

$$\pi^*_j - \frac{\pi_j \, \text{prob}(INF^*_1, \ldots, INF^*_{t-1} \mid H_j)}{\sum_i \pi_i \, \text{prob}(INF^*_1, \ldots, INF^*_{t-1} \mid H_i)}$$

where prob$(INF \mid H_i)$ is the probability of getting the particular observation if the ith hypothesis were true. We say therefore that the rational investor is a *Bayesian* or engages in *Bayesian inference*.

Implied Single-period Utility Maximization

Let us return to the original T period game as distinguished from the remaining game at some time t. It can be shown that the choice of action at each time t, given information known by then, can always be expressed as the solution to a single-period expected utility maximization problem:

$$\max E\,[U_t(INF_t; INF^*_1, \ldots, INF^*_{t-1})] \tag{3.16}$$

The form of this function may change over time and may depend on the INF^*_i already known. In particular it may depend on $C^*_1, \ldots, C^*_{t-1}$. Thus axioms

I-IV do not rule out the possibility that the rational investor's risk aversion today may properly depend on how well he or she ate yesterday.

In principle the functions U_t can be determined by the methods of dynamic programming (see Bellman, 1957). The computation, to be sketched below, would be beyond our own capabilities but, of course, not beyond those of the rational investor. Our ultimate objective will be to obtain an economically computable procedure whose expected utility for the game as a whole approximates that of the true optimum.

For a possible history through the end of $T-1$, i.e. for a possible combination of values of $INF_1 = INF_1^*, \ldots, INF_{T-1} = INF_{T-1}^*$, the remaining game is a one-period game. The problem of choosing ACT_T is then one of maximizing the expected value of a single-period utility function:

$$U_T(INF_T; INF_1^*, \ldots, INF_{T-1}^*) = U(INF_1^*, INF_2^*, \ldots, INF_{T-1}^*, INF_T) \quad (3.17)$$

The rule by which a U_i is assigned to a $(C_1^i, \ldots, C_T^i)$ may be expressed as a function $U(INF_1, \ldots, INF_T)$, as in the right-hand side of (3.17), since INF_t includes C_t. We say that U_T is a function of INF_T only, since by the end of $T-1$ the other INF_t^* are known parameters.

Let

$$U_{T-1}(INF_{T-1}; INF_1^*, \ldots, INF_{T-2}^*)$$
$$= \max E\,[U_T(INF_T; INF_1^*, \ldots, INF_{T-2}^*, INF_{T-1})] \quad (3.18)$$

i.e. U_{T-1} is the expected value of U_T in (3.17), assuming that the optimum action is chosen at the start of period T. This $U_{T-1} = \max E\,[U_T]$ is all that need be remembered from the computation for period T, in order to choose an optimum ACT_{T-1}. U_{T-1} is not a function of INF_T, since it is an expected value (of U_T) over all possible INF_T (suitably weighted by their probabilities). At the start of $T-1$, U_{T-1} depends only on INF_{T-1}, yet to be determined. The INF_t for preceding $t < T-1$ are already given, and therefore are known parameters of U_{T-1}. The optimum action at the start of $T-1$ - optimum, that is, for the game as a whole - consists in choosing ACT_{T-1} so as to maximize the expected value of U_{T-1}. Thus at the beginning of period $T-1$ the optimum strategy for the game as a whole requires only a single-period expected utility maximization - since $INF_1^*, \ldots, INF_{T-2}^*$ are (vector) parameters, already determined, and U_{T-1} in (3.18) is then a function only of INF_{T-1}, yet to be determined.

Similarly, if we define

$$U_{T-2}(INF_{T-2}; INF_1^*, \ldots, INF_{T-3}^*)$$
$$= \max E\,[U_{T-1}(INF_{T-1}; INF_1^*, \ldots, INF_{T-3}^*, INF_{T-2})]$$

as the expected value of U_{T-1} given the past values of INF_1 to INF_{T-2}, assuming that the correct action is taken at time $T-1$, then the optimum action at the start of period $T-2$ - optimum for the game as a whole - is to maximize the expected value of U_{T-2}. This again is a single-period utility function

$$U_{T-2}(INF_{T-2}; INF_1^*, \ldots, INF_{T-3}^*)$$

with parameters $INF_1^*, \ldots, INF_{T-3}^*$ already determined.

In this manner the rational investor with unlimited calculating speed and capacity can determine a sequence of single-period utility functions

$$U_T(INF_T; INF_1^*, \ldots, INF_{T-1}^*)$$

$$U_{T-1}(INF_{T-1}; INF_1^*, \ldots, INF_{T-2}^*)$$

$$\vdots$$

$$U_2(INF_2; INF_1^*)$$

$$U_1(INF_1)$$

such that the optimum action for the game as a whole, given that information $INF_1^*, \ldots, INF_{t-1}^*$ has already accumulated by time t, is to maximize the expected value of $U_t(INF_t; INF_1^*, \ldots, INF_{t-1}^*)$.

In general the shape of U_t will depend on the parameters $INF_1^*, \ldots, INF_{t-1}^*$. This is of no consequence to our argument. We will be concerned with the contents of INF_t and the nature of the relationship between U_t and INF_t. We will consider, for example, situations in which U_t depends only on C_t and W_{t+1} - consumption during t and wealth at the end of t. We will consider whether such a utility function can be maximized or almost maximized by a choice of portfolio from the mean-variance efficient set. It will be of no concern to us whether this function would have been different if $INF_1, \ldots, INF_{t-1}$ had been different. We will also consider situations in which

$$U_t(INF_t) = U_t(C_t, W_{t+1}, Y_{1t}, \ldots, Y_{kt})$$

where $Y_{1t}, \ldots, Y_{kt}$ are a small number of variables which become revealed during time t. The Y_{it} may be correlated with the return on the portfolio, and this correlation may vary from one portfolio to another. We will consider how mean-variance analysis can be extended to approximate the correct action if $U_t(C_t, W_{t+1}, Y_{1t}, \ldots, Y_{kt})$ is approximately a quadratic function in $(W_{t+1}, Y_{1t}, \ldots, Y_{kt})$ for given C_t. It will not concern us at all in this matter as to whether $U_t(C_t, W_{t+1}, Y_{1t}, \ldots, Y_{kt})$ would have had a different shape if $INF_1, \ldots, INF_{t-1}$ had been different.

Quadratic Approximations

We now write $U_t(INF_t; INF_1^*, \ldots, INF_{t-1}^*)$ as $U_t(INF_t)$, leaving implicit the fact that the shape of $U_t(INF_t)$ may depend on what has gone before. In the first instance, suppose that U_t depends only on C_t and W_{t+1}. Perhaps other information accrues during period t, like which particular companies look more promising and which less promising than appeared at the start of the period; but U_t – the expected value of the game as a whole assuming an optimum strategy is followed – is here assumed to only depend on the two numbers C_t and W_{t+1}.

In this case it can be shown that an optimum solution for the game as a whole can be obtained by treating t as two periods, t_a and t_b. Consumption C_t is determined in the first of these, t_a; then the portfolio is chosen in the second, t_b. Of course, in computing backwards from last period to first in the dynamic programming manner, U_{t_b} is determined before U_{t_a}. We will be concerned here with the choice of portfolio at the beginning of period t_b. Given our current assumptions this requires maximizing the expected value of a function only of W_{t+1}. The shape of this function may depend on past events, including the choice of C_t. Since the amount to be invested $I_t = W_t - C_t$ is already determined by the start of t_b, the single-period utility function can also be expressed as a function of return on the portfolio:

$$\tilde{U}_t(R_t) = U_{t_b}[(W_t - C_t)(1 + R_t)]$$

We will assume here that $\tilde{U}_t(R_t)$ is strictly concave. This implies that the investor will prefer a given return R_0 with certainty to a probability distribution of return with $V(R) > 0$ and $E(R) = R_0$.

Markowitz (1959) asserts that if $\tilde{U}_t(R_t)$ can be approximated closely enough by a quadratic for a sufficiently wide range of returns, then $E(U)$ will be approximately equal to some function $f(E, V)$ of mean and variance. He suggests two methods of approximating a given $\tilde{U}(R)$ by a quadratic:

$$Q_Z(R) \cong \tilde{U}(0) + \tilde{U}'(0)R + 0.5\tilde{U}''(0)R^2 \qquad (3.19a)$$

$$Q_E(R) \cong \tilde{U}(E) + \tilde{U}'(E)(R - E) + 0.5\tilde{U}''(E)(R - E)^2 \qquad (3.19b)$$

where $\cong$ stands for "is approximately equal to", and a prime here denotes a derivative. The first of these approximations (3.19a) is a Taylor expansion around $R = 0$; the second, around $R = E$. Two functions of E and V, obtained by taking expected values of (3.19a) and (3.19b), are

$$f_Z(E, V) = E[Q_Z(R)] = \tilde{U}(0) + \tilde{U}'(0)E + 0.5\tilde{U}''(0)(E^2 + V) \qquad (3.20a)$$

$$f_E(E, V) = E[Q_E(R)] = \tilde{U}(E) + 0.5\tilde{U}''(E)V \qquad (3.20b)$$

For example, when $U = \log_e(1 + R)$ then f_Z and f_E are

$$f_Z^l(E, V) = E + (E^2 + V)/2 \qquad (3.21a)$$

$$f_Z^l(E, V) = \log_e(1 + E) - V/[2(1 + E)^2] \qquad (3.21b)$$

In chapter 13 of Markowitz (1959) the reader is invited to "imagine three Rational Men, each about to select a portfolio", with $\tilde{U}(R)$ equal to $\log_e(1 + R)$,

$(1+R)^{1/2}$, and $(1+R)^{1/3}$ respectively. Markowitz (1959, chapter 6, table 2) shows that $Q_Z^l(R)$ is "almost identical" to $\log_e(1+R)$ for a range of returns from about a 30 percent loss to about a 30 or 40 percent gain. It is then shown (Markowitz, 1959, chapter 13, table 1) that the respective $Q_Z(R)$ approximations are almost identical to $U=(1+R)^{1/2}$ and $U=(1+R)^{1/3}$ for a wider range, from about a 50 per cent loss to about a 70 or 80 percent gain. The $Q_E(R)$ approximations[4] are similar, except that they fit most closely near $R=E$ rather than $R=0$ (and their range of close fit is spread out by a factor of e.g. $(1+E)^2$ for $U=\log_e(1+R)$).

The accuracy of these approximations depends on the return on the portfolio as a whole rather than the return on its individual securities. For example, as long as the return on the portfolio as a whole is between a 30 percent loss and about a 30 or 40 percent gain for $U=\log_e(1+R)$ then $\tilde{U}(R)$ is always close to $Q_Z^l(R)$, and its expected value $f_Z^l(E, V)$ must be close to $E(U)$.

To illustrate, Markowitz (1959) assumes that each of the three investors must choose from eleven portfolios, namely nine stocks (undiversified portfolios) and two particular EV efficient portfolios. The example assumes that the investors' beliefs about the future are the same (or at least have the same E, V, $E[\log_e(1+R)]$, etc. for the eleven portfolios) as observed in the preceding[5] 18 years of annual returns. Markowitz (1959, chapter 6, table 3 and figure 2) shows that $f_E^l(E, V)$ provided a much closer approximation to $E[\log_e(1+R)]$ than did $f_Z^l(E, V)$, and that the relationship between $f_E^l(E, V)$ and $E(U)$ was close to $E(U)=0+1f_E^l$. In particular, the portfolio (among the eleven) which maximized $f_E^l(E, V)$ also maximized $E(U)$.

This suggests that the first of the three rational investors would lose little by maximizing f_E^l rather than $E(U)$ in choosing among distributions "like" those of the eleven portfolios. As to the second and third investors, since their respective $Q_Z(R)$ fit their $U(R)$ over a wider range, it would seem that their respective f_Z and f_E would do at least as well as those of the first investor. Markowitz (1959) therefore argued that each would lose little if required to pick a portfolio from the EV efficient set rather than being allowed to each maximize $E(U)$. (Extensive subsequent tests of the ability of an $f(E, V)$ to approximate $E(U)$ are reported in the next section.)

Markowitz (1959) concludes that

> While it cannot be claimed that all such utility functions can be accurately approximated by a quadratic, the quadratic nevertheless shows a surprising flexibility in approximating smooth, concave curves. Whenever the individual's utility function can be reasonably approximated by a [concave] quadratic, one of the portfolios which minimizes variance for some value

[4] See Levy and Markowitz (1979) for sample tabulations.

[5] When the computation was done, in 1955.

of expected return provides almost the maximum obtainable expected utility.

Each of our Rational Men has his own utility function. Each examines the curve showing efficient combinations of mean and variance. Each selects the portfolio most appropriate to his own needs. Each obtains a portfolio almost as good as the very best available for him.

This provides a viewpoint with respect to the actual use of efficient set analyses. If the person carefully selects among the efficient combinations of mean and variance, and if his true utility function is approximately quadratic, then his final choice of portfolio is about as suitable as a portfolio can be. It is not essential for the investor to understand that he is imitating a Rational Man maximizing a quadratic approximation to his true utility function.

Markowitz (1959) does not claim that mean-variance analysis is always to be preferred to the maximization of an explicit, correctly derived $\tilde{U}(R)$. "The advantage of a utility function, as compared with an efficient set analysis, is that the utility function is a specially constructed representation of the investor's willingness to bear risk. If derived with care, it is a more accurate portrayal. . . ." On the other hand, Markowitz (1959) points out two advantages of using EV analysis:

Computation It is still true as this is written, as it was in 1959, that it is typically much more economical to trace out a mean-variance efficient set than to maximize $E[\tilde{U}(R)]$. For example, depending on the utility function and the form of the joint distribution assumed, maximization of $E(U)$ for a few or a few dozen securities can be as expensive as tracing out an EV efficient set for hundreds of securities (or thousands if sparse matrix techniques are applicable and used).[6]

Need to determine investor's utility function This does not mean persuading the investor that some prepackaged utility function has desirable features. It refers rather to soliciting the investor's preferences among various gambles and summarizing these in a utility function. Perhaps the modern investing institution with its staff of quantitative analysts and consultants is ready to undertake this task. Such was not the case in 1959.

[6] For example, Dexter, Yu, and Ziemba (1980), discussed in the next section, compare the mean-variance efficient portfolio with greatest $E(U)$ to the portfolio which actually maximizes $E(U)$ assuming joint lognormal returns on securities. They consider only cases with $n = 2$, 3, and 4. An analysis with $n = 5$ was attempted and abandoned because of the high computing costs involved in maximizing $E(U)$. Other studies – namely Pulley (1981, 1983) and Kroll, Levy, and Markowitz (1984) – consider joint distributions with a finite number of sample points (usually historical observations) and succeed in maximizing $E(U)$ for $n = 10$, 25, and 20 respectively.

To complete our summary of Markowitz (1959) on quadratic approximation, next let us suppose that U_t is a function of C_t, W_{t+1}, $Y_{t1}, \ldots, Y_{tk}$ for small k, e.g. $k = 1$ or 2. Assume that our choice of portfolio does not influence the value of Y_{ti}, but some portfolios have returns which are more correlated with Y_{ti} than are others. As before, we can determine C_t first, in subperiod t_a, and determine the portfolio second at the start of subperiod t_b. We may replace W_{t+1} by $(1+R_t)(W_t - C_t)$ in U_{t_b}, expressing utility as a function of R_t, $Y_{t1}, \ldots, Y_{tk}$. Suppose this function $\tilde{U}_t(R_t, \ldots, Y_{tk})$ can be closely approximated by a quadratic for a "large enough" region around $(R_t^0, Y_{t1}^0, \ldots, Y_{tk}^0) = (E, E(Y_{t1}), \ldots, E(Y_{tk}))$. The expected value of this quadratic depends only on the means and variances of the Y_{ik} and their correlations - which the choice of portfolio does not influence - and $E(R_t)$, $V(R_t)$, and the correlations $\rho(R_t, Y_{ti})$ which the choice of portfolio determines. Mean-variance analysis can be used to obtain efficient points in $(E, V, \rho(R, Y_1), \ldots, \rho(R, Y_k))$ space by treating the Y_i as exogenous assets.

Research on *EV* Approximations

Young and Trent (1969) investigate approximations to $E[\log_e(1+R)]$ or, equivalently, the geometric mean GM equal to $\exp\{E[\log_e(1+R)]\}$. Suppose an investor reinvested repeatedly in many independent draws from the same probability distribution, without adding or withdrawing funds. The rate of return he or she would achieve would "probably be close" to GM, at least in the sense that (for a distribution with a finite number of outcomes) if observed frequencies (of various values of R) are close to their probabilities then the "internal rate of return" achieved by these repeated investments will be close to GM.[7]

Young and Trent consider the ratio of approximate to actual GM, for five approximations, for monthly and annual distributions of returns, for 233 securities, and for various synthetic (made-up) 4-, 8-, 16-, and 32-stock portfolios. The one of their GM approximations which does the best, denoted $G(2)$, is essentially f_E^l in (3.21b). Surprisingly $G(2)$ even beat $G(5)$ based on a Taylor expansion including the third and fourth moments of the distribution.

For monthly holding period returns, $G(2)/GM$ averaged 0.9999 over the 233 stocks, with a standard deviation of 0.0028. For annual holding period returns,

[7] "Probably be close" can also be expressed as a strong or weak law of large numbers (see e.g. Markowitz, 1976). Kelly (1956), Latané (1957, 1959), Markowitz (1959), and Breiman (1960, 1961) conclude that if an investor "invests for the long run" then he or she will maximize GM or $E[\log_e(1+R)]$ each period. Samuelson (1963, 1969) argues otherwise. Markowitz (1976) rebuts.

$G(2)/GM$ averaged 0.995 with a standard deviation of 0.029. For annual returns on 392 synthetic 4-stock portfolios, $G(2)/GM$ averaged 0.998 with a standard deviation of 0.0088. Young and Trent conclude (in their opening paragraph) that "empirical evidence indicates that even though a number of the monthly and annual distributions deviate significantly from normality, the approximation involving only the mean and variance produces quite accurate estimates of the geometric means of these distributions."

Samuelson (1970) and Ohlson (1975) present conditions under which mean and variance are asymptotically sufficient for an optimum decision as the length of holding periods - i.e. the intervals between portfolio revisions - approaches zero. The Young and Trent results indicate that, as far as $E[\log_e(1+R)]$ is concerned, monthly holding periods are short enough to insure that $f(E, V)$ is virtually the same as $E(U)$.

Levy and Markowitz (1979) compare "actual" expected utility and mean-variance approximations for various utility functions, historical distributions, and mean-variance approximations. The quadratic approximations analyzed by Levy and Markowitz depend on a parameter k, and are fit through three points, namely $E-k\sigma$, E, and $E+k\sigma$. For the utility functions and historical distributions considered, the approximations improved as k approached zero. Since $f_E(E, V)$ in (3.20b) is the limit of the Levy-Markowitz approximation as $k \to 0$, Levy and Markowitz concluded that (for the given sample and utility functions) f_E is as good as any of their approximations. (In our discussion of the Levy-Markowitz results, "$f(E, V)$" will refer to their approximation with $k = 0.01$, the smallest k they considered.)

As in Markowitz (1959) and Young and Trent (1969), Levy and Markowitz (1979) assume that distributions of returns are the same as various historical distributions (or, at the least, have the same E, V, $E[\log_e(1+R)]$, $E[(1+R)^{1/2}]$, etc.) Distributions used include annual returns on 149 investment company portfolios, annual and monthly returns on 97 individual stocks, and annual returns on randomly drawn synthetic portfolios with $n = 5$ or 6. The utility functions analyzed were $\log_e(1+R)$, $(1+R)^a$ for $a = 0.1$, 0.3, 0.5, 0.7, and 0.9, and $-\exp[-b(1+R)]$ for $b = 0.1, 0.5, 1.0, 3.0, 5.0$ and 10.0.

For $U = \log_e(1+R)$ the correlation between $E(U)$ and $f_E(E, V)$, over the 149 distributions of annual returns on investment companies, was $\rho = 0.997$. That for $V = (1+R)^{1/2}$ was $\rho = 0.999$, reminiscent of the fact that $Q_Z(R)$ remains close to $U(R)$ for a greater range for $U = (1+R)^{1/2}$ than for $U = \log_e(1+R)$. For all utility functions except $-\exp[-b(1+R)]$ for $b = 3.0$, 5.0, and 10.0, the correlation between $E(U)$ and $f(E, V)$ was at least 0.997. In most cases it was 0.999.

For $-\exp[-b(1+R)]$, $b = 3.0$, 5.0, and 10.0, the correlation was respectively 0.949, 0.855, and 0.447. Levy and Markowitz make two points concerning the "misbehaved" $-\exp[-10(1+R)]$:

(1) While all utility functions satisfy the Von Neumann and Morgenstern axioms, not all will appeal to many (or any) investors.

$$U = -\exp[-10(1+R)]$$

in particular exhibits various strange preferences. For example an investor with this utility function would prefer 10 percent with certainty to a 50-50 chance of zero return (no gain, no loss) versus a gain of 1,000,000,000 percent.

(2) $U(R)$ and $Q_E(R)$ diverge almost immediately, so that the investor with this utility function should not expect an EV approximation to work well.

Correlations between $f(E, V)$ and $E(U)$ were smaller over the set of annual returns on 97 stocks. For example, for $U = \log_e(1+R)$ the correlation was 0.880 for the annual stock returns as compared with 0.997 for the annual investment company returns. When the holding period was reduced the correlations increased, as expected. For example, for monthly stock returns the correlation (for $U = \log_e(1+R)$) was 0.995. Also, a bit of diversification helped a lot. For annual returns on 19 small (nonoverlapping) portfolios ($n = 5$ or 6) drawn at random from the 97 securities, the correlation (for $U = \log_e(1+R)$) was 0.998. Similar effects (of going from investment companies to stocks, from annual stock returns to monthly stock returns, and from annual stock returns to annual returns on 5- or 6-stock portfolios) were found for the other utility functions.

Thus, for most utility functions considered, the mean-variance approximation did quite well, especially for annual returns on diversified portfolios and for monthly returns (even on undiversified portfolios). The success of the mean-variance approximation leads to an apparent anomaly: for many utility functions, if you know mean and variance you practically know expected utility; the mean-variance approximation to expected utility is based on a quadratic approximation to the single-period utility function; yet Arrow (1965) and Pratt (1964) show that *any* quadratic utility function has the objectionable property that an investor with such a utility function becomes increasingly averse to risks of a given dollar amount as his wealth increases.

Levy and Markowitz (1979) show that the anomaly disappears if you distinguish three types of quadratic approximations:

(1) Assuming that the investor has a utility-of-wealth function that remains constant through time – so that the investor moves along the curve to a new position as his or her wealth changes – fit a quadratic to this curve at some instant, and continue to use this same approximation subsequently.

(2) Fit the quadratic to the investor's current single-period utility function. For example, if the investor has an unchanging utility-of-wealth function, choose a quadratic to fit well near current wealth (i.e. near $R = 0$).

(3) Allow the quadratic approximation to vary from one portfolio to another; i.e. let the approximation depend on the mean, and perhaps the standard deviation, of the probability distribution whose expected value is to be estimated.

The Pratt-Arrow objection applies to an approximation of type (1). The $Q_Z(R)$ is of type (2) while $Q_E(R)$ and the various Levy-Markowitz approximations are of type (3). Levy and Markowitz show that, under quite general assumptions, the type (3) mean-variance maximizer has the same risk aversion in the small (in the sense of Pratt) as does the original expected utility maximizer; hence the Pratt-Arrow objection to "quadratic utility" does not apply.

The studies summarized above compare $E(U)$ and some kind of $f(E, V)$ for a finite number of probability distributions, e.g. 149 investment companies. More recent studies - namely Dexter, Yu, and Ziemba (1980), Pulley (1981, 1983), Kroll, Levy, and Markowitz (1984), and Simaan (1986) - compare $E(U)$ and one or more $f(E, V)$ for the set of portfolios available either from a standard portfolio analysis or from Black's model. Dexter et al. and Simaan each assume a particular (different in the two cases) functional form for the distribution of securities' returns, and fit its parameters to historical data. The other studies use historical returns as if they were the actual joint distributions. In addition, Pulley (1983) assumes particular functional forms, generates synthetic "histories" of joint returns from these forms, and then proceeds as if the samples were the joint distributions.

The studies differ in the period used as the joint distribution or to estimate parameters. The method of measuring the goodness of approximation differs between some of the studies. Differing lengths of holding periods - from monthly to annual - are analyzed. One thing which the studies have in common, however, is the general thrust of their conclusions.

According to Dexter, Yu, and Ziemba "it is fair to conclude that decisions based on the approximation yield expected utility values virtually identical to those obtained from the true optimal solution." Pulley (1983), analyzing the logarithmic utility function, finds that "investors maximizing expected logarithmic utility would hold virtually the same portfolios as investors maximizing certain mean-variance functions. . . . Moreover, we find the goodness of the mean-variance approximations to be robust for different holding periods, different ratios of noninvested to invested wealth, and different subjective return distributions, including non-normal distributions. . . . investors . . . could, in fact, achieve virtually identical returns . . . by maximizing functions of means and variances alone." Kroll, Levy, and Markowitz conclude that "for various utility functions and the historical returns on 3 different sets of securities, when a portfolio may be chosen from any of the infinite number of portfolios of the standard constraint set the best mean-variance efficient portfolio has almost maximum obtainable expected utility. This remained true when 50% borrowing was allowed."

Simaan assumes $U = -\exp[-b(1+R)]$ for various b, including b greater than 10. (Recall the much lower correlation between $E(U)$ and $f(E, V)$ for b as much as 10.) Simaan evaluates the goodness of the mean-variance approximation by the amount which the investor should be just willing to pay (e.g. "1/10th cent per dollar invested" is the form of the answer) to obtain an optimum portfolio rather than the best mean-variance efficient portfolio. As b increases (and if a riskless security is not available) the mean-variance approximation deteriorates. However, in terms of the Simaan criterion, as compared with the Levy-Markowitz correlations, "the results exhibit a larger domain for which mean-variance strategies lead to a fairly good approximate choice of expected utility maximization than that of Levy and Markowitz (1979)."

The universal conclusion of these studies,[8] then, was that mean-variance approximations provide almost maximum expected utility except for utility functions - such as $U = -\exp[-b(1+R)]$ for b well over 10 - which have pathological risk aversion.

Ederington (1986) evaluates mean-variance approximations in terms of "10,000 simulated years" by drawing four quarters at random from quarterly returns on 130 mutual funds. Ederington argues that these 10,000 synthetic years for each mutual fund will provide more extreme cases, and therefore provide a better test of mean-variance approximations, than the few years of actual history as used in the Young and Trent and the Levy and Markowitz analyses.

Ederington's 130 mutual funds provide (129)(130)/2 pairwise comparisons. Ederington tabulates the percent of these comparisons in which $f_E(E, V)$ ranks the pair in the wrong order (as compared with that provided by $E(U)$). He also tabulates this for approximations, derived from a Taylor expansion around E, but using (1) E only, (2) the first three moments, and (3) the first four moments of the distribution. We will refer to these approximations as f_1, f_3, and f_4, and will here refer to f_E as f_2.

For $U = \log_e(1+R)$ the percent of wrong choices made by f_1, f_2, f_3, and f_4 respectively are 10.97, 0.52, 1.32, 0.27. (Put the other way around, f_E gives the correct choice for 99.48 percent of the pairs, while f_4 raises this to 99.73.) For $U = (1+R)^{1/2}$ the error percentages are 5.03, 0.20, 0.44, and 0.07. The error rates are higher for more risk averse utility functions. For example, for $U =$

[8] In addition, Tew and Reid (forthcoming) evaluate EV approximations versus the maximization of $E(U)$ for "portfolios" of farm decisions (e.g. crop selection). They conclude that "The results of the comparison of portfolios using the actual farm level data indicated no utility loss from selecting the best portfolio from the EV set rather than directly maximizing utility over all portfolios. Similarly, results from the experimental setting in which the data were severely skewed indicated little, if any, utility loss."

$-\exp[-5(1+R)]$ the error rates for f_1, f_2, f_3, and f_4 are 36.49, 5.28, 11.56, and 1.82. Thus, assuming that ***annual*** rather than *monthly* holding period returns are appropriate,[9] an analysis based on four moments would be desirable for extremely risk averse investors (if the cost of such an analysis is not prohibitive). Such analyses are yet to be developed.

Ederington also considers whether the goodness of the mean-variance approximation is due to near quadraticness of the utility function or near normality of probability distributions. Towards this end he notes that f_E is the appropriate mean-variance approximation if U is nearly quadratic, whereas another approximation, which we will denote as $f_n(E, V)$, is appropriate if distributions are nearly normal. He compares the correlations (over the 130 mutual funds) between f_E and $E(U)$, and between f_n and $E(U)$. For the majority of utility functions considered - in particular, for the utility functions with moderate risk aversion such as $\log_e(1+R)$, $(1+R)^{1/2}$ and $-\exp[-b(1+R)]$ for $b \leqslant 4.0$ - f_E did better than f_n. For utility functions with very high risk aversion - such as $-\exp[-5(1+R)]$ - f_n did better.

Related Matters

For the sake of completeness, this section makes brief references to two matters not covered in the above synopsis of the foundations of mean-variance theory.

Distributions of returns

One can justify mean-variance analysis by assumptions concerning the joint distribution of security returns. Feldstein (1969) disputed the Tobin (1958) conjecture that two-parameter families of distributions would suffice generally. Chamberlain (1983) shows that if the joint distribution of returns is "spherically

[9] As stated in footnote 3 of this chapter, it is not possible to solve the actual dynamic portfolio selection problem with transaction costs. One can include transaction costs in a general portfolio selection model by charging for, rather than constraining, X^{I} and X^{D} in (3.13). The problem is that the single-period U function is no longer a function of (e.g.) W_{t+1} only but - strictly speaking - depends on the composition of the portfolio. It is an approximation to pretend that the optimal decision at the beginning of the period seeks a good probability distribution of return on the value of the assets (and not on the composition of assets) at the end of the period. The question here is: given that we make such an approximation, is it better (i.e. does it provide greater expected utility for the whole game) to pretend that the holding period is a month, a year, or something else? I do not know the answer. But today, with low commissions, with high transaction volumes and therefore reasonably liquid markets, and with the active use of securities (such as options and futures) whose life is a fraction of a year, perhaps a monthly (or quarterly) holding period is the better approximation. Thus far all experiments with monthly holding period returns show f_E to be extremely accurate except for pathologically risk averse utility functions.

symmetrical" then the probability distribution of a portfolio is known once its E and V are known. Joint normal is a special case of spherically symmetrical. Ross (1978) shows that an even broader class of joint distributions implies that the mean-variance capital asset pricing models are precisely right if $\Sigma X_i = 1$ is the only constraint.

There is no conflict between the Chamberlain (1983) and Ross (1978) approaches, on the one hand, and that of Markowitz (1959). If the form of the joint distribution of returns is such as to justify mean-variance analysis, then an argument based on quadratic approximation is not needed. If the joint distributions are not of the required form, then perhaps a quadratic approximation argument will apply.

Continuous trading

Merton (1969, 1971) developed portfolio theory assuming that the investor could trade continuously in time. Black and Scholes (1973) assume the Mossin (1966) model - i.e. Black's model with a riskless asset - plus continuous trading and a particular probability distribution of stock price changes. From these assumptions they derive a formula for the value of an option on the stock as a function of the stock's current price, its variance, the time until the expiration of the option, and the payoff formula for the option.

In one sense the single-period model analyzed in this book can approximate Merton's continuous time model, and may include puts, calls, or other securities derived from a given security. In another sense this book ignores the continuous time model and option pricing theory. We will briefly explain the two senses and why we ignore these fertile concepts, which have been widely used in theory and applications.

The assumption of continuous trading leads to an "instantaneous" portfolio analysis which is virtually indistinguishable from a single-period portfolio analysis where the period is, say, a second in duration. The analysis in this book applies to a single period of any duration - a year, a month, a day, a second - and, in effect, to Merton's instant. Furthermore, the securities of our analysis need not be confined to bonds and stocks, but may include derivative securities like puts, calls, and futures. The relationship between the price of one of these at the end of the period, as a function of the price of the underlying security and perhaps other things at the end of the period, may be assumed to follow the Black-Scholes formula, or may be assumed to follow some existing or yet-to-be-developed rival model. All we require is that the model provide the analysis with means and variances of return on the derivative securities, and covariances between each of these and each of the other securities of the analysis.

The single period of our single-period analysis, then, may be essentially an "instant" in a model with continuous trading, and may include derivative securities as well as stocks and bonds. But we will not attempt to derive the Black-Scholes option pricing formula. This is in contrast to other historically important formulas which we will derive, generalize, or assign as exercises. The Black-Scholes formula is deduced from an argument which – very roughly speaking – relates option price as a function of the stock price *at one instant* to that at a *nearby instant* (so to speak). In general we will ignore the connection between periods. For example, we will not rederive the results of Mossin (1968) concerning myopic utility functions for a discrete time many-period game (although our preceding remarks imply that the Mossin results plus the notion of quadratic approximation may be used as a justification for single-period mean-variance analysis). Similarly we will not rederive here the Merton or Black-Scholes "connection between instants."

We have a bookfull of material to cover in order to understand the general single-period analysis itself. We note that this single-period analysis is a component of various discrete or continuous dynamic analyses without pursuing any of these. To do otherwise would increase the size of the book substantially, especially if we attempted a rigorous account of models with continuous trading. As it is, the mathematical requirements of our current topic, beyond the calculus and matrix algebra prerequisites announced in the preface and reviewed in the appendix to the book, are presented in one chapter – chapter 4. Several more such chapters would be required for a rigorous account of stochastic integrals and related topics used in models of continuous trading.[10]

[10] See Malliaris and Brock (1982) for a survey of basic mathematical relationships with proofs or references to proofs, and applications to economic and financial models including option pricing. Also see Karatzas et al. (1986) for a rigorous derivation of the optimum solution to a large class of continuous time investment/consumption models.

Part II

Preliminary Results

4

Properties of Feasible Portfolio Sets

The present chapter assumes that the reader is familiar with the notion of a vector as a point in n dimensional space, and related ideas, covered in the appendix to the book through page 358. The remainder of the appendix will be needed for chapter 5.

Definitions We will speak of points in *EV space*, in *Eσ space*, and in *portfolio space*. *EV* space is the two-dimensional space whose points are *EV* combinations; *Eσ* space is the two-dimensional space whose points are *Eσ* combinations; and portfolio space is the n dimensional space R^n whose points are portfolios (X_1, $X_2, \ldots, X_n$). We will speak of any n component vector as a point in portfolio space or, briefly, *a portfolio*, whether or not it is a feasible portfolio given the requirements of the particular analysis.

This chapter deals with portfolio space. It presents properties of the set of feasible portfolios for any portfolio selection model as defined in chapter 2. We begin by defining and analyzing properties which some sets in R^n have and others do not, e.g. the properties of being closed, convex, or compact. We will see, for example, that every portfolio selection constraint set has the first two of these properties, and every bounded constraint set has the third. Implications of such properties as they relate to *EV* efficient sets will emerge partly in this chapter and partly in subsequent chapters.

Properties of sets - such as those of being closed, convex, or compact - are studied in the field of functional analysis. This chapter presents as much functional analysis as will be used in this book. If the reader has no prior exposure to the subject the present chapter may prove to be the most difficult of all the chapters which are essential to an understanding of the rest of the book. (Chapter 9 is difficult, but most of it can be skipped at a first reading.)

The reader is urged to pay particular attention to definitions of concepts such as sphere, ball, open set, closed set, and the like. The definitions are quite precise and, in many instances, not something one could guess accurately from the ordinary nonmathematical usage of the words.

Some concepts and results of this chapter appear frequently in following chapters. This is true in particular of convexity, affine hull, and the characterization of directions as infeasible, bounded feasible, and unbounded feasible. Other concepts appear less frequently. For example, after this chapter the notion of a cone does not appear again until chapter 12. The reader may wish to refer back to the discussion in this chapter when a concept first appears in a later chapter.

It is not essential for the reader to master every detail of this chapter before moving on to the rest of the book. In particular, the reader may wish to leave some of the longer proofs go with a superficial reading at first. Partly to facilitate this, a proof is separated from subsequent material by an end of proof mark ###.

While this chapter is intended as a self-contained introduction to as much functional analysis as we will need, the reader may wish further readings on this topic either for an alternate exposition of the material herein, or to increase his or her scope in the area. Most of what we present here on this subject may be found in chapter 3 of Dieudonné (1969). If the reader is not familiar with elementary set theory and the properties of real numbers, he or she may wish to supplement the reading of chapters 1 and 2 of Dieudonné by some other account of these same topics, e.g. that in Birkhoff and MacLane (1977). Kolmogorov and Fomin (1957) is a quite readable introduction to functional analysis. Unfortunately, Dieudonné and Kolmogorov-Fomin use slightly different definitions of the word "compact." We follow the Dieudonné usage. The notion of a recession cone, an important property of unbounded convex sets, is presented in Rockafeller (1970). The latter work assumes that the reader knows basic functional analysis, and contains an exhaustive presentation of the properties of convex sets and convex functions.

Notation

We will use the notation from logic and set theory shown in table 4.1. The symbols defined in the table allow us to express relationships involving propositions and sets in a compact manner, and to manipulate them formally. They serve a role similar to that of the symbols of arithmetic. We could express verbally that a third number is related to two others by the following relationship: the third is the first times itself added to the second times itself, this sum divided by the second less the first. But I imagine that the reader has come to prefer the notation $C=(a^2+b^2)/(a-b)$. The symbols in table 4.1 provide a similar compactness and (once learned) clarity for relationships involving propositions and sets.

Typically, the meaning of each abbreviation should be substituted in reading any statement involving the symbols in table 4.1. For example, the statement "$\exists N \forall i \geqslant N$: $|b_i - a| < \epsilon$" should be read as "there is an N such that, for every

Table 4.1 Set notation

Notation	*Meaning*	*Examples and explanation*
$\in$	is a member of; belongs to	$X \in S$ means X belongs to the set S. There should be no confusion between the use of ϵ as a variable, as in "for any $\epsilon > 0$", and the use of $\in$ as an abbreviation for "belongs to", since only one of these meanings makes sense in any given use. Moreover, the printed symbols are clearly different
$\notin$	is not a member of; does not belong to	$X \notin S$ means X does not belong to S
$\subset$	is a subset of	$S \subset T$ means S is a subset of T, i.e. every X in S is also in T. In particular $S \subset R^n$ means S is a subset of R^n
$\cap$	intersection	$A \cap B$ means the set of X such that $X \in A$ and $X \in B$. Note that $A \cap B \subset A$ and $A \cap B \subset B$
$\cup$	union	$A \cup B$ means the set of X such that $X \in A$ or $X \in B$. Note that $A \subset A \cup B$ and $B \subset A \cup B$
$A - B$	set A less set B	$X \in A - B$ means $X \in A$ and $X \notin B$
$\emptyset$	the empty set	e.g. $\{x \in R : x > 0\} \cap \{x \in R : x < 0\} = \emptyset$
I_{nt}^{+}	the set of positive integers	$I_{nt}^{+} = \{1, 2, 3, \ldots\}$
$\forall$	all; for every	$\forall\, \delta > 0$ stands for "for every $\delta > 0$"
$\exists$	exists; there is . . . such that; there exists . . . such that	$\exists\, \delta > 0$ stands for "there is a $\delta > 0$ such that"
:	serves as punctuation only	$\forall\, \epsilon > 0\ \exists\, \delta > 0 : P(x)$ should be read "for every $\epsilon > 0$ there is a $\delta > 0$ such that $P(X)$ is true", where $P(X)$ is some proposition about X (e.g. $d(X, 0) < \epsilon$). The preceding may also be written as $\forall\, \epsilon > 0\ \exists\, \delta > 0\ (P(X))$
$\sim$	not; it is false that	e.g. $\sim(\exists X \in S : P(X))$ means "it is not true that there is an X in S such that $P(X)$ is true". This proposition is true if and only if $\forall\, X \in S : \sim P(X)$
$\{A : B\}$	the set of A such that B is true	$\{X \in R^n : X \geqslant 0\}$ refers to the set of X in R^n such that $X \geqslant 0$

$i \geqslant N$, $|b_i - a| < \epsilon$" rather than read "backward E, upside down A$i \geqslant N$..." or stared at and not read at all. An exception to the rule, that the meaning of each symbol should be read in full, may be allowable when expressions involving logical symbols ($\exists$, $\forall$, $\sim$) are manipulated in a manner analogous to the manipulation of arithmetic symbols. Even then, at least the final logical expression as well as the initial logical expression should be read in full.

Parentheses can be used to define the scope of $\exists$ and $\forall$. The following illustrates the parentheses which are implied when not given explicitly with $\exists$ and $\forall$. The statement

$$\forall \epsilon > 0 \; \exists N \in I_{\text{nt}}^{+} \; \forall i \geqslant N : (\quad)$$

means the same thing as

$$\forall \epsilon > 0 (\exists N \in I_{\text{nt}}^{+} (\forall i \geqslant N : (\quad)))$$

i.e.

$\forall \epsilon > 0$ the following is true

$\exists N \in I_{\text{nt}}^{+}$ such that the following is true

$\forall i \geqslant N$ the following is true

In some cases we will prove theorems about a set without requiring that the set have members. For example, below we show that if A is closed and B is closed then so is $A \cap B$, without ruling out the possibility that $A \cap B = \emptyset$. This raises the question of the meaning of $\exists X \in S : P(X)$ and $\forall X \in S : P(X)$ when $S = \emptyset$. The statement "$\exists X \in \emptyset : P(X)$" is always false, since $\emptyset$ has no members. The statement $\forall X \in \emptyset : P(X)$ is always true, since it is the same as the statement $\sim(\exists X \in \emptyset : \sim P(X))$. Usually we prove a statement of the form $\forall X \in S : P(X)$ by assuming $X \in S$ and deducing $P(X)$. That is, we start with a statement like "suppose $X \in S$" and, after permitted inferences, end with the conclusion "proposition P is true of X". No special consideration need be given the possibility that $S = \emptyset$ in such an argument, since "$X \in \emptyset : P(X)$" is true always.

It is possible to deduce valid propositions (of logic and mathematics) by proceeding, by prescribed rules of inference, from axioms and previously proved propositions. Most mathematics texts, and even most books on logic, proceed more casually – as we shall in this book. We will use the symbols of table 4.1 as a convenient shorthand; on a small number of occasions we will manipulate logical expressions formally. But our proofs generally will leave many small steps implicit, as is the usual practice. For a monumental work on symbolic logic – and an object lesson as to why few other works attempt to make all steps explicit – see Whitehead and Russell (1910). Hilbert and Ackermann (1928) is a classic but readable exposition describing logical axioms and rules of inference. Kleene (1952) is a more modern introduction.

The Limit of a Sequence

The concept of the limit of a sequence is introduced in the calculus. For example, Courant (1937) states that "the fundamental concept on which the whole of analysis [calculus, differential equations, etc.] ultimately rests is that of the limit of a sequence." Nevertheless I find that more than half my students cannot write down the formal definition of such a limit. Since this concept and its definition will be used frequently hereafter, we review it.

Let $a_1, a_2, a_3, \ldots$ be a sequence of real numbers. The statements "$a_1, a_2, a_3, \ldots$ converges to the number b", or

$$\lim_{i \to \infty} a_i = b$$

or

$$a_1, a_2, a_3, \ldots \to b$$

or "b is the limit of the sequence $a_1, a_2, \ldots$", are defined as follows:

$$\lim_{i \to \infty} a_i = b$$

means

$$\forall \epsilon > 0 \; \exists N \in I_{\text{nt}}^{+} \; \forall i \geqslant N : |a_i - b| < \epsilon \tag{4.1}$$

In other words:

given any positive number, traditionally denoted by ϵ

then

a positive integer N can be found

so that

for any integer i which is at least as great as N

the following is true:

the absolute value of the difference between a_i and b is less than the specified ϵ

Note that the assertion is not about one particular value of ϵ, but about every possible value of ϵ, provided only that it is greater than zero. Note also that N is chosen after ϵ, and therefore may vary from one ϵ to another. Note finally that once N is chosen (for a given ϵ) then $|a_i - b| < \epsilon$ must hold for each and every i from N onward.

Consider the sequence 1, 1/2, 1/3, . . . , $1/i$, ... It seems natural to say that this sequence "approaches zero," and indeed the sequence meets the definition (4.1) of $a_i \to 0$; since given any $\epsilon > 0$ (e.g. $\epsilon = 1/1{,}000{,}000$ or $\epsilon = 1/1{,}000{,}000{,}000$) we can always choose an N (e.g. $N = 1{,}000{,}001$ or $N = 1{,}000{,}000{,}001$) such that $|1/i - 0| = 1/i$ is less than ϵ for every $i \geqslant N$.

It is not necessary for a sequence to approach its limit from one direction. For example, the sequence

$$-1, +1/2, -1/3, +1/4, \ldots, (-1)^i/i, \ldots$$

still meets the definition of $a_i \to 0$; since if $\epsilon = 1/1{,}000$ (for example) then

$$|a_i - 0| = |a_i| < \epsilon$$

provided that $i \geqslant 1{,}001$.

Any of our examples with $a_i \to 0$ can be converted to an example with $a_i \to b$ for any real b by adding b to each term of the sequence. For example,

$$6, 5.5, 5 + 1/3, \ldots, 5 + 1/i, \ldots$$

approaches 5, since $|a_i - 5| < \epsilon$ for every $i \geqslant N$ if N is chosen so that $N > 1/\epsilon$.

It is not necessary for each term in the sequence to be closer than the preceding term in order for the sequence to converge. Consider for example

$$1, 5, 1/3, 2.5, 1/5, 10/6, \ldots, \begin{Bmatrix} 1/i \text{ if } i \text{ is odd} \\ 10/i \text{ if } i \text{ is even} \end{Bmatrix}, \ldots$$

It is still true that $a_i \to 0$ by definition (4.1), since $|a_i| < \epsilon$ provided $i > 10/\epsilon$.

A sequence which is always the same number, or always the same number after some i, has this number as its limit. For example,

$$1, 2, 3, 4, 5, 5, 5, \ldots$$

has 5 as its limit, since $\forall \epsilon > 0, |a_i - 5| < \epsilon$ for $i \geqslant 5$.

Not every sequence has a limit. For example,

$$0, 1, 0, 1, \ldots, \begin{Bmatrix} 0 \text{ if } i \text{ odd} \\ 1 \text{ if } i \text{ even} \end{Bmatrix}, \ldots$$

has no limit. This seems plausible since the sequence *stays* close to neither 0, nor 1, nor any other number. We can show that, indeed, it fails to meet the definition (4.1) as follows.

We will repeatedly apply the relationships

$$\sim (\exists x \in S : P(x)) \quad \text{if and only if} \quad (\forall x \in S : \sim P(x))$$

and

$$\sim (\forall x \in S : P(x)) \quad \text{if and only if} \quad (\exists x \in S : \sim P(x))$$

For example, the negation of (4.1), i.e.

$$\sim(\forall\, \epsilon>0\ \exists\, N\in I^{+}_{\text{nt}}\ \forall\, i\geqslant N\colon |a_i-b|<\epsilon)$$

is

$$\exists\, \epsilon>0\colon \sim(\exists\, N\in I^{+}_{\text{nt}}\ \forall\, i\geqslant N\colon |a_i-b|<\epsilon) \tag{4.2a}$$

Then expanding the $\sim(\ \ )$ in (4.2a) we get

$$\exists\, \epsilon>0\ \forall\, N\in I^{+}_{\text{nt}}\colon \sim(\forall\, i\geqslant N\colon |a_i-b|<\epsilon) \tag{4.2b}$$

Expanding $\sim(\ \ )$ one more time we finally get

$$\exists\, \epsilon>0\ \forall\, N\in I^{+}_{\text{nt}}\ \exists\, i\geqslant N\colon |a_i-b|\geqslant\epsilon \tag{4.2c}$$

where we have written $|a_i-b|\geqslant\epsilon$ in place of $\sim(|a_i-b|<\epsilon)$. Since the assertion is $\exists\, \epsilon>0\ldots$, to confirm that (4.2c) holds for the sequence 0, 1, 0, 1, . . . we need only exhibit a single value of $\epsilon>0$ such that the remainder of (4.2c) holds. Whether we set $b=0$, or $b=1$, or $b=1/2$, or any other value, for $\epsilon=1/4$ it is true that for *every* N there is an $i\geqslant N$ (actually N itself or $N+1$) such that $|a_i-b|>\epsilon$. Thus this sequence converges to no b.

Another sequence without a limit is this:

$$1, 0, 0, 0, 0, 0, 0, 0, 0, 1, 0, \ldots \begin{Bmatrix} 1 \text{ if } \log_{10} i \text{ is an integer} \\ 0 \text{ otherwise} \end{Bmatrix}, \ldots$$

This sequence equals zero most of the time, and increasingly so as i increases. Nevertheless for any choice of b, if we set $\epsilon=1/4$ then, for any N no matter how great, there is eventually an $i\geqslant N$ such that $|a_i-b|>\epsilon$. Thus the sequence does not converge.

The elementary properties of limits may be deduced from definition (4.1). For example, if $a_1, a_2, \ldots \to a_0$ and $b_1, b_2, \ldots \to b_0$ are two convergent sequences with the limits noted, then

$$\begin{aligned} \lim_{i\to\infty} (a_i+b_i) &= a_0+b_0 \\ &= \lim a_i + \lim b_i \end{aligned} \tag{4.3a}$$

(When it is clear which subscript is meant - e.g. when there is only one subscript - then the "$i\to\infty$" may be omitted, as above.)

Equation (4.3a) may be shown as follows. For $\epsilon^*=\epsilon/2$ there is an N_a and an N_b such that

$$|a_i-a_0|<\epsilon^* \qquad \text{for } i\geqslant N_a$$

$$|b_i-b_0|<\epsilon^* \qquad \text{for } i\geqslant N_b$$

For $N = \max(N_a, N_b)$

$$\begin{aligned} |a_i + b_i - (a_0 + b_0)| &= |(a_i - a_0) + (b_i - b_0)| \\ &\leqslant |a_i - a_0| + |b_i - b_0| \\ &< 2\epsilon^* = \epsilon \end{aligned}$$

One can similarly verify that

$$\lim_{i\to\infty} (c + a_i) = c + \lim_{i\to\infty} a_i \tag{4.3b}$$

$$\lim a_i b_i = (\lim a_i)(\lim b_i) \tag{4.3c}$$

$$\lim (a_i)^2 = (\lim a_i)^2 \tag{4.3d}$$

(See exercise 4.1(c) concerning the last.) An immediate corollary of (4.3c) is that $\lim ba_i = b \lim a_i$.

Convergence in R^n

The concept of a convergent sequence can be extended to sequences of points in R^n. Let $X^1, X^2, X^3, \ldots$ be a sequence of points $X^i \in R^n$. Note that X^1 does not represent a first component of some vector X, but a first vector with components $X^1 = (X^1_1, X^1_2, X^1_3, \ldots, X^1_n)$. We say that X^i converges to $X_0 \in R^n$, or write

$$\lim_{i\to\infty} X^i = X_0$$

or

$$X^1, X^2, \ldots \to X_0$$

if, for every $\epsilon > 0$, there is an N such that $d(X^i, X_0) < \epsilon$ for every $i \geqslant N$, where $d(X^i, X_0)$ is the distance function defined in equation (A.15). In symbols:

$$X_0 = \lim X^i$$

means

$$\forall \epsilon > 0 \; \exists N \in I^+_{\text{nt}} \; \forall i \geqslant N : d(X^i, X_0) < \epsilon \tag{4.4}$$

The definition (4.1) of a sequence of numbers (i.e. a sequence of $a_i \in R^1$) is a special case of (4.4), since $d(X^i, X_0) = |X^i - X_0|$ for $X^i \in R^1$. Equation (4.4) requires that given any (not just some, but any) $\epsilon > 0$ there is an N - whose choice may depend on ϵ - such that from the Nth place in the sequence onward (without exception) the distance from X^i to X_0 is less than ϵ. Definition (4.4) is fundamental to the material which follows.

Closed Sets

Definitions The *open interval*

$$(a, b) = \{x \in R : a < x < b\}$$

is the set of real numbers between a and b excluding the end points of the interval. The *closed interval* is

$$[a, b] = \{x \in R : a \leqslant x \leqslant b\}$$

If $b < a$ then $(a, b) = [a, b] = \emptyset$. If $a = b$ then $(a, b) = \emptyset$, whereas $[a, b] = \{a\}$, the set containing only a. Let $a_i = 1/i$; then both of the following statements is true:

$$a_i \in (0, 1) \qquad \forall i \in I^+_{\text{nt}} \tag{4.5a}$$

$$a_i \in [0, 1] \qquad \forall i \in I^+_{\text{nt}} \tag{4.5b}$$

But since $\lim a_i = 0$,

$$\lim a_i \notin (0, 1) \tag{4.6a}$$

$$\lim a_i \in [0, 1] \tag{4.6b}$$

Equations (4.5a) and (4.6a) show that each point in a sequence can belong to a set S, the sequence can converge, yet the limit may not be in the set. The example in (4.5a) is in terms of points in R, but the same is possible for points in $S \subset R^n$ for $n > 1$.

Equation (4.6b) notes that the limit of $a_1, a_2, \ldots$ is contained in the set $[0, 1]$. Later we shall see that if $a_1, a_2, \ldots$ are points in $[0, 1]$ and if, in addition, it is known that $a_1, a_2, \ldots$ converges to some limit, say a_0, then a_0 is always in $[0, 1]$.

Definition A set $S \subset R^n$ for $n \geqslant 1$, is said to be *closed* if every sequence $X^1, X^2, \ldots$ such that

$$X^i \in S \qquad \text{for } i \in I^+_{\text{nt}}$$

and such that

$$X^1, X^2, \ldots \text{ converges}$$

has

$$\lim X^i \in S$$

The definition of a closed set S does not assert that every sequence of points in S has a limit. Rather it requires that such sequences as do converge have their limit in S. We say that a closed set S contains all its limit points. Examples of closed sets will be provided later, after we learn more about how to identify sets as closed.

Spheres, Balls, and Open Sets

Definition The *sphere* with center $X \in R^n$ and radius $r > 0$ is defined as the set

$$S_r(X) = \{Y \in R^n : d(X, Y) = r\}$$

Confirm that

(1) For $n = 1$, $S_r(X)$ consists of the two points $X + r$ and $X - r$.
(2) For $n = 2$, $S_r(X)$ is the circle with radius r and center $X = (X_1, X_2)$.
(3) For $n = 3$, $S_r(X)$ is the sphere with radius r and center $X = (X_1, X_2, X_3)$.

Frequently we use the letter S to represent an arbitrary subset of R^n. Such a set S may be, but typically is not, a sphere symbolized by $S_r(X)$. We will usually use some other letter, such as T, to designate an arbitrary set when some sphere $S_r(X)$ is also under discussion.

Definition The *open ball* $B_r(X)$ with center X and radius $r > 0$ is defined to be

$$B_r(X) = \{Y \in R^n : d(X, Y) < r\}$$

Confirm that

(1) For $n = 1$, $B_r(X)$ is the open interval $(X - r, X + r)$.
(2) For $n = 2$, $B_r(X)$ is the area within the circle $S_r(X)$, not including the circle itself.
(3) For $n = 3$, $B_r(X)$ is the set of points within the sphere $S_r(X)$, not including the sphere itself.

Consider any point in (0, 1), for example the point $x = 0.999$. For r sufficiently small, e.g. $r = 0.0005$, the entire set

$$B_{0.0005}(0.999) = (0.9985, 0.9995)$$

is contained within (0, 1). This is true for any point $X \in (0, 1)$ where the choice of r depends on X. It is not true for the set $[0, 1]$ since, for example, $(1 - r, 1 + r)$ is not contained completely in $[0, 1]$ for any choice of $r > 0$. Set (0, 1) is an example of an open set, defined more generally as follows.

Definition A set $T \subset R^n$ is said to be *open* if, for any $X \in T$ there is an r such that

$$B_r(X) \subset T$$

In symbols, T is open means

$$\forall X \in T \; \exists r > 0 : B_r(X) \subset T$$

Theorem 4.1 The following are open sets:

(i) $B_r(X) \qquad \forall X \in R^n \; \forall r > 0$
(ii) $\{X \in R^n : d(X, a) > r\} \qquad \forall r > 0 \; \forall a \in R^n$
(iii) R^n
(iv) $\emptyset$

Proof

(i) Suppose $Y \in B_r(X)$. Let $d_Y = d(Y, X) < r$. Also $r^* = (r - d_Y)/2 > 0$. If $Z \in B_{r^*}(Y)$ then

$$\begin{aligned} d(X, Z) &\leqslant d(X, Y) + d(Y, Z) \\ &\leqslant d_Y + (r - d_Y)/2 \\ &= (r + d_Y)/2 \\ &< r \end{aligned}$$

Thus $Z \in B_r(X)$. Since Z is an arbitrary point in $B_{r^*}(Y)$ we conclude

$$B_{r^*}(Y) \subset B_r(X)$$

and since Y is an arbitrary point in $B_r(X)$ we conclude $B_r(X)$ is open.

(ii) This is the set outside (as opposed to inside) the sphere $S_r(X)$. The proof is similar to (i) for $B_r(X)$ inside the sphere.

(iii) This is trivial, since for any $X \in R^n$ and any $r > 0$, $B_r(X) \subset R^n$.

(iv) Follows from the comments in the earlier section on notation concerning the truth of propositions of the form $\forall X \in \emptyset : P(X)$. ###

Theorem 4.2 If $S_1, S_2, \ldots, S_k$ are open sets, then $S_1 \cup S_2 \cup \ldots \cup S_k$ is open. In particular, if S_1 and S_2 are open then so is $S_1 \cup S_2$.

Proof If $X \in S_1 \cup S_2 \ldots \cup S_k$ then there is at least one i such that $X \in S_i$. But since S_i is open there is an $r > 0$ such that $B_r(X) \subset S_i \subset (S_1 \cup S_2 \ldots \cup S_k)$. Since X is any point in $S_1 \cup S_2 \ldots \cup S_k$, the theorem follows. ###

We will use open sets to help us identify closed sets. The connection between open and closed sets is the following.

Theorem 4.3 If S is an open subset of R^n then $C = R^n - S$ is closed. Conversely if C is a closed subset of R^n then $S = R^n - C$ is open.

Proof First we will show that if S is open then $C = R^n - S$ is closed. In light of the definition of a closed set, it suffices to show that C has all its limit points -

that is, if $X^i \in C\ \forall i \in I^+_{nt}$ and $X_0 = \lim X^i$, then X_0 is in C, not in S. Suppose, to the contrary, that $X_0 \in S$. Then, since S is open, there exists an $r>0$ such that $B_r(X_0)$ is a subset of S. Therefore there can be no $X^i \in C$ such that $d(X^i, X_0) < r$. This contradicts the assumption that $X^1, X^2, \ldots$ in C converges to X_0.

Next we assume that C is closed and show that S is open. It is sufficient to show that for any $X_0 \in S$ there is an r such that $B_r(X_0)$ is contained in S. Suppose to the contrary there were no such r for some X_0. Then for every $r>0$ there exists an $X^i \in C$ such that $d(X^i, X_0) < r$. In particular for $r_1, r_2, \ldots,$ where $r_i = 1/i$, we have $d(X^i, X_0) < 1/i$. It follows that $\forall r>0\ \exists N \in I^+_{nt}\ \forall i \geqslant N: d(X^i, X_0) < r$. Thus $X^i \to X_0$. But every X^i is in the closed set C. Hence X_0 must itself be in C, contradicting the assumption that $X_0 \in S$. ###

Corollary 4.4 For any $r>0$, $S_r(X)$ is a closed set.

Proof $R^n = S_r(X) \cup B_r(X) \cup \{Y \in R^n : d(X, Y) > r\}$, where no point is in more than one of the last three sets. Since the second and third sets are open (theorem 4.1), and therefore their union is open (theorem 4.2), it follows that $S_r(X)$ is closed (theorem 4.3). ###

Theorem 4.5 If $C_1, C_2, \ldots, C_k$ are closed, then so is $C_1 \cap C_2 \cap \ldots \cap C_n$.

Proof This follows from theorems 4.2 and 4.3, and from the fact that

$$R^n - (S_1 \cup S_2 \cup \ldots \cup S_k) = (R^n - S_1) \cap (R^n - S_2) \cap \ldots \cap (R^n - S_k)$$

The latter relationship - a basic result from elementary set theory - follows immediately from the definitions of $A \cap B$, $A \cup B$, and $A - B$. ###

In the calculus, a real-valued function of one variable is defined to be continuous at a particular number x if for any $\epsilon>0$ there is $\delta>0$ such that $|f(y)-f(x)|<\epsilon$ provided that $|x-y|<\delta$. The function is called continuous if it is continuous at every x. This definition may be extended to functions whose argument (i.e. whose "input") is a point in R^m and whose value (i.e. whose "output") is a point in R^n.

Definition A function $Y = f(X)$, $X \in R^m$, $Y \in R^n$, is *continuous* at $X_0 \in R^m$ if for every $\epsilon>0$ there is a $\delta>0$ such that the distance between $f(X)$ and $f(X_0)$ is less than ϵ provided that X and X_0 are closer than δ. In symbols

$f(X)$ is continuous at X_0

means

$$\forall \epsilon>0\ \exists \delta>0\ \forall X \in B_\delta(X_0) : f(X) \in B_\epsilon(f(X_0))$$

(*Exercise* Make sure the symbolic definition says the same thing as the verbal one.) The function is said to be *continuous* if it is continuous at every point in R^m

Theorem 4.6 Let $Y = f(X)$ for $X \in R^m$, $Y \in R^n$. The following two statements are equivalent - one is true if and only if the other is true:

(i) f is continuous.
(ii) If $X^1, X^2, X^3, \ldots$ is any sequence of points in R^m which converges to a point X_0, then $f(X^1), f(X^2), f(X^3), \ldots$ is a sequence of points in R^n which converges to $f(X_0)$.

Proof First we will suppose (i) and prove that (ii) follows, i.e. that $X^1, X^2, \ldots \to X^0$ implies $f(X^1), f(X^2), \ldots \to f(X^0)$. In other words we must show that $\forall\, \epsilon > 0\ \exists\, N \in I^+_{\text{nt}}\ \forall\, i \geq N : d(f(X^i), f(X_0)) < \epsilon$. The fact that f is continuous implies that - given the aforementioned ϵ -

$$\exists\, \delta > 0\ \forall\, X \in B_\delta(X_0) : f(X) \in B_\epsilon(f(X_0))$$

Since $\lim X^i = X_0$, given $\delta > 0$

$$\exists\, N \in I^+_{\text{nt}}\ \forall\, i \geq N : X \in B_\delta(X_0)$$

For this choice of N, then

$$\forall\, i \geq N : f(X^i) \in B_\epsilon(f(X_0))$$

as was to be shown.

Next we assume (ii) and derive (i). To show (i) it is sufficient to show that

$$\forall\, X_0 \in R^m\ \forall\, \epsilon > 0\ \exists\, \delta > 0\ \forall\, X \in B_\delta(X_0) : f(X) \in B_\epsilon(f(X_0)) \tag{4.7a}$$

We will suppose this i.e. (i) to be false and derive a contradiction; that is, we will show that (ii) cannot be true, contrary to the assumption at the beginning of this paragraph. Proceeding as with equation (4.2), we see that the negation of (4.7a) is

$$\exists\, X_0 \in R^m\ \exists\, \epsilon > 0\ \forall\, \delta > 0\ \exists\, X \in B_\delta(X_0) : f(X) \notin B_\epsilon(f(X_0)) \tag{4.7b}$$

In particular, for the X_0 and ϵ whose existence is supposed in (4.7b), and for $\delta_1 = 1$, then $\delta_2 = 1/2$, then $\delta_3 = 1/3, \ldots, \delta_i = 1/i$, etc., there is an X^i such that $X^i \in B_{1/i}(X_0)$ but $f(X^i) \notin B_\epsilon(f(X_0))$. But then $X^1, X^2, X^3, \ldots \to X^0$, but not $f(X^1), f(X^2), \ldots \to f(X_0)$. Thus the supposition that (i) is false leads to the conclusion that (ii) is false; hence if (ii) is true then (i) must be true. ###

Since (according to equations (4.3)) $\lim X^i = X_0$ implies $\lim \mu' X^i = \mu' X_0$ and $\lim (X^i)' C X^i = (X_0)' C X_0$, it follows that $\mu' X$ and $X' C X$ are continuous functions (as we knew already from the calculus).

Corollary 4.7 The following set is open: $\{X \in R^n : a'X > a_0\}$ for any fixed $a_0 \in R$ and $a \in R^n$ with $a \neq 0$.

Proof Let X be any point in the set, i.e. any point with $a'X > a_0$. Since $a'X$ is a continuous real-valued function, there is a $\delta > 0$ such that if $Z \in B_\delta(X)$

then $|a'Z - a'X| < a'X - a_0$. This implies that $a'Z > a_0$ (details left as an exercise). Since Z is an arbitrary point in $B_\delta(X)$, we see that $B_\delta(X) \subset \{X \in R^n : a'X > a_0\}$. Since X is an arbitrary point in the set, the set is open. ###

Theorem 4.8 For fixed $a_0 \in R$ and $a \in R^n$ with $a \neq 0$, the following sets are closed:

(i) $S_a = \{X \in R^n : a'X \geqslant a_0\}$
(ii) $S_b = \{X \in R^n : a'X \leqslant a_0\}$
(iii) $S_c = \{X \in R^n : a'X = a_0\}$
(iv) R^n
(v) $\emptyset$

Proof Corollary 4.7 says that $R^n - S_b$ is open; therefore S_b is closed. S_a is the same as $\{X \in R^n : (-a)'X \leqslant -a_0\}$, so case (ii) covers case (i). Since the intersection of two closed sets is closed (theorem 4.5), and $S_c = S_a \cap S_b$, cases (i) and (ii) imply case (iii). Cases (iv) and (v) follow from $R^n = R^n - \emptyset$, and $\emptyset = R^n - R^n$, and the fact that each is known to be open (theorem 4.1). ###

Corollary 4.9 The set of feasible portfolios of a portfolio selection model is a closed set.

Proof If the selection of a portfolio is subject to no constraints then the set of feasible portfolios is R^n - which is a closed set. Else, any one constraint of type (i), (ii), (iii), (iv), or (v) in equation (2.1) is satisfied by a closed set of points, according to theorem 4.8. But the set of points which satisfies two or more such constraints is the intersection of the sets which satisfy the individual constraints, and the intersection of closed sets is closed. ###

As a particular case of corollary 4.9, the "closed interval" $[a, b]$ is indeed a "closed set."

Compact Sets

Definition A set $S \subset R^n$ is *bounded* if it is contained in some ball; i.e. if there exist $X \in R^n$ and $r > 0$ such that $S \subset B_r(X)$.

The definition of boundedness can be stated in terms of some fixed center X_0; for, if a set is contained in the ball $B_r(X)$ it is also contained in the ball $B_{r+d(X,X_0)}(X_0)$. We will usually discuss boundedness in terms of $X_0 = 0$.

Some obtainable portfolio sets which satisfy the definition of the general portfolio selection model are bounded; others are unbounded. For example the standard model, and any model consisting of the standard model plus additional constraints, is bounded; for constraints (1.1a) and (1.1b) imply that $X_i \leqslant 1$ for $i = 1$ to n. Thus every feasible portfolio is in $B_n(0)$. On the other hand the Tobin-Sharpe-Lintner model and Black's model have unbounded constraint sets. In the Tobin-Sharpe-Lintner model, for example, the point $X_\lambda = (\lambda, 0, 0, \ldots, 0, \lambda - 1)$ is feasible for all $\lambda \geqslant 0$. But $d(0, X_\lambda) \geqslant \lambda$. Hence, for any $r > 0$, there is a feasible portfolio not contained in $B_r(0)$.

Definition $S \subset R^n$ is *compact* if S is closed and bounded.

In particular, in light of corollary 4.9, if the set of feasible portfolios of a portfolio selection model is bounded, then it is compact. Theorem 4.10 below shows us a property of compact sets which is sometimes used as its definition. The two definitions are equivalent if we consider only *finite* dimensional spaces, as we do in this book. This alternate definition is concerned with the notion of a convergent subsequence of a sequence of numbers.

The sequence 0, 1, 0, 1, 0, 1, ... has no limit. But if we look at only the a_i with i odd from this sequence we have the new sequence 0, 0, 0, ..., which converges to 0. Thus the sequence 0, 1, 0, 1, ... does not itself converge, but has a convergent subsequence. The same is true for

$$1, 1.5, 1/3, 1.25, 0.20, \ldots, \begin{Bmatrix} 1/i \text{ if } i \text{ odd} \\ 1 + 1/i \text{ if } i \text{ even} \end{Bmatrix}, \ldots$$

whose odd members form a subsequence which converges to 0, and whose even members form a subsequence that converges to 1. On the other hand, the sequence $1, 2, 3, \ldots, i, \ldots$ neither converges nor has a subsequence that does.

Definition Let $X^1, X^2, \ldots$ be a sequence of points in R^n. Let $i(1), i(2), i(3), \ldots$ be a sequence of positive integers such that $i(1) < i(2) < i(3) < \ldots$. (It is convenient in the present context to write $i(1)$ for the usual i_1.) The sequence consisting of $X^{i(1)}, X^{i(2)}, X^{i(3)}, \ldots$ is called a subsequence of $X^1, X^2, X^3, \ldots$. The sequence $X^1, X^2, X^3, \ldots$ is said to *have a convergent subsequence* if there is some choice of $i(1) < i(2) < i(3) \ldots$ such that $X^{i(1)}, X^{i(2)}, X^{i(3)} \ldots$ converges.

Theorem 4.10 $S \subset R^n$ is compact if and only if every sequence $X^1, X^2, X^3, \ldots$ with

$$X^i \in S \qquad \forall i \in I^+_{\text{nt}}$$

has a subsequence which converges to a point $X_0 \in S$.

The proof of this theorem is lengthy, and is presented in the appendix to this chapter.

Theorem 4.11 If $S \subset R$ is compact and nonempty ($S \neq \emptyset$) then S contains a largest number and a smallest number.

Proof We will show that the set S contains a largest member. The proof that it contains a smallest member is similar. This proof uses the following fact about the real numbers R: if a nonempty set of real numbers has an upper bound then it has a least upper bound. (An upper bound, for a set of real numbers S, is a number b such that $b \geq x$ for all $x \in S$.) That is, there exists a number, called the LUB or supremum (sup) of S, such that if b is any upper bound of S then $b \geq \sup(S)$. Suppose $S \subset R$ is compact and nonempty. Then, since a compact set is bounded, S has a least upper bound, say a_0. First suppose $a_0 \in S$. Then a_0 is the largest number in S, else it would not be an upper bound of S. Next suppose $a_0 \notin S$. We will show that a_0 is the limit of a sequence of points in S and, since S is closed, therefore must be in S - contradicting the supposition that $a_0 \notin S$. For every $i \in I^+_{nt}$, there is an $a_i \in S$ such that $a_i > a_0 - 1/i$, else S would have a smaller upper bound than a_0. But $a_1, a_2, a_3, \ldots \to a_0$, as was to be shown. ###

Definition Suppose $Y = f(X)$ is a function whose argument is $X \in R^m$ and whose value is $Y \in R^n$. Let S be any subset of R^m. Then by $f(S)$ we mean the set of Y such that $Y = f(X)$ for some $X \in S$. In other words,

$$f(S) = \{Y \in R^n : Y = f(X) \text{ for } X \in S\}$$

$f(S)$ is called the *image* of S (with respect to the function f).

Theorem 4.12 Let $Y = f(X)$ be a continuous function from $X \in R^m$ to $Y \in R^n$. If S is compact then $f(S)$ is compact.

Proof It is sufficient to show that if $Y^1, Y^2, Y^3, \ldots$ is any sequence of points in $f(S)$ then there is a subsequence $Y^{i(1)}, Y^{i(2)}, \ldots$ which converges to a point in $f(S)$. By definition of $f(S)$, there exists points $X^1, X^2, \ldots$ in S such that $Y^i = f(X^i)$, $\forall i \in I^+_{nt}$. Since S is compact there is a subsequence of $X^1, X^2, \ldots$, call it $X^{i(1)}, X^{i(2)}, \ldots$, such that $X^{i(1)}, X^{i(2)}, \ldots \to X_0$ for $X_0 \in S$. Since f is continuous, $f(X^{i(1)}), f(X^{i(2)}), \ldots \to f(X_0)$. But $f(X_0)$ is in $f(S)$ since $X_0 \in S$. Thus $f(X^{i(1)}), f(X^{i(2)}), \ldots$ is a subsequence of the Y^i which converges to a point in $f(S)$. ###

Theorem 4.13 Let S be a nonempty compact subset of R^n; let $y = f(X)$, for $y \in R$, $X \in R^n$, be a continuous function. There is an $X_{\min}$ and an $X_{\max}$ in S such that

$$f(X_{\min}) \leq f(X) \leq f(X_{\max}) \qquad \forall X \in S$$

In other words, a continuous real-valued function f achieves both a minimum and maximum on a compact set S.

Proof Theorem 4.12 assures that $f(S)$ is compact; and theorem 4.11 assures that, since $f(S) \subset R$, there exists $y_{\min}$ and $y_{\max}$ in $f(S)$ such that

$$y_{\min} \leq f(X) \leq y_{\max} \qquad \forall X \in S$$

$X_{\min}$ and $X_{\max}$ are points in S such that $y_{\min} = f(X_{\min})$ and $y_{\max} = f(X_{\max})$. ###

Convex Sets

If $\alpha' = (\alpha_1, \ldots, \alpha_n)$, and $\beta' = (\beta_1, \ldots, \beta_n)$ are constant vectors with $\beta \neq 0$, and t is a scalar variable, then the set of all portfolios X which satisfy

$$X = \alpha + \beta t \qquad \text{for all } t \in R \tag{4.8}$$

is a *straight line* in portfolio space. (This is equivalent to the definition of a straight line as a one-dimensional affine space, given in the appendix to the book (see exercise 4.2(d)), and has various properties one would expect of a straight line (see exercise 4.2(a)-(c)).) We must have $\beta \neq 0$, i.e. $\beta_i \neq 0$ for at least one i, otherwise X in (4.8) is a constant vector.

In R^n as in R^2, "two points determine a line." Given any two points in portfolio space, $X^a \neq X^b$, the straight line passing through these points satisfies

$$X = (1-t)X^a + tX^b \tag{4.9a}$$

$$= X^a + t(X^b - X^a) \tag{4.9b}$$

Note that (4.9b) is of the same form as (4.8). For $t = 0$, $X = X^a$; for $t = 1$, $X = X^b$; for $0 \leqslant t \leqslant 1$, X is on the line segment connecting X^a and X^b; for t outside the closed interval $[0, 1]$, X is on the line drawn through X^a and X^b but does not lie between them.

Definition A set S of points is *convex* if X and Y in S implies that the entire straight line segment between X and Y is also in S. In other words

$$X \in S \text{ and } Y \in S$$

implies

$$tX + (1-t)Y \in S \qquad \text{for } 0 \leqslant t \leqslant 1$$

Figures 4.1(a)-(c) illustrate convex and nonconvex sets in R^2. The area bounded by the curve in figure 4.1(a) is not convex, since the straight line connecting the particular points X and Y passes outside the set. The area on and in the circle in figure 4.1(b) is convex since a straight line connecting any two points in this set is contained in the set. Since theorem 4.8(ii) assures us that the set is closed, we may refer to it as a closed, convex set. If we exclude one or more of the boundary points from the set, the set is still convex but is not closed.

The set of points on and in the polygon *abcd* in figure 4.1(c) - that is, the set of points on or above the line passing through a and b, on or to the left of the line passing through b and c, on or below the line through c and d, and on or to the right of the line passing through d and a - is closed and convex. Corollary 4.9 showed that the set is closed. Convexity is shown in the following.

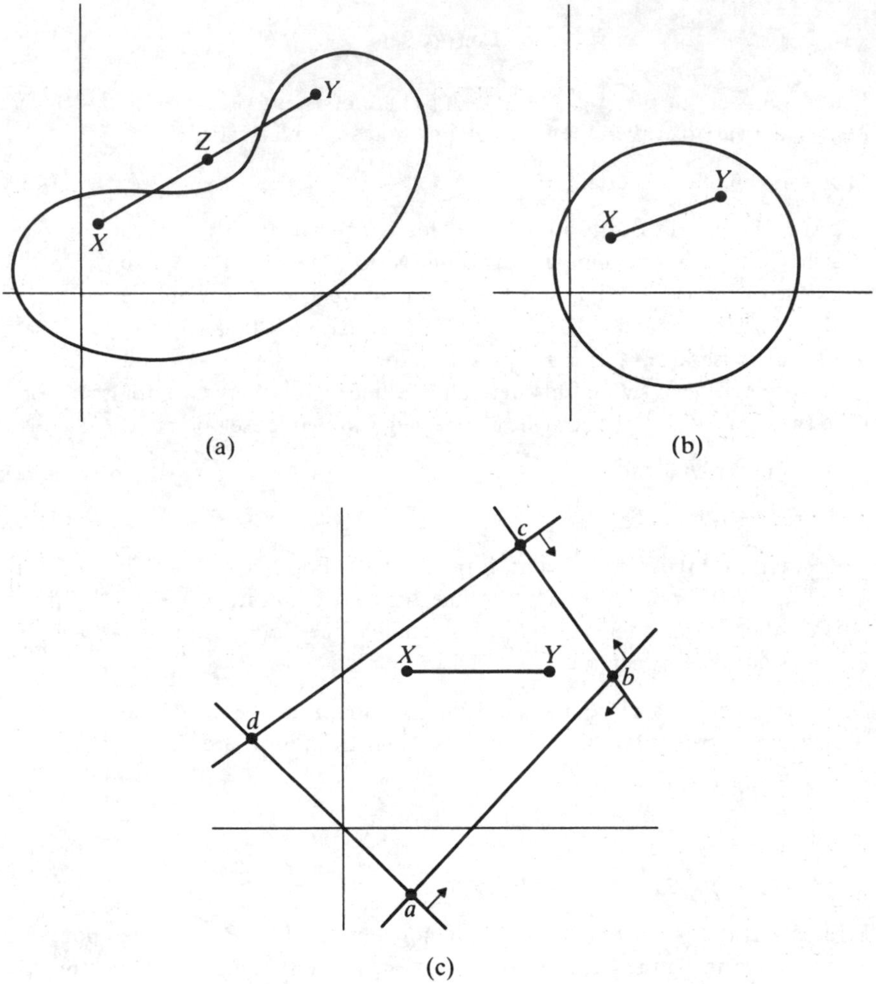

Figure 4.1 (*a*) *Nonconvex set* (*b*) *Convex set* (*c*) *Convex set*

Theorem 4.14 The set of points (portfolios) which satisfies the constraints of the general portfolio selection model, form 0, is a convex set.

Proof The notation is that of equation (2.1). Since constraint type (i) is a special case of (iii); (ii) is a special case of (iv); (iv) can be brought into type (iii) by multiplying both sides by −1; and one equation of type (v) is the same as a pair of constraints, one of type (iii) and one of type (iv); it is sufficient to prove the proposition for a constraint set of form 1. Suppose X and Y satisfy

$AX \geqslant b$ and $AY \geqslant b$. Then, for any t such that $0 \leqslant t \leqslant 1$,

$$A[tX + (1-t)Y] = tAX + (1-t)AY$$
$$\geqslant tb + (1-t)b = b$$

###

Notes on proof

(1) The theorem is trivially true if S does not contain two distinct points, either because it is empty or because S contains only one point.

(2) It would not have been sufficient to show that the result follows for models of form 2; for while there is always a model of form 2 which has the same set of obtainable EV combinations as a model of form 0, this model may change the shape – in fact, the dimensionality – of the set of feasible portfolios. In the case of the strictly equivalent model of form 1, the same set of X are feasible, though the constraints have been rewritten. Of course, now that we know that the theorem is true for all models of form 0 we know, in particular, it is true for models of form 2.

The property of convexity can be described as having every point in the set in "line of sight" of every other point. Every point can "see" every other without passing out of the set. In particular, suppose X_0 is a point in a convex set S, and $f(X)$ is a function defined on S. If for every ray starting at X_0, $f(X_0) \leqslant f(X)$, then X_0 minimizes $f(X)$ among X in S. If the reverse inequality holds, then X_0 provides a maximum.

Theorem 4.15 If $X^1, X^2, \ldots, X^k$ are in a convex set S, and if $\alpha_1, \alpha_2, \ldots, \alpha_k$ are k scalars such that

$$\Sigma\alpha_i = 1$$
$$\alpha_i \geqslant 0 \qquad i = 1, \ldots, k$$

then

$$\Sigma\alpha_i X^i$$

is in S.

Proof For $k = 2$, the theorem is the same as the definition of convexity. We will assume that the theorem is true for some $k \geqslant 2$, and prove that it is true for $k + 1$. The theorem follows by *mathematical induction* (i.e. we have shown that its truth for $k = 2$ proves its truth for $k = 3$; its truth for $k = 3$ proves its truth for $k = 4$; and so on). The proof is trivial if $\alpha_{k+1} = 1$. Else we may write

$$\sum_{i=1}^{k+1} \alpha_i X^i = \left(\sum_{i=1}^{k} \alpha_i\right)\left[\sum_{i=1}^{k}\left(\frac{\alpha_i}{\sum_{j=1}^{k}\alpha_j}\right) X^i\right] + \alpha_{k+1}X^{k+1}$$

The term in the [ ] is in S, by the inductive hypothesis; therefore the expression on the right-hand side is the nonnegative weighted average of two points in S - which is in S. ###

Definition A weighted sum $\Sigma_{i=1}^{k}\alpha_i X^i$, where $\Sigma\alpha_i = 1$ and $\alpha_i \geqslant 0$ for $i = 1, \ldots, k$, is called a *convex combination* of $X^1, \ldots, X^k$. Theorem 4.15 says that a convex combination of points in a convex set S, is itself in S.

Unbounded Constraint Sets

Theorem 4.17 stated below, and proved in the appendix to this chapter, presents an important property of closed convex unbounded sets, and hence of any unbounded set of feasible portfolios. We first illustrate this property with two two-dimensional examples, one with a convex unbounded set, the other with a nonconvex unbounded set. Consider the nonconvex region S in figure 4.2(a) bounded by

$$X_1 \geqslant 1 \qquad X_2 \geqslant 0 \qquad X_2 \leqslant 1/X_1$$

Let d be any point in the set with $X_2 > 0$. No ray starting at this point is contained completely in this set: for example, a horizontal ray will intersect the curve at $X_2 = 1/X_1$ and then move out of the set; any ray

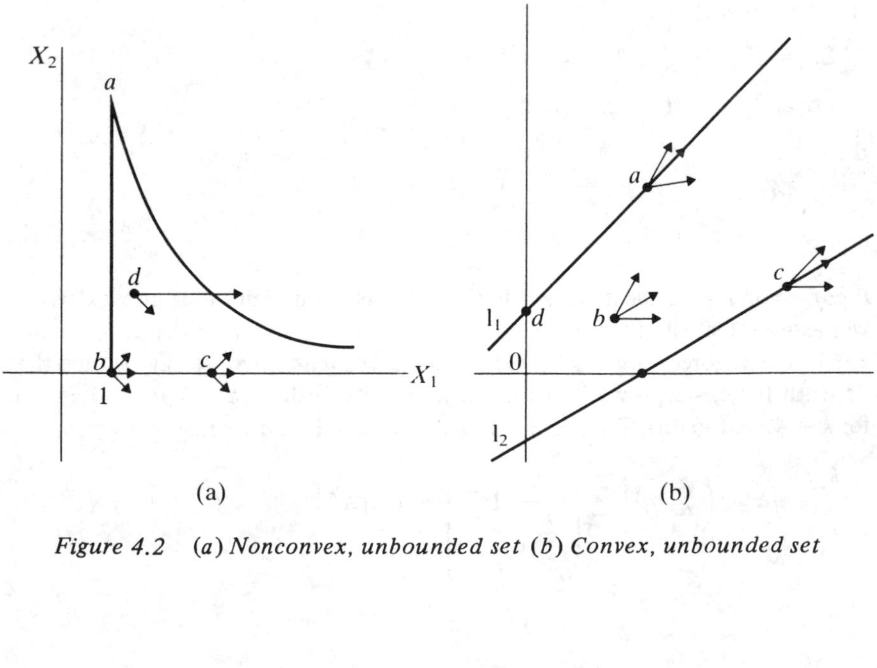

Figure 4.2 (*a*) *Nonconvex, unbounded set* (*b*) *Convex, unbounded set*

$$\begin{pmatrix} X_1 \\ X_2 \end{pmatrix} = \begin{pmatrix} X_1^d \\ X_2^d \end{pmatrix} + t\begin{pmatrix} b_1 \\ b_2 \end{pmatrix} \qquad t \geqslant 0$$

with $b_2 < 0$ will intersect the $X_2 = 0$ boundary (and perhaps pass above $X_2 = 1/X_1$, as well); and so on. On the other hand, any point c in S with $X_2 = 0$ is the start of a ray

$$X_1 = X_1^c + t \qquad t \geqslant 0$$

$$X_2 = 0$$

which stays completely within S.

In figure 4.2(a), then, some points are the start of a ray which stays completely within S while others start no such ray. Compare this with figure 4.2(b). In figure 4.2(b) the set S consists of points on or below l_1 and on or above l_2 which also have $X_1 \geqslant 0$ and $X_2 \geqslant 0$. We assume that l_1 has a positive intercept; l_2 has a negative intercept; and both have positive slopes with the slope of l_1 greater than that of l_2. Pick any point in S, such as a, b, or c. Confirm that any such point, X_0, is the start of a ray completely in S, where the ray is given by

$$\begin{aligned} X_1 &= X_1^0 + t \\ X_2 &= X_2^0 + b_2 t \end{aligned} \qquad t \geqslant 0$$

provided that b_2 has any value between the slope of l_2 and the slope of l_1, inclusive. Suppose on the other hand that b_2 exceeds the slope of l_1. Then either the ray will pass out of the set immediately - i.e. for any $t > 0$ - if X^0 is on l_1; or else it will intersect l_1 eventually and then pass out of S. A similar story applies if b_2 is less than the slope of l_2. The ray will immediately or eventually pass below l_2 and hence out of S.

In contrast to figure 4.2(a), then, every point in S in figure 4.2(b) is the start of a ray contained completely in S. More than this, all the rays which have this property and start at any point X^a in S have exactly the same directions as such rays which start at any other point X^b in S.

The property that the set in figure 4.2(b) has, and that in figure 4.2(a) does not - that there are certain "unbounded directions", that any ray which starts in the set and moves in one of these directions remains in the set, while any ray that moves in any other direction passes out of the set - holds more generally than just the set in R^2 illustrated in figure 4.2(b). Indeed, it holds for any unbounded feasible set satisfying the constraints of the general portfolio selection model. More generally still, in the appendix to this chapter we show the following lemma and theorem.

Lemma 4.16 If S is a closed convex unbounded subset of R^n, and X is any point in S, then there is a ray that starts at X and stays in S.

Theorem 4.17 Let S be a closed convex unbounded subset of R^n; let Y and Z be two points in S. Then the set of rays which start at Y and stay in S have the same directions as the rays which start at Z and stay in S.

Definition If S is a set of feasible portfolios, then a direction $\beta\,(\neq 0)$ such that $X = X_0 + \beta t$ is in S provided that $X_0 \in S$ and $t \geqslant 0$ is called an *unbounded feasible direction*.

Disallowed Directions and Bounded Feasible Directions

The appendix to the book states that a set $S \subset R^n$ is called *affine* if $X \in S$ and $Y \in S$ implies $tX + (1-t)Y$ is in S, for all $t \in R$. An affine set that includes $X = 0$ is called a *linear subspace.*

Suppose that (of the five types of constraints (i)–(v) of equation (2.1)) the constraints of a portfolio selection model consist only of equalities (v) $AX = b$. In particular there are no nonnegativity requirements or other inequalities (i) through (iv). Then the set S of points which meets these constraints is either empty, because no X satisfies all the constraints, or else it is an affine set, since if $AX = b$ and $AY = b$ then

$$\begin{aligned} A[tX + (1-t)Y] &= tAX + (1-t)AY \\ &= tb + (1-t)b = b \end{aligned}$$

It is possible that only a single point satisfies the requirements $AX = b$. This single point then is considered a zero-dimensional affine set.

A feasible set may be contained in an affine set without occupying the entire set. For example, in the standard model the feasible set is contained in the $n-1$ dimensional affine set satisfying $\Sigma X_i = 1$ without filling the entire set. If a set of constraints contains k equalities, or k pairs of inequalities each equivalent to one equality, and if these equalities are linearly independent, then the feasible set will be contained within an $n-k$ dimensional affine set.

Definition The *affine hull* of a set S is the smallest affine space A containing S. Exercise 4.6 shows that such an A always exists. When we speak of the affine hull of a portfolio selection model, we refer to the affine hull of its set of feasible portfolios.

A feasible set may have a k dimensional hull, with $k < n$, even if it does not contain linear equalities or equivalent pairs of inequalities. For example, consider the constraint set

$$X_1 \geqslant 1 \tag{4.10a}$$

$$X_2 \geqslant 1 \tag{4.10b}$$

$$X_1 + X_2 \leqslant 2 + \epsilon \tag{4.10c}$$

$$0 \leqslant X_3 \leqslant 1 \tag{4.10d}$$

For $\epsilon > 0$ any (X_1, X_2, X_3) is feasible in which the (X_1, X_2) combination lies on or in the triangle *abc* of figure 4.3 and X_3 satisfies (4.10d). For $\epsilon = 0$, the only feasible portfolios lie on the line segment between the points (1, 1, 0) and (1, 1, 1). For $\epsilon > 0$ there is no one- or two-dimensional affine set which contains the feasible set. When $\epsilon = 0$ the feasible set is a subset of the straight line (one-dimensional affine set) through (1, 1, 0) and (1, 1, 1).

Whenever a model has a k dimensional affine hull, $k < n$, it is possible to define new variables $Y = HX$ with the following properties:

> H is an orthogonal matrix, so that any vector in terms of Y has the same length as the vector expressed in terms of X, and any pair of directions have the same angle.

Any feasible portfolio has

$$Y_i = c_i \qquad \text{for } i = k+1, \ldots, n \tag{4.11}$$

for constants c_i.

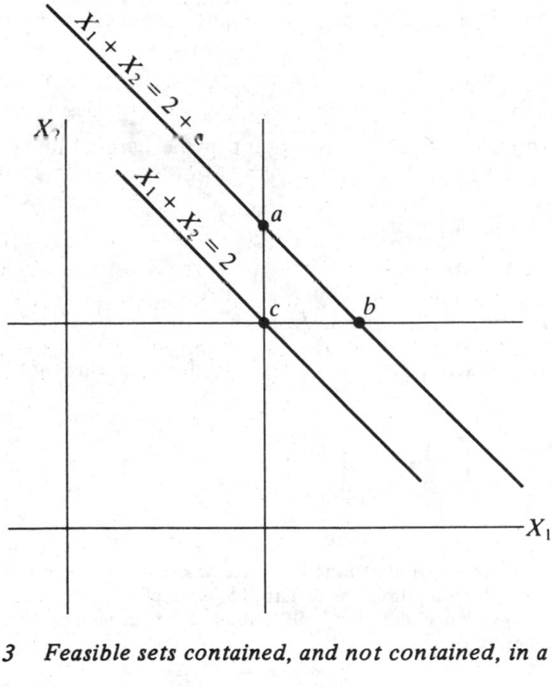

Figure 4.3 Feasible sets contained, and not contained, in a linear set

The example in figure 4.3 with $\epsilon = 0$ is already almost of this form, except that X_1 and X_2 rather than X_2 and X_3 are constant. It can be transformed into the form in (4.11) by the orthogonal transformation

$$\begin{pmatrix} Y_1 \\ Y_2 \\ Y_3 \end{pmatrix} = \begin{pmatrix} 0 & 0 & 1 \\ 0 & 1 & 0 \\ 1 & 0 & 0 \end{pmatrix} \begin{pmatrix} X_1 \\ X_2 \\ X_3 \end{pmatrix}$$

Definition Suppose that a feasible set S has a k dimensional affine hull T with $k<n$. Suppose L is the linear space parallel to T, and M is the subspace perpendicular to L. Any vector $\beta \in R^n$ can be written as $\beta = Y + Z$ in one and only one way with Y in L and Z in M. We say that β is a *disallowed direction* if $Z \neq 0$. We say that β is a *feasible direction* if $Z = 0$. β is a *bounded feasible direction* if it is a feasible direction but not an unbounded one.[1]

For example, in terms of the Y coordinate system of (4.11), any vector β with $\beta_i \neq 0$ for some $i > k$ is a disallowed direction. Any vector $\beta \neq 0$ with $\beta_i = 0$ for all $i > k$ is a feasible direction.

Theorem 4.18 Any movement from a feasible point in a disallowed direction produces an infeasible portfolio. In other words, if X is feasible and β is a disallowed direction then $X + \beta t$ is infeasible for any $t \neq 0$.

Proof Any point in a feasible set S is contained in its affine hull T. Every point in T may be written as

$$X = a + Y$$

where a is any point in T, and Y is a point in the parallel linear subspace L. In other words, $X \in T$ if and only if $(X - a) \in L$. But

$$\begin{aligned}(X + \beta t) - a &= (X - a) + \beta t \\ &= Y + \beta t\end{aligned}$$

for $Y \in L$, $\beta \notin L$, and $t \neq 0$, is not in L. ###

Suppose that the feasible set is on and in the diamond *abcd* in figure 4.4. Directions

$$\begin{pmatrix} 1 \\ 0 \end{pmatrix}, \quad \begin{pmatrix} 0 \\ 1 \end{pmatrix}, \quad \begin{pmatrix} -1 \\ 0 \end{pmatrix}, \quad \begin{pmatrix} 0 \\ -1 \end{pmatrix}$$

[1] As explained in the appendix to the book, for any scalar $\lambda > 0$ and vector $\beta \neq 0$ we will say that $\lambda\beta$ "is the same direction" as β. This, for example, will allow us to speak of any $\beta \neq 0$ as (e.g.) a "zero-variance direction," or "unbounded feasible direction," or "disallowed direction," etc., whether or not $\|\beta\| = 1$.

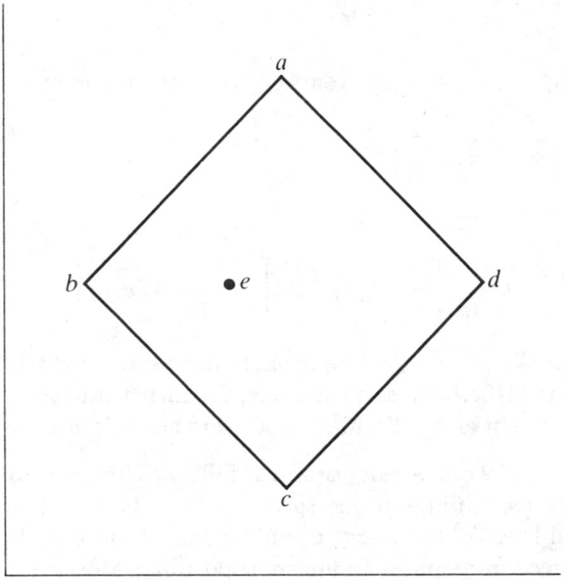

Figure 4.4 Feasible points which allow and do not allow movement in certain "bounded feasible" directions

are bounded feasible directions, since they are neither disallowed nor unbounded directions. You cannot move in all of these directions from every point. For example you cannot move in the direction $(1, 0)$ or $(-1, 0)$ from a, or in the direction $(1, 0)$ from any point on adc. However, you can move a bit from e in any of the above directions, and in any other feasible direction, and remain feasible.

Theorem 4.19 Suppose S is a set of feasible portfolios whose affine hull T has dimension $k > 0$. Then there exists a portfolio $X_0 \in S$ with the following property:

If β is a feasible direction, then there is a t such that $X_0 + \beta t$ is feasible.

(The set of points in S with this property is called the *relative interior* of S; see Rockafeller, 1970.)

Proof Since $k \geqslant 1$, there are $k + 1$ vectors in S, say $X_0, X^1, X^2, \ldots, X^k$ such that $Y^1 = X^1 - X_0$, $Y^2 = X^2 - X_0$, $\ldots$, $Y^k = X^k - X_0$ are independent feasible directions. Since L, the set of feasible directions, is a k dimensional linear space, any feasible direction β is a linear combination of the Y^i, i.e.

$$\beta = \sum_{i=1}^{k} \alpha_i Y^i = \sum_{i=1}^{k} \alpha_i (X^i - X_0)$$

where $\alpha = (\alpha_1, \ldots, \alpha_k) \neq 0$. The convexity of S, and theorem 4.15, imply that

$$X^* = \frac{1}{k+1} X_0 + \sum_{i=1}^{k} \frac{1}{k+1} X^i$$

is in S. Then

$$X^* + \beta t = \sum_{i=1}^{k} X^i \left(\frac{1}{k+1} + \alpha_i t \right) + X_0 \left[\frac{1}{k+1} - (\Sigma \alpha_i)\, t \right]$$

The weights of $X_0, X^1, \ldots, X^k$ on the right-hand side sum to 1 for all t, and are all positive for sufficiently small t; hence, for sufficiently small t, $X^* + \beta t$ is a convex combination of $X_0, X^1, X^2, \ldots, X^k$, and hence is in S. ###

Theorems 4.17–4.19 can be summarized as follows: given any portfolio selection model, every direction in portfolio space is either disallowed, bounded feasible, or unbounded feasible. Movement by any amount from a feasible portfolio in a disallowed direction produces an infeasible portfolio. Movement by any amount in an unbounded feasible direction produces a feasible portfolio. For a portfolio in the relative interior of the set of feasible portfolios (and such portfolios always exist if the set has any feasible directions) at least a bit of movement in any feasible direction is possible without leaving the set of feasible portfolios.

Conical Sets

Definition A set $S \subset R^n$ is a *cone* and $X_0 \in S$ is a *vertex* of S if the following holds: if $Y \neq X_0$ is any point in S, then the ray starting at X_0 and passing through Y lies completely in S. Sometimes the requirement that X_0 be in S is omitted from the definition of the cone. If S and X_0 satisfy the definition of a cone except that $X_0 \notin S$, we shall refer to S as a *cone with vertex deleted.*

Theorem 4.20 Every affine set S is a cone. Every point X_0 in S is a vertex of S.

Proof Let Y be any point in S such that $X_0 \neq Y$. Then the definition of vertex requires that the entire ray

$$\begin{aligned} X &= X_0 + (Y - X_0)t \qquad t \geqslant 0 \\ &= (1-t)X_0 + tY \end{aligned}$$

be in S. But this is assured because S is affine. ###

Black's model contains equalities only and is therefore an affine set. Consequently it is a cone with every point a vertex. The Tobin-Sharpe-Lintner model is a cone with vertex $(0, 0, \ldots, -1)$. This may be seen by substituting $\Sigma_{i-1}^{n} X_i - 1$ for X_{n+1} throughout. Then the constraints become

$$X_i \geqslant 0 \qquad i = 1, \ldots, n$$

$$\sum_{i=1}^{n} X_i \geqslant 0$$

The last constraint is implied by the prior n, and may be omitted. In general, constraint sets of the form

$$AX \geqslant 0$$

are cones with the origin as vertex, since

$$A(0 + Xt) = tAX \geqslant 0 \qquad \text{for all } t \geqslant 0$$

The Tobin-Sharpe-Lintner model is not an affine set since, for example, if $X' = (X_1, \ldots, X_n) \neq 0$ is feasible then

$$-X = 2\begin{pmatrix} 0 \\ \vdots \\ 0 \end{pmatrix} + (-1)X$$

is not feasible.

In chapter 12 we shall see that some of the "special" implications of the Black and the Tobin-Sharpe-Lintner models are also true, respectively, of any affine constraint set containing at least two points, and of any conical constraint set with vertex meeting certain conditions. The following theorem is not cited in subsequent chapters, but is included here as part of the characterization of the set of unbounded feasible directions.

Theorem 4.21 Let S be an unbounded closed convex subset of R^n. Let T be the set of directions such that

$$X + \beta t \qquad \text{is in } S$$

for any X in S, β in T, and any $t \geqslant 0$; e.g. if S is a set of feasible portfolios, T is the set of unbounded feasible directions. Then $T \cup \{0\}$ is a closed, convex cone with $\beta = 0$ a vertex. T itself is a cone with vertex 0 deleted.

Proof $0 \notin T$ since 0 is not a direction. To show that T is a cone with vertex 0 deleted, we must show that if β is in T so is

$$0 + t\beta = t\beta \qquad \text{for all } t > 0$$

But $t\beta$ is the same direction as β, and therefore is in T if β is in T. To see that T is convex, consider $\beta^1 \in T$, $\beta^2 \in T$, and $\beta^0 = a\beta^1 + (1-a)\beta^2$, for scalar $0 < a < 1$. We must show that $\beta^0 \in T$. Since $\beta^1 t$ and $\beta^2 t$ are in T, and therefore in S for all $t > 0$, the convexity of S implies that

$$\beta^0 t = a\beta^1 t + (1-a)\beta^2 t$$

is in S for all $t > 0$; therefore $\beta^0 \in T$.

The fact that $T \cup \{0\}$ is closed is seen by showing that $U = R^n - (T \cup \{0\})$ is open. Suppose $\beta_0 \in U$. Then $\beta_0 \neq 0$. Also, for any fixed $X_0 \in S$, there is a t_0 such that $X_0 + \beta_0 t \notin S$ for all $t > t_0$. (The convexity of S implies that $X_0 + \beta_0 t \in S$ for t in some bounded or unbounded interval of R. This plus the definition of T imply the preceding assertion.) For some fixed $t^* > t_0$, the fact that $R^n - S$ is open implies that there is a δ such that $B_\delta(X_0 + \beta_0 t^*) \subset R^n - S$; i.e.

$$\begin{aligned} Y &= X_0 + \beta_0 t^* + \gamma \\ &= X_0 + (\beta_0 + \gamma/t^*)\, t^* \end{aligned}$$

is in $R^n - S$ provided that $\|\gamma\| < \delta$. Since for any $\tilde{\beta}$ in $B_{\delta/t^*}(\beta_0)$ we have

$$\begin{aligned} Z &= X_0 + \tilde{\beta} t^* \\ &= X_0 + (\beta_0 + \gamma/t^*)\, t^* \end{aligned}$$

for $\|\gamma\| < \delta$, the preceding implies $Z \notin S$. Further, the fact that $X_0 \in S$, and the convexity of S, imply $X_0 + \tilde{\beta} t$ not in S for all $t \geq t^*$; hence $\tilde{\beta} \notin T$. Since δ can be chosen small enough so that $0 \notin B_{\delta/t^*}(\beta_0)$, there is an $r > 0$ such that $B_r(\beta_0) \subset R^n - (T \cup \{0\})$; from which the openness of $R^n - (T \cup \{0\})$ and the closedness of $T \cup \{0\}$ follow. ###

Definition The set T in theorem 4.21 is called the *recession cone* of the set S (see Rockafeller, 1970).

Appendix to Chapter 4

This appendix contains the proofs of two theorems and a lemma stated in chapter 4. For the proof of theorem 4.10 we need the concept of a Cauchy sequence, and an important result concerning real numbers.

Definition A sequence $X^1, X^2, X^3, \ldots$ of points in R^n is a *Cauchy sequence* if

$$\forall \epsilon > 0 \; \exists N \in I^+_{\text{nt}} \; \forall i \geq N \; \forall j \geq N : d(X^i, X^j) < \epsilon$$

This says that the elements of the sequence become and stay arbitrarily close to each other. As a special case, a sequence of real numbers $a_1, a_2, \ldots$ is a Cauchy sequence if

$$\forall \epsilon > 0 \, \exists N \in I_{\text{nt}}^{+} \, \forall i \geqslant N \, \forall j \geqslant N : |a_i - a_j| < \epsilon$$

One of the fundamental theorems about real numbers is that every Cauchy sequence is a convergent sequence. This uses the following (previously noted) property of real numbers: if a set S of real numbers has an upper bound then it has a least upper bound, called the LUB or supremum of S. Similarly, if S has a lower bound it has a greatest lower bound, called its GLB or infimum. (The property stated in the last two sentences is either assumed as one of the axioms defining the real numbers, as in Birkhoff and MacLane, 1977; or is proved, if an alternative definition of the real numbers is used, as in Dedekind, 1872.)

Theorem 4.22 A sequence of real numbers $a_1, a_2, \ldots$ has a finite limit b if and only if $a_1, a_2, \ldots$ is a Cauchy sequence.

Proof First let us assume $a_1, a_2, \ldots \to b$ and show that $a_1, a_2, \ldots$ is a Cauchy sequence. Since $a_1, a_2, \ldots \to b$,

$$\forall \epsilon > 0 \, \exists N \in I_{\text{nt}}^{+} \, \forall i \geqslant N : |b - a_i| < \epsilon/2$$

For this N, if i and $j \geqslant N$ then

$$\begin{aligned} |a_i - a_j| &= |a_i - b + b - a_j| \\ &\leqslant |a_i - b| + |b - a_j| \\ &< \epsilon/2 + \epsilon/2 = \epsilon \end{aligned}$$

Hence for i and $j \geqslant$ this N, $|a_i - a_j| < \epsilon$; hence $a_1, a_2, \ldots$ is a Cauchy sequence.

Next we show that if $a_1, a_2, \ldots$ is a Cauchy sequence then there is a b such that $a_1, a_2, \ldots \to b$. From the definition of a Cauchy sequence, there is a subsequence

$$a_{N_1}, a_{N_2}, a_{N_3}, \ldots$$

(where $N_{i+1} > N_i$) such that

$$\text{if} \quad m \geqslant N_i \quad \text{and} \quad n \geqslant N_i \quad \text{then} \quad |a_m - a_n| < 1/2^{i+2}$$

Define a sequence of closed intervals

$$I_i = [a_{N_i} - 1/2^i, a_{N_i} + 1/2^i]$$

Note that these intervals are nested, i.e. $I_2 \subset I_1$, $I_3 \subset I_2$, etc., since the left-hand points define an increasing sequence, and the right-hand points define a decreasing sequence; e.g. even if $a_{N_{i+1}}$ is as much below a_{N_i} as its definition permits, the left-hand point of I_{i+1} is still greater than that of I_i.

Since the left-hand points have an upper bound, they have a least upper bound c. Similarly the right-hand points have a greatest lower bound b. The definition of I_i, and the fact that the left-hand (right-hand) points are lower bounds (upper bounds) for the right-hand (left-hand) points assures us that

$$|c - b| \leqslant 1/2^{i-1}$$

for all i. This implies $b = c$. Thus $a_{N_i} \to b$; also $|a_j - a_{N_i}| \to 0$ for $j > N_i$ as $N_i \to \infty$ from the definition of a Cauchy sequence. This implies $a_1, a_2, \ldots \to b$.

###

Theorem 4.10 $S \subset R^n$ is compact if and only if every sequence $X^1, X^2, X^3, \ldots$ with

$$X^i \in S \qquad \forall\, i \in I^+_{\text{nt}}$$

has a subsequence which converges to a point $X_0 \in S$.

Proof First we assume that S is compact (i.e. closed and bounded) and show that every sequence has a convergent subsequence. Let $B_1(Y^{11}), B_1(Y^{12}), \ldots, B_1(Y^{1,n(1)})$ be a finite number of open balls of radius one, perhaps overlapping, such that S is a subset of the union $B_1(Y^{11}) \cup B_1(Y^{12}) \cup \ldots \cup B_1(Y^{1,n(1)})$. (In R^n it is always possible to "cover" a bounded set with a finite number of balls of a given size.) At least one of these balls must contain an infinite number of the terms from $X^1, X^2, X^3, \ldots$ (if $X^i = X^j$ for $i \neq j$, we still count this as two terms). Call this the subsequence $X^{11}, X^{12}, X^{13}, \ldots$. Suppose that the ball $B_1(Y^{1*})$ is the one (or one of the ones) which contains an infinite number of the terms from $X^1, X^2, X^3, \ldots$. This ball can be covered by a finite number of balls of radius 1/2; call them $B_{1/2}(Y^{21}), B_{1/2}(Y^{22}), B_{1/2}(Y^{23}), \ldots, B_{1/2}(Y^{2,n(2)})$. (The number required depends on the dimension n of the particular R^n.) At least one of these balls must contain an infinite number of the terms from the subsequence $X^{11}, X^{12}, X^{13}, \ldots$. Label this new infinite subset $X^{21}, X^{22}, X^{23}, \ldots$. Repeating the process we get subsequences

$$X^{31}, X^{32}, \ldots$$

$$X^{41}, X^{42}, \ldots$$

$$X^{51}, X^{52}, \ldots$$

where

$$X^{i1}, X^{i2}, \ldots$$

is contained in a ball, call it B^i, of radius $1/i$; also $X^{i1}, X^{i2}, \ldots$ is a subsequence of the preceding $X^{i-1,1}, X^{i-1,2}, X^{i-1,3}, \ldots$; therefore each X^{ij} is in each of the preceding balls $B^1, B^2, \ldots, B^{i-1}$. Consider the sequence $X^{11}, X^{21}, X^{31} \ldots$. The term X^{i1} is the first element of the ith sequence $X^{i1}, X^{i2}, \ldots$. Thus $X^{11}, X^{21}, X^{31}, \ldots$ is still a subsequence of $X^1, X^2, X^3, \ldots$. It is also a Cauchy sequence, since $X^{i1} \in B^n$ for all $i \geqslant n$, and hence $d(X^{n1}, X^{i1}) < 2/n$, $\forall\, i \geqslant n$. Thus $X^{11}, X^{21}, X^{31}, \ldots$ is a convergent sequence. Say $X_0 = \lim X^{i1}$. But since every X^{i1} belongs to S and S is closed, therefore $X_0 \in S$.

Next we suppose that every sequence from S has a convergent subsequence, and show that S is compact. First we show that it must be bounded. Let X^1 be any point in S. If S is not bounded then there is a point X^2 in S such that $d(X^1, X^2) \geqslant 1$. Similarly if S is unbounded then there is X^3 such that both $d(X^1, X^3) \geqslant 1$ and $d(X^2, X^3) \geqslant 1$. Proceeding in the same way we find X^1, X^2,

$\ldots, X^i$ such that $d(X^i, X^j) \geqslant 1$ for all $j < i$; and thus construct a sequence with $d(X^i, X^j) \geqslant 1$, for every $i \neq j$. Any subsequence must have the same property, therefore cannot be Cauchy, and therefore cannot be convergent. We conclude that if every sequence from S has a convergent subsequence, S must be bounded.

Finally, we continue to suppose that every sequence from S has a convergent subsequence and show S is closed. If S were not closed there would be a sequence of points $X^1, X^2, X^3, \ldots$ in S which converges to a point X_0 not in S. No subsequences of $X^1, X^2, \ldots$ can converge to any point except X_0; since $X^* \neq X^0$ implies $d(X^*, X^0) \neq 0$, hence there is an ϵ and N such that $d(X^i, X^*) \geqslant d(X^*, X^0) - d(X^0, X^i) > \epsilon > 0$ for all $i \geqslant N$. Thus no subsequence can converge to an X^* in S, contradicting the assumption that every sequence in S has a convergent subsequence. ###

Next we prove the lemma and theorem on rays in a unbounded, closed convex set. (The set called S in the previous statement of the lemma is here called T, to avoid confusion with the sphere $S_1(X)$ used in the proof.)

Lemma 4.16 If T is an unbounded closed convex subset of R^n, and X is any point in T, then there is a ray that starts at X and stays in T.

Remark This is not necessarily true if the set is unbounded but not closed (see exercise 4.3), or is unbounded but not convex as illustrated in figure 4.2(a).

Proof Since T is unbounded, for every $k = 1, 2, 3, \ldots$ there is a Y_k in T such that $d(X, Y_k) > k$. Since T is convex, all points between X and Y_k are in T, including the point $Z_k = t_k X + (1 - t_k) Y_k$ such that $d(X, Z_k) = 1$. These Z_k, $k = 1, 2, \ldots$, are in $S_1(X)$ - the sphere with radius one and center X. Since $S_1(X)$ is a compact set, the sequence $Z_1, Z_2, \ldots$ has a subsequence which converges to some point Z_0 in T. We shall show that the ray from X through Z_0 is contained in T.

Let $t_a > 0$ be any arbitrary positive number, and let

$$X^a = X + t_a(Z_0 - X)$$

We need only show that this representative point on the ray from X through Z_0 is in T. Since T is closed, we need only show that for every $\epsilon > 0$ there is an X^b in T such that $d(X^b, X^a) < \epsilon$. This will assure us that X^a is the limit of a sequence of points of T, and thus is in the closed set T.

Since Z_0 is the limit of a subsequence of $Z_1, Z_2, \ldots$, for any $\epsilon > 0$ there is a k having the following properties:

$$k > t_a \qquad \text{and} \qquad d(Z_k, Z_0) < \epsilon / t_a$$

We may write the ray from X through Z_k and Y_k as

$$Y = X + t(Z_k - X) \qquad t \geqslant 0$$

Since $d(X, Y_k) > k > t_a$,

$$X^b = X + t_a(Z_k - X)$$

lies on the line segment joining X and Y_k, both in T; hence X^b is in T. The distance between X^a and X^b is

$$\begin{aligned}\|X^b - X^a\| &= \|[X + t_a(Z_k - X)] - [X + t_a(Z_0 - X)]\| \\ &= \|t_a(Z_k - Z_0)\| \\ &= t_a\|Z_k - Z_0\| < \epsilon\end{aligned}$$

Thus for any $\epsilon > 0$ there is an X^b in T within ϵ of X^a. X^a is therefore the limit of a sequence of points of T, and hence is in T. ###

Theorem 4.17 Let S be a closed convex unbounded subset of R^n; let Y and Z be two points in S. Then the set of rays which start at Y and stay in S have the same directions as the rays which start at Z and stay in S.

Proof It will be sufficient to show that if $X = Y + bt$, $t \geqslant 0$, stays in S then so does $X = Z + bt$. The theorem then follows from the fact that Y and Z are arbitrary points in S, and b is an arbitrary direction of a ray starting at Y and staying in S.

Pick any $t_a > 0$, but hold it fixed for the present. If we can show that $Z_a = Z + bt_a$ is in S, then the theorem follows from the fact that t_a is an arbitrary positive number. Because S is closed, Z_a is in S if we can show that for any $\epsilon > 0$ there is a Z_b in S such that the distance from Z_a to Z_b is $< \epsilon$. The proof of the latter is actually two-dimensional, and is much clarified by a diagram such as that in figure 4.5. For figure 4.5, choose a new coordinate system with Z as the origin and the ray $Z + bt$, $t \geqslant 0$, as the positive horizontal axis. There is a shortest line segment from Z to the line $Y + bt$ $(t \in R)$. (If the distance between these lines is zero, i.e. they are the same line, then there is nothing to prove. We assume that the distance is positive.) The ray from Z in the direction of this segment will be used as the positive vertical axis in figure 4.5. Since $Y + bt$, $t \geqslant 0$, is parallel to $Z + bt$, $t \geqslant 0$, these lines lie in the same plane, together with all lines which connect a point in one with a point in the other. We do not know

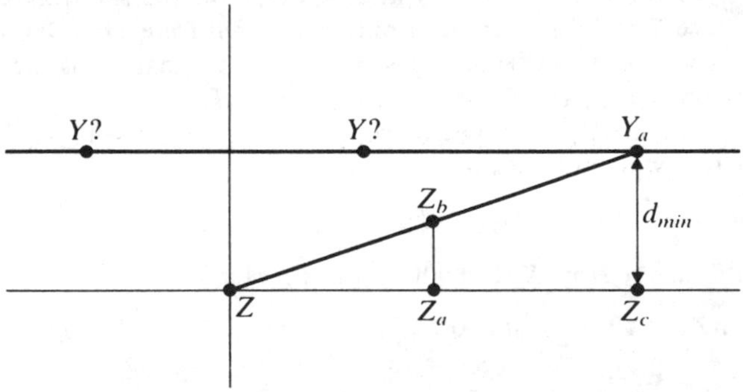

Figure 4.5 *Z_b may be chosen arbitrarily close to Z_a by choosing Y_a sufficiently far from Z*

whether Y itself has a positive, zero, or negative horizontal coordinate value. As is clear from the figure, and follows formally from

$$d(Z, Y_a) \geqslant d(Y, Y_a) - d(Y, Z)$$

since we can choose a Y_a on $Y + bt$, $t \geqslant 0$, arbitrarily far from Y (in the positive horizontal direction in the figure) we can also choose Y_a arbitrarily far from Z. Choose Y_a on $Y + bt$, $t \geqslant 0$, so that

$$d(Z, Y_a) > [d(Z, Z_a)\, d_{\min}/\epsilon] + d_{\min}$$

where $d_{\min}$ is the distance between the two lines. Let Z_b be the point on the line ZY_a with the same horizontal coordinate as Z_a, and let Z_c be the point on the horizontal axis with the same horizontal coordinate as Y_a. Then

$$\frac{d(Z_b, Z_a)}{d_{\min}} = \frac{d(Z, Z_a)}{d(Z, Z_c)}$$

$$< \frac{d(Z, Z_a)}{d(Z, Y_a) - d_{\min}}$$

$$< \frac{d(Z, Z_a)}{d(Z, Z_a)\, d_{\min}/\epsilon}$$

Thus

$$d(Z_b, Z_a) < \epsilon$$

as was to be shown. ###

Note on proof As Y_a moves to the right, Z_b approaches Z_a. Since Z and Y_a are in S, convexity assures Z_b in S. Since S is closed, the fact that Z_b approaches Z_a implies Z_a in S.

Exercises

4.1 (a) Prove equations (4.3b) and (4.3c).
(b) Suppose $\lim a_i = 0$. Show that $\lim (a_i)^2 = 0$.
(c) Suppose $\lim a_i = b$. Show that $\lim(a_i)^2 = b^2$. (Hint: write $(a_i - b)^2 = a_i^2 - 2a_ib + b^2$; note that $\lim (a_i - b) = 0$, and use part (b) as well as other results already established.)

4.2 (a) Using the definition of a straight line in R^n given in (4.8), show that $\partial X_i/\partial t$ is the same at every point on the line.
(b) Show that $\Delta X_i/\Delta X_j$ is the same for every pair of points on the line, provided $\partial X_j/\partial t \neq 0$, where ΔX_i represents (as usual) the change in X_i.
(c) Show that if X^1, X^2, X^3, and X^4 are four points on a line in R^n, with $X^1 \neq X^2$ and $X^3 \neq X^4$, then $X^1 - X^2$ and $X^3 - X^4$ are either the "same

direction" or "opposite directions" as defined in the appendix to the book.

(d) Show that the set of points satisfying equation (4.8), for fixed α and $\beta \neq 0$ and all real t, is a one-dimensional affine space as defined in the appendix to the book. Specifically, show that the set of points which satisfy (4.8) includes two points X_0 and X^1 such that $X^1 - X_0 \neq 0$; but does not include three points X_0, X^1, X^2 such that $X^1 - X_0 \neq 0, X^2 - X_0 \neq 0$, and $(X^1 - X_0)'(X^2 - X_0) = 0$.

4.3 Consider the set S of points $X = (X_1, X_2)$ such that $(0,0) \in S$ and $(1, 0) \in S$; also, $(X_1, X_2) \in S$ if $0 < X_1 < 1$ and $X_2 \geqslant 0$.

(a) Is S convex? Why?
(b) Is S closed? Why?
(c) Is it true that for any two points Y and Z in S, the rays which start at Y and stay in S have the same direction as the rays which start at Z and stay in S? Why?

4.4 (a) In R^2 show that a semicircle (perimeter only) has the entire plane as its affine hull, yet there are directions β such that you cannot move from any point on the semicircle in the direction β and find another point on the semicircle.
(b) Does (a) contradict theorem 4.19? Why?

4.5 (a) For the standard model with $n = 2$, sketch and label:

(i) The set of feasible portfolios in the $X_1 X_2$ plane
(ii) The affine hull of this feasible set
(iii) The set of feasible directions.

How many distinct feasible directions are there (i.e. directions β^1 and β^2 such that β^1 is not "the same direction as β^2" as defined in the appendix to the book)?

(b) For the standard model with $n = 3$, describe (i), (ii), and (iii) of (a). Describe a set containing every distinct feasible direction.

4.6 The definition of affine hull uses the fact that given any set $S \neq \emptyset, S \subset R^n$, there is a set A such that: A is affine; $S \subset A$; and if A^* is affine and contains S then $A \subset A^*$. Thus A is the *smallest* affine set which contains S. The existence of such an A may be seen as follows:

(a) Observe that some affine set contains A. (Hint: R^n is affine.)
(b) Show that if A_1 and A_2 are affine, $A_1 \cap A_2 \neq \emptyset$, and $A_1 \neq A_2$, then $A_1 \cap A_2$ is affine and is either identical to one of the A_i or else has a smaller dimension than either of them. (Hint: if A is affine and k dimensional then it may be described as the set of points which satisfy $n - k$ nonredundant linear equations.)
(c) Show that for any set S there is a smallest affine set A which contains S. (Hint: assume the statement false; consider what possibilities this entails; show that (a) and (b) rule out these possibilities.)

5

Sets Involving Mean, Variance, and Standard Deviation

This chapter considers the shapes of various sets involving E, V, and σ. In particular, it considers sets of constant mean and constant variance, and considers how V and σ vary with E for portfolios lying on a straight line. The latter results are needed for describing the set of efficient and obtainable EV and $E\sigma$ combinations, as we shall see in later chapters.

This chapter assumes that the reader is familiar with the transformation of coordinates in n dimensional space, and its relation to the concept of eigenvalues, as reviewed in the appendix to this book.

Relationships Involving E

If $\mu = 0$ then $E = \mu' X = 0$ is the only feasible value of E. Henceforth, unless otherwise stated, assume $\mu \neq 0$.

For any $\mu \neq 0$, the set of portfolios with a given $E = E_0$, i.e. the X satisfying

$$\mu' X = E_0 \tag{5.1}$$

is an $n-1$ dimensional affine space, also called a *hyperplane*. The set of portfolios with another $E = E_1$

$$\mu' X = E_1$$

is another hyperplane parallel to the first.

We can choose a new coordinate system, orthogonal to the original, so that $Y = (1, 0, 0, \ldots, 0)$ in the new coordinate system corresponds to

$$\mu / \| \mu \|$$

in the old. In this coordinate system

$$E = Y_1$$

The vectors $X = \mu$ and $Y = (1, 0, \ldots, 0)$ in the respective coordinate systems are called the direction of increasing E. (Recall that μ and $\mu/\|\mu\|$ are considered to be the "same direction.") In the Y coordinate system, if you move along a ray from Y_0 in a direction $b' = (b_1, \ldots, b_n)$,

$$Y = Y_0 + bt, \qquad t \geqslant 0$$

clearly E increases with t if and only if $b_1 > 0$. In the X coordinate system this corresponds to the statement that E increases along a ray $X = X_0 + bt, t \geqslant 0$, if and only if $\mu' b > 0$.

Theorem 5.1 For a feasible portfolio selection model, only one value of E is obtainable if and only if the feasible set is a subset of some affine set:

$$\{Y\colon \mu' Y = E_0\}$$

Proof The hyperplane $\{Y\colon \mu' Y = E_0\}$ contains all portfolios with $E = E_0$, and only portfolios with $E = E_0$. ###

The following two easily established results are basic.

Theorem 5.2 For any line $X = a + bt$ $(t \in R)$ we have

$$E = c_0 + c_1 t \tag{5.2a}$$

where c_0 and c_1 are the scalars

$$c_0 = \mu' a \tag{5.2b}$$

$$c_1 = \mu' b \tag{5.2c}$$

Proof Equation (5.2) follows immediately from

$$E = \mu'(a + bt) \tag{5.3}$$

###

Theorem 5.3 E may be used as the parameter of a line if and only if the direction b of the line is not orthogonal to the vector μ.

Proof If and only if

$$c_1 = \mu' b \neq 0$$

i.e. if and only if μ is not orthogonal to b, we may rewrite (5.2a) as

$$t = E/c_1 - c_0/c_1$$

Substitute this into $X = a + bt$ to obtain

$$X = [a - (c_0/c_1)\, b] + (b/c_1)\, E$$

as the new equation for the line. ###

Definitions We say that the set of obtainable E values is ***unbounded above*** if, for any number E_0, there is a feasible portfolio with greater E; it is ***unbounded below*** if, for any number E_0, there is a feasible portfolio with smaller E.

A model may have its set of obtainable E unbounded from above but not from below, vice versa, both or neither.

Theorem 5.4 The set of obtainable E values is unbounded above if and only if the model has an unbounded feasible direction b, such that $\mu' b > 0$. It is unbounded below if and only if it has an unbounded feasible direction b such that $\mu' b < 0$.

Proof We will show the result for E unbounded from above. The proof for E unbounded from below is essentially identical. Half the assertion – that if there is an unbounded feasible direction such that $\mu' b > 0$ then E is unbounded above – is a corollary of theorem 5.2. For if X_0 is feasible then any X such that

$$X = X_0 + tb \qquad t \geqslant 0$$

is also feasible, and has expected return

$$\begin{aligned} E &= \mu' X_0 + (\mu' b) t \\ &= E_0 + c_1 t \end{aligned}$$

The other half of the assertion – that if E is unbounded from above there is an unbounded direction with $\mu' b > 0$ – is a corollary of our discussion of linear programming (chapter 8) and will be shown following theorem 8.3. ###

Relationships Involving V

As discussed in the appendix to the book, given any covariance matrix C there is an orthogonal transformation

$$Y = HX \tag{5.4}$$

such that

$$V = X'CX \tag{5.5a}$$

$$= Y'DY \tag{5.5b}$$

where D is a diagonal matrix:

$$D = \begin{pmatrix} \delta_1 & & 0 \\ & \delta_2 & \\ & & \ddots \\ 0 & & & \delta_n \end{pmatrix} \tag{5.5c}$$

Thus

$$V = \sum_{i=1}^{n} \delta_i Y_i^2$$

Since H is orthogonal, $H' = H^{-1}$ and $X = H'Y$. We may assume that

$$\delta_1 \geqslant \delta_2 \geqslant \ldots \geqslant \delta_n \tag{5.5d}$$

The δ_i are the eigenvalues of C.

Lemma 5.5 The eigenvalues of a covariance matrix are nonnegative.

Proof Since $V \geqslant 0$, δ_i cannot be negative; else, if e^i is a vector with 1 in the ith place and 0 elsewhere then

$$V = (e^i)' D e^i < 0$$

###

Theorem 5.6 For the Y coordinate system described in (5.4) and (5.5), among all vectors Y of unit length the vector $e^1 = (1, 0, \ldots, 0)$ has the greatest value of V. Since the orthogonal transformation H preserves lengths, $X = H_1'$ (the first row of H and first column of H') is the vector of unit length in the original coordinate system with the greatest V. Similarly, e^2 is the vector of unit length with largest V among vectors with $Y_1 = 0$; e^3 that with largest V with $Y_1 = Y_2 = 0$, etc.

Proof Choosing $Y_1, Y_2, \ldots, Y_n$ so that $\Sigma \delta_i Y_i^2$ is maximized subject to $\Sigma Y_i^2 = 1$ is the same as choosing $W_1, W_2, \ldots, W_n$ to maximize $\Sigma \delta_i W_i$ subject to $W_i \geqslant 0$ and $\Sigma_i W_i = 1$. This is done by setting $W_1 = 1$, since δ_1 is at least as large as any other δ_i. The argument is then repeated in the subspace with $Y_1 = 0$ - essentially the $n - 1$ dimensional space $(Y_2, Y_3, \ldots, Y_n)$; and again for the $n - 2$ dimensional space with $Y_1 = Y_2 = 0$; etc. ###

For fixed $V_0 \geqslant 0$, the general shape of a set with constant variance

$$\begin{aligned} V_0 &= X'CX \\ &= Y'DY \end{aligned} \tag{5.6}$$

depends on how many δ_i are zero and how many positive.

All eigenvalues zero First consider the case in which all eigenvalues are zero. This can only happen if $C = 0$, since $D = 0$ implies

$$C = H'DH = 0$$

and $C = 0$ implies

$$D = HCH' = 0$$

In this case no X satisfies (5.6) if $V_0 > 0$, and every X satisfies (5.6) if $V_0 = 0$.

All eigenvalues positive Next consider the case in which all eigenvalues are positive. Let Z be the coordinates of a point Y relative to a new coordinate system such that

$$Z_i = (\delta_i)^{1/2} Y_i \tag{5.7}$$

This new coordinate system typically does not assign the same lengths to vectors as did the old. We have multiplied the scale of each Y_i by a factor of $\sqrt{\delta_i}$, stretching or compressing the Y_i axis. In terms of the Z_i,

$$V = \Sigma Z_i^2$$

For $n = 2$ and $V_0 > 0$, a set with constant $V = V_0$ is the circle

$$V_0 = Z_1^2 + Z_2^2$$

For $n = 3$ and $V_0 > 0$, it is the sphere

$$V_0 = Z_1^2 + Z_2^2 + Z_3^2$$

For any $n > 0$ and $V_0 > 0$ it is the n dimensional sphere $S_{\sigma_0}(0)$, where $\sigma_0 = V_0^{1/2}$; i.e. the set of Z satisfying

$$V_0 = \sum_{i=1}^{n} Z_i^2 \tag{5.8}$$

Working backwards from Z to Y to X we see that, for $V_0 > 0$, any n dimensional set with constant variance

$$V_0 = X'CX$$

may be described as the object obtained by starting with the sphere in (5.8), and stretching or compressing its axes according to the formula

$$Y_i = Z_i / \delta_i^{1/2} \tag{5.9}$$

This produces an ellipsoid - a sphere which has been uniformly stretched or compressed (or let be, if $\delta_i = 1$) in each of n orthogonal directions

$$e^1 = (1,\ 0,\ 0, \ldots, 0)$$

$$e^2 = (0,\ 1,\ 0, \ldots, 0)$$

etc. Finally the ellipsoid is rotated by an orthogonal transformation

$$X = H'Y \tag{5.10}$$

to obtain the formula

$$V_0 = X'CX \tag{5.11}$$

This is still an ellipsoid, but its axes may no longer face in the same directions as the coordinate system axes.

In the present case (with all eigenvalues positive) only $Z = 0$ satisfies

$$0 = \Sigma Z_i^2$$

and therefore only $X = 0$ satisfies

$$X'CX = 0$$

In this case, the sphere $S_{\sigma_0}(0)$ shrinks to the point $\{0\}$.

Some eigenvalues zero Finally, let us consider the case in which some but not all the $\delta_i = 0$. Specifically, suppose

$$\delta_i > 0 \qquad \text{for } i = 1, \ldots, k$$

$$\delta_i = 0 \qquad \text{for } i = k+1, \ldots, n$$

where $1 \leqslant k < n$.

In this case, (5.5b) is the sum of only k nonzero terms

$$V = \sum_{i=1}^{k} \delta_i Y_i^2 \tag{5.12}$$

Defining Z_i as in (5.7) now only for $1 \leqslant i \leqslant k$, and $Z_i = Y_i$ for $i > k$, we have

$$V = \sum_{i=1}^{k} Z_i^2 \tag{5.13}$$

In R^3, if $k = 2$ then the set with constant $V = V_0$ is

$$V_0 = Z_1^2 + Z_2^2 \tag{5.14}$$

$$-\infty < Z_3 < \infty$$

For $\sigma_0^2 = V_0 > 0$ this is a cylinder: it is the set of points in which (Z_1, Z_2) lies on the circle of radius σ_0, and Z_3 has any value whatever. It is the formula for a tin can whose base is the circle, and whose sides extend indefinitely upward and downward.

As we move from the Z to the Y, the base of the figure becomes an ellipse

$$\delta_1 Y_1^2 + \delta_2 Y_2^2 = V_0$$

but the sides still extend infinitely in both directions:

$$-\infty < Y_3 < \infty$$

This is an elliptical cylinder. We speak of Y_3 and Z_3 in this case as *zero-variance directions*, since if we change Y_3 (or Z_3) we do not change V. When we rotate the axes from Y back to X, (5.11) still représents an elliptical cylinder, except that now the zero-variance direction is not necessarily one of the coordinate axes.

In the general case with $1 \leqslant k < n$ the set of constant $V = V_0 > 0$ is again a cylinder. In terms of the Z coordinate system, the base is a k dimensional sphere. The cylinder itself is the set of all points $(Z_1, \ldots, Z_n)$ where $(Z_1, \ldots, Z_k)$ lies in the sphere (5.13), and $(Z_{k+1}, \ldots, Z_n)$ have any values whatever. In terms of the Y coordinate system, $(Y_1, \ldots, Y_k)$ lies in the ellipsoid (5.12) and has any $(Y_{k+1}, \ldots, Y_n)$ whatever. The equation

$$X'CX = Y'DY$$

$$= \sum_{i=1}^{k} Z_i^2$$

$$= 0$$

is satisfied by the $n-k$ dimensional space which has

$$Z_i = 0 \qquad \text{for } i = 1 \text{ to } k$$

Definition Any vector $(0, 0, \ldots, 0, Y_{k+1}, \ldots, Y_n)$ is called a *zero-variance direction*, since adding it to any Y will not change the variance of the portfolio. When we move back from the Y to the X coordinate system, (5.11) still describes an elliptical cylinder, with an $n-k$ dimensional subspace of zero-variance directions, except that now it may be that none of the coordinates of the X system is among the zero-variance directions.

If a covariance matrix C is nonsingular, therefore positive definite, it has no zero-variance directions. Therefore any situation which can only arise when a zero-variance direction meets some condition (as we shall encounter from time to time subsequently) is precluded if C is positive definite.

Compensating Transformations

Suppose we choose a new coordinate system for portfolio space such that

$$Y = HX$$

where X is the coordinates of a portfolio relative to the old coordinate system, and Y the coordinates relative to the new system. We insist here that H be nonsingular but not necessarily orthogonal. Thus lengths and angles may not be the same for portfolios expressed in the Y system as in the X system; but we can get back from Y to X by $X = H^{-1}Y$.

Suppose also that we choose a new coordinate system for the space of random variables $r = (r_1, \ldots, r_n)$. Specifically, in the new coordinate system the random vector s corresponding to the random vector r in the old system is to be given by

$$s = (H^{-1})'r$$

Now consider a portfolio selection model in which s is the random return vector and Y is the portfolio. Then the return on the portfolio is

$$\begin{aligned} R &= s'Y \\ &= (r'H^{-1})(HX) \\ &= r'X \end{aligned}$$

The return R on the portfolio as a whole is the same at each random point in the sample space if the return vector is given by $s = (H^{-1})'r$ and the portfolio vector by $Y = HX$ as it is when the portfolio is X and the return vector r. Since R is the same at each sample point, it follows that the expected value E and the variance V is the same for the random variable $s'Y$ as it is for the random variable $r'X$.

Definition We will speak of H as a transformation of (the description of) portfolio space, and $(H^{-1})'$ as the *compensating* transformation of (the description of) return space.

If we start with a new coordinate system for return space such that $s = Kr$, K nonsingular, and let $Y = (K^{-1})'X$, then again $s'Y = r'X$. Thus the transformation $(K^{-1})'$ in portfolio space compensates for the transformation K in return space. (We could use the terminology of physics, call one of the transformations the cogredient transformation and the other the contragredient transformation. But it seems to me clearer to speak of the transformation $s = (H^{-1})'r$ in return space as compensating for the transformation $Y = HX$ in the portfolio space, and the transformation $Y = (K^{-1})'X$ in portfolio space as compensating for the transformation $s = Kr$ in the return space.)

If H is orthogonal then $H^{-1} = H'$; thus $(H^{-1})' = H$. In the case of an orthogonal transformation, then, H is its own compensating transformation.

V along a Straight Line

This section considers how V varies as a function of the parameter t along the straight line in R^n

$$X = \alpha + \beta t \qquad t \in R$$

for α and $\beta \in R^n$ and $\beta \neq 0$. One reason for our interest in V along straight lines is that, as we shall see later, efficient EV sets are provided by piecewise linear sets in portfolio space. We may write

$$\begin{aligned} V &= X'CX \\ &= (\alpha + \beta t)' C(\alpha + \beta t) \\ &= (\alpha' C\alpha) + 2(\beta' C\alpha) t + (\beta' C\beta) t^2 \\ &= a_0 + a_1 t + a_2 t^2 \end{aligned} \tag{5.15}$$

where

$$a_0 = \alpha' C\alpha \qquad a_1 = 2\beta' C\alpha \qquad a_2 = \beta' C\beta$$

Thus V is a quadratic in t. Possible values of a_0, a_1, a_2 must be consistent with the fact that $V \geqslant 0$ for every X, and therefore for every t. On any line with $\mu'\beta \neq 0$, E may be taken as the parameter.

Lemma 5.7 If $a_2 = 0$ in (5.15) then $a_1 = 0$.

Proof If $a_2 = 0$ and $a_1 > 0$ then $V < 0$ for $t < -a_0/a_1$. If $a_2 = 0$ and $a_1 < 0$ then $V < 0$ for $t > -a_0/a_1$. Either case contradicts the fact that $V \geqslant 0$ for all t. ###

It follows immediately from (5.15) and lemma 5.7 that if $a_2 = 0$ then $a_0 \geqslant 0$, and $V = a_0$ for all points on the line $\alpha + \beta t$ $(t \in R)$.

Theorem 5.8 $a_2 = 0$ in (5.15) along the straight line $\alpha + \beta t$ $(t \in R)$ if and only if β is a zero-variance direction.

Proof By definition, if β is a zero-variance direction then adding βt to any vector - in particular adding βt to α - does not change its variance. This proves half the assertion. To prove the other half, transform coordinates to the Y system in equations (5.4) and (5.5). The line becomes

$$\begin{aligned} Y &= H(\alpha + \beta t) \\ &= (H\alpha) + (H\beta)\, t \\ &= \hat{\alpha} + \hat{\beta} t \end{aligned}$$

$\hat{\beta}$ is the same direction in the Y coordinate system as β is in the X coordinate system. If $\hat{\beta}$ were not a zero-variance direction then we would have $\hat{\beta}_i \neq 0$ for some $1 \leqslant i \leqslant k$. Then equation (5.12) implies

$$V \geqslant (\hat{\beta}_i)^2 t^2$$

for all t, which contradicts the assertion that $V = a_0$ for all t. ###

Next we investigate the case in which $a_2 \neq 0$.

Theorem 5.9 If $a_2 \neq 0$ in (5.15) then $a_2 > 0$. Also we may write V as

$$V = V_{\min} + a_2(t - t_{\min})^2 \tag{5.16a}$$

where

$$V_{min} = (a_0 - a_1^2/4a_2) \geqslant 0 \tag{5.16b}$$

is the least value of V on the line and

$$t_{min} = -a_1/2a_2 \tag{5.16c}$$

is the value of t at which $V = V_{min}$.

Proof We confirm equation (5.16) as follows:

$$\begin{aligned} V_{min} + a_2(t - t_{min})^2 &= (a_0 - a_1^2/4a_2) + a_2(t + a_1/2a_2)^2 \\ &= a_0 - a_1^2/4a_2 + a_2(t^2 + a_1 t/a_2 + a_1^2/4a_2^2) \\ &= a_0 + a_1 t + a_2 t^2 \end{aligned}$$

We must have $V_{min} \geqslant 0$ else $V < 0$ at $t = t_{min}$. We cannot have $a_2 < 0$ else V will be negative for

$$(t - t_{min})^2 \geqslant -V_{min}/a_2$$ ###

Equation (5.16) shows V to be a parabola. If $\mu'b \neq 0$ for the line, then E may be taken as the parameter and, with a_2 recomputed properly, we have

$$V = V_{min} + a_2(E - E_{min})^2 \tag{5.17}$$

The case with $a_2 = 0$ can be combined with the case of $a_2 > 0$ as follows:

Summary 5.10 Along any straight line $X = \alpha + \beta t, t \in R$, we have $V = V_{min} + a_2(t - t_{min})^2$, for $a_2 \geqslant 0$, where $a_2 = 0$ if and only if β is a zero-variance direction. If $\mu'b \neq 0$ then, perhaps with a new a_2, we can write V as in (5.17).

σ along a Straight Line

The case of $a_2 = 0$ is trivial:

$$\sigma = V^{1/2} = a_0^{1/2} \qquad \text{for all } t \in R$$

For $a_2 > 0$ the shape of the curve relating σ to t depends on whether $V_{min} = 0$ or $V_{min} > 0$. In the former case

$$\sigma^2 = V = a_2(t - t_{min})^2$$

Hence

$$\sigma = a_2^{1/2} \, |t - t_{min}|$$

As shown in figure 5.1, $\sigma(t)$ is 0 at $t = t_{min}$; $+a_2^{1/2}(t - t_{min})$ for $t > t_{min}$; and $-a_2^{1/2}(t - t_{min})$ for $t < t_{min}$. When $\mu'b \neq 0$ we may write

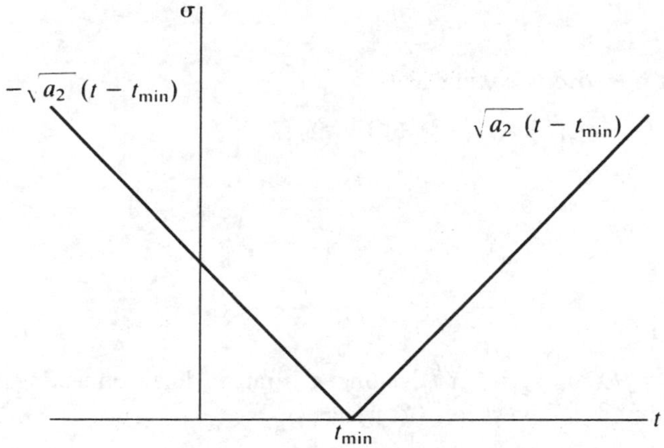

Figure 5.1 $\sigma(t)$ *when* $V_{min} = 0$

$$\sigma = a_2^{1/2}\,|E - E_{min}|$$

for the appropriate a_2.

When $V_{min} > 0$, we have the hyperbola

$$\sigma^2 - a_2(t - t_{min})^2 = V_{min}$$

The asymptotes of this hyperbola are the straight lines in figure 5.1.

Let

$$x = a_2^{1/2}(t - t_{min}) \tag{5.18a}$$

With this choice of origin and scale for the horizontal axis we get

$$\sigma^2 - x^2 = V_{min} \tag{5.18b}$$

Since $\sigma > 0$, only the upper branch of the hyperbola relates σ to t or x.

Convex Functions

Definitions Suppose $y = f(X)$ is a function which associates a number y to every vector X in S for some convex set $S \subset R^n$. We say that the function f is *convex* if for every X^a and X^b in S

$$f[tX^a + (1-t)\,X^b] \leqslant tf(X^a) + (1-t)\,f(X^b)$$

provided

$$0 \leqslant t \leqslant 1$$

We say that it is *strictly convex* if

$$f[tX^a + (1-t)X^b] < tf(X^a) + (1-t)f(X^b)$$

for any

$$X^a \neq X^b$$

and

$$0 < t < 1$$

Writing $y_a = f(X^a)$, $y_b = f(X^b)$, along a straight line connecting the points (X^a, y_a) and (X^b, y_b) the vector (X, y) has

$$X = tX^a + (1-t)X^b$$

$$y = ty_a + (1-t)y_b$$

for

$$0 \leqslant t \leqslant 1$$

Thus the definition of convexity can be restated as follows: $f(X)$ is convex if and only if for every point X between two points X^a and X^b the value of the function at the point X is less than or equal to the y on the straight line segment connecting (X^a, y_a) and (X^b, y_b). If it is actually less, except at the end points, then it is strictly convex.

The definition applies in particular when $n = 1$ and $y = f(x)$ is a function of a scalar variable.

Theorem 5.11 If $y = f(x)$, $x \in R$, has a nonnegative second derivative everywhere, then f is convex. If the second derivative is positive everywhere, then f is strictly convex.

Proof A positive second derivative implies an increasing first derivative which implies that, for $x_0 < x_1 < x_2$,

$$\frac{f(x_1) - f(x_0)}{x_1 - x_0} < \frac{f(x_2) - f(x_1)}{x_2 - x_1}$$

Transposing the negative terms in the numerators to the opposite sides of the inequality, we get

$$\frac{f(x_1)}{x_1 - x_0} + \frac{f(x_1)}{x_2 - x_1} < \frac{f(x_2)}{x_2 - x_1} + \frac{f(x_0)}{x_1 - x_0}$$

Multiplying both sides by $(x_1-x_0)(x_2-x_1)/(x_2-x_0)$, and noting that the coefficients on the left side sum to 1.0, we get

$$f(x_1) < \frac{x_2-x_1}{x_2-x_0} f(x_0) + \frac{x_1-x_0}{x_2-x_0} f(x_2)$$

The assertion concerning strict convexity follows from

$$x_1 = \frac{x_2-x_1}{x_2-x_0} x_0 + \frac{x_1-x_0}{x_2-x_0} x_2$$

and the fact that x_1 may be chosen anywhere between x_0 and x_2. A similar argument implies convexity if the second derivative is nonnegative, replacing $<$ by $\leqslant$. ###

Theorem 5.12 If $y = f(x)$, $x \in R$, is convex (strictly convex) then so is $z = a_0 + a_1 f(x)$ for $a_1 > 0$. Also, if $f(x)$ is convex (strictly convex) then so is $f(a_0 + a_1 x)$ for $a_1 \neq 0$.

Proof These follow immediately from the definition of convexity and elementary properties of inequalities. $a_1 \neq 0$ is only needed for the strictly convex case. (*Exercise* Generalize to $f(X)$, $X \in R^n$.) ###

Examples

(1) If $a_2 > 0$ then $V = V_{\text{min}} + a_2(t - t_{\text{min}})^2$ is strictly convex, since $\mathrm{d}^2 V/\mathrm{d}t^2 = 2a_2$ for all t.

(2) For $a_2 > 0$, $V_{\text{min}} > 0$, and defining x as in (5.18) we have

$$\sigma = (V_{\text{min}} + x^2)^{1/2}$$

$$\frac{\mathrm{d}\sigma}{\mathrm{d}x} = \frac{x}{(V_{\text{min}} + x^2)^{1/2}}$$

$$\frac{\mathrm{d}^2\sigma}{\mathrm{d}x^2} = \frac{V_{\text{min}}}{(V_{\text{min}} + x^2)^{3/2}}$$

This is always positive, and hence σ as a function of x is strictly convex. Theorem 5.12 then implies that σ as a function of t is strictly convex.

When $V_{\text{min}} = 0$ then $\sigma = |x|$, which is convex but not strictly convex.

(3) For X in R^n and C a positive semidefinite (or positive definite) covariance matrix, $V = X'CX$ is a convex (or respectively, a strictly convex) function. This is a corollary of equation (5.15), example (1) above, and the fact that if C is positive definite (i.e. has only positive eigenvalues) then there are no zero-variance directions.

Minimum Obtainable V and σ

Some of the properties of the lower boundaries of the sets of feasible EV and $E\sigma$ combinations follow easily from properties established in this and the preceding chapter.

Theorem 5.13 Let (E_a, V_a), (E_b, V_b), and (E_c, V_c) be three points on the lower boundary of the set of obtainable EV combinations with $E_a < E_b < E_c$ and $V_a \neq V_c$. Define t so that

$$E_b = tE_a + (1-t)E_c$$

i.e.

$$t = \frac{E_b - E_c}{E_a - E_c}$$

Then

$$V_b < tV_a + (1-t)V_c$$

and

$$\sigma_b \leqslant t\sigma_a + (1-t)\sigma_c$$

Proof Let X^a, X^b, X^c be feasible portfolios whose EV combinations are (E_a, V_a), (E_b, V_b), and (E_c, V_c) respectively. Also let

$$X^d = tX^a + (1-t)X^c$$

Because the set of feasible portfolios is convex, X^d is feasible; its E equals

$$\begin{aligned}\mu' X^d &= \mu'[tX^a + (1-t)X^c] \\ &= t\mu' X^a + (1-t)\mu' X^c \\ &= tE_a + (1-t)E_c = E_b\end{aligned}$$

Since $E_a \neq E_c$, E varies along the line through X^a and X^c and thus may be used as the parameter in the description of the line. Since $V_a \neq V_c$ we must have $a_2 > 0$ in (5.17), and thus the variance V_d of X^d is less than $tV_a + (1-t)V_c$. Since V_b is the minimum of V among feasible portfolios with $E = E_b$, it cannot be greater than that of V_d. Therefore it too has

$$V_b < tV_a + (1-t)V_c$$

According to example (2) of the previous section, the standard deviation σ_d of X^d is less than or equal to $t\sigma_a + (1-t)\sigma_c$; hence so is σ_b. ###

Theorem 5.14 If the lower boundary of the set of obtainable EV combinations contains a horizontal segment - i.e. if it has (E, V_0) for E such that $E_a \leqslant E \leqslant E_b$ with $E_a < E_b$ - then V_0 must be the minimum obtainable V.

Proof Let X^a and X^b be feasible portfolios with $E = E_a$ and E_b, respectively, and with $V = V_0$. Suppose that there was a feasible portfolio X_c with (E_c, V_c) where $V_c < V_0$. If $E_c < E_a$ then

$$t = \frac{E_b - E_a}{E_b - E_c}$$

is between 0 and 1, and

$$E_a = tE_c + (1-t)E_b$$

Let $X^* = tX^c + (1-t)X^b$. X^* has $E = E_a$. Theorem 5.13 implies that

$$V^* < tV_c + (1-t)V_0 < V_0$$

which contradicts the assumption that V_0 is the minimum obtainable V for $E = E_a$. A similar argument applies if $E_c > E_b$, with E_a and E_b exchanging roles.

###

Theorem 5.15

(i) If an unbounded feasible direction b has $\mu' b > 0$ and is also a zero-variance direction, then the lower boundary of the set of feasible EV combinations includes a horizontal ray

$$\begin{pmatrix} E \\ V \end{pmatrix} = \begin{pmatrix} E_0 \\ V_0 \end{pmatrix} + \begin{pmatrix} 1 \\ 0 \end{pmatrix} t \qquad t \geqslant 0$$

where V_0 is the minimum obtainable variance.

(ii) If an unbounded feasible direction b has $\mu' b < 0$ and is also a zero-variance direction, then the lower boundary of the set of feasible EV combinations includes a horizontal ray

$$\begin{pmatrix} E \\ V \end{pmatrix} = \begin{pmatrix} E_0 \\ V_0 \end{pmatrix} + \begin{pmatrix} -1 \\ 0 \end{pmatrix} t \qquad t \geqslant 0$$

where again V_0 is the minimum obtainable variance.

(iii) If both (i) and (ii) are true, then the lower boundary of the set of obtainable EV combinations is the horizontal line containing all EV combinations with

$$V = V_0$$

$$-\infty < E < +\infty$$

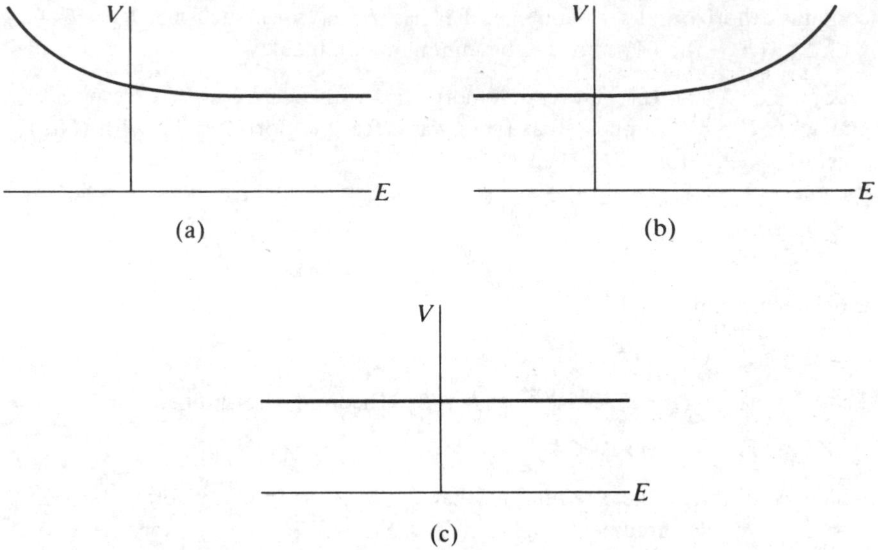

Figure 5.2 Cases with one or more unbounded, zero-variance directions b, with $\mu' b \neq 0$

Proof It will be sufficient to prove (i); (ii) is shown similarly, and (iii) is a corollary of the two. In this proof we need the fact that V achieves a minimum even if the set of feasible portfolios is unbounded. This is shown in corollary 9.16 whose proof does not depend, directly or indirectly, on the present theorem. The existence of such a portfolio will be assumed here. Let X_0 be a feasible portfolio with minimum variance and let (E_0, V_0) be its EV combination. Since b is an unbounded direction, $X = X_0 + bt$ is feasible for all $t \geqslant 0$. Since $\mu' X > 0$, E increases with t. Since b is a zero-variance direction, V remains constant as t and E increase. ###

The three cases (i), (ii), and (iii) of theorem 5.15 are illustrated in figure 5.2(a), (b), and (c). Figure 5.2(a) shows a case in which condition (i) holds but (ii) does not; figure 5.3(b) a case in which (ii) holds and (i) does not; and figure 5.3(c) a case in which both hold.

Exercises

5.1 Show that if $b'Cb = 0$ then $Cb = 0$. (Hint: argue that if $b'Cb = 0$ then along the line $X = a + bt$ we must have

$$V = a'Ca + (2a'Cb)\,t + (b'Cb)\,t^2$$
$$= a'Ca$$

for every choice of a.)

5.2 (a) Show that, on the straight line $X = a + bt$, $t \in R$, if $b'Cb > 0$ then V achieves a minimum at $t_{\min} = -a'Cb/b'Cb$, and there has the value

$$V_{\min} = a'Ca - (a'Cb)^2/b'Cb$$

(b) Use 5.2(a) to show that

$$(a'Ca)(b'Cb) \geqslant (a'Cb)^2$$

and $V_{\min} = 0$ if and only if

$$(a'Cb)^2 = (a'Ca)(b'Cb)$$

5.3 (a) Let X and Y be two portfolios. Let

$$Z = tX + (1 - t)\,Y \qquad (5.19)$$

where t is a scalar such that $0 \leqslant t \leqslant 1$. Z may be interpreted in two ways:

(i) Z is a portfolio, i.e. a vector in R^n whose components are given by (5.19) using the rules of vector addition and scalar multiplication; or

(ii) Z is a portfolio consisting of two securities. It has a fraction t invested in security X with mean E_X (which happens to equal $\mu'X$) and variance V_X (which happens to equal $X'CX$). It has the remaining fraction $1-t$ invested in security Y with mean E_Y, variance V_Y, and covariance σ_{XY} (where the latter happens to equal $X'CY$).

Show algebraically (i.e. using matrix algebra) that the two views give the same E and V for the portfolio as a whole.

(b) If we let t or $1-t$ be negative in equation (5.19) then we are "shorting" X or Y in the sense of Black's model. Confirm the equivalence of (i) and (ii) in (a) when we drop the requirement that $0 \leqslant t \leqslant 1$.

(c) For portfolios X and Y with positive variances, show that $V_{\min} = 0$ on the line through X and Y if and only if $\rho_{XY}^2 = 1$, where ρ_{XY} is the correlation between $r'X$ and $r'Y$. (Hint: use the fact that there is a $Z' = (Z_1, Z_2)$ such that $Z \neq 0$ and $Z'CZ = 0$ if and only if $CZ = 0$, and hence C is singular.)

(d) Show that on a line $X = a + bt$, every pair of portfolios X and Y (with positive variances) has $\rho_{XY}^2 = 1$ if and only if $(a'Cb)^2 = (a'Ca)(b'Cb)$. (Hint: see (c) and exercise 5.2(a).)

5.4 This exercise explores the covariance between two portfolios $X_0 = a + bt_0$ and $X = a + bt$, both on the same straight line.

(a) Assume that t_0 and therefore X_0 are fixed, while t and X are variable. Confirm that covariance is a linear function of t; specifically

$$\operatorname{cov}(r'X_0, r'X) = (a'Ca + b'Cat_0) + (a'Cb + b'Cbt_0)\,t \tag{5.20}$$

(b) Show that if b is a zero-variance direction then the covariance between X_0 and X is the same for all X on the line. In particular this covariance is the variance of X_0. (Hint: use exercise 5.1.)

(c) Show that if b is not a zero-variance direction then there is a unique choice of $X_0 = a + bt_0$ (with t_0 less than, equal to, or greater than zero) such that the covariance between X and X_0 is the same for all X on the line. (Hint: choose t_0 so that the coefficient of t in (5.20) is zero.)

(d) Use exercise 5.2(a) to show that the X_0 in (c) is the point $X_{\min} = a + bt_{\min}$, with least variance among points on the line.

(e) Show that, if b is not a zero-variance direction and $X_0 \neq X_{\min}$, then there is a point X^* on the line such that $\operatorname{cov}(r'X_0, r'X^*) = 0$.

(f) (Roll, 1977) Show that, if b is not a zero-variance direction, if $(a'Cb)^2 < (a'Ca)(b'Cb)$, and if $t_0 > t_{\min}$, then $t_Z < t_{\min}$, where $X_0 = a + bt_0$ and $X^* = a + bt_Z$ is the portfolio in (e). (Hint: show that

$$t_{\min} - t_Z = \frac{(a'Ca)(b'Cb) - (a'Cb)^2}{(b'Cb)(a'Cb + b'Cbt_0)}.)$$

6

Portfolio Selection Models with Affine Constraint Sets

This chapter derives mean-variance efficient sets for portfolio selection models with constraints

$$AX = b$$

Black's model is an example of such. In a sense to be seen in the next chapter, the solution to the current problem is a component of the solution to the general portfolio selection problem. We begin by discussing Lagrangian multipliers.

Minimization Subject to Constraints

Let S be any subset of R^n. Let $g_0(X), g_1(X), \ldots, g_m(X)$ be $m+1$ functions of $X' = (X_1, X_2, \ldots, X_n)$. Consider the following two questions:

(i) For m given numbers $b_1, b_2, \ldots, b_m$ find X in S which minimizes $g_0(X)$ subject to

$$g_i(X) = b_i \qquad i = 1, \ldots, m \tag{6.1}$$

(ii) For m given numbers $\lambda' = (\lambda_1, \lambda_2, \ldots, \lambda_m)$ find X in S which minimizes

$$L = g_0(X) - \sum_{i=1}^{m} \lambda_i g_i(X) \tag{6.2}$$

The choice in (i) is subject to m constraints in addition to the requirement that X be in S, while the choice in (ii) has no constraints other than X in S. Note that the λ in (ii), like the b in (i), are given constants as distinct from variables.

The following simple lemma is fundamental to all that follows.

Lemma 6.1 If, for given $b' = (b_1, \ldots, b_m)$ and $\lambda' = (\lambda_1, \ldots, \lambda_m)$, an optimum solution X^a to (ii) happens to satisfy (6.1), then X^a is the optimum solution to (i) as well.

Proof Suppose to the contrary that X^b in S satisfies (6.1) and has smaller g_0 than does X^a. Then

$$\begin{aligned} L(X^b) &= g_0(X^b) - \sum_{i=1}^{m} \lambda_i g_i(X^b) \\ &= g_0(X^b) - \sum_{i=1}^{m} \lambda_i b_i \\ &< g_0(X^a) - \sum_{i=1}^{m} \lambda_i b_i \\ &= g_0(X^a) - \sum_{i=1}^{m} \lambda_i g_i(X^a) \\ &= L(X^a) \end{aligned}$$

which contradicts the assumption that X^a is the solution to (ii). ###

In general, for arbitrary functions $g_0, g_1, \ldots, g_m$, there may not be λ such that the solution to (ii) gives some particular solution to (i). In figure 6.1, for example, the point in S which minimizes g_0 subject to $g_1 = b_c$ is the point c. This also minimizes $X_2 - \lambda X_1$, for λ equal to the slope of the line l. On the other hand the

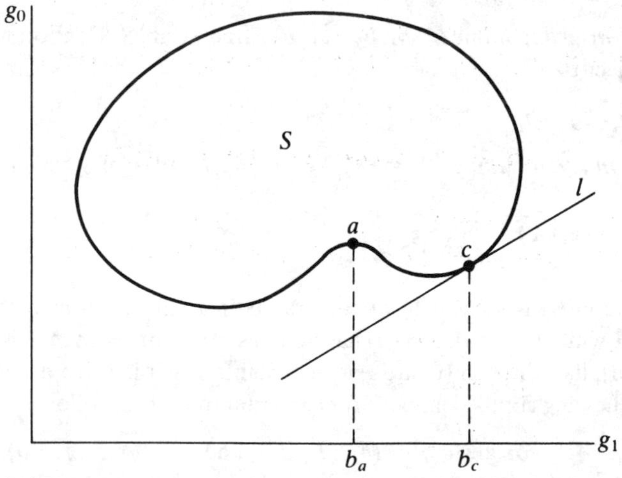

Figure 6.1 Points for which λ does and does not exist

point a minimizes g_0 subject to $g_1 = b_a$; but there is no λ such that a minimizes $X_2 - \lambda X_1$, since any straight line through a has part of S on one side of it and part of S on the other.

Definitions By a λ *point* we mean any X in S which minimizes equation (6.2) for some choice of λ. The λ are called *Lagrangian multipliers*.

The following lemma interprets the λ_i as rates of substitution.

Lemma 6.2 Let

$$Y_i = g_i(X) \qquad i = 0, 1, \ldots, m$$

If, in the neighborhood[1] of a particular λ point, the minimum value of Y_0 is a continuous function of $Y_1, \ldots, Y_m$ with partial derivatives $\partial Y_0 / \partial Y_i$, then

$$\lambda_i = \frac{\partial Y_0}{\partial Y_i}$$

Proof If Y_j is held constant for $j \neq i$ then

$$\Delta L = \Delta Y_0 - \lambda_i \Delta Y_i$$

Hence

$$\frac{\Delta L}{\Delta Y_i} = \frac{\Delta Y_0}{\Delta Y_i} - \lambda_i$$

It follows from the above, and from the definition of $\partial Y_0/\partial Y_i$ as the limit of $\Delta Y_0/\Delta Y_i$ as $\Delta Y_i \to 0$, that if $\partial Y_0/\partial Y_i > \lambda_i$ then L could be decreased - i.e. ΔL made negative - by choosing some X with smaller $Y_i = g_i(X)$, keeping $Y_j = g_j(X)$ constant for $j \neq i$; whereas if $\partial Y_0/\partial Y_i < \lambda_i$ then L could be decreased by choosing some X with larger $Y_i = g_i(X)$, keeping $Y_j = g_j(X)$ constant for $j \neq i$. ###

Efficient Portfolios with Affine Constraint Sets

In this section we will let $S = R^n$, take $V = X'CX$ for g_0 and let $g_i(X)$ be linear. Specifically, we will apply the preceding results to the following problem for given E:

minimize	$V = X'CX$	(6.3a)
subject to	$AX = b$	(6.3b)
	$\mu'X = E$	(6.3c)

[1] That is, within some ball $B_r(\hat{X})$ with $r > 0$ and $\hat{X}$ some λ point.

We will then vary E to obtain solutions for all E. The constraints in (6.3b) – those of a model of form 0 containing constraints of type (v) only (see equation (2.1)) – are satisfied by an affine set, provided they are satisfiable at all. Results are slightly simpler if we write g_0 as $V/2$ rather than V. Of course a point which minimizes $V/2$ also minimizes V. Furthermore it will be convenient to replace $-\lambda$ by λ. This only changes the signs of the given constants λ_i.

For any $m+1$ constants $\lambda_1, \ldots, \lambda_m, \lambda_E$ the function $L(X)$ in (6.2) is then

$$L(X) = \tfrac{1}{2}X'CX + \sum_{k=1}^{m} \lambda_k\left(\sum_{j=1}^{n} a_{kj}X_j\right) - \lambda_E\left(\sum_{j=1}^{n} \mu_j X_j\right) \tag{6.4}$$

$$= \tfrac{1}{2}X'CX + \lambda' AX - \lambda_E \mu' X$$

For readers accustomed to write the Lagrangian function as

$$L(X) = \tfrac{1}{2}X'CX + \lambda'(AX - b) - \lambda_E(\mu' X - E) \tag{6.5}$$

note that lemma 6.1 calls for (6.4) rather than (6.5). We will return to this matter in a postscript to this chapter.

Lemma 6.1 implies that any point obtained by minimizing L for given λ minimizes $V/2$ for some values of $\Sigma a_{kj}X_j$, $k = 1$ to m, and for some E. It does not tell us whether or not there exists λ whose solution to question (ii) gives

$$\Sigma a_{kj} X_j = b_k$$

for the given b_k and for each value of E:

$$-\infty < E < +\infty$$

We shall now explore conditions under which this is so.

For given constants $\lambda_1, \ldots, \lambda_m, \lambda_E$ a necessary condition for L to be minimized is

$$\frac{\partial L}{\partial X_i} = \sum_{j=1}^{n} \sigma_{ij} X_j + \sum_{k=1}^{m} \lambda_k a_{ki} - \lambda_E \mu_i = 0 \qquad \text{for } i = 1, \ldots, n \tag{6.6}$$

that is,

$$\sigma_{i1}X_1 + \sigma_{i2}X_2 + \ldots + \sigma_{in}X_n + a_{1i}\lambda_1 + \ldots + a_{mi}\lambda_m - \mu_i\lambda_E = 0$$
$$\text{for } i = 1 \text{ to } n$$

In matrix notation these necessary conditions are

$$CX + A'\lambda - \lambda_E \mu = 0 \tag{6.7}$$

where $\lambda' = (\lambda_1, \ldots, \lambda_m)$.

Theorem 6.3 Any X^a which satisfies (6.7) minimizes L in (6.4). In other words (6.7) is a sufficient condition, as well as a necessary one, for minimizing L for the given, fixed λ among all X in R^n.

Proof We shall suppose, to the contrary, that some point X^d provides a smaller value of L, and show that this implies a contradiction. Let

$$X = X^a + t(X^d - X^a) \qquad t \in R$$
$$= X^a + tb$$

where $b = X^d - X^a$, be the straight line through X^a and X^d. Along this line, L may be expressed as a function of t thus:

$$L = \tfrac{1}{2}X'CX + \lambda'AX - \lambda_E \mu'X$$
$$= \tfrac{1}{2}(X^a + bt)'C(X^a + bt) + \lambda'A(X^a + bt) - \lambda_E \mu'(X^a + bt)$$
$$= \tfrac{1}{2}(X^a)'CX^a + \lambda'AX^a - \lambda_E \mu'X^a + (b'CX^a + \lambda'Ab - \lambda_E \mu'b)t + \tfrac{1}{2}(b'Cb)t^2$$
$$= L(X^a) + a_1 t + a_2 t^2$$

Since C is positive semidefinite

$$a_2 = \tfrac{1}{2}b'Cb \geqslant 0$$

If $a_2 = 0$ and $dL/dt = 0$ (for any t) then L is a horizontal line, $L = L(X_a)$. If $a_2 > 0$ and $dL/dt = 0$ at $t = 0$ then the parabola has a unique minimum at $t = 0$. Thus, if we can show that L as a function of t has $dL/dt = 0$ at $t = 0$, we will have contradicted the assumption that X^d has a smaller value of L than X^a. But at $t = 0$

$$\frac{dL}{dt} = \sum_{i=1}^{n} \frac{\partial L}{\partial X_i} \frac{dX_i}{dt}$$

$$= \Sigma\, 0 \frac{dX_i}{dt} = 0 \qquad \text{###}$$

Thus any X which satisfies (6.7) minimizes L. We seek such an X which will also have $AX = b$ and $\mu'X = E$ for some particular E. That is, we seek X, λ, and λ_E which satisfy

$$\begin{pmatrix} C & A' & \mu \\ A & 0 & 0 \\ \mu' & 0 & 0 \end{pmatrix} \begin{pmatrix} X \\ \lambda \\ -\lambda_E \end{pmatrix} = \begin{pmatrix} 0 \\ b \\ E \end{pmatrix} \qquad (6.8a)$$

The trick is to solve simultaneously for X, λ, and λ_E so that the X which minimizes L for the "given" λ also satisfies $AX = b$ and $\mu'X = E$.

Theorem 6.4 If $(X', \lambda', -\lambda_E)$ satisfies (6.8a), then X minimizes V subject to $AX = b$ and $\mu' X = E$ for the given E.

Proof This is just an application of lemma 6.1. The first n equations in (6.8a) assure us that X minimizes L for given λ and λ_E. The last $m + 1$ equations assure us that X satisfies the specified constraints. ###

We have not yet determined if there are zero, one, or many solutions to (6.8a). For the moment suppose that

$$\tilde{M} = \begin{pmatrix} C & A' & \mu \\ A & 0 & 0 \\ \mu' & 0 & 0 \end{pmatrix} \tag{6.8b}$$

is nonsingular. In this case we can solve

$$\begin{pmatrix} X \\ \lambda \\ -\lambda_E \end{pmatrix} = \tilde{M}^{-1} \begin{pmatrix} 0 \\ b \\ E \end{pmatrix}$$

$$= \tilde{\alpha} + \tilde{\beta} E \tag{6.9a}$$

where

$$\tilde{\alpha} = \tilde{M}^{-1} \begin{pmatrix} 0_n \\ b \\ 0_1 \end{pmatrix} \tag{6.9b}$$

$$\tilde{\beta} = \tilde{M}^{-1} \begin{pmatrix} 0_n \\ 0_m \\ 1 \end{pmatrix} \tag{6.9c}$$

(0_k above indicates a zero vector with k components.) In (6.9), $\tilde{\alpha}$ and $\tilde{\beta}$ have $m + n + 1$ components. Since $\tilde{M}$ is nonsingular, $\tilde{\beta} \neq 0$. As E varies, $(X', \lambda', \lambda_E)$ varies linearly, since (6.9) is the formula for a straight line in $(X', \lambda', \lambda_E)$ space, with E as the parameter. Thus (6.9) provides a vector which satisfies (6.8) for every E: $-\infty < E < +\infty$. As a by-product, this shows the following.

Theorem 6.5 If

$$\tilde{M} = \begin{pmatrix} C & A' & \mu \\ A & 0 & 0 \\ \mu' & 0 & 0 \end{pmatrix}$$

is nonsingular, then for every E there are $m+1$ constants, $\lambda_1, \ldots, \lambda_m, \lambda_E$, such that an X exists which minimizes $L = (1/2)X'CX + \lambda' AX - \lambda_E \mu' X$, and this X also minimizes

$$V = X'CX$$

subject to

$$AX = b$$
$$\mu' X = E$$

The values of $\lambda_1, \ldots, \lambda_m, \lambda_E$ and the X which minimizes L are given by

$$\begin{pmatrix} X \\ \lambda \\ -\lambda_E \end{pmatrix} = \tilde{M}^{-1} \begin{pmatrix} 0 \\ b \\ E \end{pmatrix}$$
$$= \tilde{\alpha} + \tilde{\beta} E$$

for $\tilde{\alpha}$ and $\tilde{\beta}$ defined in (6.9).

Proof See preceding discussion. ###

According to equation (5.15) the relationship between V and E along the line (6.9) is a quadratic

$$V = a_0 + a_1 E + a_2 E^2 \tag{6.10}$$

with $a_2 \geqslant 0$. Both $a_2 > 0$ and $a_2 = 0$ are consistent with the assumption that $\tilde{M}$ is nonsingular. For example, if

$$C = \begin{pmatrix} 0 & 0 \\ 0 & 0 \end{pmatrix}, \qquad A = (1,\ 1), \qquad \mu = (\mu_1,\ \mu_2) \qquad \mu_1 \neq \mu_2$$

then

$$\tilde{M} = \begin{pmatrix} 0 & 0 & 1 & \mu_1 \\ 0 & 0 & 1 & \mu_2 \\ 1 & 1 & 0 & 0 \\ \mu_1 & \mu_2 & 0 & 0 \end{pmatrix}$$

has the determinant

$$(\mu_2 - \mu_1)^2 \neq 0$$

and therefore is nonsingular. Yet every point in R^n has $V = X'CX = 0$. This example shows the following.

Theorem 6.6 There are portfolio selection models which are feasible but have no efficient portfolios.

Proof In the preceding example no portfolio is efficient because there always exists another portfolio with the same variance and greater mean. (Also see exercise 1.1(d).) ###

When $a_2 > 0$, V has a unique minimum at some $E = E_{\min}$. When $a_2 = 0$ then $a_1 = 0$ (lemma 5.7). In this case the lower boundary of the obtainable set is $(E, V) = (E, a_0)$ for every E.

Next, let us assume that

$$M = \begin{pmatrix} C & A' \\ A & 0 \end{pmatrix} \tag{6.11}$$

is nonsingular. (Note the difference between M and $\bar{M}$.) Write (6.8a) as

$$\begin{pmatrix} C & A' \\ A & 0 \end{pmatrix} \begin{pmatrix} X \\ \lambda \end{pmatrix} = \begin{pmatrix} 0 \\ b \end{pmatrix} + \lambda_E \begin{pmatrix} \mu \\ 0 \end{pmatrix} \tag{6.12a}$$

or, more briefly,

$$M \begin{pmatrix} X \\ \lambda \end{pmatrix} = \begin{pmatrix} 0 \\ b \end{pmatrix} + \lambda_E \begin{pmatrix} \mu \\ 0 \end{pmatrix} \tag{6.12b}$$

leaving to the side, for the moment, the relationship

$$E = \mu' X$$

Given our current assumption that M is nonsingular we may solve (6.12b) thus:

$$\begin{aligned} \begin{pmatrix} X \\ \lambda \end{pmatrix} &= M^{-1} \begin{pmatrix} 0 \\ b \end{pmatrix} + M^{-1} \begin{pmatrix} \mu \\ 0 \end{pmatrix} \lambda_E \\ &= \alpha + \beta \lambda_E \end{aligned} \tag{6.13}$$

This provides an $(X', \lambda', \lambda_E)$ which solves (6.12) for every λ_E.

In the following chapters we show that the set of efficient EV combinations of the general model is generated by a piecewise linear set of portfolios. The pieces are given by formulas which look like equation (6.13), except that usually only a submatrix, with certain rows and corresponding columns deleted, describes a segment. We show that, even though certain submatrices of the whole M matrix are singular, all submatrices encountered in the computation are nonsingular. This is part of the reason why the critical line method, once started, "always continues to work." If instead we had used submatrices of $\bar{M}$ in (6.8b), in some cases a singular matrix would be encountered.

In part to understand the strategic difference between the use of M and $\tilde{M}$ in the critical line algorithm, and in part to complete the analysis of portfolio selection models with affine constraint sets, we consider the cases in which one or both of M and $\tilde{M}$ are singular.

Theorem 6.7 It is possible (i) for M to be singular and $\tilde{M}$ nonsingular, and (ii) vice versa.

Proof

(i) We saw that for

$$C = \begin{pmatrix} 0 & 0 \\ 0 & 0 \end{pmatrix}, \qquad A = (1,\ 1), \qquad \mu = (\mu_1,\ \mu_2) \qquad \mu_1 \neq \mu_2$$

$\tilde{M}$ is nonsingular; but

$$M = \begin{pmatrix} 0 & 0 & 1 \\ 0 & 0 & 1 \\ 1 & 1 & 0 \end{pmatrix}$$

has $|M| = 0$ and is thus singular.

(ii) Letting

$$C = \begin{pmatrix} 1 & 0 \\ 0 & 1 \end{pmatrix}, \qquad A = (1,\ 1), \qquad \mu = (1,\ 1)$$

we find that

$$|M| = \begin{pmatrix} 1 & 0 & 1 \\ 0 & 1 & 1 \\ 1 & 1 & 0 \end{pmatrix} = -2 \neq 0$$

Thus M is nonsingular, while

$$\tilde{M} = \begin{pmatrix} 1 & 0 & 1 & 1 \\ 0 & 1 & 1 & 1 \\ 1 & 1 & 0 & 0 \\ 1 & 1 & 0 & 0 \end{pmatrix}$$

has two identical rows, and therefore is singular. ###

Theorem 6.8

$$M = \begin{pmatrix} C & A' \\ A & 0 \end{pmatrix}$$

is singular if and only if at least one of the following conditions is true of the affine model with constraint set $AX = b$:

(i) The model is infeasible.
(ii) The model is feasible but at least one constraint equation is redundant.
(iii) The model contains a direction β such that β is an unbounded feasible direction, is a zero-variance direction, and has $\mu'\beta = 0$. (In this case the model has at least one redundant variable; i.e. there is an i such that if the constraint $X_i = 0$ is added to the model a strictly equivalent model is obtained).
(iv) The lower boundary of the set of obtainable EV combinations is the horizontal line

$$V = a_0$$
$$-\infty < E < \infty$$

and hence the model has no efficient portfolios.

Proof M is singular if and only if there is a $(Y', \delta') \neq (0, 0)$ such that

$$\begin{pmatrix} C & A' \\ A & 0 \end{pmatrix} \begin{pmatrix} Y \\ \delta \end{pmatrix} = \begin{pmatrix} 0 \\ 0 \end{pmatrix} \tag{6.14a}$$

We will first show that (6.14a) implies that at least one of the four conditions of the theorem is true; and then show that each of these conditions implies the existence of a $(Y', \delta') \neq (0, 0)$ such that (6.14a) holds. Suppose $Y = 0$ in (6.14a), so

$$A'\delta = 0 \tag{6.14b}$$

for some $\delta \neq 0$. This says that there is a linear combination of the rows of A, with weights not all zero, which vanishes. The theory of simultaneous linear equations implies that, in this case, either condition (i) or condition (ii) of the theorem is true.

Next suppose $Y \neq 0$. In this case (6.14a) says

$$AY = 0 \tag{6.15a}$$

$$CY = -A'\delta \tag{6.15b}$$

for some $Y \neq 0$. Equation (6.15a) implies that if X satisfies the constraints $AX = b$, then so does $X + Y$. Equation (6.15) further implies that Y is a zero-variance direction, since

$$\begin{aligned} V(Y) &= Y'CY \\ &= -Y'A'\delta \\ &= 0\delta = 0 \end{aligned}$$

For this case, in which $Y \neq 0$, we must distinguish two subcases: (a) $\mu'Y = 0$ and (b) $\mu'Y \neq 0$. Case (a) is equivalent to condition (iii), since Y is a feasible direction; unbounded, as are all feasible directions in an affine model; is a zero-variance direction and has $\mu'Y = 0$. (Concerning the parenthetical remark following condition (iii), suppose Y_i is one of the nonzero components of Y. Suppose X_0 is any feasible portfolio, and has $V_0 = X_0'CX_0$, $E_0 = \mu'X_0$. Write X_i^0 for the ith component of X_0. Then $X = X_0 - (X_i^0/Y_i)Y$ is a feasible portfolio with the same mean and variance as X_0 but with $X_i = 0$. Thus the requirement $X_i = 0$ does not alter the set of obtainable EV combinations.) In case (b), with $\mu'Y \neq 0$, let X_0 be a portfolio with minimum variance. (Its existence is shown in corollary 9.16, whose proof is not dependent on the present theorem.) Then $X_0 + tY$ provides feasible portfolios with minimum V and with every E. Thus the assumption that $\mu'Y \neq 0$, for Y in (6.14a), implies that the affine model has no efficient portfolios.

We see, then, that (6.14a) implies that at least one of the four conditions holds. We will now show that each of the four conditions implies (6.14a). Conditions (i) and (ii) imply (6.14b) for $\delta \neq 0$, and therefore (6.14a) for $(Y', \delta') = (0, \delta')$. Condition (iii) states that $Y \neq 0$ is an unbounded feasible, zero-variance direction. The fact that it is feasible implies

$$AY = 0$$

else we could not have (for X with $AX = b$)

$$A(X + tY) = b$$

for $t \neq 0$. The fact that Y is a zero-variance direction implies that $CY = 0$ as well as $Y'CY = 0$, else (feasible or infeasible) portfolios of the form

$$X = X_0 + tY$$

with variance

$$V = X_0'CX_0 + 2X_0'CYt + Y'CYt^2$$

would have negative variance for suitable t and X_0 (e.g. $X_0 = CY$). From $AY = 0$ and $CY = 0$ we conclude that (6.14a) holds for $(Y', \delta') = (Y', 0)$.

We now show that condition (iv) of the theorem implies the existence of an unbounded feasible, zero-variance direction. Equation (6.14a) then follows by the same argument as used for condition (iii). Let X^a and X^b be two feasible portfolios with different expected returns but the same, minimum feasible variance. Since the model is affine, the entire line through X^a and X^b is feasible; hence the direction $Y = X^b - X^a$ is unbounded feasible. It must also be a zero-variance direction, else V as a function of E, on the line through X^a and X^b, would be a parabola rather than a straight line; hence lower feasible V would be found between X^a and X^b, which is ruled out by assumption. ###

Theorem 6.9

$$\tilde{M} = \begin{pmatrix} C & A' & \mu \\ A & 0 & 0 \\ \mu' & 0 & 0 \end{pmatrix}$$

is singular if and only if one of the following conditions holds:

(i)–(iii) As in theorem 6.8.
(iv) Only one value of E is obtainable.

Proof $\tilde{M}$ is singular if and only if there is $(Y', \delta', \delta_E) \neq (0, 0, 0)$ such that

$$\tilde{M} \begin{pmatrix} Y \\ \delta \\ \delta_E \end{pmatrix} = 0 \tag{6.16}$$

There are various cases. If $Y = 0$, $\delta_E = 0$, and $\delta \neq 0$, then either (i) or (ii) is true, and conversely (i) or (ii) implies the existence of such a δ, as in the proof of theorem 6.8. Next suppose $Y \neq 0$. Then (6.16) and the definition of $\tilde{M}$ imply

$$\mu' Y = 0$$

$$AY = 0$$

$$\begin{aligned} V(Y) &= Y'CY \\ &= -Y'A'\delta - Y'\mu\delta_E \\ &= 0 \end{aligned}$$

This is equivalent to condition (iii), by the same argument as in theorem 6.8. Finally, assume $Y = 0$ and $\delta_E \neq 0$. This is equivalent to the assumption that only one value of E is obtainable, either because $\mu = 0$, when $\delta = 0$, or μ is a linear combination of the rows of A. In the latter case $A'\delta = -\delta_E \mu$ and $AX = b$ imply $E = -\delta' b / \delta_E$ for every feasible portfolio. ###

Definitions If $\beta \neq 0$ and $\mu'\beta = 0$ we will call β a *zero-mean direction*. If a feasible direction β is both a zero-mean and a zero-variance direction, we will call it an *irrelevant direction*.

Corollary 6.10 If a feasible affine model has neither redundant equations nor irrelevant directions then

$$M = \begin{pmatrix} C & A' \\ A & 0 \end{pmatrix}$$

is singular if and only if the lower boundary of the set of obtainable EV combinations is a horizontal line, extending infinitely in both directions, and thus has no efficient points; whereas

$$\tilde{M} = \begin{pmatrix} C & A' & \mu \\ A & 0 & 0 \\ \mu' & 0 & 0 \end{pmatrix}$$

is singular if and only if there is one and only one obtainable E.

Proof See theorems 6.8 and 6.9. ###

Assuming for the remainder of this section that the model is feasible and has neither redundant constraints nor irrelevant directions, the relationship between singular and nonsingular M and $\tilde{M}$ is illustrated in figures 6.2(a), (b), and (c).

Figure 6.2(a) illustrates the lower boundary of the set of obtainable EV combinations for two cases in which M and $\tilde{M}$ are nonsingular. In such cases all values of E are obtainable, and $a_2 > 0$ in (6.10). This is consistent with either $V_{\min} > 0$ or $V_{\min} = 0$ in equation (5.16). Thus σ as a function of E may consist of either one branch of a hyperbola or two line segments; but in either case V as a function of E a strictly convex parabola.

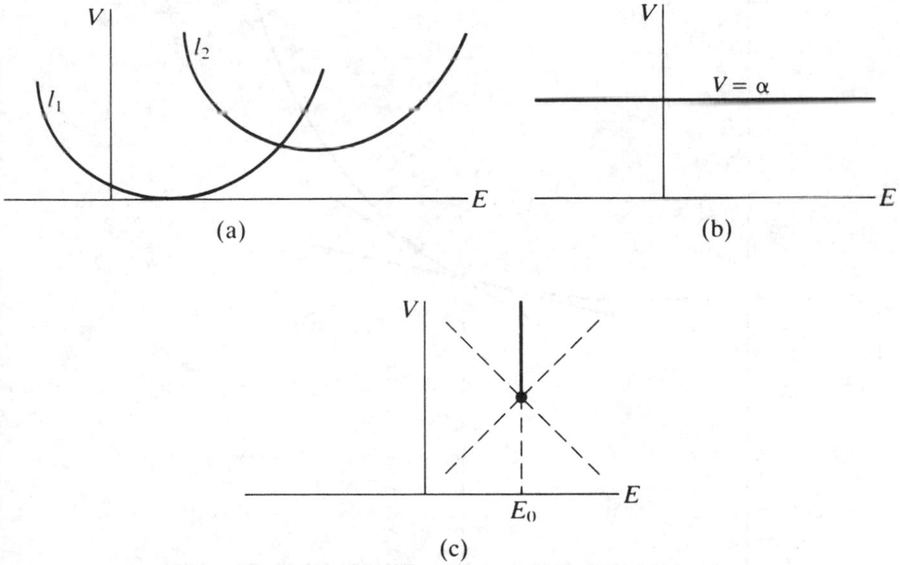

Figure 6.2 (a) Two cases in which M and $\tilde{M}$ are nonsingular (b) Case in which M is singular (c) Case in which $\tilde{M}$ is singular

Every point on either l_1 or l_2 in figure 6.2(a) is uniquely identified by its E or by its $dV/dE = 2\lambda_E$. Equation (6.9) determines X and incidentally λ and λ_E from E. Equation (6.13) uses M to determine X and λ from λ_E. E may then be determined from $E = \mu' X$.

Figure 6.2(b) illustrates the case in which M is singular and $\tilde{M}$ is nonsingular. V as a function of E is a horizontal line, which of course has $dV/dE = 0$ at all points. It is consequently impossible for (6.13) to provide an L minimizing solution for every value of $\lambda_E = 2dV/dE$.

Figure 6.2(c) represents the case in which M is nonsingular and $\tilde{M}$ is singular. In this case only one value of E is obtainable. Clearly (6.8a) cannot be solved for every E. Later we shall see that it is possible for the relationship between V and E among efficient EV combinations to have a kink in it, as illustrated in figure 6.3. The derivative from the right

$$2\lambda_E^r = \lim_{E \downarrow E_0} \Delta V/\Delta E$$

is greater than the derivative from the left

$$2\lambda_E^l = \lim_{E \uparrow E_0} \Delta V/\Delta E$$

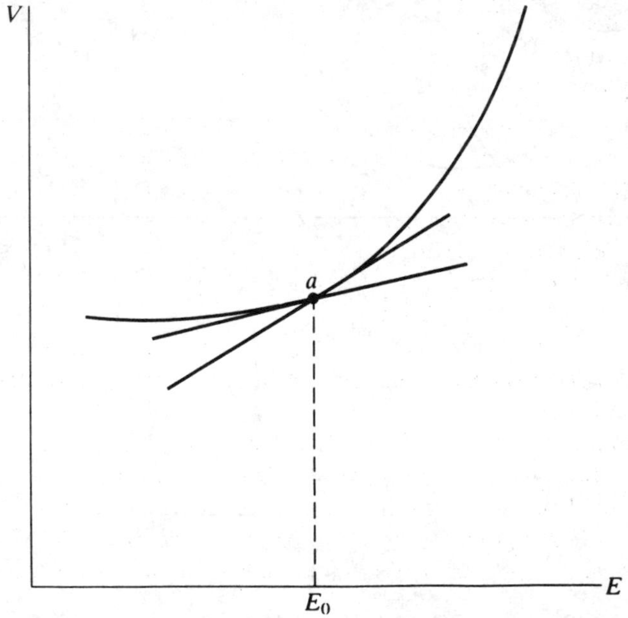

Figure 6.3 Lower boundary of obtainable EV set with kink

The set of obtainable EV combinations is supported by – that is, touches but lies completely on one side of – any line through a with slope equal to $dV/dE = 2\lambda_E$ for any λ_E in the range $\lambda_E^l \leqslant \lambda_E \leqslant \lambda_E^r$. The case of portfolio selection models with affine constraint sets and singular $\tilde{M}$ is an extreme example of this phenomenon. The set of obtainable EV combinations is supported by any straight line through (E_0, V_0) with any slope whatever. As λ_E goes, so to speak, from $+\infty$ to $-\infty$ in (6.13), X, E, and V remain constant, λ changes with λ_E, and the tangent line in figure 6.2(c) rotates clockwise from the vertical position around to the vertical again.

The case in which both M and $\tilde{M}$ are singular is not illustrated. If the model is feasible and contains neither redundant constraints nor irrelevant directions, it cannot happen that both are singular.

Postscript

Rather than as in (6.2), the Lagrangian expression is sometimes written as

$$L = g_0(X) - \sum_{k=1}^{m} \lambda_k [g_k(X) - b_k] \tag{6.17}$$

From (6.17), n equations are obtained by setting $\partial L/\partial X_i$ equal to zero. An additional m equations are obtained by setting $\partial L/\partial \lambda_k = 0$. For the problem in (6.3), for example, this procedure produces the $m + n + 1$ equations of (6.8). The procedure is justified by results in Kuhn and Tucker (1951). Kuhn and Tucker consider optimization problems in which variables may or may not be required to be nonnegative, and may be further constrained by (not necessarily linear) equalities or inequalities. They show the equivalence between the solution to our constrained minimization[2] problem and the problem of finding a minimax or saddlepoint solution to a game in which one player chooses X so as to minimize L in (6.17) for given λ, and the other player chooses λ to maximize L in (6.17) for given X. Assuming the g_i are differentiable, the condition that $\partial L/\partial \lambda_k = 0$ when the constraints are equalities (and slightly different when the constraints are inequalities) are necessary to assure that L is maximized by λ for given X.

The procedure adopted in the present chapter, using lemma 6.1 and equation (6.2), has a different basis. Suppose, by way of illustration, we sought two "goods" – two things to be maximized – in our choice of X. The amount supplied of each good is given by the functions $g_0(X)$ and $g_1(X)$. Suppose that the set of obtainable g_0, g_1 combinations provided by the choice of X in S is the area

[2] Kuhn and Tucker (1951) deal with constrained maximization rather than minimization, but their results are easily reverbalized to apply to the latter problem.

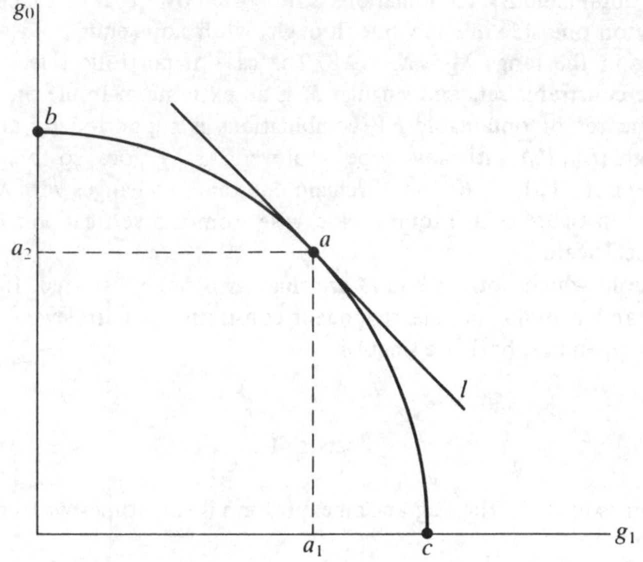

Figure 6.4 Obtainable g_0, g_1 combinations

inclosed by the curve *bac* and the two axes in figure 6.4, with g_1 on the horizontal axis and g_0 on the vertical axis. Since in this example we assume that a decision maker seeks both large g_0 and large g_1, the curve *bac* is the set of efficient g_0, g_1 combinations: given any point on *bac* it is impossible to get more g_1 without giving up g_0, and impossible to get more g_0 without giving up some g_1.

Let $a = (a_1, a_2)$ be a point on the *bac* frontier. Assume that the curve *bac* has a tangent line l at the point a with formula

$$g_0 = a_2 - \gamma(g_1 - a_1) \tag{6.18}$$

Since the tangent is negatively sloped, $\gamma > 0$ in (6.18).

The point a in the figure may be thought of as the answer to any of the following three questions:

(1) What feasible (g_1, g_0) combination maximizes g_0 for $g_1 = a_1$?
(2) What feasible (g_1, g_0) combination maximizes g_1 for $g_0 = a_2$?
(3) What feasible (g_1, g_0) combination maximizes $L = g_0 + \gamma g_1$?

The first of these questions asks us to maximize g_0 subject to X being in S plus the constraint $g_1(X) = a_1$. The second asks us to find the X in S, subject to the constraint $g_0(X) = a_2$, which maximizes $g_1(X)$. The third has no constraint other than X in S, and asks us to maximize $L = g_0 + \gamma g_1$. The answer to all three questions is provided by any X with $(g_1(X), g_0(X)) = (a_1, a_2)$.

By varying γ we can obtain each point on the frontier *bac* (including *c* if the tangent there is not vertical). Whatever values $a_1 = g_1(X)$ and $a_2 = g_0(X)$ result from maximizing L for a given γ is an efficient point, which could have been obtained by maximizing g_0 for $g_1(X) = a_1$ had we known the a_1 in advance, or by maximizing $g_1(X)$ given $g_0(X) = a_2$ had we known the a_2 in advance. The Lagrangian trick, for solving for maximum g_0 subject to a given g_1 among X in S, is to seek an X which satisfies conditions for maximizing L given any γ, and seek simultaneously the γ so that the maximizing X satisfies $g_1(X) = a_1$.

Next consider the case in which the choice of X determines $m + 1$ "quantities of interest" whose values will be denoted as $Y_0, Y_1, \ldots, Y_m$. These "quantities of interest" may be "goods" we seek to maximize such as g_0 or g_1 in the preceding example, or E in the portfolio selection problem. Instead, or in addition, the quantities of interest may include "bads" we seek to minimize, such as V in the portfolio selection model. Quantities of interest may also include such things as the difference

$$Y_k = \sum_{i=1}^{n} \beta_i X_i - X_{n+1}$$

which must equal zero for X_{n+1} to represent the beta of the portfolio, as discussed in chapter 3.

We continue to assume that X is chosen from a set $S \subset R^n$ such as $S = R^n$ in the discussion of the affine model in this chapter, or $S = \{X : X \geqslant 0\}$ in the next chapter. Given a choice of $X \in S$, the values of $Y = (Y_0, Y_1, \ldots, Y_m)$ is determined by $m + 1$ functions

$$\begin{aligned} Y_0 &= g_0(X) \\ Y_1 &= g_1(X) \\ &\vdots \\ Y_m &= g_m(X) \end{aligned}$$

or more briefly

$$Y = g(X)$$

(Note that, in the present discussion, Y_0 is a component rather than a vector.) Define

$$T = \{Y : Y = g(X), X \in S\}$$

i.e. T is the set of feasible Y, as distinct from S which is the set of feasible X.

Definition Let U be a subset of R^n. A point Z is said to be in the ***interior*** of U if there is a ball $B_r(Z) \subset U$ for some $r > 0$. A point Z is said to be in the *exterior* of U if there is a ball $B_r(Z) \subset R^n - U$ for some $r > 0$. A point Z is said to be on the *boundary* of U if it is neither a point in its interior nor a point in its exterior.

For example, if U is the set of obtainable EV combinations in figure 1.1 then the efficient EV combinations constitute part of the boundary of U.

Theorem 6.11 Let $\lambda' = (\lambda_0, \lambda_1, \ldots, \lambda_m) \neq 0$. Suppose $X^* \in S$ maximizes (or minimizes) $\lambda' Y$ among $X \in S$. Then $Y^* = g(X^*)$ must be a boundary point of $T = \{Y : Y = g(X), X \in S\}$.

Proof Since $X^* \in S$ we have Y^* in T; therefore it cannot be in the exterior of T. Thus, if it is not on the boundary of T, then Y^* must be in its interior. If it were in the interior, there would be an $r > 0$ such that $B_r(Y^*) \subset T$. Then $Y^* + \lambda r/2\|\lambda\|$ (or $Y^* - \lambda r/2\|\lambda\|) \in B_r(Y^*)$ is in T and has a greater (respectively, smaller) value of $\lambda' Y$. See exercise 6.8. ###

The part of the boundary on which an $\lambda' Y$ optimizing X^* is located depends, in an obvious way, on the signs of the λ_i and on whether we minimize or maximize. For example if we minimize (rather than maximize) $g_0 + \gamma g_1$ in figure 6.4 with $\gamma > 0$ then the minimizing X^* must provide $(g_0, g_1) = (0, 0)$. In general, if L is to be maximized and $\lambda_i > 0$ then an L maximizing X^* must provide a Y^* which maximizes Y_i among all feasible Y with the same Y_j, $j \neq i$, as Y^*; whereas if $\lambda_i < 0$ then an L maximizing X^* minimizes Y_i for the given $Y_j, j \neq i$. These statements are reversed for an L minimizing X^*. If $\lambda_i = 0$ then Y_i may or may not have either a minimum or a maximum for the given Y_j. For example, in figure 6.4, any X^* which provides a feasible g_0, g_1 with $g_1 = 0$ (i.e. any feasible g_0, g_1 on the g_0 axis) will minimize $g_0 + \gamma g_1$ if $\gamma = 0$.

If $k > 0$ then an X_0 which minimizes (or maximizes) $\lambda' X$ will also minimize (or maximize) $L = (k\lambda)' X$. Customarily this fact is used to set $\lambda_0 = 1$ where the zeroth component of $Y = (Y_0, Y_1, \ldots, Y_m)$ is chosen to assure $\lambda_0 \neq 0$.

For a given, fixed λ, (6.4) is a weighted sum of $m + 2$ "quantities of interest", namely V, E, and $\Sigma a_{ij} X_j$ for $i = 1$ to m. The first n equations in (6.8a) or (6.12a) assure us that we have minimized (6.4). This, in turn, guarantees that we have a boundary point in the space $(V, E, Y_1, \ldots, Y_m)$, where $Y_i = \Sigma a_{ij} X_j$. When $\bar{M}$ is nonsingular the last $m + 1$ equations of (6.8a) guarantee that the particular boundary point satisfies the requirements $Y_i = b_i$ and has a particular $E = \mu' X$. When M is nonsingular the $n + m$ equations of (6.12) assure that the requirements $Y_i = b_i$ are met and that $V/2 - \lambda_E E$ is minimized subject to these requirements; i.e. we have a boundary point in the space $(V/2 - \lambda_E E, Y_1, \ldots, Y_m)$ for the given λ_E.

When we consider the general portfolio selection problem in the following chapters, we will use a different set S than in the discussion of the affine model, and will therefore have different criteria for assuring that L is minimized among

X in S. But, as in the present chapter, we will use the fact that the L minimizing X_0 provides a boundary point, use additional equations to control the boundary point selected - and never define L in terms of b_k as in (6.17).

Exercises

6.1 Suppose that all investors had the same beliefs, μ and C, and each chose a portfolio subject to the same affine constraint set

$$AX^I = b$$

where $(X^I)' = (X_1^I, X_2^I, \ldots, X_n^I)$ and X_j^I is the fraction of his or her portfolio which the Ith investor holds of the jth security. It is not required that these "fractions" be nonnegative but, throughout the present exercise, we assume that $\Sigma X_i = 1$ is at least one of the constraints. We assume that M is nonsingular, and therefore the model is feasible and has efficient portfolios. Let $(X^{\mathrm{M}})' = (X_1^{\mathrm{M}}, X_2^{\mathrm{M}}, \ldots, X_n^{\mathrm{M}})$ where X_i^{M} is the total market value of the ith security divided by the total value of all securities; i.e. X_i^{M} is the proportion of the ith security in the "market portfolio." (Note that M as a superscript stands for "market" in this exercise; whereas M not as a superscript is the matrix defined in (6.11).) Let W_I be the total portfolio value of the Ith investor; let $w_I = W_I / \Sigma_j W_j$, where the sum in the denominator is taken over all investors (of which there are a finite number). Note, for use below, that $\Sigma w_I = 1$.

(a) Show that

$$X^{\mathrm{M}} = \sum_I w_I X^I$$

(Hint: first argue that the total value of the ith security is $\Sigma W_I X_i^I$.)

(b) Show that X^{M} satisfies

$$AX^{\mathrm{M}} = b$$

(c) Show that X^{M} is an efficient portfolio. (Hint: if there is only one efficient portfolio, as in figure 6.2(c), then the result is trivial. Why? Else every X^I may be written as

$$X^I = X_0 + bt_I$$

where X_0 is the efficient portfolio with minimum variance; $X = X_0 + bt$ for $t \geqslant 0$ is the ray of efficient portfolios; and $t_I \geqslant 0$ for every investor I. Show that

$$X^{\mathrm{M}} = X_0 + bt^*$$

where $t^* = \Sigma w_I t_I$ and is therefore nonnegative.)

Conclude that if all investors have the same beliefs, and the same affine constraint set with nonsingular M, then "the market is an efficient portfolio." In particular, for Black's model see Black (1972) and Merton (1972).

6.2 (Two-fund separation theorem: Sharpe, 1970, pp. 59-62; Merton, 1972.) Same assumptions as in exercise 6.1, plus the assumption that there is more than one efficient portfolio. Show that every efficient portfolio X can be written as

$$X = tX^a + (1-t)X^b$$

X^a and X^b can be chosen so that $t \geqslant 0$ but not necessarily $t \leqslant 1$. (Hint: use the fact that the efficient set is a straight line; every point on a line is of the form $X = tX^a + (1-t)X^b$ for any two distinct points $X^a \neq X^b$ on the line; also see exercise 5.3.)

6.3 We saw in this chapter that, for the model with an affine constraint set, when M is nonsingular the set of efficient portfolios is part of the line

$$\begin{pmatrix} X \\ \lambda \end{pmatrix} = M^{-1}\begin{pmatrix} 0 \\ b \end{pmatrix} + M^{-1}\begin{pmatrix} \mu \\ 0 \end{pmatrix}\lambda_E \qquad (6.19a)$$

$$= \alpha + \beta\lambda_E \qquad (6.19b)$$

In subsequent chapters we will see that, for the general portfolio selection model, we need to solve equations of the above form for various matrices related to M. For some important models, α and β can be found quickly, even when n is large. The present exercise and the next illustrate this for the simple case in which returns are uncorrelated. Exercises 6.5 and 6.6 illustrate the same for a more plausible model of covariance.

(a) Assume that there are n securities with $V_i > 0$ for $1 \leqslant i \leqslant n$, and with $\rho_{ij} = 0$ for all $i \neq j$. Assume Black's model: i.e. $\Sigma X_i = 1$ is the only constraint. Confirm that in this case equations (6.12) are

$$V_i X_i + \lambda_1 = \mu_i \lambda_E \qquad \text{for } 1 \leqslant i \leqslant n \qquad (6.20a)$$

$$\Sigma X_i = 1 \qquad (6.20b)$$

(b) From equations (6.20) infer

$$\lambda_1 = a_{n+1} + b_{n+1}\lambda_E$$

where $a_{n+1} = -1/(\Sigma 1/V_i)$ and $b_{n+1} = (\Sigma \mu_i/V_i)/(\Sigma 1/V_i)$. (Hint: solve the ith equation of (6.20a) for X_i and substitute into (6.20b).)

(c) Describe how (or, better, write a program) to find α and β given $V_i, \mu_i, 1 \leqslant i \leqslant n$.

6.4 Describe how to easily compute α and β for the model in exercise 6.3, except with $V_n = 0$. (Hint: confirm that

$$\lambda_1 = \mu_n \lambda_E$$

Use this to show that

$$X_i = \frac{\mu_i - \mu_n}{V_i} \lambda_E \qquad \text{for } 1 \leqslant i \leqslant n-1$$

Substitute this into the $(n + 1)$th equation to obtain

$$X_n = 1 - b_n \lambda_E$$

where

$$b_n = \sum_{i=1}^{n-1} (\mu_i - \mu_n)/V_i.)$$

6.5 The one-factor model of covariance (see Sharpe, 1964) assumes

$$r_i = \gamma_{0i} + \gamma_{1i} F + u_i \qquad \text{for } 1 \leqslant i \leqslant n \tag{6.21}$$

where $\text{cov}(u_i, F) = 0$ and $\text{cov}(u_i, u_j) = 0$ for $i \neq j$. (We write γ_{0i}, γ_{1i} rather than the usual α_i and β_i since α and β are preempted in this context.) As we saw in chapter 3, for this model variance may be written as

$$V = \sum_{i=1}^{n+1} X_i^2 V_i \tag{6.22}$$

where V_i in (6.22) equals V_{u_i} for $1 \leqslant i \leqslant n$; V_{n+1} of (6.22) is V_F of (6.21); and

$$X_{n+1} = \sum_{i=1}^{n} \gamma_{1i} X_i \tag{6.23}$$

This exercise and the following consider how to compute the α and β of equation (6.19b) for a model in which V is given by (6.22), $E = \sum_{i=1}^{n} X_i \mu_i$, and X is chosen subject to (6.23) and

$$\sum_{i=1}^{n} X_i = 1 \tag{6.24}$$

Note $\mu_{n+1} = 0$, and X_{n+1} does not enter the sum in (6.24).

(a) Assume $V_i > 0$ for $1 \leqslant i \leqslant n$. Confirm that equations (6.12) are

$$X_i V_i + \gamma_{1i} \lambda_1 + \lambda_2 = \mu_i \lambda_E \qquad 1 \leqslant i \leqslant n \tag{6.25a}$$

$$X_{n+1} V_{n+1} - \lambda_1 = 0 \tag{6.25b}$$

(b) Solve (6.25) for X_i $(1 \leqslant i \leqslant n + 1)$ as a linear function of the parameters λ_E and the variables λ_1 and λ_2, still to be determined.

(c) Substitute this into equations (6.23) and (6.24) to obtain equations of the form

$$c_{11}\lambda_1 + c_{12}\lambda_2 = d_{10} + d_{11}\lambda_E$$

$$c_{21}\lambda_1 + c_{22}\lambda_2 = d_{20} + d_{21}\lambda_E$$

(d) Describe how to compute α and β for this model, or write a program to do so.

6.6 This exercise uses the same assumptions as in exercise 6.5, except now assume $V_n = \gamma_{1n} = 0$. (Hint: recall the procedure in exercise 6.4.)

6.7 (a) Observe that the procedure in exercises 6.3 through 6.6 need be changed very little, to find α and β, if we replace the constraint $\Sigma X_i = 1$ by the constraint $\Sigma p_i X_i = W_0$, where p_i is the price of a share of the ith stock (or unit of other security) and W_0 is the value of the investor's portfolio. In particular the values $a_{ij} = 1$ for certain i and j in the constraint matrix A are not essential to the approach in exercises 6.3–6.6.

(b) Suppose

$$\begin{pmatrix} V_1 & & & & p_1 \\ & V_2 & & & p_2 \\ & & V_3 & & p_3 \\ & & & V_4 & p_4 \\ p_1 & p_2 & p_3 & p_4 & 0 \end{pmatrix} \begin{pmatrix} X_1 \\ X_2 \\ X_3 \\ X_4 \\ X_5 \end{pmatrix} = \begin{pmatrix} Y_1 \\ Y_2 \\ Y_3 \\ Y_4 \\ Y_5 \end{pmatrix}$$

gives Y as a function of X, where a blank in the matrix represents a zero coefficient. Describe how to compute X as a function of Y. Do not try to invert the matrix. Rather proceed as in exercise 6.3: use the first equation of the matrix to solve for X_1 as a function of Y_1 and X_5 (yet to be determined); substitute this for X_1 in the fifth equation of the matrix; and so on.

(c) Suppose that all the p_i and V_i are nonzero. The following diagram has an asterisk in each nonzero position of the matrix in (b), and a blank in each zero position:

$$\begin{pmatrix} * & & & & * \\ & * & & & * \\ & & * & & * \\ & & & * & * \\ * & * & * & * & \end{pmatrix}$$

A matrix is called *sparse* if a small fraction of its coefficients are nonzero. The above diagram is called the *sparsity diagram* of the matrix.

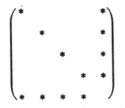

(d) What is the sparsity diagram for each of the following:

(i) M in exercise 6.3 with $n = 6$
(ii) M in exercise 6.4 with $n = 6$
(iii) M in exercise 6.5 with $n = 6$
(iv) M in exercise 6.6 with $n = 6$?

(e) For the M matrices in exercises 6.3, 6.4, 6.5, and 6.6, respectively, express the fraction f of nonzeros as a function of n. Observe that $f \to 0$ as $n \to \infty$. What is each f for $n = 100$?

(f) The diagram in (c) represents the M matrix in exercise 6.3(a) for $n = 4$. Confirm that when the first equation is used to solve for X_1, and X_1 is eliminated from the fifth equation (in the solution to exercise 6.3 or exercise 6.7(b)), the resulting matrix of four equations in four unknowns has the following sparsity diagram:

$$\begin{pmatrix} \ast & & & \ast \\ & \ast & & \ast \\ & & \ast & \ast \\ \ast & \ast & \ast & \bigstar \end{pmatrix}$$

The bold asterisk, which was not present in the fifth equation of the original, is called a *fill-in*. Confirm that there are no more fill-ins as X_2, X_3, and X_4 are eliminated.

(g) In general, it is not always necessary to use the first equation to eliminate X_1, then use the second equation to eliminate X_2, etc. Equation i can be used to eliminate X_j from the remaining equations, reducing by one the number of rows and number of columns of the remaining matrix, provided $a_{ij} \neq 0$. When this is done, one is said to *pivot* on a_{ij}. Assuming that no nonzero coefficient "accidentally" becomes zero when a variable is eliminated from a remaining equation, for a matrix with the following sparsity diagram choose a first pivot; note any fill-ins; cross out the eliminated row i and variable j; repeat with a second pivot; a third pivot, etc. Choose pivots so as to keep the number of fill-ins small.

$$\begin{pmatrix} \ast & & & & & & \ast \\ & \ast & & & & & \ast \\ & & \ast & & \ast & & \ast \\ & & & \ast & & & \ast \\ & & \ast & & \ast & & \ast \\ & & & & & \ast & \ast \\ \ast & \ast & \ast & \ast & \ast & \ast & \end{pmatrix}$$

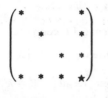

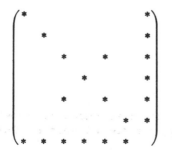

Comment The procedures in exercises 6.3–6.6 were for models whose sparsity diagrams were known in advance. It is also possible to write a program to quickly solve an arbitrary sparse matrix. The program chooses nonzero a_{ij} as pivots by a rule whose objective is to minimize fill-ins. Such sparse matrix techniques were originally proposed for large linear programming problems (Markowitz, 1957), and have been enhanced and applied extensively since (see Duff, 1977, 1981). In particular they have been applied to mean-variance analysis in Markowitz and Perold (1981b) and Perold (1984).

6.8 (a) Let S be any subset of R^n. Show that

(i) The interior of S is an open set.
(ii) The exterior of S is an open set.
(iii) The boundary of S is a closed set (therefore if X_0 is the limit of a sequence of points $X^1, X^2, \ldots$ all on the boundary of S, then X_0 is on the boundary of S).

(b) In connection with the proof of theorem 6.11, compute

(i) $d(Y^*, Y^* + \lambda r/2\|\lambda\|)$. (Hint: use $d(X, Z) = \|X - Z\|$.)
(ii) $d(Y^*, Y^* - \lambda r/2\|\lambda\|)$.
(iii) $\lambda'(Y^* + \lambda r/2\|\lambda\|) - \lambda' Y^*$. (Hint: recall $\|\lambda\|^2 = \lambda'\lambda$.)
(iv) $\lambda'(Y^* - \lambda r/2\|\lambda\|) - \lambda' Y^*$.

Part III

Solution to the General Portfolio Selection Model

7

Efficient Sets for Nondegenerate Models

This part of the book presents the solution to the general portfolio selection model defined in chapter 2. In models with only one feasible portfolio for each efficient EV combination, the solution consists of: (a) the set of efficient EV combinations; (b) the set of efficient $E\sigma$ combinations; and (c) the set of efficient portfolios. When there is more than one feasible portfolio for the same efficient EV combination, we will consider the solution to be (a) and (b), plus a set of portfolios which includes one feasible portfolio for each efficient EV combination.

Definition A set, all of whose members are efficient portfolios, which contains one and only one portfolio for each efficient EV combination, will be called a *complete, nonredundant* set of efficient portfolios. "Complete" refers to the requirement that there be one portfolio for each efficient EV combination; "nonredundant" refers to the requirement that no two portfolios provide the same EV combination.

Our objective then is to describe - and to show how to compute - the set of efficient EV combinations, the set of efficient $E\sigma$ combinations, and a complete, nonredundant set of efficient portfolios. One principal result of this and the next two chapters is that every feasible portfolio selection model has a complete, nonredundant set of efficient portfolios which is piecewise linear, and hence a set of efficient EV combinations which is piecewise parabolic, and a set of $E\sigma$ combinations which consists of linear and/or hyperbolic pieces. We will define a class of models called *nondegenerate*. We solve the nondegenerate model in this and the next chapter, and the general model in chapter 9.

In the present chapter, in chapter 8, and in most of chapter 9 we assume - usually without repeating this assumption explicitly in individual theorems, discussion, and exercises - that the portfolio selection problem is written in form 2. In other words, until otherwise stated, "portfolio selection model" means "portfolio selection model written in form 2". In theorem 9.17 we show that our results extend to any portfolio selection model in form 0, and therefore in form 1 as well as 2.

Kuhn-Tucker Conditions

Theorem 7.1 Let

$$S = \{X : X \geqslant 0\} \tag{7.1a}$$

and

$$L = \tfrac{1}{2}X'CX + \sum_{k=1}^{m} \lambda_k\left(\sum_{j=1}^{n} a_{kj}X_j\right) - \lambda_E\left(\sum_{j=1}^{n} \mu_j X_j\right) \tag{7.1b}$$

For given λ and λ_E, if X minimizes L subject to $X \in S$, and happens to have

$$AX = b \tag{7.1c}$$

$$\mu' X = E \tag{7.1d}$$

then X minimizes $V = X'CX$ subject to (7.1a, c, d). Furthermore, X minimizes $(1/2)\, V - \lambda_E E$ subject to (7.1a) and (7.1c), and if $\lambda_E > 0$ then X is an efficient portfolio. (The case in which $\lambda_E = 0$ will be considered later.)

Proof The first two assertions are applications of lemma 6.1 with $Y_0 = V$ in one case, and $Y_0 = (1/2)\, V - \lambda_E E$ in the other. Concerning the third assertion, if greater E and no more V, or less V and no less E, could be obtained subject to (7.1a, c), then X would not minimize L subject to (7.1a). ###

Let

$$\eta_i = \frac{\partial L}{\partial X_i}$$

$$= \sum_{j=1}^{n} \sigma_{ij} X_j + \sum_{k=1}^{m} a_{ki}\lambda_k - \lambda_E \mu_i \tag{7.2}$$

Or, writing $\eta' = (\eta_1, \eta_2, \ldots, \eta_n)$, equation (7.2) may be written as

$$\eta = (CA')\begin{pmatrix} X \\ \lambda \end{pmatrix} - \lambda_E \mu \tag{7.3a}$$

$$= (CA'\mu)\begin{pmatrix} X \\ \lambda \\ -\lambda_E \end{pmatrix} \tag{7.3b}$$

Theorem 7.2 For given (λ', λ_E), a necessary and sufficient condition for X_0 to minimize L among X in S is that

$$\eta_i^0 \geqslant 0 \qquad \text{for } i = 1, \ldots, n \tag{7.4a}$$

and

$$\eta_i^0 = 0 \qquad \text{for every } X_i^0 > 0 \tag{7.4b}$$

where η_0 is η evaluated at X_0.

Proof To show that (7.4) is necessary, suppose that X_0 minimizes L among $X \in S$ but does not satisfy (7.4). First, contrary to (7.4a), suppose that

$$\eta_i^0 < 0 \qquad \text{for some } i$$

Then the definition of the partial derivative as a limit of $\Delta L/\Delta X_i$ and the definition of

$$\lim_{\Delta X_i \to 0} \Delta L/\Delta X_i$$

imply that, for some $\delta = (0, 0, \ldots, \delta_i, 0, \ldots, 0)$ with ith component $\delta_i > 0$,

$$L(X_0 + \delta) < L(X_0)$$

But $X_0 + \delta \geqslant X_0 \geqslant 0$ is in S, contradicting the assumption that X_0 minimizes L among X in S. Next suppose, contrary to (7.4b), that $\eta_i^0 > 0$ for some $X_i > 0$. Then the definitions imply that there is a $\hat{\delta} = (0, 0, \ldots, -\hat{\delta}_i, 0, \ldots, 0)$ with ith component $-\hat{\delta}_i < 0$ such that

$$L(X_0 + \delta) < L(X_0)$$

for every $\delta = (0, 0, \ldots, -\delta_i, 0, \ldots, 0)$ with $\hat{\delta}_i > \delta_i > 0$. In particular, if

$$\tilde{\delta}_i = \min(X_i^0, \hat{\delta}_i)$$

and

$$\tilde{\delta} = (0, 0, \ldots, -\tilde{\delta}_i, 0, \ldots, 0)$$

then

$$X = X_0 + \tilde{\delta}$$

is in S and has $L(X) < L(X_0)$, again contradicting the assumption that X_0 minimizes L among X in S.

To show sufficiency, suppose that $X_0 \in S$ satisfies (7.4) but does not minimize L among $X \in S$. Specifically, suppose Y_0 in S has smaller L. We will derive a contradiction. The straight line segment connecting X_0 and Y_0 is

$$X = X_0 + t(Y_0 - X_0)$$
$$= X_0 + bt$$

for $0 \leqslant t \leqslant 1$. $X = X_0$ at $t = 0$; $X = Y_0$ at $t = 1$. Every point on this segment is in S, since S is a convex set. Along the entire straight line $X = X_0 + bt$, $-\infty < t < \infty$, the relationship between L and t is

$$\begin{aligned} L &= \tfrac{1}{2}X'CX + \lambda' AX - \lambda_E \mu' X \\ &= \tfrac{1}{2}(X_0 + bt)'C(X_0 + bt) + \lambda' A(X_0 + bt) - \lambda_E \mu'(X_0 + bt) \\ &= a_0 + a_1 t + a_2 t^2 \end{aligned} \tag{7.5}$$

where $a_2 = (1/2)b'Cb \geqslant 0$. If $a_2 = 0$ then (7.5) is linear, and has the same derivative everywhere. On the other hand, if $a_2 > 0$ then L has a unique minimum at some point $t_{\min}$ (not necessarily between zero and one). $\mathrm{d}L/\mathrm{d}t < 0$ for $t < t_{\min}$ and $\mathrm{d}L/\mathrm{d}t > 0$ for $t > t_{\min}$. Combining the two cases ($a_2 = 0$ and $a_2 > 0$), if $\mathrm{d}L/\mathrm{d}t \geqslant 0$ at $t = 0$ then $\mathrm{d}L/\mathrm{d}t \geqslant 0$ for all $t > 0$, and L cannot have a smaller value at Y_0 (i.e. $t = 1$) than at X_0 (i.e. $t = 0$). But indeed at $t = 0$ - since $\mathrm{d}X_i/\mathrm{d}t = b_i < 0$ is permitted only if $X_i > 0$, and hence $\eta_i^0 = 0$ - we have

$$\begin{aligned} \frac{\mathrm{d}L}{\mathrm{d}t} &= \sum_{i=1}^{n} \frac{\partial L}{\partial X_i} \frac{\mathrm{d}X_i}{\mathrm{d}t} \\ &= \sum_{i=1}^{n} \eta_i^0 b_i \\ &\geqslant 0 \end{aligned}$$

###

The requirement that X be in S and satisfy (7.4) may be written as $X \geqslant 0$, $\eta \geqslant 0$, $\eta' X = 0$. These are the *Kuhn-Tucker conditions* (1951) for minimizing V subject to (7.1c), (7.1d), and $X \in S$, or for minimizing $(1/2)V - \lambda_E E$ for fixed λ_E subject to (7.1c) and $X \in S$.

Critical Lines

In this and the next two chapters we will show that every feasible portfolio selection model has a piecewise linear complete, nonredundant set of efficient portfolios. The "pieces" of this piecewise linear set are segments of what we will call critical lines. These critical lines are the solutions to certain affine portfolio selection models related to the original model. The affine models are obtained by deleting the constraints $X \geqslant 0$, and by constraining certain of the X_i to be zero. In the present section we define critical lines in terms of variables which are allowed to vary versus variables which are required to be zero in the associated affine problem.

Let *IN* be a subset of the numbers between 1 and n, and *OUT* be those numbers between 1 and n which are not in *IN*. For example, with $n = 6$ we might have

$$IN = \{1,\ 3,\ 4\}$$
$$OUT = \{2,\ 5,\ 6\}$$

Sometimes we shall speak of "i *IN*" or "i *OUT*" as short for "i in *IN*" or "i in *OUT*".

Recall that e^i is the vector with a 1 in its ith position and zeros in its other $n-1$ positions. For a particular *IN* set we will let $\bar{C}_{IN}$ be the C matrix with its ith row and column replaced by $(e^i)'$ and e^i respectively, for every i in the *OUT* set. For *IN* and *OUT* in the preceding example,

$$\bar{C}_{IN} = \begin{pmatrix} \sigma_{11} & 0 & \sigma_{13} & \sigma_{14} & 0 & 0 \\ 0 & 1 & 0 & 0 & 0 & 0 \\ \sigma_{31} & 0 & \sigma_{33} & \sigma_{34} & 0 & 0 \\ \sigma_{41} & 0 & \sigma_{43} & \sigma_{44} & 0 & 0 \\ 0 & 0 & 0 & 0 & 1 & 0 \\ 0 & 0 & 0 & 0 & 0 & 1 \end{pmatrix}$$

We define $\bar{A}_{IN}$ as the A matrix with the ith column replaced by a 0 vector, for every i in *OUT*; and define $\bar{\mu}_{IN}$ as the μ vector with 0 for its ith component for every i in *OUT*. For the example *IN* set above, and for $m = 2$,

$$\bar{A}_{IN} = \begin{pmatrix} a_{11} & 0 & a_{13} & a_{14} & 0 & 0 \\ a_{21} & 0 & a_{23} & a_{24} & 0 & 0 \end{pmatrix}$$

$$\bar{\mu}'_{IN} = (\mu_1 \quad 0 \quad \mu_3 \quad \mu_4 \quad 0 \quad 0)$$

Usually we will write $\bar{C}, \bar{A}, \bar{\mu}$ rather than $\bar{C}_{IN}, \bar{A}_{IN}$, and $\bar{\mu}_{IN}$.

For some *IN* set, consider the affine model with variance, mean, and constraints as follows:

$$V = X'\bar{C}X \tag{7.6a}$$

$$E = \bar{\mu}'X \tag{7.6b}$$

$$\bar{A}X = b \tag{7.6c}$$

$$X_i = 0 \qquad \text{for } i \in OUT \tag{7.6d}$$

and, of course, with no requirement that $X \geqslant 0$. Let us assume - without justification for the moment - that

$$\bar{M} = \begin{pmatrix} \bar{C} & \bar{A}' \\ \bar{A} & 0 \end{pmatrix} \tag{7.7a}$$

is nonsingular. Then equation (6.12) becomes

$$\begin{pmatrix} \bar{C} & \bar{A}' \\ \bar{A} & 0 \end{pmatrix} \begin{pmatrix} X \\ \lambda \end{pmatrix} = \begin{pmatrix} 0 \\ b \end{pmatrix} + \begin{pmatrix} \bar{\mu} \\ 0 \end{pmatrix} \lambda_E \tag{7.7b}$$

Note that the ith equation of the above is $X_i = 0$ for $i \in OUT$. With $\bar{M}$ assumed to be nonsingular the solution to (7.7b) is

$$\begin{pmatrix} X \\ \lambda \end{pmatrix} = \bar{M}^{-1} \begin{pmatrix} 0 \\ b \end{pmatrix} + \bar{M}^{-1} \begin{pmatrix} \bar{\mu} \\ 0 \end{pmatrix} \lambda_E \tag{7.8}$$

X_i for i *IN* is allowed to be negative, zero, or positive in the affine model.

Definition The set of $(X', \lambda', \lambda_E)$ which satisfies (7.8) is the *critical line* of the *IN* set. We define critical lines *only* for *IN* sets with *nonsingular* $\bar{M}$. The critical line is defined as a line in the $m + n + 1$ dimensional $(X', \lambda', \lambda_E)$ space rather than in X space or (X', λ') space. (Exercise 7.5 comments on this aspect of the definition.)

Theorem 7.3 Let $(X_0', \lambda_0', \lambda_E)$ be a point on a critical line (7.8) with $\lambda_E = \lambda_E^0 > 0$. If

$$X_0 \geqslant 0 \tag{7.9a}$$

$$\eta_0 \geqslant 0 \tag{7.9b}$$

where

$$\eta_0 = (C, A', \mu) \begin{pmatrix} X_0 \\ \lambda_0 \\ -\lambda_E^0 \end{pmatrix}$$

then X_0 is efficient. (Note: the theorem makes no assertion concerning the case of $\lambda_E = 0$.)

Proof In addition to $X \geqslant 0$ and $\eta \geqslant 0$, theorem 7.2 requires that $\eta_i = 0$ if $X_i > 0$. But (7.7b) assures us that $\eta_i = 0$ for $i \in IN$, and $X_i = 0$ for $i \in OUT$.###

Equation (7.8) shows us that the relationship between X and λ_E is linear along any critical line. We shall write the critical line as

$$\begin{pmatrix} X \\ \lambda \end{pmatrix} = \alpha + \beta \lambda_E \tag{7.10a}$$

where α and β depend on the *IN* set. $\alpha_i = \beta_i = 0$ for i *OUT*, and admit other values for i *IN*. We will say that (7.10a) describes a line – in $(X', \lambda', \lambda_E)$ space – even when $\beta = 0$; see exercise 7.5. (If $\beta = 0$ then only λ_E varies on the line.)

η is also linear in λ_E, since

$$\eta = (C, A')\begin{pmatrix} X \\ \lambda \end{pmatrix} - \mu\lambda_E$$

$$= (C, A')\left\{\bar{M}^{-1}\begin{pmatrix} 0 \\ b \end{pmatrix} + \bar{M}^{-1}\begin{pmatrix} \bar{\mu} \\ 0 \end{pmatrix}\lambda_E\right\} - \mu\lambda_E$$

$$= \gamma + \delta\lambda_E \tag{7.10b}$$

where (7.7b) forces

$$\eta_i = 0 + 0\lambda_E \qquad \text{for } i \in IN$$

and admits other values of γ_i and δ_i for *i OUT*. Thus, when it is convenient to do so, one may think of a critical line as a straight line in $(X', \lambda', \lambda_E, \eta)$ space.

Efficient Segments

This section considers efficient portions of certain critical lines. Often most critical lines have no efficient portfolios. For example, in a typical standard portfolio analysis (with or without upper bounds) containing hundreds of securities, there are an astronomical number of critical lines (namely every subset of $\{1, \ldots, n\}$ whose $\bar{M}$ is nonsingular); but only a few hundred of these contain efficient portfolios. Fortunately we can find these few hundred, and their efficient portions, without enumerating all critical lines.

We begin by defining six quantities – λ_u, λ_b, λ_c, λ_a, λ_{low} and λ_{hi} associated with every critical line. Since they vary from one critical line to another, these quantities should bear a label identifying the critical line involved. We will omit such a label except when more than one critical line is under discussion. The six quantities are used – two explicitly, four implicitly – in theorem 7.4. They and the theorem are discussed and illustrated following the proof of the theorem.

The present section and the next one, on adjacent efficient segments, are the crux of the book. To a good first order of approximation, if and only if you understand these two sections you understand the book. It will take a few more sections of this chapter to prove some results summarized in the section on adjacent efficient segments; and two more chapters to tie up some loose ends. But in the end it will turn out that these two sections essentially tell the whole story of efficient sets.

For any critical line we define[1]

[1] $\max\limits_{\beta_i > 0} -\alpha_i/\beta_i$ stands for the maximum of $-\alpha_i/\beta_i$ among i such that $\beta_i > 0$.

$$\lambda_a = \begin{cases} \max\limits_{\beta_i>0} -\alpha_i/\beta_i \\ -\infty \quad \text{if } \beta_i \leqslant 0 \end{cases} \qquad \text{for } i=1,\ldots,n$$

$$\lambda_b = \begin{cases} \max\limits_{\delta_i>0} -\gamma_i/\delta_i \\ -\infty \quad \text{if } \delta_i \leqslant 0 \end{cases} \qquad \text{for } i=1,\ldots,n$$

$$\lambda_c = \begin{cases} \min\limits_{\beta_i<0} -\alpha_i/\beta_i \\ +\infty \quad \text{if } \beta_i \geqslant 0 \end{cases} \qquad \text{for } i=1,\ldots,n$$

$$\lambda_d = \begin{cases} \min\limits_{\delta_i<0} -\gamma_i/\delta_i \\ +\infty \quad \text{if } \delta_i \geqslant 0 \end{cases} \qquad \text{for } i=1,\ldots,n$$

$$\lambda_{\text{hi}} = \min(\lambda_c, \lambda_d)$$

$$\lambda_{\text{low}} = \max(\lambda_a, \lambda_b, 0)$$

where each max [min] is for $1 \leqslant i \leqslant n$.

Theorem 7.4 Consider a critical line on which:

(i) $\lambda_{\text{hi}} > \lambda_{\text{low}}$

Whether or not (i) holds, no point on a critical line can satisfy conditions (7.9) for efficiency unless, in the equation (7.10) description of the critical line,

(ii) There is no i such that $\beta_i = 0$ and $\alpha_i < 0$; and
(iii) There is no i such that $\delta_i = 0$ and $\gamma_i < 0$.

If conditions (i), (ii), and (iii) hold then all points are efficient which lie on the interval

$$\begin{pmatrix} X \\ \lambda \end{pmatrix} = \alpha + \beta\lambda_E$$

$$\lambda_{\text{low}} \leqslant \lambda_E \leqslant \lambda_{\text{hi}}$$

with the second $\leqslant$ replaced by $<$ if $\lambda_{\text{hi}} = \infty$.

Proof If $\beta_i > 0$, the set of λ_E such that $X_i = \alpha_i + \beta_i\lambda_E \geqslant 0$ is $\lambda_E \geqslant -\alpha_i/\beta_i$. Thus if any β_i is positive, we must have $\lambda_E \geqslant \lambda_a$ to assure that $X_i \geqslant 0$ for all i with $\beta_i > 0$. Similarly if $\delta_i > 0$ the set of λ_E such that $\eta_i = \gamma_i + \delta_i\lambda_E \geqslant 0$ is $\lambda_E \geqslant -\gamma_i/\delta_i$; and we must have $\lambda_E \geqslant \lambda_b$ to assure that $\eta_i \geqslant 0$ for all i with $\delta_i > 0$. For $\beta_i < 0$, we have $X_i \geqslant 0$ for $\lambda_E \leqslant -\alpha_i/\beta_i$; and for $\delta_i < 0$, we have $\eta_i \geqslant 0$ for $\lambda_E \leqslant -\gamma_i/\delta_i$. If $\beta_i = 0$ then $X_i \geqslant 0$ for all λ_E if and only if $\alpha_i \geqslant 0$; and similarly if $\delta_i = 0$. For the moment consider the case with $\lambda_{\text{low}} > 0$. Given $\lambda_{\text{hi}} > \lambda_{\text{low}}$, the conditions for efficiency in theorem 7.3 are met by (and only by) the range of λ_E prescribed in the theorem.

When $\lambda_{low} = 0$ (still assuming $\lambda_{hi} > \lambda_{low}$) theorem 7.3 does not apply to the specific point with $\lambda_E = \lambda_{low} = 0$. (It applies to the points in the interval $\lambda_{hi} \geqslant \lambda_E > \lambda_{low}$ which are therefore efficient.) The fact that the point at $\lambda_E = 0$ is also efficient may be shown as follows. Recall from chapter 5 that V as a function of E along a straight line is either horizontal or a convex parabola. It cannot be horizontal in the present instance, since we have $\lambda_E = (1/2)\, dV/dE > 0$ when $\lambda_E = \lambda_{hi}$. V is minimized at $\lambda_E = 0$, among points on the critical line and also among feasible portfolios, since it meets the Kuhn-Tucker conditions for such. It could only fail to be efficient if some other feasible portfolio had the same minimum $V = V_0$ and had $E = E^*$ greater than E_0 at $\lambda_E = 0$. But this contradicts the fact that, for sufficiently small λ_E, there are points on the critical line with $E < E^*$, $V > V_0$ and which we have already shown to be efficient. ###

Theorem 7.4 is illustrated in figure 7.1. This figure represents the straight line

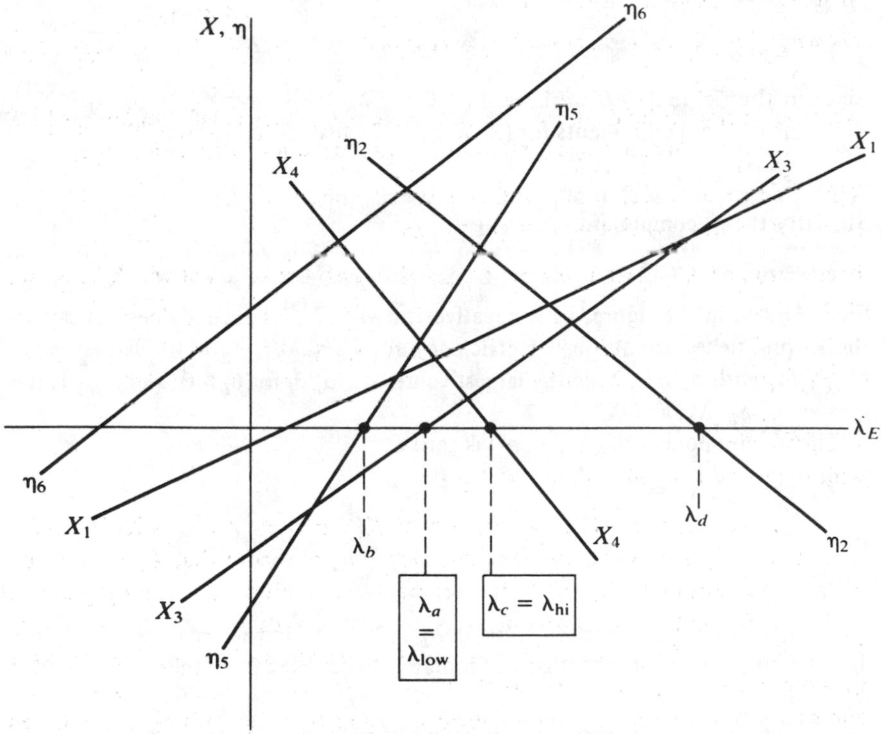

Figure 7.1 X and η along a critical line

$$\begin{pmatrix} X \\ \lambda \\ \eta \end{pmatrix} = \begin{pmatrix} \alpha \\ \gamma \end{pmatrix} + \begin{pmatrix} \beta \\ \delta \end{pmatrix} \lambda_E \tag{7.11}$$

The value of λ_E is plotted on the horizontal axis. The line labeled X_1 shows the value of X_1 as a function of λ_E in (7.11). The lines labeled X_3, X_4, η_2, η_5, and η_6 similarly show the values of each of these as a function of λ_E. Assuming $n = 6$ and $IN = \{1, 3, 4\}$, the values of X_2, X_5, X_6, η_1, η_3, and η_4 are zero everywhere on this critical line, and are omitted from the figure. The values of λ_1 and λ_2 could be plotted on the graph, but are omitted since they are not needed for the present discussion. Thus a figure such as that in 7.1 can be used to portray in two dimensions a straight line in the fourteen-dimensional space[2]

$$(X_1, X_2, X_3, X_4, X_5, X_6, \lambda_1, \lambda_2, \eta_1, \eta_2, \eta_3, \eta_4, \eta_5, \eta_6)$$

The X_1 component of the (X', λ', η') vector is zero at

$$X_1 = \alpha_1 + \beta_1 \lambda_E = 0$$

i.e. at

$$\lambda_E^{(1)} = -\alpha_1/\beta_1$$

Since in the figure $\beta_1 > 0$ we have $X_1 > 0$ for $\lambda_E > \lambda_E^{(1)}$ and $X_1 < 0$ for $\lambda_E < \lambda_E^{(1)}$. Thus one of the requirements for (X, λ, η) to be feasible is that

$$\lambda_E \geqslant \lambda_E^{(1)} = -\alpha_1/\beta_1$$

Similarly the η_5 component is zero at

$$\lambda_E = \lambda_E^{(5)} = -\gamma_5/\delta_5$$

Since $\delta_5 > 0$ in the figure, η_5 is negative for $\lambda_E < \lambda_E^{(5)}$; hence X does not satisfy the Kuhn-Tucker conditions of efficiency for $\lambda_E < \lambda_E^{(5)}$. λ_b is the largest value of $-\gamma_i/\delta_i$ with $\delta_i > 0$; λ_a is the largest value of $-\alpha_i/\beta_i$ for $\beta_i > 0$; and λ_{low} is the greatest of λ_a, λ_b, and 0.

The X_4 component of (X', λ', η') is zero at

$$X_4 = \alpha_4 + \beta_4 \lambda_E = 0$$

that is, at

$$\lambda_E^{(4)} = -\alpha_4/\beta_4$$

Since $\beta_4 < 0$ we will have $X_4 < 0$ for $\lambda_E > \lambda_E^{(4)}$. λ_c is the smallest $-\alpha_i/\beta_i$ for $\beta_i < 0$ - just $-\alpha_4/\beta_4$ in the figure. Similarly since $\delta_2 < 0$ in the figure, $\eta_2 < 0$

[2] Strictly speaking, the horizontal axis should be a parameter t, and λ_E should be one of the components of the space in which the line is drawn, for reasons illustrated in exercise 7.5. The portrayal of critical lines as in figures 7.1 and 7.2 originated with Sharpe (1963).

for $\lambda_E > -\gamma_2/\delta_2$. λ_d is the smallest value of $-\gamma_i/\delta_i$ for $\delta_i < 0$ - just $-\gamma_2/\delta_2$ in the figure. λ_{hi} is the smaller of λ_c and λ_d.

In the example, $\lambda_{low} < \lambda_{hi}$. As may be seen from the figure, for all λ_E such that

$$\lambda_{low} \leqslant \lambda_E \leqslant \lambda_{hi}$$

we have $X_i \geqslant 0$ and $\eta_i \geqslant 0$ for $i = 1, \ldots, 6$ and $\lambda_E > 0$. All points on (7.11) are therefore efficient for this range of λ_E. In general, for λ_E above λ_{hi} or below λ_{low} the portfolios on the critical line have either some $X_i < 0$ or some $\eta_i < 0$. In the former case the portfolio is not feasible; in the latter case it does not meet the Kuhn-Tucker conditions which assure efficiency.[3]

Definition We will say that a portfolio selection model is *degenerate* if it has at least one critical line such that for at least one pair of i, j with $i \neq j$, $1 \leqslant i \leqslant n$, $1 \leqslant j \leqslant n$, we have one of the following:

$$\alpha_i \neq 0, \quad \beta_i \neq 0, \quad \alpha_j \neq 0, \quad \beta_j \neq 0, \quad \alpha_i/\beta_i = \alpha_j/\beta_j$$

or

$$\alpha_i \neq 0, \quad \beta_i \neq 0, \quad \gamma_j \neq 0, \quad \delta_j \neq 0, \quad \alpha_i/\beta_i = \gamma_j/\delta_i$$

or

$$\gamma_i \neq 0, \quad \delta_i \neq 0, \quad \gamma_j \neq 0, \quad \delta_j \neq 0, \quad \gamma_i/\delta_i = \gamma_j/\delta_j$$

If a model contains no such case for any *i* and *j* on any critical line, then we call it *nondegenerate*.

An easy consequence of the above definition is that on any critical line of a nondegenerate model $\lambda_{hi} \neq \lambda_{low}$ unless both equal zero. Also, there can only be one i such that $\lambda_E^{(i)} = \lambda_{low}$ except perhaps when $\lambda_{low} = 0$; and only one i such that $\lambda_E^{(i)} = \lambda_{hi}$ except perhaps when $\lambda_{hi} = 0$. In other words, in a nondegenerate model there can be no ties for which X_i or η_i goes to zero first as λ_E increases or decreases, except possibly when $\lambda_E = 0$ (and the end of the efficient set) is reached.

Adjacent Efficient Segments

In the preceding section we saw that if $\lambda_{hi} > \lambda_{low}$ on a critical line, and conditions (ii) and (iii) of theorem 7.4 hold, then all points on the critical line are efficient for the line segment with $\lambda_{low} \leqslant \lambda_E \leqslant \lambda_{hi}$ (or with $\lambda_{low} \leqslant \lambda_E < \infty$). We now summarize how adjacent pieces of the set of efficient portfolios may

[3] As to whether or not the portfolio is in fact inefficient, see exercise 7.4.

be obtained from this piece when $\lambda_{low} > 0$ or $\lambda_{hi} < \infty$. We assume that the model is nondegenerate. Proofs are deferred until the following sections.

Our discussion breaks into several mutually exclusive parts depending on whether

(A) We move in the direction of *decreasing* λ_E, considering the adjacent critical line segment which begins at $\lambda_E = \lambda_{low}$; or

(B) We move in the direction of *increasing* λ_E, considering the adjacent critical line segment which begins at $\lambda_E = \lambda_{hi}$.

In case (A) we have the following possibilities:

(A1) λ_{low} is determined by an $X_i \geqslant 0$ constraint; that is, for some i we have $-\alpha_i/\beta_i = \lambda_a = \lambda_{low}$.

(A2) λ_{low} is determined by an $\eta_i \geqslant 0$ constraint; that is, for some i we have $-\gamma_i/\delta_i = \lambda_b = \lambda_{low}$; or

(A3) $\lambda_{low} = 0$.

The corresponding cases for (B) are:

(B1) An $X_i \geqslant 0$ constraint determines λ_{hi};

(B2) An $\eta_i \geqslant 0$ constraint determines λ_{hi}; or

(B3) $\lambda_{hi} = \infty$.

We will not discuss all these cases in equal detail since some have much in common. We start with (A1). Suppose that for $i = \omega$

$$-\alpha_\omega/\beta_\omega = \lambda_a = \lambda_{low}$$

We say that $X_\omega \downarrow 0$ ("goes downward to zero") as $\lambda_E \downarrow -\alpha_\omega/\beta_\omega$. Theorem 7.5 in the next section shows that if we move ω from the *IN* set to the *OUT* set, $\bar{M}$ stays nonsingular. Furthermore, corollary 7.7 shows that the new critical line, call it l^1, has the same (X', λ', η') at $\lambda_E = -\alpha_\omega/\beta_\omega$ as did the previous critical line, l^0, at $\lambda_E = -\alpha_\omega/\beta_\omega$. Finally, theorem 7.9 shows that as λ_E moves downward from $-\alpha_\omega/\beta_\omega$ along the new critical line l^1, the variable η_ω, now free to vary, moves upwards from zero. This implies that, in a nondegenerate model, since l^0 satisfies conditions (i), (ii), (iii) of theorem 7.4, so does l^1.

Figure 7.2 illustrates these results. For λ_E between λ_{low}^0 and λ_{hi}^0 the figure shows the values of X_1, X_3, X_4, η_2, η_5, and η_6 for the critical line l^0 as in figure 7.1. For λ_E between λ_{low}^1 and $\lambda_{hi}^1 = \lambda_{low}^0$ the figure shows the values of these same variables on l^1, except that η_3 is substituted for X_3. The value of X_3 along l^0 is shown as a dotted line for $\lambda_E < \lambda_{low}^0$. Since η_3 increases from its zero value at $\lambda_E = \lambda_{low}^0 = \lambda_{hi}^1$, the points on l^1 are efficient as λ_E decreases from λ_{hi}^1 to λ_{low}^1 where η_5 becomes zero.

$\lambda_E = \lambda_{low}^1$ in figure 7.2 illustrates case (A2) in which a requirement $\eta_i \geqslant 0$ determines λ_{low}. In case (A2) $\eta_\omega \downarrow 0$ as $\lambda_E \downarrow \lambda_{low}$. The relevant facts established

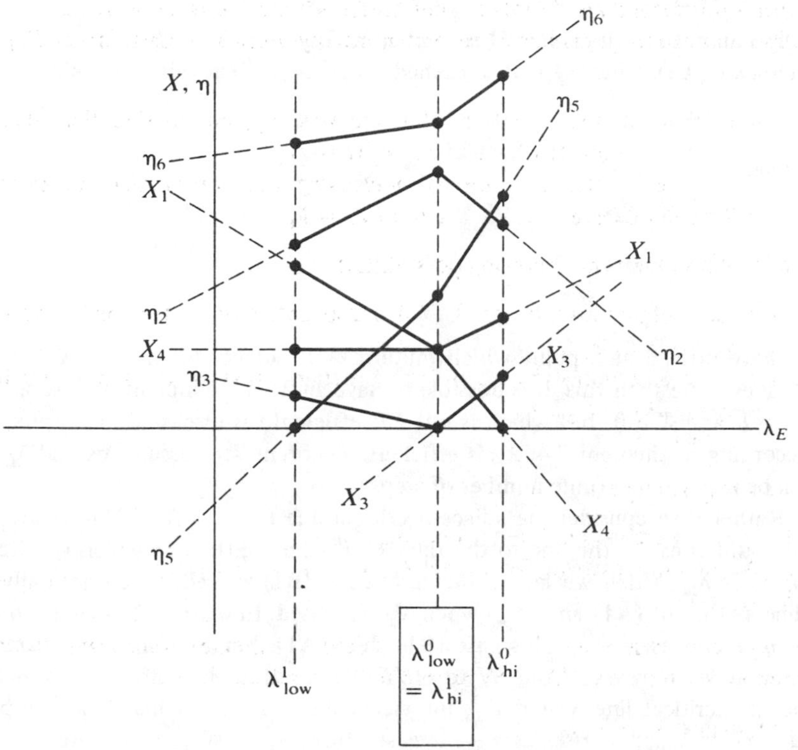

Figure 7.2 Two adjacent efficient segments

below in this case are the following: if ω is moved from the *OUT* to the *IN* set the resulting $\bar{M}$ matrix is nonsingular; the old critical line, l^1, intersects the new critical line, l^2, at $\lambda_E = \lambda^1_{\text{low}} = \lambda^2_{\text{hi}}$; on the new critical line X_ω increases from zero as λ_E decreases from $\lambda^1_{\text{low}} = \lambda^2_{\text{hi}}$. If we were to add to figure 7.2 the values of X_1, η_2, etc. for l^2, they would have the same values at $\lambda_E = \lambda^1_{\text{low}}$ as they do on l^1 at this value of λ_E. We leave such a drawing as an exercise for the reader. The broken lines to the left of $\lambda_E = \lambda^1_{\text{low}}$ are the continuation of these variables on l^1 beyond the value of λ_E for which l^1 satisfies the Kuhn-Tucker conditions.

The above process can be repeated, obtaining successive critical lines l^1, l^2, l^3, ... which are efficient for ranges of λ_E:

$$\lambda^1_{\text{low}} \leqslant \lambda_E \leqslant \lambda^1_{\text{hi}}$$

$$\lambda^2_{\text{low}} \leqslant \lambda_E \leqslant \lambda^2_{\text{hi}} = \lambda^1_{\text{low}}$$

$$\lambda_{\text{low}}^3 \leqslant \lambda_E \leqslant \lambda_{\text{hi}}^3 = \lambda_{\text{low}}^2$$

and so on until a critical line l^* is reached with $\lambda_{\text{low}} = 0$.

In case (A3), when $\lambda_E = 0$ is reached, since (X_0', λ_0') at this point minimizes

$$L = \tfrac{1}{2}V + \lambda' AX$$

among

$$X \in S = \{X : X \geqslant 0\}$$

and happens to have

$$AX = b$$

we have arrived at a point which minimizes V subject to $AX = b$, $X \geqslant 0$. But X_0 does more than this. It is possible to have an X which minimizes V subject to $AX = b$ and $X \geqslant 0$, but which is not EV efficient (as discussed in chapter 10). According to theorem 7.4, X_0 is efficient. Theorem 7.11 assures us that $\lambda_E = 0$ will be reached in a finite number of steps.

Rather than consider the adjacent critical line to the left of l^0 in figure 7.2, we could consider the one to the right of l^0; that is, the one which is efficient for $\lambda_E > \lambda_{\text{hi}}^0$. When we let λ_E increase, cases (B1) and (B2) are essentially the same as that of (A1) and (A2) when λ_E decreased. In figure 7.2, X_4 goes to zero as λ_E increases to λ_{hi}^0. This case (B1), like (A1), has the following characteristics: if we move X_4 from *IN* to *OUT* the resulting $\bar{M}$ matrix is nonsingular; the new critical line, call it l^{-1}, intersects the old critical line l^0 at the point $\lambda_E = \lambda_{\text{hi}}^0 = \lambda_{\text{low}}^{-1}$; η_4 rises as λ_E increases from $\lambda_{\text{hi}}^0 = \lambda_{\text{low}}^{-1}$, and therefore conditions (i), (ii), (iii) of theorem 7.4 hold for l^{-1} as well as for l^0.

The case (B2) in which an η_i goes to zero as λ_E increases is also essentially the same as the corresponding case (A2): i moves from *OUT* to *IN*; the new $\bar{M}$ matrix is nonsingular; the new X_i increases as λ_E increases; and the new critical line intersects the old critical line at the value of λ_E where η_i became zero.

The above process can be repeated obtaining critical lines l^{-1}, l^{-2}, l^{-3}, ... until a critical line $\hat{l}$ with $\lambda_{\text{hi}} = \infty$ is reached. This case (B3) occurs when no $\beta_i < 0$ or $\delta_i < 0$ prevents λ_E from increasing indefinitely. The critical line continues to satisfy the Kuhn-Tucker conditions as $\lambda_E \to \infty$. Case (B3) has two subcases:

(B3a) X remains constant as λ_E increases. In this case theorem 7.11 assures us that an efficient point with maximum E has been reached. A portfolio with maximum E is not necessarily efficient, as illustrated in chapter 10. But the one reached in the manner described above is indeed efficient.

(B3b) X varies as λ_E increases. In this case theorem 7.11 implies that $E \to \infty$ as $\lambda_E \to \infty$.

Theorem 7.11 further assures us that we will reach case (B3) in a finite number of steps, whether our problem has bounded E as in (B3a) or has unbounded E as in (B3b). Finally theorem 7.11 assures us that the efficient segments of the sequence of critical lines $l^*, \ldots, l^2, l^1, l^0, l^{-1}, l^{-2}, \ldots, \hat{l}$ provide a complete nonredundant set of efficient portfolios.

Thus, starting from any critical line l^0 satisfying conditions (i), (ii), (iii) of theorem 7.4, and thus far ruling out ties among the $-\alpha_i/\beta_i$ or $-\gamma_i/\delta_i$ in determining λ_{low} and λ_{hi} (except possibly when $\lambda_E = 0$ is reached), we see (or, more precisely, will have seen when the following theorems are proven) that a piecewise linear set of portfolios can be traced out in a finite number of steps, this set containing one portfolio for each efficient EV combination.

An alternate way of describing this set of efficient portfolios is as follows. Figures 7.1 and 7.2 present two-dimensional representations of lines in $2n + m + 1$ dimensional $(X', \lambda', \lambda_E, \eta')$ space. Since I cannot draw in (e.g.) sixteen-dimensional space (when $n = 6$ and $m = 3$) imagine, as best you can, critical lines drawn in this space: one such critical line for every IN set whose $\bar{M}$ is nonsingular. These critical lines intersect at many points; for example, the critical line for $IN = \{1, 3, 4\}$ will typically intersect those for $\{1, 2, 3, 4\}$, $\{1, 3, 4, 5\}$, $\{1, 3, 4, 6\}$, $\{1, 3\}$, $\{1, 4\}$, and $\{3, 4\}$. Imagine these many critical lines and their many intersections drawn in black in $(X', \lambda', \lambda_E, \eta')$ space.

We will now imagine coloring in red a complete nonredundant set of efficient portfolios. To do so we must be given an l^0 meeting conditions (i), (ii), and (iii) of theorem 7.4. (More about the finding of this l^0 in a moment.) Let $(X_s', \lambda_s', \lambda_E^s, \eta_s')$ be a point on this line with $\lambda_{\text{low}} < \lambda_E^s < \lambda_{\text{hi}}$. X_s is an efficient portfolio. Place the point of a red crayon at $(X_s', \lambda_s', \lambda_E^s, \eta_s')$ and move it along the critical line l^0 in the direction of decreasing λ_E. (λ_E varies on every critical line: on some unusual critical lines X and therefore V, E, and σ do not vary; but λ_E always varies.) As you move the red crayon along l^0 in the direction of decreasing λ_E, when you reach the *first* intersection between l^0 and another critical line – stop! Now move the crayon along the new critical line l^1 in the direction of decreasing λ_E until (again) the *first* intersection between l^1 and another critical line is encountered; then move along the new critical line l^2. In the nondegenerate case there will be no doubt as to which critical line to move on next, for there are no ties for "first intersection." Repeat this process, transferring from one critical line to the next at the first opportunity, until $\lambda_E = 0$ is reached. At this point stop (and do not continue in the direction of decreasing λ_E), for the efficient portfolio with minimum feasible V has been reached.

The job is only "half" done. Return to the starting point $(X_s', \lambda_s', \lambda_E^s, \eta_s')$ and repeat the process in the direction of increasing λ_E. As λ_E increases along l^0, stop at the *first* intersection of l^0 and another critical line l^{-1}. Move the red crayon along the new critical line in the direction of increasing λ_E until the first intersection with another critical line is reached, and so on, until a critical line is reached which intersects no other as λ_E increases (i.e. a critical line is reached with $\lambda_{hi} = \infty$). Finally imagine the entire unbounded segment of this line, for all $\lambda_E \geqslant \lambda_{low}$, marked in red.

The X of the entire piecewise linear path marked in red from $\lambda_E = 0$ to (so to speak) $\lambda_E = \infty$ provide a complete nonredundant set of portfolios. The point at $\lambda_E = 0$, and the points at which one critical line intersects another along the red (efficient) path, are called *corner portfolios*. Any segment of the efficient path could have served as l^0, including the segment with $\lambda_{low} = 0$ or the segment with $\lambda_{hi} = \infty$. It is possible for the entire path to be just one segment (with $\lambda_{low} = 0$ and $\lambda_{hi} = \infty$).

In chapter 8 we will see how to find an l^0 meeting conditions (i), (ii), (iii) of theorem 7.4 when E is bounded. In chapter 9 we will find such an l^0 when E is unbounded (as well as consider degenerate cases, with ties among the α_i/β_i and/or γ_i/δ_i). In both cases (E bounded and unbounded) l^0 is the critical line with $\lambda_{hi} = \infty$ in the approach presented here.[4] With this as a first critical line, a piecewise linear complete nonredundant set of efficient portfolios can be traced out by always moving in the direction of decreasing λ_E. An i is dropped from the IN set on each step where an $X_i \downarrow 0$, and added to the IN set when $\eta_i \downarrow 0$. The actual computation, called the ***critical line algorithm***, makes use of the fact that the $\bar{M}^{-1}$ of the adjacent critical line can be calculated without inverting the new $\bar{M}$ from scratch. Using $\bar{M}^{-1}$, the α, β, γ, δ of the critical line can be computed as in (7.8) and (7.10). From these λ_{low}, λ_{hi}, and the parameters of a quadratic relating V and E (discussed below) can be computed. A critical line code is presented in chapter 13.

The Nonsingularity of $\bar{M}$

The following theorem shows that $\bar{M}$ remains nonsingular if ω is moved from IN to OUT provided only that $\beta_\omega \neq 0$. This covers both the case in which $X_\omega \downarrow 0$ as $\lambda_E \downarrow \lambda_{low}$, which requires $\beta_\omega > 0$, and $X_\omega \downarrow 0$ as $\lambda_E \uparrow \lambda_{hi}$, which requires $\beta_\omega < 0$.

Theorem 7.5 Let $\bar{M}_a$ be as in (7.7a) for a particular $IN = IN_a$ set. For ω in IN_a let $\bar{M}_b$ be the $\bar{M}$ of the IN_b set obtained by deleting ω from IN_a. If $\bar{M}_a$ is nonsingular and $\beta_\omega \neq 0$ on the critical line l_a for IN_a, then $\bar{M}_b$ is nonsingular.

Note: the theorem does not require l_a to be one of the l^i in the sequence $\ldots, l^{-2}, l^{-1}, l^0, l^1, l^2, \ldots$. However, our application of the theorem will always be to such an l^i.

[4] The algorithm in Markowitz (1956) used for l^0 the critical line with $\lambda_{low} = 0$ in case E was unbounded above; but the algorithm essentially assumed a nonsingular C.

Proof Without loss of generality we may assume that $\omega = n$. In this case we may write

$$\bar{M}_a = \begin{pmatrix} \tilde{C} & c & \tilde{A}' \\ c' & \sigma & a' \\ \tilde{A} & a & 0 \end{pmatrix}$$

$$\bar{M}_b = \begin{pmatrix} \tilde{C} & 0 & \tilde{A}' \\ 0 & 1 & 0 \\ \tilde{A} & 0 & 0 \end{pmatrix}$$

where $\tilde{C}$ consists of the first $n-1$ rows and columns of $\bar{C}_a$; (c', σ) is the nth row of $\bar{C}_a$; $\tilde{A}$ is the first $n-1$ columns of $\bar{A}$; and a is the nth column of matrix $\bar{A}$. We will suppose, contrary to the theorem, that $\bar{M}_a$ is nonsingular and $\beta_n \neq 0$ on the critical line l_a, but nevertheless $\bar{M}_b$ is singular. We will derive a contradiction from these assumptions.

Since $\beta_n \neq 0$ along l_a, there is one and only one value of λ_E, say $\lambda_E = \lambda^*$, at which

$$X_n = \alpha_n + \beta_n \lambda_E = 0$$

This, plus the fact that (X', λ') is uniquely determined by λ_E among points that satisfy

$$\bar{M}_a \begin{pmatrix} X \\ \lambda \end{pmatrix} = \begin{pmatrix} 0 \\ b \end{pmatrix} + \begin{pmatrix} \bar{\mu} \\ 0 \end{pmatrix} \lambda_E$$

implies that there is one and only one value of $(X', \lambda', -\lambda_E) = (\tilde{X}', X_n, \lambda', -\lambda_E)$ which satisfies

$$\begin{pmatrix} \tilde{C} & c & \tilde{A}' & \tilde{\mu} \\ c' & \sigma & a' & \mu_n \\ \tilde{A} & a & 0 & 0 \\ 0 & 1 & 0 & 0 \end{pmatrix} \begin{pmatrix} \tilde{X} \\ X_n \\ \lambda \\ -\lambda_E \end{pmatrix} = \begin{pmatrix} 0 \\ 0 \\ b \\ 0 \end{pmatrix} \tag{7.12}$$

Thus the matrix in (7.12) is nonsingular, else (7.12) would have zero or many solutions.

If $\bar{M}_b$ is singular then there is $(Y', y', \delta') \neq 0$ such that

$$\begin{pmatrix} \tilde{C} & 0 & \tilde{A}' \\ 0 & 1 & 0 \\ \tilde{A} & 0 & 0 \end{pmatrix} \begin{pmatrix} Y \\ y \\ \delta \end{pmatrix} = \begin{pmatrix} 0 \\ 0 \\ 0 \end{pmatrix} \tag{7.13a}$$

The nth equation of (7.13a) requires $y = 0$, and thus implies

$$\begin{pmatrix} \tilde{C} & \tilde{A}' \\ \tilde{A} & 0 \end{pmatrix} \begin{pmatrix} Y \\ \delta \end{pmatrix} = \begin{pmatrix} 0 \\ 0 \end{pmatrix} \tag{7.13b}$$

From the definition of $\bar{M}$, for i in OUT_a the ith equation of (7.13a) reads

$$Y_i = 0 \qquad i \text{ in } OUT_a \tag{7.13c}$$

From (7.13b)

$$\tilde{A}Y = 0$$

$$\tilde{C}Y = -\tilde{A}'\delta$$

Hence

$$\begin{aligned} V(Y) &= Y'\tilde{C}Y \\ &= -Y'\tilde{A}'\delta \\ &= 0 \end{aligned}$$

Thus either $Z = (Y', 0) = 0$ or else $Z = (Y', 0)$ is a zero-variance direction (where Z has n components as compared with Y which has $n-1$ components). In the former case obviously $\mu'Z = 0$; in the latter case we can show that $\mu'Z = 0$ as follows. Recall that the X of each (X', λ') vector on l_a is the solution to the affine portfolio selection model associated with IN_a, and therefore minimizes

$$L = \tfrac{1}{2}V + \Sigma\lambda_k(\Sigma a_{kj}X_j) - \lambda_E\mu'X$$

for the particular λ and λ_E taken as constants (requiring $X_i = 0$ for i in OUT_a but not requiring $X \geqslant 0$). But if $\mu'Z \neq 0$, set $W = Z$ if $\mu'Z > 0$ or $W = -Z$ if $\mu'Z < 0$. If (X_0', λ') is a point on l_a then $X_0 + W$ has the same V, the same $\Sigma a_{kj}X_j$ for each k (this follows from $\tilde{A}Y = 0$), has $X_i^0 + W_i = 0$ for i in OUT_a (see (7.13c)) and has greater $\mu'X$ than X_0, contradicting the assumption that X_0 minimizes L for the given λ and λ_E.

Combining the information concerning Y and δ we have

$$\begin{pmatrix} \tilde{C} & c & \tilde{A}' & 0 \\ c' & \sigma & a' & 1 \\ \tilde{A} & a & 0 & 0 \\ \tilde{\mu}' & \mu_n & 0 & 0 \end{pmatrix} \begin{pmatrix} Y \\ 0 \\ \delta \\ -c'Y - a'\delta \end{pmatrix} = \begin{pmatrix} 0 \\ 0 \\ 0 \\ 0 \end{pmatrix} \tag{7.14}$$

Since $(Y', \delta') \neq 0$, the matrix in (7.14) must be singular; but this contradicts the prior conclusion that its transpose, the matrix in (7.12), is nonsingular. ###

The next theorem shows that $\bar{M}$ remains nonsingular as ω is moved from OUT to IN, provided only that $\delta_\omega \neq 0$. This covers both the case in which $\eta_\omega \downarrow 0$ as

$\lambda_E \downarrow \lambda_{\text{low}}$, which implies $\delta_\omega > 0$, and the case in which $\eta_\omega \downarrow 0$ as $\lambda_E \uparrow \lambda_{\text{hi}}$, which implies $\delta_\omega < 0$.

Theorem 7.6 Let $\bar{M}_a$ be as in (7.7a) for a particular $IN = IN_a$ set. For ω in OUT_a let $\bar{M}_b$ be the $\bar{M}$ of the IN_b set obtained by adding ω to IN_a. If $\bar{M}_a$ is nonsingular and $\delta_\omega \neq 0$ on the corresponding critical line l_a then $\bar{M}_b$ is nonsingular.

Proof Without loss of generality assume $\omega = n$. In this case

$$\bar{M}_a = \begin{pmatrix} \tilde{C} & 0 & \tilde{A}' \\ 0 & 1 & 0 \\ \tilde{A} & 0 & 0 \end{pmatrix}$$

$$\bar{M}_b = \begin{pmatrix} \tilde{C} & c & \tilde{A}' \\ c' & \sigma & a' \\ \tilde{A} & a & 0 \end{pmatrix}$$

where $\tilde{C}$, $\tilde{A}$, a, c, and σ are defined as in the proof of theorem 7.5.

By a slight variation in the argument used to show that the matrix in (7.12) is nonsingular, the fact that $\bar{M}_a$ is nonsingular and that $\delta_\omega = \delta_n \neq 0$ implies that

$$\begin{pmatrix} \tilde{C} & 0 & \tilde{A}' & \tilde{\mu} \\ 0 & 1 & 0 & 0 \\ c' & \sigma & a' & \mu_n \\ \tilde{A} & 0 & 0 & 0 \end{pmatrix} \tag{7.15}$$

is nonsingular. We shall assume that $\bar{M}_b$ is singular and derive a contradiction. If $\bar{M}_b$ were singular then there would be $(Y', y, \delta') \neq 0$ such that

$$\begin{pmatrix} \tilde{C} & c & \tilde{A}' \\ c' & \sigma & a' \\ \tilde{A} & a & 0 \end{pmatrix} \begin{pmatrix} Y \\ y \\ \delta \end{pmatrix} = \begin{pmatrix} 0 \\ 0 \\ 0 \end{pmatrix} \tag{7.16}$$

In particular

$$(\tilde{A}, \ a) \begin{pmatrix} Y \\ y \end{pmatrix} = 0 \tag{7.17a}$$

and

$$\begin{pmatrix} \tilde{C} & c \\ c' & \sigma \end{pmatrix} \begin{pmatrix} Y \\ y \end{pmatrix} = -\begin{pmatrix} \tilde{A}' \\ a' \end{pmatrix} \delta \tag{7.17b}$$

As with (7.13c) of the preceding proof,

$$Y_i = 0 \qquad \text{for } i \text{ in } OUT_a - \{\omega\} \tag{7.18}$$

Equations (7.17) imply that (Y', y) is a zero-variance direction, and that if

$$(\tilde{A}, a)\begin{pmatrix} X \\ x \end{pmatrix} = b$$

then

$$(\tilde{A}, a)\begin{pmatrix} X + Y \\ x + y \end{pmatrix} = b$$

Now, every point on the critical line l_a, associated with the matrix $\bar{M}_a$, minimizes

$$L = \tfrac{1}{2}V + \lambda' AX - \lambda_E \mu' X$$

among X with $X_i = 0$ for i in OUT_a, treating λ and λ_E as if they were constants, and ignoring $X \geqslant 0$. At the particular point $(X', \lambda', \lambda_E)$ on l_a at which $\eta_\omega = 0$, X minimizes L among X with $X_i = 0$ for i in $OUT - \{\omega\}$. But this could not be true unless

$$(\tilde{\mu}', \mu_n)\begin{pmatrix} Y \\ y \end{pmatrix} = 0$$

else

$$\begin{pmatrix} X + Y \\ x + y \end{pmatrix} \quad \text{or} \quad \begin{pmatrix} X - Y \\ x - y \end{pmatrix}$$

would have the same V and the same

$$A\begin{pmatrix} X \pm Y \\ x \pm y \end{pmatrix}$$

would satisfy $X_i + Y_i = 0$ for i in $OUT_a - \{\omega\}$, but would have greater E.

Combining our information about (Y, y) we conclude that

$$\begin{pmatrix} \tilde{C} & 0 & c & \tilde{A}' \\ 0 & 1 & \sigma & 0 \\ \tilde{A} & 0 & a & 0 \\ \tilde{\mu}' & 0 & \mu_n & 0 \end{pmatrix} \begin{pmatrix} Y \\ -\sigma y \\ y \\ \delta \end{pmatrix} = \begin{pmatrix} 0 \\ 0 \\ 0 \\ 0 \end{pmatrix}$$

Hence the above matrix is singular. But it is the transpose of (7.15) which is nonsingular. Contradiction. ###

Corollary 7.7 Let l_a and l_b be "adjacent" critical lines as described in theorem 7.5 and its note. Then the lines l_a and l_b intersect at the value of λ_E which makes $X_\omega = 0$ on l_a. This is the only value of λ_E at which $\eta_\omega = 0$ on l_b. Similarly, let l_a and l_b be the adjacent critical lines whose existence is implied by theorem 7.6. Then the lines intersect at the value of λ_E which makes $\eta_\omega = 0$ on l_a. This is the only value of λ_E at which $X_\omega = 0$ on l_b.

Proof We will treat the case of l_a and l_b as defined in theorem 7.5. The case of l_a and l_b in theorem 7.6 is essentially the same. Since only one point on l_a has $X_\omega = 0$, only one point satisfies

$$\begin{pmatrix} \tilde{C} & 0 & \tilde{A}' & \tilde{\mu} \\ c' & \sigma & a' & \mu_\omega \\ \tilde{A} & 0 & 0 & 0 \\ 0 & 1 & 0 & 0 \end{pmatrix} \begin{pmatrix} \tilde{X} \\ x \\ \lambda \\ -\lambda_E \end{pmatrix} = \begin{pmatrix} 0 \\ 0 \\ b \\ 0 \end{pmatrix}$$

If a point on l_b has $\eta_\omega = 0$ it satisfies

$$\begin{pmatrix} \tilde{C} & 0 & \tilde{A}' & \tilde{\mu} \\ 0 & 1 & 0 & 0 \\ \tilde{A} & 0 & 0 & 0 \\ c' & \sigma & a' & \mu_\omega \end{pmatrix} \begin{pmatrix} \tilde{X} \\ x \\ \lambda \\ -\lambda_E \end{pmatrix} = \begin{pmatrix} 0 \\ 0 \\ b \\ 0 \end{pmatrix}$$

But this is the same system of equations, slightly rearranged. So the unique $(\tilde{X}', x, \lambda', -\lambda_E)$ which solves one also solves the other uniquely, including the (common) value of λ_E at that point on both l_a and l_b. ###

Nonnegativity of X and η

We first prove a lemma needed later in this section, and then prove a theorem on the nonnegativity of X and η.

Lemma 7.8 For any critical line satisfying conditions (i), (ii), and (iii) of theorem 7.4 (and with $\bar{M}$ nonsingular, by definition of critical line) for $\lambda_{\text{low}} \leqslant \lambda_E \leqslant \lambda_{\text{hi}}$,

$$\begin{pmatrix} X \\ \lambda \end{pmatrix} = \bar{M}^{-1} \begin{pmatrix} 0 \\ b \end{pmatrix} + \bar{M}^{-1} \begin{pmatrix} \bar{\mu} \\ 0 \end{pmatrix} \lambda_E$$

provides a ***unique*** minimum to

$$\tfrac{1}{2} V - \lambda_E \mu' X \tag{7.19a}$$

subject to

$$AX = b \tag{7.19b}$$

$$X \geqslant 0 \tag{7.19c}$$

$$X_i = 0 \qquad i \in OUT. \tag{7.19d}$$

Proof Suppose Y also minimized (7.19a) subject to (7.19b–d). Then $A(Y-X)=0$ (obtained by subtracting $AX = b$ from $AY = b$), and $Y-X$ must be a zero-variance direction with $\mu'(Y-X)=0$; else $(1/2)X+(1/2)Y$ would provide a smaller value of (7.19a) with (7.19b–d) satisfied (since E is linear and V is either constant or strictly convex along any straight line; see theorem 5.2 and summary 5.10). Then (since $Z'CZ = 0$ implies $CZ = 0$; see exercise 5.1) we have

$$\begin{pmatrix} \bar{C} & \bar{A}' \\ \bar{A} & 0 \end{pmatrix} \begin{pmatrix} Y-X \\ 0 \end{pmatrix} = 0$$

contradicting the hypothesis that $\bar{M}$ is nonsingular. ###

Theorem 7.9 In a nondegenerate portfolio selection model, let l^0 be a critical line satisfying conditions (i), (ii), (iii) of theorem 7.4.

(A1) If $\lambda^0_{\text{low}} \neq 0$ and $X_\omega \downarrow 0$ as $\lambda_E \downarrow \lambda^0_{\text{low}}$ on l^0, then η_ω increases (from zero at $\lambda_E = \lambda^0_{\text{low}}$) as λ_E decreases on l^1.

(A2) If $\lambda^0_{\text{low}} \neq 0$ and $\eta_\omega \downarrow 0$ as $\lambda_E \downarrow \lambda^0_\omega$ on l^0, then X_ω increases (from zero at $\lambda_E = \lambda^0_{\text{low}}$) as λ_E decreases on l^1.

(B1) If $X_\omega \downarrow 0$ as $\lambda_E \uparrow \lambda^0_{\text{hi}}$ then η_ω increases (from zero at $\lambda_E = \lambda^0_{\text{hi}}$) as λ_E increases on l^{-1}.

(B2) If $\eta_\omega \downarrow 0$ as $\lambda_E \uparrow \lambda^0_{\text{hi}}$ on l^0, then X_ω increases (from zero at $\lambda_E = \lambda^0_{\text{hi}}$) as λ_E increases on l^{-1}.

In cases (A1) and (A2), l^1 satisfies conditions (i), (ii), (iii) of theorem 7.4. In cases (B1) and (B2), l^{-1} satisfies these conditions.

Proof We will consider the case (A1) in detail. The proofs for (A2), (B1) and (B2) are almost identical, changing "hi" for "low" or X for η as appropriate. Theorem 7.5 and corollary 7.7 assure us that the new $\bar{M}$ matrix is nonsingular – so there is indeed a line l^1 – that l^0 and l^1 intersect at a point, and that this is the only point on l^1 at which $\eta_\omega = 0$. This leaves two cases: either η_ω increases or it decreases on l^1 as λ_E decreases.

At the intersection of l^0 and l^1 we have $\lambda_E = \lambda^{\upsilon}_{\text{low}}$. Suppose, contrary to the theorem, that on l^1 we have $\eta_\omega < 0$ for $\lambda_E < \lambda^0_{\text{low}}$; therefore $\eta_\omega > 0$ for $\lambda_E > \lambda^0_{\text{low}}$. It follows from this and the nondegeneracy assumption that for some range of λ_E:

$$\lambda^0_{\text{low}} + \epsilon \geqslant \lambda_E \geqslant \lambda^0_{\text{low}}$$

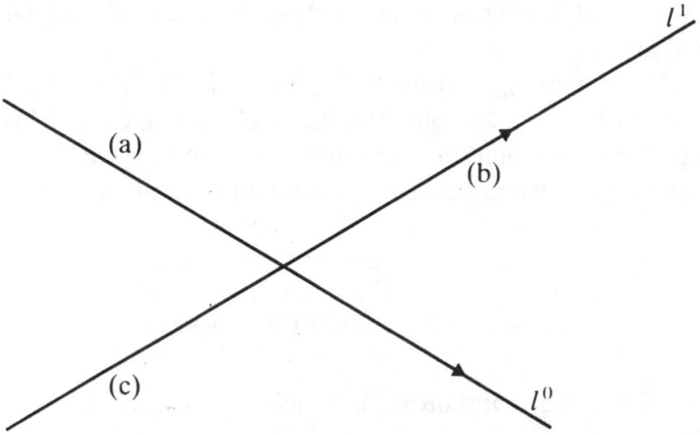

Figure 7.3 Diagram for discussion of theorem 7.9

for some $\epsilon > 0$, we have $X \geqslant 0$ and $\eta \geqslant 0$ on l^1. This in turn implies that points on l^1 with λ_E in this range minimize (7.19a) subject to (7.19b), (7.19c), and

$$X_i = 0 \text{ for } i \in OUT_0 \tag{7.19d'}$$

since (7.19d′) does not require, but does permit, $X_\omega = 0$. But points on l^0 also minimize (7.19a) subject to (7.19b), (7.19c), and (7.19d′) for the same λ_E, with $X_\omega > 0$, contradicting the uniqueness of this minimum shown in lemma 7.8.

###

The lines l^0 and l^1 of theorem 7.9 are represented in figure 7.3. Even though they are each lines in the $m+n+1$ dimensional $(X', \lambda', \lambda_E)$-space, since they intersect they are contained in a two-dimensional plane of this space. Choose a new orthogonal coordinate system so that the plane of the page is the plane determined by the two lines. The arrows on each of the lines in figure 7.3 are the directions of decreasing λ_E: the further you move on l^0 (or l^1) in the direction of the arrows the lower is λ_E.

Let IN^0 and IN^1 be the IN set associated with l^0 and l^1. In case (A1), since IN^1 is contained in IN^0 - the former is the latter with ω deleted - and OUT^0 is contained in OUT^1 we have

$$X_i = 0 \qquad \text{for } i \in OUT^0$$

$$\eta_i = 0 \qquad \text{for } i \in IN^1$$

on both l^0 and l^1. Everywhere on l^0 we have $\eta_\omega = 0$; everywhere on l^1 we have $X_\omega = 0$. Where the two lines intersect we have $X_\omega = 0$ and $\eta_\omega = 0$ on both lines. Let $\lambda_E = \lambda^*$ be the value of λ_E on both lines at their intersection. At (a) in the figure, on line l^0 on the side with $\lambda_E > \lambda_E^*$, we are given that $X_\omega > 0$. The theorem shows that at (b) in the figure, on l^1 on the side of the intersection with $\lambda_E < \lambda_E^*$, we have $\eta_\omega > 0$.

In case (A2) we have $\eta_\omega > 0$ on l^0 for $\lambda_E > \lambda_E^*$, at (a) in the figure. The theorem assures us that $X_\omega > 0$ on l^1 for $\lambda_E < \lambda_E^*$, at (b). Case (B1) is the same as (A2) except with l^1 encountered first and l^0 second as λ_E increases. Similarly (B2) is the same as (A1) when the efficient set is traced out from low to high λ_E.

Finiteness of the Critical Line Algorithm

Lemma 7.10 If X is not constant on a critical line, then E is not constant on the critical line.

Proof Suppose that the first n of the $n + m$ β_i in (7.10) are not all zero; i.e. there is an i such that $\beta_i \neq 0$ for $1 \leqslant i \leqslant n$. Suppose nevertheless that E is constant on the critical line. V must also be constant, since each point on the critical line minimizes $(1/2)V - \lambda_E E$ subject to $AX = b, X_i = 0$ for i *OUT*. Thus $\beta = (\beta_1, \ldots, \beta_n)$ is a zero-variance direction and satisfies $A\beta = 0$ (since $A(\alpha + \beta t) = A\alpha + (A\beta)t = b + 0t$ for all t). It follows that

$$\begin{pmatrix} \bar{C} & \bar{A}' \\ \bar{A} & 0 \end{pmatrix} \begin{pmatrix} \beta \\ 0 \end{pmatrix} = 0$$

for $\beta \neq 0$. This implies that $\bar{M}$ is singular, contrary to the definition of a critical line. ###

Lemma 7.10 still leaves the possibility that X may be constant on a critical line – that only λ and η vary. Examples which show that this can happen, in fact, are presented in chapters 8 and 11.

Theorem 7.11 In a feasible nondegenerate portfolio selection model the sequence of critical lines $l^0, l^1, l^2, \ldots$ will reach, in a finite number of steps, a critical line l^* on which $\lambda_{low}^* = 0$. The point X^* on l^* with $\lambda_E^* = 0$ is an efficient portfolio with minimum V. The sequence of critical lines $l^0, l^{-1}, l^{-2}, \ldots$ will reach, in a finite number of steps, a critical line $\hat{l}$ on which $\hat{\lambda}_{hi} = \infty$. If feasible E is bounded from above, X does not vary on $\hat{l}$. This X, call it $\hat{X}$, is an efficient portfolio with maximum feasible E. If feasible E is unbounded above then $\hat{l}$ provides efficient portfolios for all $E \geqslant \hat{E}_{low}$, where $\hat{E}_{low}$ is the E of the portfolio at $\lambda_E = \hat{\lambda}_{low}$.

The efficient segments from the critical lines $\hat{l}, \ldots, l^{-1}, l^0, l^1, \ldots, l^*$ constitute a complete nonredundant, piecewise linear set of efficient portfolios. (The notation here is not meant to preclude the possibility that $\hat{l} = l^0$, or $l^* = l^0$, or both.)

Proof Since $\lambda_{hi}^{k+1} = \lambda_{low}^k < \lambda_{hi}^k$ in a feasible nondegenerate model, λ_{low} decreases as we move from critical line l^0 to l^1 to l^2 etc. Similarly λ_{hi} increases as we move to l^0 to l^{-1} etc. Therefore any particular subset of 1, 2, ..., n can appear at most once as the *IN* set for any ... $l^{-2}, l^{-1}, l^0, l^1, l^2, \ldots$. This, plus the facts that: (a) there are only a finite number of subsets of 1, 2, ..., n; (b) each successive critical line intersects its neighbor at $\lambda_E = \lambda_{low}^k = \lambda_{hi}^{k+1}$; and (c) each critical line is defined for $-\infty < \lambda_E < \infty$; implies that l^* and $\hat{l}$ are reached in a finite number of steps.

Theorem 7.4 implies that the point on l^* with $\lambda_E^* = 0$ is an efficient portfolio with minimum obtainable variance, say $V = V^*$ and $E = E^*$. Since $\hat{l}, \ldots, l^0, \ldots, l^*$ provides a piecewise linear (therefore continuous) curve in X space, its EV values provide a continuous curve of efficient combinations in EV spaces. To show that the piecewise linear set in X space is a complete set of efficient portfolios, we must show that the range of E covered, when E has an upper bound, is

$$E^* \leqslant E \leqslant \hat{E}$$

where $\hat{E}$ is maximum obtainable E, and is

$$E^* \leqslant E < \infty$$

when E has no upper bound.

If feasible E is bounded above then, in particular, it must be constant on $\hat{l}$ as $\lambda_E \to \infty$. Lemma 7.10 therefore implies that X is constant on $\hat{l}$. Denote this constant value as $\hat{X}$. We will show that $\hat{E} = \mu'\hat{X}$ must be maximum feasible E. Otherwise, there would be a feasible portfolio with $\tilde{E} > \hat{E}$. Then for sufficiently large λ_E we would have

$$\tfrac{1}{2}\tilde{V} - \lambda_E \tilde{E} < \tfrac{1}{2}\hat{V} - \lambda_E \hat{E}$$

contradicting the fact that $\hat{X}$ satisfies the Kuhn-Tucker conditions assuring that it minimizes $(1/2)V - \lambda_E E$ among feasible portfolios, for all $\lambda_E \geqslant \hat{\lambda}_{low}$.

We next show that, if E is unbounded above, $\hat{l}$ has varying rather than fixed X and E. Since V is then a convex parabola, $E \to \infty$ as $\lambda_E \to \infty$ on $\hat{l}$. Suppose to the contrary that X did not vary on $\hat{l}$. Then this $\hat{X}$ with $(E, V) = (\hat{E}, \hat{V})$ must minimize $L = (1/2)V - \lambda_E E$ among feasible portfolios with $\lambda_E \geqslant \hat{\lambda}_{low}$. Since feasible E is unbounded, there is a feasible $(\tilde{E}, \tilde{V})$ combination with $\tilde{E} > \hat{E}$. But for sufficiently large λ_E we have $(1/2)\tilde{V}_E - \lambda_E \tilde{E} < (1/2)\hat{V}_E - \lambda_E \hat{E}$. Contradiction.

The fact that the set of portfolios provided by $\hat{l}, \ldots, l^*$ is nonredundant is an immediate consequence of lemma 7.10 - that E changes when X changes - and of the fact that E is a strictly increasing function of $\lambda_E = (1/2)\,dV/dE$ on any l^i on which E changes. The latter follows from the fact, shown in chapter 5, that V as a function of E on a straight line (on which E varies) is either horizontal or a strictly convex parabola. It cannot be horizontal on an l^i ###

The Efficient EV Set

From the existence of a piecewise linear, complete nonredundant set of efficient portfolios, the shapes of the EV and $E\sigma$ efficient sets follow easily. As we saw in chapter 5, and used in the preceding proof, if E is not constant along a straight line in portfolio space, the relationship between V and E for portfolios on the straight line must be a horizontal line or a convex parabola. The former is not possible on an efficient segment; therefore the set of efficient EV combinations is piecewise parabolic. This still leaves open the question of how the various parabolic pieces relate to and connect with each other. The shape of the efficient $E\sigma$ set is left as an exercise (see exercise 7.1).

Theorem 7.12 Let $V = \phi(E)$ be the value of V as a function of E along the set of efficient EV combinations for a feasible nondegenerate portfolio selection model. Let E^* be the value of E for the efficient EV combination which minimizes V. Let $\hat{E}$ be the largest obtainable value of E, or $\hat{E} = \infty$ if E is unbounded. ϕ is a continuous, strictly increasing, strictly convex function with a continuous derivative except possibly at a finite number of points $E_1, E_2, \ldots, E_k$. The latter are the values of E for each critical line (of the complete nonredundant, piecewise linear portfolio set) on which $\beta_i = 0$ for $1 \leqslant i \leqslant n$. At any such point the derivatives from the left $(\mathrm{d}V/\mathrm{d}E)_\mathrm{L}$ and from the right $(\mathrm{d}V/\mathrm{d}E)_\mathrm{R}$ exist, and

$$\left(\frac{\mathrm{d}V}{\mathrm{d}E}\right)_\mathrm{L} < \left(\frac{\mathrm{d}V}{\mathrm{d}E}\right)_\mathrm{R}$$

Proof Along any critical line on which E varies, $\mathrm{d}V/\mathrm{d}E = 2\lambda_E$. Since ϕ is a convex parabola along any critical line on which E varies, the assertions of the theorem are true for the efficient segment excluding the end points, i.e. for $\lambda_{\mathrm{low}} < \lambda_E < \lambda_{\mathrm{hi}}$, for any critical line on which E varies.

Since $\lambda_E = \lambda^0_{\mathrm{low}} = \lambda^1_{\mathrm{hi}}$ where two such critical lines intersect, then $(\mathrm{d}V/\mathrm{d}E)_\mathrm{R} = (\mathrm{d}V/\mathrm{d}E)_\mathrm{L} = \mathrm{d}V/\mathrm{d}E = 2\lambda_E$ at this point. Also, $\mathrm{d}V/\mathrm{d}E$ is continuous at this point since $\mathrm{d}V/\mathrm{d}E \to 2\lambda^0_{\mathrm{low}} = 2\lambda^1_{\mathrm{hi}}$ both on the parabola to the left and on that to the right.

Now, consider the case in which a critical line l^0 (on which E varies) is adjacent to a line l^1 on which E does not vary, which in turn is adjacent to a line l^2 on which E varies again. (Given our current nondegeneracy assumptions, it cannot happen that two adjacent critical lines are such that E varies on neither; show as an exercise.) Suppose l^0, l^1, l^2 satisfy the Kuhn-Tucker conditions for efficiency for, respectively,

$$\lambda_{\text{low}}^{0} \leqslant \lambda_E \leqslant \lambda_{\text{hi}}^{0}$$
$$\lambda_{\text{low}}^{1} \leqslant \lambda_E \leqslant \lambda_{\text{hi}}^{1} = \lambda_{\text{low}}^{0}$$
$$\lambda_{\text{low}}^{2} \leqslant \lambda_E \leqslant \lambda_{\text{hi}}^{2} = \lambda_{\text{low}}^{1}$$

where

$$\lambda_{\text{low}}^{2} < \lambda_{\text{low}}^{1} < \lambda_{\text{low}}^{0} < \lambda_{\text{hi}}^{0}$$

Let E^1 be the value of E everywhere on l^1. Then, at $E = E^1$,

$$\begin{aligned} \frac{1}{2}\left(\frac{\mathrm{d}\phi}{\mathrm{d}E}\right)_{\mathrm{L}} &= \lambda_{\text{hi}}^{2} = \lambda_{\text{low}}^{1} \\ &< \lambda_{\text{hi}}^{1} \\ &= \lambda_{\text{low}}^{0} = \frac{1}{2}\left(\frac{\mathrm{d}\phi}{\mathrm{d}E}\right)_{\mathrm{R}} \end{aligned}$$

The fact that $(\mathrm{d}\phi/\mathrm{d}E)_{\mathrm{L}} \leqslant (\mathrm{d}\phi/\mathrm{d}E)_{\mathrm{R}}$ everywhere, and each is strictly increasing in E, implies the strict convexity of ϕ. ###

At a point at which two critical lines l^0 and l^1 intersect, both lines having E varying, both the parabola for l^0 and that for l^1 have the same V and the same $\mathrm{d}V/\mathrm{d}E$ at the intersection. Whichever parabola has X_ω *IN* rather than *OUT* has the smaller $\mathrm{d}^2V/\mathrm{d}E^2$, since the other line minimizes V subject to an additional constraint $X_\omega = 0$, and therefore cannot have smaller V for given E. The two parabolas touch but do not cross, like P_a and P_b in figure 7.4. The set of efficient EV combinations moves along one parabola to the right of their common point and on the other to the left.

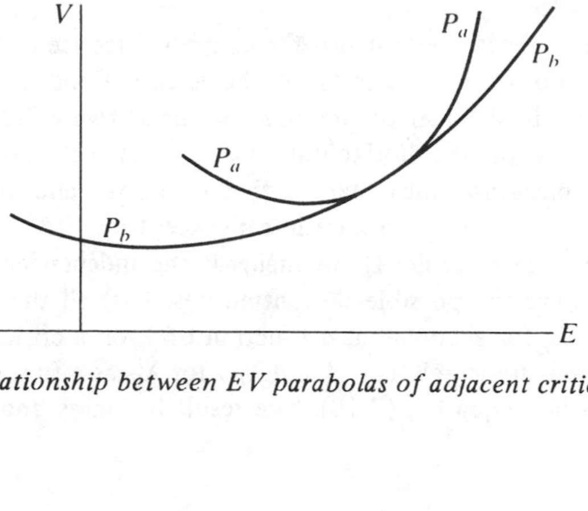

Figure 7.4 Relationship between EV parabolas of adjacent critical lines

Choice of Axes

At this point we will consider a matter deferred from chapter 1, namely why throughout this book E or λ_E are used as the independent variables and placed on the horizontal axis, whereas the current practice is to place V or σ on the horizontal.

Figure 7.2 illustrates that, for any feasible portfolio selection model, there is a complete nonredundant efficient set which is piecewise linear. It will take us two more chapters to find that this is true for arbitrary, possibly degenerate models, and to learn how to find l^0. But, in the end, we will see that figure 7.2 essentially tells the whole story. In some cases there may be only one piece, or only a single point, but these are special cases of "piecewise linear."

Figure 7.2 is incomplete in two ways. First, to show the whole efficient set the figure would have to be extended to the left and right to cover the range $0 \leqslant \lambda_E < \infty$. In principle this is possible to do, since there are only a finite number of pieces, including an unbounded linear piece on the right (only part of which would appear in an actual drawing).

A second way in which figure 7.2 is incomplete is that it omits some quantities of interest, namely E, V, σ, and $\lambda_1, \ldots, \lambda_m$. Except for the fact that the figure is already cluttered, we could add E, V, σ, and λ_k as functions of λ_E. It is an easy exercise to show that these are respectively piecewise linear, piecewise parabolic, piecewise hyperbolic and/or linear, and piecewise linear. The pieces for E, V, and σ will be horizontal on segments in which X is constant and only λ and η vary as λ_E varies.

A reasonable alternate way of drawing figure 7.2 is with E as the independent variable and with λ_E - as well as X, η, λ, V, and σ - as dependent variables. This would show V as a function of E as in figure 1.1 and, in addition, would show X, η, λ, σ, λ_E as functions of E. X would still be a piecewise linear function, but η, λ, and λ_E (as functions of E) would be discontinuous wherever X is constant as λ_E varies.

We noted in chapter 1 that it is the common practice to draw figure 1.1 with V or σ on the horizontal axis and E on the vertical. Consider what would happen if - to conform to the current practice - we drew figure 7.2 with V as the independent variable on the horizontal. With λ_E as the independent variable all relations are piecewise linear except that of $V(\lambda_E)$ and $\sigma(\lambda_E)$. With E as the independent variable all pieces are linear (except for $V(E)$ and $\sigma(E)$) albeit now discontinuities are possible. If we make V the independent variable then (not only do we have the possible discontinuities, but) all the pieces become nonlinear. X and λ, for example, as a function of V on a critical line are found by solving (the quadratic relating V and λ_E) for λ_E as a function of V, then substituting this into equation (7.10). The result is a mess, and no less a mess if we use σ as the independent variable, certainly as compared with using λ_E or E as the independent variable.

A different way of remaining consistent with current practice is to think of λ_E or E as the independent variable, but represent the independent variable on the vertical axis. The effect of this may be seen by turning figure 7.2 sideways. My preference is to leave the independent variable on the horizontal. A third way to conform to current practice is to draw E on the vertical when only V and E (or σ and E) appear, and to draw it (or λ_E) on the horizontal when other variables appear. I prefer the practice of consistently placing E (or λ_E, whichever is the "independent variable" or "parameter" of the equations portrayed) on the horizontal.

Exercises

7.1 Show that the relationship between E and σ is a continuous curve consisting of a series of pieces, each piece being a segment of a hyperbola or a segment of a straight line. When is it the former versus the latter? When does the relationship between E and σ contain a kink? (Hint: see theorem 7.12 and the section in chapter 5 on σ along a straight line.)

7.2 Consider a standard four-security model with

$$V = X_1^2 + X_2^2 + X_3^2 + X_4^2$$

$$E = X_1 + 2X_2 + 3X_3 + 4X_4$$

(a) Compute the set of efficient portfolios starting with $IN = \{4\}$. (Hint: see exercise 6.3 with regard to the finding of α and β. Confirm that the critical line for this IN set is the $\hat{l}$ of theorem 7.11.)

(b) Compute the set of efficient portfolios starting with $IN = \{1, 2, 3, 4,\}$. (Hint: confirm that the critical line for this IN set is l^* of theorem 7.11.)

7.3 The following method for computing critical lines for portfolio selection problems with upper bounds is based on those for linear programming developed by Dantzig (1963).

(a) Let

$$S = \{X\colon 0 \leqslant X_i \leqslant U_i\}$$
$$= \{X\colon 0 \leqslant X \leqslant U\}$$

where U is a vector of upper bounds. Let the constraint set for a portfolio selection problem require

$$X \in S \tag{7.20a}$$

and

$$AX = b \tag{7.20b}$$

As previously, define the Lagrangian equation as

$$L = \tfrac{1}{2}V + \lambda' AX - \lambda_E E \tag{7.21}$$

Show that a feasible portfolio X minimizes L among X in S if and only if

$$\eta_i \geqslant 0 \qquad \text{if } X_i = 0 \tag{7.22a}$$

$$\eta_i \leqslant 0 \qquad \text{if } X_i = U_i \tag{7.22b}$$

$$\eta_i = 0 \qquad \text{if } 0 < X_i < U_i \tag{7.22c}$$

(b) Divide $\{1, 2, \ldots, n\}$ into three sets *DOWN*, *IN*, and *UP*, with each i in one and only one of these sets. Define $\bar{M}$ by replacing the ith row and column by $(e^i)'$ and e^i for every i in either *DOWN* or *UP*. For every *DOWN-IN-UP* partition with nonsingular $\bar{M}$, define a critical line as a set which minimizes $(1/2)V - \lambda_E E$ for various λ_E in the affine model in which $X_i = 0$ for i in *DOWN*, $X_i = U_i$ for i in *UP*, and X is otherwise constrained only by $AX = b$. For what range of λ_E do the portfolios on a given critical line satisfy the Kuhn-Tucker conditions for efficiency?

(c) Starting with a given critical line l^0 containing an efficient segment, how do you find (i) adjacent segments $l^1, l^2, \ldots, l^*$, where l^* contains the efficient portfolio at $\lambda_E = 0$, and (ii) adjacent segments $l^{-1}, l^{-2}, \ldots, \hat{l}$, where $\hat{l}$ remains efficient as $\lambda_E \to \infty$?

(d) Suppose A is m by n, and every X_i has an upper bound. How many rows and columns are in the equivalent form 2 model? ($X_i \leqslant U_i$ is not allowed (as is) in a model of form 2.) Compare the sizes of the M, α, β, γ, δ of the equivalent form 2 model and the model as computed in (a)-(c).

7.4 For a nondegenerate model, consider a critical line which satisfies conditions (i), (ii), and (iii) of theorem 7.4, and has $\lambda_{low} > 0$. Suppose $\eta_i \downarrow 0$ as $\lambda_E \downarrow \lambda_{low}$. We know that the critical line no longer satisfies the Kuhn-Tucker conditions when $\lambda_E < \lambda_{low}$. But are the points on this critical line actually inefficient for $\lambda_E < \lambda_{low}$? (Hint: distinguish the cases (a) in which X does not change on the critical line, and (b) X does vary. In the latter case, use lemma 7.8.)

7.5 In the definition preceding theorem 7.3, a critical line was defined as a line in $(X', \lambda', \lambda_E)$ space. But (7.8) and (7.10a) are written as if the line were in (X', λ') space with λ_E as the parameter of the line.

(a) Construct an example in which the β of equation (7.10a) is zero on a critical line. (Hint: consider a standard portfolio analysis model in which $\mu_1 = 0$ and all other μ_i are negative. Compute the critical line for $IN = \{1\}$. If this seems like an "unrealistic" example: (i) we are concerned in chapters 7–9 with covering all mathematical possibilities whether or not they are "realistic"; and (ii) it is not inconceivable that in some portfolio analysis of *real* rather than nominal returns, the security with maximum μ_i is expected to just keep up with inflation, and has a positive standard deviation of real returns.)

(b) Show that (7.10a) may always be rewritten as

$$\begin{pmatrix} X \\ \lambda \\ \lambda_E \end{pmatrix} = \begin{pmatrix} \alpha \\ 0 \end{pmatrix} + \begin{pmatrix} \beta \\ 1 \end{pmatrix} t$$

where t is the parameter of the line. Since $(\beta', 1) \neq 0$ always, this is always a line in $(X', \lambda', \lambda_E)$ space. Thus we may speak of a critical line in $(X', \lambda', \lambda_E)$ space even when $\beta = 0$ in (7.10a).

(c) Note that none of the theorems of this chapter either requires that, or asserts that, $\beta \neq 0$ in (7.10a). In particular, $\beta = 0$ does not imply that the model is degenerate or alter the computation of λ_{low} and λ_{hi}.

7.6 Dybvig (1984) shows, for the standard portfolio selection model, that a kink in the efficient EV set occurs at a particular IN set if and only if the affine model associated with this IN set has only one feasible value of E. Show that the same holds true for the general nondegenerate portfolio selection model. (Hint: from theorem 7.12 we know that X, and therefore E, does not vary on a critical line at a kink. Show that this implies that $\tilde{M}$ (defined in chapter 6) is singular for the associated affine model, while $\bar{M}$ (i.e. the M matrix of the associated affine model) is nonsingular. These two facts, combined with theorems 6.8 and 6.9, imply that only one value of E is feasible for the affine model associated with this IN set.)

7.7 We will say here that a portfolio selection model is of form 2′ if portfolio $X' = (X_1, \ldots, X_n)$ is to be chosen subject to

$$AX = B$$

$$X_i \geqslant 0 \qquad \text{for } i = 1 \text{ to } k$$

where $0 \leqslant k \leqslant n$. If $k = 0$ we have the affine model; if $k = n$ we have a model of form 2.

(a) Show that a portfolio X is efficient for this model if there exists $\lambda_E > 0$ and $\lambda' = (\lambda_1, \ldots, \lambda_m)$ such that

$$X_i \geqslant 0 \qquad \text{for } i = 1 \text{ to } k \tag{7.23}$$

$$\eta_i \geqslant 0 \qquad \text{for } i = 1 \text{ to } k \tag{7.24}$$

$$\eta_i = 0 \quad \text{if } X_i > 0 \qquad \text{for } i = 1 \text{ to } k \tag{7.25}$$

$$\eta_i = 0 \qquad \text{for } i = k+1 \text{ to } n \tag{7.26}$$

As in theorem 7.3, this part makes no assertion about the case of $\lambda_E = 0$. (Hint: set up the appropriate Lagrangian; invoke lemma 6.1; show that a portfolio satisfying (7.23)–(7.26) minimizes the Lagrangian. Argue as in the proof of theorem 7.2, except that now X_i, $i > k$, is always free to move down as well as up.)

(b) Define an *IN* set to be the union of a subset of $\{1, 2, \ldots, k\}$ and the set $\{k+1, \ldots, n\}$. Thus X_i, $i > k$, is always *IN*. Define a critical line as in the text; and define a degenerate model in terms of α_i, β_i, γ_i, δ_i for $1 \leqslant i \leqslant k$, but otherwise as in the text. Define an adjacent critical line in terms of the first $X_i \downarrow 0$ or $\eta_i \downarrow 0$ for $1 \leqslant i \leqslant k$; i.e. X_i for $i > k$ remains *IN*.

Let l^0 be a critical line such that, for $\lambda^0_{\text{low}} \leqslant \lambda_E \leqslant \lambda^0_{\text{hi}}$, $X_i \geqslant 0$ and $\eta_i \geqslant 0$ for $i \leqslant k$. Show that the points on l^0 are efficient for these λ_E.

(c) Show that, for a nondegenerate model of form 2′, given an l^0 as in (b) there are a finite number of adjacent critical lines $\hat{l}, \ldots, l^0, \ldots, l^*$ whose efficient segments constitute a complete nonredundant piecewise linear set of efficient portfolios. (Hint: in most cases the theorems needed to prove this for a model of form 2 can be cited (rather than modified and proved again) for a model of form 2′.)

7.8 (Black (1972) second model, generalized.) Consider a portfolio selection model whose constraints are

$$(A, \alpha)\begin{pmatrix} X \\ X_{n+1} \end{pmatrix} = b \tag{7.27a}$$

$$X_{n+1} \geqslant 0 \tag{7.27b}$$

where A is $m \times n$, α is $m \times 1$, X is an $n \times 1$ variable vector, and X_{n+1} is a scalar variable.

$$V = X'CX \tag{7.28}$$

i.e. r_{n+1} has zero variance. We will assume that

$$\alpha \neq 0 \tag{7.29}$$

and there is no $Y \neq 0$ such that both

$$AY = 0 \tag{7.30a}$$

and

$$Y'CY = 0 \tag{7.30b}$$

In the Black (1972) second model,

$$(A, \alpha) = (1, 1, \ldots, 1)$$

If C is nonsingular then (7.30b) will hold, since then the model has no zero-variance directions and therefore none that satisfies (7.30a).

(a) Except for relabeling variables, this model is in form 2′ (see exercise 7.7). Show that, in this form, it has only two *IN* sets.

(b) Show that, given the assumptions specified above, $\bar{M}$ is nonsingular for both *IN* sets, and therefore the model has two critical lines. (In exercise 12.9 we will see that these critical lines may or may not intersect and, even when they intersect, the set of efficient portfolios may lie on one or two of the critical lines.) (Hint for the present exercise: show, for example, that the assumption that there exists (Y', Y_{n+1}, δ') such that

$$\begin{pmatrix} C & 0 & A' \\ 0 & 0 & \alpha' \\ A & \alpha & 0 \end{pmatrix} \begin{pmatrix} Y \\ Y_{n+1} \\ \delta \end{pmatrix} = \begin{pmatrix} 0 \\ 0 \\ 0 \end{pmatrix}$$

leads to a contradiction given our assumptions.)

8

Getting Started

Theorem 7.11 asserts that there exists (and, in effect, shows us how to compute) a complete nonredundant, piecewise linear set of efficient portfolios provided two conditions are met. First, there exists (and we are able to find) an *IN* set, IN_0, with nonsingular $\bar{M}$, meeting conditions (i), (ii), and (iii) of theorem 7.4. Second, there are no ties in computing λ_{hi} or λ_{low} in the sequences of critical lines $l^0, l^1, \ldots$ and $l^0, l^{-1}, \ldots$. To assure the second condition, we assumed that the model is nondegenerate. In the present chapter we show a set of circumstances under which the IN_0 set described above exists, and show how to find it under these circumstances. Specifically, we assume here that there is a unique feasible portfolio which maximizes E, and continue to assume that the model is nondegenerate. In chapter 9 we consider the general model, without requiring a unique E maximizing portfolio. Chapter 9 also removes the assumption that E necessarily has an upper bound and that the model is nondegenerate.

The problem of maximizing a linear function such as $E = \mu' X$ subject to $AX = b, X \geqslant 0$, is called a *linear programming* problem. The next two sections of this chapter describe G. B. Dantzig's simplex method for solving this problem. We refer the reader to Dantzig (1963) for some proofs and for extensive references to prior literature.

Historically, the simplex method has played two roles. The first role is an analytic one. The fact that the simplex algorithm solves the linear programming problem relies on certain properties of linear programming problems and their solution. Indeed, the description of the simplex algorithm and proof that it works is as good a way as any to organize a description of these mathematical properties. The second role which the simplex algorithm has played is that for many years it was the fastest available means for solving arbitrary linear programming problems. As this is written there is a considerable controversy as to whether the second role is about to be taken over by variants of a method proposed by Karmarkar (1984).

Our interest in the simplex method is primarily in its analytic role. For example, in the present chapter we will use the fact – central to the simplex algorithm – that if there is a unique E maximizing portfolio then this portfolio satisfies certain algebraic "pricing" relationships. These relationships will allow us to prove that a particular critical line, obtained from the E maximizing portfolio, has properties (i), (ii), and (iii) of theorem 7.4, and therefore can be the l^0 needed to start the critical line algorithm.

It is also of value to know that the E maximizing portfolio can be computed economically in large portfolio selection problems. But it is of no concern to us whether this solution is obtained by the simplex method, by Karmarkar's method, or by some algorithm yet to be devised.

When there is more than one E maximizing portfolio, the simplex algorithm finds one which satisfies the pricing relationships. It was reported from the audience at a session of the 12th International Symposium on Mathematical Programming[1] that, when there is more than one solution to the linear programming problem, the Karmarkar method will not necessarily converge to a solution satisfying the pricing relationships. However, one could start with a Karmarkar solution and then use the simplex method to obtain a solution satisfying the pricing relationships if one desired. The method of starting the critical line algorithm when E has an upper bound but the E maximizing solution is not unique, described in the next chapter, requires an E maximizing portfolio satisfying the simplex pricing relationship; but it is of no concern as to how this solution is obtained.

The Simplex Method of Linear Programming

The simplex method has two phases. Phase I has one of the following three outcomes:

I(a) It determines that there is no X which satisfies $AX = b$, $X \geqslant 0$; i.e. the model is infeasible.

I(b) It determines that the model is feasible, and the system $AX = b$ has no redundant equations. Further, it produces a feasible X with the following characteristics: there is a subset of $\{1, 2, \ldots, n\}$ which we will call the *IN* set, and its complement which we call the *OUT* set, such that $X_j = 0$ for $j \in OUT$. The *IN* set has m members. The submatrix obtained by deleting all the columns of A whose j is *OUT*, leaving only the columns of A whose j is *IN*, is nonsingular.

I(c) It determines that the model is feasible but contains one or more redundant equations; it deletes redundant equations, producing an equivalent model without such equations. (Chapter 13 explains and uses an alternate method for producing an equivalent model; but deleting redundant

[1] August 1985, Massachusetts Institute of Technology, Cambridge, Massachusetts.

equations will suffice, and is simplest for the present discussion.) For the new equivalent model, it produces a first feasible X with the properties described in I(b).

Definitions Any X which satisfies $AX = b$, $X \geqslant 0$, is called a *feasible solution*. A *basic* feasible solution is one with the properties of the feasible solution in case I(b) above. A basic feasible solution is called *nondegenerate* if $X_i > 0$ for $i \in IN$. Otherwise, it is called *degenerate*. An *optimum* solution (or *basic optimum* solution) is a feasible solution (or basic feasible solution) which maximizes E subject to the given constraints.

We may summarize I(a)-(c) as follows. The simplex phase I either finds that the linear programming problem is infeasible, or produces a basic feasible solution to it. In the latter case it may have to first substitute an equivalent problem for the original one.

Suppose that we are given a portfolio selection problem in form 2, and we perform a simplex phase I on the constraints $AX = b$, $X \geqslant 0$. If the phase I calculation finds that the constraints are infeasible, then the portfolio selection model is also infeasible, since it has the same constraints. Suppose instead that it finds that the model is feasible but has one or more redundant equations, and eliminates these. It has then provided us with a completely equivalent portfolio selection model, since an X satisfies the old constraints if and only if it satisfies the new constraints. We summarize this as a theorem.

Theorem 8.1 For any portfolio selection model of form 2, the simplex phase I determines whether or not the model is feasible. If the model is feasible but contains redundant equations, it provides a strictly equivalent model without redundant equations.

Proof This is a direct application of the results on phase I; see Dantzig (1963). ###

For some portfolio selection models - e.g. the standard model - it is easy to determine that the model is feasible and has no redundant equations, and to find a basic feasible or even an optimum solution. For these models the simplex phase I is not needed. For more complex portfolio selection models the simplex phase I is used.

Phase II of the simplex method starts with a basic feasible solution, such as that produced by phase I, and produces one of the following two outcomes:

II(a) It gives a basic optimum solution.

II(b) It determines that no optimum solution exists because the linear objective function can be increased without bounds. More than this, it produces a ray $X = X_0 + bt$ which is feasible for all $t \geqslant 0$, and on which E increases indefinitely.

Since it is shown that phase II must have one of the above two outcomes, clearly if there is an optimum solution to the linear programming problem then there is a basic optimum solution. We will next present a formula which is true for any basic optimum solution. Our discussion will make use of the following lemma.

Lemma 8.2 Suppose that $\tilde{A}$ is any square, nonsingular submatrix of A obtained by deleting all but m columns of A; then

$$GX = \tilde{b} \tag{8.1a}$$

$$X \geqslant 0 \tag{8.1b}$$

where

$$G = \tilde{A}^{-1}A \tag{8.1c}$$

$$\tilde{b} = \tilde{A}^{-1}b \tag{8.1d}$$

is equivalent to

$$AX = b \tag{8.2a}$$

$$X \geqslant 0 \tag{8.2b}$$

in that X satisfies (8.1) if and only if it satisfies (8.2).

Proof If $X \geqslant 0$ satisfies $AX = b$, multiply both sides of (8.2a) on the left by $\tilde{A}^{-1}$ to find that $GX = \tilde{b}$. Conversely, if X satisfies $GX = \tilde{b}$ - i.e. $(\tilde{A}^{-1}A)X = (\tilde{A}^{-1}b)$ - multiply both sides by $\tilde{A}$ to show that $AX = b$. ###

Suppose X_0 is a nondegenerate basic feasible solution. Without loss of generality we may assume that $IN = \{1, 2, \ldots, m\}$ and $OUT = \{m + 1, \ldots, n\}$. We may write

$$A = (\tilde{A}, \hat{A})$$

$$X = \begin{pmatrix} \tilde{X} \\ \hat{X} \end{pmatrix}$$

$$\mu = \begin{pmatrix} \tilde{\mu} \\ \hat{\mu} \end{pmatrix}$$

where $\tilde{A}$, $\tilde{X}$, and $\tilde{\mu}$ are the first m columns or components of A, X, and μ respectively, and $\hat{A}$, $\hat{X}$, and $\hat{\mu}$ contain the remaining $n-m$ columns or components. Thus the original linear programming problem may be written as

$$\text{maximize} \qquad E = (\tilde{\mu}, \hat{\mu})\begin{pmatrix} \tilde{X} \\ \hat{X} \end{pmatrix} \tag{8.3a}$$

$$\text{subject to} \qquad (\tilde{A}, \hat{A})\begin{pmatrix} \tilde{X} \\ \hat{X} \end{pmatrix} = b \tag{8.3b}$$

$$\begin{pmatrix} \tilde{X} \\ \hat{X} \end{pmatrix} \geqslant 0 \tag{8.3c}$$

Since $\tilde{A}$ is nonsingular we may write

$$\tilde{A}^{-1}\tilde{A}\tilde{X} + \tilde{A}^{-1}\hat{A}\hat{X} = \tilde{A}^{-1}b$$

i.e.

$$\begin{aligned} \tilde{X} &= \tilde{A}^{-1}b - \tilde{A}^{-1}\hat{A}\hat{X} \\ &= \tilde{b} - \hat{G}\hat{X} \end{aligned} \tag{8.4a}$$

where $\tilde{b}$ is defined in (8.1 d), and $\hat{G}$ is defined to be

$$\hat{G} = \tilde{A}^{-1}\hat{A} \tag{8.4b}$$

Table 8.1 summarizes notation introduced in this chapter for current and later reference.

Since $\hat{X} = 0$ for the given basic feasible solution, (8.4) implies

$$\tilde{X} = \tilde{b}$$

for this solution. Since we currently assume the solution to be nondegenerate we must have

Table 8.1 Summary of chapter 8 notation

Symbol	*Meaning*
$AX = b,\ X \geqslant 0$	Given linear program. A is $m \times n$
$\tilde{A}$	An $m \times m$ nonsingular subset of the columns of A
$A = (\tilde{A}, \hat{A})$ $X' = (\tilde{X}', \hat{X}')$ $\mu' = (\tilde{\mu}', \hat{\mu}')$	Partition of A, X, and μ assuming that $\tilde{A}$ contains the first m columns of A
$G = \tilde{A}^{-1}A$ $= \tilde{A}^{-1}(\tilde{A}, \hat{A})$ $= (I, \hat{G})$	Definition of G and $\hat{G}$
$\tilde{b} = \tilde{A}^{-1}b$	Definition of $\tilde{b}$
$\tilde{X} = \tilde{b} - \hat{G}\hat{X}$	Equivalent to $AX = b$
$GX = (I, \hat{G})\begin{pmatrix} \tilde{X} \\ \hat{X} \end{pmatrix}$ $= \tilde{b}$	Equivalent to $AX = b$
$\hat{\nu} = \hat{\mu} - \hat{G}'\tilde{\mu}$	Definition of $\hat{\nu}$

$$\tilde{X} = \tilde{b} > 0 \tag{8.5}$$

i.e. $\tilde{X}_i > 0$ for $i = 1$ to m.

Also, for any $(\tilde{X}', \hat{X}')$ - not just for the given current solution - we have

$$E = (\tilde{\mu}', \hat{\mu}')\begin{pmatrix}\tilde{X}\\ \hat{X}\end{pmatrix}$$

$$= (\tilde{\mu}', \hat{\mu}')\begin{pmatrix}\tilde{b} - \hat{G}\hat{X}\\ \hat{X}\end{pmatrix}$$

$$= E_0 + \hat{\nu}'\hat{X} \tag{8.6a}$$

where

$$E_0 = \tilde{\mu}'\tilde{b} \tag{8.6b}$$

$$\hat{\nu}' = \hat{\mu}' - \tilde{\mu}'\hat{G} \tag{8.6c}$$

or

$$\hat{\nu} = \hat{\mu} - \hat{G}'\tilde{\mu} \tag{8.6d}$$

It follows from lemma 8.2 that $X' = (\tilde{X}', \hat{X}')$ satisfies (8.2a) if and only if it satisfies (8.4). Equation (8.6) is an alternate way of writing $E = \mu'X$. Thus X maximizes $\mu'X$ subject to $AX = b$, $X \geqslant 0$, if and only if it maximizes (8.6) subject to (8.4) and $X \geqslant 0$.

When the linear programming problem is written as in (8.4) and (8.6), one can tell by inspection if the particular nondegenerate basic feasible solution is optimal or not. Equation (8.4) may be written out "longhand" as follows.

$$\begin{pmatrix}X_1\\ X_2\\ \vdots\\ X_m\end{pmatrix} = \begin{pmatrix}\tilde{b}_1\\ \tilde{b}_2\\ \vdots\\ \tilde{b}_m\end{pmatrix} - \begin{pmatrix}g_{1,m+1} & \cdots & g_{1,n}\\ \vdots & & \vdots\\ g_{m,m+1} & \cdots & g_{m,n}\end{pmatrix}\begin{pmatrix}X_{m+1}\\ \vdots\\ X_n\end{pmatrix} \tag{8.7}$$

We can also write (8.7) as

$$GX = \tilde{b} \tag{8.8a}$$

where

$$G = \begin{pmatrix}1 & 0 & \cdots & 0 & g_{1,m+1} & \cdots & g_{1,n}\\ 0 & 1 & & & & & \\ \vdots & & \ddots & & \vdots & & \vdots\\ 0 & & & 1 & g_{m,m+1} & \cdots & g_{m,n}\end{pmatrix} \tag{8.8b}$$

since, for simplicity of notation, we assume that $IN = \{1, \ldots, m\}$. In general, for any IN and OUT set, the IN variables appear on the left and the OUT variables on the right of (8.7), and the various unit column vectors of (8.8) are scattered through the G matrix.

Theorem 8.3 A nondegenerate, basic, feasible solution (with IN assumed to be $\{1, 2, \ldots, m\}$, without loss of generality) is an optimal solution if and only if $\hat{v}_i \leqslant 0$ for $i = m + 1, \ldots, n$.

Proof First suppose that for some ω such that $m + 1 \leqslant \omega \leqslant n$ we have $\hat{v}_\omega > 0$. We will show that this implies the existence of a feasible solution with greater E. For ease of notation suppose $\omega = m + 1$. Then, for any value of θ it is true that

$$\begin{pmatrix} 1 & 0 & \ldots & 0 & g_{1,m+1} & \cdots & g_{1,n} \\ 0 & 1 & & & & & \\ \vdots & & \ddots & & \vdots & & \vdots \\ 0 & & & 1 & g_{m,m+1} & \cdots & g_{m,n} \end{pmatrix} \begin{bmatrix} \tilde{b} - \theta \begin{pmatrix} g_{1,m+1} \\ \vdots \\ g_{m,m+1} \end{pmatrix} \\ \theta \\ 0 \end{bmatrix} = \tilde{b}$$

Thus a solution with

$$X_{m+1} = \theta \tag{8.9a}$$

$$X_i = \tilde{b}_i - \theta g_{i,m+1} \qquad \text{for } 1 \leqslant i \leqslant m \tag{8.9b}$$

$$X_i = 0 \qquad \text{for } i > m + 1 \tag{8.9c}$$

satisfies $GX = \tilde{b}$, and hence $AX = b$. Also, $\hat{v}_{m+1} > 0$ and (8.6) imply that E increases as θ increases. Thus if $X \geqslant 0$ is satisfied for any $\theta > 0$, we have found a feasible solution with greater E. If $g_{i,m+1} \leqslant 0$ for all $1 \leqslant i \leqslant m$, then $X \geqslant 0$ is satisfied for all θ. In this case E is unbounded and, in particular, there are feasible solutions with greater E than is provided by the given basic feasible solution. Next suppose $g_{i,m+1} > 0$ for one or more i between 1 and m. Then $X \geqslant 0$ for all X satisfying (8.9) with $0 < \theta < \theta^*$, where θ^* is the smallest value of $\tilde{b}_i/g_{i,m+1}$ among i with $g_{i,m+1} > 0$. Thus for $\theta = \theta^*$ in particular, we have a feasible solution with greater E. In fact this is a basic feasible solution (see exercise 8.1).

Next suppose $\hat{v}_i \leqslant 0$ for $i = m + 1, \ldots, n$. Then it follows immediately from (8.6), plus the fact that now $\hat{X} = 0$ and must remain nonnegative, that no feasible solution can have higher E. ###

Note that the above proof did more than show that $\hat{v} \leqslant 0$ is the earmark of an optimum solution. If $\hat{v}_i > 0$ for some i, it showed how to either: (1) determine that E is unbounded, or (2) find a basic feasible solution with higher E (assuming the problem to be nondegenerate). In the latter case the process can be repeated. The constraints and definition of E can be written as (8.8) and (8.6) for the new basis. (The unit vectors e^i in (8.8) need not occupy the first m columns.) The new $\hat{v}_i$ can be inspected to see if E can be increased by introducing into the basis an X_i now out of the basis; and so on. Since in the nondegenerate case each iteration increases E, no basis will appear a second time as this process is repeated. Since there is only a finite number of bases, in the nondegenerate case phase II will end (in an optimal solution or a proof that E is unbounded) in a finite number of steps. As illustrated in exercise 8.2, the G matrix and $\hat{v}$ vector of one iteration can be derived from that of the preceding iteration with relatively little computing; in particular, without inverting the new $\bar{A}$.

Completion of proof of theorem 5.4 In the proof of theorem 5.4 we showed that if an unbounded feasible direction β has $\mu'\beta > 0$ then E is unbounded from above. Theorem 5.4 also asserts the converse, that if E is unbounded there exists such a β. This is a corollary of theorem 8.3 and the fact that the simplex phase II maximizes E, or proves it unbounded above, in a finite number of iterations. If the algorithm finds E to be unbounded, then the vector

$$\beta = \begin{pmatrix} -g_{1,m+1} \\ -g_{2,m+1} \\ \vdots \\ -g_{m,m+1} \\ 1 \\ 0 \\ \vdots \\ 0 \end{pmatrix}$$

is an unbounded direction with $\mu'\beta > 0$. ###

Corollary 8.4 With notation as in (8.6), if X is a nondegenerate optimal solution it is the unique optimum if and only if $\hat{v}_j < 0$ for $j = m + 1, \ldots, n$.

Proof This follows immediately from (8.6) and the fact that nondegeneracy implies $\theta^* > 0$ for any choice of $m + 1 \leqslant \omega \leqslant n$. ###

Prices and Profitabilities

The above results can be expressed in terms of "prices" assigned to each row of $AX = b$, and profitabilities assigned to each variable X_j.

Definitions Given any basic feasible solution, define a *price vector* $\pi' = (\pi_1, \pi_2, \ldots, \pi_m)$ for this solution by

$$\pi'\bar{A} + \bar{\mu}' = 0 \qquad (8.10a)$$

and a *profitability vector* $\Pi' = (\Pi_1, \Pi_2, \ldots, \Pi_n)$ by

$$\pi' A + \mu' = \Pi' \tag{8.10b}$$

In general the $\tilde{A}$ matrix of (8.10a) consists of

$$\tilde{A} = (A_{i_1}, A_{i_2}, \ldots, A_{i_m})$$

where A_j is the jth column of A, and

$$IN = \{i_1, i_2, \ldots, i_m\}$$

From (8.10a) we derive

$$\tilde{A}'\pi = -\tilde{\mu} \tag{8.10c}$$

$$\pi = -(\tilde{A}')^{-1}\tilde{\mu} \tag{8.10d}$$

If we assume, as usual, that $IN = \{1, 2, \ldots, m\}$, we may write $A = (\tilde{A}, \hat{A})$. Substituting (8.10d) into (8.10b) we get

$$-\tilde{\mu}'\tilde{A}^{-1}(\tilde{A}, \hat{A}) + (\tilde{\mu}', \hat{\mu}') = \Pi'$$

i.e.

$$-\tilde{\mu}'(I, \tilde{A}^{-1}\hat{A}) + (\tilde{\mu}', \hat{\mu}') = \Pi' \tag{8.10e}$$

Partitioning Π' into $(\tilde{\Pi}', \hat{\Pi}')$, and using (8.6d) as well as (8.10e), we find that

$$\tilde{\Pi} = 0 \tag{8.11a}$$

$$\hat{\Pi} = \hat{\nu} \tag{8.11b}$$

Thus theorem 8.3 and corollary 8.4 can be rephrased as follows. For any given basic feasible solution define prices $\pi_1, \ldots, \pi_m$ so that, in terms of these prices, every $IN j$ has zero profit, where the profitability of the jth "activity" is defined as

$$\Pi_j = \pi' A_j + \mu_j$$

where A_j is the jth column of A. Thus the profitability of the jth activity is computed by crediting it (if $a_{ij} > 0$) or charging it (if $a_{ij} < 0$) with $\pi_i a_{ij}$; summing these credits and charges; and adding μ_j. The basic solution is optimum if the profitability of all nonbasic activities is zero or negative. In this case we say that the basis "prices out", or "satisfies the simplex pricing criteria." If the basic solution is nondegenerate, then the solution is unique if and only if all nonbasic activities have negative profit.

When $\tilde{A}^{-1}$ for the current basis is available, prices and profits can be computed from equations (8.10). $\tilde{A}^{-1}$ can also be used to compute the X of a given basis, and help determine which X_i must go out of the basis when a new X_ω comes in. The $\tilde{A}^{-1}$ of one iteration can be "updated" from that of the preceding iteration with much less computing than would be required to invert $\bar{A}$ "from scratch." One variation of the simplex algorithm maintains $\bar{A}^{-1}$ rather than transforming constraints as in (8.8). The program in chapter 13 includes a simplex algorithm of the former variety, and is described in detail there.

Starting the Critical Line Algorithm

Theorem 8.5 Suppose X_0 is a unique nondegenerate optimum basic solution to the problem of maximizing $E = \mu' X$ subject to $AX = b$, $X \geqslant 0$. Let IN_0 be the IN set for X_0. Then X_0 is an efficient portfolio, the $\bar{M}$ matrix of IN_0 is nonsingular, and for some $\lambda^* \geqslant 0$ we have $X \geqslant 0$, $\eta \geqslant 0$ for all $\lambda_E \geqslant \lambda^*$ on the associated critical line. Thus the critical line l^0 associated with IN_0 satisfies conditions (i), (ii), and (iii) of theorem 7.4 with $\lambda_{hi} = \infty$ and $\lambda_{low} = \lambda^*$.

Proof Clearly X_0 is efficient, since no other X has as large an E. It is convenient, as above, to assume that $IN_0 = \{1, 2, \ldots, m\}$. Under this assumption $\bar{A}$ is the first m columns of A, and is nonsingular. The $\bar{M}$ of the IN_0 set

$$\bar{M}_0 = \begin{pmatrix} \bar{C} & 0 & \bar{A}' \\ 0 & I & 0 \\ \bar{A} & 0 & 0 \end{pmatrix} \tag{8.12a}$$

is nonsingular since its inverse is

$$\bar{M}_0^{-1} = \begin{pmatrix} 0 & 0 & \bar{A}^{-1} \\ 0 & I & 0 \\ (\bar{A}^{-1})' & 0 & -(\bar{A}^{-1})'\bar{C}(\bar{A}^{-1}) \end{pmatrix} \tag{8.12b}$$

as may be confirmed by multiplying the two matrices. On the associated critical line l^0,

$$\begin{pmatrix} X \\ \lambda \end{pmatrix} = \alpha + \beta\lambda_E$$

where, setting $B = \bar{A}^{-1}$, we have

$$\alpha = \bar{M}_0^{-1} \begin{pmatrix} 0 \\ 0 \\ b \end{pmatrix}$$

$$= \begin{pmatrix} 0 & 0 & B \\ 0 & I & 0 \\ B' & 0 & -B'\bar{C}B \end{pmatrix} \begin{pmatrix} 0 \\ 0 \\ b \end{pmatrix}$$

$$= \begin{pmatrix} Bb \\ 0 \\ -B'\bar{C}Bb \end{pmatrix}$$

$$\beta = \bar{M}_0^{-1} \begin{pmatrix} \bar{\mu} \\ 0 \\ 0 \end{pmatrix}$$

$$= \begin{pmatrix} 0 \\ 0 \\ B'\bar{\mu} \end{pmatrix}$$

Thus

$$\begin{pmatrix} X \\ \lambda \end{pmatrix} = \begin{pmatrix} \bar{A}^{-1}b \\ 0 \\ -(\bar{A}^{-1})'\bar{C}\bar{A}^{-1}b \end{pmatrix} + \begin{pmatrix} 0 \\ 0 \\ (\bar{A}^{-1})'\bar{\mu} \end{pmatrix} \lambda_E$$

We see then that only λ changes along l^0 as λ_E changes. X remains constant, with its last $n - m$ components equal to zero. Along l^0

$$\eta = (C, A') \begin{pmatrix} X \\ \lambda \end{pmatrix} - \mu\lambda_E$$

$$= (C, A') \begin{pmatrix} Bb \\ 0 \\ -B'\bar{C}Bb \end{pmatrix} + (C, A') \begin{pmatrix} 0 \\ 0 \\ B'\bar{\mu} \end{pmatrix} \lambda_E - \mu\lambda_E$$

$$= C \begin{pmatrix} \bar{A}^{-1}b \\ 0 \end{pmatrix} - A'(\bar{A}^{-1})'\bar{C}(\bar{A}^{-1})\, b + (A'(\bar{A}^{-1})'\bar{\mu} - \mu)\, \lambda_E$$

$$= \gamma + \delta\lambda_E$$

But using (8.4b), (8.6), and corollary 8.4 it follows that

$$\delta = (A'(\bar{A}^{-1})'\bar{\mu} - \mu)$$

$$= \left(\begin{pmatrix} \bar{A}' \\ \hat{A}' \end{pmatrix} (\bar{A}^{-1})'\bar{\mu} - \mu \right)$$

$$= \begin{pmatrix} I \\ \hat{A}'(\bar{A}^{-1})' \end{pmatrix} \bar{\mu} - \begin{pmatrix} \bar{\mu} \\ \hat{\mu} \end{pmatrix}$$

$$=\begin{pmatrix} 0 \\ \hat{G}'\bar{\mu}-\hat{\mu} \end{pmatrix}$$

$$=\begin{pmatrix} 0 \\ -\hat{\nu} \end{pmatrix}$$

i.e.

$$\delta_i = 0 \qquad \text{for } i = 1 \text{ to } m$$

$$\delta_i > 0 \qquad \text{for } i = m+1 \text{ to } n$$

Thus, for sufficiently large λ_E, on l^0 we have $\eta \geqslant 0$ as well as $X \geqslant 0$. ###

As λ_E moves downward from $+\infty$ along the first critical line, the tangent (support) line rotates as in figure 8.1. One of two cases occurs: perhaps λ_E reaches zero before any η_i reaches zero. In this case the efficient portfolio with maximum E is also the efficient portfolio with minimum V. Otherwise there is an η_i which first reaches zero as λ_E is decreased. In this case the corresponding X_i is introduced into the *IN* set, and the process described in the preceding chapter begins.

Exercises

8.1 In the proof to theorem 8.3, an $i \in IN$ becomes 0 (and is the first one to do so) at $\theta = \theta^*$. Deleting this i from *IN*, and adding ω, produces an *IN*

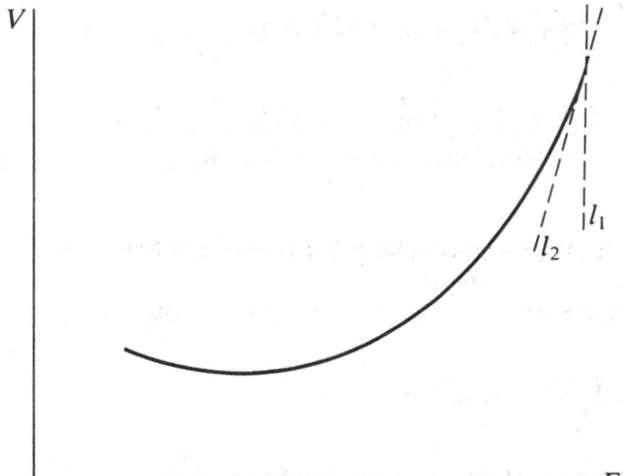

Figure 8.1 Support lines for the efficient portfolio with maximum E

set with m members. For ease of discussion in this exercise, assume that the i whose $X_i \downarrow 0$ at $\theta = \underline{\theta}^*$ is $i = m$. The proof asserts that the new *IN* set is a basis; i.e. the new $\bar{A}$ matrix

$$\bar{A}^{\text{new}} = (A_1, A_2, \ldots, A_{m-1}, A_\omega)$$

is nonsingular. Show that this is so. (Hint: assume that $\bar{A}$ is singular and derive a contradiction. Show that a singular $\bar{A}$ implies that there is an α with $\alpha_m \neq 0$ such that

$$\bar{A}^{\text{new}}\alpha = 0 \tag{8.13}$$

In particular, rule out the possibility that an $\alpha \neq 0$ with $\alpha_m = 0$ satisfies (8.13). Also show that (for the old $\bar{A}$)

$$a = \bar{A}^{-1} A_\omega$$

has $a_m \neq 0$, otherwise it could not happen that $X_m \downarrow 0$ as $\theta \uparrow \underline{\theta}^*$. Use $\alpha_m \neq 0$ and $a_m \neq 0$ to show that $\bar{A}^{\text{new}}$ singular implies that the old $\bar{A}$ is also singular.)

8.2 Consider a portfolio selection problem with the following constraints and expected value:

$$\sum_{i=1}^{7} X_i = 1 \tag{8.14}$$

$$0.9X_1 + 0.8X_2 + 0.6X_3 \leqslant 0.7 \tag{8.15}$$

$$0.3X_3 + 0.7X_4 + 0.75X_5 + 0.5X_6 \leqslant 0.7 \tag{8.16}$$

$$X_i \geqslant 0 \qquad i = 1, \ldots, 7 \tag{8.17}$$

$$E = 0.3X_1 + 0.2X_2 + 0.25X_3 + 0.2X_4 + 0.25X_5 + 0.20X_6 + 0.10X_7 \tag{8.18a}$$

Equations (8.15) and (8.16) are generalized industry constraints as described in chapter 3. Note that security 3 is in both industries and security 7 in neither.

(a) Rewrite the constraint set in form 2 by adding slack variables X_8 and X_9 to (8.15) and (8.16).

(b) Show that, because of (8.14), the definition of E can be written as

$$\sum_{i=1}^{6} (\mu_i - \mu_7) X_i - E = -\mu_7 \tag{8.18b}$$

where μ_i is the ith coefficient in (8.18a).

(c) Conclude that (8.14)–(8.16) and the definition of E can be written as follows:

X_1	X_2	X_3	X_4	X_5	
1.000	1.000	1.000	1.000	1.000	
0.900	0.800	0.600	0.000	0.000	
0.000	0.000	0.300	0.700	0.750	
0.200	0.100	0.150	0.100	0.150	
X_6	X_7^*	X_8^*	X_9^*	E	RHS
1.000	1.000	0.000	0.000	0.000	1.000
0.000	0.000	1.000	0.000	0.000	0.700
0.500	0.000	0.000	1.000	0.000	0.700
0.100	0.000	0.000	0.000	−1.000	−0.100

The first three rows of the above table are the constraint equations written in "detached coefficient" format, with variables written above their respective matrix columns, and with the right-hand side of the equations in the column labelled RHS. The fourth row is the definition of E given in (8.18b) written in detached coefficient format.

(d) Confirm that $IN = \{7, 8, 9\}$ is a nondegenerate feasible basis and that, except for the order of the columns, the constraint matrix and E equation are written as in (8.8) and (8.6).

(e) Note that $\hat{\nu}_1 = 0.2 > 0$ so that E may be increased by bringing X_1 into the basis. Use the $\bar{\beta}_i/g_{i\omega}$ criterion described in the proof of theorem 8.3 to show that if X_1 is added to the basis then X_8 must be deleted from the basis for the new basis to be feasible.

(f) Confirm that if you subtract a certain multiple of the second row in the table in (c) from the first row, you obtain the first row in the table below. What is this multiple? Similarly, if you subtract a certain multiple of the second row of the table in (c) from the fourth row, you obtain the fourth row below.

X_1^*	X_2	X_3	X_4	X_5	
0.000	0.111	0.333	1.000	1.000	
1.000	0.889	0.667	0.000	0.000	
0.000	0.000	0.300	0.700	0.750	
0.000	−0.078	0.017	0.100	0.150	
X_6	X_7^*	X_8	X_9^*	E	RHS
1.000	1.000	−1.111	0.000	0.000	0.222
0.000	0.000	1.111	0.000	0.000	0.778
0.500	0.000	0.000	1.000	0.000	0.700
0.100	0.000	−0.222	0.000	−1.000	−0.256

(g) The table in (f) expresses the constraints and E equation as in (8.8) and (8.6) for $IN = \{1, 7, 9\}$. What is the value of X and E for the basis?

(h) The largest $\hat{\nu} = \hat{\nu}_5 = 0.15 > 0$. If X_5 comes into the basis in (g), what must go out in order to remain feasible?

(i) As described in (f), transform the table in (f) for the basis $IN = \{1, 7, 9\}$ into the table below for the new basis $IN = \{1, 5, 9\}$.

X_1^*	X_2	X_3	X_4	X_5^*
0.000	0.111	0.333	1.000	1.000
1.000	0.889	0.667	0.000	0.000
0.000	−0.083	0.050	−0.050	0.000
0.000	−0.094	−0.033	−0.050	0.000

X_6	X_7	X_8	X_9^*	E	RHS
1.000	1.000	−1.111	0.000	0.000	0.222
0.000	0.000	1.111	0.000	0.000	0.778
−0.250	−0.750	0.833	1.000	0.000	0.533
−0.050	−0.150	−0.056	0.000	−1.000	−0.289

(j) The latest basis is optimal. How do we know? What are the optimal values of X and E?

(k) Suppose

$$V = 0.020X_1^2 + 0.015X_2^2 + 0.020X_3^2 + 0.010X_4^2 + 0.015X_5^2 + 0.025X_6^2$$

What is the system of equations for the first critical line (with $\lambda_{hi} = \infty$)? Determine λ_{low} for this line.

8.3 In the portfolio selection problem in exercise (8.2), change the definition of E to

$$E = 0.15X_1 + 0.2X_2 + 0.25X_3 + 0.2X_4 + 0.15X_5 + 0.20X_6 + 0.10X_7$$

Otherwise leave the problem unchanged. Find the E maximizing X and the critical line with $\lambda_{hi} = \infty$ for this new problem. (Don't worry about the tie for determining λ_{low} on this line. The next chapter considers how to proceed with degenerate models.)

9

Degenerate Cases

The preceding two chapters assume that either the portfolio selection model is infeasible, or

(1) E is bounded from above;
(2) One and only one feasible portfolio provides maximum E;
(3) The E maximizing portfolio is a nondegenerate basic solution (as this is defined in chapter 8); and
(4) The model is a nondegenerate portfolio selection model (as this is defined in chapter 7).

Given these assumptions it is concluded that a particular computing procedure, the critical line algorithm, determines a piecewise linear, complete nonredundant set of efficient portfolios. The present chapter shows that, with one exception, the existence of a piecewise linear, complete nonredundant set of efficient portfolios follows without any of the above assumptions (except feasibility). Furthermore, the critical line algorithm will calculate this set, provided that ties for determining λ_{low} are resolved "properly." The critical line algorithm, extended to resolve ties "properly", will be called the *extended critical line algorithm*. The exceptional case is that the extended algorithm may determine that the model is feasible but has no efficient portfolios, because feasible portfolios can be found with minimum V and ever increasing E.

We first consider the case in which E is bounded, but the E maximizing portfolio may be degenerate or not unique, or the model may be a degenerate portfolio selection model. After that we deal with the case in which E is not bounded.

In one sense the topics of this chapter are crucial: they show how our analysis applies to arbitrary A, b, C, and μ, without restrictive (nondegeneracy and boundedness) assumptions. In another sense this chapter adds nothing to the solution already derived in chapters 7 and 8. Except for the case in which efficient portfolios do not exist, there is still a piecewise linear, complete nonredundant efficient set in portfolio space; hence the efficient set in EV space is piecewise parabolic and that in $E\sigma$ space has pieces which are hyperbolic and/or linear. When E is unbounded above then the piece with $\lambda_{low} \leqslant \lambda_E < \infty$ has X

varying rather than X fixed; but X fixed or varying on a piece was already a possibility encountered in chapter 7.

The present chapter is long and rather difficult. Since it arrives at essentially the same solution as that in chapters 7 and 8, the reader may prefer to postpone reading it until after chapters 10-12.

Simpler "Good Enough" Methods

Simpler methods than the extensions described in the following sections will probably work, or work "well enough" in practice. This section describes such simple, but usually good enough, solutions to the problems of ties for max E, degeneracy, and unbounded E.

Ties for maximizing E

One approach to the problem encountered when two or more feasible portfolios maximize E is to change the μ_i slightly so that only one portfolio is the E maximizer. A small change can always achieve this, and usually leaves the problem practically unchanged (i.e. does not alter the problem for practical purposes).

Degeneracy

In linear programming it is known that the presence of degeneracy can prevent some versions of the simplex algorithm from finding an optimum solution. When a degenerate basic feasible solution is encountered, one or more basic variables have zero values. When a new variable is introduced into the basis, one (or more) of the current basis variables may "go out" immediately, without increasing payoff E. This produces another degenerate basic solution. For this solution too it is possible for the new variable introduced into the basis to immediately force out one or more of the variables at zero level, without any increase in E. (If more than one variable at zero level wants to go out, only one is dropped from the basis, since a basis requires m variables.) The latest solution is again degenerate.

This raises the possibility that, after proceeding this way for several steps without increasing E, one of the degenerate basic solutions B^* which was encountered before will be reached again. If the same deterministic (nonrandom) rule is used to pick a variable to go out of the basis among variables which are at zero value and could go out immediately (and the rule depends only on the composition of the basis and the incoming variable - not on iteration number, time of day, or the like) then the same sequence of bases will be encountered after the second appearance of B^* as was encountered after the first, until B^* appears a third time, and so on for an infinite loop.

The following is the situation in linear programming with respect to this possibility:

(1) Examples have been constructed in which the above *cycling* of the simplex algorithm actually occurs (see Hoffman, 1953; Dantzig, 1963).
(2) Such cycling happens rarely, if ever, in practice (i.e. in problems not specifically constructed to show its existence).
(3) Deterministic procedures for deciding which one of two or more variables at zero level should "go out" have been developed which guarantee against cycling.

Because of point (2), a version of the simplex algorithm which does not include anticycling procedures will probably work in all practical problems encountered. It is a corollary of point (3) that if a variant of the simplex method breaks ties randomly among basic variables at zero level which want to go out immediately then, with probability one, the algorithm will reach an optimal solution in a finite number of steps.

Examples have not been produced which show that the (unextended) critical line algorithm for mean-variance portfolio selection does, in fact, cycle in degenerate cases. Experience with actual problems shows that, as in linear programming, cycling is rare (or nonexistent) in practice. Subsequent sections of this chapter present procedures which guarantee that a complete nonredundant efficient set will be produced in a finite number of steps. A corollary of the existence of such a procedure is that the random choice of X_i or η_i to "go to zero first" will generate a complete nonredundant, piecewise linear efficient set with probability 1. In fact, critical line algorithms which break ties arbitrarily usually (always?) work in practice.

Unbounded E

For practical purposes the problem of unbounded E could be handled by imposing a very large upper bound on E, say $E \leqslant 1{,}000{,}000$. If this upper bound is achieved then the problem is "unbounded" for all practical purposes. If a minimum variance portfolio is arrived at with this maximum allowed E, then it will be the only efficient portfolio for the bounded problem, and suggests that the unbounded problem has no efficient portfolios, providing ever increasing E for the same minimum V. Theorem 9.15 assures us that, if the upper bound on E is chosen large enough, this approach produces essentially the correct answer.

Efficient Sets when E is Bounded

The methods used in this chapter are adaptations of the methods used to handle degeneracy in the simplex algorithm (see Dantzig, Orden, and Wolfe, 1955; or Dantzig, 1963). We will not discuss these methods as they apply to linear programming. We simply assume that (perhaps after removing redundant equations) the simplex or other algorithm hands us an optimum basic solution (that prices out), or informs us that E is unbounded (and provides us with a direction of increasing E), or informs us that the model is infeasible. The optimum E maximizing basic solution may or may not be unique or nondegenerate.

We first consider the case in which E is bounded above, but perhaps more than one feasible portfolio has this maximum value of E; perhaps the E maximizing portfolio is degenerate; and perhaps ties for λ_{low} are encountered in tracing out the set of efficient portfolios.

We will make use of an important property of polynomials:

$$p(x) = a_0 + a_1 x + a_2 x^2 + \ldots + a_n x^n$$

$$= \sum_{i=0}^{n} a_i x^i$$

as $x \downarrow 0$. The property will be stated as a lemma for ease of reference.

Lemma 9.1 If $p(x) = \Sigma_{i=0}^{n} a_i x^i$ and $a_i \neq 0$ for at least one value of i, then there is an $x^* > 0$ such that:

(i) Either $p(x) > 0$ for all x such that $0 < x < x^*$
(ii) Or else $p(x) < 0$ for all x such that $0 < x < x^*$.

If ω is the smallest value of i such that $a_i \neq 0$, then case (i) holds if $a_\omega > 0$; otherwise case (ii) holds.

Proof We may write $p(x)$ as

$$p(x) = a_\omega x^\omega (1 + x a_{\omega+1}/a_\omega + \ldots + x^{n-\omega} a_n / a_\omega)$$

(The notation here is not meant to exclude the case, for example, in which $\omega = n$ and hence $p(x) = a_n x^n$.) Since

$$1 + x a_{\omega+1}/a_\omega + \ldots + x^{n-\omega} a_n / a_\omega$$

is a continuous function of x which approaches one as $x \downarrow 0$, the sign of $p(x)$ is the same as that of a_ω for sufficiently small positive x. ###

When a linear programming problem is degenerate it is possible for a basis to be optimum but not "price out." In such a case, however, if we continue the simplex algorithm variables will enter and leave the basis until a basis is reached which not only is optimum but prices out. This is guaranteed as long as the objective E is bounded provided that the previously cited anticycling provisions are used (and typically happens without them anyway). When E is bounded we start the critical line portfolio selection algorithm with a basis which is not only E maximizing but also prices out.

Let $\tilde{A}$ be an E maximizing basis - not necessarily unique, not necessarily nondegenerate, but one which prices out. If we relabel the variables so that $IN = \{1, \ldots, m\}$ and use the notation of chapter 8 as summarized in table 8.1, we may write the E maximization problem as

$$\text{maximize} \quad E = \mu' \begin{pmatrix} \tilde{X} \\ \hat{X} \end{pmatrix} \tag{9.1a}$$

$$\text{subject to} \quad \tilde{X} = \tilde{b} - \hat{G}\hat{X} \tag{9.1b}$$

$$\begin{pmatrix} \tilde{X} \\ \hat{X} \end{pmatrix} \geqslant 0 \tag{9.1c}$$

We define the *perturbed E-maximization problem* as follows:

$$E = (\mu - v^{\epsilon})' X \tag{9.2a}$$

$$(I, \hat{G}) \begin{pmatrix} \tilde{X} \\ \hat{X} \end{pmatrix} = \tilde{b} + w^{\epsilon} \tag{9.2b}$$

$$\begin{pmatrix} \tilde{X} \\ \hat{X} \end{pmatrix} \geqslant 0 \tag{9.2c}$$

where

$$v^{\epsilon} = (\epsilon^{n}, \epsilon^{n-1}, \ldots, \epsilon)' \tag{9.2d}$$

$$w^{\epsilon} = (\epsilon^{n+1}, \epsilon^{2(n+1)}, \ldots, \epsilon^{m(n+1)})' \tag{9.2e}$$

Recall that the constraints (9.1b) are obtained by multiplying the constraints

$$(\tilde{A}, \hat{A}) \begin{pmatrix} \tilde{X} \\ \hat{X} \end{pmatrix} = b \tag{9.3a}$$

by $\tilde{A}^{-1}$ on the left, on both sides of course, producing the alternate way of writing the same constraints, namely

$$(I, \tilde{A}^{-1}\hat{A}) \begin{pmatrix} \tilde{X} \\ \hat{X} \end{pmatrix} = \tilde{A}^{-1} b \tag{9.3b}$$

The form (9.3a) may be recovered from (9.3b) by multiplying both sides of (9.3b) on the left by $\tilde{A}$. Similarly, multiplying both sides of (9.2b) by $\tilde{A}$ we find that an alternate way of expressing the equations in (9.2b) is

$$AX = b + \bar{A}w^{\epsilon} \tag{9.2b$'$}$$

where X is still ordered so that $IN = \{1, \ldots, m\}$. For the present discussion, (9.2b) will usually be the more convenient of the two equivalent forms of the constraint equations. In the remainder of this section, unless otherwise specified, we assume that the model has been thus rewritten. When we speak of the $\bar{A}$ associated with a given IN set, this is derived from the A matrix in (9.2b) in the manner defined for equation (7.6). As we consider alternate IN sets, the $\bar{A}$ in (9.3) does not change but remains the E maximizing basis.

Theorem 9.2 Using the above notation - in particular, assuming that variables have been reordered so that $IN = \{1, 2, \ldots, m\}$ is an E maximizing basis which prices out - there is an $\epsilon^* > 0$ such that $\tilde{X}$ in (9.2b) with $\hat{X} = 0$ provides the unique, nondegenerate solution to the perturbed problem in (9.2) for all models with ϵ in the range $0 < \epsilon < \epsilon^*$.

Proof Since $\bar{b} \geqslant 0$ and $w^{\epsilon} > 0$, for any $\epsilon > 0$ we have $\tilde{X} > 0$. Hence $\tilde{X}$ is still feasible and, in fact, nondegenerate. To show that $\tilde{X}$ is still optimum, and now the unique optimum, we will determine prices π^{ϵ} for this basis of the perturbed problem, and price out the variables not in the basis.

Since the first m columns of $(I, \hat{G})$ are the identity matrix, from (8.10a) we know that

$$\pi^{\epsilon} + \tilde{\mu} - \tilde{\epsilon} = 0$$

i.e.

$$\pi^{\epsilon} = -\tilde{\mu} + \tilde{\epsilon}$$

where $\tilde{\mu}$ and $\tilde{\epsilon}$ are vectors containing the first m components of μ and v^{ϵ} respectively. Note that $\tilde{\epsilon}$ is a vector, short for $\tilde{v}^{\epsilon}$, rather than a scalar like ϵ and ϵ^*. For j *OUT*, the profitability of A_j' - the jth column of $(I, \hat{G})$ - is

$$\begin{aligned} A_j'\pi^{\epsilon} + \mu_j - \epsilon^{n+1-j} &= A_j'(-\tilde{\mu} + \tilde{\epsilon}) + \mu_j - \epsilon^{n+1-j} \\ &\leqslant A_j'\tilde{\epsilon} - \epsilon^{n+1-j} \end{aligned}$$

since $-A_j'\tilde{\mu} + \mu_j \leqslant 0$ - else $(\tilde{X}', 0)$ would not have at least tied for the optimum solution to (9.1). But, since $j > m, A_j'\tilde{\epsilon}$ is a polynomial with powers of ϵ exceeding ϵ^{n+1-j}. Therefore the lowest power of the polynomial $-\epsilon^{n+1-j} + A_j'\tilde{\epsilon}$ has a negative coefficient; hence, by lemma 9.1, for $j > m$ there is an $\epsilon_j^* > 0$ such that the profitability of the jth vector is negative for positive $\epsilon < \epsilon_j^*$. The theorem follows by choosing ϵ^* to be any positive number no greater than the smallest such ϵ_j^*. ###

If we add $V = X'CX$ to (9.1a, b, c) we have what we will refer to as the *original* or *unperturbed* portfolio selection model. If we add $V = X'CX$ to (9.2a, b, c) we have the *perturbed portfolio selection model*. The constraints of this model could be written using (9.2b′), but (9.2b) will be more convenient.

If a particular $IN \subset \{1, 2, \ldots, n\}$ defines a critical line - that is, has a non-singular $\bar{M}$ - in the original model, then it defines a critical line in the perturbed model for all ϵ; since ϵ does not affect $\bar{M}$.

With the constraint equations written as in (9.2b) rather than (9.2b′), the (X', λ') values on a critical line are given by

$$\begin{pmatrix} X \\ \lambda \end{pmatrix} = \bar{M}^{-1}\begin{pmatrix} 0 \\ \tilde{b} + w^{\epsilon} \end{pmatrix} + \bar{M}^{-1}\begin{pmatrix} \bar{\mu}^{\epsilon} \\ 0 \end{pmatrix} \lambda_E \tag{9.4a}$$

where $\mu^{\epsilon} = \mu - v^{\epsilon}$, and the relationship between μ^{ϵ} and $\bar{\mu}^{\epsilon}$ is defined in chapter 7 preceding equation (7.6).

The element in the ith row, jth column of $\bar{M}^{-1}$ will be denoted by a_i^j. This is commonly denoted by $\bar{a}^{ij}$, but the complexity of the superscripts to be used below makes the adopted notation more convenient. While the bar has been omitted from a_i^j, since it is an element of $\bar{M}^{-1}$ it does depend on the IN set.

For i IN, the ith equation of (9.4a) may be written as

$$X_i = \sum_{k=1}^{m} a_i^{n+k}[\tilde{b}_k + \epsilon^{k(n+1)}] + \lambda_E\left[\sum_{k=1}^{n} a_i^k(\bar{\mu}_k - \bar{\epsilon}^{n+1-k})\right] \tag{9.4b}$$

where $\bar{\epsilon}^{n+1-k} = 0$ if k is OUT and equals ϵ^{n+1-k} if k is IN. Equation (9.4b) may also be written as

$$X_i = \alpha_i^0 + \sum_{k=1}^{m} a_i^{n+k}\epsilon^{k(n+1)} + \lambda_E\left(\beta_i^0 - \sum_{k=1}^{n} a_i^k\bar{\epsilon}^{n+1-k}\right) \tag{9.4c}$$

where

$$\alpha_i^0 = \sum_{k=1}^{m} a_i^{n+k}\tilde{b}_k \tag{9.4d}$$

$$\beta_i^0 = \sum_{k=1}^{n} a_i^k\bar{\mu}_k \tag{9.4e}$$

α_i^0 and β_i^0 are the α_i and β_i of the unperturbed model. More generally we define

$$\begin{aligned} \alpha_i^{\epsilon} &= \alpha_i^0 + \sum_{k=1}^{m} a_i^{n+k}\,\epsilon^{k(n+1)} \\ &= \alpha_i^0 + p_i(\epsilon) \end{aligned} \tag{9.4f}$$

$$\beta_i^\epsilon = \beta_i^0 - \sum_{k=1}^{n} a_i^k \bar{\epsilon}^{n+1-k} \tag{9.4g}$$
$$= \beta_i^0 + q_i(\epsilon)$$

for $i = 1, \ldots, m+n$.

Since α_i^ϵ, β_i^ϵ are the α_i and β_i for the given ϵ, we have (for the given critical line)

$$X_i = \alpha_i^\epsilon + \beta_i^\epsilon \lambda_E \qquad \text{for } i = 1, \ldots, n \tag{9.5a}$$

$$\lambda_k = \alpha_{n+k}^\epsilon + \beta_{n+k}^\epsilon \lambda_E \qquad \text{for } k = 1, \ldots, m \tag{9.5b}$$

Strictly speaking α_i^ϵ and β_i^ϵ should have a subscript or superscript denoting the particular *IN* set for which they apply. We leave this implicit.

The formula for η on a given critical line of the perturbed problem is

$$\eta = (C, A')\begin{pmatrix} X \\ \lambda \end{pmatrix} - (\mu - v^\epsilon)\lambda_E$$
$$= (C, A')(\alpha^\epsilon + \beta^\epsilon \lambda_E) - (\mu - v^\epsilon)\lambda_E$$
$$= (C, A')\alpha^\epsilon + ((C, A')\beta^\epsilon - \mu + v^\epsilon)\lambda_E$$
$$= \gamma^\epsilon + \delta^\epsilon \lambda_E \tag{9.6a}$$

where

$$\gamma_i^\epsilon = \gamma_i^0 + \sum_{k=1}^{n} \sigma_{ik} \sum_{l=1}^{m} a_k^{n+l} \epsilon^{l(n+1)} + \sum_{k=1}^{m} a_{ki} \sum_{l=1}^{m} a_{n+k}^{n+l} \epsilon^{l(n+1)} \tag{9.6b}$$

$$\delta_i^\epsilon = \delta_i^0 + \epsilon^{n+1-i} - \sum_{k=1}^{n} \sigma_{ik} \sum_{l=1}^{n} a_k^l \epsilon^{n+1-l} - \sum_{k=1}^{m} a_{ki} \sum_{l=1}^{n} a_{n+k}^l \bar{\epsilon}^{n+1-k} \tag{9.6c}$$

where γ_i^0 and δ_i^0 are the γ_i and δ_i of the unperturbed model.

Crucial results concerning the perturbed model are that for sufficiently small positive ϵ^* the model is nondegenerate, and the sequence of *IN* sets which provides the efficient set for the perturbed model is the same for all ϵ in the range $0 < \epsilon < \epsilon^*$. These results follow easily from the facts, to be shown below, that:

(1) If neither α_i^ϵ, β_i^ϵ, α_j^ϵ, nor β_j^ϵ is identically zero - i.e. zero for all values of ϵ - then either $\alpha_i^\epsilon/\beta_i^\epsilon < \alpha_j^\epsilon/\beta_j^\epsilon$ or $\alpha_j^\epsilon/\beta_j^\epsilon < \alpha_i^\epsilon/\beta_i^\epsilon$ for all ϵ in an interval $0 < \epsilon < \epsilon^*$.

(2) If neither γ_i^ϵ, δ_i^ϵ, γ_j^ϵ, nor δ_j^ϵ is identically zero then either $\gamma_i^\epsilon/\delta_i^\epsilon < \gamma_j^\epsilon/\delta_j^\epsilon$ or $\gamma_j^\epsilon/\delta_j^\epsilon < \gamma_i^\epsilon/\delta_i^\epsilon$ for all ϵ in some interval $0 < \epsilon < \epsilon^*$.

(3) If neither α_i^ϵ, β_i^ϵ, γ_j^ϵ, nor δ_j^ϵ are identically zero then either $\alpha_i^\epsilon/\beta_i^\epsilon < \gamma_j^\epsilon/\delta_j^\epsilon$ or $\gamma_j^\epsilon/\delta_j^\epsilon < \alpha_i^\epsilon/\beta_i^\epsilon$ for all ϵ in some interval $0 < \epsilon < \epsilon^*$.

Unfortunately the establishment of (1)-(3) is rather tedious. In chapter 4 we put certain more advanced or tedious material in an appendix. Here we may think of the following material, through theorem 9.11, as one long appendix. Exercise for the advanced reader: find a simpler way to prove theorems 9.12-9.14.

We begin with the proofs of (2) and (3), which are easier than (1).

Lemma 9.3 Suppose j is *OUT*. Then among all the polynomials in ϵ:

α_i^ϵ for $i = 1, \ldots, m+n$

β_i^ϵ for $i = 1, \ldots, m+n$

γ_i^ϵ for $i = 1, \ldots, n$

δ_i^ϵ for $i = 1, \ldots, n$

only δ_j^ϵ has a nonzero coefficient for ϵ^{n+1-j}.

Proof This follows from (9.4f), (9.4g), (9.6b), (9.6c), and the fact that $\bar{\epsilon}^{n+1-j} = 0$ for j *OUT*. ###

Theorem 9.4 For $i \neq j$, if neither γ_i^ϵ, δ_i^ϵ, γ_j^ϵ, nor δ_j^ϵ is identically zero, then there is $\epsilon^* > 0$ such that $\delta_i^\epsilon \neq 0$ and $\delta_j^\epsilon \neq 0$ for positive $\epsilon < \epsilon^*$. Furthermore, either

$$\gamma_i^\epsilon/\delta_i^\epsilon < \gamma_j^\epsilon/\delta_j^\epsilon \qquad \text{for all } 0 < \epsilon < \epsilon^*$$

or else

$$\gamma_j^\epsilon/\delta_j^\epsilon < \gamma_i^\epsilon/\delta_i^\epsilon \qquad \text{for all } 0 < \epsilon < \epsilon^*$$

Proof Since δ_i^ϵ is a polynomial in ϵ and is not zero for all ϵ, lemma 9.1 implies the existence of an ϵ^{*1} such that δ_i^ϵ is either always positive or always negative for all $0 < \epsilon < \epsilon^{*1}$. There is similarly an $\epsilon^{*2} > 0$ such that δ_j^ϵ is either always positive or always negative for positive $\epsilon < \epsilon^{*2}$. The ϵ^* of the theorem is chosen no greater than $\min(\epsilon^{*1}, \epsilon^{*2})$, and perhaps smaller depending on the following considerations.

For $\delta_i^\epsilon \neq 0$ and $\delta_j^\epsilon \neq 0$, the condition

$$\gamma_i^\epsilon/\delta_i^\epsilon < \gamma_j^\epsilon/\delta_j^\epsilon \tag{9.7a}$$

is equivalent to the condition

$$\gamma_i^\epsilon \delta_j^\epsilon - \gamma_j^\epsilon \delta_i^\epsilon < 0 \tag{9.7b}$$

Similarly

$$\gamma_i^\epsilon/\delta_i^\epsilon > \gamma_j^\epsilon/\delta_j^\epsilon \tag{9.7c}$$

is true if and only if

$$\gamma_i^\epsilon \delta_j^\epsilon - \gamma_j^\epsilon \delta_i^\epsilon > 0 \tag{9.7d}$$

If we can show that the polynomial in ϵ on the left-hand side of (9.7b) and (9.7d) is not identically zero, it follows from lemma 9.1 that there is an ϵ^* such that either (9.7b) or (9.7d), and therefore either (9.7a) or (9.7c), holds for all ϵ in the interval $0 < \epsilon < \epsilon^*$. The polynomial in (9.7b) and (9.7d) is identically zero if and only if all its coefficients are zero, which is true if and only if the polynomial (in ϵ) $\gamma_i^\epsilon \delta_j^\epsilon$ is the same as the polynomial $\gamma_j^\epsilon \delta_i^\epsilon$.

Since $\delta_i^\epsilon \neq 0$ we must have *i OUT*; thus lemma 9.3 assures us that, of the four polynomials γ_i^ϵ, γ_j^ϵ, δ_i^ϵ, δ_j^ϵ, only δ_i^ϵ has a nonzero coefficient for ϵ^{n+1-i}. Since γ_j^ϵ is a polynomial in powers of $\epsilon^{k(n+1)}$ for $k = 0, 1, \ldots, m$, and γ_j^ϵ is not identically zero, $\gamma_j^\epsilon \delta_i^\epsilon$ has a nonzero coefficient for $\epsilon^{k(n+1)+(n+1-i)}$ for some k. But, since γ_i^ϵ is a polynomial in $\epsilon^{k(n+1)}$ for $k = 0, 1, \ldots, m$ and δ_j^ϵ is a polynomial in $\epsilon^0, \epsilon^1, \ldots, \epsilon^n$ (excluding ϵ^{n+1-i}) $\gamma_i^\epsilon \delta_j^\epsilon$ cannot have a nonzero coefficient for $\epsilon^{k(n+1)+(n+1-i)}$. ###

Theorem 9.5 If neither γ_i^ϵ, δ_i^ϵ, α_j^ϵ, nor β_j^ϵ is identically zero, then there is an $\epsilon^* > 0$ such that $\delta_i^\epsilon \neq 0$ and $\beta_j^\epsilon \neq 0$ for positive $\epsilon < \epsilon^*$. Furthermore, either

$$\gamma_i^\epsilon / \delta_i^\epsilon < \alpha_j^\epsilon / \beta_j^\epsilon$$

or

$$\alpha_j^\epsilon / \beta_j^\epsilon < \gamma_i^\epsilon / \delta_i^\epsilon$$

for all $0 < \epsilon < \epsilon^*$.

Proof The proof of the first sentence is the same as the proof of the first sentence of theorem 9.4. The proof of the second sentence of theorem 9.4 rests on the fact that, among the four terms that appear in (9.7a), only δ_i^ϵ has a nonzero coefficient for ϵ^{n+1-i}. In the present theorem, two of the terms are α_j^ϵ and β_j^ϵ rather than γ_j^ϵ and δ_j^ϵ. It is still true that of the four terms only δ_i^ϵ has a nonzero coefficient for ϵ^{n+1-i}. The proof of the present theorem can therefore be carried out almost exactly like the proof of the preceding theorem, using for example the fact that α_j^ϵ (like γ_j^ϵ of the prior proof) is a polynomial in powers of $\epsilon^{k(n+1)}$. ###

$p_i(\epsilon)$ and $q_i(\epsilon)$, defined in (9.4f) and (9.4g), are homogeneous polynomials. If α_i^ϵ is not identically zero than either $\alpha_i^0 \neq 0$ or else $p_i(\epsilon)$ is not identically zero, or both. A similar statement applies to β_i^ϵ, β_i^0, and $q_i(\epsilon)$.

Define

$$p_{ij}(\epsilon) = \alpha_i^\epsilon \beta_j^\epsilon - \alpha_j^\epsilon \beta_i^\epsilon \tag{9.8a}$$

$$= [\alpha_i^0 + p_i(\epsilon)]\,[\beta_j^0 + q_j(\epsilon)] - [\alpha_j^0 + p_j(\epsilon)]\,[\beta_i^0 + q_i(\epsilon)] \tag{9.8b}$$

$$= [\alpha_i^0 \beta_j^0 - \alpha_j^0 \beta_i^0] + [\beta_j^0 p_i(\epsilon) - \beta_i^0 p_j(\epsilon)] + [\alpha_i^0 q_j(\epsilon) - \alpha_j^0 q_i(\epsilon)] + [p_i(\epsilon)\, q_j(\epsilon) - p_j(\epsilon)\, q_i(\epsilon)] \tag{9.8c}$$

Our next task is to show that (for $i \neq j$) if none of the four component polynomials α_i^ϵ, β_i^ϵ, α_j^ϵ, β_j^ϵ is identically zero then $p_{ij}(\epsilon)$ is not identically zero. We shall distinguish various cases depending upon which subset of the constants α_i^0, β_i^0, α_j^0, β_j^0 is zero. Lemmas 9.6 through 9.10 each show that if the component polynomials are not identically zero, yet the $p_{ij}(\epsilon)$ polynomial is identically zero, then certain cases cannot occur. In total these lemmas will show that no such case can occur.

Lemma 9.6 For $i \neq j$, if neither α_i^ϵ, β_i^ϵ, α_j^ϵ, nor β_j^ϵ is identically zero, whereas $p_{ij}(\epsilon)$ is identically zero, then it cannot be true that $\alpha_i^0 = 0$ and $\alpha_j^0 \neq 0$.

Proof We will assume $\alpha_i^0 = 0$ and $\alpha_j^0 \neq 0$, as well as the premises of the lemma, and derive a contradiction. Since the constant term of $p_{ij}(\epsilon)$ is $\alpha_i^0\beta_j^0 - \alpha_j^0\beta_i^0$, and this constant term must be zero for $p_{ij}(\epsilon)$ to be identically zero, $\alpha_i^0 = 0$ and $\alpha_j^0 \neq 0$ imply $\beta_i^0 = 0$; therefore $q_i(\epsilon)$ is not identically zero; therefore (from (9.4g)) there is an $a_i^k \neq 0$ for some k: $1 \leqslant k \leqslant n$. Equations (9.8c) and (9.4g) imply that the coefficient of the term ϵ^{n+1-k} in $p_{ij}(\epsilon)$ is $-(\alpha_i^0 a_j^k - \alpha_j^0 a_i^k)$. But this term must be zero for $p_{ij}(\epsilon)$ to be identically zero; therefore $\alpha_i^0 = 0$ and $a_i^k \neq 0$ imply $\alpha_j^0 = 0$, contradicting the assumption that $\alpha_j^0 \neq 0$. ###

Lemma 9.7 For $i \neq j$, if neither α_i^ϵ, β_i^ϵ, α_j^ϵ, nor β_j^ϵ is identically zero, whereas $p_{ij}(\epsilon)$ is identically zero, then it cannot be true that $\beta_i^0 = 0$ and $\beta_j^0 \neq 0$.

Proof The proof is essentially the same as that for lemma 9.6. In particular the assumptions that $\beta_i^0 = 0$, $\beta_j^0 \neq 0$, and $p_{ij}(\epsilon)$ is identically zero imply that $\alpha_i^0 = 0$; therefore $p_i(\epsilon)$ is not identically zero; therefore (9.4f) implies that there is an $a_i^{n+k} \neq 0$ for some k: $1 \leqslant k \leqslant m$. Equations (9.8c) and (9.4f) imply that the coefficient of $\epsilon^{k(n+1)}$ in $p_{ij}(\epsilon)$ is $(\beta_i^0 a_j^{n+k} - \beta_j^0 a_i^{n+k})$; but this and the preceding considerations imply that $\beta_j^0 = 0$, contradicting the assumption that $\beta_i^0 = 0$ and $\beta_j^0 \neq 0$. ###

Lemmas 9.6 and 9.7 leave open the following possibilities:

(1) $\alpha_i^0, \alpha_j^0, \beta_i^0, \beta_j^0$ are all nonzero
(2) $\alpha_i^0, \alpha_j^0, \beta_i^0, \beta_j^0$ are all zero
(3) α_i^0, α_j^0 are zero but β_i^0, β_j^0 are nonzero
(4) β_i^0, β_j^0 are zero but α_i^0, α_j^0 are nonzero.

The following three lemmas will dispose of these four possibilities.

Lemma 9.8 For $i \neq j$, if neither α_i^ϵ, β_i^ϵ, α_j^ϵ, nor β_j^ϵ is identically zero, whereas $p_{ij}(\epsilon)$ is identically zero, then it cannot be true that $\alpha_i^0 \neq 0, \beta_i^0 \neq 0, \alpha_j^0 \neq 0$, and $\beta_j^0 \neq 0$.

Proof Suppose it were true that $\alpha_i^0 \neq 0, \beta_i^0 \neq 0, \alpha_j^0 \neq 0, \beta_j^0 \neq 0$. Since the terms $[\alpha_i^0\beta_j^0 - \alpha_j^0\beta_i^0]$, $[\beta_j^0 p_i(\epsilon) - \beta_i^0 p_j(\epsilon)]$, and $[\alpha_i^0 q_j(\epsilon) - \alpha_j^0 q_i(\epsilon)]$ must each be zero for $p_{ij}(\epsilon)$ to be identically zero, (9.8c) and the assumption that $p_{ij}(\epsilon)$ is identically zero imply that

$$\frac{\alpha_i^0}{\alpha_j^0} = \frac{\beta_i^0}{\beta_j^0} = r \neq 0 \tag{9.9a}$$

$$p_i(\epsilon) = rp_j(\epsilon) \tag{9.9b}$$

$$q_i(\epsilon) = rq_j(\epsilon) \tag{9.9c}$$

From (9.4f) and (9.4g) we may rewrite (9.9b) and (9.9c) as

$$a_i^k = ra_j^k \qquad \text{for } k = 1, \ldots, m + n$$

This says that the ith row of $\bar{M}^{-1}$ is proportional to its jth row; hence $\bar{M}^{-1}$ is singular. But this is impossible since $\bar{M}$ is its inverse. ###

Lemma 9.9 For $i \neq j$, if neither α_i^ϵ, β_i^ϵ, α_j^ϵ, β_j^ϵ is identically zero whereas $p_{ij}(\epsilon)$ is identically zero, then it cannot be true that $\alpha_i^0 = \alpha_j^0 = 0$ and $\beta_i^0 \neq 0$, $\beta_j^0 \neq 0$. Also it cannot be true that $\beta_i^0 = \beta_j^0 = 0$ and $\alpha_i^0 \neq 0, \alpha_j^0 \neq 0$.

Proof We will prove the first of these two assertions. The second can be shown in an almost identical manner. Since the term $[\beta_i^0 p_j(\epsilon) - \beta_j^0 p_i(\epsilon)]$ in (9.8c) must be identically zero for $p_{ij}(\epsilon)$ to be identically zero, we have

$$p_i(\epsilon) = p_j(\epsilon)\, \beta_i^0/\beta_j^0$$

or, from (9.4f),

$$a_i^{n+k} = ra_j^{n+k} \qquad \text{for } k = 1, \ldots, m \tag{9.10}$$

where $r = \beta_i^0/\beta_j^0$. From $\alpha_i^0 = 0$, whereas α_i^ϵ is not identically zero, we infer from (9.4f) that there is a k $(1 \leqslant k \leqslant m)$ such that $a_i^{n+k} \neq 0$, and from (9.10) that $a_j^{n+k} \neq 0$ for the same k. But this implies that, for the particular k, the kth equation of (9.10) may be written as

$$\frac{a_i^{n+k}}{a_j^{n+k}} = \frac{\beta_i^0}{\beta_j^0} = r \tag{9.11}$$

Also, the coefficient of $\epsilon^{k(n+1)+(n+1-l)}$ in $p_{ij}(\epsilon)$, namely

$$a_j^l a_i^{n+k} - a_i^l a_j^{n+k}$$

must equal zero for $l = 1, \ldots, n$. This implies that for the k in (9.11)

$$a_i^l = \frac{a_i^{n+k}}{a_j^{n+k}} a_j^l$$

i.e.

$$a_i^l = r a_j^l \qquad \text{for } l = 1, \ldots, n \tag{9.12}$$

Combining (9.10) and (9.12) we see that our assumptions imply that the ith row of $\bar{M}^{-1}$ is proportional to the jth which, as in lemma 9.8, implies a contradiction.

###

Lemma 9.10 For $i \neq j$, if $\alpha_i^\epsilon, \beta_i^\epsilon, \alpha_j^\epsilon, \beta_j^\epsilon$ are not identically zero whereas $p_{ij}(\epsilon)$ is identically zero, then it cannot be true that $\alpha_i^0 = \beta_i^0 = \alpha_j^0 = \beta_j^0 = 0$.

Proof We will assume $\alpha_i^0 = \beta_i^0 = \alpha_j^0 = \beta_j^0 = 0$ and derive a contradiction. Since α_i^ϵ is not identically zero but $\alpha_i^0 = 0$, there is a k $(1 \leqslant k \leqslant m)$ such that $a_i^{n+k} \neq 0$. Similarly, since β_j^ϵ is not identically zero but $\beta_j^0 = 0$, there is an l $(1 \leqslant l \leqslant n)$ such that $a_j^l \neq 0$. Since the coefficient $(a_i^{n+k} a_j^l - a_j^{n+k} a_i^l)$ must be zero for $p_{ij}(\epsilon)$ to be identically zero, we infer that none of the four terms is zero, and that

$$\frac{a_i^{n+k}}{a_j^{n+k}} = \frac{a_i^l}{a_j^l}$$

$$= r \neq 0$$

for the particular k and l. From $a_i^{n+k}/a_j^{n+k} = r \neq 0$, and

$$a_i^{n+k} a_j^q - a_j^{n+k} a_i^q = 0$$

for $1 \leqslant q \leqslant n$, we infer

$$a_i^q = r a_j^q \qquad \text{for } 1 \leqslant q \leqslant n$$

Similarly $a_i^l / a_j^l = r \neq 0$ and

$$a_i^{n+s} a_j^l - a_j^{n+s} a_i^l = 0$$

for $1 \leqslant s \leqslant m$ imply

$$a_i^q = r a_j^q \qquad \text{for } n+1 \leqslant q \leqslant n+m$$

Thus the ith row of $\bar{M}^{-1}$ is proportional to the jth – implying a contradiction.

###

Theorem 9.11 For $i \neq j$ on any critical line of the perturbed model, if neither $\alpha_i^\epsilon, \beta_i^\epsilon, \alpha_j^\epsilon$, nor β_j^ϵ is identically zero then $p_{ij}(\epsilon)$ is not identically zero.

Proof Lemmas 9.7 through 9.10 imply that no assignment of values to $\alpha_i^0, \beta_i^0, \alpha_j^0, \beta_j^0$ is consistent with the assertion that neither $\alpha_i^\epsilon, \beta_i^\epsilon, \alpha_j^\epsilon$, nor β_j^ϵ is identically zero, whereas $p_{ij}(\epsilon)$ is identically zero. Therefore the present theorem follows.

###

Theorem 9.12 For any perturbed portfolio selection model there is an $\epsilon^* > 0$ such that for all ϵ in the interval $0 < \epsilon < \epsilon^*$ the perturbed model is nondegenerate.

Proof For any given portfolio selection model, such as the perturbed model for a particular $\epsilon > 0$, degeneracy is defined in terms of those α_i and β_i such that $\alpha_i \neq 0$ and $\beta_i \neq 0$, and those γ_i and δ_i such that $\gamma_i \neq 0$ and $\delta_i \neq 0$. Thus if either α_i^ϵ or β_i^ϵ is identically zero then the values of α_i^ϵ and β_i^ϵ will not enter into the determination of the degeneracy or nondegeneracy of the model; and similarly if either γ_i^ϵ or δ_i^ϵ is identically zero then the values of γ_i^ϵ and δ_i^ϵ will not enter into the determination of the degeneracy of the model. For every critical line l, and every α_i^ϵ not identically zero, there is an $\epsilon_{li}^* > 0$ such that, for all positive ϵ less than this value, α_i^ϵ is either always negative or else always positive. Similar statements apply for every critical line and every β_i^ϵ, γ_i^ϵ, and δ_i^ϵ which is not identically zero. Since there are a finite number of combinations of l and i we may choose ϵ^* small enough so that all α_i^ϵ, β_i^ϵ, γ_i^ϵ, and δ_i^ϵ which are not identically zero are of one or the other sign for all positive $\epsilon < \epsilon^*$.

With ϵ^* thus chosen, no α_i^ϵ, β_i^ϵ, γ_i^ϵ, δ_i^ϵ will equal zero unless it is identically zero - for all positive $\epsilon < \epsilon^*$. Theorem 9.11 further assures us that for suitably chosen $\hat{\epsilon}$, perhaps smaller than ϵ^* but still positive, it will not happen that

$$\alpha_i^\epsilon/\beta_i^\epsilon = \alpha_j^\epsilon/\beta_j^\epsilon$$

$$\alpha_i^\epsilon/\beta_i^\epsilon = \gamma_j^\epsilon/\delta_j^\epsilon$$

$$\gamma_i^\epsilon/\delta_i^\epsilon = \gamma_j^\epsilon/\delta_j^\epsilon$$

for any $\hat{\epsilon} > \epsilon > 0$, for any $(\alpha_i^\epsilon, \beta_i^\epsilon)$ and $(\gamma_i^\epsilon, \delta_i^\epsilon)$ pairs in which neither member of the pair is identically zero. Thus the definition of nondegeneracy is fulfilled for all ϵ in the interval $\hat{\epsilon} > \epsilon > 0$. ###

Since the perturbed model is nondegenerate for sufficiently small ϵ, if E is bounded above then theorem 7.11 assures us that there is a complete non-redundant piecewise linear set of efficient portfolios. The following theorem compares the *IN* sets of the solution for one ϵ with that of another small ϵ.

Theorem 9.13 In any perturbed portfolio selection model with E bounded above, there exists an $\epsilon^* > 0$ such that for ϵ in the interval $0 < \epsilon < \epsilon^*$ there is a unique sequence of *IN* sets - $IN_1, IN_2, \ldots, IN_L$ - which provides a piecewise linear nonredundant set of efficient portfolios, and this sequence of *IN* sets is the same for all such ϵ. (Note that we now number the *IN* sets and their critical lines 1, 2, 3,... rather than 0, 1, 2,.... In particular there are L, rather than $L + 1$, pieces in the complete nonredundant set.)

Proof IN_1 is unique for sufficiently small $\epsilon^* > 0$ by theorem 9.2. Repeatedly using theorem 9.12 we see that (unless $\lambda_E = 0$ is reached on l^1) a unique $\eta_i \downarrow 0$ determines IN_2; a unique $X_i \downarrow 0$ or $\eta_i \downarrow 0$ determines IN_3; and so on until the critical line is reached on which $\lambda_E \downarrow 0$. ###

Theorem 9.14 In a feasible portfolio selection problem with E bounded above, let $IN_1, IN_2, \ldots, IN_L$ be the IN sets in theorem 9.13 for the perturbed model for small ϵ. Let $l^1, l^2, \ldots, l^L$ be the corresponding critical lines. For some K: $0 \leqslant K < L$, the first K critical lines have $\lambda_{\text{low}} \to \infty$ as $\epsilon \to 0$. On the following $L-K$ critical lines λ_{low} remains finite as $\epsilon \to 0$. The efficient set for the original problem consists of the IN sets $IN_{K+1}, \ldots, IN_L$ and the corresponding critical lines with $\epsilon = 0$. In particular, the portfolio on l^L at $\lambda_E = 0$ is an efficient portfolio with minimum feasible variance.

Proof Let $\lambda_{\text{low}}^k(\epsilon)$ be the value of λ_{low} on the kth critical line with $0 < \epsilon < \epsilon^*$ in theorem 9.13. Always $\lambda_{\text{low}}^L(\epsilon) = 0$. For $k < L$ we have either

$$\lambda_{\text{low}}^k(\epsilon) = -\alpha_i^\epsilon / \beta_i^\epsilon$$

or

$$\lambda_{\text{low}}^k(\epsilon) = -\gamma_i^\epsilon / \delta_i^\epsilon$$

for some i for which neither α_i^ϵ nor β_i^ϵ (or neither γ_i^ϵ nor δ_i^ϵ) is identically zero. Since for ϵ in the interval $0 < \epsilon < \epsilon^*$ we do not have $\beta_i^\epsilon = 0$ (or $\delta_i^\epsilon = 0$, as appropriate), $\lambda_{\text{low}}^k(\epsilon)$ is a continuous function of ϵ and, as a ratio of two polynomials, has a (finite or infinite) limit as $\epsilon \downarrow 0$. Let

$$\hat{\lambda}^k = \lim_{\epsilon \downarrow 0} \lambda_{\text{low}}^k(\epsilon)$$

(It may happen that $\hat{\lambda}^k = \hat{\lambda}^{k+1}$ in one or more instances.) Since $\lambda_{\text{low}}^1(\epsilon) > \lambda_{\text{low}}^2(\epsilon)$ for all $0 < \epsilon < \epsilon^*$, it follows that $\hat{\lambda}^1 \geqslant \hat{\lambda}^2$. In particular, if $\hat{\lambda}^2 = \infty$ then $\hat{\lambda}^1 = \infty$. Repeated application of this argument implies that for some $K \geqslant 0$

$$\hat{\lambda}^i = \infty \qquad \text{for } i \leqslant K$$

Now let us consider some (finite) $\lambda_E = \bar{\lambda} \neq \hat{\lambda}^k$ for $k = K+1, \ldots, L$. In other words, let $\bar{\lambda} > \hat{\lambda}^{K+1}$ or strictly between $\hat{\lambda}^h$ and $\hat{\lambda}^{h+1}$ for $h \geqslant K+1$. Because of theorem 9.13 and the continuity of the $\lambda_{\text{low}}^k(\epsilon)$, there is a sufficiently small $\epsilon^* > 0$ such that the efficient portfolio with $\lambda_E = \bar{\lambda}$ is on the same critical line (i.e. has the same IN set) for all ϵ in the interval $0 < \epsilon < \epsilon^*$. If we fix this critical line (call it $k = \bar{k}$) and fix $\lambda_E = \bar{\lambda}$, but let ϵ vary, we get $X(\epsilon)$ and $\eta(\epsilon)$ as a function of ϵ. Since $\alpha^\epsilon, \beta^\epsilon, \gamma^\epsilon$, and δ^ϵ are continuous so are $X(\epsilon)$ and $\eta(\epsilon)$ as a function of ϵ at $\lambda_E = \bar{\lambda}$. Since $X(\epsilon)$ and $\eta(\epsilon)$ are continuous, including at $\epsilon = 0$, and $X(\epsilon) \geqslant 0$ and $\eta(\epsilon) \geqslant 0$ for $\epsilon^* > \epsilon > 0$, it follows that $X(0) \geqslant 0$, and $\eta(0) \geqslant 0$. (See exercise 9.2 concerning this "extension of inequalities.") Thus the critical line $k = \bar{k}$ is efficient in the original model with $\epsilon = 0$ for $\lambda_E = \bar{\lambda}$. But $\bar{\lambda}$ is any λ_E such that $\hat{\lambda}_E^h < \lambda < \hat{\lambda}^{h-1}$ if $h > K+1$ or else $\bar{\lambda} > \hat{\lambda}^{K+1}$.

Next let $\epsilon = 0$ and let $\lambda_E \downarrow \hat{\lambda}^k$ along any critical line l^k for $k \geqslant K+1$. We now consider $X(\lambda_E)$ and $\eta(\lambda_E)$ as functions of λ_E along this line. Since we have just seen that $X(\lambda_E) \geqslant 0$ and $\eta(\lambda_E) \geqslant 0$ for $\hat{\lambda}^k < \lambda_E < \hat{\lambda}^{k-1}$, and for $\lambda_E > \hat{\lambda}^{K+1}$, another application of the extension of inequalities implies that $X \geqslant 0$ and $\eta \geqslant 0$ for the relevant segments of $l^{K+1}, l^{K+2}, \ldots, l^L$ for $\lambda_E \geqslant 0$.

In particular, the point X_0 on l^L at $\lambda_E = 0$ provides minimum feasible V, and is shown to be efficient by an argument like that in the second paragraph of the proof of theorem 7.4. ###

In theorem 9.14, since E is bounded the fact that l_{K+1} remains efficient as $\lambda_E \to \infty$ shows that l_{K+1} provides one portfolio, and that this is the efficient portfolio which minimizes V subject to $\mu' X = \max E$, $AX = b$, $X \geqslant 0$ (see theorem 7.11). As to $l^1, \ldots, l^K$ (if $K > 0$), their portfolios have higher V for the same $\max E$.

Theorem 9.13 assures us that $IN_1, \ldots, IN_L$ is unique for a given perturbed problem. But there is more than one way to associate a perturbed problem (9.2) with a given original problem. First, if the E maximizing portfolio is not unique, it is possible that more than one optimum basis may price out. Any one of these may be chosen for the $\tilde{A}$ in (9.3). Second, the rows of the original problem could have been reordered arbitrarily; also the columns of $\tilde{A}$ and $\hat{A}$ could each be reordered to produce an alternate perturbed model. Since such reordering alters the powers of ϵ assigned to given constraint equations and securities, it may alter which X_i or η_i (in terms of the original ordering) is deemed to go to zero first. Theorems 9.13 and 9.14 do not assert that only one sequence of IN sets provides a complete nonredundant set of efficient portfolios. In fact, we shall see in chapter 11 that more than one such set can exist in degenerate models.

Lexicographical Ordering

It is not necessary to determine ϵ^* (of theorem 9.13) in order to determine $IN_1, IN_2, \ldots, IN_L$. IN_1 is the IN set of any E maximizing basis which prices out. Given IN_i we need to know (among other things to be discussed shortly) whether or not $\beta_i^\epsilon > 0$ for sufficiently small ϵ. This can be determined from the sign of the first nonzero coefficient of

$$\beta_i^\epsilon = \beta_i^0 + q_i(\epsilon)$$

i.e. the coefficient of the lowest power of ϵ. If this coefficient is positive then, for sufficiently small ϵ, $\beta_i^\epsilon > 0$. In this case, following terminology adapted from linear programming (see Dantzig, Orden, and Wolfe, 1955; or Dantzig, 1963), we will say that β_ϵ is *lexicographically* greater than zero, and write $\beta_i \succ 0$. Similarly we write $\beta_i \prec 0$ when, for sufficiently small ϵ, $\beta_i^\epsilon < 0$; and we write $\beta_i \not\approx 0$ when either $\beta_i \succ 0$ or $\beta_i \prec 0$.

To determine IN_{k+1} given IN_k, if i and j are members of IN_k, and if $\beta_i > 0$ and $\beta_j > 0$, we must determine whether

$$\alpha_i^\epsilon/\beta_i^\epsilon < \alpha_j^\epsilon/\beta_j^\epsilon$$

or

$$\alpha_j^\epsilon/\beta_j^\epsilon < \alpha_i^\epsilon/\beta_i^\epsilon$$

for sufficiently small ϵ. In the former case we write $\alpha_i/\beta_i \prec \alpha_j/\beta_j$, and say that α_i/β_i is lexicographically less than α_j/β_j. Theorem 9.13 assures us that if $\alpha_i \not\approx 0$, $\beta_i \not\approx 0$, $\alpha_j \not\approx 0$, and $\beta_j \not\approx 0$ then either $\alpha_i/\beta_i \prec \alpha_j/\beta_j$ or $\alpha_j/\beta_j \prec \alpha_i/\beta_i$. Whether the first or the second prevails is indicated by the sign of the first nonzero coefficient of $p_{ij}(\epsilon)$.

We may write

$$p_{ij}(\epsilon) = \sum_{k=0}^{m} \sum_{l=0}^{n} c_{kl}\epsilon^{k(n+1)+l} \tag{9.13}$$

where the c_{kl} can be inferred from (9.8c), (9.4f), and (9.4g). For example, $c_{00} = \alpha_i^0\beta_j^0 - \alpha_j^0\beta_i^0$. (In actually constructing the c_{kl} watch out for the difference in the sequence of terms between (9.13) and (9.4g).) If we check the c_{kl} in a certain order, namely in the order encountered in the following BASIC computer program

```
FOR  k = 0 TO m
     FOR l = 0 TO n
        ⟨check c_kl⟩
     NEXT l
NEXT k
```

then the first nonzero c_{kl} encountered determines whether $p_{ij}(\epsilon) > 0$ or $p_{ij}(\epsilon) < 0$. (This test need only be made for i and j such that i and j are IN, $X_i = X_j = 0$ at $\lambda_E = \lambda_{low}$ and both $\beta_i > 0$ and $\beta_j > 0$.)

Similarly if i is a member of IN_k and j is not, it can be determined whether

$$\alpha_i/\beta_i \succ \gamma_j/\delta_j$$

or

$$\alpha_i/\beta_i \prec \gamma_j/\delta_j$$

from the first nonzero coefficient of the polynomial

$$\alpha_i^\epsilon\delta_j^\epsilon - \gamma_j^\epsilon\beta_i^\epsilon$$

Again, if i and j are not members of IN_k then

$$\gamma_i/\delta_i > \gamma_j/\delta_j$$

or

$$\gamma_i/\delta_i < \gamma_j\delta_j$$

is indicated by the first nonzero coefficient of the polynomial

$$\gamma_i^\epsilon\delta_j^\epsilon - \gamma_j^\epsilon\delta_i^\epsilon$$

(See exercise 9.3.) The above tests need only be made for "appropriate" i and j; e.g. for j OUT, $\eta_j = 0$ at $\lambda_E = \lambda_{\text{low}}$, and $\delta_j > 0$.)

Unbounded E

It remains only to remove the assumption that E is bounded from above. For the case in which E is unbounded above, we define a new problem in which E is bounded, but whose solution will tell us the solution to the original problem with unbounded E. The *bounded problem* is

$$V = X'CX \tag{9.14a}$$

$$E = \mu'X \tag{9.14b}$$

$$AX = b \tag{9.14c}$$

$$\mu'X + X_{n+1} = b_{m+1} \tag{9.14d}$$

$$X \geqslant 0 \tag{9.14e}$$

$$X_{n+1} \geqslant 0 \tag{9.14f}$$

where b_{m+1}, the upper bound on $\mu'X$, is a large number in a sense to be defined.

For any given b_{m+1}, a perturbed problem (9.2) may be associated with the bounded problem (9.14). This perturbed problem may be solved, for small ϵ, by the critical line algorithm with lexicographical choice of i to go IN or OUT. The following theorem shows us that - for sufficiently large b_{m+1} - the solution to the perturbed bounded problem indicates the solution to the original unbounded problem.

Theorem 9.15 For any feasible (original) portfolio selection problem with E unbounded from above, there exists a b^*_{m+1} such that (in the associated bounded problem) for any $b_{m+1} \geqslant b^*_{m+1}$ the following is true: (i) the same IN_1 set, and therefore the same perturbed model, may be associated with the bounded model for all such b_{m+1} (in particular, there is an IN_1 set which maximizes E and prices out, for all $b_{m+1} \geqslant b^*_{m+1}$); and (ii) for this perturbed model the number K and the IN sets $IN_1, IN_2, \ldots, IN_L$ of theorems 9.13 and 9.14 are independent of the choice of b_{m+1}. If $L > K + 1$ then the critical lines $l^{K+2}, l^{K+3}, \ldots, l^L$ provide a complete nonredundant, piecewise linear efficient set for the original problem; i.e. the problem without constraints (9.14d) and (9.14f). In this case, in the set of efficient EV combinations, V is a strictly convex, piecewise parabolic function of E. If $L = K + 1$ then the original model has feasible portfolios but no efficient portfolios.

Proof First we will show that for sufficiently large b_{m+1}, IN_1 may be chosen independently of b_{m+1}. Then we will show that for sufficiently large b_{m+1}, if IN_k is independent of b_{m+1} (in the given perturbed model) then so is IN_{k+1}. For any b_{m+1}, IN_1 must be a basic solution to the problem of maximizing E subject to (9.14c–f). Given any choice of $m + 1$ variables with nonsingular $\tilde{A}$, the portfolio X is linear in b_{m+1}. It follows that a particular basis either will be feasible for all b_{m+1} greater than some b^*_{m+1}, or will be infeasible for all b_{m+1} greater than some b^*_{m+1}. Since there are only a finite number of bases, there is a b^*_{m+1} such that for $b_{m+1} \geqslant b^*_{m+1}$ the set of feasible versus infeasible bases is independent of b_{m+1}. Since the "pricing" criterion which identifies a feasible solution as optimum does not depend on b, the same basis, IN_1, will price out and therefore be optimum (uniquely so, for small ϵ in theorems 9.2 and 9.13) for all $b_{m+1} \geqslant b^*_{m+1}$. (This paragraph assures us of the existence of IN_1; exercise 9.4 tells how to compute it.)

On any critical line, α and γ depend linearly on the components of b while β and δ do not depend on b. Thus, for the model in (9.14) we may write

$$\alpha_i = \phi_i + \theta_i b_{m+1} \tag{9.15a}$$

where ϕ_i and θ_i are constants on any critical line, but vary from one critical line to another. Similarly γ_i may be written as

$$\gamma_i = \psi_i + \xi_i b_{m+1} \tag{9.15b}$$

where ψ_i and ξ_i depend on the choice of critical line. Consider i and j with i and j IN. From 9.4 f and g we see that $p_i(\epsilon)$ and $q_i(\epsilon)$ do not depend on b_{m+1}. Therefore

$$p_{ij}(\epsilon) = [\phi_i + \theta_i b_{m+1} + p_i(\epsilon)]\ [\beta_j^0 + q_j(\epsilon)]$$

$$- [\phi_j + \theta_j b_{m+1} + p_j(\epsilon)]\ [\beta_i^0 + q_i(\epsilon)]$$

This is of the form

$$p_{ij}(\epsilon) = \sum_{k=0}^{L} (c_k + d_k b_{m+1})\epsilon^k$$

Lemma 9.1 tells us that $p_{ij} > 0$ (< 0) for sufficiently small positive ϵ if its smallest power of ϵ with nonzero coefficient has a positive (negative) coefficient. We know that p_{ij} is not identically zero for all b_{m+1}, since the proof of theorem

9.2 implies that it is not identically zero in ϵ for b_{m+1} equal to any feasible E. Let ω be the smallest k with $c_\omega \neq 0$ or $d_\omega \neq 0$ (or both). If $d_k = 0$ then the sign of p_{ij} for small positive ϵ is the same as the sign of c_k, for all b_{m+1}. If $d_k \neq 0$ then there is a value b^*_{ij} such that the sign of p_{ij} for small positive ϵ is the sign of d_k, for all $b_{m+1} \geqslant b^*_{ij}$. If i and j are *OUT*, or if i is *IN* and j *OUT*, then similar considerations define a b^*_{ij}, with $\gamma_i^\epsilon \delta_j^\epsilon - \gamma_j^\epsilon \delta_i^\epsilon$ and $\alpha_i^\epsilon \delta_j^\epsilon - \gamma_j^\epsilon \beta_i^\epsilon$ serving as $p_{ij}(\epsilon)$. The b^* of the theorem must exceed the largest b^*_{ij}.

Not only is the list of *IN* sets $IN_1, IN_2, \ldots, IN_L$ the same for all sufficiently large b_{m+1}, but the subset $IN_1, IN_2, \ldots, IN_K$ on which $\hat{\lambda}_{\text{low}}(\epsilon) \to \infty$ is the same. For

$$-\frac{\alpha_i^\epsilon}{\beta_i^\epsilon} = -\frac{\phi_i + \theta_i b_{m+1} + p_i(\epsilon)}{\beta_i^0 + q_i(\epsilon)} \to \infty$$

as $\epsilon \to 0$ if and only if the smallest power of ϵ with a nonzero coefficient in the numerator is less than that of the denominator, and this "leading" coefficient in the numerator has the sign opposite that of the leading coefficient in the denominator. Sometimes for all b_{m+1}, in any case for b_{m+1} exceeding some b^*, the necessary and sufficient condition either holds for all $b_{m+1} \geqslant b^*$ or else fails to hold for all $b_{m+1} \geqslant b^*$. For any fixed $b_{m+1} \geqslant b^*_{m+1}$, (9.14) is a portfolio selection problem with bounded E; therefore l^{K+1} is a critical line on which $X = \bar{X}$ is constant while λ and η vary with λ_E. Consider first the case in which $\lambda_{\text{low}}^{K+1} > 0$. In this case the point on l^{K+2} with $\lambda_E = \lambda_{\text{hi}}^{K+2} = \lambda_{\text{low}}^{K+1}$ also has $X = \bar{X}$. This is the efficient portfolio which minimizes V among portfolios with $E = b_{m+1}$ subject to $AX = b$, $X \geqslant 0$. Since this is true for all $b_{m+1} \geqslant b^*_{m+1}$, the critical line l^{K+2} provides minimum obtainable V for given E for all sufficiently large E. It follows that $l^{K+2}, l^{K+3}, \ldots, l^L$ provide a piecewise linear, complete nonredundant efficient set. The critical line l^{K+2} is unbounded in a direction with increasing E. The strict convexity of the piecewise parabolic function relating V to E among efficient EV combinations is shown as in theorem 7.12.

In case $L = K + 1$, $\lambda_E = 0$ is reached on l^{K+1}. In this case l^{K+1} provides a portfolio which (1) has $E = b_{m+1}$, and (2) has minimum V among all feasible portfolios. Since this remains true as b_{m+1} increases, we have a feasible, zero-variance direction along which E increases. The problem therefore has feasible portfolios but no efficient portfolios. ###

Corollary 9.16 Every feasible portfolio selection model has a portfolio X_0 with minimum obtainable variance.

Proof The algorithm in theorem 9.15 either provides a complete nonredundant efficient set - which contains a portfolio with minimum variance at $\lambda_E = 0$ - or else it provides a ray, all of whose points have minimum variance. ###

The following theorem summarizes major results of the last three chapters, and asserts that they are true for any model of form 0, and therefore for any model of form 1 as well as form 2.

Theorem 9.17 Any portfolio selection model of form 0 which has at least one efficient portfolio has a piecewise linear, complete nonredundant set of efficient portfolios. There is an efficient portfolio X_0 with minimum variance V_0. Let $E_0 = \mu' X_0$. If feasible E has an upper bound then there is an efficient portfolio X^* which maximizes E. Let $E^* = \mu' X^*$. In this case the set of efficient EV combinations includes an EV combination for each E in the range $E_0 \leqslant E \leqslant E^*$. Otherwise, if feasible E is unbounded above, the set of efficient EV combinations includes an EV combination for each E in the range $E \geqslant E_0$. In the set of efficient EV combinations, V is a strictly convex, piecewise parabolic function of E.

Proof In the case of a model of form 2, the above is a corollary of theorems 9.14 and 9.15. The assertion about EV combinations follows from the definition of equivalent models and the fact, shown in chapter 2, that for every model of form 0 there is an equivalent model of form 2. The assertion about efficient portfolios follows from the manner in which an equivalent model of form 2 is constructed from a model of form 0, and hence the possibility of going back from a piecewise linear set of efficient portfolios in the model of form 2 to a piecewise linear set of efficient portfolios with the same EV combinations in the model of form 0. One way in which the form 2 model differs from its equivalent form 0 model is that every X_i which is allowed to be negative in the form 0 model is replaced by $Y_i - Z_i$, where $Y_i \geqslant 0, Z_i \geqslant 0$. It follows from the fact that $\bar{M}$ is nonsingular in the form 2 solution that Y_i and Z_i cannot both be IN. In any case, let X_i in the original model equal $Y_i - Z_i$ from the form 2 equivalent. The only other difference between the form 0 model and its form 2 equivalent is that the inequalities in the former are made into equalities in the latter by the introduction of slack variables. Delete the introduced slack variables from the form 2 portfolios to obtain the form 0 portfolios. With these two linear transformations (substitution of X_i for $Y_i - Z_i$ and the dropping of some variables) a piecewise linear set of portfolios in the model of form 2 becomes a piecewise linear set in the model of form 0, and supplies the same EV combinations. ###

Theorem 9.17 includes models of form 1, since any model of form 1 is already in form 0.

Related Matters

The present section discussed two topics related to the materials in chapters 7-9.

Roundoff error

The results of the present and two preceding chapters may be summarized as follows. Suppose that the simplex (or other linear programming) algorithm determines that a given portfolio analysis problem is feasible and, if necessary, supplies a strictly equivalent problem with no redundant equations. Then the critical line algorithm, extended to handle possibly degenerate models with possibly unbounded E, will always produce a piecewise linear, complete nonredundant set of efficient portfolios.

Our proof of this ignores roundoff error. Thus the above must be considered to be a truth about real numbers rather than a truth about a computer program which maintains a fixed (finite) number of decimal places.

In practice A, b, μ, and C contain rational numbers (i.e. fractions; e.g. decimal numbers). For such data it is feasible, albeit a bit slow and space consuming, to perform the critical line calculations with unlimited accuracy. This requires us to store separately the numerator and denominator of each rational number - e.g. 1/3 is stored as "numer. = 1, denom. = 3" rather than "number = 0.333333 . . ." - using some kind of bookkeeping system which allows us to store integers of arbitrary length. This approach will succeed (if we do not run out of storage space) since the critical line computation requires only a finite number of rational operations (addition, subtraction, multiplication, and division), and a rational operation on rational operands always produces a rational number as a result (provided that you do not attempt to divide by zero, and we do not).

In fact it is much more economical, and usually of sufficient accuracy even for very large problems, to use the double-precision arithmetic of the computers upon which the critical line algorithm is currently run. With a state-of-the-art coding of the critical line algorithm, such as described in Perold (1984), mean-variance analyses will typically run successfully for hundreds of securities with a dense covariance matrix or thousands of securities with a sparse covariance matrix. Professor Perold has kindly supplied the following additional observations concerning roundoff error (private communication):

> In practice, there is always roundoff error because of finite machine precision. Roundoff errors are present initially in the problem inputs and accumulate as the critical line algorithm wends its way from one end of the frontier to the other. Most of the time, roundoff error is not a problem, in that the critical line algorithm will produce answers correct to at least six figures when calculations are done in 64 bit double precision. However, there will be occasions when roundoff errors cause difficulty.
>
> First, it is possible that, due to roundoff error, the calculated covariance matrix is indefinite. For example, with 500 securities and 60 observations, the exact covariance matrix will always be positive semidefinite (never definite). Small perturbations can thus make it indefinite, and, with or without some of the additional problems described below, cause the critical line algorithm to fail.
>
> Second, the covariance matrix may be ill-conditioned. That is, it may be near singular in the sense that small perturbations in the inputs will

result in the selection of very different corner portfolios. This may cause the critical line algorithm to fail, or produce unreliable results, even when some of the most robust numerical techniques are used for inversion purposes, such as Gaussian elimination with complete pivoting.

Third, even with a well-conditioned covariance matrix the resulting basis matrix may be difficult to invert as a result of bad scaling. For example, when the covariance matrix is estimated with the use of daily data, the matrix entries are typically of the order of 0.001 to 0.0001. The vector of ones in the budget constraint, on the other hand, is of a substantially different order of magnitude. This is an easy problem to solve, however, since the covariance matrix can always be scaled to be of order unity.

All three of these can interact with one another and compound the problem. Happily, they do not arise as often as one might imagine, provided one scales the problem sensibly, and one uses numerically stable techniques for solving the requisite equations at each of the corners. Yes, at least here, the numerical analyst's nightmare of Murphy's law (if anything can go wrong it will go wrong) is alive, but not very well.

Complementarity problems

Lemke and Howson (1964) and Lemke (1965) use an algorithm which is essentially the same as the critical line algorithm to solve the two-person nonzero sum game. Scarf (1973, 1983) uses the same algorithm to solve for economic equilibria. The Lemke algorithm traces out a piecewise linear path as a parameter, corresponding to our λ_E, goes from ∞ to 0. This path is traced out in a space containing complementary variables corresponding to our X_i and η_i. Everywhere on this path $X \geqslant 0$ and $\eta \geqslant 0$. As in the critical line algorithm, along any linear piece of this path, if X_i is *IN* then $\eta_i = 0$ and, conversely, if η_i is free to vary then $X_i = 0$. If some $X_i \downarrow 0$ then the linear piece ends (at what we would call a corner portfolio). On the succeeding piece $X_i = 0$ and η_i is free to vary. A similar statement applies when $\eta_i \downarrow 0$: on the succeeding piece that $\eta_i = 0$ and X_i is free to vary.

There are two major differences between the Lemke algorithm and the critical line algorithm as described in Markowitz (1956, 1959) and the three preceding chapters:

(1) The matrices describing the linear pieces, corresponding to our $\bar{M}$, are not necessarily of the form in equation 7.7 for positive semidefinite C. In other words, Lemke shows that the algorithm "works" - in the sense that $\bar{M}$ remains nonsingular, η_i increases on the succeeding piece when $X_i \downarrow 0$, and X_i increases on the succeeding piece when $\eta_i \downarrow 0$ - for a wider class of matrices than dealt with in the preceding chapters.

(2) The solution to the problem posed by Lemke occurs when (what corresponds to our) $\lambda_E = 0$. The preceding part of the path, for $\lambda_E > 0$, is not

part of the solution. In our case the entire piecewise linear path is the solution. Thus if a short-cut could be found for arriving at the point at $\lambda_E = 0$, this would be a better algorithm for Lemke's problem but not for ours.

Lemke's problem is one of a class called *complementarity problems*, in which a solution to a systems of equations is sought in complementary variables (such as our X_i and η_i). These problems frequently arise from the Kuhn-Tucker conditions for constrained optimization. Historically, interest in complementarity problems was stimulated by Wolfe (1959) who showed that the Markowitz (1956) critical line algorithm entailed the same computing steps as the simplex algorithm for linear programming, except for one amendment to the latter: when a variable (e.g. X_i or η_i) is in the basis then its complement (η_i or X_i) must be out of the basis. (Wolfe was primarily concerned with minimizing a quadratic, and incidentally noted that the amended simplex algorithm would solve the portfolio selection problem; as compared with Markowitz, who was primarily concerned with the portfolio selection problem and incidentally noted that the critical line algorithm would minimize a quadratic.) Pioneering work on complementarity problems is presented or reviewed in Dantzig and Cottle (1967), Cottle and Dantzig (1968), and Lemke (1968, 1970), including the recognition of problems which take this form and procedures for solving such problems.

If we are concerned only with the portfolio selection problem as defined in chapter 2, then general results on complementarity problems add nothing to our capabilities. The critical line algorithm provides the whole solution, nothing but the solution, and (in the nondegenerate case) the only solution to the portfolio selection problem. On the other hand, we do not have to stray far from the portfolio selection problem defined in chapter 2 before we need to draw on more general complementarity results. For example, Perold (1984) includes an investment problem in which it is desirable to minimize an inhomogeneous quadratic $Q = (1/2)X'CX + \nu'X$ with positive semidefinite C, for various values of $E = \mu'X$ subject to $AX = b$, $X \geqslant 0$. If his problem had been to minimize Q subject to the constraints, ignoring E, then he could have traced out the mean-variance efficient set using ν for μ. The efficient point at $\lambda_E = 1$ would then be the solution to the problem. But the Perold problem requires finding the efficient combinations of E and Q. It is easy to set up the appropriate Lagrangian for this problem, and find the Kuhn-Tucker conditions. But, if you trace out the efficient set in the manner of the critical line algorithm, under some circumstances $\bar{M}$ may become singular. Under these circumstances it is necessary to "double pivot" - make two changes to the *IN* set - before proceeding. Graves (1967), cited by Perold, shows that double pivoting is the worst case; e.g. you will not need to triple pivot. In the Lemke problem, the Scarf problem, and the portfolio selection problem of chapter 2, single changes to the *IN* set suffice.

Exercises

9.1 There are sixteen ways to assign "zero" or "nonzero" to α_i^0, β_i^0, α_j^0, β_j^0. Make a table listing these sixteen cases and, for each case, indicate which lemma shows that the case cannot be true if neither α_i^ϵ, β_i^ϵ, α_j^ϵ, nor β_j^ϵ is identically zero whereas $p_{ij}(\epsilon)$ is identically zero. (Hint: by interchanging i and j, lemma 9.6 rules out $\alpha_j = 0$ and $\alpha_i \neq 0$ as well as $\alpha_i = 0$ and $\alpha_j \neq 0$. This accounts for eight cases, since β_i and β_j may each be either zero or nonzero.)

9.2 Prove the following version of the "extension of inequalities" used in theorem 9.14: if $f(x)$ is a continuous function such that $f(x) \geqslant b$ for all $x > a$ then $f(a) \geqslant b$. (Hint: assume to the contrary that $f(a) < b$, and show that there must be some $c > a$ such that $f(c) < b$.) See also Dieudonné (1969) for a more general version.

9.3 (a) Show that when $m = 3$ and $n = 10$, the value of $c_{2,8}$ is

$$c_{2,8} = -a_i^{12} a_j^3 + a_j^{12} a_i^3$$

(Hint: $c_{2,8}$ is the coefficient of $\epsilon^{2(11)+8}$ in (9.13). From (9.8c), (9.4f), and (9.4g) we see that this coefficient is $-a_i^{10+2} a_j^{11-8} + a_j^{10+2} a_i^{11-8}$.)

(b) In terms of the coefficients of $\bar{M}^{-1}$, what are the values of: $c_{2,0}$; $c_{0,8}$; $c_{3,6}$?

9.4 If $g_{i\omega} \leqslant 0$ for $1 \leqslant i \leqslant m$ in the proof of theorem 8.3, then feasible E may be increased without bound by increasing $X_\omega = \theta$ without bound. Suppose this to be the final outcome of a simplex calculation.

(a) Add a constraint

$$\mu' X + X_{n+1} \leqslant b_{m+1}$$

to the original E maximization problem, where $b_{m+1} > E_0 =$ the E of the last basis (before introducing X_ω). Show that if IN was the IN set of either the last basis B, or a previous feasible basis for the problem without the $(m + 1)$th equation, then $IN \cup \{n + 1\}$ is a feasible basis with the same E for the problem with the $(m + 1)$th equation. Show also that, for any one of these bases, the profitabilities of all nonbasis variables are the same in the original problem and the new bounded problem. In particular, $\hat{v}_\omega > 0$ in the bounded problem for basis B with IN set equal to $IN_B \cup \{X_{n+1}\}$.

(b) If X_ω is introduced into basis B in the bounded problem then $X_{n+1} \downarrow 0$ and the basis produced by the simplex algorithm is $IN_B \cup \{\omega\}$. Show that not only does this new basis have maximum E allowed in the bounded problem, but it prices out in the sense that all profitabilities are nonpositive. Thus $IN_B \cup \{\omega\}$ may be used as the IN_1 set whose existence is assured in theorem 9.15.

9.5 Compare (a) the set of efficient portfolios in Black's model when written as in equation (1.13), i.e. when considered as a model with an affine constraint set, and (b) the set of efficient portfolios for the equivalent form 2 model. Conclude that while both are piecewise linear, the former may have fewer critical lines (because two or more efficient segments of the latter may coalesce into one in the former). Also analyze the degeneracy of the form 2 version.

10

All Feasible Mean-Variance Combinations

Preceding chapters describe the set of efficient EV combinations and show how to compute this set economically. The present chapter describes the balance of the EV obtainable set. In particular it describes the shape of the *top* or *upper boundary* of the set - those combinations which maximize V for given E. It also considers the *bottom* or *lower boundary* of the obtainable EV set - those combinations which minimize V for given E, of which the efficient EV combinations are a subset. The first theorem of the chapter assures us that if we know the upper and lower boundaries of the obtainable EV set, we know all obtainable EV combinations.

Theorem 10.1 If (E_0, V_1) and (E_0, V_2) are obtainable then so is every (E_0, V) with $V_1 \leqslant V \leqslant V_2$.

Proof Suppose that X^a is a feasible portfolio which provides (E_0, V_1), and X^b is one which provides (E_0, V_2). Then the convexity of the set of obtainable portfolios implies that

$$X = tX^a + (1-t)X^b$$

$$0 \leqslant t \leqslant 1$$

is also feasible. The expected return of X is

$$E = \mu'[tX^a + (1-t)X^b]$$

$$= t\mu'X^a + (1-t)\mu'X^b = E_0$$

V is a quadratic in t; hence, like any continuous function, it passes through all values of V between V_1 (at $t=1$) and V_2 (at $t=0$). ###

If X^a and X^b are arbitrary feasible points with the same E, it is possible to have $V < V_1$ for some $0 \leqslant t \leqslant 1$. The theorem does not claim otherwise. This is ruled out if V_1 is the minimum obtainable value of V among feasible portfolios with $E = E_0$.

It is possible for the set of obtainable V for given $E = E_0$ to be unbounded. For example, consider Black's model with $n = 2$, $\mu_1 = \mu_2$, $V_1 > 0$, $V_2 > 0$, and $-1 < \rho_{12} < 1$. In this particular case all feasible portfolios have the same E, but V has no upper bound. Since V_2 need not be the maximum obtainable V given $E = E_0$ in theorem 10.1, the theorem is applicable when the set of obtainable EV combinations is unbounded above.

Theorem 10.2 Suppose E_1 and E_2 are obtainable values of E for a given portfolio selection model. If there is an unbounded set of V such that (E_1, V) is obtainable, then there is also an unbounded set of V such that (E_2, V) is obtainable. In other words, if feasible (E, V) is unbounded for any E then it is unbounded for every obtainable E.

Proof The proof is easy if we can show that unbounded V for some $E = E_1$ implies that there is an unbounded feasible direction β such that $\mu'\beta = 0$ and β is not a zero-variance direction. In this case we can start with any point, move in direction β, stay feasible, keep E constant, and increase V without bounds. To show that there is an unbounded direction with these attributes, it is sufficient to show the following lemma:

If constraints $AX = b$, $X \geqslant 0$ have unbounded feasible V, then they admit an unbounded feasible direction which is not a zero-variance direction.

The theorem follows immediately if A and b of the lemma are set to

$$\begin{pmatrix} A \\ \mu' \end{pmatrix} \quad \text{and} \quad \begin{pmatrix} b \\ E_1 \end{pmatrix}$$

of the theorem.

To prove the lemma, we will use mathematical induction on the dimensionality of the affine hull of the model. If the model has a one-dimensional affine hull then the result is trivial. For then, if we take the horizontal axis as the one-dimensional subspace, either the direction to the right or that to the left (or both) must be unbounded feasible, and the axis must not be a zero-variance direction, in order for feasible variance to increase without bounds.

Next assume that the theorem is true for a $K-1$ dimensional affine hull. We will show that this implies that it is true for a K dimensional affine hull, thus completing the induction.

Suppose then that $AX = b$, $X \geqslant 0$ be given with a K dimensional affine hull. Let X_0 be a feasible point with $V = V_0$. Let $X^1, X^2, X^3 \ldots$ be feasible points with $V_1, V_2, V_3 \ldots$ such that $V_0 < V_i$, $i = 1, 2, \ldots,$ and the V_i increase without bounds. Then $\beta^i = X^i - X_0$ is not a zero-variance direction. If one of these β^i is an unbounded feasible direction, then the lemma is proven. If not, for each ray

$$X = X_0 + \beta^i t$$

there is a smallest t at which some component of X, say X_h, equals zero among components with $\beta^i_h < 0$. Write $j_i = h$. At least one k, $1 \leqslant k \leqslant n$, must appear an infinite number of times in the sequence $j_1, j_2, \ldots$. Let Y^1, Y^2, $Y^3 \ldots$ be the points on $X = X_0 + \beta^i t$ at which $X_k = 0$, for only those i such that $j_i = k$. Since the original $V_1, V_2, V_3 \ldots$ sequence was unbounded it follows that $V(Y^1)$, $V(Y^2)$, $V(Y^3) \ldots$ is unbounded. (This uses the fact that, on $X = X_0 + \beta^i t$, the t for Y^i is at least as great as the t for X^i; and $V^i > V^0$ implies V increases with t beyond the t for X^i.) But the model $AX = b$, $X_k = 0$, $X \geqslant 0$ has a $K-1$ dimensional affine hull, since we know that feasible portfolios are not confined to $X_k = 0$ in the given model $AX = b$, $X \geqslant 0$ with its K dimensional affine hull (recall $X_k \downarrow 0$ on many lines starting at X_0). By the inductive assumption we know that $AX = b$, $X_k = 0$, $X \geqslant 0$ has an unbounded feasible nonzero-variance direction β - which is also such a direction for $AX = b, X \geqslant 0$. ###

We see, then, that the top of the EV set is either bounded for all obtainable E or unbounded for all obtainable E. For the moment we leave the top and re-examine the bottom of the set of obtainable EV combinations. The following example shows that there can be a horizontal segment with minimum obtainable V. Theorem 5.14 showed that this is the only place on the lower boundary where a horizontal EV segment can occur. Theorem 10.3, a corollary of theorem 9.17, assures us that elsewhere on the lower boundary V is strictly convex and piecewise parabolic.

Consider the standard three-security model with

$$\mu' = (1,\ 2,\ 3) \tag{10.1a}$$

$$C = \begin{pmatrix} 1 & 0 & 1 \\ 0 & 2 & 0 \\ 1 & 0 & 1 \end{pmatrix} \tag{10.1b}$$

We could rescale μ and C to make the numbers more realistic, i.e. more like historical means and covariances, but the present values are more convenient. $\rho_{13} = 1$ is essential to the example. The combinations of E and V obtained by letting

$$X_1 = 1 - X_2 \qquad 0 \leqslant X_2 \leqslant 1$$

$$X_3 = 0$$

is the arc ab in figure 10.1; the combinations obtained by letting

$$X_3 = 1 - X_2 \qquad 0 \leqslant X_2 \leqslant 1$$

$$X_1 = 0$$

is the arc bc. The fact that V may be written as

$$V = 2X_2^2 + (X_1 + X_3)^2 \tag{10.2}$$

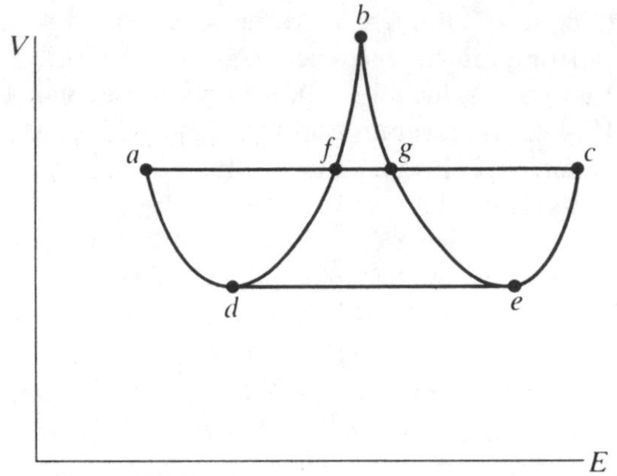

Figure 10.1 *Obtainable EV combinations for a particular standard model*

and

$$\mu_3 > \mu_2 > \mu_1$$

implies that in order to maximize E for given V we must have $X_1 = 0$; else we could trade X_3 for X_1, increasing E and keeping V constant. Thus the set of efficient EV combinations consists of the arc *ec*. Similarly it follows that the portfolios which (a) minimize V for given E, and (b) *minimize* E for given V make up the arc *ad*. The set of portfolios of the form

$$X = (X_1, 1/3, (2/3) - X_1) \qquad \text{for } 0 \leqslant X_1 \leqslant 2/3$$

have constant variance, and an E value which increases from that at the point *d* to that at the point *e*. It follows from (10.2) that no other feasible portfolios can have a lower variance than these, and therefore the flat segment *de* is part of the bottom of the set of obtainable EV combinations.

Theorem 10.3 If the lower boundary of the set of feasible EV combinations contains a linear segment, this segment must be horizontal with minimum variance. If the lower boundary has no such horizontal region, then it is strictly convex and piecewise parabolic for all feasible E. If the lower boundary has a horizontal region and this horizontal region has a largest (smallest) $E = E_0$ ($E = E^*$) then the lower boundary is strictly convex above E_0 (below E^*).

Proof Theorem 9.17 assures that the set of efficient EV combinations is strictly convex, and therefore cannot have any linear segments. This efficient set provides an EV combination with minimum V for given E for every feasible $E \geqslant E_0$, where (E_0, V_0) is the efficient EV combination with minimum V_0. There may be other feasible EV combinations with $V = V_0$, but E_0 has higher E. Replacing μ by $-\mu$, thus seeking to maximize $-E$, i.e. to minimize $+E$, the same theorem implies that the set of points which minimize V for given E must be strictly convex and piecewise parabolic for all $E \leqslant E^*$, where E^* is the smallest obtainable E among portfolios with $V = V_0$ = minimum obtainable V. Thus the only EV combinations on the lower boundary of the feasible EV set which can be part of an interval with $a_2 = 0$ are portfolios which minimize V. ###

The procedure in chapter 9 for E without upper bound admits the possibility that the horizontal segment may extend to the right without bound. A similar argument, with $-\mu$ replacing μ, shows that it may also, or instead, extend indefinitely to the left. This was illustrated in figure 5.2. (*Exercise* Provide examples of models with one-dimensional affine hulls which illustrate each of the possibilities in figure 5.2.)

The Top of the Obtainable EV Set

For a given obtainable E, the set of obtainable V may be bounded or unbounded. If the set of obtainable portfolios is bounded, then so is the set of obtainable V (since a continuous function always achieves a maximum on any compact set). Two-security examples show that when the obtainable set is unbounded, V may be bounded or unbounded; and may be bounded among obtainable portfolios with a given E, although unbounded among all obtainable portfolios with any E.

Definition Because of theorem 10.2 we may speak of any feasible portfolio selection model as having either *bounded V for given E* or *unbounded V for given E*.

If a model is feasible but contains one or more redundant equations, these facts will be discovered in phase I of the simplex algorithm, and a completely equivalent model with no redundant equations will be substituted for the original model. Conclusions concerning the shape of the top of the obtainable EV set which are true for this completely equivalent model are also true for the original model. In the theorems below concerning the shape of the top of the obtainable EV set we may therefore assume, without loss of generality, that the model contains no redundant equations, i.e. A has rank m.

Among feasible models with A of rank m, we may distinguish the following two cases:

$$\begin{pmatrix} A \\ \mu' \end{pmatrix} \quad \text{has rank } m \tag{10.3a}$$

$$\begin{pmatrix} A \\ \mu' \end{pmatrix} \quad \text{has rank } m+1 \tag{10.3b}$$

Before we explore these two cases we establish a lemma for an "m by n matrix A of rank m". We will apply this lemma once to the matrix A in case (10.3a) and once to the matrix

$$\begin{pmatrix} A \\ \mu' \end{pmatrix}$$

in case (10.3b). In the latter case, "m" of the lemma stands for $m+1$ of the application.

Lemma 10.4 Suppose that A is an m by n matrix of rank m, that the constraint set

$$AX = b \tag{10.4a}$$

$$X \geqslant 0 \tag{10.4b}$$

is feasible, and that V is bounded on (10.4). Then there is a basic feasible solution which provides maximum V.

Proof Suppose $X' = (X_1, \ldots, X_n)$ satisfies (10.4). Further suppose for convenience of notation that $X_1, X_2, \ldots, X_k$ are positive and $X_{k+1}, \ldots, X_n$ are 0. Let $A_1, \ldots, A_k$ denote the first k columns of the A matrix. Our first step will be to show that if the vectors $A_1, \ldots, A_k$ are not independent, then the same or higher V is provided by a feasible portfolio with X_i still 0 for $k+1 \leqslant i \leqslant n$, but with at least one $X_i = 0$ for $1 \leqslant i \leqslant k$. (If $k = n$, the set of i such that $n+1 \leqslant i \leqslant n$ is the empty set.) Our current assumption, then, is that there is a vector $\alpha \neq 0$ such that

$$(A_1, \ldots, A_k)\alpha = 0$$

If necessary, permute the indices so that $\alpha_1 \neq 0$. Then

$$A_1 = -\sum_{i=2}^{k} \frac{\alpha_i}{\alpha_1} A_i$$

$$= -\sum_{i=2}^{k} \beta_i A_i$$

where $\beta_i = \alpha_i/\alpha_1$. Therefore

$$A_1(X_1 + \theta) + \sum_{i=2}^{k} A_i(X_i + \theta\beta_i) = b$$

for all real θ. Let $\beta = (1, \beta_2, \ldots, \beta_k)$. Since V is assumed here to be bounded on (10.4), it cannot be true that $\beta \geqslant 0$ and is not a zero-variance direction. The following two cases cover the remaining possibilities: β is a zero-variance direction, or $\beta_i < 0$ for some i (or both). If β is a zero-variance direction, let

$$\theta^* = \min_{\beta_i > 0} X_i/\beta_i$$

We know that such a θ^* exists since $\beta_1 = 1$. Then

$$X^* = X - \beta\theta^*$$

satisfies (10.4) and provides the same V as X, but has at least one $X_i = 0, 1 \leqslant i \leqslant k$. If β is not a zero-variance direction, then we must have $\beta_i < 0$ for some i, as well as $\beta_1 > 0$. Thus we may define

$$\theta_{\text{low}} = \max_{\beta_i > 0} - X_i/\beta_i$$

$$\theta_{\text{hi}} = \min_{\beta_i < 0} - X_i/\beta_i$$

and note that $\theta_{\text{hi}} > 0 > \theta_{\text{low}}$. Then

$$X^* = X + \beta\theta \tag{10.5a}$$

remains feasible for exactly those θ which satisfy

$$\theta_{\text{low}} \leqslant \theta \leqslant \theta_{\text{hi}} \tag{10.5b}$$

Since V is a parabola with $d^2V/d\theta^2 > 0$ along the line segment defined by (10.5a) and (10.5b), it reaches its maximum at one or the other of the end points of the interval. But at the end points, with $\theta = \theta_{\text{low}}$ or $\theta = \theta_{\text{hi}}$, some $X_i = 0$ for $1 \leqslant i \leqslant k$.

Repeated application of the same argument shows that for every feasible solution X there is another feasible solution X^* with at least as great a V, and with A_i independent for i with $X_i^* > 0$. Reorder the indices so that $X_i^* > 0$ for $i = 1, \ldots, h$, and $X_i^* = 0$ for $i > h$. If $h = m$ then $(A_1, \ldots, A_h)$ is a basis. Else, since $A = (A_1, \ldots, A_n)$ has rank m (i.e. the n column vectors of A span the space of m dimensional vectors), $m - h$ vectors can be chosen from $A_{h+1}, \ldots, A_n$ so that these vectors plus $A_1, \ldots, A_h$ form a basis. Reorder indices so that the original and the selected vectors are now labeled $A_1, \ldots, A_m$, still with $X_i^* > 0$ only for $i \leqslant h$. Since this $(A_1, \ldots, A_m)$ is nonsingular, and

$$(A_1, \ldots, A_m)\begin{pmatrix} X_1^* \\ X_2^* \\ \vdots \\ X_m^* \end{pmatrix} = b$$

$$X^* \geqslant 0$$

we have a basic feasible solution with at least as great a V as the given solution X, as the lemma asserts. ###

Theorem 10.5 If a portfolio selection model (written in form 2)

(i) Is feasible
(ii) Has A of rank m, and
(iii) Satisfies condition (10.3a)

then only one value of E is obtainable. Maximum obtainable V (for this E) is either unbounded or is achieved by some basic feasible solution.

Proof Assumptions (ii) and (iii) imply that μ' is a linear combination of the rows of A; that is,

$$\mu' = \beta' A$$

for some row vector $\beta' \neq 0$. This in turn implies that all X which satisfy $AX = b$ have

$$\begin{aligned} E &= \mu' X \\ &= \beta' A X = \beta' b \end{aligned}$$

If obtainable V is unbounded, nothing remains to be shown. If obtainable V is bounded we must show that some obtainable portfolio has a maximum V (i.e. it is not true that obtainable portfolios have V which are arbitrarily close to, but not equal to, the greatest lower bound of V). There are a finite number of basic feasible portfolios. Let V^* be the maximum V among these. Lemma 10.4 assures us that no feasible portfolio has higher V. Thus V^* is the maximum obtainable V and is provided by some basic feasible portfolio. ###

Theorem 10.6 Suppose that a feasible portfolio satisfies (10.3b) and has bounded V for given E. If E_0 is an obtainable value of E, then there is a feasible portfolio which maximizes V for $E = E_0$, and which has the following characteristics:

(i) $m + 1$ securities are *IN*
(ii) $X_i = 0$ for i *OUT*
(iii) The subset of

$$\begin{pmatrix} A \\ \mu' \end{pmatrix}$$

obtained by deleting *OUT* securities, leaving $m + 1$ *IN* columns, is nonsingular.

Proof Apply lemma 10.4 to the constraint set

$$AX = b$$
$$\mu' X = E_0$$
$$X \geqslant 0$$

###

If equation (10.3b) holds, theorem 10.6 assures us that the following procedure can be used to calculate the upper boundary of the set of EV combinations. While this procedure is finite, it is not economical for large problems. It does, however, show us the shape of the top of the EV set, just as the critical line algorithm shows us the shape of the efficient set within the lower boundary of the EV set.

First, make a list of all combinations of $m+1$ out of the n indices $(1, \ldots, n)$. From this list delete combinations whose subset of

$$\begin{pmatrix} A \\ \mu' \end{pmatrix}$$

is singular. By arguments similar to those in chapters 6 and 7, for any combination still on the list, if we set $X_i = 0$ for i not in the combination, and require $AX = b$, $\mu' X = E$, then

(1) X is a uniquely determined linear function of E.
(2) V is a quadratic function of E with $d^2V/dE^2 \geqslant 0$, where $d^2V/dE^2 = 0$ only if V is constant on the line.
(3) X is feasible - i.e. satisfies $X \geqslant 0$ - either (a) nowhere, (b) on a closed interval $X_{\text{low}} \leqslant X \leqslant X_{\text{hi}}$, or (c) on a half-line $X \geqslant X_{\text{low}}$ or $X \leqslant X_{\text{hi}}$.

If a combination is feasible nowhere, delete it from the list. Item (2) says that the relationship between V and E for a combination is either a parabola or a horizontal line. It will be convenient here to refer to a horizontal line as an honorary "parabola."

The parabola (or horizontal line) which relates V to E for one combination on the list may intersect (or touch) that for another combination at 0, 1, or 2 points. The only other possibility is that the two parabolas are identical. Figure 10.2 shows some of the possible relationships between the EV parabolas of two IN sets still on our list. The portfolios associated with the IN_1 set, giving rise to the EV parabola P_1, are infeasible for $E < E_a$; those associated with IN_2, giving rise to the P_2 parabola, are infeasible for $E < E_b$. Restricting ourselves only to the portions of the parabolas associated with feasible portfolios, P_1 is "on top" in the interval $E_a \leqslant E < E_b$; then P_2 is on top in the interval $E_b \leqslant E < E_c$. At $E = E_c$, P_1 and P_2 provide the same V; for $E_c < E < E_d$, P_1 is on top; P_1 and P_2

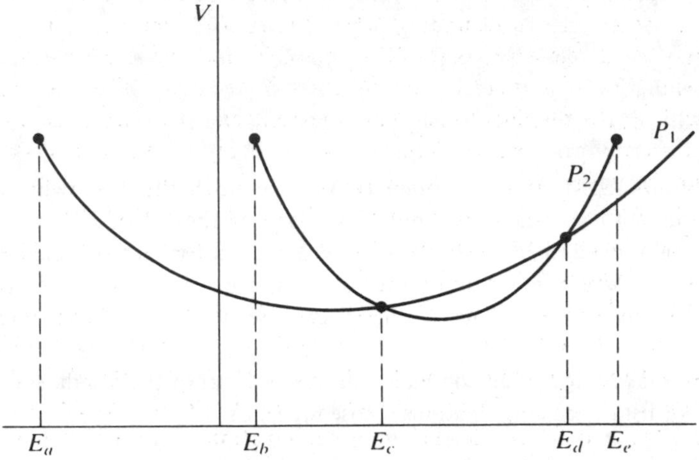

Figure 10.2 Feasible portions of two EV parabolas

tie for max V at E_d; for $E_d < E \leqslant E_e$, P_2 is on top. Beyond E_e, P_2 is no longer feasible, so P_1 is on top for $E > E_e$.

If we delete the points E_a, E_b, E_c, E_d, E_e we are left with a finite number of open intervals:

$$E_a < E < E_b$$

$$E_b < E < E_c$$

$$E_c < E < E_d$$

$$E_d < E < E_e$$

$$E_e < E$$

such that throughout any one of these intervals, one of the parabolas is strictly above the other.

The comparison of the feasible portion of pairs of such parabolas produces various cases depending, for example, on whether one or both the parabolas are feasible for E bounded above only, below only, or both above and below; whether the parabolas intersect 0, 1, or 2 times; whether the range of E for which one parabola is feasible overlaps that for the other parabola; and so on. But in every case if you delete a finite number of values of E - namely the zero, one, or two end points of the intervals in which each parabola is feasible, and the values of E at which the parabolas intersect (or touch) - you are left with a finite number of open intervals (one or two of which may be unbounded) such that, in any given interval, one of the parabolas is strictly above all the others.

(If two combinations give rise to the same parabola we consider this the same parabola, rather than two parabolas which "intersect" everywhere.)

It may be possible to delete fewer E values and still have the same result. For example, in a particular case it may be unnecessary to delete the smallest E for which P_1 is feasible, because P_2 is feasible and provides greater V. We will not concern ourselves with deleting a few too many E values, or insist that the particular parabola which is on top change from one interval to the next. We need only the fact that by deleting some finite number of E values, we are left with a finite number of open intervals such that, for any particular interval, one and only one parabola is on top.

Consider all the parabolas associated with combinations of variables on our list. For each of these with feasible E bounded on the left, delete the lowest feasible E value; for those bounded on the right, delete the highest E value. In particular, if a combination is feasible for only one point, this E value is deleted. (We could have deleted such combinations from our list in the first place.) From the preceding considerations, and the fact that "being on top" is transitive - if P_1 is on top of P_2 throughout an interval, and P_2 is on top of P_3 throughout the same interval, then P_1 is on top of P_3 throughout this interval - it follows that, for each of the open intervals, one parabola is on top throughout the interval. This result is summarized in the following theorem, which also includes results concerning which is on top at deleted points, and on the continuity of the top of the EV set.

Theorem 10.7 Suppose that a portfolio selection model (written in form 2) has an A of rank m, and has more than one feasible value of E. Then there will be $k \geqslant 1$ combinations, each combination consisting of $m+1$ variables, such that the subset of

$$\begin{pmatrix} A \\ \mu' \end{pmatrix}$$

obtained by deleting all but these $m+1$ columns is nonsingular. For a given such combination, V is a "parabola" in E with $\mathrm{d}^2V/\mathrm{d}E^2 \geqslant 0$, where $\mathrm{d}^2V/\mathrm{d}E^2 = 0$ only if V is constant for the combination. (Here we include horizontal line as a special case of "parabola.") Let I be the (bounded or unbounded) interval of feasible E for the model. Delete from I the E values at which any two of the aforementioned EV parabolas intersect or touch, and those E values which are the highest or lowest E values feasible for some combination. The interval I less these deletions consists of a finite number of open intervals $I_1, I_2, \ldots, I_L$, perhaps including one or two unbounded intervals. For each of these intervals there is one and only one parabola which is on top (has highest V for given E) throughout the interval. However, more than one combination may give rise to this same parabola.

Each of the deleted points is the end point of one or two of the intervals $I_1, \ldots, I_L$. A parabola which is on top on an adjacent interval, at least ties for max V at a deleted point. In particular, if a deleted point p is adjacent to two intervals, one to its left and one to its right, then the V maximizing parabola P_ℓ on the interval to the left and that P_r to the right are both feasible at p, and both have the same V maximizing value at the deleted point p. Thus the top of the obtainable EV set is continuous.

Proof The first paragraph of the theorem summarizes the preceding discussion. We shall prove the assertions in the second paragraph. Suppose that P_ℓ is a parabola to the left of a deleted point p whose E is E_p. We will show that the limit, as $E \to E_p$, of V on the parabola P_ℓ is the same as the maximum feasible V at E_p. A similar proof applies for a parabola P_r to the right of a deleted point. The continuity of the top of the EV set is then a corollary.

Since any feasible IN set with nonsingular

$$\begin{pmatrix} A \\ \mu' \end{pmatrix}$$

is feasible on a closed E set, P_ℓ is feasible at E_p. Thus maximum obtainable V at E_p cannot be less than that provided by P_ℓ. We shall show that it cannot be greater. Suppose, to the contrary, that there is a feasible portfolio X^* with expected value E_p and variance $V^* > V_\ell$, where V_ℓ is the limit of V on P_ℓ as $E \uparrow E_p$. Let X_ℓ be any feasible point of the IN set which generates P_ℓ, with $E_\ell < E_p$. Then by convexity of the constraint set

$$X = cX^* + (1-c)X_\ell$$

is feasible for $0 \leqslant c \leqslant 1$. But by continuity of E and V, $E_X \uparrow E_p$ and $V_X \to V^*$ as $c \uparrow 1$. But this means that, for E_X sufficiently close to (but below) E_p, we have

$$\begin{aligned} V_X &> V^* - \tfrac{1}{2}(V^* - V_\ell) \\ &= \tfrac{1}{2}V^* + \tfrac{1}{2}V_\ell \end{aligned}$$

Also, for E_X sufficiently close to E_p the point on P_ℓ has V less than

$$V_\ell + \tfrac{1}{2}(V^* - V_\ell) = \tfrac{1}{2}V^* + \tfrac{1}{2}V_\ell$$

These two inequalities contradict the assertion that P_ℓ provides maximum V for given E for at least a small interval to the left of E_p. ###

Comparison of the Top and Bottom of the EV Set

In this section we compare the shape of the top and the bottom of the obtainable EV set. One difference is that the top of the EV set may be unbounded –

in which case it is unbounded for every feasible E - whereas the bottom is always bounded. From this point on in this section, we will be concerned exclusively with comparing the top and the bottom when the top is bounded. We have seen in the case of a bounded top that the top, like the bottom, of the obtainable EV set is continuous and consists of pieces of parabolas and/or horizontal lines. The present section shows, on the other hand, that some of the properties of the bottom are not true of the top.

We saw in chapter 5 that the lower boundary of the obtainable EV set is convex. An example will show that the top may be neither convex nor concave.

We have seen that, if a particular *IN* set provides minimum V for some E, then it does so for a closed (bounded or unbounded) interval. It cannot, for example, provide minimum V for E in two disjoint intervals without doing so in the interval which lies between. The example mentioned in the previous paragraph will also show that the top of the feasible EV set differs in the present matter. It is possible for a given *IN* set to provide maximum V for given E for two disjoint E intervals without also doing so for the intervening interval.

The example which serves the two purposes described above also shows that, while the set of EV combinations on top is always continuous, the curve in portfolio space which provides this top may necessarily be discontinuous; that is, for a given model no continuous curve $X(E)$ may exist which provides the top. An example in an exercise will further illustrate the discontinuity of the curve in portfolio space which provides the (continuous) top of the feasible EV set.

Let us reconsider the standard model with μ and C in (10.1), as illustrated in figure 10.1. Theorem 10.7 assures us that in order to determine the top of the obtainable EV set, we need only consider *IN* sets with $m+1 = 2$ members. The feasible segment of the EV parabola for the *IN* set (1, 2) is the curve *ab*; that for the *IN* set (2, 3) is the curve *bc*; that for the *IN* set (1, 3) is the straight line *ac*. As the reader can confirm algebraically, the line *ac* intersects the curve *ab* at the point *f* where $E = 1.667$, and intersects the line *bc* at the point *g* where $E = 2.333$. (*ac* also intersects *ab* at *a*, and *bc* at *c*.) The line *ac* provided by the *IN* set (1,3) is on top in the open intervals

$$1.0 < E < 1.667$$

$$2.333 < E < 3.0$$

but not in the intermediate interval

$$1.667 < E < 2.333$$

Thus a given *IN* set can provide the top of the EV set for two (or more - see exercise 10.1) nonadjacent intervals.

The top of the EV set in figure 10.1 is *afbgc*. This is neither convex nor concave.

Except at the points *f* and *g*, only one portfolio provides maximum V for given E. Whether we choose the point from the (1,2) *IN* set or that from the

(1,3) as the efficient portfolio at $E = 1.667$, there will be a discontinuity in the set of efficient portfolios either as $E \downarrow 1.667$ or as $E \uparrow 1.667$. A similar discontinuity occurs at g.

In the three-security example of figure 10.1, one security "jumps" to zero from a positive number at f while another security jumps to a positive number from zero. To dispel any notion that things happen "one security at a time" on the top of the feasible EV set, as they do on the bottom, exercise 10.2 provides a four-security example in which two securities jump from zero to positive values, while the two others jump from positive values to zero.

The Sides of the Feasible EV Set

Definitions If a portfolio selection model has a minimum obtainable E, say $E_{\min}$, then the *left side* of the EV obtainable set is the set of obtainable EV combinations with $E = E_{\min}$. If the model has a maximum obtainable E, say $E_{\max}$, then the *right side* of the EV obtainable set is the set of obtainable EV combinations with $E = E_{\max}$.

Consider, for example, the standard three-security portfolio analysis with

$$C = \begin{pmatrix} 1 & 0 & 0 \\ 0 & 1 & 0 \\ 0 & 0 & 1 \end{pmatrix}$$

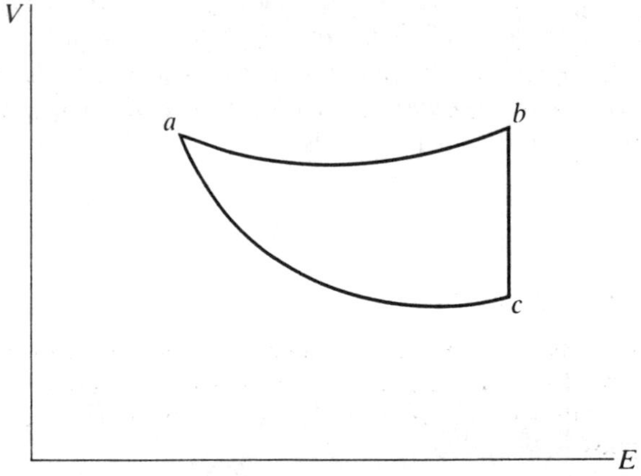

Figure 10.3 Example in which the right side of the obtainable EV set is a vertical line

$\mu' = (1, 2, 2)$

The minimum value of E is provided by (1, 0, 0), whereas the maximum value of E is provided by any feasible portfolio with $X_1 = 0$, $X_2 + X_3 = 1$. Among these, the portfolio (0, 1/2, 1/2) provides minimum variance; either (0, 0, 1) or (0, 1, 0) provides maximum variance. If the reader sets up and solves the equations for the critical line l_{123} he or she will find that it passes through the points (1, 0, 0) and (0, 1/2, 1/2), and is feasible at these points (and between). Thus l_{123} provides the entire bottom of the set of the obtainable EV set. Thus the feasible EV set is as shown in figure 10.3. Points a, b, and c are the EV combinations associated with (1, 0, 0), with either (0, 1, 0) or (0, 0, 1), and with (0, 1/2, 1/2), respectively. The left side of the obtainable EV set is a single point, whereas the right side in this instance is the line bc.

Other possibilities concerning left and right sides include the following. If E is unbounded above (below) then the EV set has no right (left) side; if E has an upper (lower) bound but V is unbounded for given E, then the right (left) side is unbounded above. If E is bounded from above and below then either, neither, or both the left and right boundary may be a single point depending on whether a unique portfolio maximizes (minimizes) E. If more than one portfolio maximizes (minimizes) E it is still possible (though not usual) for all E maximizing (minimizing) portfolios to have the same V, and thus provide a single point as the right (left) boundary.

Exercises

10.1 In a standard four-security model, suppose $\mu' = (1, 2, 3, 4)$; $V_1 = V_4 = 1$; $V_2 = V_3 = 1.5$; $\rho_{14} = 1$; all other $\rho_{ij} = 0$ for $i \neq j$. Determine and sketch the top of the EV set. How many times is the (1, 4) "parabola" on top? (Hint: first show that if $\rho_{ij} = 0$ and $X_i + X_j = 1$, then V has a minimum of

$$V_i V_j / (V_i + V_j)$$

at

$$X_i = V_j / (V_i + V_j)$$

Sketch the six "parabolas" obtained by taking pairs of securities. The symmetry of the problem, and the fact that the feasible ranges of some of the parabolas do not overlap, reduces the number of intersections which must be computed.)

10.2 In a standard four-security model, suppose $\mu' = (1, 2, 3, 4)$; $V_1 = V_2 = V_3 = V_4 = 1$; $\rho_{ij} = 0$ for $i \neq j$. Show that at $E = 2.5$ the top of the EV set jumps from the (1, 3) to the (2, 4) parabola.

Part IV

Special Cases

11

Canonical Form of the Two-Dimensional Analysis

The preceding part of this book contains the solution to the general portfolio selection model defined in chapter 2. The present part considers various special cases and applications.

For example, in the general solution we saw that any feasible model with efficient portfolios has a piecewise linear, complete nonredundant set of efficient portfolios. When efficient portfolios are unique for given E, this may be stated simply as: the set of efficient portfolios is piecewise linear. In the particular case of an affine constraint set investigated in chapter 6, such as Black's model, the set of efficient portfolios is typically a ray starting at a portfolio with minimum V and extending indefinitely in a direction of increasing E. As a consequence, if all investors had the same μ and C then the market portfolio would be an efficient portfolio (exercise 6.1). We will see in chapter 12 that, as Tobin, Sharpe, and Lintner showed, in the Tobin-Sharpe-Lintner model the set of efficient portfolios is also typically a straight line starting at a minimum variance (actually, a zero-variance) portfolio and extending indefinitely in a direction of increasing E. Consequently, as with the Black model, the market portfolio is an efficient portfolio.

More generally, in the next chapter we will show that the market portfolio is an efficient portfolio in any model whose constraint set is a cone whose vertex minimizes variance among portfolios in the model's affine hull. We will also investigate other generalizations of capital asset pricing model (CAPM) results.

In the present chapter we principally consider the two-dimensional analysis, i.e. the case in which the portfolio selection model has a two-dimensional affine hull. This includes the standard three-security analysis, Black's model with three securities, and the Tobin-Sharpe-Lintner analysis with two risky and one riskless security. A *canonical* method of graphical analysis is presented here which is frequently much more revealing than the original (Markowitz, 1952, 1959) method. (The canonical analysis is generalized to the k dimensional case in the last section of this chapter.)

The two-dimensional analysis is a fertile source of examples and counter-examples such as the following:

(1) The critical line algorithm admits the possibility that the set of efficient EV combinations may have a kink. Such cases are easy to construct in the two-dimensional case.

(2) In trying to generalize the Tobin-Sharpe-Lintner result to more general conical constraint sets, the thought occurred that perhaps the result follows as long as the vertex of the feasible cone has minimum feasible variance. A two-dimensional example shows that this is not the case.

(3) We noted that if all investors believed the same μ and C, all chose portfolios subject to the same constraint set, and this constraint set is affine or Tobin-Sharpe-Lintner, then the market portfolio is an efficient portfolio. Two-dimensional examples show that this conclusion is not true for arbitrary constraint sets, and illustrate why it is typically not true for most bounded constraint sets.

The Standard Three-security Analysis

In the standard three-security analysis we may substitute $1-X_1-X_2$ for X_3 to obtain the constraints

$$X_1 \geqslant 0$$

$$X_2 \geqslant 0$$

$$1-X_1-X_2 \geqslant 0$$

i.e.

$$X_1+X_2 \leqslant 1$$

The feasible set in the X_1X_2 plane, as illustrated in figure 11.1, consists of those points which are above the X_1 axis, to the right of the X_2 axis, and below the line $X_1+X_2=1$.

If we also substitute $1-X_1-X_2$ for X_3 in the formula for portfolio return we get

$$\begin{aligned} R &= X_1r_1+X_2r_2+X_3r_3 \\ &= r_3+X_1(r_1-r_3)+X_2(r_2-r_3) \end{aligned}$$

Define

$$u_0=r_3 \tag{11.1a}$$

$$u_1=r_1-r_3 \tag{11.1b}$$

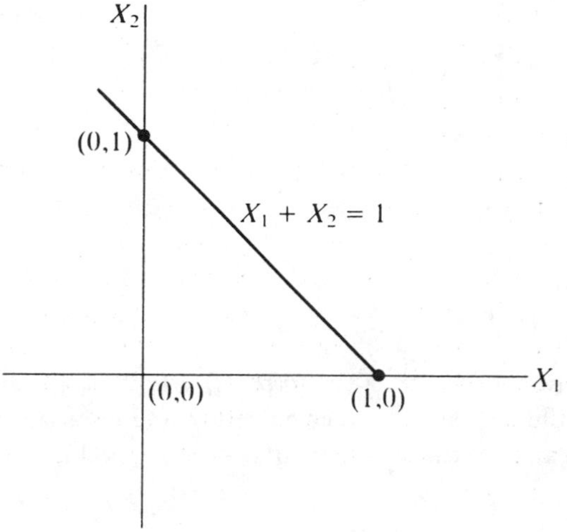

Figure 11.1 Feasible set for the standard three-security analysis

$$u_2 = r_2 - r_3 \tag{11.1c}$$

Then

$$R = u_0 + u_1 X_1 + u_2 X_2 \tag{11.2a}$$

Therefore

$$E = \nu_0 + \nu_1 X_1 + \nu_2 X_2 \tag{11.2b}$$

where

$$\nu_i = E(u_i) \tag{11.2c}$$

and

$$V = (1, X_1, X_2) \begin{pmatrix} \tau_{00} & \tau_{01} & \tau_{02} \\ \tau_{10} & \tau_{11} & \tau_{12} \\ \tau_{20} & \tau_{21} & \tau_{22} \end{pmatrix} \begin{pmatrix} 1 \\ X_1 \\ X_2 \end{pmatrix} \tag{11.2d}$$

where

$$\tau_{ij} = \text{cov}(u_i, u_j) \tag{11.2e}$$

The relationship between $u' = (u_0, u_1, u_2)$ and $r' = (r_1, r_2, r_3)$ is

$$u = Hr \tag{11.3}$$

where

$$H = \begin{pmatrix} 0 & 0 & 1 \\ 1 & 0 & -1 \\ 0 & 1 & -1 \end{pmatrix}$$

This is nonsingular; in fact,

$$H^{-1} = \begin{pmatrix} 1 & 1 & 0 \\ 1 & 0 & 1 \\ 1 & 0 & 0 \end{pmatrix}$$

Using the notation $Er = E(r_1, r_2, r_3) = [E(r_1), E(r_2), E(r_3)]$, given any μ and a positive semidefinite C as the expected return and covariance matrix of r, the expected return and covariance matrix of $u = (u_0, u_1, u_2)$ is

$$\begin{aligned} \nu &= EHr \\ &= HEr \\ &= H\mu \end{aligned} \tag{11.4a}$$

and

$$\begin{aligned} (\tau_{ij}) &= E\{[H(r-\mu)]\,[H(r-\mu)]'\} \\ &= HCH' \end{aligned} \tag{11.4b}$$

Conversely, given any ν and positive semidefinite (τ_{ij}) we can find the μ and C to which these correspond by

$$\mu = H^{-1}\nu \tag{11.5a}$$

$$C = (H^{-1})\,(\tau)\,(H^{-1})' \tag{11.5b}$$

Thus if we explore all the cases which can arise by arbitrary choice of ν and positive semidefinite (τ_{ij}) we also explore all the cases that arise by arbitrary choice of μ and positive semidefinite C.

Suppose that a three-security portfolio selection model consists of the equation

$$\Sigma X_i = 1$$

and inequalities

$$a_{i1}X_1 + a_{i2}X_2 + a_{i3}X_3 \geqslant b_i \qquad i = 1, \ldots, I \tag{11.6a}$$

where the inequalities in (11.6a) may or may not include inequalities $X_j \geqslant 0$, $j = 1, 2, 3$. Substituting $X_3 = 1 - X_1 - X_2$ into (11.6a) we get inequalities in the

X_1X_2 plane

$$\tilde{a}_{i1}X_1 + \tilde{a}_{i2}X_2 \geqslant \tilde{b}_i \qquad i = 1, \ldots, I \tag{11.6b}$$

Possibilities encompassed by (11.6b) include: the model is infeasible; only a single point satisfies all the inequalities in (11.6b); an unbounded region satisfies all the constraints; the feasible portfolios constitute a line, a ray or a line segment; or the feasible portfolios constitute a K sided convex polygon such as those in figure 11.2. We will deal principally with the standard model, but will illustrate how our methods apply to models with constraints (11.6b).

Theorems 11.8-11.10 in the last section of this chapter show that our present discussion applies, not only to three-security models subject to $\Sigma X = 1$, but to

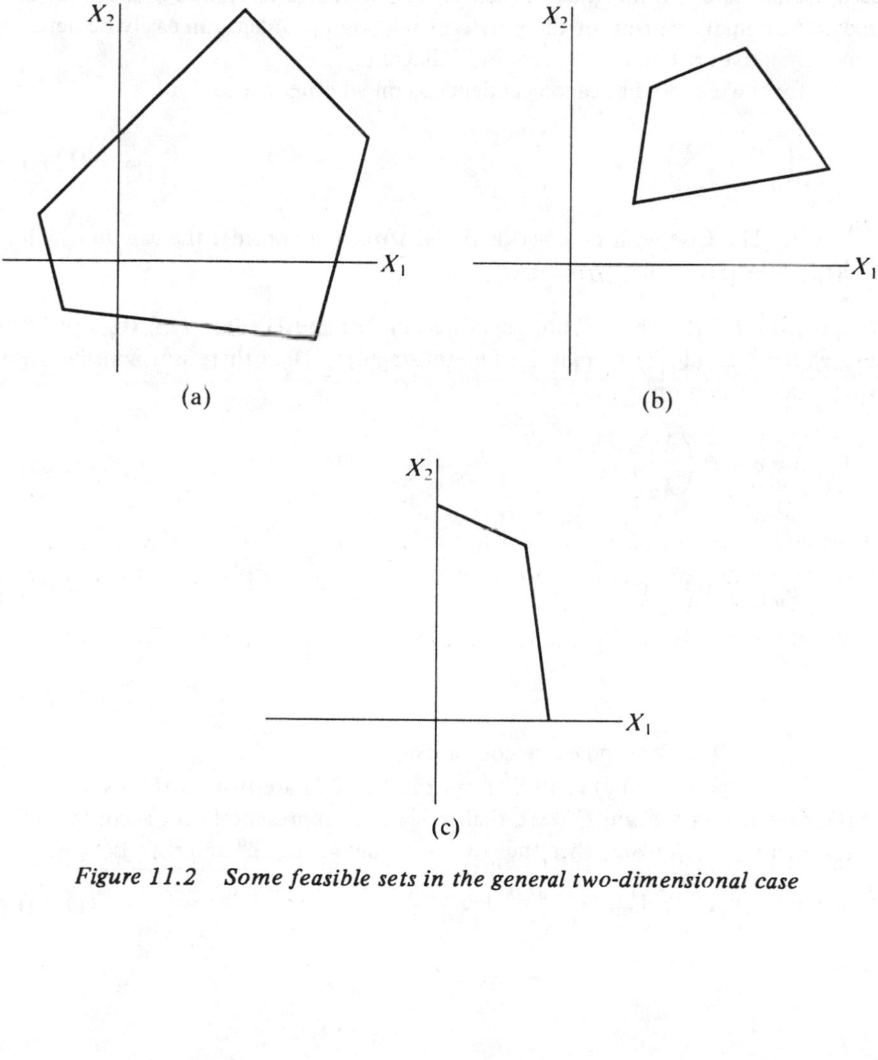

Figure 11.2 Some feasible sets in the general two-dimensional case

any model with a two-dimensional affine hull not containing $X=0$. More generally, these theorems analyze arbitrary portfolio selection models with k dimensional affine hulls. They treat slightly differently the case when $X=0$ is in the hull from that in which it is not.

Canonical Form when Rank is 2

We next consider certain affine transformations of the (X_1, X_2) coordinate system. The purpose of these transformations is to reduce the two-dimensional portfolio selection problem to a simple canonical form in which the set of efficient portfolios can be seen immediately from a diagram, diagrams can be easily constructed to illustrate the existence of various usual and unusual cases, and an "original" version of the portfolio selection problem can easily be determined that gives rise to a given canonical diagram.

The form we choose as canonical depends on whether the rank of

$$\tau^* = \begin{pmatrix} \tau_{11} & \tau_{12} \\ \tau_{21} & \tau_{22} \end{pmatrix} \tag{11.7}$$

is 1 or 2. (The case with rank $=0$ is trivial.) We first consider the case in which τ^* has rank $=2$.

Theorem 11.1 If E and V are given by (11.2b) and (11.2d) with $(\nu_1, \nu_2) \neq 0$ and with τ^* in (11.7) of rank 2 - i.e. nonsingular - then there is a nonsingular affine transformation

$$\begin{pmatrix} Y_1 \\ Y_2 \end{pmatrix} = a + G \begin{pmatrix} X_1 \\ X_2 \end{pmatrix} \tag{11.8a}$$

such that

$$V = V_{\min} + Y_1^2 + Y_2^2 \tag{11.8b}$$

and

$$E = a_0 + a_1 Y_1 \tag{11.8c}$$

where $V_{\min} \geqslant 0, a_1 > 0$ and a_0 are constants.

If $(X^a)' = (X_1^a, X_2^a, X_3^a)$ and $(X^b)' = (X_1^b, X_2^b, X_3^b)$ are two portfolios satisfying $\Sigma X_i = 1$, and Y^a and Y^b are their respective representations, according to (11.8a), in the $Y_1 Y_2$ plane, then the covariance between $r'X^a$ and $r'X^b$ is

$$\operatorname{cov}(r'X^a, r'X^b) = V_{\min} + Y_1^a Y_1^b + Y_2^a Y_2^b \tag{11.8d}$$

Proof Equation (11.2d) expresses V as a (not necessarily homogeneous) quadratic function of X_1 and X_2. The appendix to the book reviews the fact that there is a nonsingular affine transformation such that

$$V = V_{\min} + Z_1^2 + Z_2^2$$

If B is any orthogonal transformation and

$$Y = BZ$$

then $Y_1^2 + Y_2^2 = Z_1^2 + Z_2^2$ since B preserves lengths; therefore

$$\begin{aligned} V &= V_{\min} + Y_1^2 + Y_2^2 \\ &= (1, Y_1, Y_2) \begin{pmatrix} V_{\min} & 0 & 0 \\ 0 & 1 & 0 \\ 0 & 0 & 1 \end{pmatrix} \begin{pmatrix} 1 \\ Y_1 \\ Y_2 \end{pmatrix} \\ &= (1, Y_1, Y_2)\, D \begin{pmatrix} 1 \\ Y_1 \\ Y_2 \end{pmatrix} \end{aligned}$$

To assure (11.8c), choose B so that $Y = (1, 0)$ is the same direction as the (assumed nonzero) expected return vector. Since

$$\begin{aligned} X'CX &= (1, X_1, X_2)\, \tau \begin{pmatrix} 1 \\ X_1 \\ X_2 \end{pmatrix} \\ &= (1, Y_1, Y_2)\, D \begin{pmatrix} 1 \\ Y_1 \\ Y_2 \end{pmatrix} \\ &= \tilde{Y}' D \tilde{Y} \end{aligned}$$

where $\tilde{Y}' = (1, Y_1, Y_2)$, we have

$$\begin{aligned} &(X^a + X^b)'C(X^a + X^b) - (X^a - X^b)'C(X^a - X^b) \\ &\qquad = (\tilde{Y}^a + \tilde{Y}^b)'D(\tilde{Y}^a + \tilde{Y}^b) - (\tilde{Y}^a - \tilde{Y}^b)'D(\tilde{Y}^a - \tilde{Y}^b) \end{aligned}$$

But the left-hand side of the equality equals $4\,\mathrm{cov}(r'X^a, r'X^b)$ while the right equals $4(\tilde{Y}^a)'D\tilde{Y}^b$, from which (11.8d) follows. ###

Definition For a two-dimensional portfolio analysis with τ^* of rank 2, a coordinate system in terms of which E and V are given by (11.8c) and (11.8b) will be called a *canonical form* of the analysis.

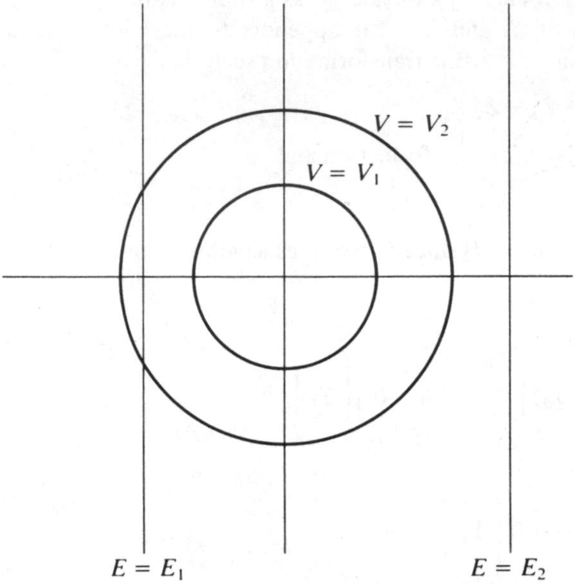

Figure 11.3 Isomean lines and isovariance circles in the canonical two-dimensional analysis with τ^* of rank 2

Figure 11.3 shows the isomean lines and isovariance curves in Y_1Y_2 space. The isomean lines are vertical, and the isovariance sets are circles with the origin $Y = (0, 0)$ as center. The transformation

$$\begin{pmatrix} Y_1^* \\ Y_2^* \end{pmatrix} = \begin{pmatrix} 1 & 0 \\ 0 & -1 \end{pmatrix} \begin{pmatrix} Y_1 \\ Y_2 \end{pmatrix}$$

reverses the positive and negative direction of Y_2, but leaves unchanged lengths, angles, isovariance circles, and isomean vertical lines. Therefore the Y^* as well as the Y coordinate system is canonical.

While nonsingular affine transformations do not necessarily preserve lengths and angles, they do transform straight lines into straight lines, triangles into triangles and, generally, K sided convex polygons into K sided convex polygons. In particular, the affine transformation described in theorem 11.1 transforms the constraint set of the standard model into a triangle; but not necessarily a right triangle, not necessarily an isosceles triangle, and not necessarily one with vertex at the origin. Figures 11.4(a)–(c) each contain an isovariance set for the transformed model, an arrow in the direction of increasing E, and a triangle. We know that the set of obtainable portfolios for the standard three-security

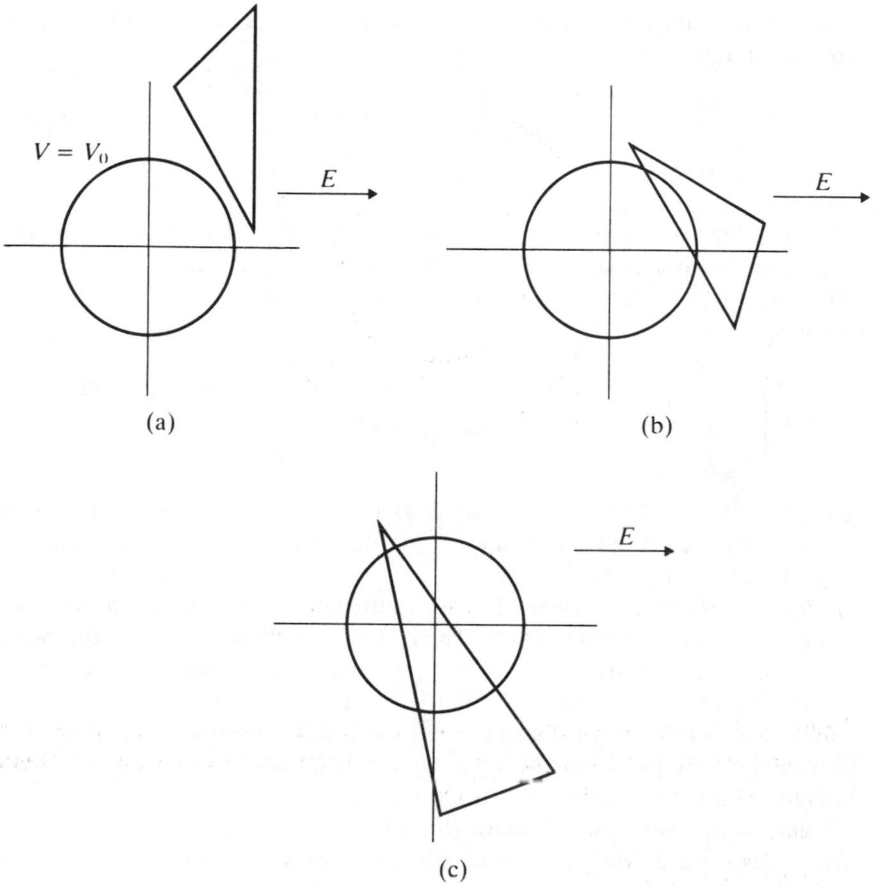

Figure 11.4 *Which triangle(s) can represent a transformed standard constraint set?*

analysis is transformed from its original triangular shape to a new triangle. Which of the triangles in figures 11.4(a)-(c) could be the transformed feasible set for the standard model? The following theorem assures us that any of them can be.

Theorem 11.2 With notation as previously introduced in this chapter, given any triangle T in the Y_1Y_2 plane there exists a covariance matrix C and expected return vector μ such that, when the standard portfolio selection model is transformed into one of its canonical forms, the set of feasible portfolios is transformed into the given triangle T.

Proof Equation (11.3) is a nonsingular transformation of the returns: $u = Hr$. The compensating transformation of the portfolio vector, $\tilde{X} = (H^{-1})'X$ according to chapter 5, is

$$\tilde{X} = \begin{pmatrix} X_0 \\ X_1 \\ X_2 \end{pmatrix} = \begin{pmatrix} 1 & 1 & 1 \\ 1 & 0 & 0 \\ 0 & 1 & 0 \end{pmatrix} \begin{pmatrix} X_1 \\ X_2 \\ X_3 \end{pmatrix}$$

This nonsingular transformation maps the $X_1 + X_2 + X_3 = 1$ plane into the $X_0 = 1$ plane, and leaves X_1 and X_2 unchanged. $V = (\tilde{X})'\tau\tilde{X}$ for τ in (11.2d). Theorem 11.1 can be restated as showing the existence of a nonsingular *linear* mapping

$$\tilde{Y} = \begin{pmatrix} Y_0 \\ Y_1 \\ Y_2 \end{pmatrix} = \tilde{G}\tilde{X}$$

such that $V = \tilde{Y}'D\tilde{Y} = X'CX$, for the D in the proof of theorem 11.1 (also $E = \mu'X = (a_0, a_1, 0)\,\tilde{Y})$ for X and $\tilde{Y}$ in the affine hull, where $\tilde{G}$ maps the $X_0 = 1$ plane into the $\tilde{Y}_0 = 1$ plane.

The vertices of the triangle T may be thought of as three points (not in a straight line) in the $\tilde{Y}_0 = 1$ plane. There is a nonsingular linear transformation which maps these three points into e^1, e^2, and e^3 of X space. The covariance matrix D (in terms of $\tilde{Y}$) and the expected return vector ν map into C and μ in terms of X in the manner illustrated in (11.5). But if we start with this C and μ and transform X into $\tilde{Y}$ so that e^1, e^2, and e^3 map into the vertices of T then we find that $\tilde{Y}$ is in canonical form, by construction.

Since D is positive semidefinite (for any choice of $V_{\min} \geqslant 0$) the C derived from it, as in the previous paragraph, is also positive semidefinite. ###

Given any triangle in the Y_1Y_2 plane, it is easy to determine an expected return vector $\mu' = (\mu_1, \mu_2, \mu_3)$ and a covariance matrix C for the original r_1, r_2, r_3 such that the given triangle is the constraint set for the canonical form of the standard analysis with this μ and C. Arbitrarily choose $V_{\min} \geqslant 0$, any a_0, and any $a_1 > 0$. Arbitrarily assign the numbers 1, 2, 3 to the vertices of the triangle. For the ith vertex, compute μ_i using (11.8c), V_i using (11.8b), and σ_{ij} using (11.8d). This provides the desired μ and C.

Thus if we find a canonical example whose efficient sets have noteworthy properties (and if the properties are not changed by an affine change in the coordinate systems) then we can use (11.8b), (11.8c), and (11.8d) to easily determine an "original" standard model with the same properties. It is usually more difficult to start with the μ and C of a standard model and find the triangle of its canonical form. A procedure for this is given in the appendix to this chapter.

Efficient Sets in the Canonical Analysis (Rank 2)

If we define

$$E^* = (E - a_0)/a_1 \tag{11.9a}$$

then

$$E^* = Y_1 \tag{11.9b}$$

The set of E^*V efficient portfolios is the same as the set of EV efficient portfolios. The shapes of the EV and $E\sigma$ efficient sets are unchanged, except for the choice of unit and scale on the E axis. Below we refer to E in statements which are true for any choice of unit and scale, and to E^* for statements which require (11.9b).

Let l_1 be any straight line in the $Y_1 Y_2$ plane. The point on l_1 with minimum V is the point with smallest $Y_1^2 + Y_2^2$, i.e. the point closest to the origin. The Pythagorean theorem of plane geometry implies that, unless l_1 actually passes through the origin, the point with minimum V on l_1 is the point P such that $0P$ is perpendicular to l_1 as in figures 11.5(b), (c), and (d).

Since the isomean lines are the vertical lines of the plane (for either E or E^*) the point which has minimum V for given E is the point where the isomean line crosses the Y_1 axis, such as the point P in figure 11.5(d). The Pythagorean theorem implies that given two points with the same E, and therefore with the same value of Y_1, the one with the smaller $|Y_2|$ has the smaller V.

The affine transformation that brings the standard triangle to the triangle T in the $Y_1 Y_2$ plane does not preserve lengths and angles. Nevertheless one can tell the proportions invested in the three securities for any portfolio P in triangle T. The vertices of the triangle, such as points a, b, and c in figure 11.6, correspond to the vertices of the standard triangle, and therefore represent undiversified portfolios. For the moment it is of no concern to us as to which vertex of the original triangle mapped into a, b, or c. We will refer to vertex a as having a 100 percent investment in security a; and similarly for b and c. A point on the line segment between a and b represents a portfolio with no security c, but with some of both securities a and b. If the point is one-fourth of the way from a to b then the portfolio consists of 75 percent a and 25 percent b.

If the point is within the triangle, it represents a portfolio with some of all three securities. The proportion of security a in the portfolio may be determined by drawing a line parallel to bc. This line will cut ab at the point b' and ac at the point c' in figure 11.6.

$$\frac{b'b}{ab} = \frac{c'c}{ac}$$

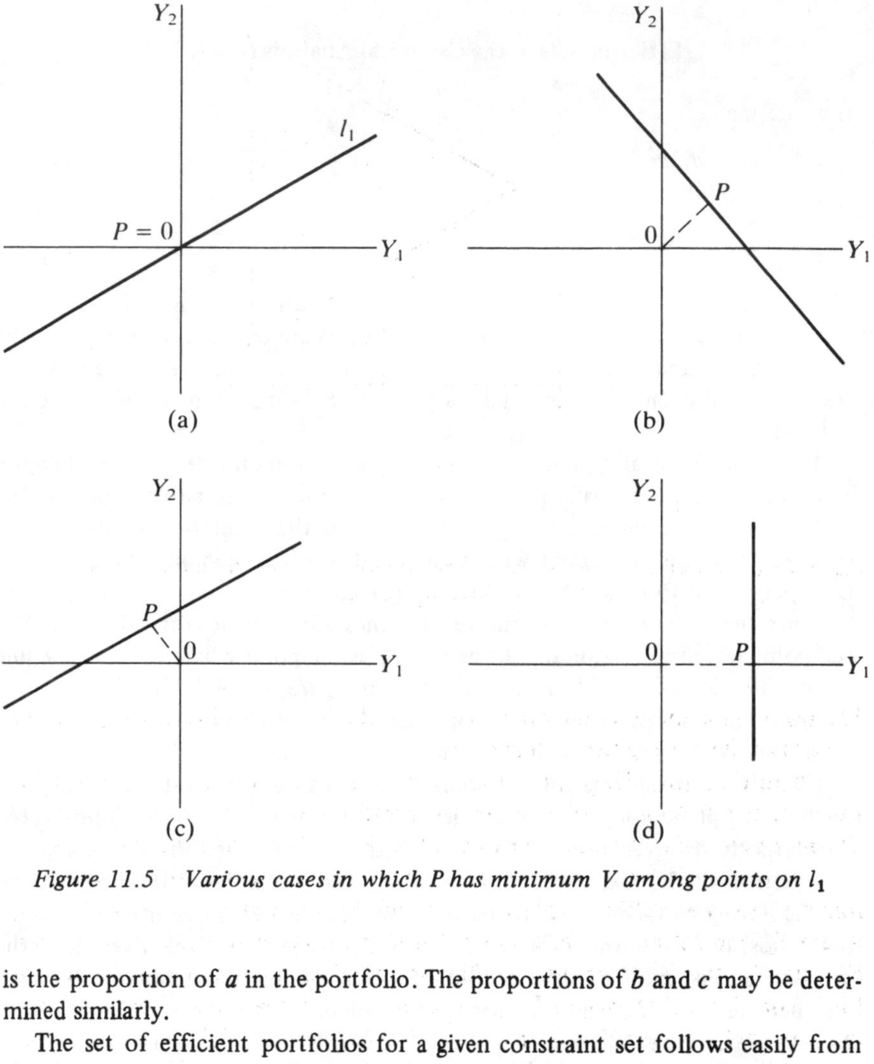

Figure 11.5 Various cases in which P has minimum V among points on l_1

is the proportion of a in the portfolio. The proportions of b and c may be determined similarly.

The set of efficient portfolios for a given constraint set follows easily from the above considerations. Figure 11.7 shows efficient sets for various triangular feasible sets. In each figure the set of feasible portfolios is the triangle abc. In figure 11.7(a) the point d on ab, such that $0d$ is perpendicular to ab, has less variance than any other point on the line through ab. It is also the feasible portfolio with minimum variance, since all other feasible portfolios lie above the line through a and b. The portfolio c has maximum E (and E^*). There is an efficient portfolio for every value of E (and E^*) between that at d and that at c; i.e. for $Y_1 = \underline{E}^*$ through $Y_1 = \bar{E}^*$. Since all feasible portfolios have positive Y_2 in figure

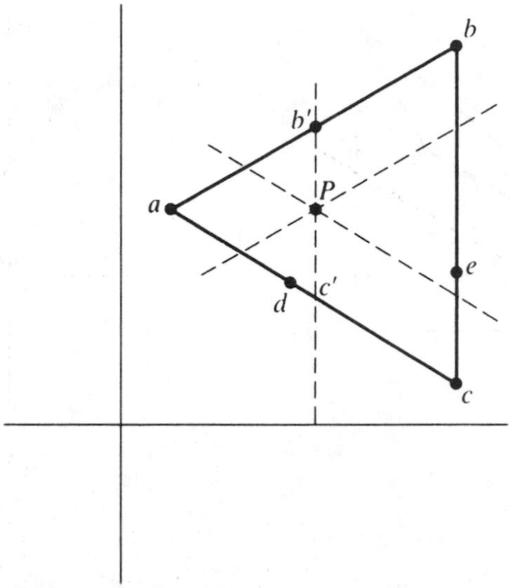

Figure 11.6 Portfolios represented by points in the transformed standard triangle

11.7(a), $|Y_2|$ is minimized by minimizing Y_2. Thus the set of efficient portfolios consists of the line segments *db* and *bc*.

In figure 11.7(b) the point *d* again minimizes V on the line through *a* and *b*. But *d* is not feasible. The undiversified portfolio at *a* has minimum variance. The set of efficient portfolios consists of the segment *ab* plus the segment *bc*.

In figure 11.7(c) the point at *d* minimizes variance among all feasible portfolios. There is one efficient portfolio for each Y_1 between $Y_1 = E_d^*$ and $Y_1 = E_c^*$, where E_d^* and E_c^* are the values of E^* at *d* and *c* respectively. For Y_1 between E_d^* and E_e^*, the point on the line through *ab* gives minimum feasible value of $|Y_2|$. For $Y_1 = E_e^*$ through E_f^* the horizontal axis is feasible and provides minimum (namely zero) $|Y_2|$ for given Y_1. For E_f^* through E_c^* the points on the segment *fc* give minimum $|Y_2|$ for given Y_1. Thus the set of efficient portfolios in figure 11.7(c) consists of the segments *de*, *ef*, and *fc*.

In figure 11.7(d) the point *d* has less variance than any other point on the line through *b* and *c*. *d* is not feasible; *c* is the closest feasible point to *d* on the line through *bc*; therefore *c* has minimum variance among feasible points on *bc*. It can be argued similarly, letting *e* play the role of *d*, that *c* has lower variance than any other feasible point on the line through *ac*. Since any line from the origin to a feasible portfolio which is not on *bc* or *ac* must cross one of these

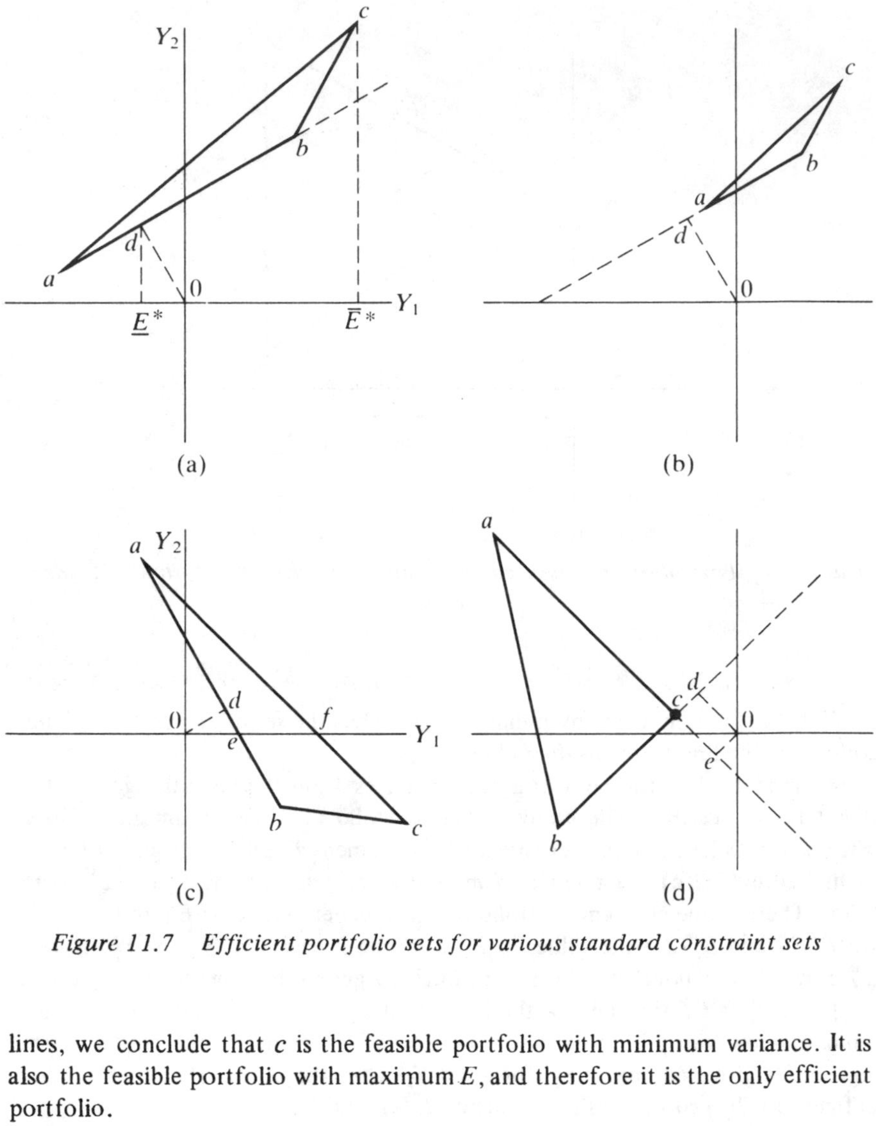

Figure 11.7 Efficient portfolio sets for various standard constraint sets

lines, we conclude that c is the feasible portfolio with minimum variance. It is also the feasible portfolio with maximum E, and therefore it is the only efficient portfolio.

Figure 11.8 illustrates the set of efficient portfolios for a nonstandard constraint set. The set of feasible portfolios in the Y_1Y_2 plane comprises the points on and in the polygon *abcefgha*. The feasible portfolio with minimum variance is the point d. That with maximum E is the point f. There is one efficient portfolio for each value of Y_1 between E_d^* and E_f^*. Between the point i where bc intersects the horizontal axis and the point j where ce intersects the hori-

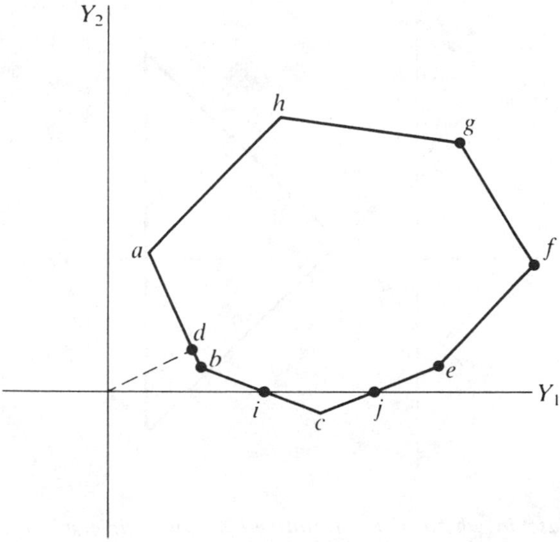

Figure 11.8 Efficient portfolios for a nonstandard constraint set

zontal axis, $Y_2 = 0$ is feasible for each Y_1. Otherwise, in this particular figure, $|Y_2|$ is minimized by minimizing Y_2. The set of efficient portfolios therefore comprises the segments *db*, *bi*, *ij*, *je*, and *ef*.

Figure 11.9 illustrates a novel possibility. Usually we expect the E maximizing portfolio to be undiversified in the standard analysis, and the V minimizing portfolio to be diversified. In the figure, V is minimized by a portfolio consisting of only security *a* (based on the same argument used with figure 11.7(d)), while the portfolio at *f*, including some *b* and some *c*, is the only efficient portfolio with $E_b^* = E_c^* = \max E$. Note that $E_b = E_c$ is essential to this illustration, but there is a considerable latitude in the placing of the point *a*.

Kinks in the Set of Efficient *EV* Combinations

The critical line algorithm allows for the possibility that only λ, not X, will vary on a critical line and, therefore, there is a kink in the set of efficient *EV* combinations. Among the examples in figures 11.7 through 11.9, some have kinks in their efficient *EV* set and some do not, as we shall now see.

In the $Y_1 Y_2$ plane, a line has constant E if and only if it is vertical. Any other line may be written as $Y_2 = c_0 + c_1 Y_1$. Since $E^* = Y_1$, $dV/dE^* = dV/dY_1$. There-

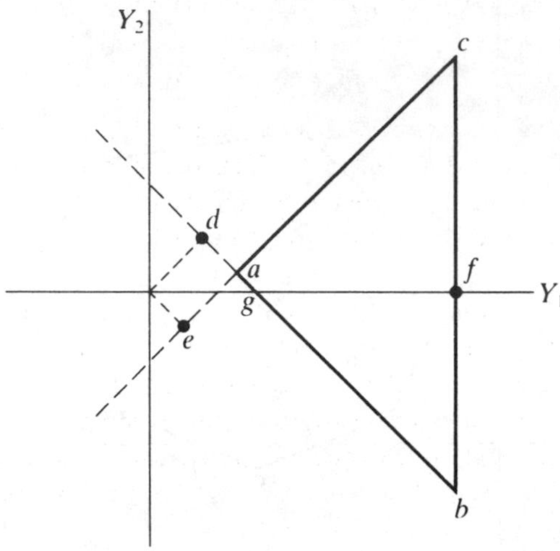

Figure 11.9 *Case in which V is minimized by an undiversified portfolio, and the efficient portfolio with maximum E is diversified*

fore V as a function of E^* (or E) will have a kink if and only if V as a function of Y_1 has a kink. From (11.8b) we compute

$$\frac{\mathrm{d}(1/2)V}{\mathrm{d}Y_1} = Y_1 + Y_2 \frac{\mathrm{d}Y_2}{\mathrm{d}Y_1}$$

$$= Y_1 + c_1 Y_2 \qquad (11.10)$$

Theorem 11.3 Suppose that two lines $Y_2 = c_0^a + c_1^a Y_1$ and $Y_2 = c_0^b + c_1^b Y_1$ intersect at a point $(Y_1, 0)$. At their point of intersection both lines have the same $\mathrm{d}V/\mathrm{d}E$.

Proof Equation (11.10) implies that $\mathrm{d}V/\mathrm{d}E^* = 2Y_1$ on both lines. ###

Theorem 11.4 If two lines $Y_2 = c_0^a + c_1^a Y_1$ and $Y_2 = c_0^b + c_1^b Y_1$ intersect at a point with $Y_2 > 0$ then the one with the larger c_1 has the greater $\mathrm{d}V/\mathrm{d}E$; e.g. $c_1^a > c_1^b$ implies $\mathrm{d}V/\mathrm{d}E$ is greater on the first line than on the second at their intersection. If $Y_2 < 0$ then the line with the smaller c_1 has the greater $\mathrm{d}V/\mathrm{d}E$.

Proof The theorem follows immediately from equation (11.10). ###

Corollary 11.5 If critical line l_1 is efficient for $E_0 \leqslant E \leqslant E_1$ and l_2 is efficient for $E_1 \leqslant E \leqslant E_2$, with $Y^b = (Y_1^b, Y_2^b)$ at the intersection of the two lines, then there is a kink at $E_1^* = Y_1^b$ if and only if $Y_2^b \neq 0$.

Proof There is a kink at $E^* = E_b^* = Y_1^b$ if and only if dV/dE at Y^b is not the same on l_1 and l_2. The two lines must have different slopes, else they would be the same line. Theorems 11.3 and 11.4 then imply the corollary. ###

Corollary 11.5 shows, for example, that there is a kink in the set of efficient EV combinations at portfolio b in figure 11.7(a), and at b in 11.7(b). It shows that there is no kink at either the points e or f in figure 11.7(c). In figure 11.8 there is a kink at b, no kink at either i or j, and a kink at e. In figure 11.9 there is no kink at g.

One should not conclude, from the ease with which one can draw three-security examples with kinks, that kinks in the set of efficient EV combinations are common in practice. A kink occurs at a given *IN* set if and only if the associated affine model has only one feasible E (see exercise 7.6). In the standard analysis, for example, often all efficient portfolios are diversified except the one with maximum E. If *IN* has more than one member in the standard model, a kink occurs if and only if all *IN* securities have the same μ_i. This is certainly a possible, but not a frequent, case.

In the examples of figures 11.7 and 11.9, the kink in the EV set occurs in a subspace in which only one X is feasible; e.g. a subspace in which X_2 and X_3 are out, hence $X = (1, 0, 0)$ is the only feasible X. In the preceding paragraph we spoke as if it were possible for X to not vary, and therefore a kink to occur in the efficient EV set, even if the subspace allows more than one X (though only one value of E is obtainable in the subspace). It is not possible to supply a standard three-security example of this, but it is possible to supply a standard four-security example; see exercise 11.2.

Linear Segments in the Set of Efficient $E\sigma$ Combinations

We saw in chapter 5 that, on any line along which E and V vary, σ is a linear function of E on a segment of a straight line if and only if: (1) the straight line passes through a point Z_0 with zero variance, and (2) the segment does not include Z_0, other than perhaps as an end point. (If the segment includes Z_0 then $\sigma(E)$ along the line is piecewise linear, with two pieces as described in chapter 5.) If the line contains no zero-variance portfolio, then $\sigma(E)$ is hyperbolic.

In the two-dimensional case, if $V_{\min} > 0$ no portfolio in the model's affine hull has zero variance, and therefore no feasible line segment can have σ as a linear function of E. For the remainder of the present section we assume $V_{\min} = 0$. For the case with τ^* of rank 2, the only portfolio with $V = 0$ is $(Y_1, Y_2) = (0, 0)$. Thus a straight line segment passes through a zero-variance portfolio if and only if it passes through the origin. Except for the vertical line $Y_1 = 0$, all such lines are of the form $Y_2 = bY_1$.

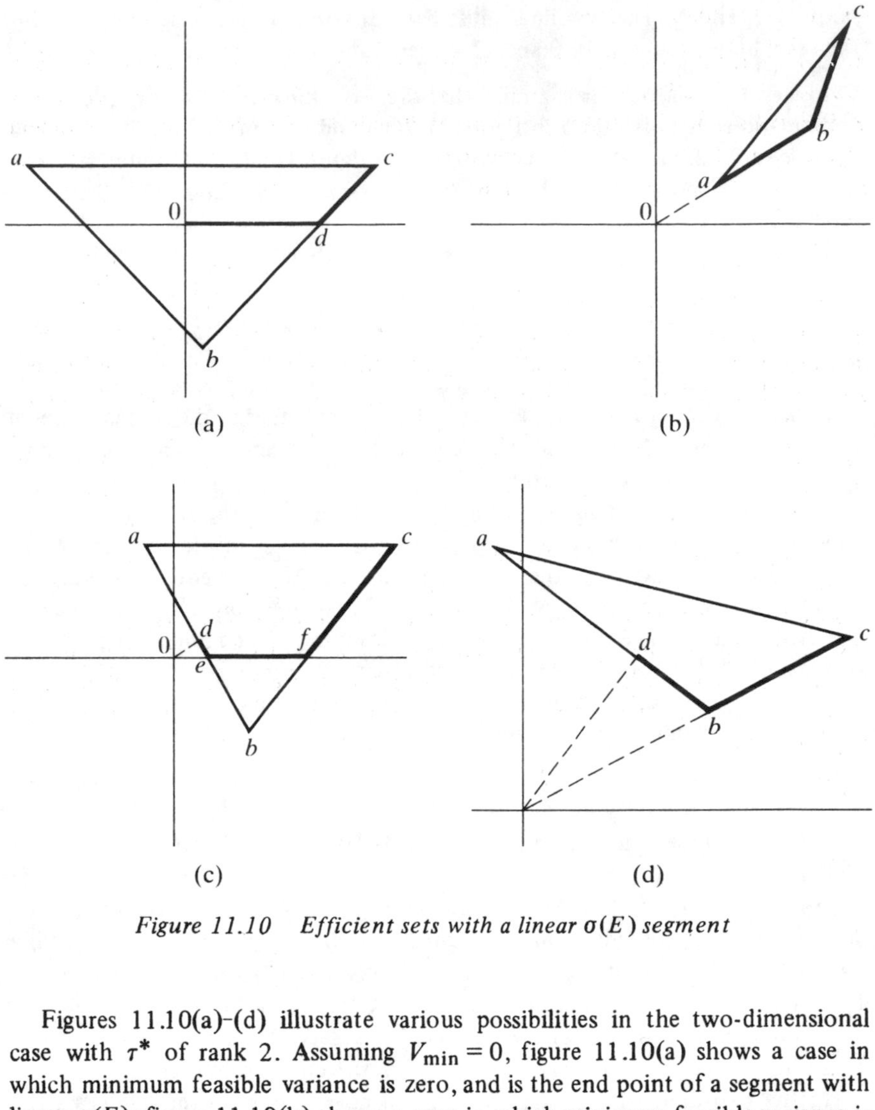

Figure 11.10 Efficient sets with a linear $\sigma(E)$ segment

Figures 11.10(a)–(d) illustrate various possibilities in the two-dimensional case with τ^* of rank 2. Assuming $V_{\min} = 0$, figure 11.10(a) shows a case in which minimum feasible variance is zero, and is the end point of a segment with linear $\sigma(E)$; figure 11.10(b) shows a case in which minimum feasible variance is positive, and is the end point of a segment with linear $\sigma(E)$; figure 11.10(c) shows an efficient set consisting of three line segments of which the middle one has linear $\sigma(E)$; figure 11.10(d) shows an efficient set with two segments of which the one with higher E has the linear $\sigma(E)$. In the two-dimensional case with τ^* of rank 2, it is not possible for more than one segment of the efficient set to have linear $\sigma(E)$. This is an application of the following more general result concerning any portfolio selection model whose affine hull has one zero-variance portfolio.

Theorem 11.6 In any portfolio selection model whose affine hull has one and only one zero-variance portfolio X_0, there is at most one linear segment in the efficient $E\sigma$ set. This linear segment, if it exists, is provided by the efficient segment of exactly one critical line. (In case of degenerate or unbounded problems we assume that the critical lines are chosen as prescribed in theorems 9.14 or 9.15.)

Proof Theorems 9.14 and 9.15 show that the sequence of critical lines for a degenerate model, with bounded or unbounded E, is the same as that of a subsequence $(l_{K+1}, \ldots, l_L)$ of critical lines for a related nondegenerate model with bounded E. It is sufficient therefore to prove the present theorem for nondegenerate models with bounded E. Suppose l_h and l_k, $h<k$, are critical lines with linear segments of $\sigma(E)$. Each line must pass through X_0, though perhaps neither of their efficient segments includes X_0. Thus both $\sigma_h(E)$ and $\sigma_k(E)$ must be segments of lines that pass through $(E_0, 0)$, where E_0 is the expected return of X_0. Since $h<k \leqslant L$, the lines l_h and l_{h+1} intersect at a point $\tilde{X} \neq X_0$, with $E = \tilde{E}$. Since l_h is the only line containing both $\tilde{X}$ and X_0, and theorem 7.9 implies that l_{h+1} is not the same line, we conclude that $\sigma(E)$ is not linear on l_{h+1}. Since $\sigma(E)$ is strictly convex on l_{h+1}, and convex everywhere, for $j>h$ we have $\sigma_j(E)$ above the straight line of which $\sigma_h(E)$ is a segment. In particular a feasible portfolio on l_k has (E, σ) above that on the line through $\sigma_h(E)$; e.g. see point P in figure 11.11. This implies that $\sigma_k(E)$, a segment from a straight line connecting P and $(E_0, 0)$, must have greater slope than $\sigma_h(E)$. But a convex function cannot have a greater derivative at E_1 than E_2 if $E_1 < E_2$. ###

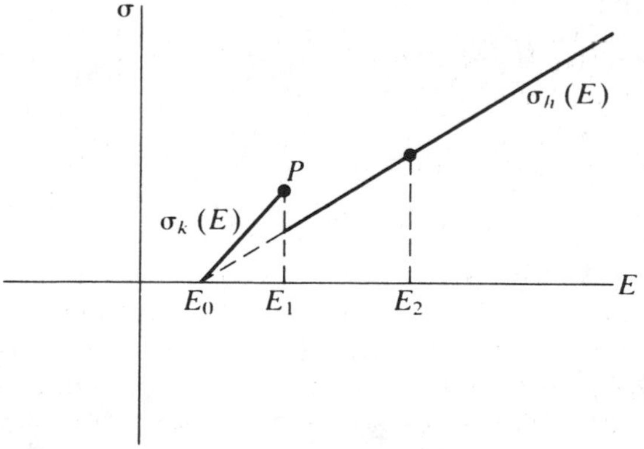

Figure 11.11 *Used in proof of theorem 11.6*

τ^* of Rank 1

Theorem 11.7 When

$$\tau^* = \begin{pmatrix} \tau_{11} & \tau_{12} \\ \tau_{21} & \tau_{22} \end{pmatrix}$$

has rank 1 there is an affine transformation

$$\begin{pmatrix} Y_1 \\ Y_2 \end{pmatrix} = \begin{pmatrix} a_1 \\ 0 \end{pmatrix} + H \begin{pmatrix} X_1 \\ X_2 \end{pmatrix} \tag{11.11}$$

such that H is orthogonal and

$$V = V_{\min} + \tilde{\tau}_{11} Y_1^2 \tag{11.12a}$$

The covariance between two portfolios Y^a and Y^b is

$$\operatorname{cov}(Y^a, Y^b) = V_{\min} + \tilde{\tau}_{11} Y_1^a Y_1^b \tag{11.12b}$$

Note: the theorem does not assert that $Y_1 = E^*$. In general (11.11) transforms E into a new affine function

$$E = \bar{\nu}_0 + \bar{\nu}_1 Y_1 + \bar{\nu}_2 Y_2 \tag{11.13}$$

$(\nu_1, \nu_2) \neq 0$ implies $(\bar{\nu}_1, \bar{\nu}_2) \neq 0$.

Proof Using the notation of (11.1) and (11.2), we first seek an orthogonal transformation

$$\begin{pmatrix} \tilde{u}_1 \\ \tilde{u}_2 \end{pmatrix} = H \begin{pmatrix} u_1 \\ u_2 \end{pmatrix}$$

such that the covariance matrix of $\tilde{u}$ is

$$\begin{pmatrix} \tilde{\tau}_{11} & 0 \\ 0 & 0 \end{pmatrix}$$

In case $\tau_{22} = 0$ then $H = I$; if $\tau_{11} = 0$ then

$$H = \begin{pmatrix} 0 & 1 \\ 1 & 0 \end{pmatrix}$$

Otherwise we have

$$\begin{pmatrix} \tau_{11} & \tau_{12} \\ \tau_{21} & \tau_{22} \end{pmatrix} = \begin{pmatrix} \tau_1^2 & \rho\tau_1\tau_2 \\ \rho\tau_1\tau_2 & \tau_2^2 \end{pmatrix}$$

where τ_i is the standard deviation of u_i, and $\rho = -1$ or $+1$ is the correlation between u_1 and u_2. In this case

$$H = \begin{pmatrix} \tau_1/(\tau_1^2 + \tau_2^2)^{1/2} & \rho\tau_2/(\tau_1^2 + \tau_2^2)^{1/2} \\ -\rho\tau_2/(\tau_1^2 + \tau_2^2)^{1/2} & \tau_1/(\tau_1^2 + \tau_2^2)^{1/2} \end{pmatrix}$$

will serve. This may be shown by confirming that

$$\tilde{u}_2 = (-\rho\tau_2 r_1 + \tau_1 r_2)/(\tau_1^2 + \tau_2^2)^{1/2}$$

has zero variance. (Use the formula for the variance of a weighted sum, the fact that $\tau_{12} = \rho\tau_1\tau_2$, and the fact that $\rho^2 = 1$ in this case.)

Writing the compensating transformation as $\tilde{X} = HX$, we have

$$V = \tau_{00} + 2\tilde{\tau}_{01}\tilde{X}_1 + \tilde{\tau}_{11}(\tilde{X}_1)^2$$

where, as in (11.2d),

$$\tilde{\tau}_{01} = \text{cov}(u_0, \tilde{u}_1)$$

Defining

$$\begin{pmatrix} Y_1 \\ Y_2 \end{pmatrix} = \begin{pmatrix} \tilde{X}_1 \\ \tilde{X}_2 \end{pmatrix} + \begin{pmatrix} \tilde{\tau}_{01}/\tilde{\tau}_{11} \\ 0 \end{pmatrix}$$

we have

$$V = V_{\text{min}} + \tilde{\tau}_{11} Y_1^2$$

where

$$V_{\text{min}} = \tau_{00} - \tilde{\tau}_{01}^2/\tilde{\tau}_{11}$$

Equation (11.12b) is obtained from (11.12a) exactly as (11.8d) is obtained from (11.8b) in the proof of theorem 11.1. ###

Since H is orthogonal in theorem 11.7, and the translation $(a_1, a_2)'$ has $a_2 = 0$, (11.11) leaves the standard three-security constraint set as a right triangle with its right angle somewhere on the Y_1 axis. We leave it as an exercise to show the converse – that any such triangle may be the result of transforming a two-dimensional analysis with τ^* of rank 1 by an affine transformation of the form in theorem 11.7.

Definition The standard model as transformed by (11.11) will be considered the *canonical form when τ^* has rank 1*.

Triangle *abc* in figure 11.12 is a possible transformed standard constraint set T. Equation (11.12a) implies that the vertical line through the origin is the iso-

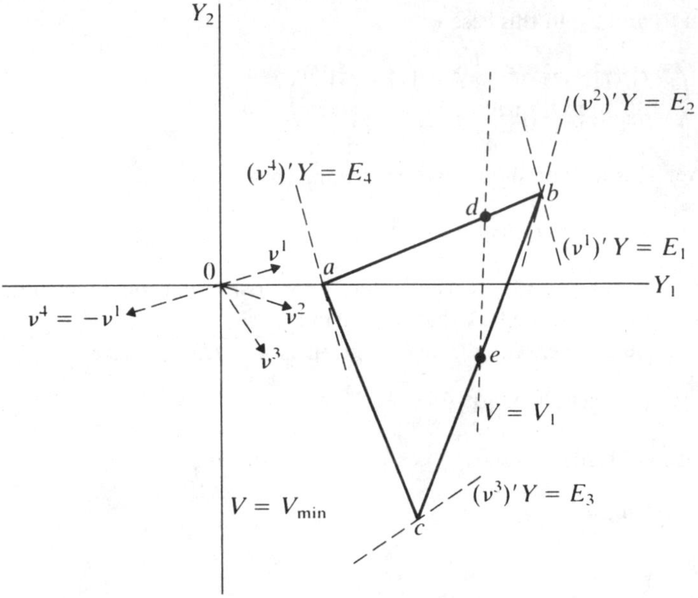

Figure 11.12 Standard three-security analysis with τ^* of rank 1 in canonical form, with various (ν_1^a, ν_2^a) vectors

variance set for $V = V_{min}$. For $V > V_{min}$, (11.12a) implies that the isovariance line for the given V is a pair of vertical lines, such as the vertical line labeled $V = V_1$ in the figure plus another as far to the left of the origin as the line shown is to the right. In the present instance the line $V = V_{min}$ does not intersect T and, as it happens, portfolio a has minimum variance.

The figure shows arrows from the origin to various possible $\bar{\nu} = (\bar{\nu}_1, \bar{\nu}_2)$ vectors such as $\bar{\nu} = \nu^1 = (\nu_1^1, \nu_2^1)$. Isomean lines are perpendicular to the respective arrows (ν vectors). For example if $\bar{\nu} = \nu^1$ then the line labeled $(\nu^1)'Y = E_1$ is the isomean line with $E = E_1$ passing through the point b. No feasible portfolio has higher E when $\bar{\nu} = \nu^1$. Thus portfolio b maximizes $E = (\nu^1)'Y$. Similarly c maximizes $E = (\nu^3)'Y$ and a maximizes $E = (\nu^4)'Y$. In the latter case a is the only efficient portfolio.

If $\bar{\nu}_2 > 0$, as in the case of $\bar{\nu} = \nu^1$ in the figure, then E increases with Y_2 if Y_1 - and therefore V - is held constant. In particular, the portfolio d in the figure has greater E than any other feasible portfolio with $V = V_1$. Indeed, if $\bar{\nu} = \nu^1$ then the line segment ab is the set of efficient portfolios.

If $\bar{\nu}_2 < 0$, as is the case of $\bar{\nu} = \nu^2$ or $\bar{\nu} = \nu^3$, then E increases as Y_2 decreases if Y_1, and therefore V, is held constant. In particular if $\bar{\nu}_2 < 0$ the portfolio e has greatest E among feasible portfolios with $V = V_1$.

If $\bar{\nu} = \nu^3$ then the set of efficient portfolios is the line segment *ac* - since *a* has minimum V, *c* has maximum E, and the portfolios on *ac* minimize V for each value of E between E_a and E_c.

If $\bar{\nu} = \nu^2$ then *b* has maximum E, *a* still has minimum V, and the efficient set consists of the two segments *ac* and *cb*. The shape of the efficient $\sigma(E)$ in this case depends on whether $V_{\min} = 0$ or $V_{\min} > 0$. In case $V_{\min} = 0$, since both the line containing *ac* and that containing *cb* intersect the $V = V_{\min} = 0$ line, $\sigma(E)$ is linear on both *ac* and *cb*. Thus the conclusion of theorem 11.6 does not necessarily hold when τ^* has rank 1. In case $V_{\min} > 0$, no portfolio in the $Y_1 Y_2$ plane has zero variance, and $\sigma(E)$ is a hyperbola on both *ac* and *cb*.

Finally, assume $\bar{\nu} = \nu^5 = (\bar{\nu}_1, 0)$ with $\bar{\nu}_1 > 0$ (not shown in the figure). In this case *d* and *e*, and every portfolio between them, have the same E as well as the same V. In the example in the figure, if $\bar{\nu} = \nu^5$ *every* portfolio is efficient. Not every portfolio has nonsingular $\bar{M}$. If we were to start the critical line algorithm at *b*, at which E is maximized, it would trace out either the segment *ba*, or else the pair of segments *bc* and *ca*, as the set of efficient portfolios. Either set provides a complete nonredundant set of efficient portfolios; however, one set contains more pieces than the other. The path taken depends on how the perturbation described in chapter 9 tilts the $\bar{\nu}$ vector; i.e. it depends on the (arbitrary) ordering of variables in the E maximizing basis.

Given the three vertices of the transformed triangle and the $\bar{\nu}$ arrow of a standard three-security canonical diagram for the case of τ^* with rank 1, a μ and C for the original r_1, r_2, r_3 which gives rise to this canonical diagram may be determined as follows. Choose $V_{\min} \geqslant 0$ and ν_0 arbitrarily. For each vertex of the triangle, and therefore each r_i, determine V_i by (11.12a), σ_{ij} by (11.12b), and $E(r_i)$ by (11.13). Conversely, given a $\mu \neq 0$ and C whose τ^* has rank 1, the $\bar{\nu}, \bar{\tau}_{11}$, and constraint triangle of canonical form can be determined by the procedure in the proof of theorem 11.7.

The *k* Dimensional Canonical Analysis

The following theorems generalize the two-dimensional analysis.

Theorem 11.8 Suppose that a given portfolio selection model, with $V = X'CX$ for given C, has a k dimensional affine hull. Then there exists a nonsingular affine transformation (and its inverse)

$$Y = a + HX$$

$$X = b + KY$$

such that

(i) In the Y coordinate system the affine hull is

$$\{Y: Y_i = 0 \qquad \text{for } k < i \leqslant n\}$$

(ii) For Y in the affine hull,

$$V = V_{\min} + Y'DY$$

where D is a diagonal matrix whose diagonal elements d_{ii} are zero or one.[1]

Proof Let $\tilde{a}$ and $\tilde{H}$ be the vector and matrix of an affine transformation

$$\tilde{X} = \tilde{a} + \tilde{H}X$$

such that the affine hull is

$$\{\tilde{X}: \tilde{X}_i = 0 \qquad k < i \leqslant n\}$$

Write

$$\tilde{X} = \begin{pmatrix} X^1 \\ X^2 \end{pmatrix}$$

where $(X^1)' = (\tilde{X}_1, \ldots, \tilde{X}_k)$ and $(X^2)' = (\tilde{X}_{k+1}, \ldots, \tilde{X}_n)$. For points in the affine hull, $X^2 = 0$, and we may write

$$V = V_0 + \tilde{b}'X^1 + (X^1)'\tilde{C}(X^1)$$

for suitable $\tilde{b}$ and $\tilde{C}$. Let $X^1_{\min}$ be the value of X^1 at which V is minimized among points in the affine hull. We know $X^1_{\min}$ exists, though it may not be unique. Let

$$Z^1 = X^1 - X^1_{\min}$$

be the translation which places the V minimizing portfolio at the origin, $Z^1 = 0$. Then, for points in the affine hull,

$$V = V_{\min} + (Z^1)'\tilde{C}(Z^1)$$

In particular, the linear term $(\Sigma b_i Z^1_i)$ is zero, else for some $i \leqslant k$ we would have $\partial V / \partial Z^1_i \neq 0$ at $Z^1 = 0$, contradicting the assumption that $Z^1 = 0$ minimizes V among points in the affine hull.

Next choose a nonsingular linear transformation

$$Y^1 = H^* Z^1$$

$$Z^1 = K^* Y^1$$

such that $D = (K^*)'\tilde{C}(K^*)$ is a diagonal matrix with diagonal elements equal to zero and one. Since this is a nonsingular transformation of the Z^1 subspace into the Y^1 subspace, the affine hull remains the set of points with $X^2 = 0$.

[1] Because of condition (i) in the theorem, d_{ii} may be chosen arbitrarily for $k < i \leqslant n$. If we choose $d_{ii} = 0$ for such i, then V is not changed if we add $(0, 0, \ldots, 0, c_{k+1}, \ldots, c_n)$ to every Y. Thus the theorem still holds if we require $Y_i = c_i$ for $k < i \leqslant n$ in condition (i), for any given constants c_i.

Defining

$$Y = \begin{pmatrix} Y^1 \\ Y^2 \end{pmatrix} = \begin{pmatrix} H^* & 0 \\ 0 & I \end{pmatrix} \begin{pmatrix} Z^1 \\ X^2 \end{pmatrix}$$

and combining the preceding affine transformations (e.g. the last linear transformation, the preceding translation, etc.) we obtain an affine transformation from X to Y with the characteristics asserted in the theorem. ###

If the affine hull includes $X = 0$, we have $X_{\min} = 0$, and a linear transformation may be used as the affine transformation in the theorem.

The preceding theorem assures us that - for a given C - there is an affine transformation $Y = a + HX$ such that $V = V_{\min} + Y'DY$. The following theorem goes in the reverse direction: it assumes that an affine transformation (among other things) is given, and shows that there is a C such that the given transformation changes $V = X'CX$ into $V = V_{\min} + Y'DY$. Specifically, the following theorem assures us that

Given: any $V_{\min} \geqslant 0$, any D as described in theorem 11.8, any affine transformation $Y = a + HX$ with $a \neq 0$ and nonsingular H such that the model's affine hull is $\{Y: Y_i = 0 \text{ for all } i > k\}$

Then: there is a positive semidefinite C such that $Y = a + HX$ changes $V = X'CX$ into $V = V_{\min} + Y'DY$ for Y in the affine hull.

If $a = 0$, theorem 11.10 proves a similar statement for $V_{\min} = 0$ and $Y = HX$ any nonsingular linear transformation.

The difference between theorems 11.8 and 11.9 may be illustrated in terms of the standard two-dimensional analysis with τ^* of rank 2. Theorem 11.8 assures us that (as we have seen in this particular case) any three-security standard analysis can be reduced to the form defined as canonical for τ^* of rank 2. Theorem 11.9 assures us that (as we have also seen in this case) given any three distinct points P_1, P_2, and P_3 in the plane, not lying on the same straight line, there is a C such that the given affine transformation - namely, one which sends the vertices e^1, e^2, and e^3 into the points P_1, P_2, and P_3 of the plane with $Y_3 = 0$ - transforms $V = X'CX$ into

$$V = V_{\min} + Y'DY$$

where $D = I$ in this case.[2] (As a separate matter, we can choose μ so that E becomes $E = a_0 + a_1 Y_1$.)

Similarly, exercise 11.2 considers a standard four-security model, specifies four points Y^a, Y^b, Y^c, Y^d, and implicitly assumes that there is a C matrix such

[2] As explained in the preceding footnote, we may require $Y_3 = c_3$ for arbitrary c_3. In the proof of theorem 11.2 it was convenient to label the coordinates (Y_0, Y_1, Y_2) and require $Y_0 = 1$.

that a particular affine transformation - i.e. the one which transforms e^1, e^2, e^3, and e^4 into Y^a, Y^b, Y^c, Y^d - also transforms $V = X'CX$ into $V = V_{min} + Y'DY$, where $D = I$. Theorem 11.9 assures us that such a C exists.

In the above examples, it is required that C transforms into $D = I$. The theorem allows the required D to be any diagonal matrix containing ones and zeros. For example, let $n = 3$ and

$$D = \begin{pmatrix} 1 & 0 & 0 \\ 0 & 0 & 0 \\ 0 & 0 & 0 \end{pmatrix}$$

Let P_1, P_2, and P_3 be any three points in the plane, not in a straight line; and let

$$Y = a + HX$$

be the affine transformation such that: (1) the set

$$\{X: \Sigma X_i = 1\}$$

corresponds to the set

$$\{Y: Y_3 = 0\}$$

and (2) the unit vectors e^1, e^2, and e^3 in the X space become the points with (Y_1, Y_2) equal to P_1, P_2, and P_3 respectively. Then theorem 11.9 assures us that there is a covariance matrix C such that $V = X'CX$ becomes $V = V_{min} + Y'DY$ in the new coordinate system for Y in the affine hull.[3]

Theorem 11.9 Suppose that a given portfolio selection constraint set has a k dimensional affine hull not containing $X = 0$. Let

$$Y = a + HX$$

$$X = b + KY$$

be nonsingular affine transformations such that the affine hull is

$$\{Y: Y_i = 0 \qquad \text{for } k < i \leqslant n\}$$

Let V_{min} be any nonnegative number and D be any diagonal matrix whose entries are zero or one. Then there is a covariance matrix C such that

[3] For this D, and for any $V > V_{min}$, the set of (Y_1, Y_2) with this V is a pair of vertical lines equidistant from the origin. If D were a matrix with any value of $d_{11} > 0$ and all other $d_{ij} = 0$, rather than the above D with $d_{11} = 1$, then the set of (Y_1, Y_2) with given $V > V_{min}$ would again be a pair of vertical lines equidistant from the origin. In the canonical analysis with τ^* of rank 1, earlier in this chapter, we did not insist on $d_{11} = 1$, but only on vertical isovariance lines. This allowed us to require that the transformation satisfy equation (11.11) with H orthogonal.

$$V = X'CX = V_{\min} + Y'DY$$

for points in the affine hull.

Proof Partition Y and D into k and $n-k$ rows and/or columns thus:

$$Y = \begin{pmatrix} Y^1 \\ Y^2 \end{pmatrix} \qquad D = \begin{pmatrix} D^{11} & D^{12} \\ D^{21} & D^{22} \end{pmatrix}$$

The affine hull is the set of all points with $Y^2 = 0$. The point $Y = a$ corresponds to $X = 0$. Since this point is not in the affine hull we must have $k < n$ and an $a_i \neq 0$ for some $i > k$. Without loss of generality we may assume $a_n \neq 0$. Since the theorem requires $V = V_{\min} + Y'DY$ only for $Y^2 = 0$, it suffices to prove the theorem for a D with D^{11} as given and a D^{12}, D^{21}, D^{22} of our choosing. Suppose V were given by

$$V = V_{\min} + c_n Y_n + \sum_{i=1}^{k} d_{ii} Y_i^2 + 2 \sum_{i=1}^{k} d_{in} Y_i Y_n + d_{nn} Y_n^2 \tag{11.14}$$

where

$$d_{in} = -d_{ii} a_i / a_n \qquad i = 1 \text{ to } k$$

$$d_{nn} = (V_{\min}/a_n^2) + \sum_{i=1}^{k} d_{ii} a_i^2 / a_n^2$$

$$c_n = 2\left[\left(\sum_{i=1}^{k} d_{ii} a_i^2 / a_n\right) - d_{nn} a_n\right]$$

Since (11.14) satisfies $V = V_{\min} + Y'DY$ when Y is in the affine hull (therefore $Y_n = 0$) we need only show that (11.14) is the result of substituting the given $X = b + KY$ into a homogeneous positive semidefinite quadratic form, $V = X'CX$. This is equivalent to the statement that V in (11.14) has a minimum at $Y = a$, and at that point has $V = 0$. (Since the substitution $Y = a + HX$ expresses V in (11.14) as some kind of quadratic in X, the question is: is it homogeneous and positive definite, i.e. is $V = 0$ when $X = 0$, and $V \geqslant 0$ always?) Take partials and set to zero to confirm that V in (11.14) meets the first-order conditions for a minimum at $Y = a$. (In particular for $i < n$, $\partial V/\partial Y_i = 0$ when $Y_i = (a_i/a_n) Y_n$ for $d_{ii} = 1$, whereas any value of Y_i satisfies $\partial V/\partial Y_i = 0$ when $d_{ii} = 0$. The latter is applicable, in particular, for $k < i < n$. Finally, $Y_n = a_n$ satisfies $\partial V/\partial Y_n = 0$.) Substitute $Y = a$ into (11.14) to confirm that $V = 0$ at this point.

Finally we must, in effect, check the second-order conditions for a minimum at $Y = a$; e.g. we must check that if we move from $Y = a$ along any line $Y =$

$a+\beta t$, V has a minimum at $t=0$. The first-order conditions assure that $dV/dt=0$ at $t=0$. From (11.14) we see that everywhere along the line

$$\frac{1}{2}\frac{d^2V}{dt^2} = \sum_{i=1}^{k} d_{ii}\beta_i^2 - 2\sum_{i=1}^{k} (d_{ii}a_i/a_n)\beta_i\beta_n + \left[\sum_{i=1}^{k} (d_{ii}a_i^2/a_n^2) + V_{\min}/a_n^2\right]\beta_n^2$$

$$= \sum_{i=1}^{k} d_{ii}(\beta_i - a_i\beta_n/a_n)^2 + (V_{\min}/a_n^2)\beta_n^2$$

$$\geqslant 0$$

Thus V is indeed minimized at $t=0$ for all directions β ###

Theorem 11.10 Consider a portfolio selection model whose affine hull includes $X=0$. Let $Y=HX$ be a nonsingular linear transformation such that the affine hull is

$$\{Y: Y_i = 0 \qquad k < i \leqslant n\}$$

Let D be any diagonal matrix whose entries are zero and one. Then there is a covariance matrix C such that $V = X'CX = Y'DY$ for Y in the affine hull.

Proof Let $C = H'DH$. Then $Y'DY = X'H'DHX = X'CX$. ###

Appendix to Chapter 11

This appendix shows how to derive a canonical form for a given standard three-security analysis with $(\nu_1, \nu_2) \neq 0$ and nonsingular τ^*. With u as defined in (11.1), let

$$\begin{pmatrix} u_1^a \\ u_2^a \end{pmatrix} = \begin{pmatrix} [2V_1(1+\rho)]^{-1/2} & [2V_2(1+\rho)]^{-1/2} \\ [2V_1(1-\rho)]^{-1/2} & -[2V_2(1-\rho)]^{-1/2} \end{pmatrix} \begin{pmatrix} u_1 \\ u_2 \end{pmatrix}$$

$$= H^a \begin{pmatrix} u_1 \\ u_2 \end{pmatrix} \tag{11.15}$$

where $V_i = V(u_i)$ and $\rho = \text{corr}(u_1, u_2)$. Confirm that u_1^a and u_2^a are uncorrelated and each has $V(u_i^a) = 1$.

The compensating transformation is

$$\begin{pmatrix} X_1^a \\ X_2^a \end{pmatrix} = \begin{pmatrix} [V_1(1+\rho)/2]^{1/2} & [V_2(1+\rho)/2]^{1/2} \\ [V_1(1-\rho)/2]^{1/2} & -[V_2(1-\rho)/2]^{1/2} \end{pmatrix} \begin{pmatrix} X_1 \\ X_2 \end{pmatrix}$$

$$= (H^a)'^{-1} X \tag{11.16}$$

which can be confirmed directly. Since H^a is nonsingular, $(\nu_1, \nu_2) \neq 0$ implies $[E(u_1^a), E(u_2^a)] \neq 0$.

From

$$R = u_0 + u_1^a X_1^a + u_2^a X_2^a$$

we infer

$$V = \tau_{00} + 2\tau_{01}^a X_1^a + 2\tau_{02}^a X_2^a + (X_1^a)^2 + (X_2^a)^2$$

where

$$\tau_{0i}^a = \text{cov}(u_0, u_i^a)$$

Define $X^b = (X_1^b, X_2^b)$ by the affine transformation

$$\begin{pmatrix} X_1^b \\ X_2^b \end{pmatrix} = \begin{pmatrix} X_1^a \\ X_2^a \end{pmatrix} + \begin{pmatrix} \tau_{01}^a \\ \tau_{02}^a \end{pmatrix} \tag{11.17}$$

Confirm that

$$V = V_{\min} + (X_1^b)^2 + (X_2^b)^2 \tag{11.18}$$

where

$$V_{\min} = \tau_{00} - (\tau_{01}^a)^2 - (\tau_{02}^a)^2 \tag{11.19}$$

Since

$$\begin{aligned} R &= u_0 + u_1^a(X_1^b - \tau_{01}^a) + u_2^a(X_2^b - \tau_{02}^a) \\ &= (u_0 - u_1^a\tau_{01}^a - u_2^a\tau_{02}^a) + u_1^a X_1^b + u_2^a X_2^b \end{aligned} \tag{11.20}$$

the linear transformation in return space

$$\begin{pmatrix} u_0^b \\ u_1^b \\ u_2^b \end{pmatrix} = \begin{pmatrix} 1 & -\tau_{01}^a & -\tau_{02}^a \\ 0 & 1 & 0 \\ 0 & 0 & 1 \end{pmatrix} \begin{pmatrix} u_0 \\ u_1^a \\ u_2^a \end{pmatrix} \tag{11.21}$$

is a compensating transformation for the affine transformation (11.17) in portfolio space.

From (11.20) it follows that

$$E = v_0^b + v_1^b X_1^b + v_2^b X_2^2 \tag{11.22}$$

where

$$\begin{aligned} v_0^b &= E(u_0) - \tau_{01}^a E(u_1^a) - \tau_{02}^a E(u_2^a) \\ v_1^b &= E(u_1^a) \\ v_2^b &= E(u_1^b) \end{aligned}$$

Equation (11.18) shows that the isovariance curves in (X_1^b, X_2^b) are concentric circles with center $X^b = (0, 0)$. If we rotate the axes the isovariance curves will remain circles with the origin as their center. Our final transformation chooses a rotation which makes all isomean lines vertical.

Specifically, since $(\nu_1, \nu_2) \neq 0$ implies $\nu^b = [E(u_1^a), E(u_2^a)] \neq 0$ and therefore $\| \nu^b \| \neq 0$, we may let

$$\begin{pmatrix} Y_1 \\ Y_2 \end{pmatrix} = \begin{pmatrix} \nu_1^b/\| \nu^b \| & \nu_2^b/\| \nu^b \| \\ -\nu_2^b/\| \nu^b \| & \nu_1^b/\| \nu^b \| \end{pmatrix} \begin{pmatrix} X_1^b \\ X_2^b \end{pmatrix}$$

$$= H^c \begin{pmatrix} X_1^b \\ X_2^b \end{pmatrix} \tag{11.23}$$

Since H^c is orthogonal, it is its own compensating matrix. Thus $R = v_0 + v_1 Y_1 + v_2 Y_2$, where

$$\begin{pmatrix} v_0 \\ v_1 \\ v_2 \end{pmatrix} = \begin{pmatrix} 1 & 0 & 0 \\ 0 & \nu_1^b/\| \nu^b \| & \nu_2^b/\| \nu^b \| \\ 0 & -\nu_2^b/\| \nu^b \| & \nu_1^b/\| \nu^b \| \end{pmatrix} \begin{pmatrix} u_0^b \\ u_1^b \\ u_2^b \end{pmatrix}$$

Since

$$X^b = \begin{pmatrix} X_1^b \\ X_2^b \end{pmatrix} = \begin{pmatrix} \nu_1^b/\| \nu^b \| & -\nu_2^b/\| \nu^b \| \\ \nu_2^b/\| \nu^b \| & \nu_1^b/\| \nu^b \| \end{pmatrix} \begin{pmatrix} Y_1 \\ Y_2 \end{pmatrix}$$

$$= (H^c)^{-1} Y$$

we see that $Y = (1, 0)$ has the same direction as the expected return vector, namely (ν_1^b, ν_2^b) in the X_1^b, X_2^b coordinate system; whereas $Y = (0, 1)$ is a direction in which E remains constant.

Transformations (11.16), (11.17), and (11.23), applied to $X = (0, 0)$, $(1, 0)$, and $(0, 1)$, provide the vertices of the constraint triangle in Y space; i.e. in a canonical form for the given ν and τ.

Exercises

11.1 The μ and C requested below refer to the means, variances, and covariances of the original r_1, r_2, r_3. The easy way to solve the problem is to find the answer in canonical form, then determine the μ and C which give rise to this form.

(a) Give an example of a μ and C of a standard three-security analysis which has a kink in the set of efficient EV combinations. Sketch the set of efficient portfolios in $Y_1 Y_2$ space and in $X_1 X_2$ space.

(b) As in (a), except provide an example whose set of efficient portfolios contains two line segments and no kink in the set of efficient EV combinations.

(c) As in (a), except provide an example in which the set of efficient portfolios has three line segments, the relationship between σ and E

is linear on the middle segment, and there is no kink in the set of efficient EV (or $E\sigma$) combinations.

11.2 Consider a standard four-security example with nonsingular τ^* and $(\nu_1, \nu_2, \nu_3) \neq 0$. Suppose that in canonical form, with $V = V_{\text{min}} + Y_1^2 + Y_2^2 + Y_3^2$ and $E^* = Y_1$, the vertices of the constraint set are

(2, 0, 1)

(1, 1, 0.5)

(1, −1, 0.5)

(0, 0, 1)

Show that the set of corner portfolios (i.e. end points of the linear segments of the set of efficient portfolios) are (2, 0, 1), (1, 0, 0.5), and (0.4, 0, 0.8). Show also that the set of efficient EV combinations has a kink at the portfolio (1, 0, 0.5); that this is the constant X on a critical line on which only λ changes; and that the affine model corresponding to this critical line allows more than one X, but has only one feasible E. (Hint: for $1 \leqslant E^* \leqslant 2$, feasible V is minimized by a portfolio of the form $(Y_1, 0, Y_3)$.)

11.3 (a) When $n = 3$ and the rank of $\tau^* = 2$, describe the canonical analysis of Black's model, including the sets of feasible and efficient portfolios.

(b) As above, when rank of $\tau^* = 1$. In particular for this case, when are there no efficient portfolios? When is there a half-plane of efficient portfolios?

11.4 What is the μ and C (of the original r_1, r_2, r_3 variables) of a standard portfolio analysis in which every nonnull subset of $\{1, 2, 3\}$ is the IN set of an efficient segment? For example, $\{3\}$ has the highest E; $IN = \{2, 3\}$ is the next efficient segment; then $X_3 \downarrow 0$ and only λ varies on the critical line with $IN = \{2\}$; $\eta_1 \downarrow 0$ and therefore $IN = \{1, 2\}$ on the next efficient segment; then $\eta_3 \downarrow 0$ and $IN = \{1, 2, 3\}$; then $X_2 \downarrow 0$ and $IN = \{1, 3\}$; finally $X_3 \downarrow 0$ and $IN = \{1\}$ provides minimum V. (Hint: with $E_3 > E_2 > E_1$, place security 1 in the first quadrant of $Y_1 Y_2$ and place securities 2 and 3 in the fourth quadrant with the point for 2 above the line connecting 1 and 3. Be sure that security 1 has less variance than any feasible point on the line connecting 1 and 3.)

11.5 (G. Hawawini) This question is concerned with the canonical representation of three uncorrelated securities. Part (a) considers a special case; part (b) considers the general case. It is helpful in this problem to recall from the appendix to the book that $Y_1^a Y_1^b + Y_2^a Y_2^b$ in (11.8d) equals $\cos(Y^a, Y^b) \| Y^a \| \| Y^b \|$.

(a) Let the constraint triangle T in Y_1Y_2 space be an equilateral triangle with center at the origin. Show that there is a V_{min} such that $\sigma_{ij}=0$ for $i \neq j$. (Hint: let P_1, P_2, P_3 be the three vertices. Use the facts that lengths $0P_1$, $0P_2$, and $0P_3$ are equal and that the angles $<P_1 0P_2$, $<P_2 0P_3$, and $<P_3 0P_1$ are all equal (to $2\pi/3$) and have a negative cosine.)

(b) Let θ_{12}, θ_{23}, θ_{31} be three angles each greater than $\pi/2$, such that $\theta_{12}+\theta_{23}+\theta_{31}=2\pi$. Show that, given any such θ_{12}, θ_{23}, θ_{31} and any $V_{min}>0$, there are three lengths d_1, d_2, d_3 such that if the ith vertex P_i of the constraint triangle is placed at a distance d_i from the origin, and if $<P_1 0P_2=\theta_{12}$, $<P_2 0P_3=\theta_{23}$, $<P_3 0P_1=\theta_{31}$ then $\sigma_{ij}=0$ for $i \neq j$. (Hint: choose d_1, d_2, d_3 so that $\cos(\theta_{ij})\, d_i d_j = -V_{min}$ for every $i \neq j$. $\cos(\theta_{ij})$ is given and negative. Multiply both sides by -1, and take logarithms to solve for the d_i.)

11.6 This exercise explores the relationship between two straight lines in the Y_1Y_2 plane on the one hand, and the corresponding pair of parabolas in EV space on the other hand. Throughout this exercise assume that τ^* is of rank 2.

(a) Consider two horizontal lines in the Y_1Y_2 plane. In which cases will their EV parabolas be identical even though the lines do not intersect? In which cases will the EV parabolas intersect nowhere? Show that these are the only two possibilities for pairs of horizontal lines.

(b) Consider two parallel lines which are not horizontal and not vertical. Show that their parabolas intersect at one and only one point.

(c) Consider the Y_1 axis and any line l not parallel to it and not vertical. Show that their two parabolas are tangent where l crosses the Y_1 axis, and the parabola of the Y_1 axis is below that of l everywhere else.

(d) Consider two lines which are not parallel, and of which neither is vertical. When will their parabolas intersect twice, namely once where the lines intersect and once where they do not? (Hint: write the two lines as $Y_2=a+bY_1$ and $Y_2=\alpha+\beta Y_1$. They intersect when $a+bY_1=\alpha+\beta Y_1$. The lines do not intersect but have the same V (and E) at the Y_1 which solves $a+bY_1=-(\alpha+\beta Y_1)$. When can both of these equalities be solved for Y_1 with two different values of Y_1 as the result?)

(e) Why are vertical lines excluded in (a)-(d)?

(f) How do the answers to (a)-(d) change if we consider curves in $E\sigma$ space rather than EV space (i) when $V_{min}=0$, (ii) when $V_{min}>0$?

(g) Assuming $V_{min}=0$, sketch the set of efficient $E\sigma$ combinations for a set of efficient portfolios which satisfies exercise 11.4. Be mindful of the relationships between the various hyperbolic or linear curves in $E\sigma$ space for the different lines whose segments make up the set of efficient portfolios. For example, note which curves are hyperbolic and which linear, which curves are tangent and which intersect, and for which values of $E^*=Y_1$ each has its minimum.

12

Conical Constraint Sets and the Efficiency of the Market Portfolio

The capital asset pricing models (CAPMs) of Sharpe (1964) and Lintner (1965) assume that all investors seek mean-variance efficiency, all have the same beliefs, and each chooses a portfolio subject to the same constraint set, namely what we call the Tobin-Sharpe-Lintner constraint set. From these premises Sharpe and Lintner conclude that the *market portfolio* $X^{\mathrm{M}} = (X_1^{\mathrm{M}}, X_2^{\mathrm{M}}, \ldots, X_n^{\mathrm{M}})$ - where X_i^{M} is the ratio of the total value of the ith security to the value of all securities - is an efficient portfolio. They further conclude that the *excess return* on the ith security - $\mu_i - r_0$, where r_0 is the risk-free rate - is proportional to β_i, the regression coefficient of r_i against the return on the market portfolio.

Black (1972) also assumes that all investors have the same beliefs, and seek mean-variance efficiency. In contrast to Sharpe and Lintner, however, Black assumes that each investor chooses a portfolio subject to what we call Black's constraint set. Black concludes that the market portfolio is an efficient portfolio, and that μ_i is a linear function of β_i.

In the present chapter, as in Sharpe, Lintner, and Black, we assume that all investors have the same beliefs, have the same constraint set, and seek mean-variance efficiency. On the other hand, we will consider more general portfolio selection constraint sets than in Sharpe, Lintner, or Black. We saw in exercise 6.1 that if the common constraint set is affine and if the M matrix is nonsingular then the market portfolio is an efficient portfolio. We begin the present chapter by showing that the latter conclusion - that the market portfolio is an efficient portfolio - follows more generally for a class of models which include the affine model and the Tobin-Sharpe-Lintner model as special cases. But the conclusion is typically false for bounded constraint sets (and not always true for unbounded constraint sets, as illustrated in exercise 12.7). Thus one of the central conclusions of traditional CAPMs - that the market portfolio is an efficient portfolio - does not generalize to arbitrary portfolio selection constraint sets.

We also consider the relationship between the expected return of individual securities and their betas for general portfolio selection constraint sets. Here an altered version of the standard CAPM result does generalize.

The Market Portfolio

If we write the common constraint requirements in form 2 then X^I - the portfolio of the Ith investor - is chosen subject to $AX^I = b$, $X^I \geqslant 0$. Let W_I be the equity in, or "net asset value" of, the Ith portfolio. Define $w_I = W_I/\Sigma_J W_J$. We will define the *market portfolio* as

$$X^{\mathrm{M}} = \sum_I w_I X^I \tag{12.1}$$

This definition of X^{M}, used below, may or may not agree with that given previously, e.g. in the first paragraph of this chapter, as we will now illustrate.

If the constraint set to which all investors are subject is the standard portfolio selection constraint set, or the standard constraints plus upper bounds, and we take W_I as the dollar value of the Ith portfolio, then $W_I X_i^I$ is the dollar value of the ith security held in the Ith portfolio. It follows that $X^{\mathrm{M}} = \Sigma_I w_I X^I$ has as its ith component X_i^{M} the ratio of the total value of the ith security to the total value of all securities. In this case the present and previous definitions are in accord.

If we assume Black's model as the constraint set to which all investors are subject, then X_i^I may be negative, $W_I X_i^I$ may be negative (where W_I is the net value of the Ith portfolio, subtracting negative holdings from positive holdings), and $X^{\mathrm{M}} = \Sigma w_I X^I$ again has as its ith component the ratio of the total value of the ith security to the total value of all securities. In this case as well, the present and prior definitions are in accord.

In the Tobin-Sharpe-Lintner model, if W_I is taken as the equity in the account then $W_I X_i^I$ is the (nonnegative) amount of the ith security held in the Ith portfolio. X_i^{M} $(1 \leqslant i \leqslant n)$ will no longer be the ratio of the value of the ith security to that of all securities. Rather we will have

$$\sum_{i=1}^{n} X_i^{\mathrm{M}} = 1 + X_{n+1}^{\mathrm{M}}$$

where X_{n+1}^{M} is the ratio of the total amount borrowed (or lent if $X_{n+1}^{\mathrm{M}} < 0$) to the total equity of all accounts. We now speak of $X^{\mathrm{M}} = (X_1^{\mathrm{M}}, X_2^{\mathrm{M}}, \ldots, X_{n+1}^{\mathrm{M}})$ as the market portfolio. If X^{σ} represents the market portfolio by our prior ("old") definition and X^{ν} by the current ("new") definition, then $X_i^{\sigma} = X_i^{\nu}/(1 + X_{n+1}^{\nu})$ for $1 \leqslant i \leqslant n$. Both X^{ν} and X^{σ} (or, strictly speaking, $((X^{\sigma})', 0)$) are efficient portfolios.

We assume $W_I \geqslant 0$ for every I, and therefore $w_I \geqslant 0$ as well as $\Sigma w_I = 1$. Since the common constraint set $(AX^I = b,\ X^I \geqslant 0)$ is convex, $X^{\mathrm{M}} = \Sigma w_I X^I$ is a feasible portfolio by theorem 4.15. We will see that X^{M} may or may not be efficient, even though all X^I are efficient.

Conical Constraint Sets

In this section we derive properties of any model which meets the following two conditions:

(i) The set of feasible portfolios is a cone; and
(ii) The vertex of the cone minimizes V among portfolios in the affine hull of the feasible set. (Other portfolios in the affine hull may also have this minimum V.)

Examples

(1) An affine set is a cone with every point a vertex. Since corollary 9.16 assures us that some point at least ties for minimum variance in this set, such a point may serve as the required vertex. Thus conditions (i) and (ii) apply for any model with an affine constraint set, such as Black's model.
(2) We saw in chapter 4 that the constraint set of the Tobin-Sharpe-Lintner model is a cone. Since the vertex has zero variance, the model meets conditions (i) and (ii).
(3) Koopmans (1951) analyzes a class of production models with resource inputs, product outputs, and conical linear programming constraint sets. If we add random output and/or input prices to any of these models, seek mean-variance efficiency, and note that the vertex of any of these models has zero variance, we obtain a class of portfolio selection models satisfying assumptions (i) and (ii).

Theorem 12.1 Suppose that (i) a portfolio selection model has a conical feasible set, and (ii) some portfolio X_0 is a vertex of the cone of feasible portfolios and minimizes variance among portfolios in the affine hull of the feasible set. Then either X_0 is an efficient portfolio, or else no portfolio is efficient.

Note: we saw in chapter 10 that, in general, there can be two feasible portfolios, X^* and $\tilde{X}$, both with minimum feasible variance, where X^* is efficient and $\tilde{X}$ is not. The present theorem rules out the possibility that X_0 is inefficient.

Proof If X_0 is the only portfolio with mimimum variance, then clearly it is efficient. Otherwise we distinguish two cases:

(1) All other feasible portfolios with the same V have the same or lower E. Then again X_0 is efficient.

(2) There is a feasible portfolio X^* with the same V and higher E. Since X_0 is the vertex of the feasible cone, every point on the ray

$$X = X_0 + (X^* - X_0)\,t \qquad t \geqslant 0$$

is feasible. Since X_0 and X^* both have minimum V, this ray must be a zero-variance direction, else a feasible portfolio with smaller variance would lie between X_0 and X^*. Thus every portfolio on this (everywhere feasible) ray has the same V. But E increases with t everywhere on this ray; thus for every feasible portfolio with minimum V, there is another feasible portfolio with the same V and higher E. Therefore the model has no efficient portfolios. ###

Theorem 12.2 Suppose that:

(i) A portfolio selection model has a conical feasible set;
(ii) There is a vertex X_0 of the feasible cone which minimizes variance among portfolios in the affine hull of the feasible set; and
(iii) X_0 is an efficient portfolio.

Then the set of all efficient portfolios is a convex cone with X_0 a vertex. (Note that this is an assertion about all efficient portfolios, not just a complete non-redundant subset.)

Proof It is possible that X_0 is the only efficient portfolio, perhaps because it is the only feasible portfolio, or because it uniquely minimizes V and has greater E than any other feasible portfolio. In this case the efficient set is trivially a (zero-dimensional) convex cone with X_0 as vertex. Otherwise, in order to show that the set S of efficient portfolios is a cone, we must show that if X^* is in S then so is the entire ray

$$X = X_0 + (X^* - X_0)\,t \qquad t \geqslant 0 \tag{12.2}$$

First suppose that X^* has the same E, and therefore the same V, as X_0. Then, by an argument as in the proof of theorem 12.1, $(X^* - X_0)$ must be a zero-variance direction. Thus every point on the ray from X_0 through X^* must have the same E and V as X_0, and therefore is efficient.

Next suppose that X^* is an efficient portfolio with higher E and V than X_0. Since X_0 is a vertex of the feasible cone, every X satisfying (12.2) is feasible. We must show that each such X is efficient. Suppose otherwise. Then there is a feasible $\tilde{X}$ with $V = \tilde{V}$ smaller than the V of the portfolio on the ray in (12.2) with the same $E = \tilde{E}$ as that of $\tilde{X}$. Again, since X_0 is a vertex of the feasible cone, the entire ray

$$X = X_0 + (\tilde{X} - X_0)\,t \qquad t \geqslant 0 \tag{12.3}$$

is feasible. The relationships between V and E - call them $V^*(E)$ and $\tilde{V}(E)$ - on the rays in (12.2) and (12.3) are both parabolas with $V = V_{\min}$ and $dV/dE = 0$

at $t = 0$. Thus if one of these parabolas is less than the other at any point, it is less than the other at every point except $t = 0$. Therefore it is not possible for $\tilde{V}(E)$ to be below $V^*(E)$ at some point, and for X^* to be efficient as assumed.

We conclude that S is a cone. Before we show that it is convex we will prove the following lemma:

Lemma Suppose that X^* is an efficient portfolio with $E^* > E_0$. We have seen that the entire ray in (12.2) is efficient, and clearly it provides one X for each $E \geqslant E_0$. Suppose $\tilde{X}$ is any efficient portfolio not on this ray. Then $\tilde{X}$ may be written as

$$\tilde{X} = X^{**} + b \tag{12.4}$$

where X^{**} is a point on the ray in (12.2) with the same E as $\tilde{X}$, and b is a zero-mean, zero-variance direction.

Proof of lemma Since $\tilde{X}$ is efficient it must have $\tilde{E} \geqslant E_0$. Some point on the ray must have this same $E = \tilde{E}$. Call it X^{**}. Let $b = X^{**} - \tilde{X}$. Then $\mu' b = \mu'(X^{**} - \tilde{X}) = 0$; and b must be a zero-variance direction else some X between X^{**} and $\tilde{X}$ would have the same $E = \tilde{E}$ and smaller V.

Returning to the proof of the convexity of the efficient set, suppose that X^* and $\tilde{X}$ are two distinct efficient portfolios. We must show that

$$X = tX^* + (1-t)\tilde{X}$$

is efficient for any $0 \leqslant t \leqslant 1$. If one of the portfolios (say X^*) has $E^* > E_0$, write $\tilde{X}$ as in (12.4) whether or not $\tilde{E} > E_0$. Else if both portfolios have $E = E_0$ then we have $X^* = X_0 + b^*$ and $\tilde{X} = X_0 + \tilde{b}$, where b^* and $\tilde{b}$ are zero-mean, zero-variance directions. Hence

$$\tilde{X} = X^* + b$$

where $b = \tilde{b} - b^*$ is a zero-mean, zero-variance direction. In this case the argument below applies with $X^{**} = X^*$.

In either case we have

$$\tilde{X} = X^{**} + b$$

Then

$$\begin{aligned} X &= tX^* + (1-t)\tilde{X} \\ &= tX^* + (1-t)(X^{**} + b) \\ &= tX^* + (1-t)X^{**} + (1-t)b \end{aligned}$$

Since X^* and X^{**} are both on the ray from X_0 through X^*, so is $tX^* + (1-t)X^{**}$ and hence is efficient. But, since b is a zero-mean, zero-variance direction, adding $(1-t)b$ changes neither E nor V; hence X is an efficient portfolio. ###

Assumption (ii) of theorem 12.2 cannot be replaced by the weaker assumption that X_0 has minimum feasible variance: see exercise 12.7.

Corollary 12.3 Given the assumptions and notation in theorem 12.2, plus the following assumptions:

(iv) There exists feasible $E > E_0$; and
(v) There is only one efficient portfolio for each $E \geqslant E_0$.

Then the set of efficient portfolios is a ray

$$X = X_0 + bt \qquad t \geqslant 0$$

Proof Let X^* be any efficient portfolio with $E^* > E_0$. According to theorem 12.2, if we let $b = X^* - X_0$, then every X on the ray in the corollary is efficient. But since there is an X on this ray for every $E \geqslant E_0$, the corollary follows. ###

In financial theory, the conclusion that the efficient set for some model is a ray - as in corollary 12.3 or for a model with an affine constraint set and non-singular C - is referred to as a *two-funds separation theorem*, since two points (portfolios, mutual funds) determine a straight line in accordance with equation (4.9); see for example exercise 6.2. For ease of reference, we state the following as a numbered theorem.

Theorem 12.4 Suppose that a finite number of investors each choose a mean-variance efficient portfolio X^I subject to the same constraint set. Define the market portfolio as

$$X = \sum_I w_I X^I \tag{12.5}$$

where $\Sigma w_I = 1$, $w_I \geqslant 0$ for all I. If the set of efficient portfolios is convex, then the market portfolio X is an efficient portfolio.

Proof This is an application of theorem 4.15. ###

Efficiency of the Market Portfolio

Theorem 12.4 notes that if an efficient portfolio set is convex then the market portfolio is efficient. Theorem 12.2 presents conditions which assure that the efficient set is convex.

But mean-variance efficient portfolio sets are not inevitably convex, and in practice are typically not convex. In figures 11.7 through 11.10 the set of efficient portfolios is piecewise linear. When this set consists of one linear segment, as may be constructed as an exercise, then the set is convex. If the set contains two or more linear segments, and if there is at most one efficient portfolio for any given E, then it is not convex. In this case the market portfolio need not be an efficient portfolio.

Figures 12.1(a)-(c) illustrate such cases for the standard portfolio analysis in canonical form. In figure 12.1(a), V is minimized at d, E is maximized at c, and the efficient set consists of three line segments de, ef, and fc. Suppose first that the market contains two kinds of investors. Both kinds have the same beliefs and must choose a portfolio subject to the same constraints. Specifically, both kinds face a model whose canonical analysis is shown in the figure. The difference between the two kinds of investors is that the first seeks to maximize one particular function of mean and variance, $f_a(E, V)$, while the second seeks to maximize a different function, $f_b(E, V)$. (See chapter 3 concerning the relationship between such functions, and a one-period utility function of the Von Neumann-Morgenstern type.)

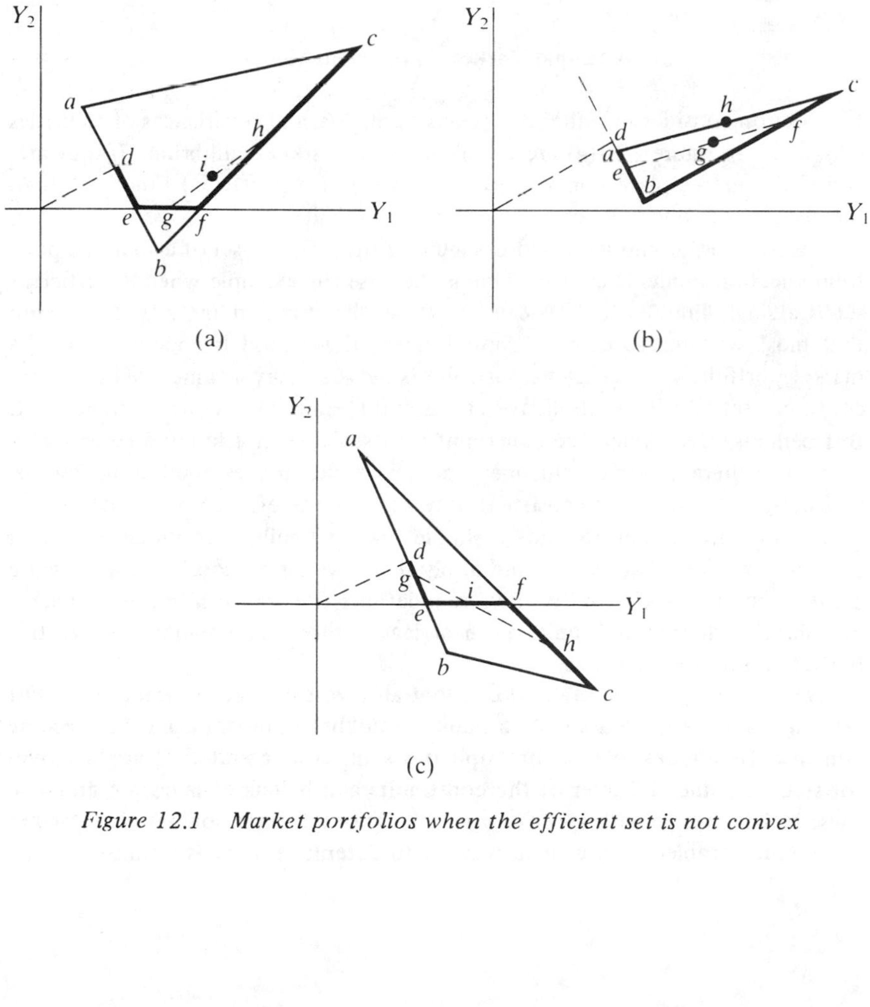

Figure 12.1 Market portfolios when the efficient set is not convex

We assume that the investors who seek to maximize $f_a(E, V)$ choose g as their optimum portfolio, whereas those who seek to maximize $f_b(E, V)$ choose h. The essential assumption here is that g and h lie on different lines.

The market portfolio i is a weighted average of g and h. The point i will lie closer to g or closer to h depending on whether the sum of the portfolio values of the first kind of investor is less or greater than that of the second kind. In either case, as long as both kinds hold portfolios, the market portfolio i will be between g and h on the segment connecting them. It will not lie on either *de*, *ef*, or *fc* and hence will not be an efficient portfolio.

Next let us assume that, rather than two kinds of investors, there are many - each kind with its own objective function $f_a, f_b, f_c, \ldots$. Perhaps some investors choose a portfolio on the segment *de*, some on *ef*, and others on *fc*. As long as portfolios are selected from more than one segment, the market portfolio will lie to the right of *de*, above *ef*, and to the left of *fc* - and will not be an efficient portfolio.

A Simple Market Equilibrium Model

This section considers whether the means, variances, and covariances of securities a, b, and c in figure 12.1(a) are consistent with market equilibrium. If they are, and if the marketplace contains investors with diverse $f(E, V)$ functions, then the market portfolio will not be an efficient portfolio.

It is possible to choose μ and C such that the efficient set of a standard portfolio selection model is convex. This is the case for example when the efficient set is a single line segment, as can happen in the standard analysis. The reason that most writings to date on capital asset pricing models conclude that the market portfolio is an efficient portfolio is because they assume one or another constraint set which - in itself, for any μ and C - implies a convex efficient set. But perhaps - even when the constraint set itself does not imply a convex efficient set - there is some adjustment process which makes equilibrium means, variances, and covariances consistent only with convex efficient portfolio sets.

The present section contains a simple market equilibrium model which, if the world worked that way, would imply that covariances consistent with figure 12.1(a) - in fact, any μ and positive semidefinite C - are consistent with market equilibrium: the market could reach at least a short run equilibrium with this μ and C as everyone's beliefs.

Even assuming, as is usually done, that all investors face the same constraint set and share the same μ and C, a market equilibrium model can easily become complex. It requires explicit or implicit assumptions about the supply curves for securities, the character of the constraints and beliefs of investors, and how these beliefs change with security prices. It is not our intention here to solve the equilibrium problem in a general way, or to determine what is a realistic model and solve this specific one. Rather we shall select assumptions partly to make it easy to derive an equilibrium solution; to show that any μ and C are consistent with equilibrium given these assumptions; to remind the reader that the prior conclusion (that the efficient portfolio set is convex) is based on special and quite unrealistic assumptions about constraint sets; and to invite the reader to postulate and solve a more general or more realistic model of equilibrium. The assumptions of our model are these:

(i) *Fixed supply of each investment* We will speak as if all investment were common stocks, and there were a fixed number of shares of each. This is an almost reasonable assumption for stocks (and bonds, here called stocks) in the short run. It is less reasonable for "cash," but we do not want to open that Pandora's box here.

(ii) *Arbitrary portfolio selection constraint set* (but the same for each investor).

(iii) *Arbitrary but fixed μ and C*, and the same for all investors, where μ and C contain the means, variances, and covariances of r_i - the rate of return on the ith security per dollar invested. An alternate simple assumption is that the investors have given beliefs, μ and C, concerning returns per share. The assumption used - in terms of returns per dollar invested - is the one more commonly adopted (see for example Sharpe, 1963; Cohen and Pogue, 1967; King, 1966).

(iv) Investors seek to maximize $f_I(E, V)$ *which may differ from one investor I to another*. We assume

$$\partial f_I/\partial E > 0 \text{ and } \partial f_I/\partial V < 0.$$

(v) *Market equilibrium prices* are those at which the *number of shares demanded* by investors in (ii), (iii), and (iv) *equals the number of shares supplied* in (i).

(vi) We will compute the number of shares of the ith security demanded by the Ith investor by

$$W_I X_i^I / p_i$$

where p_i is the price per share of the ith security, X_i^I is the ratio of the value of security i in the Ith portfolio to the value of the portfolio, and W_I is the value of the Ith portfolio at the *beginning* of the period (before returns r_i are drawn).

(vi′) Since investors typically enter a period already holding a portfolio of securities, it might be more reasonable to compute the W^I and p_i simultaneously, requiring

$$W_I = \sum_i p_i S_i^I$$

where S_i^I is the initial number of shares of i held by I. The solution of the system is more complex assuming (vi′) than (vi), particularly if we are to do more than count the number of equations and unknowns. We will solve the system using assumption (vi), then briefly compare this solution with the requirements of (vi′).

We will now show that market equilibrium conditions (i)-(vi) are consistent with any μ and positive semidefinite C. According to assumption (iv), each investor chooses a mean-variance efficient portfolio $X^I = (X_1^I, \ldots, X_n^I)$ from the set offered by (ii) and (iii). (It is possible that more than one X maximizes $f_I(E, V)$. In this case we assume that X^I is an arbitrary choice from the set of f_I maximizing portfolios.) Then assumption (vi) implies that D_i^I, the number of dollars' worth of i demanded by investor I, is

$$D_i^I = W_I X_i^I \tag{12.6a}$$

The total dollar demand D_i for the ith security by all investors is therefore determined:

$$D_i = \sum_I D_i^I \tag{12.6b}$$

Since the total number of shares S_i for the ith security is assumed fixed, the market equilibrium prices follow:

$$p_i^e = D_i / S_i \tag{12.6c}$$

Concerning the stability of this equilibrium, equation (12.6b) implies a demand for shares as a function of price,

$$S_i^D = D_i / p_i \tag{12.6d}$$

If $p_i < p_i^e$ then $S_i^D > S_i$. More shares will be demanded than are available and, presumably, the price of a share will be bid up. If $p_i > p_i^e$ then $S_i^D < S_i$ and the price will be bid down. Thus, assuming that the adjustment mechanism does not overshoot p_i^e (or just does not overshoot p_i^e too much, so that the process converges) the equilibrium is a stable one.

If we assume (vi′) rather than (vi), the W_I in (12.6a) would depend on the prices p_i. Then W_I, D_i^I, D_i, p_i^e are determined simultaneously by a system of equations. If the W_I which are part of this solution are close to the initial portfolio values, the solution to (i)-(vi) will be close to that of (i)-(vi′) (since the W_I do not affect the X_i^I or S_i in this model - only the D_i^I by (12.6a) and thence the D_i and p_i^e via (12.6b) and (12.6c) by continuous relationships).

How Inefficient can the Market Portfolio Be?

The preceding section shows that, in a market satisfying assumptions (i)-(vi), any μ and C are consistent with market equilibrium. Figure 12.1(a) illustrates that the market portfolio, being a weighted average of efficient portfolios, need not itself be an efficient portfolio unless the efficient portfolio set is convex. Figures 12.1(b) and (c) illustrate some further possibilities along these lines.

In figure 12.1(b) the efficient set consists of the two segments *ab* and *bc*. Every point on and in the feasible triangle *abc* can be expressed as a weighted average of efficient portfolios. Suppose, for example, that there are two types of investors. The first find the efficient portfolio at *e* best for them; the second find portfolio *f* to be best. The market portfolio is then a weighted average, i.e. a convex combination of *e* and *f*, such as *g*.

The value of security *b* makes up a small fraction of the market portfolio *g*. This does not mean that *b* is a cheap security, in the sense that either it has a low price per share or has a market value less than the value of its company's assets. For all we can tell from the figure, *b* may be a smaller company than *a* or *c*, have fewer shares outstanding, and sell at a price which is about the same as that of *a* and *c*. Equation (12.6c) requires only that the product $D_b = p_b S_b$ have the relationship to D_a and D_c implied by the figure. Thus, *a*, *b*, and *c* can sell for reasonable values, given the nature of the respective companies, yet the market portfolio can be far from efficient - in fact, can nearly *maximize* rather than minimize V for given E.

We could have assumed that the two kinds of investors preferred *a* and *c* rather than *e* and *f* in the figure. (Note that the figure is drawn so that the investor can have some interest in high mean as opposed to low variance, i.e. can have $\partial f_I(E, V)/\partial E > 0$, and still choose *a*.) In this case the market portfolio would be a point *h* on the line segment *ac*. However, portfolio *h* contains none of security *b*. Thus if $S_b > 0$ then *h* implies $p_b = 0$. If *b* is the stock of a viable company, presumably assumption (iii) will fail as $p_b \downarrow 0$. In particular someone, or everyone, will decide to increase their estimated μ_b per dollar invested. Thus the assumption that investors have fixed probability beliefs concerning returns per dollar invested, and these beliefs are independent of current price, is convenient, precedented, but not invulnerable to *reductio ad absurdum*.

One scenario which would be consistent with market portfolio *h* is the following. Suppose that, until now, only securities *a* and *c* existed. Now someone is about to market a "synthetic" security (like an option on an index) involving the returns on *a*, *c*, and some other event (like the flip of a coin). The synthetic security is constructed so that each unit sold (at a fixed price p_b) has the mean, variance, and covariance characteristics per dollar invested represented by *b* in the figure. (Here we assume that p_b is fixed and S_b varies.) The introduction of the synthetic security changes the efficient set from *ac* to *ab*, *bc*. But because of the preferences of the two groups of investors, no one buys *b*; $S_b = 0$. (This is just one of those cases in which a synthetic security is brought to market and is a disappointment to its promoters.) In the present example the market portfolio, which remains unchanged when security b is introduced, goes from efficient to inefficient and, indeed, *maximizes* V for given E.

If investors select portfolios from two adjacent critical lines, and only from these two, then the market portfolio cannot be efficient. But suppose that investors choose from three or more critical lines, or from two critical lines which are not adjacent; can it "accidentally" happen that the market portfolio will be efficient? Figure 12.1(c) answers this question affirmatively. The efficient set in the figure consists of the three segments *de*, *ef*, and *fc*. If some investors choose portfolio g and the remainder choose h, it is possible for the market portfolio to be the efficient portfolio i.

Expected Returns and Betas

One of the most influential conclusions of the Sharpe-Lintner capital asset pricing model is that a security's excess return - its expected return less the riskless rate - is proportional to β_i, the least square regression of r_i on market return R_M. That is,

$$(\mu_i - r_0) = k\beta_i \qquad \text{for } i = 1, \ldots, n \tag{12.7a}$$

where $k > 0$, and

$$\beta_i = \text{cov}(r_i, R_M)/V(R_M) \tag{12.7b}$$

Equation (12.7) holds not only for each security, but also for all portfolios with zero investment in the riskfree security, and therefore $\Sigma_{i=1}^{n} X_i = 1$. Since the beta of R_M itself is 1.0, equation (12.7a) implies $k = E(R_M) - \mu_0$.

Black (1972) showed that if the constraint set which all investors face is what we call Black's model, then there is a linear relationship between μ_i and β_i:

$$\mu_i = a_0 + a_1\beta_i \qquad \text{for } i = 1, \ldots, n \tag{12.8}$$

with $a_1 > 0$. Equation (12.8) for Black's model, like (12.7) for the Sharpe-Lintner model, holds for all portfolios with $\Sigma_{i=1}^{n} X_i = 1$. In the case of Black's model, therefore, it holds for all feasible portfolios. Note that (12.7a) is a special case of (12.8).

In the present section we consider whether or not a formula of the form (12.8) is true for other constraint sets. We continue to assume that all investors face the same constraint set and have the same μ and C. We will see that typically (12.8) is true if we define β_i as

$$\beta_i = \text{cov}(r_i, R_P)/V(R_P) \tag{12.9}$$

where R_P is the return on any (feasible or infeasible) portfolio P chosen from a certain two-dimensional affine subspace of R^n. However, it can easily happen that the market portfolio is not in this two-dimensional affine subspace, and indeed that no P in this subspace is feasible. In the standard model, for example, it can easily happen that every portfolio P in this subspace has some $X_i < 0$; nevertheless it is these, and only these, portfolios for which (12.8) holds.

Using (12.9) we see that (12.8) is true for all i, if and only if

$$\text{cov}(r_i, R_P) = c_0 + c_1\mu_i \qquad \text{for all } i$$

for $c_1 > 0$, where $c_0 = -a_0V(R_P)/a_1$ and $c_1 = V(R_P)/a_1$. We begin with a general result, for any n, concerning the existence of c_0 and c_1 such that the above holds, and then illustrate this result in terms of the standard three-security model. Note that the following theorem makes no distinction between feasible and infeasible portfolios, and therefore is not dependent on the choice of constraint set.

Theorem 12.5 Let P be any point (feasible or infeasible) in R^n. Let e^i be the vector (portfolio) with $X_i = 1$ and $X_j = 0$ for $j \neq i$. No claim is made that e^i is feasible. Let c_0 and c_1 be any real numbers. Then

$$\begin{aligned}\text{cov}(r_i, R_P) &= (e^i)'CP \\ &= c_0 + c_1\mu_i \qquad \text{for } i = 1, \ldots, n\end{aligned} \tag{12.10}$$

if and only if P provides an unconstrained minimum for

$$L = (1/2)V - c_0(\Sigma X_i) - c_1(\Sigma X_i\mu_i) \tag{12.11}$$

In particular, P minimizes V among portfolios with its same E_P and ΣX_i^P (whether or not ΣX_i is constrained).[1]

Proof Setting partials of L equal to zero, we see (by theorem 6.3) that P provides an unconstrained minimum for L if and only if

$$CP = c_0 e + c_1 \mu \tag{12.12}$$

where $e' = (1, 1, \ldots, 1)$. We will show that (12.10) holds if and only if (12.12) holds. If P satisfies (12.12) then any portfolio X which satisfies $X'e = 1$ also satisfies

[1] This theorem is a generalization of results in Roll (1978). In Black's model, to which Roll's results apply, the property of (1) being an efficient portfolio implies (2) the property of providing an *unconstrained minimum* to $V - \lambda_E\mu'X + \lambda_1\Sigma X_i$ for some λ_1, λ_E. Conversely, for suitably chosen λ_1 and λ_E, property (2) implies property (1) in Black's model. In the general model (even in the standard model) property (1) neither implies nor is implied by (2). The present theorem shows that it is property (2), not property (1), that assures (12.10).

$$X'CP = c_0 X'e + c_1 X'\mu$$
$$= c_0 + c_1 E$$

In particular, setting $X = e^i$, we see that (12.10) holds. Conversely, suppose that (12.10) holds. From equations (1.22) and (1.26) it follows that any portfolio which satisfies $X'e = 1$ also has covariance with R_P equal to

$$X'CP = c_0 + c_1 X'\mu$$

i.e.

$$X'(CP - c_1\mu) = c_0 \qquad (12.13)$$

One possibility is that $CP - c_1\mu = 0$, and therefore $c_0 = 0$. In this case (12.12) follows immediately. In the other case $CP - c_1\mu \neq 0$. Then the set of X which satisfy (12.13) is a hyperplane. But since every point of the hyperplane $X'e = 1$ is a point of the hyperplane in (12.13), these must be the same hyperplane; therefore we must have

$$CP - c_1\mu = c_0 e$$

from which (12.12) again follows. ###

When the standard three-security analysis is represented in canonical form, the set $\{X: \Sigma X_i = 1\}$ is no more or less than the entire $Y_1 Y_2$ plane. Thus a point in this plane minimizes V for given E and ΣX_i if and only if it minimizes V for given E among points in the plane. When τ^* is of rank 2, the set of points which do so is precisely the Y_1 axis. Thus, in this case, for every point on the Y_1 axis there exists c_0 and c_1 such that (12.10) is satisfied, and these are the only points on the plane for which this is true. We have seen that, in the standard three-security analysis with rank 2, the feasible set may or may not intersect the Y_1 axis. If it does not, then any portfolio (or index) which satisfies $\Sigma X_i = 1$ and (12.10) must have some $X_i < 0$. We have also seen that, even if the feasible set intersects the Y_1 axis, the market portfolio may not lie on the Y_1 axis. Then (12.10) does not hold for P equal to the market portfolio.

Exercises

12.1 Elton, Gruber, and Padberg (1976) show that for the Tobin-Sharpe-Lintner constraint set, and for certain special covariance matrices, the set of EV efficient portfolios can be calculated by a simple algorithm. The proof in Elton et al. is rather complicated, parts of it being relegated to a tough appendix. The following exercise provides a simple derivation of the Elton, Gruber, and Padberg result.

The Tobin-Sharpe-Lintner constraint set may be written as

$$X_i \geqslant 0 \qquad i = 1, \ldots, n \qquad (12.14)$$

with no constraint equations, as shown in the remarks following theorem 4.20. Here we let $i = 0$ represent borrowing, reserving $i = n+1$ for another purpose. Defining

$$\nu_i = \mu_i - r_0$$

it follows (from $\mu_0 = -r_0$ and $X_0 = \Sigma_{i=1}^n X_i - 1$) that $E^* = E - r_0$ is

$$E^* = \sum_{i=1}^{n} X_i \nu_i \tag{12.15a}$$

A portfolio is EV efficient if and only if it is E^*V efficient.

In the present exercise, assume that returns are generated by a one-factor model (see equation (3.3)). Thus

$$V = \sum_{i=1}^{n+1} X_i^2 V_i \tag{12.15b}$$

where

$$\sum_{i=1}^{n} \beta_i X_i - X_{n+1} = 0 \tag{12.16}$$

Also assume

$$V_i > 0 \qquad \text{for } 1 \leqslant i \leqslant n+1 \tag{12.17}$$

The problem is to find EV efficient sets subject to (12.14) and (12.16) where E^* and V are given by (12.15a) and (12.15b). Note that X_{n+1} is not constrained with respect to sign.

(a) Show that, given the above assumptions, either: (i) the only efficient portfolio is $X = 0$, or else (ii) the set of efficient portfolios is a single ray starting at $X = 0$. (Hint: note that C is nonsingular and use corollary 12.3.) Conclude that we will have solved the problem if we can determine when case (i) is true, and, in case (ii), can determine one efficient portfolio $X^* \neq 0$.

(b) Show that in case (ii), the problem

$$\text{minimize } (1/2)V - \lambda_E E \tag{12.18a}$$

subject to (12.14) and (12.16), where $\lambda_E > 0$ is a fixed parameter, is solved by an EV efficient portfolio $X^* \neq 0$. In case (i), (12.18a) is minimized subject to (12.14) and (12.16) by $X = 0$. Letting $\lambda_E = 1$, conclude that we have solved the problem if we can find the X which minimizes

$$(1/2)V - E \tag{12.18b}$$

subject to (12.14) and (12.16).

(c) Set up the Lagrangian, take partial derivatives, and conclude from the Kuhn-Tucker conditions that we have minimized (12.18b) subject to

(12.14) and (12.16) if we find $X_1, X_2, \ldots, X_{n+1}, \lambda$ such that (12.14) and (12.16) hold and

$$V_i X_i - \nu_i + \lambda\beta_i = 0 \qquad \text{for } 1 \leqslant i \leqslant n \text{ with } X_i > 0 \tag{12.19a}$$

$$V_i X_i - \nu_i + \lambda\beta_i \geqslant 0 \qquad \text{for } 1 \leqslant i \leqslant n \text{ with } X_i = 0 \tag{12.19b}$$

$$V_{n+1} X_{n+1} = \lambda \tag{12.19c}$$

(d) From (12.19a) and (12.19b) infer that $X_i (1 \leqslant i \leqslant n)$ can be expressed as a function of λ as follows:

$$\text{if } \beta_i > 0, \qquad X_i = \begin{cases} 0 & \text{for } \lambda \geqslant \hat{\lambda}_i = \nu_i/\beta_i \\ (\nu_i - \lambda\beta_i)/V_i & \text{for } \lambda < \hat{\lambda}_i \end{cases} \tag{12.20a}$$

$$\text{if } \beta_i < 0, \qquad X_i = \begin{cases} 0 & \text{for } \lambda \leqslant \hat{\lambda}_i = \nu_i/\beta_i \\ (\nu_i - \lambda\beta_i)/V_i & \text{for } \lambda > \hat{\lambda}_i \end{cases} \tag{12.20b}$$

$$\text{if } \beta_i = 0, \qquad X_i = \max(0, \nu_i/V_i) \qquad \text{for all } \lambda \tag{12.20c}$$

Note that X_i is piecewise linear in every case (including a horizontal piece in every case). X_i is a nonincreasing function of λ if $\beta_i > 0$ and a nondecreasing function if $\beta_i < 0$. Conclude that the product $\beta_i X_i$ is a piecewise linear and nonincreasing function in every case.

(e) From (d) infer that $\Sigma_1^n \beta_i X_i$ is a piecewise linear (therefore continuous) nonincreasing function of λ, for $-\infty < \lambda < \infty$. Conclude that there is a $\lambda = \lambda^*$ such that

$$\Sigma \beta_i X_i = \lambda^* / V_{n+1}$$

Because of (12.16), at this value of λ equation (12.19c) as well as (12.19a) and (12.19b) are satisfied, and the problem is solved.

(f) Write out an algorithm – better still, write a computer program – which finds λ^*, then computes the X_i from (12.19). (Hint: note that $\Sigma \beta_i X_i$ as a function of λ is piecewise linear with its corners at the $\hat{\lambda}_i$. Sort the $\hat{\lambda}_i$. Compute the slope and intercept of the $\Sigma \beta_i X_i$ line above the largest $\hat{\lambda}_i$ (or below the smallest: you can work from either direction.) How does $\Sigma \beta_i X_i$ change as λ crosses each $\hat{\lambda}_i$ in turn? How can you tell if (and for what value of λ) $V_{n+1}(\Sigma \beta_i X_i) = \lambda$ above the highest $\hat{\lambda}_i$; between two successive $\hat{\lambda}_i$; or below the lowest $\hat{\lambda}_i$?)

12.2 Modify exercise 12.1 to permit constraints of the form $0 \leqslant X_i \leqslant U_i$ (Elton, Gruber, and Padberg, 1977). See exercise 7.3 regarding the Kuhn-Tucker conditions in exercise 12.1(c) when $X_i \leqslant U_i$ is required. Find that, as in exercise 12.1, the X_i are piecewise linear functions of λ, that $\Sigma \beta_i X_i$ is a nonincreasing function of λ, etc.

12.3 Assume that all correlation coefficients are positive and identical, i.e. $\rho_{ij} = \rho > 0$ for $i \neq j$. Then

$$V = \sum_{i \neq j} \rho \sigma_i \sigma_j X_i X_j + \sum_{i=1}^{n} V_i X_i^2$$

$$= \sum_{i=1}^{n} \sum_{j=1}^{n} \rho \sigma_i \sigma_j X_i X_j + (1-\rho) \sum_{i=1}^{n} V_i X_i^2$$

$$= \rho \left(\sum_{i=1}^{n} X_i \sigma_i \right)^2 + (1-\rho) \Sigma X_i^2 V_i$$

This may be written as

$$V = \sum_{i=1}^{n+1} \tilde{V}_i X_i^2 \qquad (12.21)$$

where

$$\sum_{i=1}^{n} X_i \sigma_i - X_{n+1} = 0 \qquad (12.22)$$

and where

$$\tilde{V}_i = (1-\rho) V_i \qquad 1 \leqslant i \leqslant n$$

$$V_{n+1} = \rho$$

Compare (12.21) and (12.22) with (12.15b) and (12.16). How may the present problem be solved? For alternate assumptions concerning the covariance matrix and constraint set, see Elton, Gruber, and Padberg (1976, 1977, 1978).

12.4 The present exercise explores the canonical two-dimensional analysis of the Tobin-Sharpe-Lintner model; i.e. the case with two risky as well as one risk-free asset. Write the constraints as in (12.14) with $n = 2$.

(a) We start with the case in which C has rank 2. Since the origin already has minimum variance, a linear (rather than a more general affine) transformation of coordinates can be used to bring the model into the canonical form for the two-dimensional model with rank 2. In particular, the origin remains the vertex of the feasible cone. Since the transformation is not necessarily orthogonal, the two rays which bound the cone do not necessarily remain orthogonal. Show that the angle between the two rays, measured so as to include the cone, can become any value strictly greater than 0 and strictly less than π; see figure 12.2. (Hint: a nonsingular linear transformation maps a convex cone with the origin as its only vertex into another

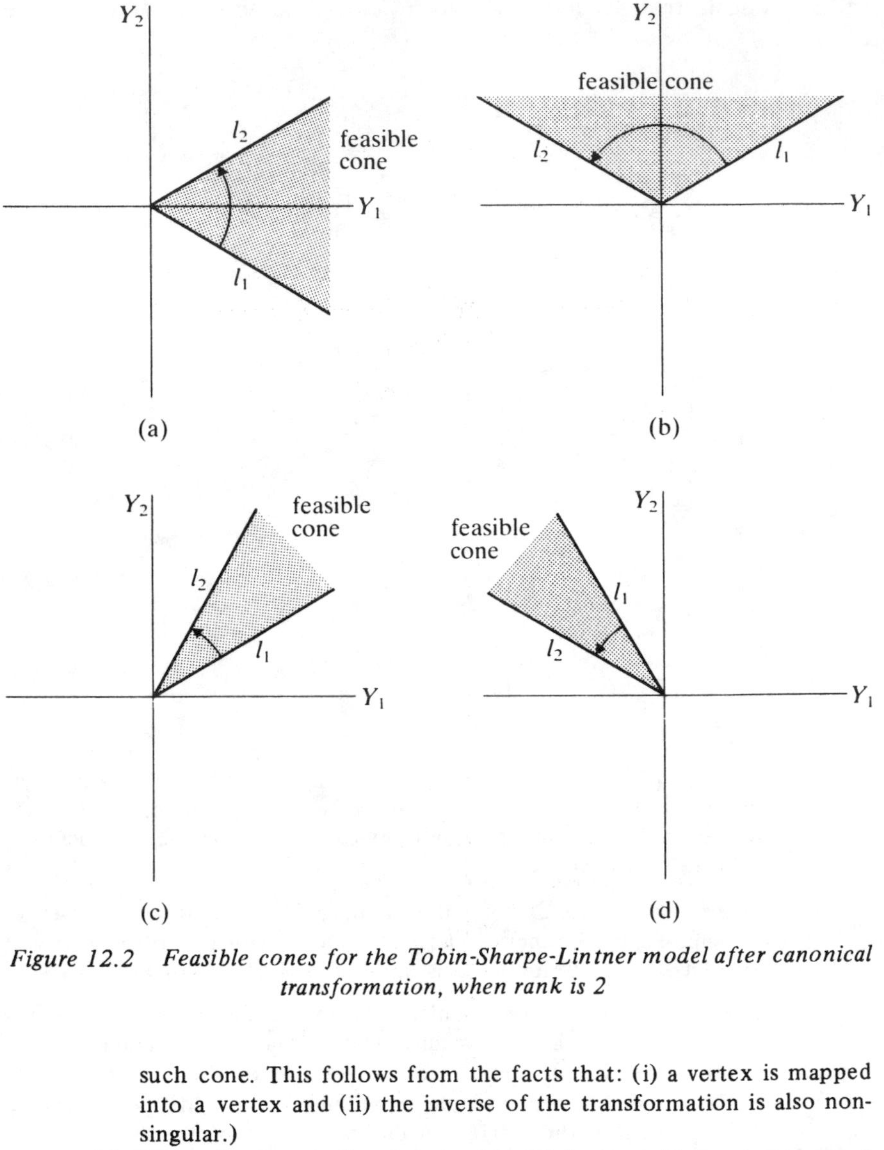

Figure 12.2 Feasible cones for the Tobin-Sharpe-Lintner model after canonical transformation, when rank is 2

such cone. This follows from the facts that: (i) a vertex is mapped into a vertex and (ii) the inverse of the transformation is also non-singular.)

(b) With τ^* of rank 2, what is the efficient set if the transformed feasible cone includes the Y_1 axis, as in figure 12.2(a)? What if it does not include the Y_1 axis, but some part of the efficient cone has points with $Y_1 > 0$; i.e. if only one boundary line has $Y_1 > 0$ (figure 12.2(b)), or if both have points with $Y_1 > 0$ (figure 12.2(c))? What if neither boundary ray has points with $Y_1 > 0$ as in figure 12.2(d)?

(c) Figures 12.3(a) and (b) consider the canonical form for rank 1. In particular, vertical lines are lines of constant variance, with the line

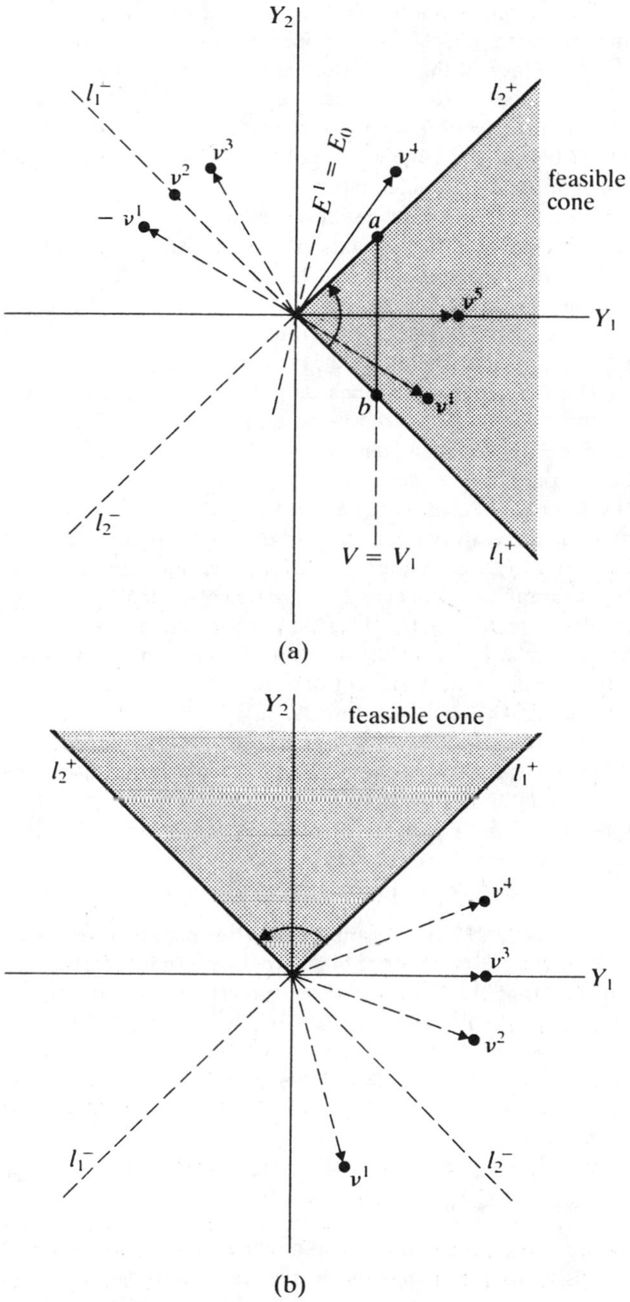

Figure 12.3 Two-dimensional analysis of the Tobin-Sharpe-Lintner model with rank 1

$Y_1 = 0$ having minimum (in the present case, zero) variance. In the analysis with rank 1, the expected return vector need not be the Y_1 axis. Since in the present case the vertex of the cone is one of the zero-variance portfolios, it remains at the origin. The transformation to canonical form is orthogonal when rank is 1; hence the two rays which bound the cone (originally the X_1 and X_2 axes) remain orthogonal in the $Y_1 Y_2$ coordinate system.

Figure 12.3(a) analyzes the case in which the feasible cone contains no part of the Y_2 axis other than the origin. The rays which bound the feasible cone are labeled l_1^+ and l_2^+. The ray labeled l_1^- lies in the same line as l_1^+, but has the opposite direction; and similarly for l_2^- and l_2^+. Various possible return vectors such as $\nu^1 = (\nu_1^1, \nu_2^1)$ are labeled $\nu^1, \nu^2, \nu^3, \nu^4, \nu^5$, and $-\nu^1$.

The efficient set depends on ν. First, analyze the following cases: (i) the ν vector is located between l_1^- and l_2^-, such as is $-\nu^1$ (the line labeled $E^1 = E_0$ is an isomean line for this case); and (ii) the ν vector lies on the l_1^- ray, as does ν_2.

(d) If ν lies above l_1, as is the case with ν^3, ν^4, ν^5, and ν^1, then E increases as you move away from the origin on l_2^+. If, in addition, $\nu_2 > 0$ as in ν^3 and ν^4, then E increases as Y_2 increases along any vertical line. For example, in this case E is greater at a than b on the vertical line labeled $V = V_1$. What is the efficient set in this case?

(e) Show that if ν lies on the positive Y_1 axis then every portfolio in the feasible cone is an efficient portfolio.

(f) Figure 12.3(b) analyzes the case in which the feasible cone includes the positive Y_2 axis. l_1^+, l_2^+, l_1^-, l_2^- are defined as in figure 12.3(a). What are the efficient sets: (i) if the expected return vector ν lies between l_1^- and l_2^-, as does ν^1; (ii) if ν lies on l_2^- (not shown); (iii) if ν lies between l_2^- and the positive Y_1 axis, as does ν^2; and (iv) if ν is on the positive Y_1 axis, as is ν^3?

(g) Show that if $\nu_1 > 0$ as in the case of ν^4, no portfolio is efficient.

12.5 (Based on Black, 1972) Assume that all investors have the same beliefs and select their portfolio subject to the same affine constraint set. Assume also that there is more than one efficient portfolio, but only one efficient portfolio for any $E \geqslant E^\dagger$ (where $E^\dagger$ is the E of the portfolio with minimum V). We have seen that, under these assumptions, the set of efficient portfolios is a ray, $X = X^* + \beta t$, $t \geqslant 0$, and the market portfolio

$$X^{\mathrm{M}} = \Sigma w_I X^I$$

is an efficient portfolio. Let X^* be the feasible portfolio which minimizes V. We will assume that $X^{\mathrm{M}} \neq X^*$; i.e. some $X^I \neq X^*$.

(a) Under these assumptions, the covariance between $X = X^* + \beta t$ and X^{M} is a (nonconstant) linear function of t, for all $t \in R$. (See the results of exercise 5.4; but watch out for differences in notation from that used here.) The same is true for the beta (regression coefficient) of $r'X$ against $r'X^{\mathrm{M}}$. Infer that for some value of t, call it t_0,

$$X_0 = X^* + t_0\beta$$

has zero covariance with $r'X^{\mathrm{M}}$, and therefore $r'X_0$ has a zero beta against $r'X^{\mathrm{M}}$.

(b) Let $E_0 = \mu' X_0$, for the X_0 in (a). Assume that the constraint requirements include $\Sigma X_i = 1$, perhaps together with other equality constraints. Show that

$$(\mu_i - E_0) = k \operatorname{cov}(r_i, r'X^{\mathrm{M}})$$

for every security i, where k is some constant independent of i. Also,

$$(\mu_i - E_0) = k^* \beta_{i,M}$$

where $\beta_{i,M}$ is the regresssion of r_i on $r'X^{\mathrm{M}}$ and k^* is another constant. (Hint: use theorem 12.5.)

12.6 (a) Assume that all investors seek mean-variance efficiency, and that all investors have the same beliefs with C nonsingular and with some $\mu_i \neq \mu_j$; that $\Sigma X_i^I = 1$ is the only constraint on the choice of the Ith portfolio; and that there is a riskless security. Conclude, as did Mossin (1966), that (as in the case of the Sharpe-Lintner model) every efficient portfolio lies on a straight line segment that starts at a portfolio X^{C} consisting of the riskless security only ($X_i^{\mathrm{C}} = 0$ for all other securities) and passes through a portfolio X^{N} not containing the riskless security. (We continue to define C, μ, and X as in the chapter. This differs from Mossin's setup, but we arrive at the same result.)

(b) Show that for Mossin's model defined in (a) – i.e. Black's model with a riskless asset – the market is an efficient portfolio, and equation (12.7) holds.

(c) In equilibrium, C and μ must be such that the amount held by all investors of the ith security, $\Sigma_I X_i^I$, is nonnegative. Show that, given the assumptions of (a), all investors hold nonnegative amounts of all assets.

(d) Contrast the above result with those of the model whose constraints are $\Sigma_i X_i^I = 1, X_i^I \geqslant 0$ for all i and I. Mossin's model does not require $X_i^I \geqslant 0$, but concludes that this will hold in equilbrium. Nevertheless its other conclusions – e.g. the necessity of market efficiency and equation (12.7) – is qualitatively different from those of the standard model in which each investor takes $X_i^I \geqslant 0$ as a constraint.

12.7 (a) Draw four figures of the form defined to be canonical in chapter 11 when τ^* has rank 2. In each of these figures let the (nonstandard) constraint set be a cone with one vertex, where this vertex has minimum feasible V, but is not on the Y_1 axis (and therefore not at the origin). Construct the respective figures so that:

(i) The vertex is the only efficient portfolio.
(ii) The set of efficient portfolios is a single straight line.
(iii) The set of efficient portfolios is a pair of straight line segments (one of them an unbounded segment of the Y_1 axis).
(iv) The set of efficient portfolios consists of three straight line segments (one of them a bounded portion of the Y_1 axis).

(b) From (a) (iii) and (iv) conclude that assumption (ii) of theorem 12.2 - that X_0 has no greater variance than any other point in the affine hull - cannot be replaced by the assumption that X_0 has minimum feasible variance.

12.8 Suppose that all investors seek mean-variance efficiency, and that all have the same beliefs, but that they have different constraint sets. Specifically, for this exercise suppose that some have a standard constraint set and the others have the constraint set of Black's model. Consider the three-security case with τ^* of rank 2. Since the two types of investors have the same beliefs, the same canonical diagram can be used for both. The constraint set for one type will be a triangle; for the other, the whole $Y_1 Y_2$ space.

(a) Draw a figure illustrating the following fact: if the weighted average $\Sigma_{I \in S} w_I^* X^I$ of the portfolios of investors with standard constraint sets does not lie on the Y_1 axis, then the weighted average $\Sigma_I w_I X^I$ will not lie on the Y_1 axis. Here $\Sigma_{I \in S}$ indicates a sum over investors with standard constraint set, and $w_I^* = W_I / \Sigma_{J \in S} W_J$.
(b) For the case in (a), conclude that the market portfolio X^{M} will not be an efficient portfolio for investors with Black's constraint set, and will not satisfy equation (12.10). Draw an example in which the market portfolio X^{M} is an efficient portfolio for an investor with a standard constraint set.

12.9 (Black (1972) second model, with two risky and one riskless asset.) Consider the three-security portfolio analysis with constraints

$$X_1 + X_2 + X_3 = 1 \tag{12.23}$$

$$X_3 \geqslant 0 \tag{12.24}$$

where r_3 has zero variance.

(a) Show that τ^* cannot have rank 2 in this model if some portfolio with $X_1 + X_2 = 1$, $X_3 = 0$, has zero variance. (Hint: it cannot be that two points (in the canonical (Y_1, Y_2) plane for τ^* of rank 2) have $V = V_{\min}$.)
(b) Assume τ^* has rank 2. Let P_1 and P_2 be the points in canonical Y space corresponding to e^1 and e^2 in the original X space. Show that the set of feasible portfolios is the closed half-plane consisting of all

points on and to one side of the line through P_1 and P_2. This line corresponds to the line $X_3 = 0$ in the original space. Show that the feasible half-plane for this model always includes the origin.

(c) Assuming that τ^* has rank 2, draw canonical diagrams having each of the following properties. (For perhaps greater realism and a bit more challenge, construct cases in which $\mu_i > \mu_3$, $i = 1, 2$.)

(i) The two critical lines of the model (see exercise 7.8) do not intersect.

(ii) The two critical lines intersect, but only one has efficient portfolios. Specifically, the set of efficient portfolios is the Y_1 axis for $Y_1 \geqslant 0$. (Hint: the critical line on which $X_3 = 0$ intersects the Y_1 axis where $Y_1 < 0$.)

(iii) The set of efficient portfolios consists of a finite portion of the Y_1 axis and an unbounded portion of the critical line on which X_3 is *OUT*.

(iv) $\mu_1 = \mu_2 > \mu_3$.

(d) Consider the Black (1972) second model for any n (as defined in (2.22)). Consider a case in which the efficient set has two segments (see exercise 7.8 as well as part (c) of this exercise). Assume investors select portfolios from each of the segments. Then the market portfolio $(X^{\text{M}})' = (X_1^{\text{M}}, X_2^{\text{M}}, \ldots, X_{n+1}^{\text{M}})$ will be on neither segment and thus will not be an efficient portfolio. Furthermore, show that in this model a portfolio P must be on the critical line with X_{n+1} *IN* in order to minimize L in (12.11). Therefore equation (12.10) does not hold for X^{M}. Black (1972), on the other hand, asserts that the market portfolio $\tilde{X}^{\text{M}} = (X_1, X_2, \ldots, X_n)$, as defined in the first paragraph of this chapter such that $\Sigma_{i=1}^{n} X_i = 1$, is efficient and (12.10) is satisfied for $i = 1$ to n. Resolve this apparent contradiction (for any n; illustrate for $n = 2$). (Hint: there is no contradiction since theorem 12.5 gives necessary and sufficient conditions for (12.10) to hold for *all* securities, i.e. for $i = 1$ to $n + 1$ in the present case. In general, a portfolio with $\Sigma_{i=1}^{n} X_i = 1$ lies on the $X_{n+1} = 0$ hyperplane; e.g. on the $X_3 = 0$ line when $n = 2$. Show that, for any n, $(X_1^{\text{M}}, X_2^{\text{M}}, \ldots, X_n^{\text{M}}, 0)/\Sigma_{i=1}^{n} X_i^{\text{M}}$ lies on the efficient portion of the critical line for the *IN* set with $n + 1$ *OUT*; i.e. it lies on the efficient set for Black's (first) model (without X_{n+1}). The proof of this is two-dimensional, since all efficient portfolios (for Black's second model) lie in the plane determined by the two intersecting critical lines (see discussion following theorem 7.9 for an example using a two-dimensional subset of a higher dimensional space). Black's result for the second model then follows from the result from Black's (first) model.)

12.10. (a) Suppose that the set of feasible portfolios is a cone with a vertex with minimum variance among portfolios in the affine hull. (Other portfolios in the affine hull may have the same minimum variance.)

Suppose also that there is more than one efficient EV combination. What is the shape of the set of efficient $E\sigma$ combinations? Distinguish between the case in which minimum variance is zero and that in which it is positive. (Hint: a single ray provides a complete nonredundant set of efficient portfolios. Recall the discussion in chapter 5 of $\sigma(E)$ along a straight line.)

(b) Let S_0 be the set of $E\sigma$ combinations for a standard model. The standard model may be viewed as a Tobin-Sharpe-Lintner model (equations (1.12)) in which $X_{n+1} = 0$ is required. Assume that $\sigma = 0$ is not feasible for the standard model under consideration, and that $\mu_i > r_0 = -\mu_{n+1}$ for some i. Let S_1 be the set of efficient $E\sigma$ combinations if we allow $X_{n+1} \geqslant -1$ (i.e. if we add a risk-free asset to the standard model and allow lending and unlimited borrowing at this rate, as in the Tobin-Sharpe-Lintner model). Show that S_1 is a ray that starts at $(r_0, 0)$ and touches but does not intersect S_0. Now assume in addition that only one portfolio P_0 provides the $E\sigma$ combination at the point of tangency between S_0 and S_1. Conclude (the *Tobin separation theorem*) that all efficient portfolios consists of P_0 plus perhaps more or less borrowing or lending. Draw a figure illustrating why combining cash with any other portfolio (even any other portfolio giving rise to a point on S_0) is inefficient. (Hint: recall that $\sigma(E)$ is linear on a straight line when the line contains a point with $\sigma = 0$; or see figure I of Lintner, 1965, or almost any introductory text in finance.)

(c) How could the answer in (b) be different if we had not assumed (i) $\mu_i > r_0$ for some i, and (ii) $\sigma = 0$ was not feasible for the standard model under consideration?

(d) In chapter 1 we indicated that in Black's model the bottom of the set of feasible EV combinations was typically a single parabola. Why is this true? In the Tobin-Sharpe-Lintner model, on the other hand, we said it was possible to have two different parabolas on the bottom, meeting at $(r_0, 0)$. How can this happen? Are there any other possibilities for the bottom of the feasible EV set for the Tobin-Sharpe-Lintner model? (Hints: in Black's model, if more than one E is feasible, a straight line provides a complete nonredundant set of portfolios with minimum V for *all* E. Assuming $\mu_i < r_0$ for some i, extend the Tobin-Sharpe-Lintner analysis in (b) to the entire bottom of the set of feasible EV combinations. S_0 and S_1 now have two tangencies, one to the right and one to the left of $E = r_0$. Now suppose these tangencies are provided by unique portfolios P_0 and P_1. Distinguish the cases in which P_0 and P_1 are (i) on the same critical line, and (ii) on different critical lines. Concerning other possibilities, note that if $\mu_i \geqslant r_0$ for all i then only $E \geqslant r_0$ is feasible. Then what does the bottom of the set of feasible EV combinations look like? Next, what if $\mu_i = r_0$ for all i; or if $\mu_i < r_0$ for all i?)

Part V

A Portfolio Selection Program

13

Program Description

By Peter Todd

The first printing of this book presented a program for solving the general portfolio selection problem, or portfolio optimizer, that was written in an experimental programming language called EAS-E (Markowitz, Malhotra, and Pazel, 1984). In this printing we wanted to present a program in a programming language that would be widely known to and useable by readers. We first thought of using C++ since it is widely used and I had already written 3 different versions of such a program in C or C++. However, we realized that we could better meet our goals by choosing Microsoft Visual Basic for Applications (VBA). This way the program can be executed by anyone with access to Microsoft Excel. If faster execution is required, then the program could easily be ported to Microsoft Visual Basic (VB), or possibly another version of Basic, and compiled to an executable file.

The program presented here is a descendent of the original EAS-E program presented in the first printing of this book, which is the main source for the algorithms described here. My first experience in writing portfolio selection programs was to translate the EAS-E program in the first printing to the C programming language. I later added a number of features to improve efficiency and flexibility[1]. Along the way I converted the program to C++. These programs have grown far too large and complex for inclusion in a book chapter such as this. In order to avoid excessive complexity, and to keep the program size relatively small, most of these added features were removed from the Basic version of the program presented here. However, two noteworthy features that were not in the original EAS-E program remain:

1. The ability to specify upper limits and non-zero lower limits on holdings of individual securities (without adding constraint equations and slack variables).
2. Inequality constraints can be specified, with the program adding the necessary slack variables automatically. In the EAS-E program the user had to convert any inequality constraints to equality constraints, adding the required slack variables manually.

These two features allow the portfolio selection problem to be specified directly in "*form 0*", as described on page 24. This is generally more convenient than "*form 2*", as was required by the original program.

In all, the Basic program is considerably longer that the original EAS-E program. This is partly because of the additional features, and partly because EAS-E contains certain constructs that allow for very concise code. The program presented here is

[1] Other programmers also worked on versions of the C program from time to time, including Yuji Yamane, Jun Murofushi, and Kazuyoshi Tanaka.

implemented as 7 code "modules", which are listed in the appendix to this chapter. The appendix also contains sample inputs and outputs. To avoid retyping the program, readers can obtain the program via email by sending a request to the author at pete@riverviewinc.com.

Two of the modules contain input and output code that is specific to Microsoft Excel. The other modules are all independent of the specific environment. The modules are:

1. Module *Main*. Contains all global data declarations, and the optimizer top-level subroutine (*Optimize*).
2. Module *Simplex*. Implements the Simplex algorithm to find the portfolio with the maximum expected return (E) subject to the constraints.
3. Module *CLA*. Implements the critical line algorithm to trace out the efficient frontier.
4. Module *Inputs*. Reads inputs from an Excel spreadsheet.
5. Module *Output*. Outputs corner portfolios to an Excel spreadsheet.
6. Module *Utility*. Utility functions and subroutines.
7. Class module *cSet*. A simple implementation of a "set" data type used to keep track of the sets of *IN* and *OUT* variables.

Notation

I have made certain extensions and modifications in notation in this Chapter, relative to earlier chapters. Hopefully the notation used here is clear from the context, but to avoid possible confusion a few clarifications are in order:

1. Superscript "*T*" is used to indicate matrix or vector transposition, rather than a "prime" symbol (*e.g.*, A^T rather than A').
2. Besides the *IN* and *OUT* sets, as defined in Chapter 7, we also define the *LO* and *UP* sets—the sets of variables fixed against their lower and upper limits, respectively. Then $OUT = LO \cup UP$.
3. The subscripts I and O, are used to indicate sub-vectors or sub-matrices based on the *IN* and *OUT* sets. For example X_I represents the *IN* elements of vector X, and M_{IO} represents the *IN* rows and *OUT* columns of matrix M.
4. When only a single subscript is used with the A matrix, we are referring to columns of A. Thus the notations A_I and A_O refer to the *IN* columns and *OUT* columns of A, respectively. Note that with A_I we are not replacing the *OUT* columns of A with zeros (as in the definition of $\overline{A}_{IN}$ on page 155), but simply dropping the *OUT* columns.
5. The notation M_{II}^{-1} refers to the inverse of matrix M_{II}, or $(M_{II})^{-1}$ rather than $(M^{-1})_{II}$. When we refer to specific rows, columns or elements of M_{II}^{-1}, the subscripts refer to the corresponding rows in the full M matrix. For example, if M is a 10 by 10 matrix, and variables 3, 4, 9, and 10 are *IN*, then M_{II}^{-1} is a 4 by 4 matrix, and $(M_{II}^{-1})_{3,3}$ refers to the element in the first row and column of M_{II}^{-1}, since this is the element that corresponds to $M_{3,3}$.

Statement of the Problem

Our problem in portfolio optimization is to find the *efficient frontier*, subject to constraints. The efficient frontier is the set of all portfolios that maximize the portfolio expected return (E) for a given level of variance (V), or equivalently, minimize V for a given level of E. Portfolios are defined by X, the n-vector of security weights, where n is the number of securities in our universe. In practice, some elements of X may not represent real securities, but slack variables or artificial basis variables introduced for convenience of solution—see below. Portfolio E and V are given by

$$E=\mu^{T}X \tag{13.1}$$

and

$$V=X^{T}CX \tag{13.2}$$

where μ is an n-vector of security expected returns, and C is an n by n security covariance matrix. Constraints on the choice of X are of the form

$$AX=b \tag{13.3}$$

and

$$L\leq X\leq U \tag{13.4}$$

where A is an m by n matrix of constraint coefficients, b is an m-vector of constraint right-hand sides, and U and L are n-vectors of upper and lower limits of X[2]. Normally equation (13.3) would contain at least a *budget constraint*, which constrains the sum of the security weights to equal 1.0. A wide variety of other constraints can be used.

Upper and lower limits could be implemented through equation (13.3) and a lower limit of zero, but it is much more efficient to handle them separately in equation (13.4). If an upper limit is not desired it can be omitted. Lower limits are always required, but may be set to a large negative number so that the limit will not be binding.

In order to conform with equation (13.3), inequality constraints must be converted to equality constraints by the introduction of *slack variables* (the program handles this automatically). For example, for a 3-variable problem ($n = 3$), the constraint

$$3X_1+2X_2-X_3\geq 0.5 \tag{13.5}$$

is first converted to "less than" constraint by multiplying through by –1 to get

$$-3X_1-2X_2+X_3\leq -0.5$$

(skip this step for "less than" constraints). Then slack variable X_4 is introduced and the constraint is replaced with

$$-3X_1-2X_2+X_3+X_4=-0.5 \tag{13.6}$$

$$X_4\geq 0 \tag{13.7}$$

Equations (13.6) and (13.7) are together equivalent to the original constraint equation (13.5). Equation (13.7) is implemented by setting the lower limit on X_4 (L_4) to zero. The number of variables (n) is increased by one, μ_4 is set to zero, and the covariance matrix C is extended with a row and column of zeroes for the slack variable.

---

[2] Note that L was used to represent the Lagrangian function in Chapters 6 and 7.

Program Inputs

The inputs to the program are as follows:

1. The number of securities in the "universe" (*NumSecs*). This can be anywhere from 2 to a large number depending on the environment. When running under the Excel interface, this is limited to 255, since that is the maximum number of columns in a spreadsheet. The program runs relatively slowly when run under Excel since the program is not compiled to native code. However, if the same program were complied under the standalone version of Visual Basic, then it should be practical to run with up to several thousand variables. Note that we will use n to refer to the total number of variables, including any slack variables.
2. The number of constraint equations (m). Usually at least one constraint equation that specifies a "budget" should be used (see Constraint Equations below). There is no specific limit to the number of constraint equations.
3. The ending value of λ_E (*EndLambdaE*). The Critical Line Algorithm will stop iterating when λ_E reaches this value. To generate a complete efficient frontier a small value such a 0.00001 should be used. Recall that $\lambda_E = 2dV/dE$ (see page 138).
4. The maximum number of corner portfolios to be generated (*MaxCPs*). This equals the maximum number of iterations of the Critical Line Algorithm. This is a failsafe mechanism to stop the program if something goes wrong. For example, if an invalid covariance matrix is input, sometimes the Critical Line Algorithm may fail and iterate endlessly. Some number that is several times *NumSecs+m* is reasonable.
5. The vector of security expected returns (μ or *mu*, length *NumSecs*). The units are arbitrary, but annual percentage is typically used.
6. The vector of lower limits on the holdings of each security (L, length *NumSecs*). Zero is the usual value. Use a positive value to force the holding of a security. Use a negative value to allow shorting.
7. The vector of upper limits on the holdings of each security (U, length *NumSecs*). If an upper limit is not desired then leave the input cell empty.
8. The securities covariance matrix (C or *Cov*, *NumSecs*×*NumSecs*). Since the covariance matrix always must be symmetric about the main diagonal, only the lower triangular portion of the covariance matrix is required by the Excel spreadsheet interface. A valid covariance matrix is always positive semidefinite (see pages 42-43).
9. The set of m constraint equations. This includes the matrix of constraint coefficients (A, size m×*NumSecs*), the vector of constraint "right-hand sides" (b, length m), and an array specifying the type of each constraint as "equality", "greater than" inequality, or "less than" inequality (*ConType*, length m). In the Excel interface these are specified as "=", ">", and "<", respectively. Some kind of "budget" constraint limiting the total investment should normally be used[3]. Typically, the budget is specified so that all security weights must add up to 1.0 (see the first constraint

---

[3] Otherwise, unless every variable has an upper limit, E will be unbounded. This program does not handle the case of "unbounded E". In practical problems this should probably never occur. Page 201 describes a method to handle this situation.

equation in the sample inputs). There is no specific limit to the number of constraint equations.

The Main Module

The program listings are presented in exhibit A. The listings include “bookmarks” in the comments of the form <M*n*>, <S*n*>, <C*n*>, <I*n*>, or <U*n*>, where *n* is an integer, so that we can refer to specific sections of the program in the description below. Bookmarks starting with “M”, “S”, "C", "I" and “U” refer to modules *Main*, *Simplex*, *CLA*, *Inputs*, and *Utility*, respectively.

Public Data Declarations

Main contains public constant and variable declarations, which are accessible to all modules of the program. Many of the constants would be “enumerations”, except that this feature is missing from VBA (it is available in VB). The constant *EPSILON* is defined as a small number to be used in comparisons to “zero”, which can help to avoid numerical instability caused by round-off error. Thirteen of the variables declared here contain inputs that must be read by subroutine *Inputs.Read.*<M1> The remaining variables are internal to the optimizer. Public arrays are allocated by subroutine *AllocatePublicArrays* in module *Main* (*Main.AllocatePublicArrays*), except for *ConType*, which is allocated in *Inputs.Read.* Arrays that depend on the number of variables are allocated to be large enough to accommodate added slack variables, and artificial bases variables added during the first phase of the simplex algorithm (see below). After the first phase of the simplex such arrays can be reallocated to drop the artificial basis variables.

Main Routine

The entry point and main routine of the optimizer is subroutine *Main.Optimize*. The high-level program operation can be summarized as follows:

Call *Inputs.Read* to read the inputs.
Add slack variables.
Call *Output.Setup* to set up for outputting corner portfolios.
Call *Simplex.Run* to get top point of efficient frontier.
Call *CLA.Setup* to set up for CLA.
While not at end of efficient frontier:
    Call *CLA.Iteration* to get next corner portfolio.
    Call *Output.CornerPortfolio* to output corner portfolio.
End While.

Optimize first calls *Inputs.Read* to read the inputs into global variables.<M2> *Optimize* then converts inequality constraints to equality constraints by adding slack variables.<M3> *Optimize* next calls *Output.Setup* to set up for outputting the results.<M4> Then *Optimize* calls *Simplex.Run* to execute the simplex algorithm, which finds the portfolio with the highest expected return subject to the constraints.<M5> If the simplex algorithm cannot find such a portfolio, then *Optimize* displays an error message and exits.<M6> Otherwise, *Optimize* calls *CLA.Setup* to set up for the Critical Line Algorithm,<M7> and then iteratively calls *CLA.Iteration* to calculate the next corner portfolio on the efficient frontier, and *Output.OutputCornerPortfolio* to output each corner portfolio.<M8> CLA iteration ceases when either the bottom of the efficient frontier has been reached (according the *EndLambdaE*) or the iteration limit has been reached.

Reading Inputs

The program is designed so that all code dependent on the particular source of inputs is located in module *Inputs*. The implementation presented here is to read the inputs from named "ranges" (actually named single cells) in a Microsoft Excel spreadsheet. For example, the number of securities is read from named range *NumSecs*.

Inputs.Read first reads the scalar inputs, including the number of securities (*NumSecs*) and the number of constraint equations (*m*).<I1> *Read* then allocates and reads the array of contraint types (*ConType*) to determine the number of inequality constraints, which equals the number of slack variables to be added (*NumSlackVars*).<I2> The total number of *X* variables for the Critical Line Algorithm (*n*) is then

$$n = NumSecs + NumSlackVars$$

Read then calls *Main.AllocatePublicArrays* to allocate all public arrays (other than *ConType*) and sets.<I3> *Read* then reads the remaining inputs into the just-allocated public arrays.<I4> The covariance matrix (*C*) is read into the *M* matrix (*MMat*)—recall that *M* is defined as (see page 132)

$$M = \begin{pmatrix} C & A^T \\ A & 0 \end{pmatrix} \tag{13.8}$$

The Simplex Algorithm

The purpose of the simplex algorithm is to find the portfolio (*X*) that maximizes the portfolio expected return $E = \mu^{\mathrm{T}} X$ (the objective function) subject to the constraints $L \le X \le U$ and $AX = b$. The simplex algorithm relies on the fact that if there are one or more *E*-maximizing solutions to a problem, then at least one such solution must be a *basic solution*[4]. Thus we can restrict our search for an *E*-maximizing solution to basic solutions. Basic solutions occur at *extreme feasible points* of the solution space defined by the *m* constraints. At such points there must be exactly *m* *IN* variables, with the remaining variables *OUT*. We can start with any basic solution. Then in each iteration we determine which *OUT* variable would give the most rapid increase in *E* as it comes *IN*, and bring that variable *IN* until a variable is driven *OUT* by reaching its upper or lower limit. We continue iterating until no further increase in *E* can be obtained by bringing any *OUT* variable *IN*.

Since the simplex algorithm requires a basic solution to get started, and since finding such a solution may be non-trivial, we run the algorithm in 2 phases. The first phase solves a modified problem for which we can easily find a starting basic solution, and

---

[4] Non-basic solutions may tie for maximum *E*.

which yields a basic solution to our original problem. The second phase then finds an optimal basic solution to the original problem.

Simplex Phase 1

In phase 1 we start all of the variables from the original problem *OUT* at their lower limits.<S1> We add *m* "artificial basis" or "infeasibility" variables that start *IN*.<S2> We also use an objective function that results in forcing the artificial basis variables *OUT*, yielding a desired feasible solution to the original problem. Using a dot to indicate the modified arrays, the substitutions required for our modified problem are

$$\dot{X} = \begin{pmatrix} X \\ Y \end{pmatrix},\ \dot{\mu} = \begin{pmatrix} 0 \\ -1 \end{pmatrix},\ \dot{A} = (A, B),\ \dot{L} = \begin{pmatrix} L \\ 0 \end{pmatrix},\ \text{and}\ \dot{U} = \begin{pmatrix} U \\ \infty \end{pmatrix}$$

where *Y* represents the added artificial basis variables, and *B* is an *m*×*m* matrix defined as follows:

$$B_{i,j} = \begin{cases} 0 & i \neq j \\ 1 & (i = j)\ \text{and}\ (b_i \geq (AL)_i) \\ -1 & (i = j)\ \text{and}\ (b_i < (AL)_i) \end{cases}$$

Since *B* provides the starting *IN* columns of our modified constraint coefficient matrix, it is the starting A_I.

In our modified objective function we assign negative values for the artificial basis variables, and zeros for other variables (we use vector *z* in the code to represent the objective function for the simplex).<S1><S2> Then maximizing the objective function drives the artificial basis variables to their lower limits.

Of course, we still need a feasible solution to our modified problem to start phase one. Starting *X* fixed at *L* our constraint equation becomes

$$(A, B)\begin{pmatrix} L \\ Y \end{pmatrix} = b$$

Solving for *Y* we get

$$Y = B^{-1}(b - AL) = \text{abs}(b - AL)$$

Note that B^{-1} equals *B*. Therefore, the starting value of $A_I^{-1} = A_I = B$.

After executing the basic simplex algorithm on the phase 1 problem (see below), we obtain one of three results:

1. All *m* of the added artificial basis variables are *OUT*, and *m* of the *X* variables are *IN*. Then *X* is a valid starting feasible solution for phase 2. We drop the artificial basis variables<S4>, and continue with phase 2.
2. One or more of the artificial basis variables are still *IN* and non-zero. Then no feasible solution to our problem exists, and the problem must be reformulated.

3. One or more of the artificial basis variables are still *IN*, but all equal zero. In this case, our constraint set (including upper and lower limits) is *degenerate.*[5] *X* is still a valid starting feasible solution for phase 2, but we cannot simply drop the artificial basis variables since they are not all *OUT*. If we continue without dropping these variables, then we must ensure that none of these leftover artificial basis variables can ever become non-zero during the simplex phase 2 and critical line algorithm (which would mean the violation of our original set of constraints). We can do this by setting the upper limits of these variables to zero<S5>. Note that with degenerate problems the chance of problems such as cycling during simplex phase 2 is increased (though still rare). The program warns when a degenerate problem is encountered.

Simplex Phase 2

The results of simplex phase 1 give us a basic solution to our original problem. We set our objective function (z) to our original expected returns (μ), and then run the simplex phase 2 to find the optimal solution.<S6> After executing the simplex algorithm (see below), we obtain one of two results:

1. We have a valid *E*-maximizing solution. Continue on to critical line algorithm!
2. The problem is "unbounded", meaning that we can increase *E* without limit.<S15> This indicates that there are no upper limits or budget constraint effecting some variables. The problem must be reformulated.

One further check is made before continuing on to the critical line algorithm. The *E*-maximizing solution we have obtained may tie with other solutions for maximizing *E*. In this case our solution may not be efficient, since there is no reason to expect that it would have the lowest *V* among the *E*-maximizing solutions. Since the critical line algorithm requires that the starting portfolio be a unique *E*-maximizing solution (see Chapter 9), we check for non-uniqueness, and if necessary, alter the problem slightly to make our solution the unique *E*-maximizing solution. We do this by checking the profitability of each *OUT* variable from the last simplex iteration. Variables with zero profitability could have come *IN* with no decrease in *E*, and thus indicate the existence of another *E*-maximizing solution. We make our solution unique by slightly increasing such variable's expected return if the variable is at its upper limit, or decreasing its expected return if at its lower limit.<S7><S30>

The Steps of the Simplex Algorithm (Phases 1 and 2)

1. **Determine which *OUT* variable should come *IN*.** We select the *OUT* variable that produces the most rapid increase in *E* as it comes *IN* (*i.e.*, maximizes $\partial E/\partial X_j$ for $j \in LO$, or $-\partial E/\partial X_j$ for $j \in UP$). We can derive the formula for $\partial E/\partial X_j$ by starting with $E = \mu^{\mathrm{T}} X$, and partitioning into *IN* and *OUT* variables, as follows:

---

[5] The definition of degenerate must be modified from that given in Chapter 8 (page 186) since we are now allowing upper limits and non-zero lower limits. A basic feasible solution is now nondegenerate if $X_i > L_i$ and $X_i < U_i$ for $i \in IN$.

$$E = \left(\mu_I^{\mathrm{T}}, \mu_O^{\mathrm{T}}\right)\begin{pmatrix} X_I \\ X_O \end{pmatrix} = \mu_I^{\mathrm{T}} X_I + \mu_O^{\mathrm{T}} X_O \tag{13.9}$$

Partitioning $AX = b$ similarly, and solving for X_I

$$\left(A_I, A_O\right)\begin{pmatrix} X_I \\ X_O \end{pmatrix} = b$$

$$X_I = A_I^{-1}\left(b - A_O X_O\right) \tag{13.10}$$

Substituting this result for X_I in equation (13. 9)

$$E = \mu_I^{\mathrm{T}} A_I^{-1}\left(b - A_O X_O\right) + \mu_O^{\mathrm{T}} X_O$$

Partitioning the *OUT* variables to separate variable *j* from the other *OUT* variables:

$$E = \mu_I^{\mathrm{T}} A_I^{-1}\left(b - A_{O-j} X_{O-j} - A_j X_j\right) + \mu_{O-j}^{\mathrm{T}} X_{O-j} + \mu_j X_j$$

$$\frac{\partial E}{\partial X_j} = -\mu_I^{\mathrm{T}} A_I^{-1} A_j + \mu_j = -\left(A_j\right)^{\mathrm{T}}\left(A_I^{-1}\right)^{\mathrm{T}} \mu_I + \mu_j$$

where A_j is the *j*-th column of *A*, A_{O-j} is the *OUT* columns of *A* excluding column *j*, and X_{O-j}, and μ_{O-j} are the *OUT* elements of *X* and μ, excluding element *j*. Define ***m***-vector π, the "price" of each *IN* variable, as<S10>

$$\pi = -\left(A_I^{-1}\right)^{\mathrm{T}} \mu_I$$

Also define ***n***-vector Π, the "profitability" of each *OUT* variable coming *IN*, as<S11>

$$\Pi_j = \begin{cases} \dfrac{\partial E}{\partial X_j} = \left(A_j\right)^{\mathrm{T}} \pi + \mu_j & j \in LO \\ -\dfrac{\partial E}{\partial X_j} = -\left(A_j\right)^{\mathrm{t}} \pi - \mu_j & j \in UP \\ 0 & j \in IN \end{cases}$$

Determine j_{max}, the subscript of the *OUT* variable with the largest profitability. If $\Pi_{j_{max}} \le 0$, then there is no profit for any *OUT* variable coming *IN*.<S12> If this happens during simplex phase 2 then we have found the optimal solution (end of algorithm). If it happens during phase 1, then either the problem is infeasible (at least one of the *IN* ABVs is non-zero) or degenerate (all *IN* ABVs are zero). Otherwise $\left(\Pi_{j_{max}} > 0\right)$, variable j_{max} comes *IN* (continue with next step).

2. **Determine which variable should go *OUT*.** First compute α (*AdjRate* in the code), the rate of adjustment for each *IN* variable as $X_{j_{max}}$ comes *IN* ($\partial X_j / \partial X_{j_{max}}$ if $j_{max} \in LO$, or $-\partial X_j / \partial X_{j_{max}}$ if $j_{max} \in UP$). The formula for $\partial X_j / \partial X_{j_{max}}$ can be derived starting from constraint equation $AX = b$ and partitioning for *IN* variables, *OUT* variables excluding j_{max}, and j_{max}:

$$\left(A_I, A_{O-j_{max}}, A_{j_{max}}\right)\begin{pmatrix} X_I \\ X_{O-j_{max}} \\ X_{j_{max}} \end{pmatrix} = b$$

$$X_I = A_I^{-1}\left(b - A_{O-j_{max}} X_{O-j_{max}} - A_{j_{max}} X_{j_{max}}\right)$$

$$\frac{\partial X_I}{\partial X_{j_{max}}} = -A_I^{-1} A_{j_{max}}$$

α is then computed from:<S13>

$$\alpha = \begin{cases} -A_I^{-1} A_{j_{max}} & j_{max} \in LO \\ A_I^{-1} A_{j_{max}} & j_{max} \in UP \end{cases} \tag{13.11}$$

Next compute θ, the amount that $X_{j_{max}}$ can come *IN* (absolute value) before an *IN* variable hits a lower or upper bound:<S14>

$$\theta = \min \begin{pmatrix} U_{j_{max}} - L_{j_{max}} & \\ \left(U_{j(i)} - X_{j(i)}\right)/\alpha_i & i = 1...m,\ \alpha_i > 0 \\ \left(L_{j(i)} - X_{j(i)}\right)/\alpha_i & i = 1...m,\ \alpha_i < 0 \end{pmatrix} \tag{13.12}$$

where $j(i)$ is the index of the variable (1 to *n*) that corresponds to the *i*-th *IN* variable (1 to *m*). The value of *i* that produces θ in (13.12) is i_{out}, and the corresponding variable index is j_{out}.

For variables that have no upper limit, the first 2 lines in equation (13.12) are not applicable. If no variable can provide a value for θ (the variable coming *IN* and all currently *IN* variables have no upper limits, and all α_i's are positive), then the problem is "unbounded", meaning that *E* can be increased without limit. This cannot happen during simplex phase 1. For simplex phase 2 this would indicate that besides being no upper limits for at least some variables, there is no effective budget constraint (exit algorithm).<S15>

The variable that contributes the minimum value for θ in equation (13.12) is the first variable to hit an upper or lower bound as $X_{j_{max}}$ comes *IN*, and is therefore the variable that must go *OUT*. If θ is from the first line in equation (13.12), then the variable coming *IN* ($X_{j_{max}}$) is also the variable that goes *OUT* (from *UP* to *LO*, or from *LO* to *UP*). Otherwise, θ is from the second or third line, and the corresponding *IN* variable is going *UP* or *LO*, respectively.

3. **Determine the new values of the *IN X*'s.** The new values of the *IN* variables are computed from:<S16>

   $$X_I = X_I + \theta\alpha$$

4. **Update the *IN*, *OUT*, *UP*, and *LO* sets.** Delete j_{max} from the *OUT* and *UP* or *LO* sets, add it to the *IN* set.<S17><U1> Delete j_{out} from the *IN* set and add it to the *OUT*

and *UP* or *LO* sets.<S18><U2> In the program we use array *State* to record whether *OUT* variables are *UP* or *LO*.

5. **Update A_I^{-1} for the new *IN* set.**<S19> Rather than recompute A_I^{-1} from scratch when the *IN* set changes, we update the existing matrix, which is much more efficient.<S20> If $X_{j_{max}}$ is going *OUT*, no update is required, since the set of *IN* variables is not changing. We can derive the formula to update A_I^{-1} as follows: Assume we are replacing the *i*-th column of A_I with vector *V*. Define the updated versions of A_I and A_I^{-1} to be $\dot{A}_I$ and $\dot{A}_I^{-1}$. Define vector *v* equal to $A_I^{-1}V$. Also define matrix *E* as the matrix obtained by replacing the *i*-th column of the identity matrix with *v*. For example, if $m = 4$ and $i = 3$:

$$E = \begin{pmatrix} 1 & 0 & v_1 & 0 \\ 0 & 1 & v_2 & 0 \\ 0 & 0 & v_3 & 0 \\ 0 & 0 & v_4 & 1 \end{pmatrix}$$

Then $\dot{A}_I = A_I E$ and $\dot{A}_I^{-1} = E^{-1} A_I^{-1}$. In our example we can compute E^{-1} as

$$E^{-1} = \begin{pmatrix} 1 & 0 & -v_1/v_3 & 0 \\ 0 & 1 & -v_2/v_3 & 0 \\ 0 & 0 & 1/v_3 & 0 \\ 0 & 0 & -v_4/v_3 & 1 \end{pmatrix}$$

Generalizing this and replacing vector *v* with α as defined in (13.11) we obtain the desired formula:

$$\left(\dot{A}_I^{-1}\right)_{i,j} = \left(A_I^{-1}\right)_{i,j} - \frac{\alpha_i}{\alpha_{i_{out}}}\left(A_I^{-1}\right)_{i_{out},j} \qquad i \neq i_{out}$$

$$\left(\dot{A}_I^{-1}\right)_{i_{out},j} = \begin{cases} -\left(A_I^{-1}\right)_{i_{out},j}/\alpha_{i_{out}} & j_{\max} \in LO \\ \left(A_I^{-1}\right)_{i_{out},j}/\alpha_{i_{out}} & j_{\max} \in UP \end{cases}$$

After replacing column i_{out} of A_I with column $j_{\max}$ of *A*, we re-order the columns in A_I so that they remain in the same order as in *A*, which results in the same re-ordering of the *rows* of A_I^{-1} <S21> (in practice, it may be more efficient to do this re-ordering by remapping indices).

This completes a simplex iteration. If this is phase 1, and all artificial basis variables have gone *OUT*, then we have found a starting feasible solution, and we are finished with simplex phase 1. Otherwise, return to step 1 for another iteration.

The Critical Line Algorithm

In each iteration of the CLA we start with a corner portfolio from the efficient frontier, and a set of *IN* and *OUT* variables. In the first iteration, these are provided by the simplex algorithm. In subsequent iterations, they are provided by the previous CLA iteration. In each iteration we determine how much we can decrease λ_E until a variable needs to go *IN* or *OUT*, which determines the next corner portfolio. As λ_E decreases, we check for the first *IN* variable for which X_i would cross a lower or upper bound, or the first *OUT* variable for which η_i would cross zero. The point at which a variable must go *IN* or *OUT* is the next corner portfolio. The critical line algorithm iterates until λ_E has decreased below the value *EndLambdaE* indicating that we have effectively reached the bottom of the efficient frontier.

Changes to the Algorithm

In order to accommodate non-zero lower limits and upper limits, certain minor changes must be made to the critical line algorithm as presented in Chapter 7. For variables that are *UP* the value of η_i must be positive. Therefore, equations (7.4a) and (7.4b) are replaced by

$$\eta_i \geq 0 \quad i \in LO$$

$$\eta_i = 0 \quad i \in IN$$

$$\eta_i \leq 0 \quad i \in UP$$

In Chapter 7 variables that were *OUT* were necessarily equal to zero, so certain terms conveniently dropped out of various equations. Now variables that are *OUT* may not be zero so such terms must be considered. Equation (7.7b) becomes

$$\begin{pmatrix} C_{II} & A_I^T \\ A_I & 0 \end{pmatrix}\begin{pmatrix} X_I \\ \lambda \end{pmatrix} = \begin{pmatrix} 0 \\ b \end{pmatrix} - \begin{pmatrix} C_{IO} \\ A_O \end{pmatrix} X_O + \begin{pmatrix} \mu_I \\ 0 \end{pmatrix} \lambda_E$$

Equation (7.8) becomes

$$\begin{pmatrix} X_I \\ \lambda \end{pmatrix} = M_{II}^{-1}\bar{b}_I + M_{II}^{-1}\begin{pmatrix} \mu_I \\ 0 \end{pmatrix}\lambda_E \tag{13.13}$$

where we define

$$\bar{b}_I = \begin{pmatrix} 0 \\ b \end{pmatrix} - M_{IO}X_O \tag{13.14}$$

Based on (13.13) we define

$$\alpha_I = M_{II}^{-1}\bar{b}_I\,, \qquad \beta_I = M_{II}^{-1}\begin{pmatrix} \mu_I \\ 0 \end{pmatrix} \tag{13.15}$$

Also we define

$$\alpha_O = X_O\,, \qquad \beta_O = 0 \tag{13.16}$$

With the changes just described, equations (7.10a) and (7.10b) still apply. We use these equations to check how far λ_E can be decreased before an *IN* variable needs to go *OUT*, or an *OUT* variable needs to come *IN*. We see from (7.10a) that for *IN* variables, if $\beta_i < 0$ then X_i increases as λ_E decreases. Therefore, if X_i has an upper limit we must check for X_i reaching U_i, which will occur at

$$\lambda_E = \frac{U_i - \alpha_i}{\beta_i} \qquad \beta_i < 0, \ i \in IN$$

Similarly, if $\beta_i > 0$ then X_i decreases as λ_E decreases, so we must check for X_i reaching L_i, which will occur at

$$\lambda_E = \frac{L_i - \alpha_i}{\beta_i} \qquad \beta_i > 0, \ i \in IN$$

For *LO* variables, since $\eta_i \geq 0$, we see from (7.10b) that if $\delta_i > 0$ then η_i decreases as λ_E decreases, so we must check for η_i reaching zero, which will occur at

$$\lambda_E = \frac{-\gamma_i}{\delta_i} \qquad \delta_i > 0, \ i \in LO$$

Similarly for *UP* variables, since $\eta_i \leq 0$, we see from (7.10b) that if $\delta_i < 0$ then η_i increases as λ_E decreases, so we must check for η_i reaching zero, which will occur at

$$\lambda_E = \frac{-\gamma_i}{\delta_i} \qquad \delta_i < 0, \ i \in UP$$

Thus in place of the definitions of λ_a and λ_b on page 158 we have

$$\lambda_a = \max \begin{pmatrix} \dfrac{L_i - \alpha_i}{\beta_i} & \beta_i > 0, \ i \in IN \\ \dfrac{U_i - \alpha_i}{\beta_i} & \beta_i < 0, \ i \in IN \\ -\infty & \text{otherwise} \end{pmatrix} \tag{13.17}$$

and

$$\lambda_b = \max \begin{pmatrix} \dfrac{-\gamma_i}{\delta_i} & \delta_i > 0, \ i \in LO \\ \dfrac{-\gamma_i}{\delta_i} & \delta_i < 0, \ i \in UP \\ -\infty & \text{otherwise} \end{pmatrix} \tag{13.18}$$

Setting Up for the CLA

After successful completion of the simplex algorithm, we have a starting *X* and *IN* set for the Critical Line Algorithm (CLA). The main subroutine *Main.Optimize* calls *CLA.Setup* to set up various variables and arrays for the CLA. *Setup* does the following tasks:

1. Allocate additional arrays needed for the CLA.<C1>
2. Initialize *OUT* elements of α and β in accordance with (13.16).<C2>
3. Add the λ variables to the *IN* set, since they are always *IN*.<C3>
4. Compute the initial $\bar{b}$ vector in accordance with (13.14).<C4>
5. Add A and A^T to matrix M in accordance with (13.8). <C5> M already contains C since *Inputs.Read* put it there.
6. Compute the initial M_{II}^{-1} matrix. M_{II} is defined as

$$M_{II} = \begin{pmatrix} C_{II} & A_I^T \\ A_I & 0 \end{pmatrix}$$

At this point A_I is a square ($m \times m$) matrix for which we know the inverse from the simplex algorithm (during the *CLA* A_I becomes non-square as variable go *IN* and *OUT*). We can compute the inverse of M_{II} from<C6>

$$M_{II}^{-1} = \begin{pmatrix} 0 & A_I^{-1} \\ \left(A_I^{-1}\right)^{\mathrm{T}} & -\left(A_I^{-1}\right)^{\mathrm{T}} C_{II} A_I^{-1} \end{pmatrix} \tag{13.19}$$

which can be confirmed by multiplying $M_{II}\, M_{II}^{-1}$ to obtain the identity matrix *I*. After computing M_{II}^{-1} we can delete A_I^{-1}.

CLA Iteration

The subroutine *CLA.Iteration* is called repeatedly by *Main.Optimize* to trace out the efficient frontier—one corner portfolio at a time. In each iteration other than the first, we start by calling *CLA.AddVariable* or *CLA.DeleteVariable* to add or delete the variable that was determined in the previous iteration (see below).<C10> We next calculate α and β in accordance with (13.15) and (13.16), and use the result to compute λ_a in accordance with (13.17).<C11> Then we calculate γ_O and δ_O in accordance with (7.10b), and use the result to compute λ_b in accordance with (13.18).<C12> We next compute the λ_E for the next corner portfolio as the greater of λ_a and λ_b.<C13> If λ_a is greater, then a variable first goes OUT as λ_E is decreased. If λ_b is greater, then a variable first comes IN is as λ_E is decreased. Now that we have determined λ_E for the next corner portfolio we can compute X_I for the new corner portfolio in accordance to (7.10a).<C14><C40> Lastly, we calculate the *E* and *V* for the new corner portfolio, as well as the coefficients describing the relationship between *E* and *V* for the critical line connecting the new and previous corner portfolios (see equation 6.10).<C42><C43>

Adding a Variable

Subroutine *CLA.AddVariable* is called during the critical line algorithm to add a variable. *AddVariable* must update M_{II}^{-1}, $\bar{b}_I$, *InVars*, *OutVars*, and *State*. We can derive the algorithm for updating M_{II}^{-1} as follows:

For simplicity of notation we will represent the variable being added, variable j, as occupying the last row and column of the new M_{II} matrix. In practice we can add the new variable in any position using the same algorithm. We will also represent the new *IN* set including variable j with subscript $\dot{I}$ (with dot). Thus we have

$$(M_{II})^{New} = M_{\dot{I}\dot{I}} = \begin{pmatrix} M_{II} & M_{Ij} \\ M_{jI} & M_{jj} \end{pmatrix}$$

We can decompose $M_{\dot{I}\dot{I}}$ into 3 easily-invertable matrices as follows:

$$M_{\dot{I}\dot{I}} = \begin{pmatrix} I & 0 \\ M_{jI}M_{II}^{-1} & \sqrt{M_{jj} - M_{jI}M_{II}^{-1}M_{Ij}} \end{pmatrix} \begin{pmatrix} M_{II} & 0 \\ 0 & 1 \end{pmatrix} \begin{pmatrix} I & M_{II}^{-1}M_{Ij} \\ 0 & \sqrt{M_{jj} - M_{jI}M_{II}^{-1}M_{Ij}} \end{pmatrix}$$

This equality can be verified by matrix multiplication. Now for convenience let us substitute

$$\xi = M_{II}^{-1}M_{Ij}$$

and

$$\xi_j = \sqrt{M_{jj} - M_{jI}M_{II}^{-1}M_{Ij}}$$

to get

$$M_{\dot{I}\dot{I}} = \begin{pmatrix} I & 0 \\ \xi^T & \xi_j \end{pmatrix} \begin{pmatrix} M_{II} & 0 \\ 0 & 1 \end{pmatrix} \begin{pmatrix} I & \xi \\ 0 & \xi_j \end{pmatrix}$$

Using the fact that if A, B, and C are nonsingular matrices, then

$$(ABC)^{-1} \equiv C^{-1}B^{-1}A^{-1}$$

we can write

$$(M_{\dot{I}\dot{I}})^{-1} = \begin{pmatrix} I & \xi \\ 0 & \xi_j \end{pmatrix}^{-1} \begin{pmatrix} M_{II} & 0 \\ 0 & 1 \end{pmatrix}^{-1} \begin{pmatrix} I & 0 \\ \xi^T & \xi_j \end{pmatrix}^{-1}$$

$$(M_{\dot{I}\dot{I}})^{-1} = \begin{pmatrix} I & -\xi/\xi_j \\ 0 & 1/\xi_j \end{pmatrix} \begin{pmatrix} M_{II}^{-1} & 0 \\ 0 & 1 \end{pmatrix} \begin{pmatrix} I & 0 \\ -\xi^T/\xi_j & 1/\xi_j \end{pmatrix}$$

$$(M_{\dot{I}\dot{I}})^{-1} = \begin{pmatrix} M_{II}^{-1} + \xi\xi^{\mathrm{T}}/\xi_j^2 & -\xi/\xi_j^2 \\ -\xi^{\mathrm{T}}/\xi_j^2 & 1/\xi_j^2 \end{pmatrix}$$

We can state this algorithm more concisely as follows:<C20>

$$\xi = M_{II}^{-1}M_{Ij}$$

$$\xi_j^2 = M_{jj} - \xi^{\mathrm{T}}M_{Ij}$$

$$(M_{II}^{-1})^{New} = (M_{\dot{I}\dot{I}})^{-1} = \begin{pmatrix} M_{II}^{-1} + \xi\xi^{\mathrm{T}}/\xi_j^2 & -\xi/\xi_j^2 \\ -\xi^{\mathrm{T}}/\xi_j^2 & 1/\xi_j^2 \end{pmatrix} \qquad (13.20)$$

The algorithm for updating $\bar{b}_I$ when adding a variable can be derived from the definition of $\bar{b}_I$ (13.14). For the newly added variable *j* we get<C21>

$$\bar{b}_j = -M_{j\dot{O}} X_{\dot{O}} \tag{13.21}$$

where subscript $\dot{O}$ represents the new *OUT* set (after deleting variable *j*). For the other elements of $\bar{b}_I$ we have

$$\left(\bar{b}_I\right)^{New} = \begin{pmatrix} 0 \\ b \end{pmatrix} - M_{I\dot{O}} X_{\dot{O}}$$

$$\left(\bar{b}_I\right)^{New} = \begin{pmatrix} 0 \\ b \end{pmatrix} - M_{I\dot{O}} X_{\dot{O}} - M_{Ij} X_j + M_{Ij} X_j$$

$$\left(\bar{b}_I\right)^{New} = \left(\bar{b}_I\right)^{Old} + M_{Ij} X_j \tag{13.22}$$

Thus we update the existing elements of $\bar{b}_I$ adding $M_{Ij} X_j$.<C23>

AddVariable also updates the *IN* and *OUT* sets by calling *Utility.GoIn.*<C22> This call is actually done before the new element of $\bar{b}_I$ is computed (13.21) since this requires the new *OUT* set.

Deleting a Variable

Subroutine *CLA.DeleteVariable* is called during the critical line algorithm to delete a variable. Since the *OUT* elements of α and β are fixed by (13.16) we only need to update them when a variable goes *OUT.*<C30> *DeleteVariable* then calls *Utility.GoOut* to update *InVars, OutVars,* and *State.*<C31> *DeleteVariable* then updates M_{II}^{-1}.<C32> As when adding a variable, rather than re-computing these arrays from scratch according to their definitions, we use a more efficient procedure to update them.

We can derive the algorithm for updating M_{II}^{-1} to delete a variable by rewriting (13.20) to reverse the sense of "*New*":

$$\left(M_{\dot{I}\dot{I}}\right)^{-1} = \begin{pmatrix} \left(M_{II}^{-1}\right)^{New} + \xi\xi^{\mathrm{T}}/\xi_j^2 & -\xi/\xi_j^2 \\ -\xi^{\mathrm{T}}/\xi_j^2 & 1/\xi_j^2 \end{pmatrix}$$

Here $\dot{I}$ represents the *IN* set before deleting variable j. Partitioning the left-hand side like the right hand side

$$\begin{pmatrix} \left(M_{II}^{-1}\right)^{Old} & M_{Ij}^{-1} \\ M_{jI}^{-1} & M_{jj}^{-1} \end{pmatrix} = \begin{pmatrix} \left(M_{II}^{-1}\right)^{New} + \xi\xi^{\mathrm{T}}/\xi_j^2 & -\xi/\xi_j^2 \\ -\xi^{\mathrm{T}}/\xi_j^2 & 1/\xi_j^2 \end{pmatrix}$$

Now we can see from inspection that $\xi_j^2 = 1/M_{jj}^{-1}$ and $\xi = -M_{Ij}^{-1}/M_{jj}^{-1}$. Thus we can get

$$\left(M_{II}^{-1}\right)^{Old} = \left(M_{II}^{-1}\right)^{New} + M_{Ij}^{-1} M_{jI}^{-1} / M_{jj}^{-1}$$

or

$$\left(M_{II}^{-1}\right)^{New} = \left(M_{II}^{-1}\right)^{Old} - M_{Ij}^{-1}M_{jI}^{-1}/M_{jj}^{-1}$$

The algorithm for updating $\bar{b}_I$ can be obtained from the formula for adding a variable (13.22) by reversing "New" and "Old". Thus we update $\bar{b}_I$ by subtracting $M_{Ij}X_j$.<C33>

Calculation of Outputs from the Critical Line Algorithm

In each iteration of the critical line algorithm a new corner portfolio is determined. The linear interpolates between adjacent corner portfolio are also efficient portfolios. *CLA.Iteration* calls *CLA.CalcCornerPortfolio*<C14> to calculate the new corner portfolio, the E and V for the new corner portfolio, and coefficients for the function

$$V = a_0 + a_1 E + a_2 E^2 \tag{13.23}$$

(see 6.10), which applies between the new corner portfolio and the previous one.

We compute the value of X_I from<C40>

$$X_I = \alpha_I + \beta_I \lambda_E$$

(see 6.13). X_O is of course fixed and already known. We also compute<C41>

$$\frac{dE}{d\lambda_E} = \sum_{i \in IN} \frac{\partial E}{\partial X_i}\frac{dX}{d\lambda_E}$$
$$= \mu_I^T \beta_I$$

Since the elements of μ are only non-zero for the X variables, not the m λ variables, we can exclude the λ variables in the computation of $dE/d\lambda_E$.

If $dE/d\lambda_E$ is very small (the program assumes less than 10^{-9}), then E is essentially constant for the critical line as λ_E decreases, indicating a discontinuous slope or "kink" for the functions $E = f(\lambda_E)$ and $E = f(V)$. In this case the length of the critical line is essentially zero, and we cannot accurately compute the coefficients of (13.23), so we simply compute E and V from X according to (13.1) and (13.2).<C42>

If $dE/d\lambda_E$ is not small, then we proceed to calculate the coefficients of (13.23).<C43> Taking the second derivative of (13.23) we get

$$\frac{\mathrm{d}^2 V}{\mathrm{d}E^2} = 2a_2$$

or

$$a_2 = \frac{1}{2}\frac{\mathrm{d}^2 V}{\mathrm{d}E^2} = \frac{\mathrm{d}}{\mathrm{d}E}\left(\frac{1}{2}\frac{\mathrm{d}V}{\mathrm{d}E}\right) = \frac{\mathrm{d}\lambda_{\mathrm{E}}}{\mathrm{d}E} = \frac{1}{\mathrm{d}E/\mathrm{d}\lambda_{\mathrm{E}}}$$

since

$$\lambda_E = \frac{1}{2}\frac{\mathrm{d}V}{\mathrm{d}E}$$

(see page 176). Having a_2 we can now calculate a_1 from the first derivative of (13.23) as

$$\frac{\mathrm{d}V}{\mathrm{d}E} = a_1 + 2a_2 E$$

or

$$a_1 = \frac{\mathrm{d}V}{\mathrm{d}E} - 2a_2 E = 2\lambda_E - 2a_2 E$$

Since we have not yet computed E for the current corner portfolio, we can instead use the λ_E and E from the previous corner portfolio (λ_E^{Old} and E^{Old}), since a_0, a_1, and a_2 are constant between the previous corner portfolio and the new corner portfolio. Having a_1 and a_2 we can easily calculate a_0 from (13.23). Then we efficiently calculate the new value of E from from the previous value using

$$E^{New} = E^{Old} + \frac{\mathrm{d}E}{\mathrm{d}\lambda_E}\left(\lambda_E - \lambda_E^{Old}\right)$$

Lastly, we calculate V for the new corner portfolio from (13.23).

Outputting the Results to the Spreadsheet

The program is designed so that all code dependent on the particular output destination is located in module *Output.* The implementation presented here writes all outputs to a named range in Microsoft Excel. *Output.Setup* is first called to do any required setup prior to outputting the corner portfolios. In this implementation it just outputs column headers. In other implementations it might open the output file, for example. *Output.CornerPortfolio*, is that called after each iteration of the Critical Line Algorithm to output the corner portfolio and related information.

Appendix A to Chapter 13: Program Listing

Module Main

```
Option Explicit

Public Const EPSILON As Double = 0.00000001       'close to zero
Public Const INFINITY As Double = 1E+30
Public Const INVALID As Double = 9.999E+99

'Enumerate "directions"
Public Const Lower As Integer = -1
Public Const Higher As Integer = 1

'Enumerate Constraint Types
Public Const ctEqualTo As Integer = 1
Public Const ctGreaterThan As Integer = 2
Public Const ctLessThan As Integer = 3

'Enumerate variable states
Public Const vsIn As Integer = 0
Public Const vsUp As Integer = 1
Public Const vsLo As Integer = 2

'Enumerate Simplex error codes
Public Const SimplexInfeasible As Integer = -1
```

```
Public Const SimplexUnboundedE As Integer = -2
Public Const SimplexDegenerate As Integer = -3

'<M1> Input variables--must be set by Inputs.Read
Public NumSecs As Integer      'Number of securities
Public NumSlackVars As Integer 'Number of slack variables
Public n As Integer           'Number of variables (NumSecs+NumSlackVars)
Public m As Integer           'Number of constraints
Public mu() As Double         'Expected returns vector
Public L() As Double          'Lower Limits vector
Public U() As Double          'Upper Limits vector
Public MMat() As Double       'M matrix
Public A() As Double          'Constraint coefficients matrix
Public ConType() As Integer 'Constraint types array
Public b() As Double          'Constraint right-hand sides
Public EndLambdaE As Double 'Stop after this lambdaE (min 1E-5).
Public MaxCPs As Integer      'Stop after this many corner portfolios.

'Internal optimizer variables.
Public X() As Double          'Portfolio weights
Public InVars As cSet         'Set of In variables
Public OutVars As cSet        'Set of Out variables
Public State() As Integer     'Variable states
Public Ai() As Double         'Inverse of IN columns of A (Simplex)
Public E As Double            'Portfolio expected return
Public V As Double            'Portfolio variance
Public LambdaE As Double
Public a0 As Double, a1 As Double, a2 As Double 'V = f(E)
Public CLAcount As Integer 'Count of CLA iterations

Public Sub Optimize()         'main routine
   Dim rc As Integer, i As Integer, j As Integer, k As Integer

    '<M2> Read the inputs
    rc = Inputs.Read()
    If rc <> 0 Then
        MsgBox "Error Reading Inputs", vbExclamation, "Optimizer Error"
        Exit Sub
    End If

    '<M3> Set up inequality constraints and slack variables
    j = NumSecs + 1      'index to next slack variable
    For i = 1 To m
        If ConType(i) <> ctEqualTo Then
            If ConType(i) = ctGreaterThan Then
                'convert "greater than" constraint to "less than"
                For k = 1 To NumSecs
                    A(i, k) = -A(i, k)
                Next k
                b(i) = -b(i)
            End If
            A(i, j) = 1      'slack variable coefficient
            j = j + 1
        End If
    Next i

    Output.Setup          '<M4> Set up for outputs

    rc = Simplex.Run()  '<M5> run simplex algorithm
    If rc <> 0 Then
        '<M6> fatal error in Simplex
        If rc = SimplexInfeasible Then
            MsgBox "Infeasible problem. ", _
                    "Check constraints and limits", _
```

```
                vbExclamation
        ElseIf rc = SimplexUnboundedE Then
            MsgBox "Unbounded E. " + _
                "Make sure you have a valid budget constraint", _
                vbExclamation
        ElseIf rc = SimplexDegenerate Then
            'Message box was already displayed by Simplex.Run
        End If
        Exit Sub
    End If

    CLA.Setup   '<M7> Set up for critical line algorithm.
    '<M8> Trace out the efficient frontier.
    For CLAcount = 1 To MaxCPs
        CLA.Iteration
        Output.CornerPortfolio
        If LambdaE < EndLambdaE Then Exit For
    Next CLAcount
End Sub

Public Sub AllocatePublicArrays()
    'Allocate all public arrays except ConType(), which is
    'allocated by Inputs.Read. For variables
    'used in Simplex phase 1 we increase the number of
    'variables by m for artificial basis variables.
    ReDim mu(1 To n) As Double
    ReDim L(1 To n + m) As Double
    ReDim U(1 To n + m) As Double
    InitVector U, INFINITY
    ReDim MMat(1 To n + m, 1 To n + m) As Double
    ReDim A(1 To m, 1 To n + m) As Double
    ReDim b(1 To m) As Double
    ReDim X(1 To n + m) As Double
    ReDim State(1 To n + m) As Integer
    ReDim Ai(1 To m, 1 To m) As Double

    Set InVars = New cSet
    InVars.Initialize n + m
    Set OutVars = New cSet
    OutVars.Initialize n + m
End Sub
```

Module Simplex

```
Option Explicit

'Arrays for Simplex
Private z() As Double         'objective function coefficients
Private Price() As Double     'price vector
Private Profit() As Double    'profitability vector
Private AdjRate() As Double   'rate of adjustment of IN variables
Private nIABV As Integer      'Number of IN ABVs (artificial basis
                              '    variables)


Public Function Run() As Integer
    Dim i As Integer, j As Integer, temp As Double
    Dim ReturnCode As Integer, rc As Integer

    ReDim z(1 To n + m) As Double
    ReDim Price(1 To m) As Double
    ReDim Profit(1 To n) As Double
    ReDim AdjRate(1 To m) As Double
```

```
'<S1> Initialize all variables other than ABVs
'to be OUT at their lower limits.
For j = 1 To n
    OutVars.Add j
    State(j) = vsLo
    X(j) = L(j)
    z(j) = 0          'objective function "expected return"
Next j

'<S2> Set up ABVs.
For i = 1 To m
    temp = b(i)
    For j = 1 To n
        temp = temp - A(i, j) * L(j)
    Next j
    If temp >= 0 Then
        A(i, n + i) = 1
    Else
        A(i, n + i) = -1
    End If
    Ai(i, i) = A(i, n + i)
    InVars.Add n + i
    State(n + i) = vsIn
    X(n + i) = Abs(temp)
    z(n + i) = -1   'objective function "expected return"
Next i
nIABV = m             'starting number of IN ABVs

'<S3> Run simplex phase 1
ReturnCode = SimplexPhase(1)

If ReturnCode = 0 Then
    '<S4> No ABVs are IN (not degenerate).
    'Reallocate arrays to delete elements for ABVs.
    ReDim Preserve L(1 To n) As Double
    ReDim Preserve U(1 To n) As Double
    ReDim Preserve A(1 To m, 1 To n) As Double
    ReDim Preserve X(1 To n) As Double
    ReDim Preserve State(1 To n) As Integer
ElseIf ReturnCode = SimplexDegenerate Then
    '<S5> Degenerate problem--One or more ABVs still IN.
    rc = MsgBox("Degenerate Problem. " + _
                "Program will continue", _
                vbExclamation + vbOKCancel)
    If rc = vbOK Then
        ReturnCode = 0  'Allow program to continue
        n = n + m       'Add in ABVs to variable count.
        ReDim Preserve mu(1 To n) As Double
        ReDim Profit(1 To n) As Double
        'Set upper limits on ABVs to zero
        For i = 1 To m
            U(n - m + i) = EPSILON
        Next i
        'Increase size of MMat() while preserving contents.
        ReDim Mtemp(1 To NumSecs, 1 To NumSecs) As Double
        For i = 1 To NumSecs
            For j = 1 To NumSecs
                Mtemp(i, j) = MMat(i, j)
            Next j
        Next i
        ReDim MMat(1 To n + m, 1 To n + m)
        For i = 1 To NumSecs
            For j = 1 To NumSecs
                MMat(i, j) = Mtemp(i, j)
```

```
                Next j
            Next i
            InVars.Resize n + m
            OutVars.Resize n + m
        End If
    End If

    If ReturnCode = 0 Then
        '<S6> Run simplex phase 2
        'Objective is now to maximize expected return
        For j = 1 To n
            z(j) = mu(j)
        Next j
        ReturnCode = SimplexPhase(2)
        If ReturnCode = 0 Then AlterMu  '<S7> Ensure unique solution
    End If

    Erase z, Price, Profit, AdjRate
    Run = ReturnCode
End Function

Private Function SimplexPhase(Phase As Integer) As Integer
    Dim i0 As Integer, i As Integer, j0 As Integer, j As Integer
    Dim k As Integer, jMax As Integer, InDirection As Integer
    Dim ProfitMax As Double, sum As Double

    SimplexPhase = 0
    Do While True
        '<S10> Compute price for each constraint.
        For i = 1 To m
            sum = 0
            For j = 1 To InVars.Count
                sum = sum - Ai(j, i) * z(InVars.Member(j))
            Next j
            Price(i) = sum
        Next i

        '<S11> Compute profit for each OUT variable coming IN.
        ProfitMax = 0#
        For j0 = 1 To OutVars.Count
            j = OutVars.Member(j0)
            sum = z(j)
            For i = 1 To m
                sum = sum + A(i, j) * Price(i)
            Next i
            If (IsUp(j)) Then sum = -sum
            Profit(j) = sum
            If Profit(j) >= ProfitMax Then
                jMax = j
                ProfitMax = Profit(j)
            End If
        Next j0

        If ProfitMax < EPSILON Then
            '<S12> No profit from any OUT variable coming IN.
            If Phase = 1 Then
                'degenerate or infeasible problem.
                For j0 = 1 To nIABV
                    j = InVars.Member(InVars.Count + 1 - j0)
                    If X(j) > EPSILON Then
                        'An IN ABV is not zero--infeasible problem
                        SimplexPhase = SimplexInfeasible
                        Exit Function
                    End If
```

```
            Next j0
            'All IN ABVs are zero--degenerate problem
            SimplexPhase = SimplexDegenerate '(nIABV > 0)
        End If
        Exit Do
    End If

    If IsUp(jMax) Then
        InDirection = Lower
    Else
        InDirection = Higher
    End If

    '<S13> Compute rate of adjustment for each IN variable as
    'variable jMax comes IN (AdjRate = - Ai * A(ALL,jMax)).
    For i = 1 To m
        sum = 0
        For k = 1 To m
            sum = sum - Ai(i, k) * A(k, jMax)
        Next k
        If InDirection = Lower Then sum = -sum
        AdjRate(i) = sum
    Next i

    '<S14> Compute theta, the maximum amount that variable jMax
    'can change before another IN variable hits a limit and is
    'forced OUT. Also determine which variable is forced OUT.
    'Here we compute theta such that it will always be positiive.
    Dim theta As Double, TempTheta As Double
    Dim iOut As Integer, OutDirection As Integer
    iOut = 0     '0 indicates variable coming In also goes Out.
    OutDirection = InDirection
    If U(jMax) = INFINITY Then
        theta = INFINITY
    Else
        theta = U(jMax) - L(jMax)
    End If
    For i = 1 To m
        j = InVars.Member(i)
        If AdjRate(i) < -EPSILON Then
            'Check for variable hitting lower limit
            TempTheta = (L(j) - X(j)) / AdjRate(i)
            If TempTheta < theta Then
                theta = TempTheta
                iOut = i
                OutDirection = Lower
            End If
        ElseIf AdjRate(i) > EPSILON And U(j) <> INFINITY Then
            'Check for variable hitting upper limit
            TempTheta = (U(j) - X(j)) / AdjRate(i)
            If TempTheta < theta Then
                theta = TempTheta
                iOut = i
                OutDirection = Higher
            End If
        End If
    Next i

    '<S15> Check for failure to find a variable to go OUT.
    If theta = INFINITY Then
        SimplexPhase = SimplexUnboundedE
        Exit Function
    End If
```

```
        'Get "j" index of variable going OUT.
        Dim jOut As Integer
        If iOut >= 1 Then
            jOut = InVars.Member(iOut)
        Else
            jOut = jMax    'variable coming IN is also going OUT.
        End If

        '<S16> Update the IN variables (X's).
        For i0 = 1 To m
            j = InVars.Member(i0)
            X(j) = X(j) + theta * AdjRate(i0)
        Next i0
        If InDirection = Higher Then
            X(jMax) = X(jMax) + theta
        Else
            X(jMax) = X(jMax) - theta
        End If

        GoIn jMax                          '<S17> variable jMax goes IN
        GoOut jOut, OutDirection           '<S18> variable jOut goes OUT

        '<S19> Update AInverse If var going OUT is not var coming IN.
        If jMax <> jOut Then UpdateAInverse iOut, jMax, InDirection

        If Phase = 1 And jOut > n Then
            'Artificial basis variable went out
            nIABV = nIABV - 1
            If nIABV = 0 Then Exit Do    'All ABVs OUT--End of phase 1
        End If
    Loop
End Function

'<S20> Update Ai (inverse if A(ALL,IN)) for new IN set.
Private Sub UpdateAInverse(iOut As Integer, jMax As Integer,
InDirection As Integer)
    Dim temp As Double, i As Integer, k As Integer
    For i = 1 To m
        If i <> iOut Then
            temp = AdjRate(i) / AdjRate(iOut)
            For k = 1 To m
                Ai(i, k) = Ai(i, k) - Ai(iOut, k) * temp
            Next k
        End If
    Next i

    If InDirection = Higher Then
        temp = -AdjRate(iOut)
    Else
        temp = AdjRate(iOut)
    End If
    For k = 1 To m
        Ai(iOut, k) = Ai(iOut, k) / temp
    Next k

    '<S21> Reorder rows of Ai to stay consistent with InVars.
    ReorderAiRows iOut, InVars.Position(jMax)
End Sub

'Reorder the rows of Ai to stay consistent with InVars (ascending
'order). In C or C++ this is more efficiently handled by manipulating
'pointers to rows.
Private Sub ReorderAiRows(DelRow As Integer, AddRow As Integer)
    Dim i As Integer, j As Integer, temp As Double
```

```
    If AddRow > DelRow Then
        For j = 1 To m
            temp = Ai(DelRow, j)
            For i = DelRow To AddRow - 1
                Ai(i, j) = Ai(i + 1, j)
            Next i
            Ai(AddRow, j) = temp
        Next j
    ElseIf AddRow < DelRow Then
        For j = 1 To m
            temp = Ai(DelRow, j)
            For i = DelRow To AddRow + 1 Step -1
                Ai(i, j) = Ai(i - 1, j)
            Next i
            Ai(AddRow, j) = temp
        Next j
    End If
End Sub

'<S30> Alter mu's as required to ensure unique solution.
Private Sub AlterMu()
    Dim j0 As Integer, j As Integer
    For j0 = 1 To OutVars.Count
        j = OutVars.Member(j0)
        If Profit(j) > -0.000001 Then
            If IsLo(j) Then
                mu(j) = mu(j) - 0.000001
            Else
                mu(j) = mu(j) + 0.000001
            End If
        End If
    Next j0
End Sub
```

Module CLA

```
Option Explicit

Private alphav() As Double, betav() As Double, xi() As Double
Private bbar() As Double, Mi() As Double

Public Sub Setup()
    Dim j0 As Integer, j As Integer
    Dim k0 As Integer, k As Integer, i As Integer
    Dim sum As Double

    '<C1> Allocate arrays for CLA
    ReDim alphav(1 To n + m) As Double
    ReDim betav(1 To n + m) As Double
    ReDim xi(1 To n + m) As Double
    ReDim bbar(1 To n + m) As Double
    ReDim Mi(1 To n + m, 1 To n + m) As Double

    '<C2> Initialize OUT elements of alpha and beta
    For j0 = 1 To OutVars.Count
        j = OutVars.Member(j0)
        alphav(j) = X(j)
        betav(j) = 0
    Next j0

    '<C3> Add the lambda variables to the IN set
    For j = n + 1 To n + m
        InVars.Add j
    Next j
```

```
    '<C4> Add A and A' to MMat (already contains C)
    For i = 1 To m
        For j = 1 To n
            MMat(n + i, j) = A(i, j)
            MMat(j, n + i) = A(i, j)
        Next j
    Next i

    '<C5> Compute bbar vector.
    For j0 = 1 To InVars.Count
        j = InVars.Member(j0)
        If j <= n Then
            sum = 0
        Else
            sum = b(j - n)
        End If
        For k0 = 1 To OutVars.Count
            k = OutVars.Member(k0)
            sum = sum - MMat(j, k) * X(k)
        Next k0
        bbar(j) = sum
    Next j0

    '<C6> Set up initial Mi (M-bar-inverse)
    '   Mi = | 0             Ai               |
    '        | Ai'   -Ai' * C(IN,IN) * Ai |
    'First copy Ai and Ai'
    For j0 = 1 To m
        j = InVars.Member(j0)
        For i = 1 To m
            Mi(n + i, j) = Ai(j0, i)
            Mi(j, n + i) = Mi(n + i, j)
        Next i
    Next j0
    'T = Ai' * C(IN,IN)
    Dim T() As Double
    ReDim T(1 To m, 1 To m) As Double
    For i = 1 To m
        For j0 = 1 To m
            j = InVars.Member(j0)
            sum = 0
            For k = 1 To m
                sum = sum - Ai(k, i) * MMat(InVars.Member(k), j)
            Next k
            T(i, j0) = sum
        Next j0
    Next i
    'Lower right portion of Mi is then T * Ai
    For i = 1 To m
        For j = 1 To m
            sum = 0
            For k = 1 To m
                sum = sum + T(i, k) * Ai(k, j)
            Next k
            Mi(n + i, n + j) = sum
        Next j
    Next i

    Erase Ai, T
End Sub

Public Sub Iteration()
    Static jMaxA As Integer, OutDirection As Integer, lambdaA As Double
```

```
Static jMaxB As Integer, InDirection As Integer, lambdaB As Double
Dim j0 As Integer, j As Integer, k0 As Integer, k As Integer
Dim tempLambdaA As Double, tempLambdaB As Double
Dim alpha As Double, beta As Double
Dim gamma As Double, delta As Double

'<C10> If this is not the first iteration, then add or delete the
'variable determined in previous iteration.
If CLAcount > 1 Then
    If lambdaA > lambdaB Then
        DeleteVariable jMaxA, OutDirection
    Else
        AddVariable jMaxB, InDirection
    End If
End If

'<C11> Determine which IN variable wants to go OUT first.
jMaxA = -1: lambdaA = 0: OutDirection = 0
For j0 = 1 To InVars.Count
    'Compute alpha and beta for variable.
    j = InVars.Member(j0)
    alpha = 0: beta = 0
    For k0 = 1 To InVars.Count
        k = InVars.Member(k0)
        alpha = alpha + Mi(j, k) * bbar(k)
        If k <= n Then beta = beta + Mi(j, k) * mu(k)
    Next k0
    alphav(j) = alpha: betav(j) = beta
    If j < n Then
        'For non-lambda variable check for going OUT.
        If beta > EPSILON Then
            'Check for hitting lower limit.
            tempLambdaA = (L(j) - alpha) / beta
            If tempLambdaA >= lambdaA Then
                jMaxA = j
                lambdaA = tempLambdaA
                OutDirection = Lower
            End If
        ElseIf U(j) < INFINITY And beta < -EPSILON Then
            'Check for hitting upper limit.
            tempLambdaA = (U(j) - alpha) / beta
            If tempLambdaA >= lambdaA Then
                jMaxA = j
                lambdaA = tempLambdaA
                OutDirection = Higher
            End If
        End If
    End If
Next j0

'<C12> Determine which OUT variable wants to come IN first.
jMaxB = -1: lambdaB = 0: InDirection = 0
For j0 = 1 To OutVars.Count
    'Compute gamma and delta for variable.
    j = OutVars.Member(j0)
    gamma = 0: delta = -mu(j)
    For k = 1 To n + m
        gamma = gamma + MMat(j, k) * alphav(k)
        delta = delta + MMat(j, k) * betav(k)
    Next k
    If IsLo(j) Then
        If delta > EPSILON Then
            'Check for variable comong off lower limit.
            tempLambdaB = -gamma / delta
```

```
                If tempLambdaB >= lambdaB Then
                    jMaxB = j
                    lambdaB = tempLambdaB
                    InDirection = Higher
                End If
            End If
        Else    'at upper limit
            If delta < -EPSILON Then
                'Check for variable coming off upper limit.
                tempLambdaB = -gamma / delta
                If tempLambdaB >= lambdaB Then
                    jMaxB = j
                    lambdaB = tempLambdaB
                    InDirection = Lower
                End If
            End If
        End If
    Next j0

    '<C13> The new lambda-E is the greater of lambda-A and lambda-B.
    'If lambda-A is greater, then a variable first goes OUT as
    'lambda-E is decreased. If lambda-B is greater, then a
    'variable first comes IN is as lambda-E is decreased.
    LambdaE = Max(lambdaA, lambdaB)
    LambdaE = Max(LambdaE, 0)

    '<C14> Calculate the new corner portfolio, the E and V for
    'new corner portfolio, and a0, a1, and a2 between this and
    'previous corner portfolio.
    CalcCornerPortfolio
End Sub

'Do updates required for variable jAdd to come IN.
Private Sub AddVariable(jAdd As Integer, Direction As Integer)
    Dim j0 As Integer, j As Integer, i As Integer
    Dim k0 As Integer, k As Integer
    Dim sum As Double, xij As Double

    '<C20> update Mi for variable coming IN.
    'xi = Mi(IN,IN) * M(IN,jAdd);
    For j0 = 1 To InVars.Count
        j = InVars.Member(j0)
        sum = 0
        For k0 = 1 To InVars.Count
            k = InVars.Member(k0)
            sum = sum + Mi(j, k) * MMat(k, jAdd)
        Next k0
        xi(j) = sum
    Next j0
    'xij = M(jAdd,jAdd) - M(jAdd,IN) * xi
    xij = MMat(jAdd, jAdd)
    For k0 = 1 To InVars.Count
        k = InVars.Member(k0)
        xij = xij - MMat(jAdd, k) * xi(k)
    Next k0
    'Mi(IN,IN) += xi*xi.T/xij
    'Mi(jAdd,IN) = Mi(IN,jAdd) = -xi / xij
    For j0 = 1 To InVars.Count
        j = InVars.Member(j0)
        For k0 = 1 To j0 - 1
            k = InVars.Member(k0)
            Mi(j, k) = Mi(j, k) + xi(j) * xi(k) / xij
            Mi(k, j) = Mi(j, k)
        Next k0
```

```
        Mi(j, j) = Mi(j, j) + xi(j) * xi(j) / xij
        Mi(j, jAdd) = -xi(j) / xij
        Mi(jAdd, j) = Mi(j, jAdd)
    Next j0
    Mi(jAdd, jAdd) = 1 / xij

    '<C21> Update bbar for the current IN variables
    '  bbar(IN) = bbar(IN) + M(IN,jAdd) * X(jAdd)
    For j0 = 1 To InVars.Count
        j = InVars.Member(j0)
        bbar(j) = bbar(j) + MMat(j, jAdd) * X(jAdd)
    Next j0

    GoIn jAdd       'Variable jAdd goes IN

    '<C22> Compute bbar for new IN variable.
    '  bbar(jAdd) = -M(jAdd,OUT) * X(OUT)
    sum = 0
    For j0 = 1 To OutVars.Count
        j = OutVars.Member(j0)
        sum = sum - MMat(jAdd, j) * X(j)
    Next j0
    bbar(jAdd) = sum
End Sub

'Do updates required for variable jDel to go OUT.
Private Sub DeleteVariable(jDel As Integer, Direction As Integer)
    Dim j0 As Integer, j As Integer, k0 As Integer, k As Integer

    '<C30> update alpha and beta vectors for variable going OUT
    alphav(jDel) = X(jDel)
    betav(jDel) = 0

    GoOut jDel, Direction   '<C31> Variable jDel goes OUT

    '<C32> Update Mi and bbar for variable going OUT.
    For j0 = 1 To InVars.Count
        j = InVars.Member(j0)
        For k0 = 1 To InVars.Count
            k = InVars.Member(k0)
            Mi(j, k) = Mi(j, k) _
                    - Mi(j, jDel) * Mi(jDel, k) / Mi(jDel, jDel)
        Next k0
    Next j0

    '<C33> Update bbar(IN)
    For j0 = 1 To InVars.Count
        j = InVars.Member(j0)
        bbar(j) = bbar(j) - MMat(j, jDel) * X(jDel)
    Next j0

End Sub

'Calculate the new corner portfolio and statistics.
Private Function CalcCornerPortfolio()
    Static OldLambdaE As Double, dEdLambdaE As Double
    Dim j As Integer, j0 As Integer, k As Integer

    '<C40> Calculate the new corner portfolio.
    For j0 = 1 To InVars.Count - m
        j = InVars.Member(j0)
        X(j) = alphav(j) + betav(j) * LambdaE
    Next j0
```

```
    '<C41> Calculate dE_dLambda
    dEdLambdaE = 0
    For j0 = 1 To InVars.Count - m
        j = InVars.Member(j0)
        dEdLambdaE = dEdLambdaE + betav(j) * mu(j)
    Next j0

    If dEdLambdaE < 0.000000001 Then
        '<C42> "kink" in curve, compute E and V from scratch
        a0 = INVALID: a1 = INVALID: a2 = INVALID
        E = 0: V = 0
        For j = 1 To NumSecs
            E = E + mu(j) * X(j)
            V = V + MMat(j, j) * X(j) * X(j)
            For k = 1 To j - 1
                V = V + 2 * MMat(j, k) * X(j) * X(k)
            Next k
        Next j
    Else
        '<C43> compute a0, a1, a2, E, and V.
        a2 = 1# / dEdLambdaE
        a1 = 2# * (OldLambdaE - a2 * E)
        a0 = V - a1 * E - a2 * E * E
        E = E + (LambdaE - OldLambdaE) * dEdLambdaE
        V = a0 + a1 * E + a2 * E * E
    End If
    OldLambdaE = LambdaE
End Function
```

Module Inputs

```
Option Explicit

Public Function Read() As Integer
    '<I1> Read scalar inputs
    NumSecs = Range("NumSecs").Value
    m = Range("m").Value
    EndLambdaE = Range("EndLambdaE").Value
    If EndLambdaE < 0.00000001 Then EndLambdaE = 0.00000001
    MaxCPs = Range("MaxCPs").Value

    '<I2> Read the constraint types and count number of slack
    'variables required (one per inequality constraints).
    Dim r As Range, i As Integer
    ReDim ConType(1 To m) As Integer
    NumSlackVars = 0
    Set r = Range("ConType")
    For i = 1 To m
        Select Case Left(r(i).Text, 1) 'branch on first char
        Case "=":   ConType(i) = ctEqualTo
        Case "<":   ConType(i) = ctLessThan
                    NumSlackVars = NumSlackVars + 1
        Case ">":   ConType(i) = ctGreaterThan
                    NumSlackVars = NumSlackVars + 1
        Case Else:  Read = -1
                    Exit Function
        End Select
    Next i

    n = NumSecs + NumSlackVars  'Number of variables
    Main.AllocatePublicArrays   '<I3> Allocate arrays

    '<I4> Read the other arrays from spreadsheet.
    ReadVector Range("mu"), mu(), NumSecs
```

```
    ReadVector Range("L"), L(), NumSecs
    ReadVector Range("U"), U(), NumSecs
    ReadSymMatrix Range("Cov"), MMat(), NumSecs
    ReadMatrix Range("A"), A(), m, NumSecs
    ReadVector Range("b"), b(), m
    Read = 0
End Function

'Read a column vector from range r to V()
Private Sub ReadVector(r As Range, V() As Double, _
                       NumElements As Integer)
    Dim i As Integer
    For i = 1 To NumElements
        If IsNumeric(r(i).Formula) Then V(i) = r(i)
    Next i
End Sub

'Read a symmetric matrix from range r to Matrix().
Private Sub ReadSymMatrix(r As Range, Matrix() As Double, _
                          NumRows As Integer)
    Dim i As Integer, j As Integer
    For i = 1 To NumRows
        For j = 1 To i
            Matrix(i, j) = r(i, j)
            If j <> i Then Matrix(j, i) = Matrix(i, j)
        Next j
    Next i
End Sub

'Read a matrix from range r to Matrix().
Private Sub ReadMatrix(r As Range, Matrix() As Double, _
            NumRows As Integer, NumCols As Integer)
    Dim i As Integer, j As Integer
    For i = 1 To NumRows
        For j = 1 To NumCols
            Matrix(i, j) = r(i, j)
        Next j
    Next i
End Sub
```

Module Output

```
Option Explicit

Private OutRange As Range

Public Sub Setup()
    Dim r As Range
    Set OutRange = Range("Output")
    Set r = Range(OutRange(1, 1), OutRange(1 + MaxCPs, 8 + NumSecs))
    r.ClearContents
    r.NumberFormat = "0.000"
    OutRange(1, 1).Value = "CP Num"     'Output column headings...
    OutRange(1, 2).Value = "E"
    OutRange(1, 3).Value = "SD"
    OutRange(1, 4).Value = "LambdaE"
    OutRange(1, 5).Value = "a0"
    OutRange(1, 6).Value = "a1"
    OutRange(1, 7).Value = "a2"
    Dim j As Integer
    For j = 1 To NumSecs
        OutRange(1, j + 7).Value = "X(" & j & ")"
    Next j
End Sub
```

```
Public Sub CornerPortfolio()
    OutRange(CLAcount + 1, 1).Value = CLAcount
    OutRange(CLAcount + 1, 2).Value = E
    OutRange(CLAcount + 1, 3).Value = Sqr(V)
    OutRange(CLAcount + 1, 4).Value = LambdaE
    If a0 <> INVALID Then
        OutRange(CLAcount + 1, 5).Value = a0
        OutRange(CLAcount + 1, 6).Value = a1
        OutRange(CLAcount + 1, 7).Value = a2
    Else
        OutRange(CLAcount + 1, 5).Clear
        OutRange(CLAcount + 1, 6).Clear
        OutRange(CLAcount + 1, 7).Clear
    End If
    Dim j As Integer
    For j = 1 To NumSecs
        OutRange(CLAcount + 1, j + 7).Value = X(j)
    Next j
End Sub
```

Module Utility

```
Option Explicit

'Initialize elements of vector V to Val.
Public Sub InitVector(V() As Double, Val As Double)
    Dim i As Integer
    For i = LBound(V) To UBound(V)
        V(i) = Val
    Next i
End Sub

'Return True if variable j is Out at upper limit.
Public Function IsUp(j As Integer) As Boolean
    IsUp = (State(j) = vsUp)
End Function

'Return True if variable j is Out at lower limit
Public Function IsLo(j As Integer) As Boolean
    IsLo = (State(j) = vsLo)
End Function

Public Function Max(A As Double, b As Double) As Double
    If A >= b Then
        Max = A
    Else
        Max = b
    End If
End Function

'<U1> Variable jIn goes IN.
Public Sub GoIn(jIn As Integer)
    OutVars.Delete jIn       'Delete from OUT set
    InVars.Add jIn           'Add to IN set
    State(jIn) = vsIn
End Sub

'<U2> Variable jOut goes OUT.
Public Sub GoOut(jOut As Integer, OutDirection As Integer)
    InVars.Delete jOut       'Delete from IN set
    'Add to OUT set if security or slack variable (not ABV).
    If jOut <= NumSecs + NumSlackVars Then OutVars.Add jOut
    If OutDirection = Higher Then
```

```
        State(jOut) = vsUp
    Else
        State(jOut) = vsLo
    End If
End Sub
```

Class Module cSet

```
Option Explicit

Private Items() As Integer
Private mCount As Integer

Public Property Get Count() As Integer
    Count = mCount
End Property

Public Sub Initialize(MaxCount As Integer)
    ReDim Items(1 To MaxCount)
    mCount = 0
End Sub

Public Sub Resize(MaxCount As Integer)
    ReDim Preserve Items(1 To MaxCount) As Integer
End Sub

Public Function Member(Index As Integer) As Integer
    Member = Items(Index)
End Function

Public Sub Add(Member As Integer)
    Dim i As Integer
    For i = mCount + 1 To 2 Step -1
        If Member > Items(i - 1) Then
            Exit For
        Else
            Items(i) = Items(i - 1)
        End If
    Next i
    Items(i) = Member
    mCount = mCount + 1
End Sub

Public Sub DeleteByIndex(Index As Integer)
    Dim i As Integer
    mCount = mCount - 1
    For i = Index To mCount
        Items(i) = Items(i + 1)
    Next i
End Sub

Public Sub Delete(Member As Integer)
    Dim i As Integer
    i = Position(Member)
    DeleteByIndex i
End Sub

Public Function Position(Member As Integer) As Integer
    Dim i As Integer
    For i = 1 To mCount
        If Items(i) = Member Then Exit For
    Next i
    Position = i
End Function
```

Appendix B to Chapter 13: Integration with Spreadsheet

Readers may obtain an operating copy of this program embedded in a Microsoft Excel spreadsheet by emailing a request to the author at pete@riverviewinc.com. For readers that prefer to integrate the program into a spreadsheet themselves, or who are interested in how to do this, this appendix provides some additional details.

Using the Visual Basic Editor (Alt+F11 to open), under the "VBAProject" for your spreadsheet create six "modules" named *Main*, *Simplex*, *CLA*, *Inputs*, *Outputs*, and *Utility*, and one "class module" named *cSet*. Enter the code from the above listings into these modules and class module. Save your work!

As described earlier, the inputs are read from single-cell "named ranges" in the spreadsheet. Similarly, the outputs are written to a named range. For scalar inputs, these named ranges designate the cell the input is read from. For vector inputs, which must be input as column vectors, the named ranges designate the first element of the vector. For matrix inputs, the named ranges designate the top-left element of the matrix. The 11 named input ranges are as follows: *NumSecs*, *m*, *EndLambdaE*, *MaxCPs*, *mu*, *L*, *U*, *Cov*, *A*, *ConType*, and *b*. See "Program Inputs" on page 304 for descriptions of these inputs. The output range is *Output*.

To enter a named range, select the desired cell and type the name into the "Name Box" on the "Formula Bar". You can enter the ranges in any location you wish, even on different worksheets, as long as sufficient space is allotted for the vectors, matrices, and the output range so they do not overlap. The output range requires *NumSecs*+7 columns, and up to *MaxCPs*+1 rows.

Lastly, to execute the optimizer, run the "optimize" macro (Alt+F8, select "optimize", then click on the "Run" button. Alternatively, you can insert a command button in the spreadsheet and assign this macro to the button (select "button" from the "Forms" toolbar).

Appendix C to Chapter 13: Sample Problem

This sample problem is for 10 securities with 3 constraints, and includes non-zero lower limits and upper limits.

Sample Problem Inputs

Number of Securities:	10
Number of Constraints:	3
End LambdaE:	1.00E-05
Max Corner Portfolios:	100

Security ID	Expected Returns	Lower Limits	Upper Limits
1	1.175	0.1	0.3
2	1.190	0	0.3
3	0.396	0	0.3
4	1.120	0	0.3
5	0.346	0.1	0.3
6	0.679	0	0.3
7	0.089	0	0.3
8	0.730	0	0.3
9	0.481	0	0.3
10	1.080	0	0.3

Sample Problem Inputs (continued)

Covariance Matrix (C):

0.4075516									
0.0317584	0.9063047								
0.0518392	0.0313639	0.1949090							
0.0566390	0.0268726	0.0440849	0.1952847						
0.0330226	0.0191717	0.0300677	0.0277735	0.3405911					
0.0082778	0.0093438	0.0132274	0.0052667	0.0077706	0.1598387				
0.0216594	0.0249504	0.0352597	0.0137581	0.0206784	0.0210558	0.6805671			
0.0133242	0.0076104	0.0115493	0.0078088	0.0073641	0.0051869	0.0137788	0.9552692		
0.0343476	0.0287487	0.0427563	0.0291418	0.0254266	0.0172374	0.0462703	0.0106553	0.3168158	
0.0224990	0.0133687	0.0205730	0.0164038	0.0128408	0.0072378	0.0192609	0.0076096	0.0185432	0.1107929

Constraint: Coefficients (A):										Constraint Type (CT)	Right-Hand Side (b)
1	1	1	1	1	1	1	1	1	1	=	1
1	1	1	0.5	0	0	0	0	0	0	>	0.2
0	0	0	0.5	1	1	1	0	0	0	<	0.5

Sample Problem Outputs

The following table shows the output for the sample problem.

CP Num	E	SD	Lambda E	a0	a1	a2	X(1)	X(2)	X(3)	X(4)	X(5)	X(6)	X(7)	X(8)	X(9)	X(10)
1	1.080	0.406	2.928				0.300	0.300	0.000	0.300	0.100	0.000	0.000	0.000	0.000	0.000
2	1.080	0.406	2.928	243.315	-456.093	213.346	0.300	0.300	0.000	0.300	0.100	0.000	0.000	0.000	0.000	0.000
3	1.080	0.406	2.495				0.300	0.300	0.000	0.300	0.100	0.000	0.000	0.000	0.000	0.000
4	1.067	0.336	1.412	90.261	-171.818	81.348	0.300	0.180	0.000	0.300	0.100	0.000	0.000	0.000	0.000	0.120
5	1.064	0.326	1.244	71.888	-137.377	65.707	0.300	0.163	0.000	0.282	0.100	0.000	0.000	0.000	0.000	0.155
6	1.051	0.281	0.747	38.804	-75.207	36.500	0.214	0.119	0.000	0.267	0.100	0.000	0.000	0.000	0.000	0.300
7	1.049	0.277	0.528	120.293	-230.321	110.316	0.193	0.107	0.000	0.300	0.100	0.000	0.000	0.000	0.000	0.300
8	1.049	0.277	0.229	6110.519	-11654.376	5557.064	0.197	0.103	0.000	0.300	0.100	0.000	0.000	0.000	0.000	0.300
9	1.045	0.274	0.203	6.268	-12.265	6.066	0.190	0.100	0.000	0.300	0.100	0.000	0.000	0.009	0.000	0.300
10	1.001	0.246	0.130	1.502	-3.139	1.697	0.130	0.073	0.000	0.300	0.100	0.078	0.000	0.018	0.000	0.300
11	0.956	0.226	0.073	1.052	-2.240	1.249	0.100	0.057	0.000	0.248	0.100	0.165	0.000	0.030	0.000	0.300
12	0.946	0.223	0.059	1.252	-2.659	1.468	0.100	0.053	0.000	0.231	0.100	0.184	0.000	0.032	0.000	0.300
13	0.918	0.217	0.035	0.688	-1.468	0.838	0.100	0.043	0.000	0.190	0.100	0.203	0.000	0.034	0.029	0.300
14	0.909	0.216	0.031	0.371	-0.777	0.462	0.100	0.041	0.008	0.181	0.100	0.204	0.000	0.034	0.032	0.300
15	0.854	0.211	0.010	0.303	-0.626	0.379	0.100	0.029	0.050	0.125	0.100	0.202	0.017	0.033	0.045	0.300
16	0.815	0.210	0.000	0.221	-0.434	0.266	0.100	0.024	0.076	0.103	0.100	0.209	0.028	0.034	0.054	0.271

Appendix

Elements of Matrix Algebra and Vector Spaces

Mathematical Prerequisites

It has been assumed, as prerequisite to this book, that the reader has had a course in matrix algebra and two semesters of the calculus. Partly because not all matrix algebra texts cover the same material in the same way, and partly because some students complain of being rusty in their matrix algebra, this appendix presents, without proofs, a synopsis of requisite matrix algebra and vector space analysis. For proofs and further discussion, the student should have at hand one or more texts on the subject. Some texts, such as Aitken (1956), have primarily an algebraic point of view. Others, such as Halmos (1948), have a geometric point of view. Both views are useful in our work.

Concerning the calculus, it is assumed that the reader knows that if a function $f(X_1, X_2, \ldots, X_n)$ is defined and has partial derivatives for all values of $X_1, X_2, \ldots, X_n$ then a necessary condition for f to have a minimum at $X_0 = (X_1^0, X_2^0, \ldots, X_n^0)$ is that

$$\frac{\partial f}{\partial X_i} = 0 \qquad \text{for } i = 1, \ldots, n$$

at $X = X_0$. This is also a necessary condition for f to reach a maximum, and can occur at points at which f is neither a minimum nor a maximum. We will not refer to the sufficient conditions which assure a minimum since any easy, alternative argument will apply for our problem.

Uses of Matrix Notation

It is assumed that the reader is familiar with matrix notation including matrix addition, scalar multiplication, and matrix multiplication. In particular, a system of m equations in n unknowns

$$\begin{aligned} a_{11}X_1 + a_{12}X_2 + \ldots + a_{1n}X_n &= b_1 \\ a_{21}X_1 + a_{22}X_2 + \ldots + a_{2n}X_n &= b_2 \\ \vdots \qquad\qquad & \quad \vdots \\ a_{m1}X_1 + a_{m2}X_2 + \ldots + a_{mn}X_n &= b_m \end{aligned} \tag{A.1a}$$

can be expressed in matrix notation as

$$AX = b \tag{A.1b}$$

where

$$A = \begin{pmatrix} a_{11} & a_{12} \dots a_{1n} \\ a_{21} & a_{22} \dots a_{2n} \\ \vdots & \vdots \\ a_{m1} & a_{m2} \dots a_{mn} \end{pmatrix} \qquad X = \begin{pmatrix} X_1 \\ X_2 \\ \vdots \\ X_n \end{pmatrix} \qquad b = \begin{pmatrix} b_1 \\ b_2 \\ \vdots \\ b_m \end{pmatrix}$$

We will let A' denote the *transpose* of the matrix A. In particular,

$$X' = (X_1, X_2, \dots, X_n)$$
$$b' = (b_1, b_2, \dots, b_m)$$

are the row vectors whose transposes are the column vectors X and b. Unless transposition is indicated, all vectors in this book are column vectors. The matrix A is said to be *symmetric* if $m = n$ and $A = A'$.

A (homogeneous) linear combination (i.e. weighted sum) of variables

$$E = \mu_1 X_1 + \mu_2 X_2 + \mu_3 X_3 + \dots + \mu_n X_n$$
$$= \sum_{i=1}^{n} \mu_i X_i \tag{A.2a}$$

is written as

$$E = \mu' X \tag{A.2b}$$

where $\mu' = (\mu_1, \mu_2, \dots, \mu_n)$. A homogeneous quadratic form

$$\begin{aligned} V = {} & \sigma_{11} X_1^2 + \sigma_{12} X_1 X_2 + \dots + \sigma_{1n} X_1 X_n \\ & + \sigma_{21} X_2 X_1 + \sigma_{22} X_2^2 + \dots + \sigma_{2n} X_2 X_n \\ & \vdots \\ & + \sigma_{n1} X_n X_1 + \sigma_{n2} X_n X_2 + \dots + \sigma_{nn} X_n^2 \end{aligned} \tag{A.3a}$$

is written as

$$V = X' C X \tag{A.3b}$$

where

$$C = \begin{pmatrix} \sigma_{11} & \sigma_{12} & \dots & \sigma_{1n} \\ \sigma_{21} & \sigma_{22} & \dots & \sigma_{2n} \\ \vdots & & & \vdots \\ \sigma_{n1} & \sigma_{n2} & \dots & \sigma_{nn} \end{pmatrix}$$

Any homogeneous quadratic function can be written so that C is symmetric – and we shall henceforth assume that (A.3b) is so written. If $V \geqslant 0$ for any X in

(A.3b), then C is said to be *positive semidefinite*. If $V > 0$ except when $X = 0$, C is called *positive definite*. A nonhomogeneous quadratic form may be written as

$$L = a_0 + a'X + X'CX \tag{A.4}$$

where a_0 is a scalar, $a' = (a_1, a_2, \ldots, a_n)$, and X and C are as above. In particular we assume C to be symmetric.

The notation

$$A = B \tag{A.5a}$$

means that each component of the A matrix is equal to the corresponding component of the B matrix: $a_{ij} = b_{ij}$ for all i, j. Similarly

$$A \geqslant B \tag{A.5b}$$

means that each component of the A matrix is as least as great as the corresponding component of the B matrix: $a_{ij} \geqslant b_{ij}$ for all i, j.

A *linear function*, also called a *linear transformation*, is of the form

$$Y = AX \tag{A.6a}$$

If Y has m components and X has n then A is an m by n matrix. If X equals the (n component) 0 vector then Y equals the (m component) 0 vector. An *affine function* or *affine transformation* is of the form

$$Y = a + AX \tag{A.6b}$$

where a is an m component vector of constants. In this case when $X = 0$, $Y = a$. If x, y are scalar variables and c_0, c_1 are scalar constants we usually speak of

$$y = c_0 + c_1 x \tag{A.6c}$$

as a linear relationship between y and x. Strictly speaking it is an affine relationship. The distinction between a linear function and an affine function is standard in vector analysis.

Matrix Operations

If we multiply the matrices A and B, and then multiply this product by C (on the right), the result $(AB)C$ is the same as if we multiplied B and C and then this product by A (on the left); that is,

$$(AB)C = A(BC) \tag{A.7a}$$

Multiplication of A and B is allowed, of course, only if A has the same number of columns as B has rows; multiplication of B and C requires that B has the same number of columns as C has rows. If these conditions are met then the operations on both the left- and right-hand sides of (A.7a) are allowed, and give the same result. The expression ABC therefore may be interpreted as either $(AB)C$ or $A(BC)$. Other relationships among matrices and scalars c, c_1, c_2, are

$$A(B+C) = AB + AC \tag{A.7b}$$

$$c(A+B) = cA + cB \tag{A.7c}$$

$$(c_1 + c_2)A = c_1 A + c_2 A \tag{A.7d}$$

$$(AB)' = B'A' \tag{A.7e}$$

$$(A+B)' = A' + B' \tag{A.7f}$$

Note that B' is to the left of A' in (A.7e).

It is not always true that $AB = BA$. For example,

$$\begin{pmatrix} a_{11} & a_{12} \\ a_{21} & a_{22} \end{pmatrix} \begin{pmatrix} 1 & 0 \\ 1 & 1 \end{pmatrix} = \begin{pmatrix} a_{11} + a_{12} & a_{12} \\ a_{21} + a_{22} & a_{22} \end{pmatrix}$$

whereas

$$\begin{pmatrix} 1 & 0 \\ 1 & 1 \end{pmatrix} \begin{pmatrix} a_{11} & a_{12} \\ a_{21} & a_{22} \end{pmatrix} = \begin{pmatrix} a_{11} & a_{12} \\ a_{11} + a_{21} & a_{12} + a_{22} \end{pmatrix}$$

A *zero matrix* is one whose components all equal zero. We sometimes speak of *the* zero matrix; but clearly there is a different zero matrix for each choice of number of rows m and columns n. We denote the zero matrix by the character 0 and expect the reader to know by context whether we speak of the scalar zero or a zero matrix - just as we expect the reader to know by context the shape of the zero matrix when not specified. Usually, either there is no ambiguity, or the resolution of the ambiguity is without consequence. For example, the relationship

$$A + 0 = A \tag{A.7g}$$

assumes that the zero matrix has the same number of rows and columns as does A; while the relationship

$$0A = 0 \tag{A.7h}$$

is true whether the zero on the left represents a zero scalar or an appropriately shaped zero matrix. Where there is an ambiguity of any consequence we will take special note or use special notation.

We let I represent the *identity matrix* - a square matrix with ones on the diagonal and zeros elsewhere:

$$I = \begin{pmatrix} 1 & 0 & 0 & \dots & 0 \\ 0 & 1 & 0 & \dots & 0 \\ 0 & 0 & 1 & \dots & 0 \\ \vdots & & & & \vdots \\ 0 & 0 & 0 & \dots & 1 \end{pmatrix} \tag{A.7i}$$

This is sometimes referred to as *the* identity matrix, although there is one such matrix for every value of n. It is usually left to the reader to understand which

I matrix is intended. When the shapes of the matrices or vectors are compatible,

$$AI = A \tag{A.7j}$$

$$IA = A \tag{A.7k}$$

The relationships in (A.7g, h, j, and k) apply in particular to 1 by n and n by 1 matrices, i.e. to row and column vectors.

A *diagonal matrix* has zeros everywhere except possibly on its diagonal, as for example in

$$D = \begin{pmatrix} d_1 & 0 & 0 & \dots & 0 \\ 0 & d_2 & 0 & \dots & 0 \\ 0 & 0 & d_3 & \dots & 0 \\ \vdots & & & & \vdots \\ 0 & 0 & 0 & \dots & d_n \end{pmatrix}$$

If $d_i = c$, for $1 \leqslant i \leqslant n$, multiplication on the left or right by D is the same as multiplication by the scalar c. In this case $AD = DA = cA = Ac$. In particular, note that

$$cA = Ac \tag{A.7l}$$

If the d_i differ then usually $DA \neq AD$.

Inverses

If A and B are square matrices such that $AB = I$ then also $BA = I$. We say that B is the *inverse* of A (and A is the inverse of B). The inverse of A is frequently denoted A^{-1}, just as 4^{-1} is a synonym for 0.25.

Some matrices have inverses; others do not. If A does have an inverse, and if

$$AX = b \tag{A.8a}$$

then

$$A^{-1}(AX) = A^{-1}(b)$$

i.e.

$$X = A^{-1}b \tag{A.8b}$$

It follows that if $AY = b$ as well as $AX = b$ then $X = Y$. Thus if A has an inverse, there is one and only one X such that $AX = b$, for any b. Or, to put it another way, if A has an inverse

$$Y = AX$$

is a one-one mapping from R^n onto R^n.

If A has an inverse, A is said to be *nonsingular*; otherwise it is called *singular*. Since $X = 0$ satisfies the equation $AX = 0$, the preceding discussion implies that if any nonzero vector X also satisfies this equation then A must be singular. We therefore have the following criterion which we will use frequently to determine if a matrix is nonsingular:

A matrix A is singular if and only if there is a vector $X \neq 0$ such that $AX = 0$.

Another criterion for determining whether or not a matrix is singular is that $|A| = 0$ if and only if A is singular, where $|A|$ denotes the *determinant* of A. Our only use of determinants in this book will be to show that certain matrices are singular or nonsingular. For this purpose we need only the following few facts about determinants:

$$\begin{vmatrix} a_{11} & a_{12} \\ a_{21} & a_{22} \end{vmatrix} = a_{11}a_{22} - a_{21}a_{12} \tag{A.9a}$$

$$\begin{vmatrix} a_{11} & a_{12} & a_{13} \\ a_{21} & a_{22} & a_{23} \\ a_{31} & a_{32} & a_{33} \end{vmatrix} = a_{11}\begin{vmatrix} a_{22} & a_{23} \\ a_{32} & a_{33} \end{vmatrix} - a_{21}\begin{vmatrix} a_{12} & a_{13} \\ a_{32} & a_{33} \end{vmatrix} + a_{31}\begin{vmatrix} a_{12} & a_{13} \\ a_{22} & a_{23} \end{vmatrix} \tag{A.9b}$$

If A and C are square matrices then

$$\begin{vmatrix} C & A' \\ A & 0 \end{vmatrix} = |A|^2 \tag{A.9c}$$

The last equation follows easily from the definition of the determinant as a sum of products. The reader is referred to a text such as Aitken (1956) for the definition of the determinant.

If A and B are nonsingular then

$$(A')^{-1} = (A^{-1})' \tag{A.10a}$$

$$(AB)^{-1} = B^{-1}A^{-1} \tag{A.10b}$$

Equation (A.10b) follows easily from $AB(B^{-1}A^{-1}) = A(BB^{-1})A^{-1} = I$.

Substitution of Variables

Suppose H is a nonsingular matrix and $K = H^{-1}$. Let

$$Y = HX \tag{A.11a}$$

Therefore

$$X = KY \tag{A.11b}$$

If we substitute KY for X in $AX = b$, $E = \mu'X$, and $V = X'CX$ of (A.1), (A.2), and (A.3) we get

$$AKY = b$$

Therefore

$$\bar{A}Y = b \tag{A.12a}$$

Also

$$\begin{aligned} E &= \mu' KY \\ &= \bar{\mu}' Y \end{aligned} \tag{A.12b}$$

and

$$\begin{aligned} V &= Y'K'CKY \\ &= Y'\bar{C}Y \end{aligned} \tag{A.12c}$$

where $\bar{A} = AK$, $\bar{\mu} = K'\mu$ and $\bar{C} = K'CK$. If C is symmetric, as we assume, then (A.7e) implies that $\bar{C}$ is also symmetric.

Thus linear equations, homogeneous linear functions, and homogeneous symmetric quadratic functions retain their respective forms under the linear substitution (A.11).

One of the most remarkable and useful facts about linear substitution into a quadratic form is this: if C is symmetric and positive definite then there exists nonsingular H and K such that $\bar{C} = I$. More generally, if C is symmetric and positive semidefinite then there exists nonsingular H and K such that $\bar{C}$ is a diagonal matrix with ones and/or zeros on the diagonal. $\bar{C}$ will have less than n ones – and therefore not be the identity I – if and only if C is positive semidefinite but not positive definite.

With H and K as in (A.11), and with α any vector, we may define

$$Y = \alpha + HX \tag{A.13a}$$

Therefore

$$X = \beta + KY \tag{A.13b}$$

where $\beta = -K\alpha$. If we substitute $\beta + KY$ for X in $AX = b, E = \mu'X$, $V = X'CX$, and $L = a_0 + a'X + X'CX$, we get:

$$A(\beta + KY) = b$$

i.e.

$$\bar{A}Y = \bar{b} \tag{A.14a}$$

where $\bar{b} = b - A\beta$;

$$\begin{aligned} E &= \mu'(\beta + KY) \\ &= \bar{\mu}_0 + \bar{\mu}Y \end{aligned} \tag{A.14b}$$

where $\bar{\mu}_0 = \mu'\beta$;

$$\begin{aligned} V &= (\beta + KY)'C(\beta + KY) \\ &= \beta'C\beta + 2\beta'CKY + Y'K'CKY \\ &= V_0 + \bar{\beta}'Y + Y'\bar{C}Y \end{aligned} \tag{A.14c}$$

where $V_0 = \beta' C\beta$ and $\bar{\beta}' = 2\beta' CK$; and finally

$$L = a_0 + a'(\beta + KY) + (\beta + KY)'C(\beta + KY)$$
$$= (a_0 + a'\beta + \beta' C\beta) + (K'a + 2K'C\beta)'Y + Y'\bar{C}Y$$
$$= \bar{a}_0 + \bar{a}'Y + Y'\bar{C}Y \qquad \text{(A.14d)}$$

where $\bar{a}_0 = a_0 + a'\beta + \beta' C\beta$ and $\bar{a} = K'a + 2K'C\beta$. For arbitrary choice of H and α, then, E and V do not necessarily remain homogeneous. If C is symmetric and positive semidefinite, for suitable choice of H and α, L becomes

$$L = Y'DY \qquad \text{(A.14e)}$$

where D is a diagonal matrix whose entries contain only zeros and ones.

n Dimensional Geometry

Just as a vector with two components $X' = (X_1, X_2)$ may be represented by a point in a plane, and $X' = (X_1, X_2, X_3)$ by a point in space, so $X' = (X_1, X_2, \ldots, X_n)$ may be imagined as a point in an n dimensional space R^n. We will represent a point in R^n by either a column vector X or its transpose, the row vector X'. The distance d between two points X and Y is given by the Pythagorean formula

$$d(X, Y) = \left[\sum_{i=1}^{n} (X_i - Y_i)^2 \right]^{1/2} \qquad \text{(A.15)}$$

Often we do not need formula (A.15), but only a few of the properties of the d function. It can be shown that d satisfies the following properties. For every X, Y, and Z in R^n:

$$d(X, Y) \geqslant 0 \qquad \text{(A.16a)}$$

$$d(X, Y) = 0 \qquad \text{if and only if } X = Y \qquad \text{(A.16b)}$$

$$d(X, Y) = d(Y, X) \qquad \text{(A.16c)}$$

$$d(X, Z) \leqslant d(X, Y) + d(Y, Z) \qquad \text{(A.16d)}$$

The last is referred to as the *triangle inequality*. Equations (A.16a-d) are properties we expect of distance, as well as consequences of (A.15). Specifically, distance is never negative; a point is at zero distance only from itself; the distance from a point X to a point Y is the same as that from the latter to the former; and it is shorter to go directly from X to Z than to go from X to Y and then to Z. Equations (A.16a-d) may be thought of either as properties of the algebraic equation in (A.15) as applied to row vectors or column vectors, or as properties of the points in space which the row or column vectors represent.

One sometimes speaks of a vector as if it were an arrow drawn from the origin to a particular point. For the moment let us call this a *geometric* vector and distinguish it from an *algebraic* row or column vector. We also distinguish the geometric vector from the *geometric point* which lies at one of its ends, though both the geometric vectors and the geometric points are represented by the same algebraic (row or column) vector.

Let X be an (algebraic) column vector. The length of the geometric vector represented by X is the same as the distance from the origin to the geometric point which X represents. We denote this length by $\|X\|$ and refer to it as the *norm* of X. Thus

$$\|X\| = d(0, X) \tag{A.17}$$

Relationships (A.17) and (A.16) imply

$$\|X\| \geqslant 0 \tag{A.18a}$$

$$\|X\| = 0 \qquad \text{if and only if } X = 0 \tag{A.18b}$$

$$\|X + Y\| \leqslant \|X\| + \|Y\| \tag{A.18c}$$

The formula for d in (A.15) implies

$$\|cX\| = |c|\,\|X\| \tag{A.18d}$$

for any scalar c (where $|c|$ stands for the absolute value of c). Equation (A.17) describes the norm of a vector in terms of the distance function. Conversely distance can be described in terms of norm as

$$d(X, Y) = \|X - Y\| \tag{A.19}$$

It would be a great nuisance, for the reader as well as for the writer, to constantly distinguish between (1) the algebraic vectors X, Y, and Z, (2) the points represented by these algebraic vectors, and (3) the geometric vectors which they represent. Thus when we say

(1) $X_i \geqslant 0$ for $i = 1, \ldots, n$;
(2) X, Y, and Z lie on the same straight line (not necessarily through the origin); or
(3) The cosine of the angle between X and Y is $X'Y/(\|X\|\,\|Y\|)$;

the first statement applies to the components of the algebraic vector; the second applies to the points which X, Y, and Z represent; and the third applies to the geometric vectors which X and Y represent. Alternatively, the second and third may be considered as statements about algebraic vectors that rely on definitions concerning "the angle between two algebraic vectors," or when three algebraic vectors "lie on the same straight line." These definitions for algebraic vectors are constructed so that the statements (using words like "line" and "angle") about algebraic vectors will also apply - where appropriate - to geometric points and geometric vectors. (We will sometimes use the statement "X is in R^n" to mean that X is an algebraic (row or column) vector with n components, or is the name of a point in an n dimensional space, or both.)

It is often said that a geometric vector has magnitude and direction. We will speak of norm (or length) rather than magnitude. As to direction, it will be most convenient to speak of any vector $\beta \neq 0$ as "a direction," any vector $\lambda\beta$ (where

λ is a positive scalar) as "the same direction" as β, and the vector $-\lambda\beta$ as "the opposite direction." Thus $(1, -3, 5)$ is the same direction as $(2, -6, 10)$, whereas $(-3, 9, -15)$ is the opposite direction, while $(0, 1, 0)$ is a different direction, and $(0, 0, 0)$ is not a direction. If it seems strange to say that β and $\lambda\beta$ are the same direction, recall that we refer to any ratio of integers i/j as a rational number (i.e. fraction) provided $j \neq 0$, but say that certain ratios, such as 1/2 and 4/8, are "the same" rational number.

Orthogonality

In the plane R^2, if $\|X\| = \|Y\| = 1$ then the cosine between (the geometric vector represented by) X and (that of) Y is

$$\cos(X, Y) = X'Y$$

If these vectors are not necessarily of unit length but $\|X\| \neq 0$ and $\|Y\| \neq 0$ then

$$X'Y = \cos(X, Y)\,\|X\|\,\|Y\|$$

When two vectors are perpendicular (*orthogonal*) the cosine of the angle between them is zero; therefore $X'Y = 0$. More generally, in R^n we say that two vectors X and Y are orthogonal if $X'Y = 0$. In particular the zero vector is orthogonal to every vector.

Let e^i be the vector in R^n with a 1 in its ith place and 0 elsewhere; e.g. $(e^3)' = (0, 0, 1, 0, \ldots, 0)$. Then $(e^i)'e^j = 0$ for $i \neq j$. $e^1, e^2, \ldots, e^n$ are n orthogonal vectors in R^n. Since $X'e^i = X_i$, the ith component of X, only the zero vector is orthogonal to all the e^i. Thus one cannot find an $(n+1)$th $X \neq 0$ orthogonal to all $e^1, \ldots, e^n$.

Let $X^1 \neq 0$ be a nonzero vector. (Note that X^1 does not represent a first component of some vector, but a first vector: $(X^1)' = (X_1^1, X_2^1, \ldots, X_n^1)$.) Then it is possible to find $n-1$ more nonzero vectors $X^2, X^3, \ldots, X^n$ in R^n such that $(X^i)'X^j = 0$, but it is impossible to find an $(n+1)$th $X \neq 0$ orthogonal to these. Thus in R^n there are many ways of finding n orthogonal nonzero vectors. In fact, given any k orthogonal vectors, $n-k$ can be found so that the entire set of n is orthogonal. But it is impossible to find $n+1$ nonzero orthogonal vectors. If the X^i has $\|X^i\| = 1$, as well as $(X^i)'(X^j) = 0$ for $i \neq j$, then $X^1, \ldots, X^n$ is called an *orthonormal system* of vectors. In particular, the coordinate vectors $e^1, e^2, \ldots, e^n$ are an orthonormal system.

Independence and Subspaces

For the set of vectors $X^1, X^2, X^3, \ldots, X^k$, the vectors are said to be *independent* if there are no scalars $a_1, a_2, \ldots, a_k$ such that

$$\sum_{i=1}^{k} a_i X^i = 0$$

except $a_1 = a_2 = \ldots = a_k = 0$. Otherwise $X^1, X^2, \ldots, X^k$ are called *dependent*. If we let A be the matrix formed by setting the k column vectors side by side, i.e.

$$A = (X^1, X^2, \ldots, X^k)$$

then $X^1, \ldots, X^k$ are independent if there is no vector $a \neq 0$ such that

$$Aa = 0$$

In particular, if $k = n$, the n vectors are independent if and only if A is non-singular.

A non-empty set S of points in R^n is said to be a *linear subspace* if, for any X and Y in S and any two numbers a_0 and a_1,

$$Z = a_0 X + a_1 Y$$

is also a point in S. Since $a_0 = a_1 = 0$ is allowed, every linear subspace contains $X = 0$. Examples of linear subspaces include the following:

(1) The set consisting of the zero vector only. This subspace is said to be zero-dimensional. Since $c0 = 0$ for any scalar c, this set contains no independent vectors.
(2) The set of X of the form $X = cX_0$, for some fixed X_0 in R^n with $X_0 \neq 0$, and for *all* scalars c. This set is a straight line through the origin. It contains one, but not two, independent vectors and is called one-dimensional.
(3) The set X of the form $X = c_1 X^1 + c_2 X^2$, for every pair of scalars c_1 and c_2, where X^1 and X^2 are two fixed vectors in R^n such that $X^1 \neq X^2$ and neither equals the zero vector. This set is a two-dimensional plane containing the origin. It contains two, but not three, independent vectors.
(4) R^n itself satisfies the definition of a subspace. It is the one and only n dimensional subspace of R^n.

Suppose that $X^1, \ldots, X^k$ are k independent vectors in some linear subspace S, and there is no nonzero X^{k+1} in S which is independent of the preceding. Then S is k dimensional. This defines the dimension of S in terms of one particular set of vectors $X^1, \ldots, X^k$; but the value of k for a subspace S does not depend on the set of vectors chosen. That is, if $Y^1, Y^2, \ldots, Y^h$ are h independent vectors in S, then it cannot happen that $h > k$; if $h < k$ there exist $k - h$ more vectors in S to make up a set $Y^1, Y^2, \ldots, Y^h, \ldots, Y^k$ of k independent vectors. Thus the dimension of a subspace is well defined.

If S is a k dimensional subspace of R^n, then there is an $n - k$ dimensional subspace T in R^n with the following property: if X is in S and Y is in T then $X'Y = 0$. Every Z in R^n can be written in one and only one way as $Z = X + Y$ for some X in S and Y in T. S and T are said to be *orthogonal subspaces*. In R^3, if S is a plane (containing the origin) then T is the line through the origin perpendicular to the plane.

If S_L is a linear space and a is any point in R^n, then

$$S_a = \{X : X = a + Y \quad \text{for } Y \text{ in } S_L\} \tag{A.20}$$

is called an *affine subspace* of R^n. (The notation $\{P : q\}$ is read "the set of P such that q". For example, $\{X \in R^n : X \geqslant 0\}$ is read "the set of X in R^n such that $X \geqslant 0$". The right-hand side of (A.20) is read "the set of X such that $X = a + Y$ for Y in S_L, i.e. X such that $X - a \in S_L$.) S_L is the *linear space parallel* to the affine space S_a. For example, in R^3 if S_L is a line through the origin then S_a is either the same line or a parallel line not through the origin, depending on the choice of a. If S_L is a plane containing the origin then S_a is either the same plane or a parallel plane.

If S_L is the linear subspace parallel to the affine subspace S_a, and S_L is k dimensional, then we say that S_a is k dimensional. If S_a is a k dimensional affine space, then it contains $k + 1$ vectors $X_0, X^1, X^2, \ldots, X^k$ such that

$$\begin{aligned} Y^1 &= X^1 - X_0 \\ Y^2 &= X^2 - X_0 \\ \vdots \quad & \quad \vdots \\ Y^k &= X^k - X_0 \end{aligned}$$

are independent. There is no X^{k+1} in S such that $Y^{k+1} = X^{k+1} - X_0$ is independent of $Y^1, \ldots, Y^k$. If b is in S_a then

$$S_b = \{X : X = b + Y \qquad \text{for } Y \text{ in } S_L\}$$

is the same as S_a in (A.20), since X in S_b implies that there is a Y^1 in S_L such that

$$X = b + Y^1 \tag{A.21a}$$

and b in S_a implies that there is a Y^2 in S_L such that

$$b = a + Y^2 \tag{A.21b}$$

Hence, substituting (A.21b) into (A.21a), we get

$$X = a + (Y^1 + Y^2)$$

But $Y^1 + Y^2$ is in S_L; therefore X is in S_a.

Change of Coordinate Systems

The algebraic vector assigned to a point in space depends on the coordinate system chosen. When we substitute $Y = HX$ as in (A.11a) we are, in effect, expressing the same point in terms of a new coordinate system. Frequently in the main text we express financial ideas in algebraic terms, interpret algebraic equations as figures in n dimensional space, choose a new coordinate system so that equations simplify and the nature of the figures becomes clear, analyze the figures and equations in this coordinate system, and finally interpret the results back in the original coordinate system.

To clarify the relationships between figures and formulas in different coordinate systems, this section presents a two-dimensional example; the next section states the general case in R^n. The curve in figure A.1 satisfies the equation

$$13X_1^2 - 10X_1X_2 + 13X_2^2 = 72 \tag{A.22a}$$

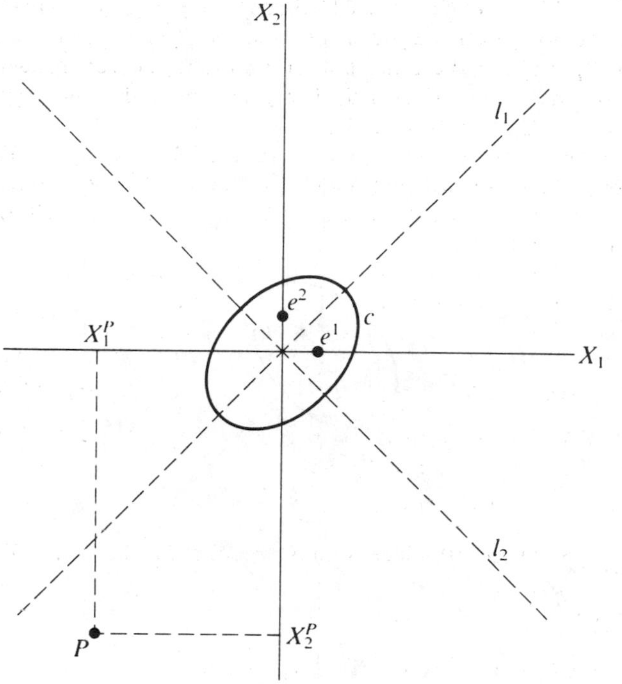

Figure A.1 Ellipse in X_1X_2 space

i.e.

$$(X_1, X_2)\begin{pmatrix} 13 & -5 \\ -5 & 13 \end{pmatrix}\begin{pmatrix} X_1 \\ X_2 \end{pmatrix} = 72 \qquad \text{(A.22b)}$$

This is an ellipse whose major and minor axes - l_1 and l_2 - make 45° angles with the X_1 and X_2 coordinate axes.

A unit length in the X_1 direction is denoted by the (geometric) vector e^1 and in the X_2 direction by e^2. The X_1 coordinate assigned to any point P in the plane is determined, as we know, by dropping a perpendicular from P to the X_1 axis, then measuring the number of e^1 (or $-e^1$ or fraction thereof) vectors required to reach this projection X_1^P. The X_2 value of P is similarly determined by a projection of P onto the X_2 axis.

In figure A.2 a new set of axes, Y_1 and Y_2, have been drawn so that the major and minor axes of the ellipse lie along Y_1 and Y_2 respectively. The unit vectors f^1 and f^2 in the Y_1 and Y_2 directions have been drawn with the same length as the e^1 and e^2 vectors. The Y_1 coordinate of the point P is determined by dropping a perpendicular from P to the Y_1 line, then counting how many units of f^1 (or $-f^1$ or fraction thereof) vectors are required to reach Y_1^P; and similarly

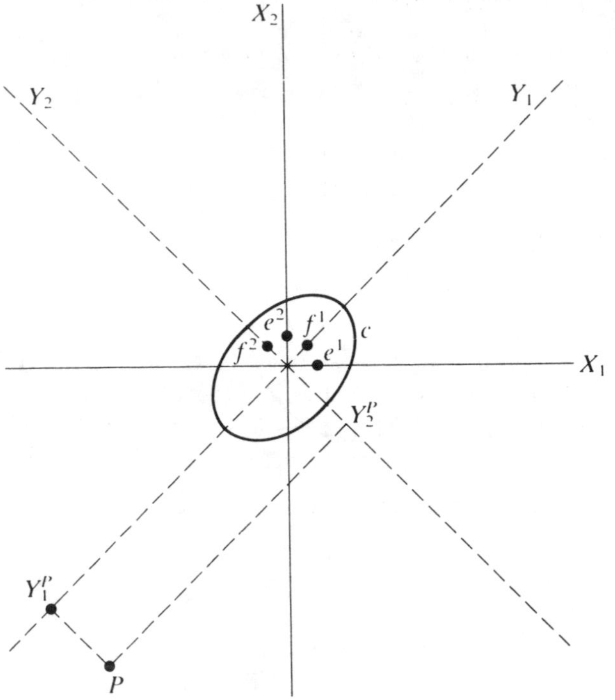

Figure A.2 Ellipse with both X_1X_2 and Y_1Y_2 coordinate systems

for the Y_2^P coordinate of the point P. It can be shown that the relationships between the X_1, X_2 coordinates of any point and the Y_1, Y_2 coordinates of the same point are given by

$$\begin{pmatrix} Y_1 \\ Y_2 \end{pmatrix} = \begin{pmatrix} 2^{-1/2} & 2^{-1/2} \\ -2^{-1/2} & 2^{-1/2} \end{pmatrix} \begin{pmatrix} X_1 \\ X_2 \end{pmatrix} \tag{A.23a}$$

$$\begin{pmatrix} X_1 \\ X_2 \end{pmatrix} = \begin{pmatrix} 2^{-1/2} & -2^{-1/2} \\ 2^{-1/2} & 2^{-1/2} \end{pmatrix} \begin{pmatrix} Y_1 \\ Y_2 \end{pmatrix} \tag{A.23b}$$

For example, the e^1 vector represented by $X' = (1, 0)$ has, according to (A.23a), $Y' = (2^{-1/2}, -2^{-1/2})$. Conversely the f^1 vector, which equals $Y' = (1, 0)$ in the Y coordinate system, according to (A.23b) corresponds to $X = (2^{-1/2}, 2^{-1/2})$. As an exercise, compute the lengths of the e^1 and e^2 vectors and the cosine of the angle between them when these are expressed in terms of the Y coordinate system. Note that e^1 and e^2 continue to have length 1 and are still orthogonal. More generally the transformation in (A.23) preserves the lengths of vectors and the angles between them. Such a transformation is referred to as an *orthogonal transformation*.

If we substitute (A.23b) for X in the formula for the ellipse we obtain

$$Y'K'CKY = 72 \tag{A.24a}$$

i.e.

$$(Y_1, Y_2)\begin{pmatrix} 8 & 0 \\ 0 & 18 \end{pmatrix}\begin{pmatrix} Y_1 \\ Y_2 \end{pmatrix} = 72 \tag{A.24b}$$

or

$$8Y_1^2 + 18Y_2^2 = 72 \tag{A.24c}$$

In terms of the Y coordinate system, chosen so that the axes of the ellipse correspond to those of the coordinate system, the equation has no cross-product Y_1Y_2 term. Figure A.3 is the same as figure A.2 except that the Y_1 axis is horizontal.

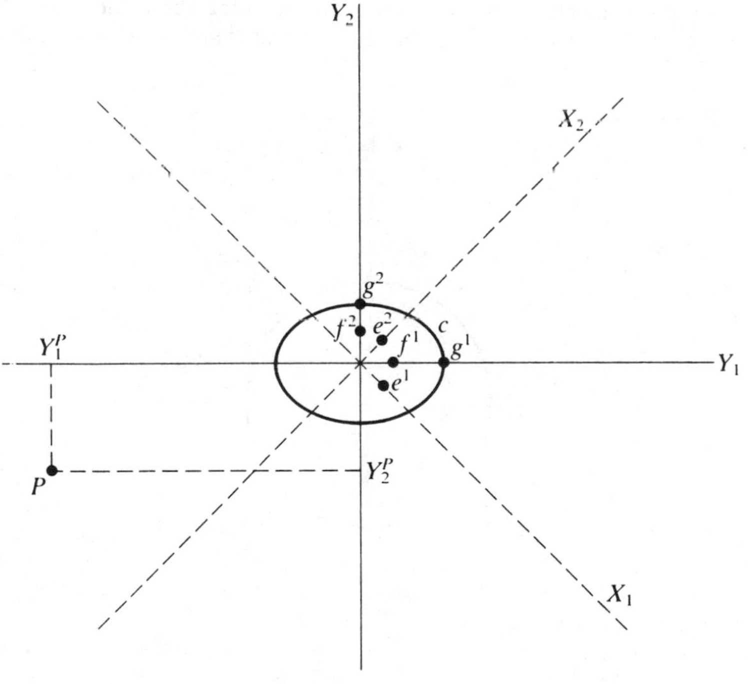

Figure A.3 As in figure A.2, with the page rotated

We define Z such that

$$\begin{pmatrix} Z_1 \\ Z_2 \end{pmatrix} = \begin{pmatrix} 1/3 & 0 \\ 0 & 1/2 \end{pmatrix} \begin{pmatrix} Y_1 \\ Y_2 \end{pmatrix} \tag{A.25a}$$

i.e.

$$\begin{pmatrix} Y_1 \\ Y_2 \end{pmatrix} = \begin{pmatrix} 3 & 0 \\ 0 & 2 \end{pmatrix} \begin{pmatrix} Z_1 \\ Z_2 \end{pmatrix} \tag{A.25b}$$

Substituting (A.25) into (A.24) we get

$$72Z_1^2 + 72Z_2^2 = 72 \tag{A.26a}$$

or

$$Z_1^2 + Z_2^2 = 1 \tag{A.26b}$$

This may be interpreted geometrically in two ways. In figure A.3 we have drawn a vector g^1 in the same direction as f^1 but three times the length. Similarly, g^2 is drawn in the same direction as f^2 but with twice the length. Thus constructed, the curve c passes through the end points of g^1 and g^2. We measure the Z_1 coordinate of a point P by dropping a perpendicular to the Y_1 axis, then measuring the number of g^1 (or $-g^1$ or fraction thereof) vectors required to reach from the origin to the projection. Alternatively, we can plot the same point P on a diagram such as that in figure A.4 in which g^1 and g^2 are drawn with unit length.

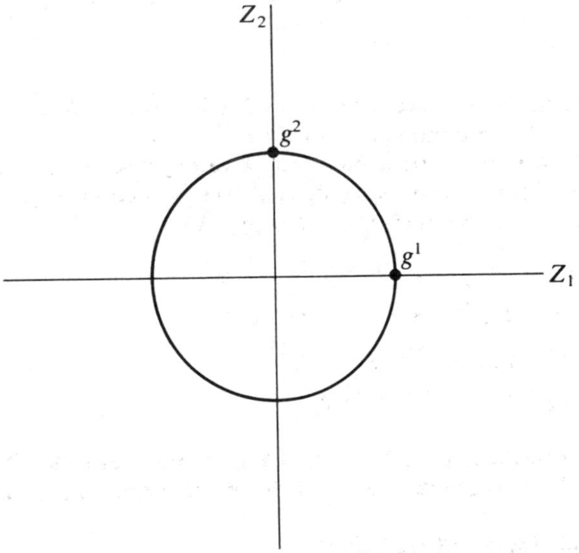

Figure A.4 As in figure A.3, except with g^1 and g^2 as the unit vectors

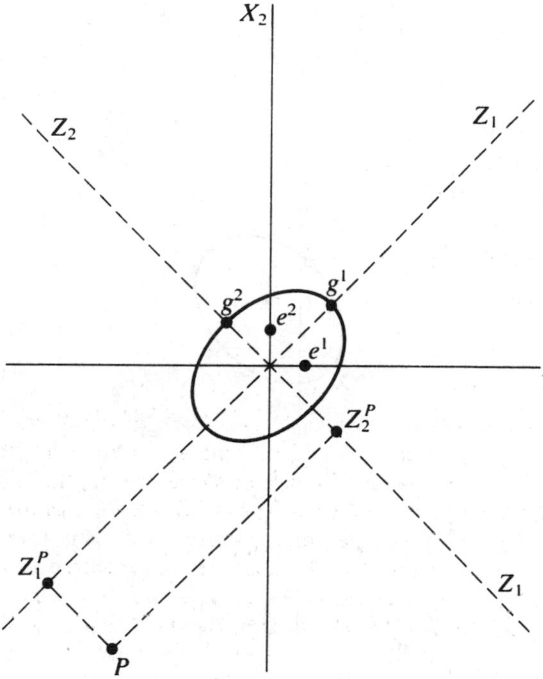

Figure A.5 From X to Z, bypassing step Y

In this figure the curve – expressed in (A.22) in terms of X, in (A.24) in terms of Y, and in (A.26) in terms of Z – is a circle.

We could have moved from the X coordinate system to the Z coordinate system in a single step without going through the Y coordinate system, as in figure A.5. The relationship between X and Z is given by

$$\begin{pmatrix} Z_1 \\ Z_2 \end{pmatrix} = \begin{pmatrix} 1/3 & 0 \\ 0 & 1/2 \end{pmatrix} \begin{pmatrix} 2^{-1/2} & 2^{-1/2} \\ -2^{-1/2} & 2^{-1/2} \end{pmatrix} \begin{pmatrix} X_1 \\ X_2 \end{pmatrix}$$

$$= \begin{pmatrix} (2^{-1/2})/3 & (2^{-1/2})/3 \\ -2^{-3/2} & 2^{-3/2} \end{pmatrix} \begin{pmatrix} X_1 \\ X_2 \end{pmatrix} \qquad \text{(A.27)}$$

obtained by substituting (A.23a) into (A.25a). Equation (A.27) "maps" each point of the X_1X_2 plane (figure A.1) into the corresponding point of the Z_1Z_2 plane (figure A.4).

The formula for the ellipse in figure A.6 is

$$13X_1^2 + 13X_2^2 - 10X_1X_2 - 6X_1 - 16X_2 = 27 \qquad \text{(A.28a)}$$

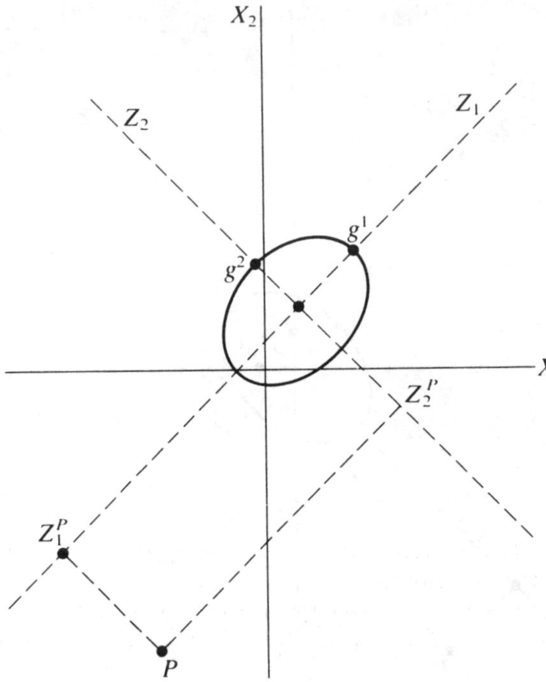

Figure A.6 Ellipse requiring an affine change in coordinates to express in simplest form

The ellipse in figure A.6 is the same as that in figure A.1, except that its center is located at $(X_1, X_2) = (1, 2)$. This may be confirmed by deriving (A.28a) from

$$13(X_1 - 1)^2 + 13(X_2 - 2)^2 - 10(X_1 - 1)(X_2 - 2) = 72 \quad \text{(A.28b)}$$

The *translation* of the origin

$$\begin{pmatrix} \tilde{X}_1 \\ \tilde{X}_2 \end{pmatrix} = \begin{pmatrix} X_1 \\ X_2 \end{pmatrix} - \begin{pmatrix} 1 \\ 2 \end{pmatrix} \quad \text{(A.29)}$$

changes (A.28b), and therefore (A.28a), into

$$13\tilde{X}_1^2 + 13\tilde{X}_2^2 - 10\tilde{X}_1\tilde{X}_2 = 72 \quad \text{(A.30)}$$

By shifting the origin to the center of the ellipse we have eliminated the linear terms – the terms in $\tilde{X}_1$ and $\tilde{X}_2$ – but not the cross-product term $\tilde{X}_1\tilde{X}_2$. If instead of shifting the origin as in (A.29) we rotate the origin 45° by substituting $Y = HX$ as in (A.23), we would eliminate the cross-product $\tilde{X}_1\tilde{X}_2$, but $\tilde{X}_1$ and $\tilde{X}_2$ would still have nonzero (but changed) weights. This statement can be confirmed here by performing the substitution, or left as an application of the discussion of R^n to follow. If we both rotate the axes and shift the origin by the affine transformation

$$\begin{pmatrix} W_1 \\ W_2 \end{pmatrix} = H\left[\begin{pmatrix} X_1 \\ X_2 \end{pmatrix} - \begin{pmatrix} 1 \\ 2 \end{pmatrix}\right]$$

$$= HX - Ha$$

where $a' = (1, 2)$, we eliminate both linear and cross-product terms, arriving at

$$8W_1^2 + 18W_2^2 = 72 \tag{A.31}$$

as in (A.24c).

If we substitute

$$\begin{pmatrix} Z_1 \\ Z_2 \end{pmatrix} = \begin{pmatrix} 1/3 & 0 \\ 0 & 1/2 \end{pmatrix}\begin{pmatrix} W_1 \\ W_2 \end{pmatrix} \tag{A.32}$$

we obtain

$$Z_1^2 + Z_2^2 = 1$$

as the equation of the ellipse. The Z_1 coordinate of any point P in figure A.6 can be determined by dropping a perpendicular from P to the line labeled Z_1, then measuring the distance to this point in g^1 units. If the Z_1, Z_2 coordinates of every point are plotted in a figure with g^1 and g^2 as unit vectors as in figure A.4, then the ellipse again becomes a circle. The mapping between a point in figure A.6 and that in figure A.4 is given by the affine transformation

$$\begin{pmatrix} Z_1 \\ Z_2 \end{pmatrix} = (\tilde{H}H)X - \tilde{H}Ha$$

where $\tilde{H}$ is the matrix in (A.32).

Change of Coordinates in R^n

The nonsingular linear transformation

$$Y = HX \tag{A.33a}$$

or, with $K = H^{-1}$,

$$X = KY \tag{A.33b}$$

corresponds to a change in coordinates in R^n. With e^i continuing to represent the (algebraic) vector with a one in its ith place and zeros elsewhere,

$$X^i = Ke^i$$

namely the ith column of K, shows the X coordinates $(X_1^i, X_2^i, \ldots, X_n^i)'$ of the vector corresponding to $Y = e^i$. If $X^1, X^2, \ldots, X^n$ are orthogonal and of unit length – i.e. comprise an orthonormal set – then (A.33a) and (A.33b) are called *orthogonal transformations*, and H (and K) is called an orthogonal matrix. This requires

$$K'K = I \tag{A.34a}$$

(since the ith row of K' is the ith column of K). In other words

$$K' = K^{-1} = H \tag{A.34b}$$

We noted above that if C is a symmetric, positive semidefinite matrix then

(1) There are *nonsingular* transformations

$$Z = \tilde{H}X$$
$$X = \tilde{K}Z$$

such that

$$V = X'CX$$
$$= Z'\tilde{D}Z$$

where $\tilde{D}$ is a diagonal matrix whose entries are zeros and ones. It is no less remarkable that

(2) There are *orthogonal* transformations

$$Y = HX$$
$$X = KY$$

such that

$$V = X'CX$$
$$= Y'DY$$

where D is a diagonal matrix whose entries are (not necessarily zeros and ones, but are) nonnegative.

The entries d_{11}, d_{22}, ... on the diagonal of D are called the *eigenvalues* of the matrix C. The transformation in (1) is easily derived from that in (2). For example, the orthogonal transformation in (A.23) changed the matrix on the left-hand side of (A.22b) into that in (A.24b). The transformation in (A.25) changed the matrix into

$$\begin{pmatrix} 72 & 0 \\ 0 & 72 \end{pmatrix}$$

in (A.26a). If instead we had defined

$$W = \begin{pmatrix} 8^{1/2} & 0 \\ 0 & 18^{1/2} \end{pmatrix} Y \tag{A.35a}$$

i.e.

$$Y = \begin{pmatrix} 8^{-1/2} & 0 \\ 0 & 18^{-1/2} \end{pmatrix} W \tag{A.35b}$$

then

$$(X_1, X_2)\begin{pmatrix} 13 & -5 \\ -5 & 13 \end{pmatrix}\begin{pmatrix} X_1 \\ X_2 \end{pmatrix} = (Y_1, Y_2)\begin{pmatrix} 8 & 0 \\ 0 & 18 \end{pmatrix}\begin{pmatrix} Y_1 \\ Y_2 \end{pmatrix} \tag{A.36a}$$

$$= (W_1, W_2)\begin{pmatrix} 1 & 0 \\ 0 & 1 \end{pmatrix}\begin{pmatrix} W_1 \\ W_2 \end{pmatrix} \tag{A.36b}$$

The linear transformation from X to Y is the orthogonal transformation whose existence is asserted in (2), and the linear transformation from X to W is the nonsingular transformation whose existence is asserted in (1).

An orthogonal transformation leaves any inner product[1] unchanged, since if $\hat{X}$ and $\tilde{X}$ are any two vectors before the transformation and $\hat{Y} = H\hat{X}$ and $\tilde{Y} = H\tilde{X}$ are the corresponding vectors after the transformation, we have

$$\hat{Y}'\tilde{Y} = \hat{X}'H'H\tilde{X} = \hat{X}'\tilde{X}$$

Thus the length of each vector and the angle between vectors, being defined in terms of inner product, are unchanged by an orthogonal transformation.

In R^n the affine transformation

$$X = b + KY \tag{A.37}$$

(for b in R^n) substituted into the nonhomogeneous quadratic form

$$V = c_0 + \alpha' X + X'CX \tag{A.38a}$$

(where c_0 is a scalar and α a vector) gives

$$\begin{aligned} V &= c_0 + \alpha'(b + KY) + (b + KY)'C(b + KY) \\ &= [c_0 + \alpha' b + b'Cb] + [\alpha' K + 2b'CK]Y + Y'[K'CK]Y \end{aligned} \tag{A.38b}$$

Note that the quadratic term $Y'K'CKY$ does not depend on b. In particular, the linear transformation $Y = HX$ which reduces $V = X'CX$ to a diagonal matrix will remove the cross-product terms from (A.38a).

A nonsingular transformation (and, in particular, an orthogonal transformation) $Y = HX$ changes linear subspaces into linear subspaces and affine subspaces into affine subspaces of the same dimension. That is, if S is a set of X values, and T the corresponding set of Y values (each Y in T equals HX for some X in S, and each X in S equals $H^{-1}Y$ for some Y in T) then S is a k dimensional linear (or affine) subspace if and only if T is a k dimensional linear (or affine) subspace. In particular, S is a line containing the origin (not containing the origin) if and only if T is a line containing (not containing) the origin.

[1] That is, the product of a row vector times a column vector.

Certain relationships involving linear and affine subspaces, described previously, are most easily seen by suitable transformation of coordinates. If S is a k dimensional linear subspace then there is an orthogonal transformation $Y = HX$ such that, in terms of the new coordinate system, the set S becomes

$$\{Y : Y_i = 0 \qquad i > k\} \tag{A.39}$$

In other words, in the new coordinate system the k dimensional linear subspace S consists of all Y whose first k components may take on any value, and whose last $n-k$ components are zero. The subspace T orthogonal to S is the set

$$\{Y : Y_i = 0 \qquad i \leqslant k\}$$

whose first k components are zero and whose last $n-k$ components may take on any value. Clearly any point Y may be written as the sum of $U+W$, U in S, W in T, in one and only one way.

If S is an affine subspace then there is an orthogonal transformation $Y = HX$ such that the set S in the new coordinate system is

$$\{Y : Y_i = a_i \qquad i > k\}$$

That is, the last $n-k$ elements have fixed values, not necessarily zero, while the first k components may take on any value. The points

$$Y_0 = (0, 0, \ldots, 0, a_{k+1}, a_{k+2}, \ldots, a_n)$$
$$Y^1 = (1, 0, \ldots, 0, a_{k+1}, a_{k+2}, \ldots, a_n)$$
$$\vdots \qquad\qquad \vdots$$
$$Y^k = (0, 0, \ldots, 1, a_{k+1}, a_{k+2}, \ldots, a_n)$$

are $k+1$ points in S such that

$$Z^1 = Y^1 - Y_0$$
$$Z^2 = Y^2 - Y_0$$
$$\vdots \qquad \vdots$$
$$Z^k = Y^k - Y_0$$

are independent.

References

Aitken, A. C. (1956), *Determinants and Matrices*, 9th edn, Oliver and Boyd, Edinburgh and London; Interscience, New York

Arrow, K. (1965), *Aspects of the Theory of Risk Bearing*, Helsinki

Baumol, W. J. (1963), "An expected gain-confidence limit criterion for portfolio selection", *Management Science*, October, pp. 174–82

Bellman, R. E. (1957), *Dynamic Programming*, Princeton University Press, Princeton, New Jersey

Birkhoff, G., and MacLane, S. (1977), *A Survey of Modern Algebra*, 4th edn, Macmillan

Black, F. (1972), "Capital market equilibrium with restricted borrowing", *Journal of Business*, July

Black, F., and Scholes, M. (1973), "The pricing of options and corporate liabilities", *Journal of Political Economy*, May/June, pp. 637–54

Blume, M. (1971), "On the assessment of risk", *Journal of Finance*, March, pp. 1–10

Borch, K. (1969), "A note on uncertainty and indifference curves", *Review of Economic Studies*, 36, January, pp. 1–4

Breiman, L. (1960), "Investment policies for expanding business optimal in a long run sense", *Naval Research Logistics Quarterly*, 7(4), pp. 647–51

Breiman, L. (1961), "Optimal gambling systems for favorable games", *Fourth Berkeley Symposium on Probability and Statistics*, pp. 65–78

Chamberlain, G. (1983), "A characterization of the distributions that imply mean variance utility functions", *Journal of Economic Theory*, June

Cohen, K. J., and Pogue, J. A. (1967), "An empirical evaluation of alternative portfolio-selection models", *Journal of Business*, April

Cottle, R. W., and Dantzig, G. B. (1968), "Complementary pivot theory of mathematical programming". In *Linear Algebra and its Applications*, vol. 1, American Elsevier, pp. 103–25.

Courant, R. (1937), *Differential and Integral Calculus*, vol. 1, new revised edn, translated by E. J. McShane, Interscience, New York

Dantzig, G. B. (1963), *Linear Programming and Extensions*, Princeton University Press, Princeton, New Jersey

Dantzig, G. B., and Cottle, R. W. (1967), "Positive (semi-)definite programming". In J. Abadie (ed.), *Nonlinear Programming*, North-Holland, Amsterdam, pp. 57–73

Dantzig, G. B., Orden, A., and Wolfe, P. (1955), "The generalized simplex method for minimizing a linear form under linear inequality restraints", *Pacific Journal of Mathematics*, 5(2), June

Dedekind, R. (1872), "Continuity and irrational numbers". Reprinted (1963) in *Essays on the Theory of Numbers*, translated by W. W. Beman 1901, Dover

Dexter, A. S., Yu, J. N. W., and Ziemba, W. T. (1980), "Portfolio selection in a lognormal market when the investor has a power utility function: computational results". In M. A. H. Dempster (ed.), *Stochastic Programming*, Academic Press, New York, pp. 507-23

Dieudonné, J. (1969), *Foundations of Modern Analysis*, Academic Press, New York and London

Duff, I. S. (1977), "A survey of sparse matrix research", *Proceedings IEEE*, 65, pp. 500-35

Duff, I. S. (ed.) (1981), *Sparse Matrices and their Uses*, Academic Press, New York and London

Dybvig, P. H. (1984), "Short sales restrictions and kinks on the mean-variance frontier", *The Journal of Finance*, 39(1), March

Ederington, L. H. (1986), "Mean-variance as an approximation to expected utility maximization", working paper 86-5, School of Business Administration, Washington University, St Louis, Missouri

Elton, E. J., Gruber, M. J., and Padberg, M. W. (1976), "Simple criteria for optimal portfolio selection", *The Journal of Finance*, 31(5), December, pp. 1341-57

Elton, E. J., Gruber, M. J., and Padberg, M. W. (1977), "Simple criteria for optimal portfolio selection with upper bounds", *Operations Research*, 25(6), November/December, pp. 952-67

Elton, E. J., Gruber, M. J., and Padberg, M. W. (1978), "Simple criteria for optimal portfolio selection: tracing out the efficient frontier", *The Journal of Finance*, 33(1), March, pp. 296-302

Fama, E. F. (1970), "Multiperiod consumption – investment decisions", *The American Economic Review*, 60, pp. 163–74

Farrell, J. L., Jr (1983), *Guide to Portfolio Management*, McGraw-Hill, New York

Feldstein, M. (1969), "Liquidity preference and portfolio selection", *Review of Economic Studies*, January

Fishburn, P. C. (1969), "A general theory of subjective probabilities and expected utilities", *The Annals of Mathematical Statistics*, 40, pp. 1419-29

Graves, R. L. (1967), "A principal pivoting simplex algorithm for linear and quadratic programming", *Operations Research*, 15, pp. 482-94

Hadar, J., and Russell, W. R. (1969), "Rules for ordering uncertain prospects", *American Economic Review*, 59, March, pp. 25-34

Hakansson, N. H. (1971), "On optimal myopic portfolio policies, with and without serial correlation of yields", *The Journal of Business of the University of Chicago*, 44(3), July

Halmos, P. R. (1948), *Finite Dimensional Vector Spaces*, Princeton University Press, Princeton, New Jersey

Halmos, P. R. (1950), *Measure Theory*, Van Nostrand, Toronto, New York, London

Hanoch, G., and Levy, H. (1969), "The efficiency analysis of choice involving risk", *Review of Economic Studies*, 36, July, pp. 335–46

Hicks, J. R. (1935), "A suggestion for simplifying the theory of money", *Economics*, February, pp. 1–19

Hicks, J. R. (1962), "Liquidity", *Economic Journal*, 72, December, pp. 787–802

Hilbert, D., and Ackermann, W. (1928), *Grundzuge der Theoretischen Logik*; Springer, Berlin, 2nd edn (1938): reprinted (1946) Dover, New York; 3rd edn (1949) Springer, Berlin. English translation of the 2nd edn by L. M. Hammond, G. G. Leckie, and F. Steinhardt, ed. with notes by R. E. Luce (1950), *Principles of Mathematical Logic*, Chelsea, New York

Hobman, R. J. (1975), "Setting investment policy in an ERISA environment", *Journal of Portfolio Management*, Fall, pp. 17–21

Hoffman, A. J. (1953), "Cycling in the simplex algorithm", National Bureau of Standards, report 2974

Kallberg, J. G., and Ziemba, W. T. (1981), "An algorithm for portfolio revision: theory, computational algorithm and empirical results", *Applications of Management Science*, 1, pp. 267–91

Karatzas, I., Lehoczky, J. P., Sethi, S. P., and Shreve, S. E. (1986), "Explicit solution of a general consumption investment problem", *Mathematics of Operations Research*, May, pp. 261–94

Karmarkar, N. (1984), "A new polynomial-time algorithm for linear programming", *Combinatorica*, 4(4), pp. 373–95

Kelly, J. L., Jr (1956), "A new interpretation of information rate", *Bell System Technical Journal*, pp. 917–26

King, B. F. (1966), "Market and industry factors in stock price behavior", *Journal of Business*, January Supplement

Kiviat, P. J., Villanueva, R., and Markowitz, H. M. (1983), *The Simscript II.5 Programming Language*, ed. E. Russell, CACI

Kleene, S. C. (1952), *Introduction to Metamathematics*, Van Nostrand, New York

Kolmogorov, A. N., and Fomin, S. V. (1957), *Elements of the Theory of Functions and Functional Analysis*, vol. 1, *Metric and Normed Spaces*, translated from the first Russian edition (1954) by Leo F. Boron, Greylock Press, Rochester, New York

Koopmans, T. C. (1951), "Analysis of production as an efficient combination of activities". In T. C. Koopmans (ed.) (1971), *Activity of Production and Allocation*, 7th edn, Yale University Press, New Haven and London

Kroll, Y., Levy, H., and Markowitz, H. M. (1984), "Mean variance versus direct utility maximization", *Journal of Finance*, 39(1), March

Kuhn, H. W., and Tucker, A. W. (1951), "Nonlinear programming", *Proceedings of the Second Berkeley Symposium on Mathematical Statistics and Probability*, ed. J. Neyman, University of California Press, Berkeley, pp. 481–92

Latané, H. A. (1957), "Rational decision making in portfolio management", Ph.D. dissertation, University of North Carolina

Latané, H. A. (1959), "Criteria for choice among risky ventures", *Journal of Political Economy*, April

Leavens, D. H. (1945), "Diversification of planning", *Trusts and Estates*, 80, May, pp. 469–73

Lemke, C. E. (1965), "Bimatrix equilibrium points and mathematical programming", *Management Science*, 11(7), May, pp. 681-9

Lemke, C. E. (1968), "On complementary pivot theory". In G. B. Dantzig and A. F. Veinott, Jr (eds), *Mathematics of the Decision Sciences*, part 1, American Mathematical Society, Providence, Rhode Island, pp. 95-135

Lemke, C. E. (1970), "Recent results on complementarity problems". In J. B. Rosen, O. L. Mangasarian and K. Ritter (eds), *Nonlinear Programming*, Academic Press, New York, pp. 349-84

Lemke, C. E., and Howson, J. T., Jr (1964), "Equilibrium points of bimatrix games", *Journal of The Society for Industrial and Applied Mathematics*, 12(2), June, pp. 413-23

Levy, H. (1985), "Efficiency analyses and equilibrium of risky assets prices: the lognormal case", working paper, Hebrew University

Levy, H., and Markowitz, H. M. (1979), "Approximating expected utility by a function of mean and variance", *American Economic Review*, June

Lintner, J. (1965), "The valuation of risk assets and the selection of risky investments in stock portfolios and capital budgets", *Review of Economics and Statistics*, February, pp. 13-37

Malliaris, A. G., and Brock, W. A. (1982), *Stochastic Methods in Economics and Finance*, North-Holland

Markowitz, H. M. (1952), "Portfolio selection", *The Journal of Finance*, 7(1), March, pp. 77-91

Markowitz, H. M. (1956), "The optimization of a quadratic function subject to linear constraints", *Naval Research Logistics Quarterly*, 3, pp. 111-33

Markowitz, H. M. (1957), "The elimination form of the inverse and its application to linear programming", *Management Science*, 3, pp. 255-69

Markowitz, H. M. (1959), *Portfolio Selection: Efficient Diversification of Investments*, Wiley, Yale University Press, 1970

Markowitz, H. M. (1976), "Investment for the long run: new evidence for an old rule", *The Journal of Finance*, 31(5), December, pp. 1273-86

Markowitz, H. M., and Perold, A. F. (1981a), "Portfolio analysis with factors and scenarios", *The Journal of Finance*, 36(14), September

Markowitz, H. M., and Perold, A. F. (1981b), "Sparsity and piecewise linearity in large portfolio optimization problems". In I. S. Duff (ed.), *Sparse Matrices and their Uses*, Academic Press, pp. 89-108

Markowitz, H. M., Malhotra, A., and Pazel, D. P. (1984), "The EAS-E application development system: principles and language summary", *Communications of the Association for Computing Machinery*, 27(8), August, pp. 785-99

Merton, R. C. (1969), "Lifetime portfolio selection under uncertainty: the continuous-time case", *The Review of Economic Statistics*, August, pp. 247-59

Merton, R. C. (1971), "Optimum consumption and portfolio rules in a continuous-time model", *Journal of Economic Theory*, 3, pp. 373-413

Merton, R. C. (1972), "An analytic derivation of the efficient portfolio frontier", *Journal of Financial and Quantitative Analysis*, September, pp. 1851-72

Mossin, J. (1966), "Equilibrium in a capital asset market", *Econometrica*, 34(4), October, pp. 768-83

Mossin, J. (1968), "Optimal multiperiod portfolio policies", *Journal of Business*, April

Ohlson, J. A. (1975), "The asymptotic validity of quadratic utility as the trading interval approaches zero". In W. T. Ziemba and R. G. Vickson (eds), *Stochastic Optimization Models in Finance*, Academic Press, New York

Perold, A. F. (1984), "Large-scale portfolio optimization", *Management Science*, 30(10), October, pp. 1143-60

Pratt, J. W. (1964), "Risk aversion in the small and in the large", *Econometrica*, 32, January, pp. 122-36

Pulley, L. M. (1981), "A general mean-variance approximation to expected utility for short holding periods", *Journal of Financial and Quantitative Analysis*, 16, pp. 361-73

Pulley, L. M. (1983), "Mean-variance approximations to expected logarithmic utility", *Operations Research*, 31(4), pp. 685-96

Rockafeller, R. T. (1970), *Convex Analysis*, Princeton University Press, Princeton, New Jersey

Roll, R. (1977), "A critique of the asset pricing theory's tests. Part I: On past and potential testability of the theory", *Journal of Financial Economics*, 4, pp. 129-76

Roll, R. (1978), "Ambiguity when performance is measured by the securities market line", *The Journal of Finance*, 33(4), September

Rosenberg, B. (1974), "Extra-market components of covariance in security returns", *Journal of Financial and Quantitative Analysis*, March

Ross, S. A. (1978), "Mutual fund separation in financial theory - the separating distributions", *Journal of Economic Theory*, 17, pp. 254-86

Roy, A. D. (1952), "Safety first and the holding of assets", *Econometrica*, 20, pp. 431-49

Samuelson, P. A. (1963), "Risk and uncertainty: a fallacy of large numbers", *Scientia*, April/May

Samuelson, P. A. (1969), "Lifetime portfolio selection by dynamic stochastic programming", *The Review of Economics and Statistics*, 51, pp. 239-46

Samuelson, P. A. (1970), "The fundamental approximation theorem of portfolio analysis in terms of means, variances and higher moments", *The Review of Economic Studies*, 37, pp. 537-42

Savage, L. J. (1954), *The Foundations of Statistics*, Wiley; 2nd edn (1972), Dover

Scarf, H. E. (1973), *The Computation of Economic Equilibria*, with the collaboration of Terje Hansen, Cowles Foundation for Research in Economics at Yale University, monograph 24, Yale University Press

Scarf, H. E. (1983), "Fixed-point theorems and economic analysis", *American Scientist*, May/June, pp. 289-96

Schreiner, J. (1980), "Portfolio revision - a turnover constrained approach", *Financial Management*, 9(1), Spring, pp. 67-75

Sharpe, W. F. (1963), "A simplified model for portfolio analysis", *Management Science*, January

Sharpe, W. F. (1964), "Capital asset prices: a theory of market equilibrium under conditions of risk", *The Journal of Finance*, 19(3), September

Sharpe, W. F. (1970), *Portfolio Theory and Capital Markets*, McGraw-Hill, New York

Simaan, Y. (1987), "Portfolio selection and capital asset pricing for a class of non-spherical distributions of assets returns", dissertation, Baruch College, The City University of New York

Tew, B. V., and Reid, D. W. (forthcoming 1987), "A test of the effectiveness of the expected value variance criterion in making risk efficient choices", *American Journal of Agricultural Economics*

Tobin, J. (1958), "Liquidity preference as behavior towards risk", *Review of Economic Studies*, February, pp. 65-86

Tsiang, S. C. (1972), "The rationale of the mean-standard deviation analysis, skewness preference, and the demand for money", *American Economic Review*, 62, June, pp. 354-71

Vasicek, O. (1973), "A note on using cross-sectional information in Bayesian estimation of security betas", *Journal of Finance*, 28, December, pp. 1233-9

Von Neumann, J., and Morgenstern, O. (1944), *Theory of Games and Economic Behavior*, 3rd edn (1953), Princeton University Press

Weston, J. F., and Baranek, W. (1955), "Programming investment portfolio construction", *Financial Analysts Journal*, May

Whitehead, A. N., and Russell, B. (1910), *Principia Mathematica*, vol. 1 (2nd edn 1925); (1912), vol. 2 (2nd edn 1927); (1913), vol. 3 (2nd edn 1927); Cambridge University Press

Wolfe, P. (1959), "The simplex method for quadratic programming", *Econometrica*, 27(3), July, pp. 382-98

Young, W. E., and Trent, R. H. (1969), "Geometric mean approximation of individual security and portfolio performance", *Journal of Financial Quantitative Analysis*, 4, June, pp. 179-99

Ziemba, W. T., and Vickson, R. G. (eds) (1975), *Stochastic Optimization Models in Finance*, Academic Press, New York

Index

Page numbers in italics refer to figures, those followed by 'n' refer to notes.

Ackermann, W. *see* Hilbert, D. and W. Ackermann
adjacent efficient segments 157, 161-6, *177*, 286
affine functions *see* affine transformations
affine hull 94
affine model 39, 94, 98-9, 127-48, 277
  associated with critical line 154
  exercises 143-8
  feasible directions in 135
  lower boundary sets 137-8
affine subspace 349
affine transformations 253, 266-8, 341, *356*, 357
  nonsingular 248-51, 252, 265
Aitken, A. C. 339, 361
algebraic vector 346, 347
anticycling 201, 203
Arrow, K. 53, 65-6, 361
artificial basis variables 303
assets
  exogenous 48-9
  riskless 37, 43, 69
  see also capital asset pricing model
axes, choice of 178-9

ball 82, 127n, 141
Baraneck, W. *see* Weston, J. F. and W. Baranek
basic solutions
  degenerate 200
  feasible 186, 190
  optimum: prices out and 202, 203
Baumol, W. J. 37, 361
Bayesian inference 56-7
Bellman, R. E. 53, 58-9, 361
beta regression coefficient 19-20
betas, expected returns and 286-8
Birkhoff, G. and S. MacLane 74, 101, 361
Black, F. 11, 39, 43-4, 144, 182, 275, 294, 296-7, 361
Black, F. and M. Scholes 69-70, 361
Black-Scholes formula 69,70
Black's model 11, 23, 38, 43-4, 125, 224, 243
  constraint set 99, 226, 275, 276, 286
  nominal and real returns 13-4
  riskless asset in 43, 69
  Roll's theorem 287n
  unbounded sets 87
Blume, M. 46, 361
Borch, K. 53, 361
borrowing
  limited 10
  non-linear model 28-31; cost of borrowing *28*
boundaries
  bottom or lower 225
  efficient subset 142
  horizontal segment, minimum V 227-9
  parabolas 6, 8, 233-6
  top or upper 225
bounded E 199, 202-14
boundedness 86-7

bounded sets 86
bounded *V* 229, 232
Breiman, L. 63n, 361
Brock, W. A. *see* Malliaris, A. G. and W. A. Brock
budget constraint 303

C programming language 302
C++ 302
calculus 339
canonical form 243-74
  definition 249
  derivation 270-2
  exercises 272-4
  k dimensional analysis 265-70
  kinks in *E V* combinations 244, 257-9
  τ^* of rank 1 262-5
  rank 2 248-52; efficient set 253-7
  standard three-security analysis 244, 265, 281
  see also two dimensional analysis
capital asset pricing model 243, 275, 282
  equilibrium pricing 38
  excess returns 275, 286
  exercises 288-98
  market equilibrium 282-4
Cauchy sequence 100-2
Chamberlain, G. 68-9, 361
closed interval 81
closed sets 81-2
  closed interval 81
  feasible portfolios 86
Cohen, K. J. and J. A. Pogue 46, 48, 361
collateral for short positions 11-3, 40n
column vector 346, 347
compact sets 86-8, 102
  image 88
compensating transformation 271
  of return space 114
complementarity problems 221-2
complete set
  efficient portfolios, of 151
  nonredundant 176, 184
computer program 301-37
  main module 305-6
  main routine 305-6
  notation 302
  program inputs 304-5
  public data declarations 305
  reading inputs 306
  statement of problem 303
  steps of the simplex algorithm 308-12
cone 98
  recession 74, 100
  with vertex deleted 98
conical sets 98-100, 277-80
constraints
  conical set 277-80
  economic analysis 43-4
  industry 44-5
  minimization subject to 125-48
    Lagrangian multipliers 125-7
    minimax or saddlepoint 139
  money management 44
  turnover 51
  upper bounds 7-8, 44, 45
  see also individual models
continuous function 84-5, 213
continuous time model 69
continuous trading 69-70
convergence in R^n 80
convergent sequence 101
  subsequence 87
convex combination 92
convex function 36, 117-9
  strictly convex 118, 119
convexity 118, 119
convex sets 89-92, 279, 280, 282-3
  unbounded, recession cone in 74
corner portfolios 166

correlation coefficient 16
Cottle, R. W. *see* Dantzig, G. B. and R. W. Cottle
Cottle, R. W. and G. B. Dantzig 222, 361
Courant, R. 77, 361
covariance 16
  applied to random variables 17
  historical 43, 46
  matrix 16, 269
    dense 220, ill-conditioned 220; orthogonal transformation 109-10; scaling 221; semidefinite 42-3; sparse 48, 220; well-conditioned 221
  models 45-8
    combination 48; one-factor 46, 47, 48; scenario 48
  no zero-variance directions 113
  singular 42-3
critical line algorithm 166, 199, 303, 312
  adding a valriable 311
  calculation of outputs 317
  deleting a variable 316
  extended 199
  finiteness of 174-6
  iteration 314
  Lemke algorithm and 221-2
  outputting results to spreadsheet 318
  "properly" resolve ties 199
  roundoff errors 219
  setting up program 313
  starting 193-5
  see also linear programming
critical lines 132-3, 154-7
  adjacent *177*, 286
  efficient segments 157-61
    adjacent 157, 161-6
  exercises 179-83
  Kuhn-Tucker conditions 164
  nonsingular $\overline{M}$ 156, 166-7
  support lines, with maximum *E 195*
  X and η *159*
    nonnegativity of 171-4
cycling 201, 203

Dantzig, G. B. 184-6, 201-2, 361
  see also Cottle, R. W. and G. B. Dantzig
Dantzig, G. B. and R. W. Cottle 222, 361
Dantzig, G. B., A. Orden and P. Wolfe 202, 362
Dantzig's simplex method 185-91
  see also simplex method
Dedkind, R. 101, 362
DEFINE statements 30-6
degeneracy 200-1
degenerate 308
degenerate cases 199-224
  E bounded 199, 202-14
  E unbounded 201, 216-20
  exercises 223-4
  "good enough" methods 200-1
  lexicographic ordering 214-6
degenerate model 161
degenerate solution 186
dense covariance matrix 220
dependent vector 349
deviation, standard 16
Dexter, A. S., J. N. W. Yu and W. Ziemba 62n, 66, 362
diagonal matrix 343
Dieudonné, J. 74, 362
directions
  disallowed 96-8
  feasible 96, 97, 121, 135
  increasing *E,* of 108
  irrelevant 136
  unbounded 93, 135
    feasible 94, 96n, 121, 226
  zero-mean 136, 279
  see also zero variance directions

disallowed directions 96-8
diversification
across industries 45
risk elimination and 37
stock returns and 65
"double pivot" 222
Duff, I. S. 148, 362
Dybvig, P. H. 181, 362

E
bounded, degenerate cases 199, 202-14
maximization
perturbed problem 203, 206, 211-2; ties for 200; unique feasible portfolios 184
relationships involving 107-8
unbounded 201, 216-20
EAS-E program 302
economic analysis, constraints set 43-4
Ederington, L. H. 67-8, 362
efficiency
exercises 288-98
of market portfolio 280-2
efficient *E*σ combinations 6
linear and/or hyperbolic 151
linear segments in set 259-62
shape of sets 176-7
efficient *EV* combinations 6
boundary of subset 142
computation of 151-83
equivalence and 25-6, 34
exercises 18-22
kinks in 244, 257-9
shape of sets 176-7
efficient frontier 302
efficient portfolios 6
piecewise linear 151,176
complete nonredundant set 176, 184
weighted average 285
efficient segments 157-61
adjacent 157, 161-7
efficient sets 179-83
canonical form
non-standard constraints 257; standard constraints 256; transformed standard triangle *255*; *V* minimized 257, *258*
convex 279, 280
E bounded above 202-14
Kuhn-Tucker conditions 152-4
nondegenerate models 151-83
nonnegativity of *X* and η 171-4
nonsingularity of $\overline{M}$ 156, 166-71, 184
not convex 280, *281*
piecewise linear 280
rays 280
see also critical lines
eigenvalues 107
nonnegative 110
positive 111-2
some zero 112
zero 110
Elton, E. J., M. J. Gruber and M. W. Padberg 288-91, 362
equilibrium pricing 38
equivalent models 25-6, 34
strictly 25, 34
*E*σ combinations *see* efficient, inefficient *and* obtainable *E*σ combinations; *see also E and* σ (sigma)
*E*σ efficient sets
canonical analysis 252
hyperbolic or/and linear pieces 19
see also efficient sets
*E*σ space 73
EV approximations
research on 63-8
EV combinations *see* efficient, inefficient *and* obtainable *EV* combinations; *see also E and V*
EV efficient sets
canonical analysis 253
see also efficient sets

EV obtainable sets *see* obtainable *EV* sets
EV space 73
Excel Spreadsheet 303
excess returns 275, 286
exogenous assets 48-9
expected returns 286-8
extended critical line algorithm 199
"extension of inequalities" 213, 223
extensive form of game 56
exterior of subset 142
extreme feasible points 303

Fama, E. F. 53, 362
farm decisions 67n
Farrell, J. L. Jr 46n, 362
feasible bases 217
feasible directions
  affine model 135
  bounded 96, 97
  unbounded 96n, 121
feasible $E\sigma$ combinations *see* obtainable $E\sigma$ combinations
feasible *EV* combinations *see* obtainable *EV* combinations
feasible portfolio sets 73-106
  closed sets 86
  contained in affine set 94, 95
  standard model 4
feasible solution 186
  basic 186
    nondegenerate 190
Feldstein, M. 68, 362
finite sample space 15-8
Fishburn, P. C. 54, 362
FLAG 315
Fomin, S. V. *see* Kolmogorov, A. N. and S. V. Fomin
four security model, standard 267-8
functions
  continuous 84-5, 213
  convex 36, 117-9

general portfolio selection model 22-41
  capabilities and assumptions 42-7
  constraints 43-5
  covariance models 45-8
  exogenous assets 48-9
  index tracking 50
  mean and variance use 52-6
  nonlinear 28-36
  three forms of 24-7
  see also portfolio selection mode: *and also individual models, e.g.,* Black's model geometric point 347
geometric vector 346
goods
  maximization 139-41
  obtainable combinations *140*
  quantities of interest 141, 142
Graves, R. L. 222, 362
Gruber, M. J. *see* Elton, E. J., M. J. Gruber and M. W. Padberg

Hadar, J. and W. R. Russell 38, 362
Hakansson, N. H. 53, 362
Halmos, P. R. 18, 347, 362
Hanoch, G. and H. Levy 38, 363
Hicks, J. R. 36-7, 363
Hilbert, D. and W. Ackermann 76, 363
historical covariance 43, 46
Hobman, R. J. 48, 363
Hoffman, A. J. 201, 363
Howson, J. T. Jr *see* Lemke, C. E. and J. T. Howson Jr. hull, affine *see* affine hull hyperplane 107-8, 288

identity matrix 342
ill-conditioned covariance matrix 220-21
image of set 88
implied single-period utility maximization 57-9
IN sets 155, 156
income, non-portfolio 48-9

independent vectors 348, 349
index tracking 50
industry constraints 44-5
inefficient $E\sigma$ combination *6*
inefficient EV combination *6*
inequalities, extension of 213, 223
infeasible model 8
"instant" 69-70
interior of subset 141
intermediate model 26
internal rate of return 63
interval
  closed 81
  open 81
inverses 343-4
investors' beliefs 275, 282-3, 285
irrelevant direction 136
isomean lines 250, 253, 264
  vertical 271
isovariance curves 250, 271
  vertical lines 264

JOUT 317

Kallberg, J. G. and W. T. Ziemba 51n, 363
Karatzas, I., L. P. Lehoczky, S. P. Sethi and S. E. Shreve 70n, 363
Karmarkar, N. 185, 363
Karmarkar's method 184-5
Kelly, J. L. Jr. 63n, 363
King, B. F. 46, 363
kinks 244, 257-9
Kiviat, P. J., R. Villanueva and H. M. Markowitz 363
Kleene, S. C. 76, 363
Kolmogorov, A. N. and S. V. Fomin 74, 363
Koopmans, T. C. 277, 363
Kroll, Y., H. Levy and H. M. Markowitz 62n, 66, 363
Kuhn, H. W. and A. W. Tucker 139, 139n, 154, 363
Kuhn-Tucker conditions 152-4, 164, 222

Lagrangian multipliers 125-7, 128
  existence of λ *126*
  rates of substitution, λ as 127
Latané, H. A. 63n, 363
least square regression coefficient 19-20
Leavens, D. H. 37, 363
Lebesgue integral 20, 22
left side (obtainable set) 238
legitimate portfolio *see* feasible portfolio sets
Lehoczky, L. P. *see* Karatzas, I., L. P. Lehoczky, S. P. Sethi and S. E. Shreve
Lemke, C. E. 221-2, 364
Lemke, C. E. and J. T. Howson Jr. 221, 364
Lemke algorithm 221-2, 364
Levy, H. 38, 364
  see also Hanoch, G. and H. Levy; Kroll, Y., H. Levy and H. M. Markowitz
Levy, H. and H. M. Markowitz 53, 61n, 64-7, 364
lexicographical ordering 214-6
limited borrowing 10
linear functions *see* linear transformation
linear mapping 252
linear programming 27, 184-5
  cycling of algorithm 201
  degeneracy 200-1
  exercises 195-8
  "good enough" method 200-1
  notation 188
  see also simplex method
linear segments 280
  efficient E_σ combinations 259-62
linear sets, piecewise *see* piecewise linear sets

linear subspace 94, 349
linear transformation 341, 357, 359
  nonsingular 270
  return space, in 271
Lintner, J. 9, 38, 39-40, 243, 275, 364
liquidity preference 38
long positions 11
lower boundary set, affine model 137-8

$\overline{M}$, nonsingularity 156, 166-71, 184
MacLane, S. *see* Birkhoff, G. and S. MacLane
Malhotra, A. *see* Markowitz, H. M., A. Malhotra and D. P. Pazel
Malliaris, A. G. and W. A. Brock 70n, 364
mapping, nonsingular linear 252
market equilibrium 282-4
  prices 282
market portfolio 275, 276-7
  conical constraint sets 277-80
  efficiency 280-2
  exercises 288-98
  inefficiency of 284-6
  not necessarily efficient 280-1
Markowitz, H. M. 37, 38, 46, 49, 52-4, 60-3, 63n, 69, 148, 166n, 221-2, 243, 364
  see also Kiviat, P. J., R. Villanueva and H. M. Markowitz; Kroll, Y., H. Levy and H. M. Markowitz; *and* Levy, H. and H. M. Markowitz
Markowitz, H. M. and A. F. Perold 48, 148, 364
Markowitz, H. M., A. Malhotra and D. P. Pazel 301, 364
mathematical induction 91
matrix algebra
  diagonal matrix 343
  identity matrix 342
  inverses 343-4
  nonsingular matrix 343
  notation 339-41
  operations 341-3
  positive definite and indefinite 341
  singular matrix 343
  substitution of variables 344-6
  symmetric matrix 340
  transpose of matrix 340
  zero matrix 342 *see also* covariance matrix
maximization
  E, unique feasible portfolio 184
  expected values 56
  goods, of 139-41
  linear function 184-5
  utility, implied single-period 57-9
mean and variance
  justification for 52-6
  of weighted sums 15-20
mean-variance portfolio selection
  models *see* portfolio selection models
Merton, R. C. 39, 69-70, 144, 364
Merton's continuous time model 69
Microsoft Visual Basic for Applications (VBA) 302
minimax solution 139
minimization
  subject to constraints 127-47
    Lagrange multipliers 125-7
    minimax or saddlepoint and 139
  V, undiversified portfolio and *258*
minimum feasible variance 213
money management
  constraints 44
  index tracking 50
Morgenstern, O. *see* Von Neumann, J. and O. Morgenstern
Mossin, J. 39, 43-4, 56, 69-70, 364, 365
Mossin's dynamic analysis value 56

η
along critical line 159
nonnegativity of 171-4
nominal returns 13-5
non-convex set 90
unbounded 92
nondegenerate model
definition 161
efficient sets for 151-83
nondegenerate solution 186, 190
nonlinear model 28-36
equivalent general model 31-6
obtainable *EV* combinations *31*
nonnegativity of X and η 171-4
non-portfolio income 48-9
nonredundant set 185, 212, 217
complete 176
efficient portfolios, of 151
see also piecewise linear set
nonsingularity of $\overline{M}$ 156, 166-71, 184
nonsingular linear mapping 252
nonsingular matrix 343
nonsingular transformations 248-51, 252, 265, 358-9
linear 270, 357
see also affine transformations
normalized form of game 56
notation
linear programming 188
matrix algebra 339-41
sets 74, 75, 76

obtainable $E\sigma$ combinations
inefficient 6
lower boundaries 120-2
standard model 4, 6
obtainable *EV* combinations
boundary shape 225
exercises 20-2
horizontal *EV* segment 227-9
inefficient 6
lower boundaries 120-2
affine model 137-8
non linear model *31*
standard model 4, 5, 6
strictly equivalent and 25-6, 34
Tobin-Sharpe-Lintner model 9
unbounded above 226
upper bounds on 8
obtainable *EV* sets
boundary shape 225-39
comparison of top and bottom 236-8
left side 238
right side 238
top of 229-36
obtainable portfolio *see* feasible portfolio sets
Ohlson, J. A. 64, 365
one-factor model 46, 47, 48
open interval 81
open sets 82-6
optimum basic solution 186, 187
nondegenerate, feasible 190
price out and 202, 203
option pricing theory 69, 70
Orden, A. *see* Dantzig, G. B., A. Orden and P. Wolfe
original model 26, 204, 214
orthogonality 348
orthogonal subspace 349
orthogonal transformations 353, 358, 359
covariance matrix 109-10
outcomes 54, 56
utility of 55

Padberg, M. W. *see* Elton, E. J., M. J. Gruber and M. W. Padberg
parabolas 6, 8, 233-6
feasible portions of 234
Pazel, D. P. *see* Markowitz, H. M., A. Malhotra and D. P. Pazel
Perold, A. F. 51, 148, 220, 222, 365
see also Markowitz, H. M. and A. F. Perold

perturbed portfolio selection model 205-6, 211-2
  E-maximization problem 203
  original problem and 214
  nondegenerate for small ε 212-3
  piecewise linear nonredundant set 212
piecewise linear sets 114, 132, 151, 154, 176, 184
  complete nonredundant 199, 212, 217
  efficient 280
Pogue, J. A. *see* Cohen, K. J. and J. A. Pogue
portfolio
  corner 323
  efficient *see* efficient portfolio
  feasible *see* feasible portfolio sets
  market *see* market portfolio space 73
    straight line in 89; transformation of 114
  theory
    historical development of 36 40
  see also portfolio selection models
portfolio selection models 3-22
  bounded *V* for given *E* 229
  collateral for short positions 11-3, 40n
  degenerate 161
  feasible, with no efficient portfolios 132
  infeasible 8
  nominal and real returns 13-5
  non degenerate
    definition 161; efficient sets 151-83
  original or unperturbed model 204
  perturbed *see* perturbed portfolio selection model
  two-dimensional affine hull 243-65
  unbounded *V* for given *E* 229
  with constraints 127-48
  see also general portfolio selection model *and individual models e.g.* Black's model
positions *see* long *and* short positions
Pratt, J. W. 53, 65-6, 365
Pratt-Arrow objection 65-6
price vector 191
prices 191-2
  market equilibrium 283
  prices out 192, 202, 203
pricing 185, 217
  equilibrium, of capital assets 38
  see also capital asset pricing model
probability
  exercises 22
  finite sample space 15-20
  general sample spaces 20
  two-parameter families 52-3, 68
  vector 192
  weighted sums 15-20
Pulley, L. M. 62n, 66, 365

quadratic approximations 53, 59-63, 64
  risk aversion in 65-6, 67
quadratic utility function 53
of interest" 141, 142

random return vector 114
rays 280
real returns 13-5
recession cone 74, 100
regression coefficient 19-20
returns
  distributions of 64, 68-9
  excess 275, 286
  expected 286-8
  forthcoming, covariances among 46
  historical 66
  holding period 63-5, 66
  index of 50n

investors' beliefs 283, 285
joint distribution of 68-9
joint lognormal, on securities 62n
nominal versus real 13-5
real 13-5
risk free rate 9, 15
return space 114
linear transformations in 271
return vector
expected 251-9
random 114
Riemann integral 20, 22
right side (obtainable set) 238
risk
aversion
quadratic approximations and 65-6, 67; variation in 58
diversification and 37
risk free assets 37
Black's model 43,69
risk free rate 9, 15, 37
riskiness 37
Rockafeller, R. T. 74, 365
Roll, R. 124, 287n, 365
Rosenberg, B. 46, 46n, 48, 365
Rosenberg model 46n
Ross, S. A. 69, 365
roundoff errors 219-21
Roy, A. D. 37, 365
Roy's model 37
Russell, B. *see* Whitehead, A. N. and B. Russell
Russell, W. R. *see* Hadar, J. and W. R. Russell

saddlepoint solution 139
safety-first portfolio 37-8
sample space
finite 15-20
general 19-20
Samuelson, P. A. 53, 63n, 64, 365
Savage, L. J.53-4, 365
scaling of covariance matrix 221
Scarf, H. E. 221-2, 365
Scarf problem 221, 222
scenario model 48
Scholes, M. *see* Black, F. and M. Scholes
Schreiner, J. 51n, 365
security, synthetic 285
segments, efficient 157-61
adjacent 157, 161-7
horizontal *EV* 227-9
minimum *V* 227-9
linear 259-62, 280
semidefinite covariance matrices 42-3
separation theorem
Tobin 38-9
two-funds 39, 280
sequences
Cauchy 100-2
convergent 101
subsequence 87
limit of 77-8
see also sets
Sethi, S. P. *see* Karatzas, I., L. P. Lehoczky, S. P. Sethi and S. E. Shreve
sets
affine 94, 98-9, 127-48
see also affine models
ball 82, 127n, 141
bounded 86
closed 81-2, 86
compact 86-8, 102
complete efficient 151, 176, 184, 199
conical 98-100
constraint 277-80
convergence in R^n 80
convex 74, 89-92, 279, 280, 282
efficient *see* efficient sets
exercises 105-6
feasible *see* feasible portfolio sets
IN sets 155,156

lower boundary 137-8
non-convex *90*, *92*
nonredundant efficient 151, 184, 199, 212, 217
notation 74, 75, 76
open 82-6
OUT 155
relationships involving *E* 107-9
sphere 82
unbounded
above 109; below 109; closed convex 103; constraint 92-4
see also piecewise linear sets, sequences, *and* subsets
Sharpe, W. F. 9, 38,39, 46, 144, 160n, 243, 275, 365, 366
short positions 11, 39-40
collateral for 11-3, 40n
Shreve, S. E. *see* Karatzas, I., L. P. Lehoczky, S. P. Sethi and S. E. Shreve
σ (sigma)
along straight line 116-7
see also efficient *E*σ combinations, *E*σ efficient sets, *E*σ space, obtainable *E*σ combinations
Simaan, Y. 66-7, 366
simplex algorithm 303-11
simplex method 184,185-91
cycling of algorithm 201
outcomes 185-7
pricing criteria 192
roundoff errors 219-20
solution definitions 186
see also linear programming
single-period utility maximization 57-9
singular matrix 343
slack variable 27, 43, 45, 302, 303
solutions
degenerate 186
feasible 186, 190
see also basic solutions
space
EV 73
portfolio 73, 89, 114, 237
random variables, of 113-4
return 114, 271
sample
finite 15-20; general 20
see also subspace *and* vector space
sparse covariance matrix 48, 220
sphere 82
Standard and Poor's 500 50
standard deviation 16
standard four-security model 267-8
standard portfolio model 3-7
bounded set 86
constraint set 276
feasible portfolio 4
nominal and real returns 13-4
simplex not needed 186
transformed to canonical form 252-3, 263
with upper bounds 7-8
standard three-security analysis 244-8
canonical form 281, 288
derivation 270-2
feasible set for 245
τ* of rank 1 *264*
transformed constraint set 251
strategy 54
ranking of *d* matrices 55
strictly convex 118, 119
strictly equivalent 25-6, 34
subsequence, convergent 87
subset
boundary of 14
exterior 142
interior 141
subspace
affine 349
linear 94, 349
orthogonal 349
vector 349-50

symmetric matrix 340

taxes 51n
Taylor expansion 63
Tew, B. V. and D. W. Reid 67n, 366
three-security analysis *see* standard three-security analysis
Tobin, J. 9, 37, 38, 52-3, 68, 243, 366
Tobin separation theorem 38-9
Tobin-Sharpe-Lintner model 8-10, 52
  canonical form 243, 244
  constraint set 275, 276, 277
  limited borrowing 10
  nominal and real returns 15
  risk free rate 9, 15, 37
  unbounded set 87
transaction costs 51n, 68n
transformations
  affine *see* affine transformations
  compensating 271
  of return space 114
  linear *see* linear transformation
  nonsingular 357, 358-9
  linear 270, 357
  orthogonal 262, 353, 358, 359
  portfolio space 114
  standard model in canonical form 263
transpose of matrix 340
Trent, R. H. *see* Young, W. E. and R. H. Trent
triangle inequality 346
Tucker, A. W. *see* Kuhn, H. W. and A. W. Tucker
Tsiang, S. C. 49, 366
turnover constraints 51
two-dimensional analysis
  canonical form 243-65
  feasible sets 247, 248
  kinks 244
  τ^*
    of rank 1 262-5; of rank 2 260, 267
  reduced to simple canonical 248-52
  see also canonical form 248-52
two-funds separation theorem 39, 280
two-parameter families 52-3, 68

unbounded directions, 93
  feasible 94, 96n, 121, 226
    in affine model 135; zero variance 135
unbounded sets 226, 229
  above 109
    EV combinations 226
  below 109
  constraint sets 92-4
  convex sets, recession cone 74
  degenerate cases 201, 216-9
uncertainty, behavior under 51
unperturbed portfolio selection model 204
utility
  implied single-period maximization 57-9
  of outcome 55
utility function need to determine investors 62
quadratic approximations 52-3, 59-63

V
  along straight line 114-6
  bounded, for given *E* 229, 232
  convex
    piecewise parabolic 217
    strictly convex 218, 219
  minimized 120-2, 227-9, 258
  relationships including 109-13
  unbounded set 226, 229
  see also efficient *EV* combinations *and* obtainable *EV* combinations
variable, slack 27, 43, 45
variance
  measure of riskiness 37
  minimum obtainable 120-3

of weighted sum 263
zero 43, 261, 263
see also zero variance directions
Vasicek, O. 46, 366
vectors
algebraic or column 346, 347
dependent 349
geometric 346
independent 348, 349
vector space
coordinate system changes 350-9
origin translation 356
independence 348-9
n dimensional geometry 346-7
orthogonality 348
subspaces 349-50
vertex 98
Vickson, R. G. *see* Ziemba, *W.* T. and R. G. Vickson
Villanueva, R. *see* Kiviat, P. J., R. Villanueva and H. M. Markowitz
Visual Basic 303
Von Neumann, J. and O. Morgenstern 53-4, 366
Von Neumann and Morgenstern axioms 54-5, 65, 281

weighted average 285
weighted sums 15-20
well-conditioned covariance matrix 221
Weston, J. F. and W. Baranek 38, 366
Whitehead, A. N. and B. Russell 76, 366
Wolfe, P. 222, 366
see also Dantzig, G. B. A. Orden and P. Wolfe

X
along critical line *159*
nonnegativity of 171-4

Young, W. E. and R. H. Trent 63-4, 67, 366
Yu, J.N.W. see Dexter,A.S., J.N.W. Yu and W. T. Ziemba

zero matrix 342
zero-mean direction 136, 279
zero variances 43, 261, 263
affine hull with one 261
see also zero variance directions
zero variance directions 96n, 112, 113, 115, 168, 170, 279
affine model 135
unbounded 122
Ziemba, W. *T. see* Dexter, A. S., J. N. W. Yu and W. T. Ziemba
Ziemba, W. T. and R. G. Vickson 53, 366

Original index by Moira Greenhalgh. Revised by Frank J. Fabozzi Associates.

Real bugs
Dr Polic
abc
20/20
Deborah Roberts